THE
SERVICE
EDGE

THE
SERVICE
EDGE

101 Companies
That Profit From
Customer Care

by RON ZEMKE
with DICK SCHAAF

Foreword by TOM PETERS

NAL BOOKS

NEW AMERICAN LIBRARY

NEW YORK
PUBLISHED IN CANADA BY
PENGUIN BOOKS CANADA LIMITED, MARKHAM, ONTARIO

Acknowledgments

The title THE SERVICE EDGE is used with permission from Lakewood Publications Inc. (50 South Ninth St., Minneapolis, MN 55402), which publishes the monthly newsletter, *The Service Edge: Creating and Maintaining Distinctive Customer Service*, edited by Ron Zemke.

 NAL TRADEMARK REG. U.S. PAT. OFF. AND FOREIGN COUNTRIES
REGISTERED TRADEMARK—MARCA REGISTRADA
HECHO EN CHICAGO, U.S.A.

SIGNET, SIGNET CLASSIC, MENTOR, ONYX, PLUME, MERIDIAN
and NAL BOOKS are published *in the United States* by NAL PENGUIN INC.,
1633 Broadway, New York, New York 10019,
in Canada by Penguin Books Canada Limited,
2801 John Street, Markham, Ontario L3R 1B4

Library of Congress Cataloging-in-Publication Data

Zemke, Ron.
   The service edge : 101 companies that profit from customer care /
by Ron Zemke with Dick Schaaf.
     p.   cm.
   Includes index.
   ISBN 0-453-00647-7
   1. Customer service—United States.   2. Service industries—United
States—Management.   I. Schaaf, Dick.   II. Title.
HF5415.5.Z46   1989
658.8′12—dc19   88-28869
                                                                      CIP

Designed by Gilfacto Rumas

First Printing, March, 1989

   2   3   4   5   6   7   8   9

PRINTED IN THE UNITED STATES OF AMERICA

Contents

CONTENTS

Part 2: The Service 101

Travel

Airlines

Delta Air Lines
American Airlines
Piedmont Airlines (USAir)

Services

American Automobile Association
Club Med
SuperShuttle

Hotels

Marriott Hotels and Resorts
Embassy Suites
Four Seasons Hotels
Hyatt Hotels & Resorts
Mississippi Management

Health Care

Hospitals

Riverside Methodist Hospital
Beth Israel Hospital
Mayo Clinic and Hospitals

Support

Merck & Company
LensCrafters
Bergen Brunswig Drug Company
Shared Medical Systems
    Corporation

Financial

Personal

American Express
H&R Block

Banking

Citicorp
First Union Corporation
First Wachovia Corporation
First Federal/Osceola
Amalgamated Bank of New York

Brokerage

Goldman Sachs & Company
Fidelity Investments
A. G. Edwards & Sons

Insurance

Northwestern Mutual Life
  Insurance Company
Chubb Group of Insurance
  Companies
Amica Mutual Insurance
  Company
USAA

Wheels

Automotive

Acura Automobile Division
Don Beyer Volvo
Longo Toyota
Jiffy Lube International

Trucking

Ryder System
Wheaton Van Lines
United Van Lines
NW Transport Service

Food Service

Restaurants

Shoney's Restaurants
Pizza Hut
Bob Evans Farms

Fast Food   McDonald's
                   Domino's Pizza
                   Wendy's

Food Sales

Retail   Stew Leonard's Dairy
                   Vons Grocery Company
                   Ukrop's Super Markets
                   SuperAmerica

Wholesale   Procter & Gamble Company
                   Super Valu
                   Frito-Lay

Retailing

General   Nordstrom
                   Parisian
                   Wal-Mart

Specialty   Liz Claiborne
                   Avon Products
                   Home Depot
                   Florsheim Shoe Company

Catalog   L. L. Bean
                   Lands' End
                   Williams-Sonoma

Technology

Electronics   Amdahl
                   Digital Equipment Corporation
                   3M
                   AMP

Support   American Management Systems
                   Businessland
                   Dataserv

Communications	*Southern Bell*
	Southern New England Telephone
	CompuServe

Manufacturing
Deluxe Corporation
Caterpillar
General Electric
H. B. Fuller
Pioneer Hi-Bred International
Armstrong World Industries

Business-to-Business

Delivery
Federal Express Corporation
United Parcel Service
Sun Distributors

Expertise
Dun & Bradstreet Corporation
Battelle Memorial Institute
Shop'n Chek

Duplicating
Quad/Graphics
Xerox
Kinko's

Support
Safety-Kleen Corporation
Miller Business Systems
ServiceMaster

Pacesetters

Entertainment
Walt Disney World/Disneyland
Cineplex Odeon Corporation

Information
The Wall Street Journal
USA Today

Public
Montgomery County, Ohio
Arizona Public Service Company
Emerald People's Utility District

Care
Kinder-Care Learning Centers
Chicken Soup
Mini Maid Services Company

Foreword

by Tom Peters

FIRST WE HAD *THE 100 BEST COMPANIES TO WORK FOR IN AMERICA*. THEN *The Best Companies for Women* and another subtitled *The 100 Best Companies in America to Sell for Today*. Do we really need another, the Service 101, which is the heart of *The Service Edge*? My answer is unequivocal: Yes.

This is an important book. Superb service has always paid—just ask IBM, Walt Disney, Boeing, or L. L. Bean. But it was the exception, as the untoward service events of everyday personal and professional life so regularly demonstrate. Moreover, alternate strategies for business success existed.

Now, superb service is becoming a requirement for survival in our fragmenting, fast-changing, quality-conscious, and ever more competitive markets. "Service added"—unheard-of responsiveness, "smarter" products, and consultative service add-ons—is redefining almost every industry, including plumbing (American Standard makes a wonderful "smart bathtub"), trucks (Navistar's new expert systems allow extensive customization of every vehicle), and mail delivery (Federal Express et al. are redefining their huge industry).

For most of us, the same few companies come to mind when we think about unparalleled service, usually the Frito-Lays, Fed Exes, and McDonald'ses. But it's a short list, and the same old list at that—and our knowledge is often limited to a few "fantastic" (albeit true) service events. This unique book rectifies all those shortfalls. It gives us a full menu of exemplars to examine as we consider the new role of service as a—if not *the*—premier weapon for tomorrow in any industry you can name, starting with old-line manufacturing.

Yes, many of the old friends (L. L. Bean, Disney, Frito-Lay) are here, as should be the case. But I, who have followed these companies for a decade, learned afresh from each of the examples as they were reexamined and laid out by Ron Zemke and Dick Schaaf.

But most interesting (to me) were the wonderful surprises. Do you know why Don Beyer Volvo of Falls Church, VA, (one of the Service 101 included in these pages) has an 80 percent repeat business rate, while the industry norm is about a third of that? Read the answer here. Interested in the sheet- and towel-folding olympics at Mississippi Management, a firm that operates exceedingly successful Holiday Inns, Ramada Inns, etc.? Want to understand how Cineplex Odeon can afford—via service and its payoff—to invest $2.75 million in a theater in which others would invest, at most, a million dollars less? I was mesmerized by these examples and bet that you will be too.

You'll also learn from H&R Block, Kinko's (the copy superstars), stellar printer Quad/Graphics (and its Camp/Quad for customers), airport transportation specialist SuperShuttle, Jiffy Lube, Deluxe (the checkmakers), Riverside Methodist Hospital, and other well-known firms like Four Seasons (hotels), American Airlines, and American Express.

The whys and wherefores of service practices in these diverse companies are set out with rich detail. It would be difficult to imagine reading about any one story without picking up at least a useful tip or two—and, more important, a feel for how the service philosophy has become the linchpin of sustained success.

The cases are reason enough to read, and then review, this book. But there is more. The first several chapters provide a very helpful framework for thinking through the service issue in a strategic way. Full chapters are devoted to listening to customers, defining a service vision, setting precise service performance standards, training and empowering frontline people, and rewarding and recognizing success. Each topic, of course, has been covered in other management texts, but never exclusively in the context of developing an overriding commitment to service as the distinctive strategic advantage for the firm.

The book, by design, is chockablock with examples. But the point, as I see it, is not the provision of nifty anecdotal evidence (although this is a unique collection of such evidence): The real objective is to goad managers at the top, and throughout any firm, to appreciate just what an unstinting dedication to service can amount to—and to challenge each and every one of us to think about making such a commitment in our own outfits.

About This Book—and the Selection of the Service 101

THIS BOOK IS BOTH A CONTINUATION AND A UNIQUE NEW EFFORT. AS A RESULT, we present it in two parts. Part 1, the first seven chapters, continues the work of defining the basics of good service begun in 1985 in *Service America!: Doing Business in the New Economy*, by Ron Zemke and Dr. Karl Albrecht. Part 2 breaks new ground in attempting, for the first time, to choose and analyze a significant number of bona fide service leaders representing the full spectrum of the American economy.

Service America! set out to determine what superior service organizations were doing that so distinguished them in their customers' eyes. In 1985 the conventional wisdom—backed up by sound research and virtually everybody's personal experience—held that service in America was bad, and getting worse. Some observers wondered aloud whether American companies were capable of providing even mediocre service. Those few organizations that could be considered exemplars of high-quality service delivery were viewed as anomalies; dismissed as the product of special conditions or circumstances.

Yet we still believed that good service was possible—we could all agree that we'd know it if and when we ever experienced it—and significant to the consumer. Our goal in 1985 was to help American businesses plot a course for service quality improvement, drawing our guidance from those few companies—those service stars—that were, despite the odds and the alibis, serving their customers well, satisfying their customers' needs and expectations, and doing it in a consistent and financially profitable way.

In the years since *Service America!* was written, there have been a number of noteworthy changes, and many of them, we're happy to say, have been for the better. A significant amount of insightful research has been conducted on service and service management. The marketplace increasingly is rewarding companies for paying attention to their customers' wants and needs. The number of organizations taking a concerted run, however belatedly, at service quality improvement is staggering! As a result, there is much more to say because so much more is known about the basic principles of running a successful, service-focused organization than in 1985. There are so many more examples to point to and talk about. Suddenly, it seems, the sky is full of stars.

Today more organizations than ever before have taken up the challenge of providing superior service to their customers. They are listening, responding, and taking new, even novel, approaches to creating and managing high-quality service. And that means there are just that many more organizations doing things we can all learn from. Granted, the battle to eradicate mundane, lackadaisical, ineffective service is far from over. But we are finally getting a handle on how it should be waged. The idea that service improvement is a process, and a never-ending one at that, is sinking in, taking hold.

Part 1 of this new book lays out the operating principles for service quality improvement as they are being employed at the frontline by successful organizations in every sector and segment of the U.S. economy. It synthesizes what researchers, consultants, and managers across the country—ourselves included—have learned about creating high-quality customer service and using it effectively as a marketplace distinguisher.

This isn't a presentation of some bold new theory, mind you. Rather it's a distillation of what we've learned from ten years of asking and reasking the core question: "*How* do they do what they do, these service-excellent organizations, and do it so well and so much better than others in their industries?" With more companies learning to do it well, more pieces of the service improvement puzzle have now been put in place. A more detailed picture of what good service is, and how it is delivered, has emerged.

This book offers proof positive that things can, and do, change for the better. And our evidence of that is the individual case studies of service success that make up Part 2. We offer the Service 101 as role models for the new American manager trying to systemize and improve service as a competitive edge. And not content simply to name names, we examine the specific tactics each employs (from which come the key principles presented in Part 1) and the results each achieves.

The conventional wisdom may still maintain that service in America stinks. To that blanket indictment, we reply: Not always. Not everywhere. And not necessarily.

A Word about Organization

The profiles of those we consider exemplars of service superiority offer a cross-section of America's service-centered economy. Some names will be obvious and familiar, the ones that come quickly to mind when the topic is distinctive service—Disney, Marriott, Federal Express, Delta Air Lines, L. L. Bean, Nordstrom, McDonald's, and Domino's. Some, through service above and beyond the norm, have pioneered or come to dominate industry niches large and small—Ryder, Citicorp, Dun & Bradstreet, Fidelity Investments, and Xerox fit this description, as do Pizza Hut, Jiffy Lube, Kinder-Care, and CompuServe.

Others may not, at first blush, seem to be service providers at all, at least not by traditional definitions; nonetheless, Deluxe Corporation, the Battelle Memorial Institute, Caterpillar, Pioneer Hi-Bred, Frito-Lay, *The Wall Street Journal*, and the government of Montgomery County, Ohio, are on our list. And there are those that will, we suspect, be a bit surprising—organizations virtually unknown outside their industries or regions: Bob Evans restaurants, Ukrop's Super Markets, Miller Business Systems, Southern New England Telephone, USAA, A. G. Edwards & Sons and H. B. Fuller, Sun Distributors and NW Transport Services, First Wachovia and the Chubb Group, Shop'n Chek and Chicken Soup.

What unites them is their commitment to high-quality service, the service-based enhancements they add to conventional product quality, their innovativeness, their responsiveness, their involvement of people at the frontline—and the way their customers have come to see them as service leaders.

We have arranged the Service 101 according to industry niche and service commonality rather than by Standard Industrial Code or alphabetically. (The government's broad-brush categorization of service might as easily be labeled "miscellaneous," and when your names start with *Z* and *S*, you tend to take a dim view of alpha listings.) Consequently, in the section headed "Travel" you'll find three pacesetting airlines (Delta, American, and Piedmont—the last now part of USAir) and three providers of travel-related services (the American Automobile Association, Club Med, and SuperShuttle). Under "Health Care" are three hospitals of markedly different descriptions (Riverside Methodist, Beth Israel, and the Mayo Clinic) plus four companies (Merck, LensCrafters, Bergen Brunswig, and Shared Medical Systems) that offer products or services to health care providers.

Introducing each cluster of companies is a brief analysis of the conditions that influence service delivery in that specific industry or niche. Based on this stage setting, the choice of service leaders should be more understandable and the lessons they offer more instructive.

How the Service 101 Were Chosen

Naming the best of anything—be it ice cream, hotels, doctors, or pizzas—is asking for trouble. The U.S. economy is alive, diverse, and wondrously varied. Our chosen organizations are not 100-percent perfect each and every time they come out of the blocks. We found none of those. The members of the Service 101 attracted us because of their belief that they can *approach* perfection if they just keep at it, and impressed us with their audacity in trying, and succeeding, so often. It is their focus on, dedication to, and sometimes obsession with the effort that makes them worth learning from. These are not the *only* 101 organizations in America that provide noteworthy service. These are the 101 that impressed us as having the most to offer as good examples.

We made three basic assumptions in our research. First, against a backdrop of mediocre, lackluster, or downright unsatisfactory treatment, we expected providers of good service to be plainly visible. Such proved to be the case.

Second, we expected that customers in the many and various subsectors of the economy would already have "discovered" our service leaders, even if the public at large had not. Customers vote with their feet. They go where they find the kind of service they want. Research shows that companies that hit on winning service formulas are profitable, grow in market share, and inspire a lot of highly positive word-of-mouth commentary among the people they satisfy. We looked for evidence of that, and it was there in abundance.

Finally, we assumed that exemplary service providers would not only be known as such to their customers, but also to their own employees. Good performance in the service marketplace is no more an accident than is any other kind of business success. As in any other kind of endeavor, the activities of an outstanding service organization have to be planned, managed, measured, and modified to keep them on target. That means the employees have to be in on the secret—they have to be selected, trained, empowered, and rewarded appropriately. We expected to find plenty of evidence of that among the Service 101, and we weren't disappointed there, either.

Sifting the Evidence

Our quest began with an intensive review of over one hundred pieces of service quality research conducted in more than twenty industries. Some of the research we reviewed is very public and very good. Other materials were proprietary: in-company studies conducted by organizations researching their own customers or benchmarking themselves against their competition, and third-party research with an industrywide scope.

Many times the information shared with us wasn't all that flattering to those doing the sharing. It was shared nonetheless. That so many organizations were willing to let us "inside the walls" was both a measure of confidence in our confidential use of their data and evidence of their determination to acknowledge their service quality warts and do something about them—a commitment sadly lacking in many companies just four years ago. (It's not all sweetness and light: In far too many organizations, we still found management taking the position that if the customers say the company isn't performing up to their expectations, stop asking them—what do they know, anyway!)

A second source of information was expert opinion. We asked people who, because of their writing or consulting or teaching, have developed special insights into service delivery to tell us which industries, and which companies within those industries, they considered trendsetters. Then we made them explain why. Karl Albrecht, Ken Johnston, Herb Cohen, Tom Peters, James Heskett, and Bob Desatnick provided both information and likely candidates for our research. Their input was augmented by the suggestions of industry experts with perspective or insight on conditions in specific niches. Through them we gained access to additional data and found many a noteworthy enterprise.

A third invaluable source was the business, and especially the trade, press. The evolution and travails of America's service economy have not gone unremarked in the business media. In many industries, in fact, service has become *the* major story as companies struggle against each other, foreign challengers, and larger economic forces.

We realize, of course, that there are trends in press reporting. And having been subjected to it ourselves, we also are well aware that corporate communications and public relations professionals live and die on the basis of how often their employers are mentioned in various forums. But, as noted, we never assumed we'd have to invent the evidence of outstanding service. It's still so rare, so out of the ordinary, that there's no hiding it. We also found that those who regularly cover success and failure in the marketplace are more than adept at poking holes in smug claims of superiority and challenging the self-important and self-aggrandizing publicity release.

External sources helped us identify and discriminate among organizations. For the operating details on which the profiles are based, we pored over as much company-specific information as we could acquire. Through interviews, data base searches, and following the "paper trail" of internal documentation—annual reports, company publications and video magazines, corporate policy manuals, frontline training materials, and proprietary performance measures—we tried to see each company as it sees itself, its market, and its customers.

Finally, inevitably, there were our own judgment calls. Our research team met regularly to argue the case for including Company A, or against profiling Company B—or, in some cases, for or against naming any organization as exemplary of superior service in a given industry. That accounts for a number of obvious omissions, including car rentals, legal and accounting services, HMOs and nursing homes, and computer software. In some of those areas, we decided that customer-centered service was not an imperative; in others, we could find no consistent evidence of service superiority.

The omission of the education industry is deserving of a further note. Some members of our team felt that any similarity between the behavior of institutions of public and private education and a customer-conscious, service-centered organization was purely coincidental. Others of us were not so sure. When we looked at industrial training and human resources development—a $40 billion industry with which we're very familiar—we found there to be no real "best of show" research, and our own personal biases are too strong and too subjective to allow for objective, refereed judgment. So, reluctantly, we offer no one from the field of education, even though it is one of the most vital services for the future of the American economy and society at large.

The toughest decisions involved balance. Sometimes a commendable organization from one industry had to be passed over to allow us to include an equally commendable exemplar from another. In banking, for example, we found the state of service quality being advanced by a large number of local, regional, and national institutions. In the end we settled on but five of the more than a dozen organizations we considered. Superior service is also a noteworthy priority for far more hospitals than the three we could profile.

The final roster reflects our determination to select organizations that exemplify specific, service-centered responses to conditions in as many industry sectors and segments as possible—and the self-imposed limits of a list with only 101 spaces. We think we've captured the essence of the best service providers in the country. We hope you agree. But if you don't, that's fine. That's what makes horse races, beauty pageants, and diving competitions so much fun.

Inevitably, there are those who will disagree with our selections. And there are those who will be sure we've overlooked a near-perfect example of greatness. So it goes. And so it should, especially in the evaluation of service quality. As a customer, your experiences with an organization are the best measure you have of how good that organization is at creating and managing good, even memorable service.

If you feel strongly that we missed one of the best, most exquisite examples of an organization that delivers distinctive customer service in whatever field, don't keep it to yourself. Write us: P.O. Box 10068, Minneapolis, MN 55458. After all, there's always the 1999 edition.

THE
SERVICE
EDGE

PART 1

THE PRINCIPLES OF DISTINCTIVE SERVICE

The Customer Service Dilemma

SERVICE IN AMERICA TODAY IS TERRIBLE. EVERYBODY SAYS SO, RIGHT?

If true, that's ironic, because today's consumers are willing to pay a premium to have their basic needs met in a timely and efficient manner, and they'll be pleasantly surprised if they're treated with a little dignity and respect in the bargain. In principle they're not asking for much. In practice it seems that today's consumers—be they wholesale, retail, commercial, or trade—might as well ask for the moon as for a modicum of responsive, respectful treatment.

In setting out to find 101 bona fide service leaders, our work would appear to be cut out for us. It's an even bet that your day-to-day experience as a consumer bears out the general observation on the unhappy state of service quality in America today. Stories of rude, unhelpful clerks, telephone conversations put on hold until the next century, and organizations that can't be bothered to fix what they sell—much less apologize for the inconvenience of the malfunction—are much too commonplace. Indeed, such stories scarcely stir a murmur of surprise from listeners. More likely they are greeted with head-nodding agreement.

The Bad News

There is, to be sure, plenty of evidence beyond the aforementioned general assertion and your specific experience to validate the conclusion that service in America leaves a lot to be desired.

A study conducted by National Family Opinion for the Consumer Research Center of the Conference Board asked consumers in six thousand households to assess the value received for money spent on almost forty different products and services. Its conclusion: "The vast majority of consumers believe that they receive good value for their dollar when they purchase [products]. But there is a rather pervasive discontent with what they get for the money they pay for [services]." Key culprits include

3

repair work of all sorts and services indifferently rendered by banks, credit card companies, doctors, dentists, lawyers, and hospitals.

When Cambridge Reports of Cambridge, Massachusetts, asked fifteen hundred people, "How well do service companies meet your needs and concerns as a consumer?" only 8 percent rated them "excellent." Fifty percent reported "good," but 42 percent said "fair," "poor," or "depends on the service." And more than one in three agreed with the statement that "service industries care less than they did a few years ago about meeting my needs."

In 1979 and again in 1986, the Technical Assistance Research Programs Institute of Washington, D.C., conducted landmark studies of consumer complaint handling in America. TARP found that at any given moment, one in four customers of the average American organization is upset enough to stop doing business with it if they can find a reasonable alternative. Yet of those upset customers, only 5 percent will actually register a complaint, the other 95 percent preferring to switch rather than fight.

Why? According to TARP, consumers overwhelmingly believe that "complaining won't do any good; no one wants to hear about [my] problem." The TARP National Consumer Survey report goes on to conclude that this pessimism is well-founded: "More than 40 percent of the households experiencing consumer problems were unhappy with the action [taken] to resolve their complaints."

The news can be even more depressing when we move from general observations to specifics. Consider that in 1987 the Department of Transportation received more than 44,000 complaints from flyers about airline service, an increase of 25 percent over 1986. In 1987, airline flights arrived on time only about 66 percent of the time, losing 11 of every 1,000 pieces of luggage in the process. American Airlines bumped just 361 passengers over those twelve months, but the country's thirteen other largest air carriers delayed from 5,655 to 24,821 unwilling passengers due to overbooking. The growing mess prompted Senator Larry Pressler of South Dakota to conclude: "The quality of service, cleanliness of planes, the whole thing has deteriorated to the point where we need a national effort to upgrade it."

If flying is a chancy prospect, dining out can be a high-calorie ordeal. A 1987 Gallup Poll asked 1,045 people what makes them decide not to return to a given restaurant. Number one on the list of reasons, identified by fully 83 percent of the respondents, was poor service. Not food quality, not ambiance, not price. Poor service.

Can't go anywhere? Can't eat anywhere? Try to buy something. A 1987 *Washington Post* survey of consumers found that nearly half of all shoppers believe service is mediocre and getting worse. One in three respondents reported they had stopped going to a specific department store because of service-related problems. The biggest complaints: long waits for service, impolite salespeople, unavailability of advertised goods, salespeople who don't know the merchandise, problems with bills, and difficulty exchanging items.

What's true on the larger scale is every bit as true on a place-by-place basis. Representative of conditions around the country are statistics compiled by the Chicago/Northern Illinois Better Business Bureau. Between 1984 and 1986, complaints to it grew 26 percent, from 886 to 1,114 a day. Number one on its list: automobile service, up from 438 complaints in 1984 to 910 in 1986—an increase of 107 percent.

Like the mad anchorman in the movie *Network*, an increasing number of consumers and those who purport to speak for them have taken to throwing open the window and shouting, "I'm madder than hell and I'm not going to take it anymore!" Andy Rooney, newspaper columnist and *60 Minutes* curmudgeon, spared no feelings in a recent column when he complained: "Airlines have made travel so inconvenient, uncomfortable, unpredictable and expensive that I don't know why everyone doesn't stay home." His two most recent flights, he observed, "gave me some understanding of what slum housing must be like."

At a symposium we participated in, *CBS Morning News* consumer reporter Erin Moriarty was equally blunt. "The number one complaint I hear from viewers is about bad service," she noted. "It is shameful." A *Time* magazine cover pleads: "Puleeze! Will Somebody Help Me?" A feature in *Forbes* wonders: "It's Supposed To Be a Service Economy . . . Where's the Service?"

Upon returning to the U.S. in 1987 after eight years on assignment as Tokyo bureau chief for *Time*, Edwin Reingold wrote that he was "stunned" by the sharp decline in American service during his absence. His Rip Van Winkle accounting of the culture shock he experienced says it all much more eloquently than a book full of statistics:

"To a returning American grown accustomed to the civility and efficiency of modern Japan, the U.S. seems to have become a quagmire of bureaucracy, ineptitude, mean spirit and lackadaisy. In Los Angeles, New York, Miami and other cities, the repatriate is appalled and depressed by the lack of efficiency and of simple courtesy and caring.

"The deterioration of service is apparent almost immediately. When a new customer tries to open an account at the Wells Fargo Bank, an officer haughtily sniffs that it will not be possible until his signature has been verified and his banking history thoroughly checked. Then she simply turns away.

"At what used to be called a service station, the attendant, who sits behind bulletproof glass, can do nothing to help a novice learn the new greasy, smelly routine of pumping his own gas.

"The sign in the lobby of the West Los Angeles city hall says the planning department opens at 8 a.m. On a recent morning a clerk finally shows up at 9, without apology. As the petitioner pays the application fee for home-improvement permits, the clerk says the process will take 75 to 120 days. It is 132 days and still counting.

"When a clerk at an appliance store does not know how to turn on the tape recorder he is trying to sell a customer, something seems terribly wrong. The mind flicks back to Tokyo again, to the electronics center called Akihabara, where every clerk is knowledgeable and unfailingly polite, eager to make a sale.

"Nowhere is the malaise of American service more obvious than in the airline business. Cabin attendants often stand by unconcerned, aloof and bored, while old folks and children struggle with their bags. Untended airplane toilets reek. Every flight seems to be late and/or overcrowded.

"To an American old enough to remember American competence, work well done and pride in fine service swiftly rendered, it is jarring to realize how much Americans have forgotten, and how quickly."

Consumers without a column or television show with which to bludgeon offenders are finding other recourse. Satisfied people don't litigate, but the dissatisfied are going to court in ever-growing numbers over everything from medical treatment to investment advice. And the courts aren't the only forum. On September 27, 1987, dozens of passengers, irate that Eastern Airlines had cancelled their flight, stormed a ticket counter in Miami. Five were arrested and the brouhaha was widely reported. But it was only the number of people involved that made the incident unusual. Police were called out to handle angry passengers at the Miami airport thirty times in 1987.

Lights in the Darkness

The experiences and statistics are irrefutable. On the whole, service in America *is* bad. But there is a growing body of evidence that can no longer be ignored—significant, important data that says things are changing. There are companies, associations, and, yes, even governmental bodies that not only care about customer satisfaction but go to great lengths to provide it.

Montgomery County Administrator Claude Malone has a pact with his department directors: "Anything we are doing that inadvertently works to make our clients feel victimized rather than served by our system must change." Empowering managers with agreements like that is only one of the ways Malone's five-year "Service Excellence" program has begun to energize the men and women who serve the half a million people who live in his county. "I have a vision," he says. "Montgomery County—the best there is in providing service." Okay, it's not poetry. But it is a clear mandate to make a governmental body responsive to the needs of the governed. And Malone, as you'll see a little farther on, backs it up.

At Maryland National Bank, president Bill Daiger and his management team are determined to be viewed as the premier service provider in their regional market. So MNB ties its service to this pledge: "Maryland National Bank backs up your checking and money market accounts with the Performance Guarantee—absolute accuracy, all the time. If you ever find an account error, we'll make it right, right away . . . refund any MNB fees incurred . . . send letters of apology to anyone inconvenienced . . . and even pay you $10!" Initiated as a one-year program, the Performance Guarantee has become a permanent fixture. Customers love it, employees are proud of it, and the competition is afraid of it.

Mission Oaks Hospital in Los Gatos, California, has a service guarantee of another sort: no waiting. If a patient has to wait longer than five minutes for emergency room care, the bill is reduced by 25 percent. According to Jerry Boyle, the hospital's marketing director, the discount has to be delivered in just two cases per thousand. Meanwhile, Mission Oaks attributes a 25-percent increase in its acute-care business to the policy, and it has seen significant growth in "industrial volume"—people coming in from local businesses—as well. Both forms of growth are considered important to the hospital's ultimate success.

What are these people and hundreds others like them up to? Why do they go to such lengths? Are they unaware that this is the era of the hostile takeover, the leveraged buyout, and voracious cost containment? Don't they realize what's really important today?

The answer is yes on all counts. What's more, they know, and believe, two things about customer service that provide the marching orders for their organizations. First, "the dollars": Attending to superior customer service, doing whatever it may take to create high levels of customer satisfaction, and building a reputation for distinctive service into a competitive edge, pays bottom-line dividends. Second, "the sense": Being a little obsessed with creating a reputation for superior service is a lot more fun than running a business on the assumption that customers are creeps and that treating them well simply encourages their unreasonable demands.

Greenbacks for Gold Stars

These are not isolated instances. Service quality has indeed become a significant marketplace force, and the degree of its significance can be measured.

Sixty percent of Cambridge Reports' respondents say having their needs met is more important to them than price: "With the exception of Northeasterners, majorities in all population groups say customer satisfaction is more important than cost when purchasing a service." And what characteristics define high-quality customer service to this group? "The most frequent response was personal attention, [followed by] dependability, promptness, and employee competence."

Working with a three-thousand-company data base called "Profit Impact of Marketing Strategy," or PIMS for short, researchers at the Strategic Planning Institute, also in Cambridge, have compared the bottom-line results of companies rated superior service providers by their customers with the results of companies rated below average by *their* customers. They conclude that organizations with high service satisfaction ratings distinguish themselves on several bottom-line factors as well.

For starters the service leaders charge, on average, 9 to 10 percent more for their basic products and services. Yet, price notwithstanding, they grow twice as fast as their low-service competition and improve market share by an average of 6 percent per year. By contrast, the low flyers lose market share by as much as 2 percent annually. And that's not all. The organizations rated superior service providers in the PIMS study had an average return on sales of 12 percent compared to 1 percent for the bottom feeders.

The 1986 TARP study also speaks to the positive payoff for good customer service. According to John Goodman, TARP's president, complaining customers can turn into extremely loyal customers. Depending on the dollar value of their problems, only 9 to 37 percent of unhappy customers who *do not* complain will do business with the offending company a second time. But from 50 to 80 percent of those who *do* complain and subsequently have their complaint fully resolved (even if it doesn't turn out in their favor) report that they will ring the company's cash register again. Based on complaint resolution and repurchase records from a number of industries, TARP has even calculated a return on investment for successful complaint handling. The lowest ROI range is 15 to 75 percent for packaged goods companies; the highest, for retailers, is 35 to 400 percent.

Given this kind of evidence, we should expect to find our Service 101 firmly in the black. They are. Some, in fact, are business as well as service leaders. Safety-Kleen, for example, is the only business in U.S. corporate history to roll up 20-percent-per-year growth for seventeen straight years. Its business? Taking care of other businesses' environmentally sensitive garbage.

Shared Medical Systems and American Management Systems have built multi-million-dollar enterprises by making someone else's computers and information management systems work effectively. Shoney's restaurants can boast of nearly 30 years of consecutive quarterly increases in revenues and pretax operating income. Embassy Suites hotels have a gross profit margin significantly higher than competitors such as Hilton and Sheraton.

The obvious conclusion is that those organizations willing to commit to superior customer service profit on the bottom line. Those unwilling or unable to meet that standard do not and will not thrive—and possibly may not even survive. And therein lies the most troubling question: If service is so bloody important, and good service pays off so terrifically well, why has service in this country been so undeniably bad for so long?

Why Service Is Bad

It's a fair question. Any number of interesting answers have been proposed. There undoubtedly is more than a little truth in all of them.

One answer is that times and tastes have changed, but too many organizations have failed to stay abreast. Thanks at least in part to the rise of the two-income family and an unprecedented level of discretionary income, the consumer of the 1980s is a different breed of cat from the consumer of the 1960s.

Bernard Fauber, chairman of K mart, America's second largest retailer, contrasted the mindsets then and now for *U.S. News & World Report*: "In the 1960s came the throwaway generation—use a product awhile and throw it out, since it came cheaply. That's not the case now. Cheap, cheap, cheap, is not what they want. People demand products that will last, but for a low price. [Today] everything about the shopping trip, from the time you get to the parking lot until you reach the checkout lane, goes into making a store competitive—a place someone is naturally drawn back to. Low price is only one leg of a three-legged stool. Price and quality give you value, and atmosphere draws you back."

A study of service quality in the property and casualty insurance business conducted by the consulting firm Temple, Barker & Sloane sounds much the same theme. The report observes that many companies try to make up for poor service quality in the field through low pricing. But a study of the financial success experienced by insurance industry service leaders prompts this sobering judgment of "price flexible" insurers: "These firms will discover the importance of quality, not as a competitive weapon, but as an imperative for survival."

A second explanation of poor service quality has to do with the image and idea of working at a service job. The contention is that a lot of people find it somehow un-American to work at a job that requires one to "serve" others. Service jobs haven't the raw machismo of pouring steel, building automobiles, inventing computers, and taming the land. Service connotes "servant." Our forebears left the old country to divorce themselves from a world of immutable class distinctions and servitude, to grab for a piece of the American Dream.

For many Americans, cab-driving, table-waiting, and baby-sitting are perfectly acceptable ways to finance the becoming of something important like a lawyer or a doctor or a banker (all, by the by, "service" occupations), but they are unacceptable as a permanent station in life. An attitude common to such temporary service people is, "I'm not really doing this. I'm actually an actor-dancer-author-college student doing this for spending money. I'll quit as soon as I qualify for a real job."

We once listened in fascination as a congressman argued for changing representative's terms from two years to four. "It's so degrading and humiliating to have to go begging for money and votes every two years," he grumped. Ruling, we gathered, is less humiliating—and, of course, less accountable.

What it boils down to is the reality that people doing a job they view as beneath them generally do it poorly. And as often as not, unfortunately, they take out their frustrations on those they are expected to serve.

A third scenario holds that service has, for many years, been something "those people at the frontline do." It has not been seen as a critical management responsibility. Customer satisfaction certainly wasn't the sort of thing with which a person holding an Ivy League MBA would want or need to be concerned—not enough leverage. When service issues demanded attention, managers of this mindset waved a hand and created backwater customer service or consumer relations departments to handle the problem, freeing the Mahogany Row types to get on with the "real" business of the business.

To this day, American boardrooms and executive offices are full of senior managers who are all for signing service proclamations and making bold speeches reminding "those people down in the trenches" how important customers are, but who can't seem to find the time to actually "work" the problem of improving bad service.

A fourth view is, stripped to its shorts, the old bromide, "You can't get good help around here anymore." William Kolberg, president of the National Alliance of Business, blames poor service on demographics and the school system: Fewer people are in the entry-level age range, he reasons, and those willing to apply for service jobs today have been poorly schooled.

He points out that people who deal with the public are usually the lowest-paid employees in the company. Those willing to take these minimum-wage jobs are most likely to be low-skilled as well, the young people in the twenty-one–to-twenty-five age bracket who, according to the U.S. Department of Education, can't figure the change for a two-item restaurant meal, are hard-pressed to decipher a bus schedule, and can barely read and write.

If they lack such basic skills, Kolberg asks, how many also lack the human skills necessary to make a customer feel well enough served to want to come back? His conclusion: "Not only must companies closely screen employees to select good ones, but they must pay good salaries to keep them." Lots of our chosen exemplars have long since figured that out and made it standard operating procedure.

Unraveling the Knot

We see merit in all of these explanations. And we certainly see how redressing the conditions some of them describe—low pay, for example—could, in the right circumstances, have a positive impact on service quality.

But at the same time we suggest that these theories and explanations deal with side issues. They miss the main points, the problems most in need of solution, the ones that must be addressed first if anything approaching significant improvement is to be attained in American business. It is our contention that when and where service in America today is found wanting, the primary reasons are almost always, first, a thorough lack of skill and knowledge about how to manage service and, second, an equally thorough lack of commitment to service quality as a serious organizational goal.

Service quality is an issue that can be addressed most directly through the actions of managers trained and motivated to satisfy—nay, as Armstrong World Industries says it, to delight—their customers. Though good service is most frequently seen by the consumer as a satisfactory outcome of an interaction with a company's frontline personnel, the most powerful influence on that interaction comes through those myriad things we refer to under the umbrella heading "management."

We base this logic on our research into the Service 101: Acknowledged bastions of service excellence, organizations admired and respected for the quality of service they deliver on a reliable, regular basis, exist in all geographic regions and in all industries. They come in all sizes, large, medium, and small. Some have been around for a decade or two, some for more than a century. They are in both the private and public sectors.

These are the organizations about which managers of poor-performing organizations love to say, "If we only had people like that. If only we were as flexible, as creative, as efficient, as responsive as that. If only we could be as organized, as well funded, as dominant, as innovative in our field." They can. Those organizations do exist. And since they exist, they can be studied, copied, and emulated. Their successful ideas can be adopted by others.

We've all seen it happen. Prior to 1955, when the gates of Disneyland swung open for the first time, there was no such thing as a theme park. Walt Disney and his management team pioneered the concept. Today it's a very healthy industry. The Disney parks in Florida and California are the best-known and among the very best-run of the breed, but they are far from the sole occupants of the theme park niche. And while some of these parks are managed by people who started in a Disney park, just as many are not.

An astute grasp of the obvious? Something you could have guessed without bothering to leave home? Probably. The point is that the vaunted Disney "magic"—that mystical pixie dust you may have wished from time to time you could sprinkle over your own company and employees—is no magic at all. It is, as you'll read in a bit, a set of highly transferrable, learnable principles that are portable beyond that specific industry as well.

Our premise is simple. In industry after industry there are exemplary performers. Disney, Marriott, Federal Express, Dun & Bradstreet, Amalgamated Bank, and Acura automobile dealerships thrive in the same economy we all confront, drawing people from the same labor force, facing the same day-to-day business conditions.

You can learn from them. We have. They are eminently clonable.

Creating Distinctive Service:
A Willful Management Act

MANAGING THE DELIVERY OF HIGH-QUALITY SERVICE IS AS DIFFERENT FROM MANaging the production of a product as the farm is different from the factory. Our research and our experience both support the contention that the art of designing, developing, and delivering distinctive customer service is a special practice with unique problems and opportunities. Yet most organizations still have the mindset that managing is managing is managing.

We do not suggest that managing service delivery and managing product production are so completely different as to have nothing in common. That would be too extreme an assertion, and unfair to some pretty good managers who have been quite successful without ever bothering to concern themselves with the differences.

Just the same, we firmly believe the differences between product and service are significant—that managing the stay of a patient in a hospital is clearly different from managing the assembly of the left front fender of a Chevrolet. If management is the key to systematic service improvement, it follows that managers must be aware of and understand the differences when they focus on creating distinctive service.

We're not alone here. Marketing experts such as Leonard L. Berry of Texas A&M University, Chris Lovelock of Lovelock and Associates, and Lynn G. Shostack of Joyce International have been making the same point for several years. To manage service effectively, especially if you are coming to the task from a product background, you must first understand the unique characteristics of a service, the things that distinguish it from a product.

Service vs. Product

To begin with, a product is a tangible, a service an intangible. A product takes up shelf space, has a shelf life, can be inventoried, depreciated, and taxed. A service doesn't exist until it is called for by the

13

recipient. It needs no shelf space, has no shelf life, and most certainly is not an asset that can be easily inventoried.

Quality control of a product involves weighing, measuring, and comparing the finished good against a rigorous, engineered standard. Quality control of a service entails watching a process unfold and evaluating it against the consumer's judgment. The only completely valid standard of comparison is the customer's level of satisfaction. That's a perception—something appreciably more slippery to measure than the physical dimensions of a product.

What's more, a service can't be demonstrated or sampled prior to purchase. A hospital can't put fifty thousand freeze-dried appendectomies in little envelopes and send them out to the community with the invitation, "Try this. If you like it, come on down to Murphy's Hospital. We have a whole bunch more on the shelf." The intangibility of the service means you must persuade customers that what you can do is something they want and need done, and that you can do it well. Small wonder that testimonials and performance guarantees are invaluable in service marketing.

Then there's the fact that the sale, production, and consumption of a service take place almost simultaneously—and frequently, the purchaser plays a role in the production of the service itself. Take a haircut: The service cannot and does not start until you show up, hop into the chair, and explain what you want. You participate in the service's design when you say you want the "do" you just saw in *Cosmo* or *GQ*. Give the barber/beautician some feedback—"a little more off the top, please . . . no, I would not like a green tint"—and you also are participating in the production of the service.

Your role is important. Without it the cutter would have no way of knowing exactly what you want, or how he or she is doing at pleasing you. But to play your role, you have to "know your lines." You must have some idea of what it is you want done to your current coiffure, determine whether this cutter can actually do what you want done, and figure out how to go about describing what you want. Making the customer knowledgeable enough to specify the service and give useful feedback during and after its delivery is a form of customer education. The more complex the service, the more important that education becomes.

Next, it is important to recognize that the receiver's expectations—and perceptions—of the service are integral to his or her satisfaction. Consumer desires can be very specific or very vague, but either way they become part of the service process. You walk into a McDonald's or a Wendy's with a set of expectations: "Burger, shake, fries; eat it and beat it." If you are met by a tuxedoed maitre d' with a menu and led to a table with flowers and linen, your expectations are not being met. In fact, what might at first look like superior service may actually strike you as bad service because it is so far removed from your specific, walking-in-the-door expectations.

Professor Berry puts the problem of expectations in perspective: "Consumer perceptions of service quality result from comparing expectations prior to receiving the service and actual experiences with the service. Quality evaluations derive from the service process as well as the service outcome."

In his analysis, what we, as consumers, think we are going to receive, compared and contrasted with what we perceive is being received, *and* the process we go through receiving it, determine our level of satisfaction. It is an all-or-nothing, three-factor formula based on the assumption that the level of our satisfaction with the entire process is the critical link to repeat business.

Consequently, service satisfaction is the result of a dynamic, not static, encounter. The consumer evaluates both process and outcome, and values both. Poor product can't be overcome by a good relationship with a customer, at least not for long. Nor will good product overcome poor treatment unless the situation is a unique one. A physical examination conducted by a smelly, grumpy, rude, and nasty physician is a bad physical, regardless of how technically competent the results. When you do not enjoy the experience, you are not likely to want to repeat it, nor will you recommend it to others.

The mandate is clear: To create a distinctive level of customer service, management must understand—and even on occasion shape—the customer's prepurchase expectations, influence the customer's evaluation of postpurchase quality, and ensure that the process of being served is not only painless and easy but, when possible, enjoyable. We must manage not only what we do for the customer, but the way we do it—the totality of the customer's experience with the organization.

Complicating that task is the reality that service expectations are more variable than product expectations. Two people may hear the same promise—"Yes, ladies and gentlemen, Smedly Weight-Off Clinic guarantees easy, painless weight reduction in ten days"—yet walk through Smedly's door with very different expectations of what "easy" and "painless" and "guarantee" mean.

Because a service is most frequently provided to or for one individual at a time, being able to respond to that variability is essential. The barber or hairdresser must be able to adjust to the customer's head and hair because the "raw stock," so to speak, is controlled by the customer. "I'm sorry, sir, your head is not round enough for me to work on," won't do if the barber hopes to make a living.

A more extreme case is the physician who must balance a dozen variables to make a diagnosis and play out a dozen scenarios in prescribing a course of treatment. If every appendix was like every other, or 95 percent a tolerable level of surgery survival, medicine would be an easy, inexpensive, highly automated craft. It isn't. It requires discretion, extensive and intensive preparation, and skill.

In a sense, every service provider experiences the variety of input a physician does. Every service provider is expected, by the customer anyway, to respond to the uniqueness of each special situation. Few may be expected or encouraged to respond to those uniquenesses 100 percent of the time with 100-percent accuracy, as a physician must, but the expectation is there just the same.

"Controlling" for Diversity

The range of "input variables"—essentially the customer's unique expectations—makes the industrial model of production management of limited value to service organizations concerned with providing a high-quality experience. Controlling a service delivery process for uniformity of outcome usually leads to diminished rather than enhanced customer satisfaction. People don't give you high marks for treating them in a robotized, mechanical, one-size-fits-all fashion. The service manager's task is to support diversity of response between the customer and the organization, especially between the customer and frontline contact people.

That means people are more individually important to service delivery than they have been considered in product production. Delivery of a service usually requires human interaction; seller and buyer come in contact to create the service. You don't know the thousands of people who were involved in designing and building the car you're driving, and it doesn't matter. But you do remember the salesperson who walked you around the lot and negotiated the deal. And if you don't remember that one person favorably, you'll buy your next car someplace else.

The automated teller machine (ATM) is a perfect example of a logical, reasonable, rational approach to service delivery that should work but doesn't because of the human contact factor. It was created to decrease both transaction costs and customer complaints about long lines and rude service. It has been with us for well over fifteen years. Yet nationally only 48 percent of bank customers ever use ATMs, and only one in three of us uses them for most of our transactions.

Why the low penetration? Research clearly shows that customers are distressed by their lack of trust in machines and the missing human contact. Syndicated columnist Ellen Goodman calls the ATM "the computer wall where I go for money—I refuse to call it a bank."

The point isn't about the future of ATMs, but about the human factor in service. Customers frequently expect human contact from service providers, and they value that contact. When Cambridge Reports asked people what they think of when they hear the word "service," the most frequent response was some variation of personal attention, responsiveness, politeness of employees. Service design must account for that response, that expectation, on the part of the customer.

That's especially true when something goes wrong. When a product breaks, malfunctions, or in some way fails to meet expectations, the customer gets mad, huffs and puffs, and more frequently than not brings it back for exchange or repair. He may be miffed, even upset, but the discontent is generally focused on the product. When a service fails and needs redressing, the consumer focuses squarely on the service provider. The attitude becomes, "Someone did this *to me*. This is a personal affront."

That's dangerous ground. Both buyer and seller, the server and the served, have personalities, emotions, personal experiences, and pet peeves—and neither has an on/off switch. The over-the-telephone collision of two people, both of whom have just experienced bad weekends, long commutes, and reprimands for being late, is a human situation—and as likely a service encounter as any other. Despite all the personal baggage, however, the server must remain in control and be able to cope with the situation, making that human contact turn out well for the customer and for the organization.

Finally, exerting quality control over a service requires monitoring of both processes and attitudes. Everything counts for the service customer. Eric Hoffer observes in *The True Believer*: "You can tell the novice from the journeyman carpenter not so much by products they produce, but by the sweat on their brows. One works so much harder to accomplish the same end than does the other." If you are making A-frames or automobiles, the display of effort doesn't matter. If you are delivering a service, it does, because consumers take whatever data they can find, judge it by their own personal standards and expectations, and decide whether or not they are satisfied. When the flip-down tray on the seat in front of the passenger is wobbly and coffee-stained, the passenger starts to doubt not just the cabin crew, but engine maintenance and flight deck competence as well.

Process covers a lot of territory. Picture a medical technician, trainee grade, who walks into your hospital room knees shaking, chin trembling, blood sample tray rattling in sweaty hands. How likely is it that such an entrance will instill confidence or a cooperative attitude in you? Knowing nothing about the competence of the technician to draw a blood sample, you already are finding the "service" less than satisfactory. The process as it has been unfolding—the performance viewed since the curtain went up, the door opened, and the tech walked in—is all the data you have so far. And regardless of how spurious or misleading that data may in fact be, you just don't like what you're seeing.

Yogi Berra said, "You can observe a lot by just watching." Customers do just that. Then they report what they see to other potential customers. They'll explain a memorable restaurant experience by saying things like "the food was great, the service was impeccable, and did they put on a show with the caesar salad! Just a super evening." They'll recommend a neighborhood bar because "lots of good people come in—you can always get into a good conversation or hustle up a pool game." They judge a multitude of facets in the service performance based on their observations of the process and the attitudes experienced.

Both influence service satisfaction, but attitudes are by far the trickier to control. Customers seldom *know* what a service worker's attitude is toward them, but that doesn't stop them from making a satisfaction judgment based on what they *think* it is. To them, the clerk who rings up an order with a telephone cradled in the crook of his neck, a personal conversation in progress, no eye contact, and a wad of gum in his mouth, is sending a clear message: "You're not important enough for me to treat you with even a modicum of respect. You're a duty, not a person." On the basis of that unpleasant encounter, which at most may last a minute or two, a decision is made about that store as an acceptable place to shop.

Notice that we haven't even considered what kind of store it is, or what kind of product it sells, or how wonderful the product itself might turn out to be. It doesn't matter. Somebody else sells the same product. That's where the customer is going next time.

In their book, *Contact: The First Four Minutes*, psychiatrists Leonard and Natalie Zunin observe that there is a short moment in time, a four-minute window of opportunity, when satisfying human contacts will be established or denied. This threshold exists in commercial as well as private affairs. It is as critical to customer satisfaction as it is to friendships or even marital relations.

Exemplary organizations, the 101 in this book and others like them, accept the challenge to manage the special conditions that distinguish service from product toward a successful outcome. They have a common standard of performance:

When the customer is satisfied, really pleased to be doing business with us, we will be successful and profitable.

Moments of Truth . . .

In *Service America*, we reported that successful, service-focused organizations
- Are obsessive about listening to, understanding, and responding swiftly to changing *customer* wants, needs, and expectations
- Create and communicate a well-defined, customer-inspired, service *strategy*
- Develop and maintain "customer-friendly" service delivery *systems*

and
- Hire, inspire, and develop customer-oriented frontline *people*.

These findings were explained by using a Triangle of Service, with strategy, systems, and people at the points, surrounding a customer placed dead center inside. It is still an effective model for thinking about customer service, and should inspire four relevant questions in organizations seeking to create, or extend, a competitive advantage through the delivery of high-quality service. From the deliverer's perspective, they are:

- How well do we understand our *customers* and their expectations of us?
- Have we defined our *strategy*—our mission or goal—in terms of customer expectations?
- Are our delivery *systems* accessible and approachable (designed to make us "easy to do business with," or simply for our own operational convenience)?
- Are our *people* selected, trained, empowered, and rewarded for providing exceptional service to the customer?

Finding the answers to those questions is a challenge for any organization trying to survive, let alone thrive, in today's service-oriented economy. In Scandinavia in the early 1980s, a very bright service executive figured out how to bring the fuzzy, intangible aspects of service into sharp focus so they can be identified and managed on the customer's behalf. From Jan Carlzon, CEO of Scandinavian Airlines System (SAS), comes the concept of managing the customer's "moments of truth"—the transactions the customer has with the organization.

The imagery suggests that, like the bull and the bullfighter, there are points where the customer comes eye to eye with your organization and something fundamental and memorable takes place. What customers know of you comes from those encounters. How they feel about you is a result of the quality of those encounters. Moments of truth come in many forms: advertising, telephone calls, face-to-face conversations, use of the product or service, bills, complaints, and more. In fact, *a moment of truth occurs any time the customer comes in contact with some aspect of the organization and uses that opportunity to judge the quality of service the organization is providing*.

It's important to listen to customers to find out what their moments of truth are and how well they are being managed—how the customer rates the organization's performance at each of those moments of truth. One of the greatest temptations is to believe that, because of years of experience in "the business," whatever that business is, we know what the customer wants and needs even better than the customer does. Time and again, we find this is just not the case. Our logic is not necessarily the customers' logic, nor are our perceptions of quality and value the same as theirs.

In workshops, there's an exercise we use to make the point. We ask participants to list the five most important things they expect of a coffee break—not an office or on-the-job coffee break, but one of those organized, orchestrated things that take place at meetings and seminars in hotels and convention centers. Invariably the five things that head the list are availability of hot coffee or some equivalent such as tea or soda, the ability to move through the line quickly and come back for a refill, having restrooms nearby and available in ample number for the group, the availability of telephones for quick calls back to the office, and room to stand and talk with other participants.

When we ask catering managers—the coffee break professionals—what they think of when they prepare for a coffee break, we find a much different focus. Their top five considerations are timely availability of hot and flavorful coffee, extra consumables (rolls, muffins, fresh fruit, juice, plus alternatives to coffee), an attractive display in the serving area, clean and undamaged china and silver, and clean tables and table dressings.

Who is crazy here? No one. Left to our own devices, we pay more and more attention to things of less and less importance to the customer. We simply "assume" the restrooms and the telephones because our attention is focused on setting up the tables and arranging the pastries in an attractive layout. But customers notice and are upset when the restroom is closed for cleaning just when the coffee break is called, or the nearest phone is a city block away.

Moments of truth are not created equal, however. Some have more impact than others. A few years ago a major hotel corporation surveyed people who had stayed in company properties across the country about the quality of the service they had experienced—moments of truth identified in previous research. The last question the interviewer asked was would they stay in the same hotel again. The researchers calculated that 70 percent of the difference between those who would come back to a given hotel and those who would not was attributable to customer encounters with people at the front desk.

To manage efficiently and effectively, we must have a way of deciding the rank order of impact each specific moment of truth has on overall service quality. Knowing not only the moments of truth but their relative impact on customer satisfaction is critical to the resource allocation process, the trade-offs we make as we devise a service strategy and design the delivery systems to implement it.

. . . and Cycles of Service

Once you know the the customer's moments of truth, you can lay them out and examine their interrelationships in a meaningful way. If moments of truth are the discrete points of contact the customer has with your organization, the "cycle of service" is the repeatable, closed-loop sequence of those events.

A cycle begins at the very first point of contact. It may be when the customer sees your advertisement, gets a call from a salesperson, receives a catalog in the mail, finds a story about your organization on the 6 o'clock news, or contacts you for information. It ends—temporarily, you hope—when the customer considers the service complete, only to begin anew when the customer comes back for more.

Mapping moments of truth around a cycle of service can be most revealing. When GTE North, a GTE subsidiary that provides residential telephone service in ten midwestern states, began looking at its residential repair services, it assumed that the cycle of service began with a customer contacting one of its repair answering centers for help or information. Careful study, however, revealed that from the customer's point of view the first moment of truth was the discovery that the phone wasn't working. The second moment of truth was determining *how* to contact the phone company when the phone had stopped working. Calling the repair center was actually the customer's third moment of truth—and, in fact, calling was only one of several options used to report phone trouble, according to Bill Griswald, the company's service quality guru.

Tracing the cycle of service showed that finding ways to make reporting a problem easy and positive, not just improving the way customers are handled when they have a problem with their phone service, was important to the service management process. And if managing each moment of truth is important to customer satisfaction, then the management focus had to include finding ways to have a positive impact on customers at the instant they perceived a problem.

Recovery

The blind spot in many service delivery systems is that they fail even to anticipate that something can go wrong. In production management, allowance is made for breakage, spoilage, duds, and units that simply don't meet the specs. Some of this bad product can be flagged through quality control before it ever reaches a customer. For product that fails in the field, there are repair facilities and service technicians.

Service systems, on the other hand, are too often managed as though anything other than perfection is inconceivable. Very few businesses address the redress of service errors in a preplanned, systematic fashion. The attitude seems to be, "Don't even mention it. Talking about service problems as if they can happen is likely to cause them!" Yet customers make as many mistakes as the people serving them do. (The idea that the customer is always right is wrong. You simply treat the customer as if he or she is right in those instances.)

Even if the company never flubs its lines, there will be times when needs and expectations fail to mesh to everyone's satisfaction. In those cases, it's crucial to address customer problems and service delivery glitches as quickly and as completely as possible. When the unexpected but unavoidable occurs, the Service 101 are ready, willing, and able to swing into action. They work as hard when things go wrong as they do to make things go right the first time out.

The word for that is "recovery." It originated with Donald Porter of British Airways, based on that newly privatized airline's initial efforts to understand customer expectations after years of operating as a government-run entity: "It had never occurred to us in any concrete way. 'Recovery' was the term we coined to describe a very frequently repeated concern: If something goes wrong, as it often does, will anybody make a special effort to set it right? Will someone go out of his or her way to make amends to the customer? Does anybody make an effort to offset the negative effects of a screw-up? Does anyone even know where, when, or how to deliver a simple apology?"

The word is a good one. It connotes an effort to return things to a normal state, to make whole again. Most organizations have the traditional service department—a group charged with fixing what breaks. That is a reactive and very minimal kind of recovery. More than damage control, a good recovery system is a positive, managed effort to attack a problem so thoroughly and wholeheartedly that there will be no possibility the customer might walk away discouraged, disappointed, or wishing he had never gotten involved with us in the first place.

Is it worth it? Data compiled by TARP is compelling. Its National Consumer Survey, conducted for the United States Office of Consumer Affairs, found that resolving problems quickly and efficiently had a positive impact on customer loyalty. Consumers who had problems, complained, and had their problems satisfactorily resolved were more likely to be "brand loyal" than consumers *without problems*, and significantly more loyal than customers who experienced problems but failed to register a complaint. Even in instances when the complaint was not resolved in their favor, nearly half of the customers who made the effort and were listened to indicated that they would give the offending company another try. Working to normalize relations with an unhappy customer is one of the highest-impact activities a service organization can undertake.

Building an effective service recovery system begins with two things: knowing the customer's expectations, and understanding what the service breakdown looks and feels like from the customer's viewpoint. There are two distinct levels to the latter: annoyance and victimization.

Annoyance is the minor feeling of irritation we get when the service experience falls slightly short of what we expected. Victimization is a more serious breakdown, and engenders a major feeling of ire, frustration, or pain. Recovery takes a different form depending on whether the customer feels annoyed or victimized. The difference between the two is easy to see from specific examples.

- When your flight is one hour late, you are annoyed. When being one hour late causes you to miss the last connection to your destination and you have to sleep in the airport overnight, you have been victimized.
- When one of your two phones is out of service, you are annoyed. When your only phone is out of service and you have a heart condition, you feel victimized.
- When your car breaks down and you have to ride to work with a neighbor, you're annoyed. When you are a traveling salesperson and the car breaks down because the repair shop, for the third time, failed to fix a problem, and now you're going to miss several previously scheduled calls on very short notice, you have been victimized.

Central to the difference between annoyance and victimization is the way the customer feels about the breakdown. When the customer is left dependent rather than merely inconvenienced, and truly angry rather than mildly irritated, you are dealing with a victim. Any service breakdown will require the deliverer to jump through a few hoops to get the customer back to neutral. More hoops are required to correct victimization than annoyance.

A sequence of as many as five ingredients are involved in effective recovery. The first two are imperative for annoyed customers; all five are required for working with customers who feel victimized.

Apology. Recovery absolutely demands some acknowledgment of error immediately following a breakdown in service. If the flight from Denver to Dallas is more than an hour late taking off, yet the flight attendant makes the standard FAA speech and the pilot comes on the intercom to announce the altitude with no mention of the lateness, you begin to wonder whether the airline is so accustomed to being late that its people treat it as normal.

Apology is more powerful when delivered in the first person. A corporate "We're sorry" lacks the sincerity and authenticity that comes when a person takes responsibility and acknowledges on behalf of the organization that the customer was mistreated.

Urgent Reinstatement. Because both the outcome and the process of service delivery must be managed, a sense of urgency is important even when things go as planned. It has new, more critical meaning when applied to recovery. Sometimes, an expression of gallant intent is sufficient, but the customer must perceive that the deliverer is doing the best job possible to get things back into balance without delay. There are points for good intentions and customer-driven effort. Part of the power of this ingredient is the demonstration that the deliverer has the customer's interests at heart.

If the customer is annoyed, apology and urgent reinstatement, done well, are likely to return things to normal. If the customer has been victimized, recovery is more complex, and the following three ingredients must be added to the recipe.

Empathy. Expressing compassion may be the mother lode of all service gold. Victimized customers are likely to insist that before you attempt to redress their views or feelings you first demonstrate that you understand them. Empathy is the expression of "I know how you must feel—I care about you—I can relate to your misfortune—I can identify with what has happened." In its highest form, the customer feels heard, affirmed, cared about.

Sincere expressions of empathy are quite different from expressions of sympathy. Sympathy occurs when one shares another's pain. Empathy is showing compassion for the person in pain without feeling that pain personally—it's a shoulder to cry on, a source of strength. There are great risks with sympathy because the helper joins the helpee rather than the other way around. Those who resort to sympathy are themselves "one-down" and prove the axiom misery loves company. Where sympathy is helping someone feel better about being weak, empathy is the kind of understanding that helps them feel strong again.

A Hawaiian woman who spoke limited English was en route to Roanoke, Virginia, recently to visit her daughter. After six thousand miles, eighteen hours, and four stops, she got to Charlotte, North Carolina, only to learn that the Roanoke airport was closed due to snow and ice. On her last leg of the journey, and now only one hour from her destination, she was informed she would have to stay the night in Charlotte. A Piedmont Airlines gate attendant made all the arrangements, called her daughter for her, then sat with her for a while, asking the woman questions about Hawaii and her daughter. As tears welled up in the woman's eyes, the gate attendant spontaneously embraced her and said, "You've come so far, I know you really want to see her." The woman smiled through her tears and said, "I'm glad you are my friend."

The apology tells the victimized customer that it matters there was a breakdown; empathy adds that it matters that a person was hurt in the process. A wise service expert once said, "When service fails, first treat the person, then the problem."

Symbolic Atonement. The fourth ingredient in the recovery recipe is some symbol of atonement. At its most basic level, it is a gesture that clearly says, "We want to make it up to you." Atonement is not a pound of flesh. The symbol or gesture is the key. It's the "It's on us—no charge—here's a coupon" type of demonstration.

Our colleague Chip Bell tells of walking into a crowded fast-food restaurant for a sandwich, small fries, and soft drink to take back to his office. When he placed the order, he was told it would take about three minutes for the sandwich. It was noon, lines were long, some delay was acceptable. But as the minutes stretched to nearly ten, he grew increasingly impatient.

Eventually the order was ready and service recipient came eyeball to eyeball with the provider. Before he could vent his anger, the cashier was already in tune with his feelings. "I'm very sorry," she offered. "I know you were in a hurry. I gave you a large order of fries because you had to wait. I hope you'll come back again." Apology, urgent reinstatement, empathy, symbolic atonement—right out of the recovery textbook. That kind of performance is no accident. The system was designed, the employees trained, for the eventuality of a breakdown. The cashier, Chip adds, invariably with an expression of awe, was all of seventeen years old.

Follow-up. This last ingredient may or may not be critical to quality service when the customer is only annoyed. The data are mixed. It is unequivocally important if the customer is a victim. Not only does it provide a sense of closure, it serves to affirm the authenticity of the recovery response and provides a means of feedback.

Properly managed, follow-up also can be a tool to promote the self-esteem of the service deliverer. The frontline person who takes a beating when things go wrong can walk away feeling good as a result of follow-up. "We may have messed up, but things are okay now."

Not long ago, we met up with Chip Bell on our way to check in at the Long Wharf Marriott in Boston. He couldn't wait to tell us about the recovery process he'd just observed at the hotel's front desk. A traveler had been attempting to check in, only to be told that the hotel was overbooked and no room was available for him.

"I'm sorry," Chip had heard the manager on the desk explain. "We're overbooked, and even though you have a reservation, I'm afraid we don't have a room for you this evening. I know this isn't acceptable, and we apologize for it. What I've done is taken the liberty of making a reservation for you at a hotel near here. Just take this card to the front desk at the Parker House. They're expecting you. I know you're upset. I would be too in your place. But I hope you'll find the accommodations there as acceptable as here. And here's ten dollars. That should cover the cab ride over there, plus the tip."

Hardly mollified, the guest had taken the note and the cash and walked away muttering to himself. Chip, however, had stuck around, so he saw an already good example of recovery extended to include follow-up. As the disgruntled traveler walked out to the cab stand, the desk manager turned to an associate and said, "He doesn't look like he's very happy with us yet. Give him about fifteen minutes to get over there, get registered, and up to his room. Then call him up and ask him if the accommodations are acceptable. While you're at it, invite him to come back tomorrow morning and have breakfast, as our guest, on our concierge level. Tell him we'll leave an envelope in his name with the concierge with a note for the hostess at the restaurant. That ought to do it."

We don't know if it did for that particular traveler. But it did for us. That's because when we walked up to the desk and asked for the room reserved in our name, the manager gave us a professional smile and said, "I'm sorry. We're overbooked this evening, and even though you have a reservation, I'm afraid we don't have a room. I know this isn't acceptable, and we apologize for it. What I've done is taken the liberty of making a reservation for you at the Parker House . . . " We let him work his way through the whole recovery process, and we were just as impressed when we were the object of the effort as we had been when we'd heard about it happening to somebody else.

A final note: Complaints are an asset when they are handled well. TARP's data clearly supports a well-designed, conscientious recovery effort. It also suggests, however, that a poor or grudging recovery effort may be worse than no effort at all. In the words of the study's authors, "Some companies handle complaints so poorly that they would be better off not soliciting complaints." In these cases, they note, doubly dissatisfied customers indicate less inclination to patronize a business again than those who suffered the first breakdown in silence.

What the Good Ones Do

After completing the profiles of the Service 101, we stepped back and asked ourselves what these organizations that top the customer polls, stand out in the industry studies, and are admired by peers and competitors alike have in common. Some of the commonalities we knew from our previous work and the research and reporting of others to be symptomatic of distinguished service providers. Others surprised us because they turned up so regularly in so many different industries.

Careful selection and thorough training, for instance, are both well recognized as common components in the success of many businesses, but we were impressed by how often Service 101 organizations viewed them as almost a mandatory couplet. Invariably, it seemed, those that are painstaking in the employee-selection process turned out to be equally thorough in training those employees for top performance. As the CEO of one organization put it, "If we are going to take this much care in finding talent, it behooves us to develop it to the fullest."

Some characteristics are difficult to put into words in a useful way. Take the word "earnest": It describes an attitude frequently encountered, but how do we explain that so it is helpful in your attempts to bring about change? All we can say is that one of our lasting impressions is of management people in company after company—and frontline people as well—who are *earnest* in their belief in and dedication to producing high-quality service for their customers.

We were impressed by the number of creative ways service providers are finding to serve better and please more. "Year of the Customer" and "Service Is Our Key to Success" have become seemingly universal corporate slogans for the late 1980s, but real work is in back of many of these campaigns. Far more organizations than most of us suspect are succeeding at devising unique, interesting, and effective ways to distinguish themselves in their customers' eyes—more ways, in fact, than we could ever hope to catalog. This is not an observation we reserve to the Service 101. Many of the literally hundreds of companies we looked into but did not, for one reason or another, profile have their fair share of people working hard, and succeeding, at building a competitive advantage through high-quality service.

When it comes to service quality, degree of success, degree of difficulty, and degree of intensity all serve to set the Service 101 apart. In many cases, we found important, industry-specific reasons for an organization's service leadership—unique or special positioning, executive vision, entrepreneurial zeal, even situation-based opportunism. Some organizations set the standards for their industry. Just as there is no way to evaluate theme-park entertainment *without* Disney, you cannot cover credit card services *without* considering American Express, tax preparation assistance *without* H&R Block, business information services *without* Dun & Bradstreet. These are benchmark companies against which others compare themselves.

Interestingly, we found that successful service providers typically work harder at developing the capacity of their organizations to respond to customers than on their image in the marketplace. Their success comes from skillful, sustained management that serves rather than beguiles the customer. It's not simply a matter of "putting someone in charge of service," or coming up with a nifty new slogan, or featuring customers on the cover of the annual report.

They aren't publicity shy, mind you. They have perspective. They know that strategically managing service requires a long-term, top-down, organizationwide effort that focuses the energy and resources of the business on customer satisfaction. It's a promise they must put punch behind. And they know too well that promising more than they can actually deliver, or posturing as superhuman, can easily become an albatross not gladly worn around anyone's neck. Better to underpromise and overdeliver, say many of the companies we've been studying.

Five Operating Principles

Beyond these general impressions and observations, we have identified five specific operating principles that are common, in varying degrees, to the Service 101. These five factors are fundamental tactics used to build and manage extraordinary levels of customer satisfaction and loyalty. In brief:

- The Service 101 listen to, understand, and respond—often in unique and creative ways—to the evolving needs and constantly shifting expectations of their customers.
- They establish a clear vision of what superior service is, communicate that vision to employees at every level, and ensure that service quality is personally and positively important to everyone in the organization.
- They establish concrete standards of service quality and regularly measure themselves against those standards, not uncommonly guarding against the "acceptable error" mindset by establishing as their goal 100-percent performance.
- They hire good people, train them carefully and extensively so they have the knowledge and skills to achieve the service standards, then empower them to work on behalf of customers, whether inside or outside the organization.
- They recognize and reward service accomplishments, sometimes individually, sometimes as a group effort, in particular celebrating the successes of employees who go "one step beyond" for their customers.

Before turning to the profiles of the pacesetters and the industries they lead, we believe a more detailed exploration of these operating principles will be instructive.

Operating Principle #1:
Listen, Understand, and Respond to Customers

Listening to customers must become everyone's business. With most competitors moving ever faster, the race will go to those who listen (and respond) most intently.

—Tom Peters, *Thriving on Chaos*

IN SERVICE BUSINESSES OF EVERY SIZE AND DESCRIPTION, THE PRIORITY TODAY is to continuously and carefully listen to customers, understand what they're saying as it applies to the business of serving them, and then respond creatively to what they tell you.

Listening has to have a purpose. Among the Service 101, there are four reasons to listen to customers. The first, which we've already touched on, is to understand the customer's moments of truth and map what the cycle of that experience looks like from the customer's standpoint. From that you can determine the critical contact points and measure how well your organization is managing the cycle toward a positive outcome.

The second is to keep tabs on the market's—the aggregate of individual customers'—changing wants, needs, and expectations. "Riding the customer's learning curve" is an IBM expression for this kind of listening, which is one of the mainstays of the market research business. As any restaurateur can tell you, it is critical to survival to know when the palate populi is tiring of the Cajun taste and has begun to develop a lust for wild game or New Zealand home-style cooking. In an era of constant change, customer expectations and needs are as fluid as anything else.

The third rationale for diligent listening is to hear the unexpected ideas customers and those who work with them can bring to the table. Procter & Gamble was able to anticipate the need for All-Temperature Cheer because the people answering the 800-number in its customer-service unit noticed a peculiarity in data: The average household's weekly laundry had increased from 6.4 to 7.6 loads while the average wash temperature dropped fifteen degrees. Follow-up research revealed that the many new

29

fabrics reaching the market were requiring closer sorting and better temperature control of the weekly wash.

Finally, listening carefully to customers is a valuable way to involve the customer in the business. Breaking down "them and us" barriers isn't as cosmetic a reason as it may sound. When Embassy Suites managers buttonhole guests in the hotel to ask them about their stay, or someone at Longo Toyota rings up a new-car buyer six months later to find out how the new wheels are working, they are enfolding the customer in the details of the business and heightening the perception of their responsiveness. They also are confronting head-on the unsettling statistic that says only 4 percent of unhappy customers will complain about their problems while the other 96 out of 100 switch to a competitor.

Identifying the "Real" Customer

The listening effort begins with deciding just who it is you are talking about when you say "the customer." No business can succeed by trying to be all things to all people, yet few, if any, organizations have a single, plain-vanilla customer with a single set of needs and expectations.

Typically the modern service business must respond to many different constituencies, often in different ways depending on the relative importance of each. Some customers find what they want exactly the way they want it at Wal-Mart, others swear by the likes of Nordstrom and Parisian, and still others are comfortable in either environment. Any or all could be your customers, but the mix is as unique as the service you provide. If listening to customers is to be a useful effort and not simply an activity trap, you have to decide to whom you're going to listen, what it is you should be listening for, and when, where, and how you can best acquire the information.

Identifying "which customer" is especially important in large, multilined, highly market-segmented companies. When one of the newly deregulated phone companies considered selling products and services to small and medium-sized businesses, management avoided the trap of simply retrofitting products and services designed for the *Fortune* 500 by first asking potential customers about their needs.

As it turned out, it was a good thing they did. Small businesses, the company discovered, are neither similar to large corporations and government agencies in their telecommunications requirements nor greatly similar to each other. Those with one or two phone lines differed significantly from those with three to seven lines, and neither had much in common with companies needing seven to thirty lines. Had it tried to understand "small business" as a single entity, the company's picture of the new market would have been quite distorted. Making sure it was talking to the right people about the right things prevented months, if not years, of misdirection.

Knowing what to listen for implies knowing what to ask, another consideration that isn't as simple as it sounds. Customers know what they know from uniquely personal experience. Perceptions are valid for the individual, but single incidents translated through the customer's way of telling the tale don't always instruct. The customer who says your company is "lousy at communication" may have in mind one unpleasant phone call, periodic frustration with a poorly written product manual, years of puzzling over incomprehensible bills, or any combination of a dozen other things. You only know what they mean when you ask the right questions.

How to Listen

There is no one best way to listen to customers—and no such thing as paying too much attention to customers' ideas and opinions. The cardinal sin is to believe that there is nothing more to learn. Here are some variations on the listening theme practiced by the Service 101.

Face-to-Face. The simplest way to listen to customers is across a table or desk, one on one. Asking customers what they like and dislike about doing business with you, what they like and dislike about your products, and what they can and can't depend on your organization to do for them is as valuable a tactic for a diversified corporation as it is for a mom-and-pop dry cleaner.

Edward Crutchfield, chairman and CEO of First Union Corporation, a pacesetting bank holding company based in North Carolina, found such a strategy vital to elevating service delivered under the First Union name. When his senior management group concluded that service quality could be an important marketplace distinguisher, the first place they went was into the field. They stationed themselves out in the branches, listening to tellers and customers interact, watching loan applicants fidget and pace, and developing a very personal understanding of just how much of a task they were about to undertake.

When Erie Chapman III, president of Riverside Methodist Hospitals in Columbus, Ohio, wants to know what's going on under his roof, he spends a couple of instructive hours pushing wheelchairs around and listening to the patients in them. In companies as diverse as Amdahl (a computer maker), Bergen Brunswig (drug store merchandise and management services), Cineplex Odeon (movie theaters), Shoney's (a restaurant chain), and Wal-Mart (small-scale, small-town department stores), senior managers constantly seek opportunities to meet firsthand with customers.

Formal Research. The flip side of such informal soundings is traditional research: doing focus groups, conducting surveys and service audits, studying demographic and psychographic patterns, and systematically looking at the marketplace to predict its twists and turns.

Honda launched Acura as a separate nameplate both to end-run import restrictions and to address luxury-car customers who would have viewed the Integra and Legend as high-end Civics if they were sold out of the same showroom. Lands' End selects products, prepares catalogs, and manages its mailing lists in accordance with an in-depth data base on its target market. Home Depot pitches construction, electrical, and plumbing supplies to do-it-yourselfers because demographic data shows the amateurs now account for more of the market than professional contractors do, and they will make up an ever greater share in the future.

Such research often involves bringing in a third party to do listening most companies can't objectively do for themselves. While market researchers tend to make their craft sound magical and mysterious—and they are clever people—the most important asset they bring to the table is the ability to sample your customers broadly and fairly. They make sure you aren't being unduly influenced in your view of the market by unrepresentative customers or an inbred organizational bias.

United Van Lines uses an independent research firm to survey three thousand of its recently relocated customer families each year. Mystery shoppers from independent firms visit Marriott hotels, First Union bank branches, and Cineplex Odeon theaters on a regular basis; Domino's, Shoney's, and Jiffy Lube assign their own service quality investigators (some recruited from among customers) unannounced to every location in their respective systems. Shop'n Chek's business involves deploying demographically customized mystery shopper teams to monitor service levels for its clients.

While opposite ends of an important spectrum, neither of these basic listening techniques is all-encompassing. The people charged with monitoring and finding opportunities in customer comments, complaints, and kudos are regularly fishing the stream of opinions and ideas in other ways.

Frontline Contact. Stew Leonard's Dairy makes good use of this tactic, sending groups of employees out to competitors to look and listen and report back with new and improved ways of keeping customers happy. Battelle Memorial Institute expects its research project managers to stay in touch with their clients on a regular basis, even though the scientific and technical investigations underway may not have results to report for a year or more.

Many companies invite customers in with the express intention of teaching and listening, not selling. AMP sends a corporate jet to pick up its customers' electronics engineers and bring them to Pennsylvania for technical training and product design consultations. Don Beyer Volvo holds mixers so its auto mechanics can meet the people whose cars they service. Dun & Bradstreet has made it a corporate objective that employees at every level be able to identify the customers, internal or external, for their particular work.

And some—like Emerald People's Utility District, which throws a summer picnic for employees *and* customers—just get the servers and the served together for the fun of it.

Customer Hotlines. Perhaps no single listening tactic turns up more often than the toll-free telephone number that connects a customer with someone who can answer a question, take an order, resolve a complaint, dispatch a repair person, or provide timely information. Procter & Gamble, General Electric, Armstrong, American Express, Wheaton Van Lines, Fidelity Investments, and AAA routinely use 800-numbers to give their customers easy access to their products and services—and to gather intelligence on what customers are thinking and doing. The tactic not only works for *external* customers, but also can be effective *internally*, as evidenced by Piedmont Airlines' use of toll-free numbers to answers its employees' questions and smooth the path of merger into USAir.

In many of the Service 101, senior managers regularly spend time on incoming service, complaint, and information calls. It gives them an anonymous, status-free contact with customers that helps them understand field-level frustrations and concerns direct, free of the impersonal filtering of reports and memos.

Comment and Complaint Analysis. Every organization has customer comment and complaint files. Most use them strictly as a paper trail to track business relationships and problem resolutions. The crafty ones go a couple of steps farther, encouraging and then using this raw feedback to see themselves from the customer's viewpoint.

General comments gleaned from letters, phone calls, comment cards, and follow-up satisfaction surveys provide a running index of customer attitudes and experiences for hotels, restaurants, car dealerships, and a host of other businesses. Unsolicited praise is used by companies such as Amica Mutual Insurance, LensCrafters, Delta Air Lines, and Federal Express to recognize and reward frontline workers who clearly have provided people-pleasing service. Complaints are analyzed as bellwethers on developing problems that can be nipped in the bud—and as opportunities to get back in the disgruntled customer's good graces by showing concern and responsiveness.

Consumer Advisory Panels. Difficult customers need not be painful to listen to. Several of the companies we've been studying make a point of forming inquisitive, dissatisfied, and sometimes even vociferously critical customers into advisory boards where they can play devil's advocate to their hearts' content. In the process, they provide useful insight into vexing service problems. Organizations as different as Arizona Public Service (a power company) and Don Beyer Volvo (a car dealership) make effective use of this form of listening. In a more proactive setting, the independent agents who sell policies for Northwestern Mutual Life Insurance can contribute to no fewer than three different panels that provide input on the company's products and services.

Mutual Education. Training sessions also serve as listening posts for companies that know what to listen for. Quad/Graphics invites its printing customers to "camp," where company employees explain the technical processes involved in producing magazines and other printed materials—and get to know the people who buy their services. When Minnesota-based 3M gathers printing technology executives from around the world at the company's conference center and hideaway in the north woods, the goal is much the same. Over in Milwaukee, Northwestern Mutual makes sure field agents have time to mix and mingle with the administrative and support people who back up their efforts when they're in town for training.

Whether you use any or all of these approaches, or have evolved some unique methods of your own, the point is developing multiple ways of continuously finding out about your customers and tracking their learning curves. This is what Tom Peters calls "engaged listening" in *Thriving on Chaos*—giving your organization ample opportunities to tap into customers' ideas and experiences, and then squeezing the last drop of potential out of every encounter you have with a customer who has something he or she believes is important for you to hear.

Using What You Hear

Listening is half a loaf. Doing something with what you learn feeds the multitude. Unfortunately, the corporate library chock-full of customer research no one has ever tried to find a use for is far too common. A bemused telephone company executive once told us, "There is no approach to studying customers we haven't used. The trouble is, we never do anything with what we learn. If you could study a problem out of existence, we'd be way ahead."

What good will it do you to codify your customers' moments of truth and chart their cycle of service if you don't use the information? Any employee who deals with a customer needs to know not only the moments of truth for that customer, but the *impact* of what happens at those moments of truth.

For each moment of truth, we find that three distinct factors will play a role in the customer's judgment of service quality received:
- The customer's *standard* or *nominal* expectations
- What the customer has experienced at that particular moment of . truth in the past that has *detracted* from the quality of service

and

- What the customer has experienced in the past that has *enhanced* the transaction.

Each tends to be a discrete list in the customer's mind, and by listening to the customer those lists can be compiled to provide a valuable map of the moment of truth. We call this a "Moment of Truth Impact Analysis." Figure 1 shows how we mapped the moments of truth involved when a customer contacts GTE North's repair answering service.

A lot of useful data comes out of a Moment of Truth Impact Analysis—if you're listening for it and prepared to use it. The lists of enhancers, detractors, and standard expectations tell you what the critical part of the transaction is from the customer's point of view, where the "fail points" have occurred in the past, what the customer's minimum standard of performance is, and the ways in which you can make the transaction a memorable one. All you have to do is listen effectively and act on the basis of the information.

That's how Federal Express ultimately came to terms with the surcharge it used to add for Saturday service. The surcharge applied even if the customer brought the package to a FedEx location. According to founder and CEO Fred Smith, customers complained loudly and long about having to pay extra, yet internally the company worried because taking revenue away threatened to produce a net loss. Finally, after listening inside and out, Federal Express decided its customers had a point and removed the surcharge—although not without significant misgivings. The result: Within six months, Saturday service was up to such an extent that it was generating a handsome return. "We could never prove that before we did it," says Smith.

Responding to customers is basic to our second operating principle, defining superior service and creating a service strategy, so we'll come back to it in that context.

MOMENT OF TRUTH:

The Customer Contacts the Repair Answering Center

Experience Enhancers	*Standard Expectations*	*Experience Detractors*
• The operator had a melodious, well-modulated voice.	• I will only have to call one number.	• I can't understand the operator's words.
• The operator communicated a sense of urgency.	• I will call a local number.	• I had to call more than once to get through.
• The operator really understood my problem or situation; had heard it before and knew just what to do.	• I will be treated fairly.	• I had to listen to a recording that made me feel unwelcome.
• The operator apologized sincerely.	• The operator will speak clearly.	• While I am on hold I get silence, which makes me wonder if I am disconnected.
• The operator asked me about medical emergencies or other special situations that may warrant extra attention.	• The phone will not be busy.	• The operator sounded like he or she was following a form—stock or routine questions.
• The operator made some comment that let me know he or she was aware of my area (i.e., sounded like a neighbor).	• The operator will answer within a reasonable period.	• I felt the operator rushed me; didn't really listen.
• The operator offered to have work done at my convenience.	• The operator will be a real person.	• I got mirandized: "Are you aware that there may be a charge for this service . . ."
• The operator told me how I could prevent the problem in the future.	• The operator will speak pleasantly.	• I was not able to walk into an office and talk with someone personally.
	• The operator will listen to my problems in a manner that lets me know he or she understands my problem.	• The operator sounded bored.
	• The operator will seem competent, helpful, and understanding.	
	• The operator will promise me a solution with a reasonable deadline.	
	• The operator will explain exactly what will happen next.	

Figure 1: Moment of Truth Impact Analysis

Operating Principle #2: Define Superior Service and Establish a Service Strategy

Developing a competitive strategy is developing a broad formula for how a business is going to compete, what its goals should be, and what policies will be needed to carry out those goals.

—Michael E. Porter, *Competitive Strategy: Techniques for Analyzing Industries and Companies*

EFFECTIVE LISTENING GIVES THE SERVICE 101 VALUABLE INFORMATION ABOUT their customers' experiences and expectations. It tells them what customers consider poor, good, and superior service. It provides the foundation, the words and examples, they will use to articulate what providing superior service means to the customer—and should mean to everyone else in the organization.

In addition to providing a practical definition of superior service, listening gives the information needed to invent or continue to evolve the response: an understandable, unifying idea of what the organization is trying to accomplish to make itself unique in the customers' eyes. This concept of delivering service, or *service strategy*, directs the attention of people in the organization toward the real priorities of the customer. Employees use it to guide their actions. Communicating it to customers attracts them to the organization. The definition or vision of good service is nothing less than the centerline along which customer-focused organizations are aligned.

One of the briefest but most viable definitions of superior service we've seen belongs to Deluxe Corporation, the nation's largest printer of personal checks and other financial instruments. To Deluxe's customers, superior service amounts to "forty-eight-hour turnaround, zero defects." Whether the order is for a simple red-and-black box of personal checks or revised financial forms to consolidate the operations of two merging institutions, Deluxe's employees and customers alike expect that the job will be processed, printed, and shipped within forty-eight hours of receipt, and that it will be right the first time. Similarly, McDonald's leans on its short and to the point "Q.S.V.C.—Quality, Service, Value, and Cleanliness."

Other organizations use a lot more space and words, especially those with multiple businesses and multiple product and service lines. Here's how Maryland National Bank defines its Customer First Commitment:

"MNBA is a company of people committed to . . .

- Providing the customer with the finest products backed by consistently top quality service.
- Delivering these products and services efficiently, thus ensuring fair prices to the customer and sound earnings for the corporation.
- Treating the customer as we expect to be treated—putting 'the customer first' everyday—and meaning it."

People in the retail or branch banking operation of the company refined that statement into this one, which is much more specific to their business and customers:

"We the people of Maryland National Bank are committed to being the best bank in our region, and the most worthy of the public's confidence. To meet the challenges ahead, together we pledge to:

- Provide the highest possible level of service.
- Always be courteous and professional, with customers as our top priority.
- Care about doing every part of our work as well as it can be done, taking pride in all we do.
- Help and support one another at all times and seek innovative solutions to the challenges we face.
- Strive to keep our reputation for high quality and constantly make it better.
- Maintain a strong position of leadership in the industry."

Those nicely worded but fairly general commitments became very specific and tangible when the management of the bank's retail group went to the marketplace with the Performance Guarantee related earlier. It promised to pay customers ten dollars, you'll recall, if MNB made a mistake on a checking or money market account. President Bill Daiger proposed that if and when the ten dollars ever had to be paid, it come from the operating unit that caused the error. Thus challenged, the people in the check-processing unit created their own functional service strategy in alignment with the Performance Guarantee:

"The mission of the check processing group is to deliver error free activity statements to customers in a timely fashion."

The MNB experience clearly demonstrates that a service strategy need not be a sterile, wall-cluttering piece of corporate eyewash. An effective strategy can and should serve as both a touchstone of organizational values and commitment and an inspiration for developing creative and distinctive ways to serve the customer. At Maryland National, the service strategy was a splash that created ripples throughout the organization. That is as it should be.

Anatomy of a Service Strategy

The definition of superior service is the foundation of a service strategy: the way you define what service quality is, why that quality is important to the customer, and what's at stake for the organization and its people. It's more than a slogan. Slogans can call attention to a service strategy, but the strategy is in the definition itself—the "image" of good service you want everyone to have in mind every time they face or think about the customer. Unless and until the management of an organization is able to make concrete and communicate broadly, to everyone at every level, and to the customer as well, a single vision of service quality, the organization doesn't have a service strategy.

A word about "vision." The term is in danger of becoming trivialized and battered beyond usefulness, but it is still the best description of what we are trying to convey. A vision is an idea refined through experience and thinking. You don't get it from lying on a conference room floor chanting a mantra. It evolves and matures as your understanding of customers and your experience at delivering quality service increase. It's the model, the set of guiding principles, the concept. It isn't fuzzy—or better not be—nor is it soft and mushy. It is a clear, precise understanding of what your business is all about.

During a discussion we were leading on what a service strategy should and shouldn't do and say, an executive of the Dayton Hudson Department Store Company impatiently slashed through the technical jargon for us. "In other words," he observed pointedly, "a service strategy is the 'bear any burden, pay any price promise we make to ourselves on behalf of our customer,' isn't it?" He "got it in one" as the English say, and much more succinctly than we had been able to. A service strategy is simply a statement of what you intend to do—must do, really—for the customer if you are to be successful in distinguishing yourself through service quality, whatever the business may be.

We would gladly give you a definitive formula for creating a service strategy if such a formula existed. Alas, it does not. But there is some guidance available. It is our observation that an effective service strategy has four characteristics. Specifically, an effective service strategy

- Is a nontrivial statement of intent
  that
- Noticeably differentiates you from others
- Has value in your customer's eyes

and

● Is deliverable by the organization.

That fourth characteristic is what differentiates a marketing slogan and an advertising campaign from a service strategy. It's where most organizations go wrong. Several years back, when General Motors created Mr. Goodwrench as a symbol of excellence, it took the automotive community somewhat by surprise. Not to be outdone, the denizens of a competitor's marketing department came up with a great countermove. "We'll have 'No Unhappy Owners' at Flupmobile," they decreed. Happy with themselves, they trooped off to the advertising agency in New York and ordered the "No Unhappy Owners" commercial. Not long after, during halftime of a Sunday professional football game, the commercial announced to the world, "At Flupmobile, we will have no unhappy owners."

The following Monday, in Flupmobile dealerships nationwide, owners were pulling into service bay drive-up lanes and declaring, "Guess what, baby, I *are* one—an Unhappy Owner!" But since the whole idea was to one-up Mr. Goodwrench on the airwaves, not in the drive lanes, service writers and managers in the dealerships weren't of a mind, nor had they been instructed, to do anything differently than before the advertisement blared its happy but hollow message. The most common response was some variation on, "Could it be you have me confused with someone who gives a darn?" Far from driving home a message of superior service, such cavalier treatment only further alienated the customers.

Farfetched? Hardly. The "advertise yourself into service distinction" ploy is as alive and well today as it was when Flupmobile made its faux pas. It hasn't been all that long ago that we sat through a presentation made by an advertising agency to a mutual client. Research clearly showed this large regional bank to be eighth out of ten in customer service satisfaction among the retail financials in its market. "No problem," explained the advertising account rep. "We'll just declare you the best in the market and the public's perceptions will follow along with the new positioning." Management came within two votes of accepting the cockeyed premise, the supporting marketing scheme, and the megabuck proposal to put it on the air.

Among the Service 101, a statement of service strategy functions first and foremost as an *internal* focus of effort. It is based on an understanding of a combination of organizational values, customer expectations of products and services, customer expectations of the process of doing business with the company, and an in-depth analysis of the strengths and weaknesses of the organization as it confronts the threats and opportunities in the current marketplace. That whole swirl of information and ideas must be distilled to a form that can be understood by employee and customer alike.

Putting It into Words

A workable service strategy must include a concept or mission that people can understand and support through concrete actions. It also must include benefits important to the customer that differentiate the organization from its competitors in a meaningful way.

Among the Service 101, defining and communicating the service strategy is a part of training employees, developing service delivery systems, measuring organizational performance, and managing the sales and marketing effort. A well-defined service strategy declares an organization's competitive direction and must become its gospel. That means it has to be communicated over and over again, until everyone in the organization can hum it right along.

Chip Bell suggests a simple test. A service strategy, he contends, is complete and will probably work to communicate what it needs to communicate if it answers three questions: What is our unique contribution? To whom do we provide this service? What key value do we want them to perceive about us?

He goes on to suggest this fill-in-the-blank format:

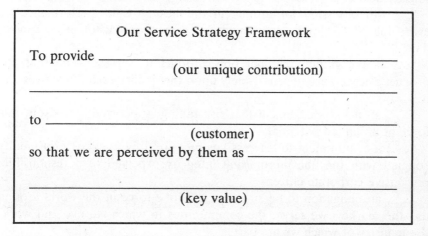

Our Service Strategy Framework

To provide _____
                     (our unique contribution)

_____

to _____
                     (customer)
so that we are perceived by them as _____

_____
                     (key value)

Keep his three questions in the back of your mind as you consider the "Statement of Philosophy" that sets the tone for operations at Super Valu, the nation's largest service-providing organization:

"The philosophy of Super Valu companies will always be a 'total commitment to serving customers more effectively than anyone else could serve them.' We believe the pursuit of this meaningful goal is the continuing and overriding responsibility from which every corporate activity must evolve. We value today's success as merely the beginning of a constantly expanding level of achievement.

"We believe that customers are most knowledgeable, skilled and capable buyers who will always seek out and do business with that supplier or store which most effectively serves their wants and needs.

"Therefore, by serving our customers more effectively than anyone else could serve them, and by efficiently managing our business with highly skilled and dedicated people, we are confident that we shall continue to increase Super Valu's sales and share of market. We believe that this philosophy and practice will result in continuing profitable growth for Super Valu and provide security and opportunity for our many thousands of loyal employees."

United Van Lines answers the same questions in a somewhat different but no less effective style when it defines "Our Guiding Values and Principles" this way:

"As a worldwide leader in providing household goods transportation and related services, United Van Lines has built its reputation upon the accomplishments of its *people* at all levels of the organization. The members of the United family—agents, van operators, and Headquarters employees—all share certain key values and principles:

". . . an appreciation of the individual's rights, responsibilities, beliefs, sensitivities, and needs.

". . . an obsession for turning in the best possible performance on every job . . . in every department . . . for every customer . . . every day.

". . . a recognition that our only product is 'service'—and that our product's acceptance depends solely upon the quality each of us invests in it.

". . . an acknowledgement that risk-taking, supported by reason, is a force of unlimited potential.

". . . a commitment to 'success,' as measured by financial profitability coupled with the uncompromising integrity expected of a responsible, responsive corporate citizen.

". . . an obligation to be an active, positive force in the world around us—the markets we serve, the communities in which we live and work, the industry of which we are part.

". . . an understanding that, regardless of our roles within the United family, we are all partners in the process of shaping tomorrow through today's accomplishments and careful planning for the future."

Alignment and Communication

Alignment is an apt description of the process of making the service strategy part of an organization—employees at all levels must be aligned with a single vision of what the organization is trying to accomplish with customers and the way customers judge or view their performance. To achieve that alignment, the service strategy must be actively communicated throughout the organization.

Two members of our Service 101 use music as a metaphor for the process of keeping all the systems and all the employees focused on superior customer service. At Four Seasons Hotels, managers are likened to conductors of a symphony—their role is to keep all the various pieces playing in proper tempo and harmony so the performance is pleasing to the customer. Similarly, Paul Orfalea, founder of Kinko's copy centers, constantly exhorts one and all to "keep the music playing," again alluding to the process of aligning the various component people and systems in the service-delivery system for maximum impact on the customer.

The internal communication effort tends to use one of two different approaches: cascading or cloning. *Cascading* begins with the crafting of a single, highly detailed message, frequently with implications for service standards built into it. Like water in an intricate, multilevel fountain, this common message flows from one operating unit in the organization to another. Employees in each successive unit are asked to commit to it. Sometimes they are challenged to create standards and criteria appropriate to their unit that will be in concert with the service strategy and against which they are willing to be measured.

Cloning works from the opposite direction. It is more appropriate in situations where a single service message must be spread through an organization characterized by diverse and unrelated professions and practices.

In Montgomery County, for example, each distinct department participates in the "Service Excellence" initiative, but in keeping with its own customer or client demands, operating mission, and unique challenges. The people in the field collecting stray dogs and cats face different demands than the counselors trying to help unwed teenage mothers learn job skills and build a future for their families. The cloning nature of the process ensures that standards will be the same, even though the specific strategies and tactics are different in each department. Each identifies its own key customers, specifies their unique needs and values, and creates specific supporting actions geared to respond to the identified client needs.

Multicare Medical Center, the holding company for Tacoma General Hospital and Mary Bridge Children's Hospital in Tacoma, also is using the cloning approach to spread a single service message to an organization characterized by diverse and unrelated professions and practices nursing, pharmacy, radiology, laboratory, housekeeping, and physical therapy as well as psychological, transportation, dietary, and intensive-care services. The vehicle it uses is a "Customer Service Action Plan" referred to as Merci, an acronym developed from *M*edical *E*xcellence *R*equires *C*oncern for the *I*ndividual.

The program begins with the exploration of a customer service philosophy that expresses the core values of the organization in terms of individual belief statements and a set of "core" caring behaviors and actions.

MERCI: Medical Excellence Requires Concern for the Individual

Philosophy of Customer Service

As an employee of Multicare Medical Center, I share with other employees in the business of caring for people:

- I believe that patients, physicians, visitors, and my fellow employees are my customers.
- I know that the way people are treated contributes to the healing process.
- I strive to balance technical skill and personal attention.
- I find value and support in myself and in my fellow employees.
- I know that my actions are important to our ability to achieve business success through high levels of customer satisfaction.

Caring Actions

Reach out. Welcome people immediately to your work area. Acknowledge their presence. Make eye contact and smile. Introduce yourself in a pleasant tone of voice. State your name and what job you perform. When the opportunity is available, use the person's name to address him/her. Be attentive, genuine, and positive.

Be friendly. If you are unsure if someone needs help . . . ask him/her. Share information willingly and honestly. If you can't help, personally find someone who can. Know what services are available and how to get them.

Be timely. Respond quickly. Explain delays.

Listen actively. Take time to listen. Give the person your full attention. Listen to the person's message: What is said, and what is not said.

Take pride in your appearance. Look appropriately well groomed. Follow the guidelines for correct attire as established by your department. There is only one chance to make a first impression.

Provide safe, clean and attractive surroundings. Maintain a neat, safe, pleasant work area. Take responsibility to keep all areas clean. Respect the need for a quiet environment.

Show courtesy. Put yourself in the other person's place. Respond quickly. Allow others to go first. Be polite and helpful in person, or on the phone.

Demonstrate your competence. Confidence comes from competence in your job skills and knowledge. Stay current. Express confidence by performing tasks accurately and with ease. Be "response able". While knowing the limits of your practice (job), solve problems within your authority. If resolving the person's problem to the fullest is beyond your reasonable limits, know how to get help.

Explain what you are doing. Make explanations brief and easy to understand. Answer questions honestly and kindly. Be willing to explain it again. Use language that the other person can understand.

Look for an opportunity to serve. You are "Multicare" to every person you encounter. Go out of your way to be helpful to others. Care enough to do your very best.

Remember to say good-by. Be sure the person has the information he/she needs before leaving. End on a friendly note. Say thank you.

Care for each other. Treat each other as we would treat our guests. We need to experience nurturing to be able to nurture. Feeling good at work helps keep us healthy. By using these caring actions, we please ourselves and our customers.

Both approaches work. We have seen other slants and variations of these two models used in other organizations, but the key components tend to be much the same. Regardless of the task chosen, however, good service organizations know that communicating a service strategy is like taking a bath: No matter how well you do it this time, you have to do it all over again, and frequently, if you are going to stay clean. Unlike repairing a heart valve or removing the tonsils, the communication of a service strategy is something that must be done over and over again to remain fresh. The message must be repeated in as many different ways and at as many different times as possible if it is to become a norm for organizational behavior.

The conflict between focus and distraction is well understood by our Service 101. So is the remedy. They are committed not only to creating distinctive service right now, but to keeping the focus on service quality for the long haul. Defining superior service is a serious, value-based business proposition. Communicating the message of service strategy, whether internally or externally, isn't a program or an event. It is a continuing effort that can never be pronounced done.

Operating Principle #3:
Set Standards and Measure Performance

Quality is not measured by me. It's not even measured by you. Quality is in the eyes of your customers. If they're not happy with you, you're not happy with us.

—John Guerra, AT&T branch manager (from a 1988 AT&T business-to-business advertisement)

IN PRODUCT MANUFACTURING, THERE ARE TWO SCHOOLS OF THOUGHT ON HOW best to improve quality. The disagreement is over beginnings. One school holds that quality improvement properly begins internally at the workgroup level, with the focus on improving the degree to which the group meets technical standards. The primary thrust is directed at decreasing the proportion and amount of rejected product, eliminating scrap and waste, and speeding production. The competing view asserts that quality improvement begins with the customer's evaluation of quality itself, and only then works backward into the organization.

When it comes to improving *service* quality, on the other hand, no debate is possible—the discussion begins and ends with the customer's assessment. Superior service quality is there if the customer says so, and it isn't there if the customer votes thumbs-down. What's more, the only true and reliable measurement of service quality is the assessment of customers' most recent experiences with the organization and their level of satisfaction with those experiences.

Companies that enjoy reputations for distinctive service quality consistently meet their customers' expectations. Far from leaving anything to chance, the Service 101 establish clear, customer-oriented performance standards throughout their organizations and then constantly and meticulously measure performance against those standards.

A commitment to service quality without a commitment to standards and measurement would be a dedication to lip service, not customer service. Only with customer-focused standards and customer-based satisfaction measurements can you create and manage dynamic, information-

47

based service delivery systems that can be tuned and refined to changing customer expectations. As J. W. "Bill" Marriott, Jr., chairman of Marriott Corporation, puts it: "Measurement of customer perception causes a lot of focus just where we want it, on the customer."

Setting Standards

When we work through the topic of standards in workshops, the discussion frequently turns technical over a basic values conflict. At some point, someone invariably groans that "customer satisfaction scores are well and good, but my people don't see the customer. We need *real* standards and *real* measurement if we are going to run this business right." In essence, the conflict turns out to be between internally generated standards and customer-centered measurement.

It's an understandable quandary. Setting standards and measuring performance in accordance with customer-centered values smacks of letting the inmates run the asylum. Surely the organization's professionals are best qualified to determine how to do whatever it is that they do?

The answer is yes. And no. Like the myopia of catering managers planning coffee breaks around pastries and china patterns instead of telephones and restrooms, personal education and experience, company policies and procedures, and the habits developed over time all conspire to insulate the process of service delivery from the customer's perception of what is really desired.

Remember Len Berry's formula for customer satisfaction: It is not only the quality of the outcome, but also the customer's expectations *and* the customer's perception of the process leading from expectations to outcome that determine the ultimate quality of the service provided. Knowing what to do and how to do it in a *technical* sense does not necessarily confer understanding of customers' wants and needs, or customers' expectations of how they would like you to satisfy those wants and needs.

To see this conflict more clearly, consider the practice of medicine. "What could a patient possibly have to tell us about the practice of medicine that would be germane?" is the typical approach of professional practitioners from a lofty perch they've gained only after years of intensive— and expensive—preparation. "How could you possibly be practicing the healing arts without taking the patients' views into consideration?" is the seemingly militant consumerist response from the frontlines. Each view is helpful only in defining the extremes.

No one questions the need for ethical standards and professional review in medicine. Nor do we contend that the layman is qualified to judge compliance with those standards. A nondoctor is no more fit to judge the *technical* quality of a hernia operation than a nonmechanic is to judge the *technical* quality of adjustments to the car's fuel-injection system.

The owner is, however, not only a competent judge of whether the tuned-up car is running well, but also the only relevant judge of whether the adjustments were worth the money paid for the service. Likewise, the hernia patient is competent to judge whether the relief sought has been obtained, and in a way that met his expectations as a patient. Those judgments of outcome are relevant to the establishment of service standards. Lack of respect for those judgments is what brings mechanics and repair shops into ill repute and dumps doctors and hospitals into malpractice litigation.

The solution is to deploy and manage the organization's technical expertise in keeping with the customer's ever-changing definition of good service. It can be done. At Riverside Methodist, no one would think of letting patients pick up a scalpel or make a diagnosis. But when two entire floors of the hospital were designated as a specialty center for women's health problems, the list of medical services to be offered and the setting in which those services were to be provided were both designed with input from the women in the community who might someday be the center's patients.

In the financial field, Citicorp launched its concerted service improvement campaign from the discovery of a gap between the technical skills it had long considered to be good *performance* and the expectations and desires its customers believed were basic to good *service*. Likewise, First Union's formula for people-pleasing financial service derives from first learning how customers define it and then measuring how well they believe the bank is providing it.

The subject need not always be approached so gingerly. For many of the Service 101, standards are straightforward, easy to set, and integrated into the service strategy. When Deluxe Corporation publicly promises "forty-eight-hour turnaround, zero defects," the standard is clear and unquestioned. The same is true of the Federal Express guarantee of "absolutely, positively overnight" delivery, or the Domino's standard that states the pizza will be at your door within thirty minutes of your order.

Notice that useful, measurable standards tend to be expressed precisely. Moving the "bear any burden, pay any price promise we make to our customers" back into the organization can lead to problems if the customer-based measures are left behind. "You'll have the best sleep ever," or "You're gonna like our place," are slogans, not standards. If customers don't have a clue to exactly what kind of service promise has been made, how will they know good service when they see it?

Nordstrom, L. L. Bean, and Lands' End all have clear satisfaction guarantees: If you don't like it, they'll take it back, no questions asked. Their customers don't have to worry that someone will decide that this particular return isn't allowable because the item is no longer on sale, or they don't have the sales slip and packaging, or the phase of the moon has changed. The standard is expressed in terms of the customer, not internal organizational concerns like inventory control.

The other jeopardy that comes from setting standards that are neither firm nor customer-focused is the idea of permitting a comfort level of allowable errors. Deluxe knows that sometimes it will make a mistake or miss the forty-eight-hour deadline. As a salve to the corporate ego, it would be easy to revise the standard from an absolute to a relative value—aiming to ship, say, 98 percent of all orders within forty-eight hours, then crowing because 99-point-whatever-percent were out the door in that amount of time.

In service, a permissible error rate is a way of saying that it is perfectly all right to turn off, disappoint, and even lose a certain percentage of customers. That's unacceptable logic to the superior service organizations. So Deluxe holds to the absolute standard because that is the definition of superior performance it wants its customers to expect and its employees to aspire to. It not only measures its rate of achievement against that standard—which, looked at from the other side, is an acknowledgment of, but not an alibi for, its failure rate—but publishes the information in the annual report every year so everybody knows how well it is doing.

James Barksdale, Federal Express's chief operating officer, is equally forthright: "If we have 98 percent overnight delivery of eight hundred thousand packages and letters [which is what FedEx handled nightly during the seasonal madness of Christmas week in 1986], then sixteen thousand— 2 percent—of our customers did not receive their package absolutely, positively overnight. I'm not inclined to brag too loudly about sixteen thousand packages gone astray."

Frank McMillan, director of quality for Shell Oil, puts the question in starker terms: "What is an acceptable error rate—what will you, as a customer, accept as acceptable failure—for airliner landings. Is 98 percent okay? 99 percent? No, of course not. How about hospital nursery care. What is the acceptable rate for dropped babies: 98 percent? 99 percent? No. One hundred percent is all you will tolerate. Are your customers any less demanding than you are? I doubt it!"

That quote should be on the desk of everyone charged with setting performance standards. High-quality service involves adherence to customer expectations, not a compromise between what the customer wants and what the organization is comfortable providing. 3M is one of a number of the companies we studied that defines quality itself as "conformance to customer requirements." That's where standards come from, and that is where meaningful measurement begins.

Why They Measure

One of the most common characteristics of the outstanding service providers is their dedication to measuring customer satisfaction and using the results to guide operations. They measure formally. They measure frequently—on average, monthly. And they attach important individual, work-group, and organizational outcomes to the results.

Because the results of quality measurements are meant to be taken seriously, the most effective systems are those that produce actionable information. The object of the data quest is more than "smile ratings," in other words. If treatment at the front desk is a high-impact variable in a hotel—and it is—you can bet that Marriott, Embassy Suites, Hyatt, Four Seasons, and Mississippi Management are all getting regular readings on front-desk treatment from their respective customers.

Their way of asking the questions may vary, but the questions asked are very specific to their particular customer profile. There's nothing immediately useful to be learned from an open-ended, global query such as, "How was the treatment at the front desk?" Instead, a carefully crafted series of questions will probe into customer assessments of all aspects of the encounter: speed, accuracy, cordiality, helpfulness, completeness of information, response to inquiries, and any other moments of truth that build the overall impression of quality.

Measurement results typically become the agenda for subsequent internal dialogue and problem-solving efforts. After all, an organization's service quality measurement system is only as good as the service improvement discussions it prompts—and that's true at all levels in the organization. Some of the most heated discussions we have seen in organizations like Marriott and Federal Express have been inspired by the results of a customer survey. As Tom Oliver, FedEx's senior vice president of sales and service, told us once, "If the customer believes he has a problem, he has a problem. Period."

While many of the Service 101 use formal, highly reliable measurement systems, none relies solely on such systems for customer feedback. For example, Marriott's regular, scientific, third-party sampling and surveying is supplemented by a less formal, more open, Guest Satisfaction Index (GSI) compiled from the in-room survey forms people voluntarily fill out and turn in. Because GSI data comes in more frequently than the results of third-party, scientifically administered surveys, it is used as a rolling indicator of how a property is doing with guests. John Dixon, general manager of the Marriott in Washington, D.C., characterizes his property's GSI as a "reality check. It answers the question, 'Are we as good as we think we are?' "

GSI results are taken every bit as seriously as the results of monthly telephone polls. Regular ratings are posted in employee work areas.

Meetings are held to discuss the scores and what they say about service quality. Written comments are posted for employees to read for themselves. And Dixon is a big believer in the value of combining the handwritten guest comments and the formal survey numbers into an overall picture of what guests are experiencing. "We dramatize and emphasize good results, the positive comments—they communicate the standard," he explains. "We use complaints and poor results to discuss improvement—they tell us how short we are of the goal."

Service measurements often benefit from a standard of comparison. One major Chicago-based specialty retailer regularly assigns its favorite market research company to track and analyze what customers think of the service in its stores. Then, to determine how that compares to service that's widely acknowledged as outstanding, the market researchers do telephone surveys of Nordstrom customers on the West Coast. Comparing the internal measurements with the external data from half a continent away allows this midwestern retailer to benchmark the way its customers feel about it against satisfaction ratings from "the best of the best."

Such benchmarking goes on more and more frequently today. Telephone companies benchmark against their regional competition, but many also compare themselves to Southern Bell. Xerox parts distribution people benchmark themselves not just against competitors, but against L. L. Bean.

One measure of just how seriously the data being generated is taken among the Service 101 is the important outcomes that increasingly are attached to the results. Information from the comment cards sent out by General Electric to follow up on major appliance service calls have salary impact for GE service technicians. Regular service quality surveys are basic to the decentralized style of management at Digital Equipment Corporation. Both United and Wheaton Van Lines confront and counsel agents and drivers rated less than satisfactory; those who cannot or will not clean up their acts are cut loose.

At Longo Toyota, negative feedback from customers gets salespeople called on the carpet, no matter how many cars they are selling. At Federal Express, Marriott, and many others, pay and promotions can hinge on good customer feedback. And service quality is now more important than profitability in the way managers of Pizza Hut restaurants are rated and rewarded.

The value of the information is only enhanced by spreading it through the organization. The more people in each functional unit of the company—be it a Wal-Mart store, a First Federal/Osceola savings and loan branch, a Club Med village, or an Embassy Suites hotel—know about the hit/miss ratio and what the causes of the hits and misses seem to be, the better able they are to improve their performance. Measurement for measurement's sake is pointless. As manufacturing quality guru Philip Crosby points out, "Building a better scale doesn't change your weight."

Determining What to Measure

"Hey! How'm I doin'?" may generate useful feedback for New York Mayor Ed Koch, but it hardly ever produces the quality or quantity of information needed to direct the creation of distinctive customer service. Likewise, knowing that from a random sample of a thousand recent customers we scored an average of 4.5 on a scale of 1 to 6 is nice, but not at all useful. It doesn't help us figure out how good or bad the customer considers 4.5-level performance, or what we have to do to get a 6.

A number of market research specialists, prominent among them Texas A&M's Len Berry, have been trying to develop measurement systems that will be universally applicable to service quality and customer satisfaction. From focus groups and survey research in a variety of industries, they offer a list of five statistically derived factors that they contend can be used—in a generic sense, at least—to assess what they label "ServQual." Their five component factors are

- Reliability. The ability to provide what was promised, dependably and accurately.
- Assurance. The knowledge and courtesy of employees, and their ability to convey trust and confidence.
- Empathy. The degree of caring and individual attention provided to customers.
- Responsiveness. The willingness to help customers and provide prompt service.
- Tangibles. The physical facilities and equipment, and appearance of personnel.

As a general litmus test, ServQual is an intriguing start. But the generic nature of any such universal index produces results that are, unavoidably, generic. And that falls far short when what's needed is specific information that can be used to confirm or correct employee or unit performance. The more general the feedback, the less effective it is for such purposes. The really useful, specific, directly applicable information comes from talking to your particular customers, constantly and often at length, to determine what you are doing that is making them happy and/or letting them down.

Among the Service 101, we found that the measurement of service performance is a systematic effort that depends on no single measure to tell all. These organizations seem to wear both belts and suspenders, just in case. Technically speaking, they value "nonrepetitive, redundant" measures of their frontline performance, customer satisfaction, and service quality—they measure the same thing in a lot of different ways. The more information, the better, they maintain.

That reinforces our own bias that the most meaningful measurement reflects an organization's unique service strategy. That strategy, you'll recall, was originally devised from listening carefully to customers and identifying the moments of truth that have the greatest impact on their service satisfaction. Logically, then, the best measurement you can devise should mirror and validate the details of your service strategy.

In the mid-1970s, we served as consultants to a medium-sized theme park in the upper Midwest, helping it evolve a measurement and feedback system for customer satisfaction and service quality. The premise of the founder was that the more "fun" people had in the park, the more likely they would be to both come back themselves and tell others. Defining fun was therefore basic to measuring satisfaction.

The original operational model coalesced around four keys to guests having fun: friendliness, cleanliness, service, and show. We then tried to find the fewest questions we could ask people exiting the park that would still reliably report on both overall satisfaction and the four component factors. Though our scales were statistically correct, frontline people and their managers smiled politely and, in essence, told us, "That's nice. So what?"

We were puzzled at their lukewarm reaction, so we asked them why. "What you have is nice for management, but it doesn't help *us*," they said. "When you ask about cleanliness, it would help to know exactly when and where they saw us doing good or bad." So we put back the detailed items on clean restrooms, clean sidewalks, clean parking lots, and so forth. And where we had created general friendliness items, we tossed them out and asked about employee friendliness by area and job type.

The refined measurement and feedback system may not have enhanced our statistical model, but because it did increase the coverage of customer encounters, an interesting thing happened. Employees and supervisors suddenly weren't satisfied knowing they had achieved a 4.8 on bathroom cleanliness. They insisted on knowing how things were perceived by shift, by type of restroom (men's or women's), and by time of day (early morning, midday, later afternoon, or evening). They simply couldn't get enough feedback.

From that experience we reached two conclusions about measurement systems. The actions of the Service 101 only serve to further reinforce them. We believe, first, that the people on the frontlines of the organization respond best to information relevant to their piece of the world—and they can tell you a lot about what will make that information relevant. And, second, we notice that when people have relevant information about things they deem important and believe they can effect, they become very committed to using that information.

Guidelines for Effectiveness

Measurement can be a confusing area, primarily because of the statistical arcanery and psychobabble the measurement experts drape about their craft. There are some statistical niceties to observe, but most involve sampling technique—making sure you survey enough people and in the right way. Yet, as Professor Michael Scriven, an eminent research design and statistics expert so aptly puts it, "Any statistical test you can't do with a simple hand calculator may be too complex to yield practical results."

Here's a quick list of pointers to help you create a top-notch performance measurement feedback system.

Begin with your service strategy. If it's well designed, you'll find a number of measurable promises in it. Deluxe, for example, posts a service strategy that says: "Our goal is to produce error free financial instruments for the banks and financial institutions of the United States and deliver them in a timely fashion." It translates that operationally as "zero defects, forty-eight-hour turnaround on all orders." The forty-eight-hour turnaround and zero-defects standards are both eminently measurable; so too is the customer's perceptions of what constitutes appropriate order handling.

The service strategy should also suggest some less obvious measurements. For instance, Deluxe's forty-eight-hour turnaround is an internal measure. How long is the order/delivery cycle from the customer's point of view? How long should it be? Where does it break down? What happens to the customer when the system breaks down? What do they do when they perceive they have been waiting too long for an order?

Measure frequently. Once a month is a minimum. In sixty to ninety days, any customer and organizational performance information you now have will be stale. Domino's, for one, formally measures performance quality weekly.

Ask customer-based questions. Tap both the customer's experience ("What happened to you?") and the customer's perception ("How do you feel about what happened to you?"). The customer's specific, personal experience and interpretations enlighten far more than open-ended, general questions such as, "On the whole, how was your stay?"

Ask fair questions. Deal with the things your people can deal with. "Do you believe the federal government should step in" type questions may be entertaining, but they don't yield information people in your organization can act upon. Collecting production figures—number of customers served, number of interviews done—should focus on people-regulated processes, not machine-regulated systems that people are powerless to change or control.

Collect group and individual data. Look for data that can be helpful to individual performers as well as work groups. The people who run the salad line in the dietary department need to know specifically how the salad went over as well as how well the entire meal was received.

Benchmark yourself. Collect information on the sales, market share, and customer satisfaction of your competitors at least three times a year. When J. C. Penney sends store managers out into the malls where its stores are located, they ask the same questions of Sears or Nordstrom customers that they do of their own in order to develop live qualitative and quantitative info on both their own stores and their competition.

Collect both quantitative and qualitative data. Your measurement system should collect numerical ratings as well as customer comments. Both need to be analyzed and discussed. As Marriott's John Dixon reminds his managers, "The specific comments explain the numbers." Both kinds of information are useful.

Make the results visible. Displaying the results emphasizes their importance and destroys the notion that customer ratings are something held in confidence and not discussed with the frontline or above a whisper. In the theme park mentioned earlier, customer satisfaction information was tracked on a giant graph painted on a fifty-foot-long by ten-foot-high wall next to the time clock. At Marriott, front-desk results are posted where front-desk people can see them, restaurant service results where kitchen and wait people will see them, and so on.

Make sure the results are employee-friendly. Simple, straightforward averages and ratios work better than artificially compiled and weighted index scores. People are more likely to understand that "87 percent rated front-desk employees as cheerful and helpful" than that "we received a 4.5 on our 10-factor, weighted average service quality and rainfall appreciation index."

Make sure the results are believable. If employees have seen the results collected, know how they are being compiled, and have evidence that it was *their* customers who gave the information, they're more likely to act on it. If the information comes down from on high, speaks of random sampling and anonymity, or in some way gives the impression that the results are abstract, employees tend to discount it. To make the data more believable, we've seen some companies successfully use their own employees to gather, compile, and post the data.

Make sure the results are used. When customer satisfaction, performance, and service quality information is widely discussed, used for problem-solving meetings, and signals a celebration of success, people see the data as important. Simply posting numbers or sending out a complaint summary memo with an "FYI" on it doesn't really call for any significant action.

How Good Ideas Go Bad

The goal of measurement is to gather information people can use to manage their efforts so they do a better job of meeting the organization's customer service standards. When the feedback system doesn't work, it's often because the information gathered is being used incorrectly. It has stopped being feedback and become a chore, a threat, or something to be avoided.

Dr. Karen Brethower, an industrial psychologist, poses six questions for any measurement system that purports to help people improve their performance, but that doesn't seem to be having the promised effect.

1. Is the information being used to embarrass, punish, or scold employees? If it is, it can be counterproductive in some surprising ways. One company used to give a "Rude Hog" award for the service rep with the lowest customer satisfaction ratings. It wasn't long before employees were vying for it. "Rude Hog" had become a badge of honor. "Way to go Harry! Don't let the SOBs push you around," was the spirit inspired. Most systems designed to punish bad performance this way go wrong in similar fashion.

2. Is the information about something that has no payoff for the people receiving it? Frontline people may be *interested* in sales volume, accounts opened, and so on, but if there is no personal relevance connected to the information, they clump it with other forms of corporate gossip and file it under "nonessential."

3. Is the information too late for employees to act on? By July, feedback about the service center team's April performance is so removed from the actions that created it as to be worthless. Too many things have changed in the interim for employees to be concerned or even remember much about the details of "way back when."

4. Is the feedback about something the people receiving it cannot change or effect? You can tell a five-foot-tall person he's short, but nothing positive will come of it. Telling the mechanics how customers perceive the attitudes of salespeople in the dealership doesn't help either. But telling them customers perceive the service bay as dirty and cluttered, and their behavior as unprofessional, can inspire some change.

5. Is the feedback about the wrong things? Salespeople can't help it if customers think the store is inconveniently located, or isn't decorated in a warm and friendly way. But information that tells them they are closing 70 percent of the sales to people who perceive *them* as easy to locate or warm and helpful against only 25 percent to those who see them as cold and aloof—or can't find them at all—is right on target.

6. Is the information difficult to collect and record? Collecting and recording data can be a positive way to involve frontline people— managers as well—in the nitty-gritty details of the business. But they won't do it if the procedure is hellishly difficult. Totalling and posting the volume of calls handled, customer feedback cards handed out, or sales made from proposals presented are manageable self-monitoring opportunities as long as they're relevant and nonintrusive.

Operating Principle #4: Select, Train, and Empower Employees to Work for the Customer

You start with good people, you train and motivate them, and you give them an opportunity to advance, then the organization succeeds.

—Bill Marriott, Jr., CEO, Marriott Corporation

WHAT HAPPENS BETWEEN YOUR FRONTLINE EMPLOYEES AND YOUR CUSTOMERS makes or breaks you at the moment of truth. Meet customers' expectations and you both win. Miss, and everyone loses. The ultimate success or failure of those critical, person-to-person transactions turns on your organization's success or failure when it comes to hiring good people, training them thoroughly, and managing them in a way that encourages them to "do what needs to be done" for customers.

Selection

To maximize performance on the frontline, start with the right kind of raw material—people who are interested in the kind of work your organization does, and who have a capacity not only for the technical or professional aspects of the job but for the "people parts" too. As we have explored company after company, we constantly have been struck by the slow, careful, calculated way they approach the hiring process for even the lowest-paying positions. The "get somebody, anybody, on those phones" mentality was nowhere in evidence.

Selectivity is a watchword, from Nordstrom department stores to the Mayo Clinic. Both are accustomed to interviewing as many as ten candidates or more for every position to be filled. At Disney, no one is hired on the basis of one interview or the recommendation of one interviewer; at least two of each are required. Piedmont Airlines faced up to the quality challenge inherent in hiring new people in a period of rapid growth by querying its experienced service employees on what *they* felt were the characteristics of good frontline personnel, then evaluating applicants against those criteria. Similarly, Federal Express selects new customer agents, couriers, and other workers on the basis of very scientifically drawn profiles of successful performers in those positions.

Four Seasons Hotels and First Federal/Osceola are notable among a number of companies that look first for evidence of the right attitude, and only then at previous experience or education. On the other hand, Home Depot prizes candidates with do-it-yourself backgrounds because they already know a lot of the things their customers will need and want to know; for the same reason, Williams-Sonoma looks for applicants with an already pronounced penchant for rattling pots and pans.

Nepotism in both the literal and figurative sense pops up in interesting ways among the Service 101. Stew Leonard's Dairy makes a point of hiring relatives of employees who have demonstrated their ability to deliver the kind of service for which the store is renowned. It figures good service runs in the family. Amica Mutual Insurance likewise considers recommendations from current employees—its corporate family—in filling vacancies, just as it respects recommendations from current customers in evaluating new policy applicants. *USA Today* drew its start-up staff from the Gannett family of newspapers coast to coast.

Often, internal recruiting takes precedence over trolling the want ads in hiring for critical frontline positions or supervisory slots. When the Travel Related Services division of American Express needs to fill a customer service position in any of its Regional Operating Centers (ROCs), recruiting is limited to people who are already on the payroll in other ROC positions. Only the cream of the cream should be directly representing the company to the customer, AmEx maintains.

Likewise, the proving ground for supervisors in Walt Disney World and Disneyland is frontline performance on the Jungle Cruise and in the shops along Main Street, U.S.A. In 1988, Nordstrom opened its first location on the East Coast with frontline employees from the area surrounding Tysons Corner, Virginia, but every manager in the store was a Nordy veteran from the West Coast.

Chain and franchise operations also look within to find qualified people to run new locations. H&R Block managers first must earn their chevrons as tax preparers. Parisian supervisors and managers start on the sales floor. With only a couple of exceptions, every Domino's franchisee was once a frontline employee.

Selection standards in the exemplary service organizations tend not to be left up to the whims of local management. On-site managers do indeed make the actual hiring decisions, but the way they arrive at those decisions is not left up to chance. Their organizations put considerable effort into equipping them with the information and tools they need to do good selection—structured interview guides, tests (both performance and paper-and-pencil), successful candidate profiles, and training in interviewing skills. They know what to look for, and they recognize that it's far better in the long run to take a little longer, and be a little pickier, than to have to go through the process all over again in a couple of months.

Training

Hiring and training are opposite sides of the same coin in most high-performing service organizations. If people are a resource, they can and should be developed and refined to increase their ultimate value. That never-ending process includes formal and on-the-job training, guided experience, effective supervision, performance review, and organizational support. Federal Express's James Barksdale only exaggerates a little when he says, "If you train your people well enough, you can just get out of the way and let them do the job."

At FedEx, that's a serious notion: The company invested six months and $5 million training people on the ins and outs of its ill-fated ZAP-mail service before it was introduced. By contrast, a random sample of companies surveyed by Zenger-Miller, a training industry consulting firm, finds that on average U.S. organizations spend a meager $2.58 per frontline employee on service quality training—and the majority of that focuses on cross-selling and handling irate complainers rather than on how to serve customers better. The Zenger-Miller conclusion is starkly eloquent: Frontline employees are "unprepared, unsupported, and unrewarded."

We didn't find that to be true among the Service 101. While we can't put a number to their training expenditures—largely because many guard information on the dollars as well as the details of their training activities as a proprietary component of their competitiveness—we estimate that these organizations dedicate from 1 to 5 percent of their employees' *working hours* (that means on the clock, paid time) to some form of training.

They do occasionally admit to the payoffs. Avon sales reps who have been through the company's training programs sell more product and last longer than those who haven't been formally trained. Much like baby ducks "imprinting" on their mothers, Parisian trainees follow high-performing salespeople around the store, gaining both selling skills and a valuable mentor in the process. Embassy Suites pays employees who are training for better positions, or cross-training for different positions, at a higher rate because the extra skills they develop are valuable inside the hotel. First Federal/Osceola's savings and loan business has been growing in double-digit fashion since everyone at the frontline is now trained and expected to sell as well as serve.

Many of the companies we studied simply refuse to turn new employees loose on unsuspecting customers until a requisite amount of training has been successfully accomplished. At Lands' End and L. L. Bean, two of the bright stars in catalog retailing, new customer service reps aren't allowed near a telephone until they have spent a week or more in training. They remain under the watchful eye of an experienced associate—who monitors calls, answers their questions, and gives feedback and support—until they are able to function on their own. No one drills harder or longer than Merck, where aspiring sales representatives spend a year or more in training before they are deemed sufficiently prepared to represent the pharmaceutical company.

Past experience and modern technology are both employed as teachers. American Express roleplays are based on real situations that have confronted operators in its ROCs. Cashiers in Vons grocery stores and SuperAmerica gas-and-goods outlets practice common and uncommon service situations in the classroom before they go out in the stores to ring up orders for customers. ServiceMaster and Mini Maid have refined cleaning techniques into detailed, step-by-step technical and operations manuals for their workers.

At Domino's, McDonald's, and Wendy's, frontline training is accomplished through store-level VCR installations whose programs introduce new items and emphasize product consistency and control standards. Domino's has gone so far as to invent an animated cartoon character—Vincent Van Dough—to carry the gospel of consistency, safety, and cleanliness to employees via videotapes. In Acura dealerships and Florsheim shoe stores, high-tech, high-end videodisc systems present both product information and training.

What gets taught in all this training? It depends on the job's requirements, but first and foremost among many of the Service 101 is product knowledge. Interestingly, a proprietary retail industry study we examined concluded that one factor capable of driving customers from department stores to discount stores is the inability of employees in the former to provide any more information about a product than the consumer has been able to learn from other sources. If there's no value difference between the two, why pay more?

Product knowledge is a necessity, not a luxury, in more than retail outlets these days. For companies such as Merck and H&R Block, such knowledge is an obvious given, but L. L. Bean trains to a comparable level. Its goal is for telephone customer service reps to be so knowledgeable that they can help the customer make informed purchase decisions, whether the product is duck-hunting boots or a complete outfit for a kayak outing.

The service reps who staff Procter & Gamble's telephone answer center have been out to the manufacturing plants to see how the company's products are made. The salespeople in the Liz Claiborne section of a department store, regardless of what name is over the store's doorway, have been trained to Liz Claiborne's exacting standards. New employees at Walt Disney World and Disneyland are steeped in Disney heritage and traditions. Each, in its own way, is a form of product knowledge training.

As an aside on the subject of product knowledge, it's worth noting how many of the companies we have been studying turn their training efforts outward toward their customers, often by capitalizing on the skills their frontline people bring to or develop on the job. Businessland stores have a classroom as well as a showroom, and customers who buy something in the latter are prone to spend time in the former learning how to use it. Quad/Graphics has its printing camp. L. L. Bean employees conduct about a hundred outdoor skills clinics each year. Home Depot and Williams-Sonoma train their customers on the right ways to use the home improvement products and kitchenwares they sell. Don Beyer Volvo's classroom and resident trainer are available to customers when they're not occupied by the dealership's mechanics. H&R Block screens for new tax preparers while offering tax preparation classes to the general public.

Given their widely varying service strategies, it's not suprising to find a great deal of differentiation in the training organizations give their frontline people in customer-contact or people-handling skills. Airline flight attendants, department store sales associates, restaurant waiters and waitresses, hotel desk and bell staffs, and office machine and computer repair people are among the first employees with whom the customer comes into contact, but the nature of that contact varies tremendously from one industry setting to another. Consequently the training that prepares frontline service people also varies greatly in everything from transactional complexity and performance criteria to duration and technique.

Yet the basic objectives of that training are predictable. The hotel desk clerk or store cashier who makes zero eye contact while sullenly demanding, "Give me nine kinds of identification . . . okay, next!" is a liability our Service 101 simply do not tolerate. Astute managers in companies from airlines and banks to restaurants and retail stores know full well the impact a smile and a thank you from a maid, or a busboy, or a ticket agent, or a parking lot attendant can have on a customer. Comments like, "What a great place—everybody was so helpful and friendly!" have clout no advertising can match.

One challenge trainers wrestle with is the general lack of preparation for the world of work that entry-level people bring to the job. Fortunately, in many customer-contact roles, the actual level of technical skill required to deliver satisfying service is not terribly high. The primary needs of most frontline people can be met with some very basic "here's how we do it here" training. It helps immensely if that training is presented in the context of understanding the importance of the human touch to the customer, which means primary customer-contact employees also need to know how to start the recovery process when things go wrong.

Suffice it to say that people on the frontlines, those whose job descriptions specify that they must meet, greet, and treat customers well, need training that reflects the degree of difficulty of the customer contact built into their job. The good companies provide that kind of training both when their workers start on the job and on a continuing basis. Encouragement from supervisors, occasional refreshers on the basics, progressive sessions added as experience and confidence grows, and timely customer feedback keep the level of performance tuned up and frontline people turned on to providing it.

Every employee has a customer, so everybody in the organization has at least basic responsibility for some level of service quality and customer satisfaction. But the good service providers also develop a cadre of highly skilled customer service specialists. Primary customer-contact employees can handle the normal business of the business—99 percent of the people they deal with are clean, pleasant, and easy to accommodate, providing the organization itself is easy to do business with.

Customer service specialists, on the other hand, work in a more rarified environment, one requiring a greater depth of both technical and product knowledge, as well as interpersonal skills. These people draw the thankless assignment of responding professionally to letters that arrive addressed "You Bunch of @%$*&*#$* Idiots" in words cut from newspaper headlines, or carrying on phone conversations with profanely nasty people seemingly determined to prove they can be ten times as rude, boorish, and insensitive as the person or treatment they have called to complain about. They must be prepared to quiet the loud, calm the outraged, untangle Aunt Martha and Uncle Hank's overdraft problems, and generally convert confused and unhappy users into satisfied customers again.

Why bother? A single sales call costs over $150 these days, and creating new customers is often a long, slow process. The TARP studies cited earlier demonstrate that the cost of satisfying—and keeping—an existing customer who is temporarily upset is marginal compared to the cost of creating a new customer. That's why so many of the Service 101 pride themselves on the skill of their customer service specialists, even as they work hard to reduce the number of times when these people have to be severely tested. Predictably, filling these critical slots requires even greater care than normal in selection, followed by extensive and sophisticated training.

Stress and the Frontline

Frontline service people, most especially the service specialists, but the primary service providers as well, must be able to "stand up"—sometimes literally—to a high level of customer contact. Not all of it will be pleasant. Dealing with customers calls for a level of maturity and self-esteem that allows one to put personal feelings and problems aside to focus on customers and their wants and problems. Service workers need social skills and an understanding of the normal rules of social behavior. A restaurateur we know in upstate Connecticut complains that it is impossible for people to provide good service in a fine dining establishment if they have never experienced good service. He teaches new waiters and waitresses to be diners first, and servers second.

Service workers also need tolerance and stamina. The strain of constant, intensive encounters with people who are essentially strangers leads to burnout. Under the constant stress and pressure, service providers need to be able to continue to perform capably and willingly without withdrawing into robotic, detached behavior or becoming aggressive and hostile.

Perceptive companies are increasingly beginning to recognize and deal with the "emotional labor" component of high-contact service jobs. That's encouraging. It isn't that long ago that managers would sniff that working a phone bank or service desk all day was a cushy job, not at all like spending a shift on the assembly line or down at the mill. Work is work. Service providers just come home feeling a different kind of tired.

Basing selection on evidence of ability to do contact-intensive service work is difficult, but not impossible. In a shrinking labor market, it's becoming trickier, however. The more adept a company becomes at extending the tenure of its current experienced and proven service workers, the more control it retains over the quality of service its customers experience. In response to this dynamic, organizations are beginning to train their frontline people in stress management and "emotional self-defense" strategies.

In addition, they are realizing the importance of training managers to accept and support the need a frontline worker may occasionally feel to walk away, if only for a moment, before overload occurs. In theme parks like Disney's, frontline people have the option of "going offstage" when the pressure gets too high, and can do so without fear of recrimination. In hospitals and airlines, frontline employees sometimes form support groups to help each other deal with the stresses and frustrations experienced on the job. It is an area of valid concern, and one we believe will grow increasingly important as the effort to improve service quality continues to heat up.

Turning the Frontline Loose

When Dorn Johnstone, vice president of planning and development for American Health Group International, a health services corporation in Kirkland, Washington, wants to explain the meaning of "empowerment," he tells a story about his local Nordstrom store. One day, quite by accident, a pair of suit pants got into the laundry pile instead of the dry-cleaning pile. They came out looking like something from Mickey Rooney's rag bag, so he stopped by Nordstrom's in hopes of purchasing a replacement pair. Two weeks passed before his salesman called to report no luck in finding a pair anywhere. He'd even called the manufacturer, thinking to have a new pair made, but there was no material left from the dye lot, so the pants wouldn't match the jacket.

Then came the kicker: The salesman said he was crediting the price of the suit to Johnstone's Nordstrom account. Not necessary, Johnstone protested—after all, it was his mistake. The store certainly wasn't responsible. The salesman conceded that point, but noted that his customer now had a worthless half of a suit, and that would never do. Oh, and he looked forward to taking care of him when he came in to use the credit to replace the suit.

"Do you have any doubts about where I do my clothes shopping today?" Johnstone asks. "Or who my salesman is?"

It's a story that both stretches credulity and makes a point: Exemplary customer care can and does create extraordinary customer loyalty. But stories like these (and where Nordstrom is concerned, they are legion) also cause people to shake their heads, throw up their hands, and lament: "Not in my organization. Not in my lifetime. Not in a thousand years." The point in telling the tale is to dramatize how taking a little initiative keeps customers coming back. Yet how seldom that initiative is taken, and how many reasons there are for not taking—and not giving permission to others to take—that initiative.

Empowerment is the next necessary step beyond simply training employees to do their jobs. It means encouraging and rewarding them for extra effort, imagination, and initiative—and tolerating their missteps when well-intentioned efforts fail to work out exactly as planned. The goal is that best of all business worlds where empowered employees confidently and capably address unique problems and opportunities when and as they occur.

At first blush, it sounds like an apple pie and motherhood idea: "In a service-focused organization, frontline employees—those people who deal most directly with the customer—should have the skill, knowledge, tools, time, and authority to do whatever it takes to meet a customer's needs." Who could be against it?

Anyone accustomed to the exercise of traditional forms of authority, that's who. And anyone unaccustomed to taking responsibility for thinking up and implementing on-the-spot solutions that aren't in the book. It's risky. It sounds like a lot of random energy is pulsing through the organization, and who knows where and how it will come out? And it smacks of that radical decentralization stuff. A lot of things can go wrong.

A frustrated bank officer told us what happened when first-line managers were instructed to let line employees make the check-cashing decisions traditionally reserved for branch management. It was supposed to free the branch managers for other things. Instead, the tellers wrote rules for check-cashing that would have made even the bank's president show three forms of ID to deposit his paycheck. So much for just "turning 'em loose" to serve the customer!

By contrast, however, you'll find evidence of empowerment is a common theme running through many, even most, of the profiles to come. The Service 101 consistently and profitably demonstrate that there is much more to empowerment than simply passing hands over previously "held-down" employees. Selection, training, tools, and management all come into play.

While sharing the dais of an executive seminar with James Barksdale of Federal Express, we heard him express, in very unflustered fashion, the FedEx mindset on empowerment. He had been asked how the company's managers had so quickly authorized the middle-of-the-night airlift that brought special rescue equipment to Texas so drillers could extricate little Jessica McClure from the well in which she'd become trapped. Barksdale's response was clear and to the point. "There *wasn't* any management authorization required. The operator who answered the call in our regional center just said yes and started the ball rolling," he explained.

How could that be, an incredulous listener persisted. "Look," Barksdale replied, "my job is to see to it that we hire, train, and pay people to make that kind of decision right there on the frontline. If that person calls me at home in the middle of the night to okay doing something that important, I've failed as a manager."

Empowerment, the act of vesting substantial responsibility in the people nearest to the problems to be solved, is an exhilarating and awesome thing for any manager with a healthy respect for Murphy's Law to contemplate. Nonetheless, the pressure for improved service quality and productivity, accentuated by the thinning of middle management ranks, is leading an increasing number of companies to accept it as a significant part of the answer to the question, "How can we get more responsibility down to the frontline, where it belongs?"

In *The Renewal Factor*, Robert H. Waterman, Jr., refers to empowerment as a matter of management adhering to and encouraging faith in the principle that "the person doing the job knows far better than anyone else the best way of doing the job, and therefore is the one best fitted to improve it." Waterman insists that the key to creating an empowered work force is the development of a style of management he calls "directed autonomy."

Here's how it looks to him: "People in every nook and cranny of the organization empowered—encouraged in fact—to do things their way. Suggestions are actively sought. But this all takes place within a context of direction. People know what the boundaries are; they know where they should act on their own and where not. The boss knows that his or her job is to establish those boundaries, and then truly get out of the way."

Empowerment in many ways is the reverse of doing things "by the book." Sometimes, in fact, it entails the elimination of the rule book. Nordstrom's company policy manual is one sentence long: "Use your own best judgment at all times." An invitation to anarchy? Not really. According to Tom Peters, it also frees management to be its best: "At Nordstrom the absence of manuals is anything but an invitation to chaos. Nordstrom supervisors are always coaching and teaching. Indeed says [Nordstrom VP] Betsy Sanders, their chief duty is to coach salespersons on exactly what it means to 'use your own best judgment.' "

If service is to succeed and satisfy, it is important, even critical, that employees know how to do their jobs and do them well. But the creation of the perfect procedural manual isn't the means to that end. If anything, it represents the antithesis of what it takes to create high-quality, responsive service.

In *The Change Masters*, Harvard Business School professor Rosabeth Moss Kanter argues that there are three basic "power tools" that must be in place before employees can actually take charge of their environment and "reach outside of and beyond the authority of position to develop ideas for change." These power tools are information (data, technical knowledge, political intelligence, expertise), resources (funds, materials, space, time), and support (endorsement, backing, approval, legitimacy).

Beyond these tools, she argues that individual employees, if they are to take grassroots responsibility for responsiveness to customers, must believe that there is an opportunity to perform in an empowered way, have a sense of personal self-esteem, accept "ownership" of the job to be done, feel part of a team, and believe that they are involved in something of importance or purpose.

Tom Peters tends to be more direct and less academic. To get the best efforts possible from people, he advises, it is necessary to "dehumiliate" work by eliminating the "policies and practices (almost always tiny) of the organization which demean and belittle human dignity. It is impossible to get people's best efforts, involvement, and caring concern for things you believe important to your customers and the long-term best interests of your organization when we write policies and procedures that treat them like thieves and paperclip bandits."

Employee as Customer

Research conducted by University of Maryland management professor Benjamin Schneider shows the impact of management practices on employee performance and customer satisfaction. He reports that *employees'* satisfaction with the way they are managed is significantly related to *customers'* satisfaction with the service they receive from the organization. In other words, he has found that when employees are satisfied with the way they are treated, with the availability of the right tools to do the job, and with management support for delivering high-quality service, customers are more likely to be satisfied with the quality of treatment they receive from those employees and more likely to continue doing business with the organization.

In many of the exemplary service organizations we profile here, employees are routinely and consciously treated with the same respect with which they are expected to treat customers. Indeed, in many organizations employees are seen as "internal customers" and managers reflect a dictum we first heard expressed by Jan Carlzon of SAS: "If you're not serving the customer, your job is to be serving someone who is." That's a simple but important acknowledgment that rudeness, disrespect, and petty tyranny flow downhill in organizations, and the last stop on the slope is directly in front of the customer.

There are two dimensions to empowerment—one organizational, one personal. Giving employees overt permission and encouragement to work creatively in the customer's best interests, providing support for their efforts, treating them as you expect customers to be treated, and rewarding and applauding their triumphs and achievements are organizational tactics necessary to convince frontline workers that they really are empowered to work for the customer. These organizational responses recognize that empowerment isn't something *given*. It is a process of *releasing* the individual employee's power or capability by removing the barriers that prevent their expression. The factors that professors Kanter and Schneider talk about and that Waterman illustrates are organizational factors. They deal with things surrounding the employee.

The personal dimension of empowerment has to do with things internal, with the capability and skill of the employee to respond appropriately when the barriers have been removed. The capacity, the potential, must be there, and it also must be nurtured and developed. Finding people with the capacity is a selection issue. Developing that capacity's potential is the training side of the coin. Neither, however, confers service wisdom. That comes from the breadth and depth of experience that empowered employees amass and continually reinvest on behalf of the customer—to the benefit of both the organization and themselves.

```
┌─────────────────────────────────────────────────────┐
│                                                     │
│              Operating Principle #5:                │
│         Recognize and Reward Accomplishment         │
║                                                     ║
└─────────────────────────────────────────────────────┘
```

Recognition and reward has to be done on a very short interval basis . . . given immediately after the service was rendered. [It's] not something that you'd get in your pension 35 years from now, but it's money you can buy bread with Monday.

—Edward E. Crutchfield, Jr., Chairman and CEO, First Union Corporation

MANAGERS IN THE EXEMPLARY SERVICE ORGANIZATION UNDERSTAND THE TWIN-engine motivation of recognition and reward. Recognizing and praising employees for a job well done isn't seen as a superfluous effort. It is understood for what it truly is, a confirmation of accomplishment and a reinforcement of commitment.

As you'll see from their profiles, in most of these organizations there is a positive payoff for employees who *meet* the service standards, and both financial rewards and psychic accolades for those who *exceed* them. Those who go one step beyond for the customers become "service heroes." They are held up as role models and rewarded accordingly, because their managers, and their managers' managers, know that the celebration of organizational, group, and individual service accomplishments is essential if the delivery of high-quality service is to be the norm, not the exception.

Compensation and Motivation

People don't work just for the fun of it. They work, first and foremost, for the money they need to buy the necessities and luxuries of life. Money is a powerful motivator—and a very generalized one. It is a means to a vast number of ends, and makes the fulfillment of an infinite number of dreams possible.

Most of us start from the need to know that the work we do will earn our minimum subsistence requirements. As pay rises, so too do organizational visibility and prestige, and personal pride and self-esteem. Those attributes can be harnessed to motivate continuing performance. Consequently, service-distinctive organizations not uncommonly pay above the average for their industry—and they make that both a point of internal pride and a prominent feature in their external recruitment efforts.

Realizing that straight pay, while it may ensure attendance, does not typically produce strategic alignment, personal enthusiasm, or outstanding performance, many of the Service 101 use the carrot of monetary incentives as well. Mississippi Management pays regular bonuses for such mundane tasks as carving prime rib properly or making more beds (in the correct way, to be sure) than the norm. SuperShuttle drivers can work toward a paid day off on which they are compensated on the basis of their own typical performance; the more they hustle and the better they serve, the more they earn on the job *and* the more valuable their time off becomes.

Federal Express employees, from the couriers on the streets each day to the parcel sorters in the Memphis hub every night, fall into this category. Sorters start at well over $9 an hour, and even part-timers are eligible for profit-sharing bonuses. At Nordstrom, salespeople earn about $2 an hour above local retail wages plus a sales commission of 6-percent or more. A top sales associate can gross $50,000 to $60,000 a year working the sales floor, the kind of money most people assume is reserved to managerial work. It's not uncommon, incidentally, for a Nordstrom sales associate to have had management experience in another retailing organization.

It's a little puzzling that more companies don't use incentive-style compensation at the frontline. Personal pay tied to organizational performance has long been a valued perk of executives, and generally with sound results. A 1983 McKinsey & Co. study found that in the most profitable companies in the $25 million sales range, for example, 40 percent of CEO compensation and 36 percent of senior management pay is tied to organizational performance. A study conducted in the late 1970s for the National Science Foundation noted that among the eleven hundred companies then listed on the New York Stock Exchange, those with formal incentive plans for managers earned on average 43.6 percent more in pretax profit than companies that did not use incentives.

But executives aren't the only ones who respond positively to such programs. The same National Science Foundation report also reviewed three hundred studies of productivity, pay, and job satisfaction and concluded that when employees' pay is linked to their performance, their motivation to work is raised, productivity is higher, and they are likely to be more satisfied with their work. One specific study the report cited had looked at four hundred companies and found that going from no measurement of work to a work measurement and performance feedback system raised productivity an average of about 43 percent. When both performance feedback and *incentives* were instituted, productivity rose 63.8 percent on average.

The study's authors concluded that increased productivity depends on two propositions. First comes motivation: arousing and maintaining the will to work effectively—having workers who are productive not because they are coerced but because they are committed. Second is reward: Of all the factors that help to create highly motivated and highly satisfied workers, the principal one, the National Science Foundation report noted, appears to be that effective performance be recognized and rewarded in whatever terms are meaningful to the individual—financial, psychological, or both.

That message traditionally has been better understood in manufacturing companies than in service organizations. *People, Performance and Pay*, a recent study by the American Productivity Center in Houston and the American Compensation Association, found that 48 percent of manufacturers, but only 19 percent of service companies, use performance incentive systems. In the service businesses using such compensation tactics, productivity gain-sharing, pay-for-knowledge, and small-group incentives were reported to be the most successful techniques.

Incentive systems aren't automatic performance generators, of course. They can even backfire and be counterproductive when they don't work out in the fashion anticipated. Several times we've seen organizations readjust a system when it became obvious that salespeople were going to greatly exceed the targets that had been set for them. The excuse always seemed to be that the program "needs some fine-tuning." But often we learned behind closed doors that someone in senior management had decided it was unseemly for the frontline people to earn so much more than others "at *their* level." We suspect that translates as, "Who do they think they are, earning as much for frontline work as I do as a manager?" Invariably, the frontline people get the message and never do anything remotely productive enough to get them "rate busted" again.

The impulse to make sure the troops don't make too much, says Harvard's Rosabeth Moss Kanter, is a fairly natural one. As she explains it: "Social psychologists have shown that the maintenance of an authority relationship depends on a degree of inequality. If the distance between boss and subordinate—social, economic, or otherwise—declines, so does automatic deference and respect.

"This is further aided by the existence of objective measures of contribution. Once high performance is established, once the measures are clear and clearly achieved, the subordinate no longer needs the good will of his or her boss quite so much. One more source of dependency is reduced, and power again becomes more equalized. Proven achievement reflected in higher earnings than the boss's produces security. Security produces risk-taking. Risk-taking produces speaking up and pushing back."

The instinct to preserve traditional forms of hierarchy and bureaucracy is well worth fighting against when the objective is superior service. As previously discussed, managers are only free to lead when they are able to free their employees to act as if they have the ability to think, understand, and do something about the legitimate problems encountered in the day-to-day conduct of the business.

It is vital, however, to think through all the implications of an incentive plan before it is instituted. Brokerage houses have long provided incentives to stockbrokers on an individual performance basis, typically calculated on measures of sales. Individual revenues build into gross revenues, of course—and when revenue records, not customer satisfaction, become the organization's overriding goal, service-centered considerations become less important than the next quarterly.

Even before the October 1987 crash, industry observers and the business press had begun to question some of the practices coming into vogue up and down Wall Street. At some houses, every sort of incentive was turned on the brokers—furs, Mercedes, yachts, dinner for two any place on the planet, you name it. The operative and far from trivial question was whether these practices—notable by their absence at Goldman Sachs and A. G. Edwards & Sons—were causing brokers to work *against* their clients' best interests, churning accounts and pushing people into questionable ventures because of the remarkable ways such activity boosted personal compensation and rewards. It's not far removed from the ethical debate in medicine over the performance of unnecessary surgery to keep the knife from getting rusty and the cash flow from drying up.

To be effective as a long-term service tactic, incentives must be based on the customer's best interests as well as their effects on the individual's and the company's sales figures. Incentives should help emphasize legitimate customer satisfaction. An incentive program that subordinates an organization's long-term relationship with the customer to consideration of an individual's selfish, short-term gain—whether that individual is a frontline salesperson, a stockholder, or a highly placed executive—is a dangerous narcotic.

Symbolic Reward

Money isn't everything—although the cynical may insist that it's an extremely close second to whatever is first. Effective incentive and reward programs can also be created from a combination of dollars, trips to exotic locales, merchandise, and purely psychic payoffs. American Airlines employs much of the same reward methodology built into its frequent-flyer program to provide an incentive framework for individual and small group service achievements. Ryder uses a similar program to reward the efforts of the dealers who rent its trucks out to customers.

Exclusivity can lend cachet to programs whose actual goods range from simple to awe-inspiring. Employees at Southern Bell often ask where they can buy the designer-style jackets and sports clothing the company awards to outstanding service providers. They're told the line's not for sale—the only way to *get* a jacket is to *earn* a jacket. By the same token, executives at Acura's U.S. headquarters in Gardena, California, can only envy the limited-edition crystal sculptures awarded to the best dealerships, because the contract calls for the creator to produce only enough for the winners.

A little spontaneity is often an effective ingredient in choosing an award or making one out of something the business already has readily at hand. With the St. Louis Cardinals playing in the 1987 World Series, a Citicorp manager in that river city knew exactly how to call attention to the service accomplishments of his branch's people. The cruise-for-two promos accumulated from wholesalers in 1987 by Ukrop's Super Markets in Richmond, Virginia, became highly sought-after prizes when they were converted to rewards for exceptional frontline performers throughout the small supermarket chain. Auto mechanics at Don Beyer Volvo regularly compete for a month's worth of driving around in a luxury model right off the showroom floor.

And little rewards can be as effective as big ones if they're used in the right way. Lapel-style pins and special nametags are tactics common to service leaders from Federal Express and Citicorp to LensCrafters and First Federal/Osceola. At Citicorp Retail Services in Denver, bright ideas for new or improved ways to serve customers warrant the awarding of a "Bright Ideas" coffee mug or similar keepsake to each and every contributor. Meanwhile, the employee submitting the best idea of the month wins temporary possession of a revolving trophy—a three-foot-high light bulb.

The thought behind the Citicorp program is no less important for the lighthearted nature of its visible aspects. According to Lauren O'Connell, assistant vice president of operations, "The point of these contests and recognition programs and service evaluations and checklists is that they make everyone feel that quality service is his or her individual responsibility. That not only leads to better service quality for the customer, it also means higher morale. People do care about their jobs when they know that their managers consider those jobs to be important. And caring about one's job and knowing that it's important is where service quality really starts."

Celebration

Often entwined with the recognition and reward is a sense of celebration. That's clearly an operative concept when American Express assembles its Great Performers in New York each year so executives and colleagues alike can glow all over them for a job exceptionally done. LensCrafters and Southern Bell's parent, BellSouth, also bring their service award winners into corporate headquarters at annual meeting time to make a big deal out of their achievements, and service awards are passed out at national meetings of managers and franchisees by Pizza Hut and Domino's alike as part of a carefully planned celebration of common efforts and successes.

Organizational development consultant Cathy DeForest writes that, like the leaders of an army, managers must "recognize that the act of celebrating provides a way to nourish the spirit of an organization as well as create a moment in time when a glimpse of a transformed organization can be seen and felt. Organizational celebration is a way, a process, of honoring individuals, groups, events, achievements, the common and extraordinary life within an organization in a creative, meaningful, and often festive manner."

Recognition and celebration also are a way of reaffirming to people, in highly human terms, that they are an important part of something that matters. They can be significant motivators for people in any organization, but especially so in a service organization, where pride of product is essentially pride in personal performance. Two recent studies make the point.

In late 1987, *Inc.* magazine and the Hay Group consulting company compared opinions and feelings of employees in the relatively smaller companies who form the "*Inc.* 500" with those of employees in the large corporations that make up the *Fortune* 500. They were more than a little surprised to find that while employees in small companies rate their pay and benefits as poorer, their opportunity for advancement as less, and company communication as worse than do their counterparts in the larger companies, their overall job satisfaction was significantly and spectacularly higher.

Why? According to the *Inc.*/Hay survey, the employees of these smaller companies believed themselves to be important to their organization, and felt their organization was doing something significant. More specifically, the employees of the smaller companies felt their work was more challenging, said their ideas were more likely to be adopted, reported a higher sense of accomplishment from what they did, and thought they were treated with more respect.

Focus group discussions validated the survey findings, *Inc.* reported: "These are employees who talk about the company in first-person plural, as in, 'We can serve our customers faster,' or 'We may look like we're disorganized, but we're not.' Said another: 'The quality is personal—the product is us.' "

The second confirmation of the importance of feeling involved in something worthwhile comes from the previously mentioned Forum Corporation study, reported in January 1988. Forum found that employees who believed that their organization served customers well were much less likely to say they planned to leave their current jobs within the next year than those who felt they worked for a company that was doing a poor job of serving the customer.

Throughout the Service 101, that vision of being part of something valuable, worthwhile, and important quite often was expressed best and most forcefully by the executives at the very top of the organization. Fred Smith, founder of Federal Express, had the fixed-jaw, fiery look of the true believer when he told us, "Our corporate philosophy is People, Service, Profit. We do something important. We carry the most important commerce in the history of the world." Significantly, we heard the same sentiment repeated over and over again by couriers and managers throughout the FedEx system.

Marriott employees told us, "We're part of a family here. The name Marriott is a person's name, and it stands for something." At Riverside Methodist, Erie Chapman makes it his responsibility to reinforce the fact that he and his hospital's employees are involved in critically important work. We heard and felt the same sense of pride and belonging from people at Lands' End, Dun & Bradstreet, United Van Lines, Southern Bell, CompuServe, Delta Air Lines, Miller Business Systems, Kinder-Care, Chubb and Northwestern Mutual insurance, 3M and H. B. Fuller, Beth Israel Hospital and the Mayo Clinic.

But the most memorable way we heard it expressed was at Walt Disney World, where we stopped one day to chat with a young groundskeeper. "How do you like being a street-sweeper in a theme park?" we asked. He stepped back, stood up tall, looked us square in the eye, and shot back: "Oh, no. I'm not a street-sweeper. I'm in show business. I'm part of the Act."

To frontline workers in any organization with ambitions of providing distinctive service to its customers, the importance of being a part of something important may be the most important operating principle of all.

PART 2

THE SERVICE 101

TRAVEL

AIRLINES

Delta Air Lines

American Airlines

Piedmont Airlines (USAir)

SERVICES

American Automobile Association

Club Med

SuperShuttle

Travel: Do Larry, Curly, and Moe
Really Run the Airlines?

REFINED TO ITS ESSENCE, AN AIRLINE HAS A SIMPLE CHARGE: TO MOVE PEOPLE from point A to point B across the face of the earth and get them there safely and on time, with their luggage in hand. In service management parlance, that is an airline's *core* service, its assumed mission. If it can't complete that mission regularly and routinely, then there is some question whether it should even purport to be an airline at all.

In 1987 the issue was not moot. According to the Federal Aviation Agency and the Department of Transportation (FAA and DOT, respectively), official government watchdogs of the airline industry, U.S. air carriers "bumped," or forced to give up their seats, 60,424 legitimately booked passengers in the first three months of 1987. They also mishandled 11 out of every 1,000 passenger bags, met their published schedules only 66 percent of the time, and were involved in a total of 1,063 "near misses" for the year. To the best of anyone's knowledge, only one commercial air flight, a Delta 737 bound from Atlanta to Lexington, Kentucky, actually landed at the wrong airport in the wrong city. The crew mistook nearby Frankfort for Lexington—slightly less embarrassing than mistaking Newark for New York City, but only slightly.

Nor do the airlines seem to be doing much better at delivering *peripheral* services: those value-added things like seat comfort, meal quality, and TLC that surround the core, and that tend to be the easiest place for one airline to distinguish itself from another. In 1987 flyers lodged 4,068 complaints about customer service—protests concerning poor treatment at the hands of airline employees—with the Department of Transportation. That made customer treatment the third most complained about aspect of air travel, immediately after flight schedule and baggage problems. In 1986, by comparison, customer treatment was only the sixth most frequently recorded DOT complaint. Overall, disgruntled airline passengers filed 44,845 complaints in 1987, an increase of 252 percent over 1986.

And now the one thing the airlines have been successful with lately, the frequent flyer free-flight come-on, is boomeranging on them. Started in

1981 by American Airlines as a way of inducing some semblance of brand loyalty, frequent flyer plans today have more than 30 million enrollees. Converted to tickets, the free flight points earned by this group in just seven years comes to a whopping IOU of about $1.24 billion, or 5.4 billion free air miles.

The most intriguing thing about frequent flyer programs is that, on a scale of 1 to 10, most frequent flyers—the 45 to 48 percent of the airline customer base that flies for business reasons and holds most of the free flight points—generally rank the mileage giveaway programs a "2" in importance.

Rod Stiefbold, a service quality researcher with Custom Research Inc., Minneapolis, has done a good number of airline studies, and he marvels that "customers by and large rate safety, schedule convenience, ticket prices, seat comfort, meal quality and treatment by crew and agents as more important than an airline's frequent flyer program. Yet where do they put their effort? On the frequent flyer programs. I guess they like majoring in the minors."

Stiefbold's assessment isn't a solitary one. When, in 1987, the International Foundation of Airline Passengers' Associations (IFAPA) asked thirty thousand frequent flyers worldwide to rank airline features in terms of importance, the researchers reported: "Convenient schedules generally take top priority, followed by safety and security, seating comfort, punctuality, in-flight service, and frequency [of flights]."

The study also reported that "priorities for improvement are basically similar around the world, with the striking exception of a massive demand for improved punctuality in North America." Other North American airline features in need of improvement, in order, were: seating comfort, safety and security, carry-on baggage space, check-in and boarding process, consistent standards between airlines, low fares, in-flight service, convenient reservations, and cabin crew performance. It seems clear that a big dose of smile training or a couple hundred gross of linen napkins won't do much to alleviate the flying public's disenchantment with the airline industry. The problems of greatest concern to the consumer are much more fundamental.

Is this any way to run an airline system, much less a single airline? No, of course not. And when asked, industry people from regulators and owners to pilots, baggage handlers, and cabin attendants agree. So what's the problem? Why don't they just shape up? As is the case with most of the newly deregulated industries we have looked at, "easier said than done" is a bona fide and appropriate answer.

Since 1978, when Congress freed airlines to compete in an essentially free market manner, air traffic has skyrocketed. In 1987, U.S. carriers lofted 17,000 flights a day and boarded a total of 450 million passengers, half again as many passengers as in any year prior to deregulation. One estimate suggests that by 2001 the total will reach 750 million a year. All this traffic increase has been accomplished, mind you, with the same airports, same air traffic control system (minus several thousand well-trained air traffic controllers sent packing by Ronald Reagan), and the same basic technology that was in place in 1974.

The airlines, for their part, haven't done anything to alleviate the pressures. In a desperate effort to garner early-morning business traffic, virtually all have published what amount to bogus schedules, promising departure and arrival times that are virtually impossible to meet due to the simple fact that all are using essentially the same departure and arrival times for the same destinations.

With Congress unwilling to spend big to improve the air traffic control system, and no new metropolitan airport closer than ten years away, the prognosis for better flying through better facilities is dim. Clearly the congressional and industry leaders who thought decontrol of the airlines would be a neat idea hadn't the foggiest notion of the fallout effects of their impulse.

Deregulation has had other effects. The airlines that went into the deregulation era in strong financial condition immediately started gobbling up weaker national and regional competitors as well as a majority of the commuter lines. The thirteen major national lines that existed before decontrol are down to nine; eight if you consider that Eastern and Continental are both owned by Texas Air, the same company that bought and absorbed Frontier and People Express airlines.

At the same time, carriers that once had required routes in marginally profitable areas quickly abandoned them to the dominant regionals, who immediately priced themselves the way most sole suppliers do. De facto monopolies now exist. Flying out of Minneapolis or Milwaukee? You have little choice but Northwest. St. Louis? TWA has 317 departing flights compared to 22 for its nearest rival. From Dallas, it's American; from Pittsburgh, it's USAir—and so on. According to University of Denver transportation law expert Paul Stephen Dempsey, Texas Air, Delta, American, TWA, and Northwest control more than 84 percent of U.S. passenger air traffic. (So much for the pre-deregulation promise of increased choice through freer competition!)

Ticket price wars on the heavily traveled routes, drastic cost-cutting measures, mounting frequent flyer indebtedness, and the inability of new era managers like Frank Lorenzo to squeeze more than a pittance of pay givebacks from employees have conspired to depress airline earnings and stock prices—none of which makes airline execs too eager to do much more to improve service than write stirring speeches or commission pretentious advertising campaigns that declare service improved. (And so much for the theory of market supply and demand!)

Yet while passengers are seething about flight delays and cancellations, lost and damaged luggage, overbooked flights, poor treatment, reservation problems, and confusing, questionable fares, they are not necessarily pining for a re-regulation of the industry. The IFAPA study found a majority of respondents agreeing that decontrol has been a success. These respondents cite decreases in fares, increases in choice, and an increase in flight frequencies as benefits of deregulation. Although 52 percent of the IFAPA respondents blame deregulation for worsened conditions at airports, an adverse impact on safety, and deterioration in both cabin service and flight-connection assurance, only one in three is willing to suggest a return to the rules of 1978.

How the Airlines Are Responding

Whether from embarrassment, consumer pressure, or fear of further congressional action, the airlines are *trying* to recoup from their gravely tarnished service images:

- American and Delta have bolstered the training of frontline people with an emphasis on dealing with customer complaints.
- Six of the nation's major airlines have vowed to publish more realistic flight schedules.
- Continental, whose strategy clearly has been to substitute low fares for decent customer treatment, has gone to its employees with a plea—and an incentive—for improved service.
- The president of Eastern took the unprecedented step of writing an open letter to frequent flyers to acknowledge and explain problems, and promise to improve. At some Eastern stations, customer service people have been granted more authority to compensate customers for cancelled and delayed flights.
- Northwest, the champ of lost luggage, hired away a competitor's baggage-moving guru. And although Northwest has in the past been one of the least-on-time airlines, it has of late experimented successfully with performance guarantees. A recent Chicago/Minneapolis "You fly on time or you fly on us" program, says a spokesman, challenged and motivated employees, pleased customers, and improved performance.
- American has developed a policy of informing passengers of alternate flights that are available when American is experiencing long delays.
- TWA has launched an upgraded in-flight quality control system. Thirty people are now paid to fly the airline and rate the service. They reward superior service on the spot.
- United, which cut over 1,200 management jobs in 1986, has hired 700 new customer service agents and more than 4,000 new ground crew mechanics.

The Better than Average

It's a fact that no U.S.-based airline gets the kind of ratings from passengers that European and Asia/Pacific airlines receive. And though much of the blame for that falls on the industry's shoulders, a goodly portion of the problem will remain unsolvable until the airline "infrastructure" is modernized in consort with contemporary air travel needs. Just the same, some American carriers have developed a discernible edge on their domestic competition and are working hard to make the best of a bad situation.

The IFAPA study found American and Delta among the preferred of the world—at least in the eyes of North American frequent flyers. A 1987 poll by *Travel-Holiday* magazine named Delta and Piedmont the numbers one and two domestic airlines. The poll's top two international airlines were Swissair and Singapore Airlines, the same two airlines favored by most IFAPA respondents (actually second was a tie between Singapore Airlines and Air New Zealand).

A poll of 150 chief executive officers and senior bankers in 26 countries conducted by *Institutional Investor* magazine rated airlines on six factors: on-time performance, cabin cleanliness, meals/beverage service, helpful flight attendants, helpful ground personnel, and sleeperette seats. While no U.S. carrier was rated in the top three in any category—only one airline, Swissair, won medals in all six categories—American and Delta were rated eleventh and fourteenth, respectively.

So our best examples of service quality for U.S. airlines are Delta and American, plus Piedmont, which is becoming part of USAir. While none is perfect, all three are, in their customers' eyes, better than the competition. And all seem to be head and shoulders above the competition in making a genuine effort—as opposed to offering purely lip service rhetoric—to improve service quality. Their employees and customers both seem to appreciate that.

It's worth noting that the four airlines with the "youngest" fleets of aircraft are, in order, Delta, Piedmont, American, and USAir. Not only are their peripherals better, but they have all been managed with an emphasis on investing in the essential equipment for the core service without which service quality issues are irrelevant.

A footnote on the selection of Delta: One airline industry old-timer we interviewed made an interesting observation. "You know," he mused, "when you look at the numbers, Delta isn't all that good. They ran seventh, eighth, and ninth in on-time performance all year, and they're not tops on baggage, or on bumping. But they have been telling themselves, and us, they are the best for so long we and *they* actually believe it."

He's right. Despite bump, on-time, and baggage statistics that are modest at best, Delta was the least complained about airline in 1987. That reminded us of a grudging compliment Donald Burr, chairman and founder of People Express—the no-service airline that no longer exists— once paid Delta in a *Wall Street Journal* interview: "The moment you're bumped from a Delta flight and you're unhappy, a little man in a red jacket rushes up and he says, 'I'll call your Aunt Minnie and tell her you're not on the flight so she won't worry, and meanwhile why don't you come over here and have a cup of coffee, and we'll get you on the next flight.' After treatment like that, few passengers complain about Delta."

Perhaps Mr. Burr was "righter" than even he suspected. In the multi-billion dollar gamble that is today's airline industry, a carrier's fate in the customer's eyes could well depend on some not so very big things, like little men in red jackets working their bottoms off to show their customers that they know what a mess contemporary air travel is, and that they dislike it as much as the passengers do.

Taking Care of the Traveler

They also profit who only *serve* those who stand and wait. Getting there is part of the travel experience. Staying there is another. What you do there is a third. We look at a couple of renowned entertainment exemplars in the Pacesetters section to come, and we'll consider the Hotel industry in the next chapter.

But there's another piece of the travel puzzle that involves service, and it's the piece that includes all those necessary but sometimes obnoxious little pieces that support the trip: making the arrangements, planning the vacation, routing the drive, checking out the accommodations, getting the traveler to and from the airport or hotel. We've been impressed by the activities of three organizations whose size, structure, and mission vary tremendously, but whose commitment to service is noteworthy.

The American Automobile Association has become a good deal more than just an "auto club"—it will plan your route, stock your glove box with maps, help you pick a hotel, arrange your airline tickets and accommodations, sell you traveler's checks, issue you an International Driving Permit, and make sure you know just who to turn to if you have car trouble along the highway. Club Med will take your entire vacation in hand, relieving you of figuring out where to go, how to get there, or what to do while you're there. And if you happen to be in or passing through one of the cities served by SuperShuttle—a West Coast hybrid of bus, limo, and taxi services that seems to have figured out how to take the best and eliminate the worst from all three—you may actually find yourself enjoying the trip from the airport into town, or back.

Bon voyage.

Delta Air Lines

ONE OF THE MOST GRAPHIC AND INSPIRING EXAMPLES OF GOOD SERVICE TURNING around an ailing corporation took place in the early 1980s at an airline: Sweden's Scandinavian Airlines System, better known as SAS. Almost simultaneously in Great Britain, British Air was successfully making the transition from government-owned entity to privatized company, in large part through a diligent emphasis on improved, high-quality service to its passengers.

During pretty much the same period, on the other hand, U.S.-based airlines have come in for miles and miles of criticism. Since deregulation clouded the skies in 1978, late flights, congested airports, endless baggage and overbooking snafus, and often rude and insensitive personnel both on and off the airplanes have come to be seen as simply a state-of-the-art experience for legions of long-suffering American air travelers.

Or so it sometimes seems from the talk in departure lounges and the commentary in the business and popular press.

But while deregulation—and, more significantly, the industrywide shift to hub-and-spoke operating profiles that funnel feeder flights into and out of centralized and congested regional air terminals—has caused disruptions and delays and undeniably aggravated weak spots in the U.S. air travel system, good service is not a lost art, nor is it a talent never known on domestic air carriers. One of the best examples of that is Delta Air Lines, where good customer service, both in-flight and on the ground, has been a point of emphasis since the mid-1950s.

The modern-day descendant of the world's first commercial crop-dusting company, Delta Air Service began passenger operations in 1929 with three five-passenger monoplanes and a mail route that stretched between Jackson, Mississippi, and Dallas, with stops at Shreveport and Monroe, Louisiana. Sixty years later, it's among the three largest U.S. airlines, serving more than 150 destinations worldwide and employing some 54,000 people. Significantly, Delta pioneered hub-and-spoke configurations out of its home base in Atlanta in the late-1970s.

Along the way, Delta has grown both by developing new business and merging with other carriers, most notably Western Airlines in 1987. It now runs major hubs through Atlanta, Los Angeles (Western's former home), Dallas/Fort Worth, Salt Lake City, and Cincinnati. On the whole, it runs them well: For the last five years (1983 through 1987), the readers of *Travel-Holiday* magazine have ranked Delta the number one U.S. air carrier. Every year since 1974, Delta has been dead last among active U.S. airlines in the government's tally of complaints per 100,000 passengers flown.

In fact, from 1984 through 1986, Delta averaged under 1 complaint per 100,000 passengers carried, the only currently active independent U.S. carrier that can make that claim. (The only other airline that *could* was Piedmont, which is being merged into USAir.) During the same period, Western (whose operations were fully merged into Delta's in early 1987) steadily improved its complaint-free performance, from seventh in 1984 (1.65 complaints per 100,000 passengers) to fifth in 1985 (1.48 complaints), and then to third (1.27 complaints) in 1986.

At Delta, it's more than southern hospitality. The airline has long encouraged a family spirit among its employees, including rewards for good customer service that date back to 1956. It also has invested relatively more in its people, and there's evidence of a cause-and-effect relationship at work. In 1987, *Fortune* calculated that of the five major carriers (American, Delta, Northwest, Texas Air—which includes Continental and Eastern—and United), Delta had the highest labor costs as a percentage of revenue: 47 percent in 1986. Northwest's labor costs were 35 percent of revenue in that year, Texas Air's just 32 percent.

Can it be just coincidence that the airlines most notorious for customer complaints are Continental, Eastern, and Northwest, all of which averaged more than 15 complaints per 100,000 passengers in 1987? We don't think so. Research consistently shows that the way employees are treated by their management has direct impact on the way those employees treat the business's customers. (In this context, it's also worth noting that Walt Disney World has changed its "official airline" from Eastern to Delta.)

At Delta, the official line is that good customer service is basic to the company's success. Without it, an airline that began passenger service just four months before the stock market collapsed in 1929, one that spent its early years serving the Deep South, the most poverty-stricken part of a distressed nation, could not have survived at all, let alone grown to a position of prominence and prestige.

The philosophy shows up in many ways. Unlike most major airlines, Delta is largely nonunion by choice (only the pilots and a few dispatchers are unionized), and it is determined to stay that way by maintaining excellent labor relations and low-key supervisory systems. It has worked hard to avoid adversarial face-offs with its labor force, regardless of job description or pay level. At Delta, flight attendants are expected to make their own decisions about the level and quality of service they provide. When a supervisor makes a check ride, the flight crew knows it. Delta takes the Japanese-like attitude that employees should be encouraged to do their best, not made paranoid by the prospect of making a mistake while someone important is looking.

Job rules are minimal. Cooperation is a watchword. Customer service agents at check-in counters and departure gates wear any number of hats, and it's not uncommon for the flight crew to pitch in and help ticket passengers if the alternative is a long and aggravating delay. Delta's tradition of no layoffs (or "furloughs," in the parlance of Delta's management) was maintained even in 1983, when the airline posted its only operating loss in the last thirty-nine years.

To take pride in who you are and what you're doing, it helps to understand and take pride in who you've been. Delta takes great pains to remember its roots, including those grafted on to it. When Northwest and Republic merged in 1986, the latter ceased to exist as anything more than a footnote in the former's history—and an excuse for poor passenger service. Delta, on the other hand, still officially remembers and credits the regional carriers that long ago became part of its culture, keeping alive the memory of Chicago and Southern Air Lines, merged in way back in 1953, and Northeast Airlines, which became part of Delta in 1972. As part of the merger with Western, Delta recently has begun weaving Western's history and status as America's oldest existing air carrier into its own heritage.

At the frontline, Delta rewards and celebrates employee achievements and contributions through two long-running programs. Delta's Customer Service Awards, more visible than ever some thirty years after their initiation, are determined by the company's senior officers on the basis of "customer-oriented service far above the normal call of duty." The Feather-in-Your-Cap Award was added in 1972 to recognize and reward individuals who perform an outstanding service for the company, a fellow employee, or even the community at large.

Do they work? How else can you explain the behavior of Susan A. Poindexter, a senior customer services agent at Delta's outpost in Cincinnati. She was on duty one day in 1987 when a woman traveling with two small children became ill during a stop in that city. The woman, who spoke no English, needed to go to the hospital. What to do? Point to the cab stand? Call a skycap? Plead ignorance of the strange language and hope someone else would take charge?

Poindexter went above and beyond. She accompanied the woman and her children to the hospital. When the woman was released, she took the travelers home with her and put them up overnight. The next day, she took them back to the airport and got them boarded for home. So there she was, face smiling out from page seven of the September 1987 issue of *Delta Digest*, the airline's internal magazine, one of eight Delta employees cited for customer service "Above & Beyond" in that issue. This, by the way, is her second award, the article noted.

The same issue told the tale of a first-time winner: Hector Justiniani, customer services agent (since promoted to station supervisor), Guadalajara. Justiniani, it seems, came across a customer of another airline who had four thousand pounds of freight that had to be in Phoenix as soon as possible. The "other airline" hadn't picked up the freight. So Hector did. On his day off. He took a personal vehicle to the company, loaded up all thirty-six boxes, and delivered them to Delta Air Cargo. The company is now a regular Delta customer.

It's basic to service excellence that first you prove you can do it, then you can advertise it. Delta is only now beginning to capitalize on decades of Susan Poindexters and Hector Justinianis. In a campaign built around the slogan, "We love to fly and it shows," Delta features real Delta people— flight attendants, pilots, customer services agents—providing real, everyday Delta services.

Characteristically, Delta incorporated the campaign into its internal culture. It auditioned and videotaped more than six hundred public-contact employees for roles in the commercials. It passed out bumper stickers with the new slogan and set up a contest with prizes to reward employees for displaying them on their cars. It distributed a media schedule with dates and times when the new ads would be broadcast. It featured the employees who starred in the commercials in the *Delta Digest*. It even had the advertising agency make a documentary videotape of the making of the commercials so everybody could see their coworkers getting the Hollywood treatment for being good at their jobs.

As the little (now merged) animated character in the Western Airlines commercials used to exult, it's the only way to fly.

Delta Air Lines, Inc.
Hartsfield Atlanta International Airport
Atlanta, GA 30320

American Airlines

A'A

BIGGER ISN'T NECESSARILY, OR EVEN USUALLY, BETTER IN SERVICE. IN FACT, WHILE sometimes bigger is irrelevant in service, quite often it gets in the way of good service. Big companies tend to develop big, cumbersome, rigid systems of getting work done, and individual customers (employees too) not only get lost in those systems, they chafe at the "take a number and wait" impersonality they experience along the way.

As illustrated by American Airlines, the third largest U.S.-based air carrier by most forms of measurement, that doesn't have to be the case. In the last few years, every time someone has thought to poll air travelers about which airlines serve them best, American has been right there at the top of the charts.

For example, frequent flyers surveyed by the International Foundation of Airline Passengers Association in 1987 put American at the top of their list of domestic airlines (Delta finished a close second) and ranked it fourth in the world (Delta was sixth). In 1985, a panel of senior international business and banking executives assembled by *Institutional Investor* magazine also picked American as best within the U.S., and for six straight years (1982-87), readers of *Executive Travel* magazine have agreed with that assessment.

In a 1987 poll of frequent flyers, readers of *Advertising Age* also pointed up the fact that only American and Delta can lay claim to any significant service accolades: American got 30 percent of the votes for favorite airline, Delta 25 percent. Two years earlier, Delta finished number one, American number two. While Delta was consistently praised for the warmth and friendliness of its people, American drew praise for overall service, on-time performance and AAdvantage, its multifaceted frequent flyer program.

American's service profile has been on a steady upswing since 1981, when it began targeting the business traveler and launched AAdvantage, the country's first frequent flyer program. AAdvantage now has more than 5 million enrollees. When passenger complaints rose to a crescendo in 1987, American was one of a handful of carriers confident enough in its service quality to urge the Department of Transportation to keep score in such areas as on-time performance, flight cancellations, and lost luggage. Not surprisingly, its confidence has been justified. On the government's scorecard, American consistently outperforms its U.S.-based competitors.

American is notable, among other things, for the quality and depth of its communications, and the number of audiences with which it maintains an active dialogue. The airline clearly believes that its people, its stockholders, and its passengers all need and want to know what's going on in the air travel industry, from safety considerations in the air to comfort and service standards on the ground. Consequently, it often goes out of its way to present its views on industry issues and business operations.

Its 1986 annual report, for instance, is a working primer on modern airline operations. Instead of the vapid president's statement and glitzy promotional copy that pass for meaningful information in many companies, American devoted twenty-eight pages to presenting clear and sometimes blunt analyses of air traffic control problems, hub-and-spoke flight systems, labor cost comparisons among the twelve major carriers then serving the U.S., and the importance of quality of working life for the airline's employees and passengers.

The 1987 edition explored additions to the airline's hub system, union issues, the cost of everything from fuel to crew training, the evolving art of yield management (getting maximum revenue from fine-tuning a constantly changing mix of fares—an American strength), and the status of SABRE, the world's largest, privately owned computer system, now in place in more than fourteen thousand subscriber locations, mostly travel agencies.

One reason for that thoroughness: Enhanced and improved communications was an area marked for improvement after a 1986 survey of employee attitudes. Nearly 70 percent of American's 55,000 people (there are now more than 65,000 employees, in large part due to the acquisition of AirCal in 1987) completed the confidential questionnaire. An overwhelming majority said they liked and took pride in their jobs. It shows, and it's a basic assumption that underlies employee relations at American.

Consequently, when American moved to reduce costs to remain competitive with lower-priced competitors, it turned to its employees for ideas. They organized themselves into nearly 3,500 seven-person teams for a three-month "InnovAAtions" campaign that offered merchandise prizes based on the cash value of suggestions implemented. As a result of the 1986 effort, which has led to a continuing employee involvement and feedback system, more than 1,600 ideas were adopted, members of 535 employee teams received merchandise worth $4.7 million—and American realized more than $20 million in cost-saving and revenue-generating improvements its employees could support.

Customers as well as costs were favorably affected. Many of the suggestions called for pushing greater responsibility out to the frontlines. American has followed through. Flight attendants and passenger service agents now receive training in "on the spot" problem-solving and many are empowered to make adjustments of up to several hundred dollars for American's passengers.

Systems have been streamlined accordingly. In the past, if a flight attendant accidentally spilled a drink on a passenger, for example, an agent had to meet the flight on arrival, fill out a form authorizing reimbursement for dry cleaning expense, then send the hapless traveler to the ticket counter where he had to stand in line and wait for someone else to accept the voucher and hand him five dollars or so. Now passenger services agents have access to their own cash drawer so they can settle small issues immediately, and without paperwork.

On the other hand, let a supervisor catch an employee doing something right on the job and that employee is likely to walk away with an "instant recognition chit" redeemable from an ever-growing catalog of free travel, merchandise, and other awards. The catalog and point system is the common denominator in American's companywide "AAchievers Program," launched in March of 1986, and no fewer than eighty-four other preexisting award and recognition programs being used in various company divisions and regions. The system operates like a frequent flyer program: The more points you accumulate, the more valuable the rewards available.

AAchievers points are also awarded for group effort. For instance, if the plane for Dallas/Fort Worth arrives late in Kansas City, it might be designated an "AAchievers flight." That means everyone from baggage handlers to gate agents to flight crews will receive AAchievers points for making up for lost time and getting the passengers to their next destination on time. It's a program that's invisible to passengers, but it wins points from them, too.

AAchievers is targeted on giving frontline supervisors a way to reward good performance. In 1988, American began adding a peer recognition system ("invented" by a pilot) that allows employees to nominate their colleagues for noteworthy efforts. Both are outgrowths of a continuing, four-year-old Quality of Work Life (QWL) initiative that is designed to spread out authority and build a culture where management takes care of the employees as if they were customers. Given the commitment of chairman and chief executive officer Robert Crandall, QWL has become a part of the entire airline's service quality commitment, not a short-term program.

As a spokesman for American told us, "Major decisions may be made at headquarters, but it isn't Bob Crandall who's running the airline. It's the agent on the ticket desk and the baggage handling crew in Des

Moines and the flight attendants and pilots on the plane to Dallas. We all have to stand behind the product."

American Airlines Inc.
Subsidiary of AMR
P.O. Box 619616
Dallas/Ft. Worth Airport, TX 75261

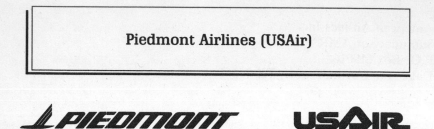

PIEDOMONT AIRLINES OFFICIALLY CEASED TO EXIST IN THE FIRST QUARTER OF 1989, when its operations finally were fully merged with USAir's to form one of the nation's five largest air carriers. The effects of that merger will take years to assess, but it's worth noting that Piedmont brought to the corporate altar a well-earned reputation as an innovative and concerned provider of customer service. USAir is no slouch on the service side either, and initially has shown every indication that it will incorporate Piedmont's quality-oriented culture into its own strong customer service philosophy without inflicting major disruptions on its passengers or employees. We hope so. Air travelers have a lot to gain from the marriage of Piedmont's customer-centered focus and USAir's strong operating standards.

When deregulation was officially pronounced in 1978, Piedmont was a small regional carrier serving primarily the Eastern Seaboard. Over the next five years, its passenger loads more than doubled and its revenues quadrupled. The reason was simply good business strategy: Rather than wade into the mess and compete toe to toe with major carriers in already saturated markets, Piedmont opted to concentrate on serving the medium and large cities the majors were largely abandoning. It located hubs in places like Charlotte, North Carolina; Dayton; Baltimore; and Syracuse; and it put its emphasis on becoming nationally known for the very things on which it had built its regional image—personal service and prompt performance.

That implied significant growth, a new challenge for a small company, and this at a time when price wars were making labor costs an extremely critical issue. Early on, Piedmont determined that the best way to keep its labor costs competitively low was to take advantage of the new growth opportunities, which would allow it to hire entry-level people at the lower end of the pay scale without taking away from the salary and benefit packages its more experienced people had earned through the years.

At the same time, Piedmont put a priority on making a lasting service impression on its passengers, deregulation notwithstanding. That meant

94

planes were kept clean, selection and training standards were kept high, and money and time were invested in nitty-gritty areas such as baggage-handling equipment and procedures. (In 1987, Northwest Airlines, one of the majors that perennially earns the unenviable distinction of leading the league in lost luggage, went so far as to hire away the architect and director of Piedmont's sophisticated baggage-handling system.)

Predictably, growth brought new problems and dilemmas, many of them service-related. One issue Piedmont debated was what to do about a service habit that had cropped up at the frontlines. Flight attendants, taking seriously the company's customer-first attitude, had begun giving passengers not just a glass of the soft drink of their choice, but the whole can, not to mention extra bags of peanuts. The pop-and-peanuts bill was growing accordingly, and in a cost-conscious environment every nickel was important. So, too, management ultimately decided, were customer and employee perceptions—rather than discouraging the practice, Piedmont made it standard operating procedure.

Because it had been paying attention to service quality before deregulation muddied the waters, Piedmont realized the importance of building on customer service skills as it grew. To do that, it turned inside and did an extensive audit of its own employees to determine what *they* thought distinguished the top service providers among their colleagues. Those characteristics were plugged into a video-based testing and verbal interview program designed to identify applicants with the kind of personality and aptitude to fit into the company's service-oriented culture.

Training doesn't accomplish much without empowerment, and Piedmont's management style reflects a thorough understanding of that dynamic. Decision-making responsibility—and authority—has been systematically pushed out to the frontlines. For example, ticket agents, not just their supervisors, can make settlements for expenses that customers incur as a result of flight problems, damaged luggage, even disagreements about ticket prices. That includes situations where Piedmont is not directly involved.

When a Continental Airlines flight crashed in Denver in November of 1987, resulting in the closing down of flight operations on a busy, pre-Thanksgiving Sunday, Piedmont employees promptly decided to help their ticketholders locate hotel rooms for the night, then wrote vouchers to pay for the rooms, plus dinner and breakfast. Passengers on other airlines were mostly left to fend for themselves.

Frontline decisions are monitored, but lightly. Both paperwork and second-guessing are deliberately kept to a minimum to encourage prompt action on customer needs. In that regard, Piedmont's philosophy is right out of the SAS model: The right person to make a decision about how to resolve a customer's problem is the person dealing directly with that customer. Every month, the airline circulates the roster of "People

Pleasers": employees whose exemplary service has prompted letters from their passengers.

In addition, in the early 1980s, at about the same time that British Air was formally discovering the idea of "recovery"—the need for an established and well-planned system to redress the mistakes that inevitably occur in service delivery—Piedmont was communicating the same operating standards to its frontline people. The emphasis was on minimizing mistakes, of course, but when something did go wrong, Piedmont's people were empowered to take immediate corrective action not only to assist the customer but also to prevent mistakes of the same nature from occuring again.

Meanwhile, more than a year before the Department of Transportation began requiring airlines to report their on-time performance in late 1987, Piedmont was already at work on that area, too, even though in relative terms it didn't seem to need attention. (The airline wasn't any worse than anyone else when it came to late arrivals, nor was it any better.) The results of the effort were quickly visible: In early 1987, when complaints about flight delays and late arrivals began to mushroom into a cause célèbre, Piedmont was conspicuous for its improved punctuality.

From initial indications, the acquisition of Piedmont by USAir (which also acquired PSA in 1987 to boost its West Coast presence) should run more smoothly than other airline marriages, notably the merger of Republic into Northwest and the acquisition of Eastern by Texas Air. Candid two-way communications—both written and via an 800-number provided to employees systemwide—have assured that the questions and fears of Piedmont's employees are dealt with quickly and openly.

For his part, USAir's chairman and president, Edwin I. Colodny, has mandated a go-slow pace since the merger was approved in late 1987, including an interregnum period during which Piedmont has continued to operate under its own name as a subsidiary. USAir's corporate culture also prizes good customer service and a positive style of employee communications (witness Colodny's eight-year-long tradition of hosting monthly lunches with USAir employees selected at random from around the company), so Piedmont's people should feel right at home.

If the combination of Piedmont and USAir (plus PSA) meshes smoothly, air travelers should be the biggest beneficiaries.

Piedmont Airlines
USAir Group, Inc.
1911 Jefferson Davis Highway
Arlington, VA 22202

American Automobile
Association

IT'S A MARK OF JUST HOW ESTABLISHED AND RESPECTED THE AMERICAN AUTO-mobile Association—better known the world over as "Triple A"—has become that most of its thirty million members still refer to it as "the auto club." It isn't. An auto club, that is. Or American, for that matter. Rather, AAA today is one of the largest, widest-ranging, and outright best travel service organizations anywhere on the planet.

The spectrum of AAA services has grown steadily, partly in response to competition from automobile clubs started by oil, insurance, and retailing companies, partly because AAA is always looking for new ways to serve its members. As a nonprofit organization, that's its only reason for being.

Consequently, AAA continues to build systematically on traditional strengths—such as providing road maps, routing automobile trips, and dispatching emergency road service—by adding authoritative ratings of hotels and motels, comprehensive travel agency services, and an ombuds-man program that mediates disputes over auto repairs. In addition, at many local AAA offices a member can buy traveler's checks without paying a service charge, cash a check, renew a driver's license or obtain license plates, have passport photos taken, arrange for an International Driving Permit, buy emergency equipment for the car and home, and purchase automobile and other kinds of insurance.

There's more. Because of its vested interest in highway safety, AAA pioneered driver's education in 1935 (up to then, there was no such thing for young drivers). It's still one of the most vigorous supporters of high school driver-training programs, many of which use its textbook, *Sportsmanlike Driving*. Nowadays, it's working on new safety and driving skills training programs aimed at experienced drivers in businesses, the military, and the nation's generally aging population.

To encourage high school students to go into automotive repair work—and, in the process, help improve the image and upgrade the performance of that notorious poor-service business—AAA offers scholarships and a national troubleshooting competition for young mechanics. At the grade school level, it sponsors the thousands of School Safety Patrol programs and works to encourage traffic safety habits from wearing seat belts to surviving pedestrian encounters with the ubiquitous American automobile.

On the community service front, its "First a Friend, Then a Host" program was one of the first to address the problem of drunk drivers at the behavioral level, encouraging hosts to be responsible in the way they serve alcoholic beverages and assertive in making sure their guests don't get behind the wheel if they can't make it home safely. AAA is also in the forefront of the movement to adapt the automobile to America's aging population, and its ambitious Handicapped Driver Research Program is helping even severely disabled people stay active and mobile.

Yet for most of its members, the most important service AAA provides is summed up in one word: security. No matter where they are or where they're going, no matter what hour of the day or night, when the family chariot breaks down AAA members know they're one phone call away from assistance. More than any other reason, that's why two out of every three Americans who join an automobile club sign up with AAA.

The network of more than 1,000 offices in the U.S. and Canada is a future no one could have envisioned when the forerunner to AAA was launched in 1902 by 9 small motor clubs in the Chicago area who between them had fewer than 1,000 members. AAA still retains one very significant legacy of its roots: It is still an "organization of organizations." With the exception of 13 regional clubs that are owned and operated by national headquarters, AAA's 159 member organizations are all locally chartered and managed.

This unique, highly decentralized organizational format allows each club to tailor national programs and develop additional services for its specific operating conditions. In New York City, that means urban survival support and extensive travel agency services. For members in Wyoming, the emphasis is on highway assistance even in unpopulated and isolated parts of the state. The "First a Friend, Then a Host" campaign was developed by a local club; Supernumber (a toll-free emergency road service number connected to a data base) came out of headquarters in Falls Church, Virginia. Other new programs are constantly being developed and refined at the local and regional level as homegrown managers look for new ways to help.

Yet because the individual clubs cooperate in providing a largely uniform menu of reciprocal core services, all this potentially confusing decentralization is invisible to AAA members. Whether you're from Alaska or Alabama, you can walk into the AAA office in Albuquerque, New Mexico, or Ames, Iowa, and they'll treat you like one of their own.

Indicative of AAA's member orientation is its trademark Emergency Road Service program. In 1987, AAA clubs responded to more than eighteen million calls for such service. Whether in their own local club's service area or miles from home, members have immediate access to help when they need it. That can involve everything from mechanical first aid (like jumping a dead battery or fixing a flat tire) to emergency assistance in the aftermath of an accident.

To make sure members know where to turn no matter where they are, more than 14,500 approved garages and service stations nationwide are programmed into a computer system accessible through Supernumber. The data base, which is updated daily, operates twenty-four hours a day and recognizes more than 30,000 telephone exchanges in about 75,000 locations—even if the member isn't sure where he's calling from, the computer will figure out where the closest assistance is to be found.

When the car needs fixing, AAA members in twenty-six states and the District of Columbia can look for the distinctive AAA emblem outside repair shops that participate in the fast-growing Approved Auto Repair program. About two thirds of the Club's members have access to the program, under which providers who meet AAA specifications for services and mechanic training can display the AAA logo. The repair shops agree to allow AAA to mediate members' disputes over repairs; AAA also arbitrates new-car customer complaints for Toyota in the U.S.

Similarly, no lodging establishment or restaurant in the U.S., Canada, Mexico, and the Caribbean can display the AAA emblem or be listed in a AAA publication—twenty-five regional TourBooks and international guidebooks, eight CitiBooks, and eleven CampBooks, more than forty million of which were distributed to members in 1987—unless and until it has been inspected and rated by a AAA representative.

For hotels, AAA inspectors revisit and update on-site reports annually, evaluating each location on more than forty different criteria, from door locks to maid service. The resulting ratings compare each participant to a national data base subdivided into four categories: hotels, motels, motor inns, and resorts. Hotels are compared to hotels, motels to motels, to determine a rating of from one to five diamonds that describes the quality of the accommodations offered. It's a very demanding system: Only forty-six of the nearly nineteen thousand lodging facilities inspected in 1987 earned the coveted fifth diamond—and six of 1986's elite lost their fifth jewel because their service profile, as determined by AAA's inspectors, declined.

Though it started with the automobile, AAA has evolved into a multidimensional travel service organization with prestige and clout both nationally and around the world. About 17 percent of the U.S. adult driving-age population belongs to AAA; 19 percent of all cars registered in the country are owned by AAA members. Under reciprocal agreements with automobile clubs in nineteen countries on five continents, AAA members traveling outside the U.S. are eligible for the same benefits and services provided by the foreign club to its own members.

Taken together, the travel agencies in its local offices book more airline tickets than any other national travel agency and sell more American Express Travelers Cheques—$2.4 billion in 1987—than any other vendor. Its TourBooks, Triptiks, maps, road atlases, and other travel-related publications—amounting to nearly 320 million documents in 1987 alone— are basic vacation-planning tools for millions of families. Its organizational voice is heard on public policy issues from drunk driving and highway funding to auto pollution control and safety equipment standards.

There are less-expensive automobile clubs (in fact, almost every one of its major competitors costs less), but the fact that almost 90 percent of all members renew their memberships annually is the clearest evidence that when it comes to service, the first name on the list is AAA.

American Automobile Association
8111 Gatehouse Road
Falls Church, VA 22047

Club Med

CLUB MED
THE ANTIDOTE FOR CIVILIZATION™

SNICKER AND WE'LL MAKE YOU TURN TO THE BACK AND READ THE INDEX. IF your immediate image of this packaged vacation operation is one of scantily packaged young singles cavorting in the sun, you're partially right. But you're also more than half wrong. In 1987, Club Med (the U.S. subsidiary of France's Club Méditerranée) played host to literally thousands of children and their parents (40 percent of its 350,000 members have children, 8 percent of its members *are* kids). Worldwide, half of Club Med's million members are married; nearly 60 percent are between the ages of thirty and sixty (median age in 1987: thirty-seven; median income: $60,000). At least half are repeat customers.

The basic service springs from the basic concept: a fully paid vacation package where you make your arrangements and pay the bill in advance in return for a well-managed program in which you don't need to worry much about money, transportation, food, activities—okay, or clothes. Skeptics scoff that it's summer camp for adults with too much money, but in many ways it's like a cruise, only on land. It's also a well-conceived and well-managed business, rated one of the ten best-managed companies in the world a couple of years ago by the *London Financial Times*. According to Club Med's research, fully 70 percent of its new members come based on a word-of-mouth recommendation; 94 percent say they plan to come back.

Club Med runs twenty-eight resort villages in North America, including the Caribbean, plus the Far East and South Pacific. There are well over a hundred in the worldwide system, the ones in Europe, Africa, and South America managed by the French parent company, which is Europe's largest tour operator. The typical village (located in a coastal or mountain area chosen for its combination of scenic seclusion and accessibility from the so-called civilized world) contains a central pool/dining/meeting area surrounded by lodging, sports facilities, and activity areas. Everything within the village is within walking distance; to visit the outside world, excursions are available.

The typical package includes air fare to and from a Club Med village,

101

ground transportation, food (including free beer and wine) and lodging in the village, and a host of activities managed by the village's friendly and capable staff. There are no television, radio, clocks, or newspapers. There's also no tipping. Club Med members are encouraged to leave the trappings of everyday life behind, including their wallets. For purchases outside the package (mostly additional food and liquor, and souvenirs), they wear strings of colorful beads that can be used in lieu of cash.

The key to Club Med's service success is careful management of each aspect of the vacation experience, in the process meeting and exceeding the expectations of customers who've grown used to constant delays, hassles, and uncertainties when they travel. Each Club Med manager is expected to run his or her own village as a separate business, recruiting most of the support staff locally and taking advantage of regional conditions and amenities.

In the Caribbean, that can mean flexible programs that teach certification-level scuba diving for those interested in developing mastery, lower-key alternatives for those who simply want to try it out—safely—just to say they've done it. Either way, the instruction, the equipment, the boat rides, the works are all included in the basic package price. In Bermuda, the club manager put in a driving range and started giving golf lessons; the overwhelming response has led other properties to work out offerings for duffers in their villages, sometimes on-site, other times involving field trips to nearby country clubs.

The customer focus at Club Med includes the organization's own special vernacular. Guests in Club Med villages are referred to as GMs (abbreviating the French *gentils membres*, or "nice people"). The approximately one hundred key staff members in each village are called GOs (*gentils organisateurs*, or "nice organizers"). Their services are augmented by another two hundred to three hundred employees recruited from the local region to handle cleaning and maintenance.

To keep close to their customers, GOs live in the village instead of going to an off-site home at the end of their workday. To respond to the ever changing wishes of a polyglot, multilingual clientele, more than a dozen different nationalities will be represented on the typical resort's staff roster. The ideal ratio of GOs to GMs is one to five, which results in a high level of personal attention in everything from tennis and windsurfing lessons to computer classes and circus skills.

GOs are invariably young, chosen for their enthusiasm, language skills, and entertainment talents (a nightly cabaret-style show is a Club Med tradition). They earn a little over a hundred dollars a week in addition to their room and board, so turnover tends to be high. Club Med, however, sees advantages in a system where frontline people pull out instead of burn out: There's a constant influx of fresh energy and a camaraderie born of people sharing a job they like to do. Toward that end, GOs receive training in both people and job skills and are given constant updates on guest comments and their village's financial performance. To keep the staff fresh and motivated, GOs are rotated to new villages every six months.

Many site-specific changes originate at the individual village level. Managers are expected to live with their guests, listen to them, and constantly experiment with new wrinkles. The goal is to keep the vacation experience stimulating and worry-free by anticipating new wishes and eliminating old irritants.

Consequently, Club Med continues to fine-tune its vacation packages in keeping with the changing desires of its customers. As swinging singles have been joined and in many cases outnumbered by married couples—an increasing number of whom bring the kids along—accommodations have been refurbished and recreational programs adjusted accordingly. In addition to communal dining rooms that promote mixing and mingling, there are now secluded restaurants at many villages. Fitness programs have been added, and there are even Mini Clubs (for children two to eleven) and Baby Clubs (ages four to twenty-three months) at some locations. In the Club Med system, those programs that continue to prove popular will spread, those that don't will be reworked or dropped. It's a form of service Darwinism.

As chairman and founder Gilbert Trigano explains, "We are convinced that vacations of the type offered by Club Med are no longer a luxury, but have become a necessity in today's world where people cannot face stress day after day without taking time off to decompress and get in shape again. The greater the stress, the greater the need for 'the antidote for civilization.' "

Club Med
40 West 57th Street
New York, NY 10019

THE CLEAN BLUE VAN WITH THE BRIGHT YELLOW TRIM GLIDES TO A STOP IN front of the departure terminal at LAX (Los Angeles International Airport). Out pops a well-dressed, remarkably unharried business traveler. A check of the watch confirms that there's still plenty of time to make the scheduled flight, time enhanced by being unencumbered with the need to find a parking space or return a rental car. There's only one discouraging note: The outbound flight isn't going to San Francisco, Phoenix, or Dallas/Fort Worth, which means there won't be another blue-and-yellow SuperShuttle van waiting there. At least, not yet. But maybe someday soon.

In 1984, a Los Angeles entrepreneur named Mitch Rouse came up with a better mousetrap. Traffic and parking around LAX was a perpetual snarl. Regional bus service in the LA Basin was virtually nonexistent, let alone attractive to busy business travelers. And taxi fares were escalating out of sight for a level of professional service that ran the gamut from bearable to horrendous. Rouse knew about that firsthand: His family has been in the taxi business since 1945. He saw a niche for a hybrid between a bus line and a cab company that would focus specifically on the needs and comfort levels of frequent fliers, yet have the capacity to provide a more ambitious level of service than the mom-and-pop limousine services that offered to group passengers together to share rides.

Like a bus line, SuperShuttle is designed to carry more than one passenger at a time along a cost-effective route, with rates predetermined rather than subject to the inexorable tick of a meter. Like a cab company, it picks up and delivers passengers portal to portal and is available when needed rather than on a clock-driven schedule. Like a limousine service, SuperShuttle caters to a demanding clientele that is accustomed to comfort, consistency, reliability, and personal attention.

Yet Rouse figures his venture isn't really competing with buses, taxis, or limos. His target market is the air passenger who drives the family car to the airport. That's about two thirds of all arriving and departing travelers passing through LAX, and the proportion is similar in the other cities to which SuperShuttle has extended service. To get those people out of their cars and into a SuperShuttle van, the service has to be faster and spiffier than a bus, cheaper and more personable than a cab, more versatile and consistently available than a limousine. It is.

Through a fast-paced combination of sophisticated computerization and customer-focused drivers and dispatchers, SuperShuttle has found a ready market for its services. In its first four years, it grew from 10 to 400 vehicles in four major markets, with passenger loads surpassing 350,000 a month and expansion continuing at a steady 13- to 15-percent annual pace. New markets are sure to follow—the company has ambitions of becoming national in scope.

SuperShuttle's service excellence involves both good people and good systems. Technology is crucial to operating on a larger scale while customizing service to each passenger's needs. SuperShuttle's well-scrubbed vans carry no more than three passengers, the efficiency of the routing coming from homemade company software specially designed for conditions in each of its four cities. By computer-matching customers with similar arrival or departure times and nearby points of origination or destination, the system reduces the time any individual traveler spends waiting or in transit. Computer terminals in each van tell the driver who to pick up and where, where each passenger is going, what order to drop them in, even what route to take to avoid traffic slowdowns or wasted time and motion.

As a result, there are none of the unpleasant suprises of airport shuttle services in other cities—like finding out the hard way that your driver has taken a slightly more expensive "scenic route." Cab fare to downtown San Francisco from the airport by the bay costs about $24; the SuperShuttle run is $8. Similarly, LAX to downtown Los Angeles is $10 via SuperShuttle, while a forty-mile trip into the outer reaches of Orange County costs about $40 compared to as much as twice that amount by cab. Drivers accept credit cards, and some businesses, airlines, and hotels in Super-Shuttle's markets have set up direct-bill accounts for their employees and guests.

Balance is important to keeping the service reliable and cost-effective, but even SuperShuttle has been surprised by the operating symmetry that has evolved. Generally, about half of its passengers are arrivals, half departures. Similarly, about half of its loads start or end at a hotel, half at personal homes. The service has become so entrenched that some hotels— among them Phoenix's prestigious Arizona Biltmore, rated five stars by Mobil—have even mothballed their own airport shuttles and use Super-Shuttle instead. In-flight service leader American Airlines has provided passengers on its flights into and out of Dallas/Fort Worth with coupons good for two dollars off on SuperShuttle service in that city, evidence of one good service provider recognizing another.

For outbound passengers heading for the airport, SuperShuttle prefers at least four hours advance notice in order to schedule and route the traveler most efficiently. For inbound passengers, advance reservations assure that a SuperShuttle van is on hand in as little as ten minutes after arrival. A central computer center in each city gets a constant readout of current flight arrival and departure times, and displays detailed information on passengers waiting for pickup. Whenever a passenger's wait exceeds the guaranteed pickup time, the screen display begins to flash, alerting dispatchers to a priority service need.

The concept of real-time management is similar to the way Federal Express processes packages from incoming to outgoing planes, according to executive vice president Dave Jacobs; in this case, however, the system is working with people instead of parcels. The goal is to drop the first of the three passengers at his or her destination almost as fast as an individual taxi ride would while delivering the third passenger within thirty minutes of the direct-service arrival time.

Drivers are carefully screened for safety record and personal commitment to meeting high service standards. In Los Angeles, SuperShuttle jobs are likely to be filled by college students and aspiring actors, both of whom are prone to take their responsibilities seriously. Drivers wear blue-and-gold blazers, white shirt or blouse, black tie and slacks. They absolutely must speak English, and it doesn't hurt their application at all if they speak a second or third language as well.

Pay is based on a commission for the number of passengers carried safely, with top drivers earning as much as $150 a day—not counting tips. Drivers who stay sharp and punctual can earn a "bonus day" each month—a day off on which they are paid on the basis of their average bookings during the month. To qualify, they have to have six months on the job, work a set number of hours in the month, and (as an added nudge toward top performance) report within thirty minutes of their scheduled start time for each qualifying shift.

The service culture may be young, but it's highly visible. Company communications materials constantly replay customer and community service anecdotes, from the traffic reports SuperShuttle drivers provide for a number of local radio stations to the fan letters received from passengers impressed by the ride they received. A much traveled Operation of the Month plaque goes to the facility rated best for superior upkeep in the preceding thirty days; it's presented based on personal inspection visits made by top company executives.

As the system has grown, new services have grown apace. Round-trip SuperShuttle vouchers are now popping up in convention registration packets, providing people arriving from all over the world with a reliable, risk-free way to get from the airport to their hotel and back. In a growing number of hotels, there's a "hotline" that rings straight through to the city's SuperShuttle dispatch center. The Los Angeles Marathon, the nation's second largest, now features SuperShuttle support for its seventeen thousand runners.

An 800-number is printed on all SuperShuttle vouchers and receipts, and every comment or complaint is followed up on. In addition, SuperShuttle periodically samples passenger reactions. "We can get a significant sample size any day of the week," notes Jacobs. As SuperShuttle expands from its western and southwestern roots into new markets, it expects a warm reception. And with good reason.

SuperShuttle International, Inc.
7001 West Imperial Highway
Los Angeles, CA 90045

HOTELS

Marriott Hotels and Resorts

Embassy Suites

Four Seasons Hotels

Hyatt Hotels & Resorts

Mississippi Management

Hotels: The Nonadventurer's Adventure

PICTURE PA INGALLS PACKING LAURA, MARY, MA, AND THE REST INTO THE FAMILY wagon (a Conestoga "woody," no doubt) and heading to sunny California for the annual family vacation. All the great mass media families take vacations. The Bradys seek adventures in Hawaii, the Griswalds head for "Wally World," even the Munsters made the trek to Death Valley.

Yet something seems amiss with the idea of the Ingalls heading down the road—because it never would have happened. A big trip for them would have been a ride over to Mankato (that's in Minnesota) for supplies. A century ago, only the very rich and the very adventurous travelled for pleasure. The family vacation didn't exist. Neither did the hospitality industry as we now know it.

Lang's Ranch in the Badlands of Dakota Territory is a good example of the traveler's lodge of yesteryear. Edmund Morris, in his biography of Theodore Roosevelt, describes a stay at Lang's during an 1883 hunting trip by the then New York assemblyman and his guide, Joe Ferris: "A cold rain began to fall, and they woke to find themselves lying in four inches of water. Shivering between sodden blankets, Ferris heard Roosevelt muttering something. To Joe's complete disbelief, the dude was saying, 'By Godfrey, but this is fun!' "

Today that odd sentiment tends to be reserved for summer camps and those trendy out-in-the-woods management leadership retreats. When we travel these days, we expect lodging that is as comfortable as the family castle we left—at minimum a room that is quiet and secure, a bed that is comfortable, a bath and toilet that are clean . . . and a television set, and room service, and a place to jog, and a good restaurant, and a lounge, and a morning paper, and, if it's not too much trouble, milk and cookies at bed time.

Where did the need for a hotel on every other corner begin? With the automobile. Almost overnight, it changed the style of travel lodging. When it became not only possible but routine to convey oneself hundreds of miles in a single day, our "next town" mentality vanished. A telephone became a mighty lever for securing reservations and the car became the

110

freedom machine. The expression "no room at the inn" was relegated to Joseph-and-Mary jokes. Successful hoteliers of the time accepted the new challenges along with their new opportunities. The hospitality industry underwent a revolution thanks largely to three men, Alexander Graham Bell, Henry Ford, and Arthur Heineman.

Arthur S. Heineman? The same. There should be a monument erected to the man who, on December 12, 1925, opened the "Milestone Motel" in San Luis Obispo, California. It was the first "motel," and Heineman claimed a copyright on the word. He foresaw the connection between motoring and lodging. More importantly, Heineman knew the traditional hotel, designed as it was to serve an upscale, entourage-trailing customer, would not satisfy the new American traveler of modest means. So, he put his motel beside the highway and provided garages for guests. It was a revolutionary service concept separated from Roosevelt's hunting trip by half a continent and a short forty-two years.

Heineman could not have foreseen the changes that another world war, a business boom, and development of a national interstate highway system would bring. As super highways connected city after city, rural properties adjacent to the concrete ribbons began to sprout suburban business centers. Once confined to the urban core, these businesses enabled whole new lodging chains to prosper. Holiday Inn, Ramada, Marriott, and Hilton became the new hospitality giants.

Post-World War II America became a nation on wheels. Deprived of gasoline and other strategic resources for several years, we literally went on a driving binge when they became available again. We learned a lot of things during the war, including how to build better machines and roads. The economy was fired up. There was money to spend again, and things to spend it on. Business prospered and expanded. Leisure time became a reality for many. Television began to teach us how to use that leisure— what we could do with time, and *where* we could go to do it.

If the 1950s and 1960s were years in which the family vacation became institutionalized, they also were the period when hospitality became a true service business. Mom-and-pop motels began to make way for hotel groups, and they in turn began to lose market share to national-scale hotel and motel chains. With so many people motoring—and, soon, flying—lodging providers found it advantageous to define serious, consistent service standards and competitively necessary to engage in amenity-upmanship.

It began with a bar of bath soap. Then there were stationery packets for teasing friends back home with picture postcards that proved how much fun we were having at this particular roadside rest. Complimentary shampoo and shower caps followed, and shoeshine paraphernalia, and sewing kits. They all contributed in some way to the positive image we had of our travel lodging. Importantly, they made us feel we were getting our money's worth. It was our "perceived value" of the hotel that made us forgive the expense.

Chains provided travelers the assurance that their amenities would be consistent from city to city. Business and pleasure travelers knew that the pool, sauna, restaurant, tennis court, bar, and game room they enjoyed in Miami would be waiting for them in Seattle. And they knew that their reservations could be made for them and that the room charges would be relatively consistent.

Just how large a business has hospitality become? U.S. Industrial Outlook estimated 1986 hotel and motel revenues at $43.9 billion, and industry experts predicted 3 million rooms by 1990, an 11 percent increase. Yet despite modest gains in the numbers of travelers, occupancy rates are flagging due to the hotel construction boom of the past decade. Everyone wanted to get into the hospitality act, at least while tax and investment laws favored the industry. Now cost-containment and controlling the effects of overbedding is as relevant in the hotel market as it is in hospitals.

A predictable correction is in evidence. As the saying goes, the legislature giveth and the legislature taketh away. The tax climate is not propelling investors into the hotel and motel industry in droves any more. For their part, property managers are looking long and hard at the nature of their business in an attempt to remain competitive. What they are learning may be at least as important to the industry as were the telephone and the auto.

Take the amenity wars, for example: The basic bar of soap that early motels graciously offered their guests as a freebie has snowballed into a contest of largess by chains hoping guest loyalty can be bought. The simple, clean, hospitable accommodations of a couple of decades past are now surrounded by lavish physical features designed to entice and entertain.

Have those tactics worked? It seems not. Forty percent of America's hotel and motel guests in 1986, according to U.S. Industrial Outlook, were business travelers. Pleasure visitors and conference attendees each accounted for 25 percent, 5.5 percent were on government business, and 4.5 percent were on other personal business.

Because they are the largest group, an assessment of business travelers' attitudes is revealing. Late in 1986, *Hotel & Motel Management* reported the results of a study that indicated that four of every ten U.S. business travelers do not stay in the same hotel on successive trips, and they often leave the choice of where to stay up to their travel agent. So much for the power of consumer advertising—and, it should be added, so much for the importance of amenities.

Industry observer Laventhol & Horwath has found that travelers like the idea of having exercise rooms, tennis courts, swimming pools, steambaths, barbers, beauty salons, game rooms, audiovisual equipment, built-in hair dryers, secretarial services, and check-cashing privileges, but they don't necessarily use them. Sometimes they don't even notice them—*Advertising Age's* 1985 hotel-motel poll found that guests of the Hyatt Hotels never mentioned the chain's notable physical features. They gave Hyatt top marks instead for the quality and consistency of its service.

As the hospitality industry matures, and as economic pressures force out the less competitive businesses, more attention is now being paid to what guests actually want. Those who can accurately gauge guest preferences stand to reap handsome profits in the multi-billion-dollar industry. Guess what research into customer wants and expectations is finding?

According to one resort developer, luxury is the single most important element sought by guests. But luxury, the Hemmeter Corporation found out, is not pink champagne for breakfast or built-in anything. A survey conducted for it by Strategic Information Research Corporation in 1987 showed that luxury is simply service.

Among those queried were travel agents and editors, civic travel bureau representatives, and large company meeting planners. By an overwhelming 73 percent, the respondents said service is the single most important consideration in rating a hotel. It is how responsive the staff is to a guest's needs that demonstrates caring and makes one feel welcome. In the end, service is the one factor that, more than anything else, makes a guest decide to return for another visit.

The way a hotel's staff anticipates guests' needs and provides for them in a personal style is the clincher in the relationship. A good friend who travels to New York on business frequently swears by the staff of the New York Helmsley and wouldn't think of staying elsewhere. The reason? One night she had an insulin reaction. The bell captain broke into the bar for a Coke to give her the needed sugar supplement and then sat with her until the house doctor arrived.

Less dramatic acts can create loyalty as well. Our colleague Chip Bell loves the Ritz-Carlton Atlanta. His affection is due, at least in part, to one memorable occasion on which the doorman was willing to conspire with him to greet Chip's wife, Nancy, with her favorite drink on a silver tray. "Dr. Bell," he told her soothingly when she pulled up at the front door, "I believe you've been looking forward to this. Just leave your keys in the ignition, and let us take care of everything for you. Please have a wonderful weekend."

Even the well-traveled and famous have favorites. We listened recently as *CBS Sunday Morning* host Charles Kuralt described Richmond's Jefferson-Sheraton as "the grandest hotel in America, a combination of Ionic, Corinthian, Rococo, Spanish, Twenties, Sixties, and revival architecture that works."

There is a lot of subjectiveness in Kuralt's rating system, but we understand why a hotel can move him like that. For our part, we have a weakness for the Royal Hawaiian in Honolulu, Marriott's Rancho Las Palmas in Palm Springs, and the Peabody hotels in Memphis and Orlando— the last having as much to do with the enthusiasm of the staff as with the ducks swimming in the lobby fountain. At the same time, and for twenty-eight dollars a night, we've found outstanding service at the Wynfield Inn in Colorado Springs.

The personal service lavished upon guests by hotels that recognize its importance can take many forms. Many rely upon a concierge to make guest feel at home and well provided for. If tickets to a show or ball game are needed, a concierge can find a way to get them, even if the event is sold out. Easy preregistration is something guests appreciate, and a quick, computerized check-out is a service they love. In the five hotels of the Fairmont family (San Francisco, San Jose, Chicago, Dallas, and New Orleans) we've found staffs whose savvy and sophistication are on a par with the best we've seen in Europe and the Orient.

Some hotels go to great lengths to instill the desire to provide service among their employees. From maids on up, all twenty-five hundred employees in the seven hotels of Boston-based Sonesta International Hotels have been playing a board game that teaches them how to handle customer service needs. Other companies have their own point systems with rewards. So seriously does the hospitality industry now view service that it is providing a thriving business for companies that send in "mystery guests" or "secret shoppers" to test employees' responsiveness to customers in both normal and stressful situations.

The objects of all this sincere attention by hotels are also the objects of a lot of study these days. Ask some managers to profile their customers, and more than a few might reply, "We wish we knew!" They would only be half kidding, but they would be more than half worried, because the manager who cannot improve his occupancy rates over the long run will, himself, not be around long.

Partly as a function of the construction spurt and a less than commensurate increase in guest nights, the watchword in the hospitality industry has become "segmentation." In marketing terms, the objective is to win back market share—steal it, if necessary—by identifying and pursuing specific clientele. By directing its marketing at a more narrowly defined audience, a hotel chain can realize substantial savings, both in marketing costs and even in unit construction. Unfortunately, as many as eighteen different, recognizable segments have been identified. The three most standard and practical segments are economy, mid-priced, and luxury (less than $40, $40-$80, and more than $80 a night).

It is not difficult for consumers to see what is happening in the lodging business. A spate of broadcast ads by a few economy motels in the mid-1980s has become a full-blown shouting war as marketers try to carve up the budget-bound tourist pie. In the 1950s, "More is good" was a common hotel pitch. Now, "Less is okay" seems to dominate. While wooing the cost-conscious vacationer or traveling businessman, a motel that once might have invested in a heated swimming pool, sauna, and glitzy piano bar now simply promises to "leave the light on for you." A forty-watter, no doubt.

Market segmentation is complicated, somewhat akin to playing chess. The philosophy behind it is based on a presumption that a pattern of guest preferences can be predicted. That is possible, but it should be remembered that the hoped-for guests are the same capricious folks who voted in the people who voted out the investment laws that put the industry in its glutted predicament.

Travelers have a fairly well-defined concept of where they fit in among the various segments. Although they may feel inclined to cross over to a higher- or lower-priced accommodation, especially if that's what is available or it's a special occasion, guests will mainly follow the pattern established by their preference and economic situation. Hoteliers are banking on that likelihood.

Segmentation makes the marketing of rooms a far simpler task. Advertising may be narrowly directed through appropriate media to prospective customers identified through exacting demographic criteria. For the upper-scale segments, additional advertising avenues are suggested by the nature of the amenities provided on-site. Swimming pools, spas, and other "health-directed" amenities, for example, can find their natural audience among readers of fitness magazines. It is not likely, however, that budget motels will advertise, "Got no money? You're our kind of guest." Instead, the low-cost rooms will draw business guests on tight budgets and vacationers en route to someplace else, and they will not require the same elaborate advertising schemes as the luxury hotels. This may explain why the budget segment is the fastest growing, having doubled in size since 1980.

For the more upscale family, and business guests with an expense account, a new phenomenon—the "all-suite" hotel—has become popular. Its larger rooms and separate bedroom make possible business meetings in the suite. Another innovation in the industry is the "residential-style" suite, which has a fully equipped kitchen and appeals to guests who need to stay for longer periods. In fact, its rates are lower the longer the guest stays. Bed-and-breakfast inns are growing in number, too. Their entrepreneurial operators understand the yearning for a simpler time when desk clerks knew and greeted their guests by name.

Another indication of the seriousness of the present revolution in the hospitality industry is the birth of creative marketing programs. The aggressive chains are leaving no stone unturned in their search for additional market share. By late 1987, the major hotel companies were claiming millions of members in "special guest" programs that used incentives to promote repeat visits, much as the airlines were doing. Like the frequent flyer programs, those millions of members undoubtedly include many who belong to several programs and whose loyalty to the hotel is less than absolute.

Among the incentives are special accommodations and credit cards whose use adds points in the hotel's member program. Days Inns of America inaugurated a "supersaver" discount program in 1985 to provide substantial savings for guests who make reservations a month in advance. Room upgrades are common in the various programs, as are free or discounted rooms. But prizes also include free airline tickets, cruises, stereo equipment, and even luxury automobiles.

Teddy Roosevelt would be amused if he could see what the marketers of today have to do to draw guests of the nonadventurous variety to their hotels. The closest he came to earning points at Lang's Ranch was for not spitting inside and for leaving his horse outside. Life was simpler then. Like the rest of the world, the hospitality business has grown up. It has gotten smarter and faster in response to the demands of competitive pressures in the late twentieth century.

There is more travel today than in Roosevelt's and the Ingalls' times because there is more need to travel. There also are more places to go, ways to travel, and things to do when we get there. For all of this diversity, there are more companies fighting tooth and nail for the privilege of helping us do it. A few are clearly better at it than others.

We've chosen five, based somewhat on segmentation, but largely based on the way their guests tend to rate them. At the head of the class is Marriott, the pacesetting lodging giant that still retains its sense of family. Embassy Suites is building the newest version of the better mousetrap, and the marketplace is clearly demonstrating its pleasure. At the high-amenity end of the spectrum, our nod goes to Canadian-based Four Seasons by a whisker over Ritz-Carlton—both are distinctive service providers. We also look at Hyatt, because of its consistency, and Mississippi Management, because it's a good example of a franchise and management company that does well under a number of signboards.

Although you won't find them profiled, we also were impressed by Red Lion and La Quinta for low-budget excellence and by Ramada, Radisson, and Quality for providing more than a roof. As the number of names we're dropping should suggest, that's good news. Wherever your travels take you, and no matter how tight or lavish your budget, you can find plenty of good service in America's hotels and motels these days.

IN THE GRAND OLD DAYS OF GRAND HOTELS, THE HOTELIER TO BE RECKONED with was Conrad Hilton. Today, in an era of specialized lodging, jet-driven business travel, and clock-conscious guests, it's J. Willard Marriott, Jr. Perhaps no chief executive in America provides a better example of how service cultures are created, nurtured, and focused from the top down.

Hotels are the most visible part of Marriott's business: With more than 400 properties in the U.S. and abroad, the comparison to Conrad Hilton is not at all outlandish. In addition to the flagship Marriott line, there are all-suite Residence Inns for stays of five days or more, and Marriott Suites for overnighters, plus the moderate-priced Courtyard by Marriott and low-budget Fairfield Inn lines. Through its various restaurant chains (most of them under the Roy Rogers, Bob's Big Boy, and original Hot Shoppes names) and airline and airport catering services, Marriott feeds more people every day than any other organization in the world.

Yet in many ways, Marriott is not a corporate name. Rather it remains a family name—one of those rare organizations that has been able to perpetuate its founders as a corporate touchstone. J. Willard Marriott, Sr., who started the company from a nine-seat root beer stand in 1927 (on the same day that Charles Lindbergh took off for glory), made a point of being able to call most of his employees by name. Today, his namesake son is as much organizational father figure as top executive. It's his vision, his sense of corporate mission, his adherence to strong personal values that drives the company.

Marriott people talk about themselves as if they really are a family, and they take an uncommon amount of pride in their work as part of the worldwide clan. Ask someone like Sam Slobovitz, a Marriott regional vice president, how an organization this large goes about creating distinctive customer service, and you get a pat answer: "It's simple. Just find a Bill Marriott to lead the organization—and I'm only partly kidding."

Here's how the management handbook explains it under the heading, The Marriott Family: "The final description or element of Marriott management is perhaps the most difficult to explain to one who has never worked for Marriott. It is something you feel in every phase of every operation and is the strongest underlying influence guiding the company. Unlike the impersonal coldness of the majority of large corporations, Marriott has a human warmth about it which transforms the whole into one large team whose members constantly work for and with each other . . . Mr. Marriott does not look at work as drudgery but as an opportunity for growth, development and accomplishment. He believes that any honest work is honorable and good for the individual, so that he or she can progress and gain satisfaction. Mr. Marriott has always looked at his organization with the same perspective as he views his family. The identical principles of cooperation, support and openness are applied to both 'families.' "

The current Mr. Marriott credits his father with the philosophy of taking care of employees as he wanted them to take care of the customer: "My father knew if he had happy employees, he would have happy customers and that would result in a good bottom line." On the evidence— one of the highest occupancy and lowest turnover rates in the hotel industry—it works.

At Marriott, there's nothing inelegant in the details. If someone finds a departed guest's galoshes, he's expected to take the initiative and make sure they're returned. Marriott looks carefully for its kind of people (the company interviewed forty thousand applicants for twelve hundred opening-day jobs at the Marriott Marquis Hotel in New York a couple of years ago), then trains, rewards, and promotes them when they do things right.

Marriott is big on promoting internally—30 percent of its managers started with the company as hourly employees. It pays well, too. Both factors encourage a lot of employee loyalty. Marriott also invests heavily in the development of frontline people, making sure they have the training and skills to carry out their jobs, whether that involves cleaning rooms or planning banquets. That promotes service quality as well as personal growth, and also engenders no small amount of employee loyalty.

As a result, customers (especially business customers) continually rate Marriott as their top choice for lodging and meeting facilities. It's the hotel name most preferred by business travelers, and the top choice of meeting planners and attendees.

Since 1985 Marriott has dominated the annual survey of business travelers conducted by *Business Travel News*. In 1987, the magazine's fourth annual study ranked Marriott tops overall, based on ratings in eleven service-related categories—the third consecutive year Marriott led the pack. Among seventy-four competitors, Marriott finished first in five categories and no worse than tenth in the other six. (What's more, its Courtyard subsidiary finished eighth overall on its own merits.) In 1986, Marriott finished first in ten of the eleven service-focused categories, including being the easiest to work with to arrange both individual and group business travel, plus having the most helpful and courteous staff, and the highest food quality.

Becoming good is one thing. Staying good is something else again. Most hotels—and, in fact, most businesses that have a lot of interaction with their customers—have a "rate-me sheet" that asks customers to evaluate the quality of the service provided to them. Marriott calls its program GSI, or Guest Service Index, and it takes the data a lot more seriously than most.

In fact, one of the few mildly annoying things that can happen to you in a Marriott is feeling almost dunned to fill out a rating form. They'll ask you at the front desk. They'll put one on the night table in your room. They'll hand you one in the restaurant. Some managers go so far as to make a contest of it—they will buy something like a two-hundred-dollar briefcase and park it on the registration counter: You fill out your rating card and toss it in the briefcase along with your business card, and every week or month or whatever they'll pull out a business card (the ratings will long since have been read and acted upon) and award the briefcase to that guest.

That level of effort is no accident. Each property has a quota of forms to pass out in order to maintain a high response rate, because the higher the response rate, the more complete and accurate the GSI reading, and the better Marriott can respond to what's happening to guests in the hotel.

It's interesting how Marriott handles the information on those forms. The data is posted in every department for employees to see. When a problem crops up, however, Marriott works very hard to focus action and attention on the ratings, not the people rated. Thus, if customers are waiting thirty seconds too long in line, those thirty seconds (and not the people who might have been working the registration desk at the time) become almost a personified villain.

In addition to the GSI program, which provides local managers with a running readout of their service quality, Marriott also attacks on another front. On a regular but unannounced cycle, every hotel is "shopped" by a third-party research company. The effort includes an nth-name survey of people who have stayed in the hotel over the past month. Those ratings go directly to corporate headquarters, where they can have profound consequences for a manager's career: Good ratings, high guest satisfaction numbers, and the property manager's star will be rising; bad ratings, poor guest-generated feedback, and a regional "swat team" may descend on the property to straighten things out.

It truly does start with Marriott himself. He knows the business inside and out, and he clearly enjoys it. Like his father before him, he reads hundreds of comment cards a month and makes innumerable site visits each year (two hundred thousand miles annually) to see how things are going out in the field. When he travels, he makes notes. The next time back he's likely to stun local personnel by remarking how much better the lobby looks since they moved the potted plants closer to the windows or replaced the wing chair by the east entrance.

He's also a hands-on executive. When a new hotel was being planned for the Walt Disney World complex, Marriott sat in on focus groups with meeting planners to find out what they wanted and needed to organize top-quality corporate meetings. One comment he heard was that the ballroom space wasn't going to be large enough for large meetings. It didn't take long for Marriott to acquire adjacent property to provide the additional space.

As the introduction to the company's Success Kit For New Managers explains, "Our success at Marriott is largely a function of our service to the guest. Quality service depends on you and the successful management of your people. If you treat your people well and guide them in a positive manner, they in turn will handle the guests with the warmth, friendliness, and efficiency that are our trademarks. If you remember little else, please remember that we are all at Marriott to make our guests' visits as comfortable as possible."

That reflects Marriott's own approach to his role as chief executive as it relates to the company's two hundred thousand employees worldwide: "My job," he explains, "is to motivate them, teach them, help them, support them, and care about them. If we take care of them, they'll take care of the guests."

Marriott Corporation
One Marriott Drive
Washington, D.C. 20058

EMBASSY
SUITES
HOTELS

A SUBSIDIARY OF HOLIDAY CORPORATION—BEST KNOWN FOR HOLIDAY INNS, THE nation's largest hotel chain—Embassy Suites has been a service leader in its own right virtually from day one. The first of the nearly one hundred Embassy Suites around the country opened its doors in Overland Park, Kansas, in 1984. That same year, Embassy purchased the 24 properties of the Granada Royale Hometel chain, the pioneer, under founder Robert E. Woolley of Phoenix back in 1969, of the all-suite hotel.

What Woolley recognized, and what Embassy Suites president Hervey Feldman has refined into a highly sophisticated business phenomenon, is that the typical hotel room was designed more for construction and housekeeping efficiency than for guest comfort, especially when that guest is a business traveler or someone seeking a leisurely way to spend a weekend.

The conventional room, the most important part of the system that serves the guest's needs, is dominated by a bed. It's a place to sleep and little more. When the basic service a hotel provides is a place to sleep, that's fine. But needs have a way of changing, especially the needs of business travelers. The interlocking of companies large and small on multiregional and national levels has changed and broadened the standard hotel's service mission to include providing meeting facilities, dining and banquet facilities, even trade show and display facilities, all of them located conveniently close to business addresses wherever they may be found, rather than centralized in a downtown core. Extended stays are also common as selling becomes more complex, which means many business travelers end up using their hotel rooms as a combination meeting room, showroom, and office-away-from-the-office.

When relatively larger numbers of people are involved, the best way to provide business-oriented facilities is in separate and distinct meeting rooms, conference and trade show areas, and restaurants. But when only a handful of people need to be involved, the hotel room can serve such a purpose—if, that is, it has been designed appropriately. Beds, unfortunately, make poor conference tables. (And in an era when women are

121

increasingly checking in as business travelers, beds provide other complications.)

Embassy Suites is a working example of a company doing something different to meet a fast-developing market need. Its success is a function of "listening sideways"—perceiving and responding to a new niche rather than competing in a straight line by replicating standard designs and services.

In the all-suite configuration, the bed is in its proper place: a bedroom that is physically separated from the rest of the space available to the guest. In the Embassy Suites design, the bedroom has its own television and telephone. In addition to bed and bath, the suite includes a living room furnished with sofa and chairs, a combination dining and work area, another television and telephone, and often a modest wet bar with refrigerator and microwave oven.

Continuing the design of Woolley's original Granada Royales (Woolley himself is the chain's largest franchisee), all Embassy Suites are built around a central atrium that provides both visual appeal and personal security—there are no long, lonely halls to walk. Included in the room rate is a free, full breakfast, cooked to order in a restaurant located in the atrium. Guests have been known to wander down to breakfast in their pajamas, and that's just fine with the management. It's the kind of "dress code" that says people feel right at home. Evenings, complimentary cocktails are served to allow guests, and their guests, to mix and mingle.

The primary service focus is the business traveler and his or her clients or prospects, and Embassy Suites properties are designed from the ground up to serve that demanding customer's needs. Although every room is a meeting room in the Embassy Suites scheme of things, each location also includes a restaurant, lounge, recreational facilities, and substantial meeting space. It also includes access to a national group and meeting services department that has been empowered to book a prospective customer's meeting into someone else's hotel if the area's Embassy Suites property can't handle it.

What elevates the Embassy Suites physical and operating design still another notch is the attention management pays to the way its people perform within those facilities. Periodically, hotels in the system poll their customers face to face to find out how they're doing. For a period of a month or more, managers will buttonhole five guests a day around the hotel and interview them about their expectations and experiences. The next day, those guest comments will be posted in the employee lounge and reviewed by the on-site management staff. They'll also be forwarded to the headquarters of Embassy Suites in Irving, Texas, just outside of Dallas. Both on-site and in Irving, those comments—and occasionally, if infrequently, complaints—will be studied and analyzed and used as a quality-control tool.

In 1987, for example, these mini-surveys were conducted with more than six thousand guests who rated everything from how long it took them to check in and out to what they thought of the free cocktails and breakfasts. The biggest improvement suggested was better free breakfasts—and Embassy Suites has responded by improving and expanding the menu.

It also involves its people at every level of the hotel. The hospitality industry, like many other service segments, depends a great deal on lower-paid, often highly transient workers. Embassy Suites is no exception. To deliver a quality experience to its guests, the chain uses a variety of tactics, prominent among them policies and procedures designed to keep employees at every level informed, involved, and motivated.

In addition to the previous day's guest comments when surveys are being taken, for example, each property posts its particular occupancy rate and estimated profits for all employees to see. When there are profits—and there usually are, since Embassy Suites, according to *Fortune*, earns a gross profit margin of 50 percent, about 20 points better than comparably priced competitors such as Hilton, Sheraton, and Westin—even the lowest-paid workers know they can take home monthly bonuses of one hundred dollars or more.

If money is one motivator, personal progress is another. Entry-level workers don't have to stay entry-level, and at Embassy Suites many don't. At any given time, between 25 and 80 percent of the firm's hourly workers are in training programs that help them upgrade or expand their skills and qualify for better-paying work. That means housekeepers can aspire to the front desk—and, on the basis of their training, will be paid a little more for making beds and cleaning bathtubs while they wait for their chance to move up. By continually cross-training themselves, employees not only learn new jobs but also can qualify for pay raises as often as every three months.

The best example of upward mobility may be Hervey Feldman himself. While he spent thirty years learning the hotel business, almost all of it in the Holiday Inn system, the first and enduring lessons in hotel service he recalls date back to his teenage years. As an errand boy at the Loon Lake Resort in upstate New York, he earned the minimum wage for everything from washing dishes to caddying on the golf course—but the $150 a week he hustled to take home was better than the paychecks that supported a lot of the families in his New Jersey neighborhood.

"It taught me the most significant lesson for my future life," he told the *Dallas Business Courier* a few years ago: "Make the employees happy, and in turn ask happy employees to do things to make customers happy. After that, it's all score keeping."

Meanwhile, day-to-day benefits show up on the frontline, where the hotel's guests stand to benefit. Because of the extensive cross-training, each Embassy Suites has a ready and willing pool of workers able to step in during peak periods, vacations, or when other workers are in training classes. That cuts down on delays and pumps up enthusiasm. A new computerized front-desk system will allow any Embassy Suites to pull up guest records systemwide, lending itself to personal service even if the traveler has never walked through the particular property's door before.

All that training has another payoff for employees and employer alike: The current directory of Embassy Suites locations is expected to more than double by the early 1990s, in keeping with company projections that foresee the all-suite segment of the market growing from about 4 percent in 1987 to 20 percent by the turn of the century. Corporate growth provides personal growth opportunities for proven achievers.

The immediate acceptance and success of Embassy Suites shows the risk-taking was well thought out and based on a sound assessment of the specifics of its chosen market segment. Two thirds of the hotel's guests are businesspeople, and women traveling on business have taken particular notice: They account for about 25 percent of all hotel business guests; they make up nearly 40 percent of Embassy Suites' clientele.

It's also indicative of a customer-centered attitude that has put this five-year-old hotel chain at the top of the service quality polls for mid- and high-priced lodging. In 1987, the experiences of 232,000 readers of *Consumer Reports* with the nation's major hotel chains ranked Embassy Suites number one for customer service in both the mid-priced and high-priced sections of the industry. And, as *Fortune* pointed out, the results of good service are showing up on the bottom line as well.

Embassy Suites, Inc.
A subsidiary of Holiday Corporation
222 Las Colinas Blvd.
Irving, TX 75039

EACH YEAR, *INSTITUTIONAL INVESTOR* MAGAZINE ASKS A PANEL OF SENIOR bankers and international financiers—each of whom spends an average of more than eighty nights per year in hotels around the world—to rate their favorite hotels. Of the thirteen North American hotels named among their top fifty choices worldwide in 1987, four of the top seven were properties operated by Four Seasons Hotels, Ltd., of Toronto. The honor roll: The Pierre, New York; Ritz-Carlton, Chicago; Four Seasons, Toronto; Four Seasons, Washington, D.C.

The company's only European entry, the Inn on the Park in London, also made the list. In fact, 1987 marked the third consecutive year that all five hotels were ranked in the top fifty, which means 10 percent of the best hotels in the world, according to the magazine read by more than 350,000 top-level financial executives in 140 countries, belong to the same family.

Institutional Investor isn't the only one to notice Four Seasons' high quality accommodations. Of the thirty-three U.S. hotels described in Rene Lecler's *The 300 Best Hotels in the World*, four are (or were) Four Seasons properties: Ritz-Carlton, Chicago (not to be confused with the hotels of the separate and nonrelated Ritz-Carlton chain, which also come highly rated); Pierre, New York; Four Seasons, San Antonio (since sold); Four Seasons-Clift, San Francisco. When *Business Travel News* asked eighteen hundred business travelers and travel agents to rate hotel chains on eleven quality categories in 1987, the runner-up to top-rated Marriott was Four Seasons (in a dead heat with the aforementioned Ritz-Carlton chain).

Well, sure, you might concede, any big hotel chain should place a few winners out of its hundreds of properties. Which is exactly the point: Four Seasons is not a big hotel chain. It operates just twenty-two hotels—fifteen in the U.S., six in Canada and one in England. It's not an old company, either. It was founded in Toronto in 1961 and didn't enter the U.S. market until its 1976 purchase of the Chicago Ritz-Carlton. That makes for a pretty high incidence of winners in a pretty short amount of time.

You could say that's by design. Four Seasons founder and chairman Isadore Sharp started out as an architect, and he's the first to admit that the first hotel he built was a less than luxurious motor court in the red-light district of downtown Toronto. Its interior design, however, was eye-catching, and its services quite a bit above and beyond the norm for a conventional motor inn. Both were indications of things to come, but in 1961 the world's great hotels were almost universally one-of-a-kind independents. The conventional wisdom was that you couldn't duplicate quality in a luxury-oriented property. Over the ensuing years, Sharp's company has become known for conclusively disproving that old bromide.

According to Canada's *Report on Business* magazine, it's "an odd brand of luxury. Call it ascetic hedonism. Ascetic because Sharp's hotels are small (average size: 340 rooms), unexceptional in their exterior design, and about as quiet as an art gallery. And they scrupulously appeal to the ascendant less-is-more mentality among upscale consumers by emphasizing on-site health and fitness clubs; low-cal, low-sodium meals; and low- and non-alcoholic beverages . . . But Sharp's hotels are also hedonistic. Fine appointments, including antique furnishings, Royal Doulton china and fresh-cut flowers . . . evoke the atmosphere of an ambassadorial residence."

Think of it as a grand hotel on a more modest scale. Four Seasons concentrates on creating an environment of understated elegance, whether in a newly built property or through the refurbishment of a fine hotel whose best years might seem to be behind it. The Pierre, for example, was an aging dowager when Four Seasons purchased it in 1981. Several million dollars later, it was reborn as one of the world's premier places to stay. Seattle's majestic Olympic Hotel was showing its age and had long since lost its prominence in the community until Four Seasons devoted $60 million to its restoration. The Inn on the Park London (the park is Hyde) was expected to be just one more pricey entry in an overbuilt luxury hotel market when it opened in 1970. Today, it's admired by hoteliers as well as travelers worldwide, as evidenced by its consistently high occupancy rate (95 percent or better in an industry where 70 percent is considered good).

Whether the property is new or old, owned by the company or operated under a management contract, Four Seasons dedicates itself to pampering guests. That's a spare-few-expenses philosophy that caters to an admittedly special clientele. Yet the way Four Seasons goes about the job of providing personal service to very demanding guests is no less noteworthy for its relatively higher price. From the room service waiter, who cheerfully and sincerely thanks you for your order as he's serving it, to the hotel's general manager, who may spend several hours a week writing letters to his own employees to share guest comments and commendations with them, the people at a Four Seasons make an uncommon impression on even the most jaded traveler. And as customers show over and over again, they will pay more to be served the way they want to be. There's something to be said for learning from the best.

What makes Four Seasons a service leader? Start with scale of operations. A typical Four Seasons property has about 350 rooms and suites compared to the 500 or more that would be found under a competitor's roof: enough to be profitable, yet not so many that the staff can't provide personal service to its guests. In contrast to the rooms, however, public facilities—ballrooms, restaurants, and the like—are commonly larger than needed for the hotel itself. That's because a Four Seasons sees itself as part of the fabric of its city and tailors itself to the needs of the local community. Consequently, the hotel itself will be centrally located, either downtown or in proximity to an area's corporate headquarters, not parked out by the airport.

Next, add staff. The average hotel, according to *Hotel & Restaurants International*, has about two employees for every three guest rooms. Four Seasons generally doubles that staffing norm: *four* employees for every three rooms. The more people on duty in the hotel, the more service they're available to provide.

And the more service they're trained and empowered to provide. From top to bottom, employees are carefully selected. Personnel policies have long favored hiring attitude over experience. If you really want to do the job right, Four Seasons believes, you can learn how. If you don't care about the quality of what you do, all the experience in the world won't make for satisfied guests.

Once good people have been found, they're supported with training and then compensated appropriately. The front office staff at a Four Seasons may be earning double to triple the industry norm through a combination of salary and bonuses; it's not at all unlikely that the uniformed doorman who welcomes you is a college graduate. To keep performance focused on guests at each hotel, not corporatewide, 80 percent of all bonuses and incentives are tied directly to the individual hotel's profitability.

Then, think about yourself. What do you like to do, to eat, to see and hear around you? You're likely to find a lot of that designed into a Four Seasons-run hotel. Though it serves what is generally termed the luxury end of the lodging market, Four Seasons isn't trying to provide luxury. Its focus is on comfort. That means a residential style that emphasizes tasteful decor, antiques, original art. It means if you need or want something, there's a true concierge available to serve you. It means if you're trying to stay healthy on the road, you can find a choice of gourmet selections with just 500 to 650 calories—outstanding food that's low in cholesterol, low in sodium, and yet doesn't look like something catered from the coffee shop out by the interstate. Four Seasons' "Alternative Cuisine" was introduced back in 1984—as a result of paying attention to guests and the way their lifestyles were changing.

Paying attention is an important, if sometimes invisible, skill. The second time you stay at a Four Seasons, you may feel as if you never left. If you enjoyed (or abhorred) the view from a certain room the last time, or requested a specific kind of soap, or wanted an extra pillow, you often find advance preparations have been made on your behalf. There's no secret involved: On your first visit, the staff took notes. Literally. And extensively. Your guest history is part of each hotel's computerized database, and it's accessible by all hotels in the Four Seasons system. It will be updated this time, too, and every time you come back.

Predictably, the top-down service imperative is also at work, beginning with Sharp in Toronto. It's his belief that the last decade of the century will find an increasingly sophisticated, better educated, and more travel-savvy customer checking in at the front desk of hotels worldwide. That customer wants not just quality, but the highest value for his or her travel dollar. To continue to succeed, Sharp maintains that Four Seasons must continue to attract the kind of people able to deliver that value.

Accordingly, general managers are recruited for their ability to act as the "conductor of a symphony," making sure all the players make the right kind of music at just the right time, and in perfect harmony. "It's important that the manager set the correct example for employees and frequently communicate to his staff," Sharp told *Hotels & Restaurants International* in 1986. "You must try to ensure that the reality in the working environment matches the rhetoric, i.e., it's no good to show your staff all sorts of audiovisuals about how to be courteous and then have management giving the wrong example."

From Sharp on down, Four Seasons managers are good examples of a thoroughgoing service-quality commitment that has paid off handsomely for the business—and for the customers who have made that business an international success.

Four Seasons Hotels, Inc.
1165 Leslie Street
Toronto, Ontario M3C 2K8

Hyatt Hotels & Resorts

HYATT✪HOTELS CORPORATION

A COURIOUS THING HAPPENS WHEN PEOPLE ARE ASKED TO RATE THEIR FAVORITE hotels. Consistently, they name a lot of Hyatt locations. Just as consistently, they can't exactly say why. It isn't the vaulted atrium lobbies—a Hyatt trademark since it took over and finished construction of what became the Hyatt Regency Atlanta in 1967—or the glass elevators, or the fancy revolving rooftop restaurants. There's something about a Hyatt, some subtle quality of the service and facilities provided, that keeps bringing people back.

Consistently, it seems, what makes Hyatt stand out in the hotel business is consistency.

"If ever there was a time when the orange juice had to be fresh or when the turndown service had to occur in every instance, it's right now," Hyatt Hotels president Darryl Hartley-Leonard told *Restaurant Business* in 1986. "If there is parity in hotels, and I think we all believe there is, then the buyer becomes very intolerant of things he had been tolerant of in the past. The customer is totally in control today. He not only has the opportunity of going to another hotel, he can go to a very similar hotel."

Hyatt Hotels & Resorts is actually two separate and distinct companies that manage or operate hotels under various Hyatt names (Hyatt, Hyatt Regency, Park Hyatt, Grand Hyatt, and Regency Club). Hyatt Hotels Corporation is the North American side of the business. It operates eighty-one hotels and twelve resorts in the U.S., Canada, and the Caribbean, including the first Hyatt near the Los Angeles International Airport, which Jay Pritzker bought in 1957 from a cash-strapped owner. Hyatt International's scope includes twenty-nine hotels and fifteen resorts in twenty-six countries. Although the company doesn't segment in the sense of maintaining different brand and price categories, its properties fall under one of four distinct forms: large commercial hotels (generally located in a downtown area, and often a key component in a given city's downtown revitalization efforts); suburban (or "smaller urban") hotels; resort and convention-oriented properties; and small-but-luxurious hotels (the Park Hyatts).

129

The holding company, Hyatt Corporation, is privately held by the Pritzker family of Chicago, but most of the hotels under the Hyatt name are owned, either entirely or substantially, by local investor groups. Hyatt serves as manager and operator, and sometimes minority stakeholder. To maintain accountability for service quality systemwide, Hyatt forgoes franchises in favor of direct, long-term management responsibility—generally twenty- to thirty-year contracts—whether or not it has an equity interest in the property.

In some respects, the Hyatt reputation for consistency is misleading. It implies a sameness of design and treatment that doesn't turn out to be the case. In fact, in marked contrast to cookie-cutter chains that promise the same familiar experience from one city to the next, no two Hyatts are alike. That's not to say that operating standards vary. They don't. But each property is designed, built, and managed to be an integral business and civic element in its particular location and for its specific clientele or market niche.

Since the original "atrium" hotel—the legendary John Portmann-designed edifice in Atlanta with its twenty-one-story central core—debuted, the company has been considered the trendsetter in the upscale hotel market for its willingness to take chances on new configurations and innovate in service areas. Its hotels are visually exciting, run by independent managers given a good deal of authority by Hyatt's decentralized operating style. At the same time, Hyatt has been slow and selective in its growth, a quality-conscious pace that has dampened the effects of an overbuilt industry's current room glut at the high end of the market.

Similarly, the segmentation that now characterizes the hotel industry has been part of Hyatt's management style for nearly two decades. But instead of building separate brand-named properties for separate segments of the traveling public, Hyatt balances their different needs under the same roof.

For example, the traditional Hyatt—five hundred or more rooms in a large metropolitan area—gets high marks from both discriminating individual travelers and business group meeting and travel planners. That's because there are facilities for each, carefully arranged and physically separated so the individual's desire for privacy and personal treatment doesn't interfere with the group's need for large-scale meeting rooms and entertainment. For the traveler seeking highly personal service and the ambience of a smaller property, Hyatt also offers the Regency Club: one or two floors set aside as a hotel-within-a-hotel, with separate key access and concierges.

Within the industry, Hyatt receives high marks for making hotel food and beverage service profitable. Of course, it wouldn't be profitable if it weren't desirable to guests and people in the community who expect the best from the restaurants in a Hyatt property. Consequently, food quality is an important part of the company's service strategy. Some Hyatts have as many as five different full-service restaurants, and many also have a gourmet deli located just off the lobby. That shows up on the bottom line: Where the average full-service hotel gets a little under a third of its operating revenues from food and beverage services, 37 percent of Hyatt's revenues come from those sources.

Hyatt's service system expertise is visible in other parts of the hotel, too. The company was the first to provide in-room amenities such as shampoo and sewing kits, the first to offer computerized guest check-in at larger (convention-scale) facilities, and has been a pacesetter in guest-appreciated services ranging from fitness and security programs to express check-out.

Achieving consistency in a decentralized service culture is also a matter of good design. Hyatt uses very few consultants: "We feel that our own people are the best consultants," one executive told *Hotels & Restaurants International* in 1987. It also pushes training and management responsibilities out to regional and property managers. In fact, all corporate-level functions, from management to marketing, are duplicated at the regional and hotel levels. The effect is much like providing identical shipments of flowers to a hundred talented gardeners: The actual plants will be the same in each garden, but each plot will display a unique flair.

For the future, Hyatt has committed itself to taking its big-city style to both flashy, upscale resorts and smaller-scale suburban hotel locations. It promises to be an interesting mix. The new Hyatt Regency Scottsdale showcases nearly $4 million worth of water wonderland: ten pools, twenty-eight fountains, forty-seven waterfalls, and even a beach. Prototype suburban metro properties with two hundred to three hundred rooms may have to forgo atriums and ballrooms to be competitive, but Hyatt executives promise the smaller size will not be accompanied by diminished service.

That, after all, wouldn't be consistent.

Hyatt Hotels Corporation
200 West Madison
Chicago, IL 60606

Mississippi Management

MISSISSIPPI MANAGEMENT INC.

THE SIGN OUT IN FRONT OF THE HOTEL IN ALABAMA MAY LOOK THE SAME AS the one back in Massachusetts, but all properties of the same brand name are not necessarily created or managed equal. Just like restaurant, car-rental, broadcasting, and other seemingly monolithic service delivery companies, many national and regional hotel corporations sell franchises to independent operators as a cost-effective way to expand their systems. Some, in fact, actually operate very few of the properties that bear their names. Consequently, while the overall design and quality standards may be the same coast to coast, there will be significant differences in day-to-day operations that reflect, at least in part, different service priorities among on-site managers and frontline workers.

Thus, Holiday Corporation will point with justifiable pride to various examples of good service management among its company-owned Holiday Inn properties. It also will point to some of its franchisees as equally noteworthy providers of top-quality service. In that context, the name Mississippi Management is sure to come up. The thirty-year-old Jackson-based company owns and operates nine well-above-average Holiday Inns in five states around the south, plus an Embassy Suites, a Ramada Inn, a Seasons Resort, and five Cabot Lodges—the last its own growing entry into the mid-level hotel market.

Mississippi Management is especially noteworthy for the importance management attaches to maintaining good service standards at the frontline, and the relatively high level of investment it routinely makes in programs to ensure and enhance the treatment it gives its guests. For example, in the name of service quality it has held an internal, company-wide Olympics—with such events as drink-mixing, egg-cracking, table-clearing, key-sorting, and sheet- and towel-folding, not to mention the grueling housekeeping cart relay. Each year, month by month, there are constant smaller-scale competitions within and among its properties, with rewards to the best reservations centers, the top front desks, the outstanding kitchens.

No phase of the operation of a modern hotel is overlooked. Mississippi

Management sends housekeepers to annual seminars and polls front-desk clerks for ways to improve check-in procedures and incorporate guest feedback into room furnishings. Every week it rewards the cooks at each property who come the closest to cutting the prime rib portions the right size with a ten-dollar bonus; there's a similar bonus for the buffet carver who comes closest to the average serving size. Housekeepers who qualify for an incentive plan can boost their hourly pay by making more beds than a property's productivity standard—provided they continue to pass quality inspections. Food and beverage managers can increase their pay by as much as 50 percent through performance bonuses.

As people stay with the company, their experience is channelled into an internal management training program, through which Mississippi Management "grows" its own general managers. The program takes six to eight months and includes extensive on-the-job training in every department from reservations and the front desk to maintenance and food service. An occasional department manager may be hired in from the outside, but most mid- and top-level managers have and continue to come up through the ranks.

One prize graduate is Cindy O'Cain, general manager of the Cabot Lodge in Nashville that she opened for Mississippi Management in 1987. O'Cain is also a graduate of the school of hotel and restaurant administration at Florida State University, but her experience with Mississippi Management predates her academic work. She started in the "hotel business" right out of high school (class of 1978) as a waitress in the company's Holiday Inn in Lake City, Florida, and worked her way up inside a succession of the company's properties while working her way through first a junior college, and later Florida State. When she picked up her degree, she had a pretty good idea who she wanted to work for—and Mississippi Management lost no time in finding a place for her.

Many hotel management companies are unwilling to make such investments, whether at the frontline or in supervision and management, even if they are able. The hospitality industry, they will note by way of explanation, is characterized by turnover rates as high as 300 percent annually, especially in low-status, low-pay jobs (a catalog that ranges from the maids in the housekeeping department to the night clerks on the front desk). Just bringing new employees up to speed is a sometimes daunting task.

With turnover among its fourteen hundred employees averaging less than a third of that industry norm, on the other hand, Mississippi Management maintains that its long-standing practice of investing heavily in training, motivation, and incentive programs at even the lowest levels of the company encourages good treatment of guests and builds loyalty and longevity among employees, no matter how low they stand on the organizational totem pole. That's why Mississippi Management bestows everything from cash awards for annual anniversaries to a trip anywhere in the United States after fifteen years (twenty-year veterans earn a Caribbean cruise for two) on everyone from property managers to maids.

To further encourage loyalty and stability among its hourly workers, Mississippi Management also has introduced a cafeteria-style benefits plan, and it plans to add to it over the next few years as opportunities present themselves. Child care is already included; a two-tier medical plan designed with an eye toward dual-earner families where the other spouse already has coverage is on the way. The reason: In a job market where the supply of entry-level workers is dwindling, the company believes it will increasingly be competing for people not just against other hotel operations, but against the full spectrum of manufacturing and service businesses. Earle Jones, Mississippi Management's president, considers the pay, the programs, the promotions, and the perks as investments in the company's very future.

The return on investment isn't always easy to measure, but there are ways to make it visible—and the customer clearly is a beneficiary. Statistically, for example, about 4 percent of Holiday Inns' guest comment cards turn up a complaint from a traveler dissatisfied with his or her stay. The Holiday Inns run by Mississippi Management consistently receive 25 percent fewer complaints than the national average for the chain. What's more, a similar comment-card feedback system at its own Cabot Lodges has turned up a continuing average of just one complaint per one hundred cards returned since that mini-chain debuted in 1985.

The hotel industry undoubtedly will continue to evolve tightly targeted pricing and property-design strategies, but the names travelers will remember will be the ones where they received the treatment they expected and desired. For Mississippi Management, the challenge is to make sure that the two Holiday Inns in Baton Rouge, Louisiana, the new Cabot Lodge in Nashville, and the other properties it operates under its own and other names continue to show up on those lists of personal favorites.

Mississippi Management, Inc.
P.O. Box 16807
Jackson, MS 39236

HEALTH CARE

HOSPITALS

Riverside Methodist Hospital

Beth Israel Hospital

Mayo Clinic and Hospitals

SUPPORT

Merck & Company

LensCrafters

Bergen Brunswig Drug Company

Shared Medical Systems Corporation

Health Care: Don't Make Them Sick While They're Trying to Get Well

YESTERDAY'S HEALTH CARE PROFESSIONALS LIVED AND WORKED IN A WORLD they dominated and controlled, a world fashioned on the assumption that there would always be sickness and disease and calamity. And the sick and injured would always need hospitals and doctors and nurses. And they would always be good little patients and do exactly as they were told. And somebody would always and without question pay the bills.

Times change.

The world they live in today is one of budgets and controls and cost containment and market positioning and competition. The result is that the hospital—the mainstay setting for the provision of major medical services—today looks and acts different from the hospital they and we grew up knowing.

- Hospitals and clinics and doctors are relearning—in some cases simply learning for the first time—that patients are people, people are markets, and markets have needs that must be met if they expect to stay in business.
- Successful hospital administrators wear three-piece suits, talk bottom line and return on investment with the best of them, and worry into the night about ways to get and stay ahead of the competition.
- Hospitals advertise, hoping to impress the increasing proportion of activist customers who insist on having a say in where and how they will be treated. The average hospital administrator is now able to talk your ear off about marketing strategy and segmentation.
- Specialty marketing has arrived. Some hospitals emulate hotels and make available luxury suites for upscale patients. They offer expectant fathers beepers so they can be paged at the office when mothers go into labor.
- On the personnel front, hospitals routinely hold people-skills training programs hoping to persuade frontliners to treat patients as individuals who happen to have an illness rather than as "the hemorrhoid in 407."

136

- On the business front, hospitals are finding ways to serve patients and make money that were unimagined ten years ago. They are engaged in taking in laundry, packaging and selling frozen meals for people with special dietary needs, and offering classes in weight reduction, smoking cessation, and fitness.

Today, more than ever before, hospitals are being managed as business enterprises—taking entrepreneurial risks, managing staff and operations in a proactive manner, and learning to specialize, specialize, specialize.

Patient as Customer

What's causing all this? Defer, for a moment, consideration of flat-rate billing, overbedding, malpractice, the doctor glut, the nursing shortage. Focus on the new driving force in medical care: the patient, a.k.a. "the customer." Gone are the days of the quiet and compliant patient who dared not speak, much less challenge the care providers. Today's better-educated, more sophisticated health care consumer can and does make judgments and discriminations about care quality.

A study of health care consumer sensitivity by Custom Research of Minneapolis found that health care customers can easily discriminate between the quality of care and the quality of caring they receive; between the way they are treated medically and treated personally. As customers, they feel competent to evaluate the quality of the caring they receive and justified in making treatment choices on that basis. They are even willing to pay more to ensure that the caring is as good as the care, the art as good as the science.

A group of Canadian researchers studying patient perceptions at Foothills Hospital in Calgary, Alberta, reached much the same conclusion recently. According to their one-year study of thirteen hundred discharged patients, "being treated as an individual" is by a considerable margin more important to their satisfaction than "getting better," and "having timely, adequate information about my condition" is more desirable than newness of facilities or the flexibility of hospital rules. The researchers add that today's patients "want to be more actively involved in the decision-making process concerning their care and treatment." The era of the patient as customer has arrived for the North American health care establishment.

How prevalent is this new consumer? No one knows for sure. Estimates of patient involvement in care provider choices run from 10 percent to 40 percent depending on the region of the country reporting, but most health care experts accept consumer involvement as a growth trend.

In one study, Russell C. Coile, Jr., and Randolph M. Grossman asked *Healthcare Forum* magazine's "Panel of 300" to anticipate what's new and what's next "in the coming 1,000 days" for American health care.

Overwhelmingly, the Delphi panel's answers revolved around quality—both quality of care and quality of caring. Coile and Grossman conclude that measurement and the ability to "prove" customer satisfaction will be increasingly important. Those organizations that cannot demonstrate successful achievement of service quality standards to potential customers, be they individual consumers, government agencies, or insurers and employers with prepaid health care benefits, will find themselves in deep trouble, even to the point of being redlined by consumers.

Not all health care administrators agree on the proportion of patients who play an active role in determining where they will receive treatment, but most agree that the trend is in the direction of patients taking a more active and informed part in determining their treatment.

Kim Wheatly, chief operating officer of St. Benedict's Hospital in Ogden, Utah, observes, "It is still not the case that the patient is the customer. Doctors and insurance companies still make most of the treatment decisions. But there clearly is a new consumer out there, one who is willing to change doctors if necessary to get health care delivered to them the way they want it delivered. We are just starting to come to grips with that phenomenon and do things for the new consumer."

What is this new health care consumer looking for? A lot of service-oriented things, yes, but *not* to play doctor or second-guess medical practices. Dawn Gideon, director of patient services at Forbes Vantage Group, Pittsburgh, sees these new consumers as patients who not only have medical needs but who also have opinions about the care they expect to receive. "Ten years ago," says Gideon, "health care was a seller's market. Regardless of how we treated a patient on the nontechnical aspects of health care, they came back to our hospital. The physician decided where they were going. We had a 100-percent occupancy rate.

"That's not the case anymore," she continues. "The result [of recent changes] is a buyer's market. Today, a growing percentage of patients indicate they are the primary decision makers at the point of determining where they want to go for treatment."

But patients, Gideon observes, are not basing their decisions on technical, care-oriented aspects such as the hospital's medical technology or the adequacy of staffing on a nursing station. They have no way to judge those things. Instead, they base their decisions on things they *do* feel qualified to judge; the room, the food, the admissions process, the questions they ask, the answers they get to their questions—everything from whether the people are smiling and friendly to how hard they have to look to find a parking space that isn't reserved for doctors only. "Those things don't necessarily have anything to do with the quality of medical care," she points out, "but they are the way patients are evaluating us."

Responding to the New Consumer

It sometimes seems as though the system itself is unable, by its very design, to provide good patient service along with medically sound patient care. And first efforts at change in many cases have only made matters worse. One of the responses to the news that patients have joined doctors and third-party payers as an influence in provider choice has been the concept of "hospital as hotel": the idea that the more like a first-class hotel a hospital can become, the more likely it will be to get good ratings from the new, discriminating patient. Some hospitals have gone on painting and carpeting and furniture-buying binges. Others have experimented with streamlined admissions procedures, valet parking, and patient escort services. Still others have seized on improving bed linen and patient garment and bath towel quality.

A few hospitals have taken the concept to its extreme and developed whole "high-amenities" wings: floors and parts of floors where, for considerable extra dollars, patients receive the sort of treatment only available on the concierge levels of luxury hotels ("Would you prefer toast or muffins for breakfast, Mr. Smith; and will that be *USA Today* or *The Wall Street Journal*; and what time would you like your wake-up call, sir?"). If the high-amenities strategy has a payoff—even momentarily—for a hospital, research like the Foothills study makes it clear that it likely won't last long.

In other words, poor food, dirty floors, and dingy rooms lead to well-deserved patient brickbats, but adequate food, clean surroundings, and tolerable rooms do not necessarily or automatically win bouquets. While poor hotel-type services in a hospital may lead to patient dissatisfaction, above-average services of the hotel genre will not necessarily, nor for very long, create a positive distinction in the average consumer's mind. The real kudos, it seems, are more clearly associated with the way the patient is treated as a person.

Thus the hot topic in health care today is "Guest Relations" training. Pioneered at Memorial Hospital of South Bend, Indiana, in the early 1980s, its object is to remind administrators, staffers, nurses, and doctors alike that Room 137 is occupied by a real person, not by "a gall bladder, a heart attack, or a burn case." In both 1986 and 1987, when *Training* magazine asked readers to pinpoint the most critical issues facing them, 43 percent of health care respondents named "improving customer service" their number one priority—a significantly higher rate of concern than for respondents from any other industry.

But it is becoming pretty clear that simply renaming patients "guests" in the Disney tradition—eschewing "customer" as too harsh and communicating the wrong image to employees—and conducting "Smile, people, smile!" courses has little effect in and of itself. Semantics and vapid grins won't change patients' perceptions unless and until hospitals become places where patients are treated as people and not as case files and symptoms. It is equally clear that a focus on treating patients as people, when done thoroughly and well, can have an impact.

William Flexner, a Minneapolis-based health care marketing consultant, says that it is unrealistic to expect customer-contact training to cure a hospital or clinic's patient satisfaction problems, but he stops short of condemning such training out of hand. "Customer-contact training can work in health care, and it can help to improve customer satisfaction. But the hospital execs have to know why they are doing it, what they can expect from it, and realize that the training is only a small part of what has to be done. They have to understand, for instance, that they are working on a retention issue, not just a customer satisfaction or customer complaint issue," he warns.

Why Change Is Difficult

It would be unfair and untrue to purport that a focus on customer satisfaction will cure all the ills bedeviling the American health care system. It is a system caught up in a complex crisis of dollars, beds, and access. As a *Business Week* writer so aptly summed up: "Too many hospitals and insurance plans are competing for too few patients. Overcapacity will undermine hospital profits, as costs rise and patient volume declines. Corporate clients will abandon insurers who can't keep their prices low. And fierce marketing wars among health maintenance organizations (HMOs) will intensify."

To that assessment we would simply add one additional, compounding, issue—the growing demand from consumers that no one be denied access to any treatment that might possibly impact their well-being.

There are abundant ironies in the situation. We in the U.S. spend more on health care—$450 billion a year, or roughly 11 percent of our GNP— than any other industrialized nation in the world; the next closest are Great Britain and Japan at about 9 percent each. The cost of medical services in this country has escalated seven times faster than the consumer price index for each of the last five years. But for all that, the American health care system is in terrible financial trouble, and it is still falling short of consumer expectations.

It's a vexing dilemma: At a time when cost containment is the watchword of the day for managers in hospitals, clinics, HMOs, government agencies like Medicare and Medicaid, and medical care insurers like Blue Cross and Blue Shield, studies by the Conference Board and Cambridge Reports routinely find the consumer disappointed in the return on his or her health care dollar. As Fabian Linden of the Conference Board Consumer Research Center summarized it in a 1985 report, "Discontent with medical services in general—doctors, dentists, hospitals and insurance—and related services, is pervasive in all age groups, in all income brackets, and in all regions of the country." The customer is losing patience with the provider while the provider is beset by and preoccupied with internal problems.

For example, we are an aging population—in 1990 our average age will be thirty-nine years—and will likely be needing more and more medical attention in the 1990s and beyond; for now, however, there is a widely acknowledged glut of hospital beds. In 1986 the occupancy rate of the average U.S. hospital—the average proportion of beds in use at any given point in time—was 63 percent, 17 points below traditional levels and the occupancy level most hospitals staff and budget for. Megatrend tracker John Naisbitt has predicted that by the turn of the century, as many as two thousand hospitals will have either closed their doors or been absorbed into other hospital systems. Meanwhile, the American health care system is experiencing a growing deficit of registered and licensed nurses that, by some predictions, will reach twenty thousand to fifty thousand in the same period.

Those factors notwithstanding, the most influential force in the way health care is provided today is the dramatic change underway in the way medical services are paid for in the United States. Not too many years ago, doctors and hospitals set their own prices for treatment. The patient received two bills, one from the doctor and one from the hospital, and, by and large, that was what patients and third parties—insurance companies, employers, and agencies like Medicare and Medicaid—paid.

All that ended in October 1983, when, in an effort to control what were viewed as runaway health care costs, the federal government instituted a plan calling for payment by Diagnostic Related Grouping. Under the DRG system, the government pays a flat rate based on the amount of time its statistics say a given procedure or treatment should take—whether it actually takes that much treatment, or less, or more.

The theory is that the time and care required for an appendectomy or a childbirth or the repair of a broken hip can be based on a statistical norm, and payment made based on that midpoint. If the statistical model is accurate, a hospital will lose money on patients who require treatment above the norm, but come out even by making money on the ones who require less. The expectation is that it will profit by learning to move patients through the system more quickly, which in turn will result in reduced health costs overall.

The prospect of gaining control over costs was too attractive to resist. Other third-party payers, primarily the insurance companies and employers who cover the medical expenses of 77.8 percent of the American population, followed along quickly, and the fix was in. Health care in the United States, at least the lion's share of it, increasingly operates on a flat-rate basis, with prices controlled by the federal government. Those providers who deliver at or below the newly established levels stay in business, those unable to bring treatment costs in line with the payment guidelines are in big trouble.

Susan Clark, vice president of education for the Minnesota Association of Hospitals and Homes for the Aged, remembers the onset of DRGs well. "I was working for a hospital at the time DRGs came into being, and within the month we had to cut costs one million dollars to stay in business. Within a year we were looking for a merger partner. Eventually, that hospital was absorbed, and in effect it no longer exists."

Contributing to the cost crunch is the growing influence of HMOs, a type of group health plan to which about 25 million Americans now subscribe. In theory, HMOs are the essence of simplicity: a bulk-purchase medical services plan that operates as a sort of health care buying club and outpatient clinic run as a for-profit business.

They are supposed to be a good deal for both employers and their employees. The employee gets easier access, low- or no-cost health care, and one-stop shopping. The employer saves 30 to 40 percent on health care benefits. In actuality, however, the people who run the HMO make money by controlling the costs of the health care services they provide or broker and by "managing" (usually limiting) Acme Widget employees' access to services.

HMOs and other third-party payers who watched and learned from them routinely require second opinions on surgical procedures, limit hospital stays, prenegogiate the fees of the doctors and hospitals they send people to, and generally worry the cost side of health care down and down. But HMOs are finding, just as have insurance companies, hospitals, and individual practitioners, that the DRG system has a big blind spot: Medicare funds, which pay 40 percent of the nation's medical bills, stubbornly refuse to rise as fast as provider costs.

In short, the pressure of too many beds, too few dollars, and a decreasing number of patients with increasing expectations and demands has shaken medicine to the core, shattering, perhaps forever, this once staid industry's proud self-image and clouding its vision of the future.

It will take more than a determined customer focus to sort out the crisis in the American health care system. As Dr. Arthur Kaplan, director of the center for Medical Ethics at the University of Minnesota put it in a recent interview, "We are going through a fundamental upheaval in health care in our society. We have expectations of health care providers that have never existed before. We have yet to come to grips with the difficult choices that go with those demands."

Beginning on the next page we profile three health care providers who, despite the pressures on the system, have been able to focus successfully on care and caring, both the dollars and the "sense" of modern medicine.

U.S. Health Corporation's Riverside Methodist Hospital is the flagship of an ambitious regional health care corporation in Columbus, Ohio. Boston's Beth Israel Hospital is a respected metropolitan teaching hospital known for its patient care creativity. The Mayo Clinic and Hospitals deservedly rank as a national treasure.

Of course, the American health care industry is more than hospitals, doctors, nurses, and pagers. It is a broad range of business from publishing to pill-making. We profile four of these related organizations: Merck & Company, a respected pharmaceutical; LensCrafters, a bright and brash purveyor of eyewear; Bergen Brunswig, a wholesaler and management support expert specializing in the needs of independent pharmacists; and Shared Medical Systems, the medical field's premier information management specialist.

Riverside Methodist Hospitals

"IT'S AN INTERESTING JOB TO BE HEAD OF AN ORGANIZATION WHICH EVERY PERSON wants to leave and no person wants to come to. On a Saturday night, when one of your friends says, 'What shall we do for fun?' no one suggests that it would be great to check into the hospital."

That wry observation is from Erie Chapman III, president and chief executive officer of U.S. Health Corporation of Columbus, Ohio. U.S. Health is a small holding company that owns or operates eight hospitals in central Ohio, six as subsidiary corporations, two under management contracts. The largest of the six is Riverside Methodist in Columbus—at 1,092 beds, the largest private general medical center in the state. Chapman also wears the hat of its president and CEO.

Occasionally, he wears other things as well: the uniform of a linen services worker or a dishwasher, for example. Chapman knows firsthand how the laundry and kitchen at Riverside Methodist operate because he periodically leaves his pin-striped suit in his office and works a few hours alongside the crews there. He's spent time in x-ray helping out the evening shift's technicians; he's also spent several shifts working as a patient escort, pushing patients around the hospital in wheelchairs (a practice he encourages his vice presidents to perform as well).

Chapman, you see, sees himself as a change agent within the American health care system, which he asserts currently has too many things in common with a prison. Like a prison, he notes, vestiges of individuality are systematically removed from those who reluctantly enter the system—starting with their clothes, which are replaced with that "degrading uniform commonly referred to as a patient gown."

How do you provide a satisfying level of service, he asks, in a situation that includes the following stark dichotomy between the service provider (doctors and nurses) and the customer (the patient):

Doctor/Nurse	*Patient*
1. I am healthy.	1. You are not.
2. I wear a uniform.	2. You're not even wearing your underwear—just a hospital gown.
3. I am standing.	3. You are sitting in a wheelchair or you are lying down.
4. I know about medical treatment.	4. You don't know anything.
5. I am confident.	5. You are scared.
6. I can probably give you your health back.	6. You probably cannot get your health back without me.
7. I am "young."	7. You are "old."

The contrasts go on and on, Chapman adds, but the single message is loud and clear: "You are my hostage. You must obey." There's more: "Your family may come to visit you (if you have a family), but they will be required to leave after visiting hours (like most American prisons). When you are finally discharged, you or your insurance company will be billed several thousand dollars for your visit (*not* like American prisons). Will you have your health back? Maybe."

Since coming on board in 1983, Chapman has committed Riverside Methodist to changing that authoritarian motif. Employees, physicians, executives, and (significantly) patients have all been enlisted in an effort that is dedicated to nothing less than remaking the hospital from top to bottom. As part of the process, about twenty service-related positions have been added to the hospital's staff of forty-seven hundred.

The list of changes in place or in progress is a little overwhelming. Start with that "degrading uniform" called the hospital gown: Riverside Methodist has replaced it with a new model designed for its patients by Ann Stevens, one of the hospital's nurse managers, and made to its specifications by a private supplier. It's better—good enough to apply for a trademark on the design—but still not good enough, so Riverside Methodist has challenged students at the Columbus School of Art and Design to have a go at further improving it.

Throughout the hospital, signage and instructions have been improved and clarified. In the radiology department, for example, patients are personally told what a normal wait may be and how to ask for assistance; a large sign near the desk counsels, "If you've been waiting more than 15 minutes, please contact the receptionist."

When you go into most emergency rooms, you're met by an admitting clerk whose primary concern is to get you registered. That's how it used to be at Riverside Methodist, but no more. Now, arriving patients are met by a triage nurse whose primary role is to determine the nature and severity of their problem. If it's heart-related, the patient is immediately taken to the Riverside Heart Institute on the hospital's campus. If it isn't, the next person they see is a primary nurse who takes personal charge of them for as long as they are in the Emergency Room. In addition, patient advocates have been added to provide information and assistance to family members, and the waiting area has been refurbished to make it more comfortable—and more comforting.

Patient advocates and liaisons are active in other parts of the hospital, too. Surgical patients and their families are served by a surgery liaison who relays information on operations, explains normal hospital procedures, and keeps everyone aware of how long it will be before the patient is returned to his or her room. Before the position was created in 1986, Riverside Methodist received an average of twenty-two surgical-related complaints a month; it received just one complaint over the next eighteen months—and more than two dozen compliments.

A volunteer has been added to the front-desk staff so someone is available to personally escort patients and visitors who need assistance or aren't sure they can find the right department or room. Patients from outside Columbus are given the name and phone number of a member of the patient-relations staff who will be available during their treatment to provide information and assistance. "Out-of-city" advocates have been asked for everything from directions to nearby restaurants and churches to recommendations on modestly priced lodging close to the hospital.

As a regional medical center, the hospital admits patients from all over central Ohio, especially rural communities without specialized medical care. For physicians in the central Ohio region who refer their patients to Riverside Methodist, there's now a special 800-number staffed from seven A.M. to eleven P.M. to provide information on treatment and prognosis. The service also can help identify and locate an appropriate specialist on staff for a long-distance consultation or provide information on hospital physicians who will take patients on referral.

The nurse who takes care of you while you're in the hospital introduces herself and hands you her business card so you know who's responsible for your care. Staff nurses from various departments also make more than two thousand follow-up phone calls each month to see how their former patients are doing. Patient-relations representatives make another thirty-five hundred visits each year to the homes of people who have been treated by Riverside Methodist in recent months, especially those who have been in for extended periods of time.

At the Heart Institute, a full-time heart care liaison provides a communication link for patients and their families and occasionally conducts focus groups with heart patients to evaluate their stays and continuing treatment needs. One outcome: Based on patient feedback, the liaison tumbled to the fact that more complaints in the heart catheterization program, which handles about four thousand procedures annually, were due to the unexplained delays often encountered (typically because physicians were responding to emergency treatment needs or spending more time with a previous patient than anticipated) than any other cause.

So now at Riverside Methodist, the liaison keeps patients and families fully informed about what's happening. Treatment isn't being provided any faster than before, but *patient perceptions* of the process have been radically altered. Where once half of the Heart Institute's patients used to express dissatisfaction over delays, now one complaint every six months is typical.

One of the unique market conditions faced by Riverside Methodist is the presence of American Honda's large automobile and motorcycle manufacturing plants in nearby Marysville. To better accommodate Japanese-speaking patients and their visitors, the hospital has provided a card for all employees that gives Japanese translations for common phrases like "When can I see my doctor?" and "Please call my family." For more extensive conversations, Japanese interpreters are on call twenty-four hours a day. Preadmission and patient-education materials also have been translated and reprinted in Japanese, and special menus are available.

Perhaps no development better illustrates Riverside Methodist's commitment to changing the way it delivers health care services than the creation in 1985 of The Elizabeth Blackwell Center, a two-floor enclave within the hospital dedicated to women's health needs. Named for America's first female physician, the Blackwell Center resulted from eighteen months of planning, during which it evolved from a conventional OB/GYN (obstetrics and gynecology) facility to a multifaceted operation that addresses the comprehensive physical, mental, and social well-being of its patients.

The change in direction resulted from listening to prospective customers: As part of the design and development process, more than five hundred women in the Columbus area participated in forums and focus groups that identified concerns from menstrual and maternity issues to sports medicine, nutrition, and lifestyle support.

The center's all-female staff is organized as a collegium rather than in a traditional hierarchy: members are all equal in rank and responsibility, and they rotate leadership functions. The management style was deliberately chosen not only for its potential to generate creative and innovative care from the staff, but also to provide a role model for patients who can observe women working professionally and productively without centralized authority figures.

What affect has all this had on the quality of medical care? Well, in 1985 Columbus-area physicians ranked Riverside Methodist fourth among the seven hospitals in the community. In 1987, they considered Riverside Methodist number one.

Riverside Methodist Hospital
U.S. Health Corporation
3555 Olentangy River Road
Columbus, OH 43214

Boston's Beth Israel Hospital
330 Brookline Avenue, Boston, MA 02215 / (617) 735-2000

WHEN YOU ASK BOSTON DOCTORS TO NAME THE BEST HOSPITAL IN TOWN, chances are they'll say Massachusetts General, the largest of the teaching hospitals affiliated with the Harvard Medical School. It's a good choice. But a funny thing happens when you rephrase the question and ask them where they would go for treatment if they or someone in their family had to be hospitalized. Then the answer you're likely to get is Beth Israel Hospital.

In *The Best Hospitals in America*, authors Linda Sunshine and John W. Wright tout sixty-four institutions, from Massachusetts General to the Mayo Clinic. Many are world-renowned research institutes. Many more are affiliated with major universities and medical schools. Beth Israel, like Mass General, is one of the major teaching facilities for Harvard, and a lot of Harvard medical research money flows through its corporate arteries. But it's a hospital, too—one with a well-earned reputation for putting an uncommon emphasis on patient care and service.

Founded in 1916 by Boston's Jewish community to serve the needs of the city's growing immigrant population, Beth Israel has become a national model not for its research breakthroughs or top-notch staff of doctors (though it can boast of both), but for its inpatient nursing programs. That's right, nursing. In a hospital, nursing is where the care—the day-to-day personal service of the business—gets delivered. Beth Israel has been doing that in an exemplary way for more than a decade.

Beth Israel's primary-nursing program, the first of its kind in a major medical center, dates back to 1975. Three years earlier, it was the first hospital in the country to issue a "Statement on the Rights of Patients," a pioneering viewpoint that inspired a Massachusetts state law and has since been replicated, in words, if not always in spirit, by hospitals and governments coast to coast.

Bills of rights are fine. No argument there. But when you wake up hurting, confused, or afraid, in a strange place, with no familiar face in sight, at 2:30 in the morning (or 2:30 in the afternoon for that matter), it's people you're looking for, not paper. Beth Israel was one of the first, and

149

still is one of the best, at making sure someone knows who you are and what you're going through, even if you aren't in good enough shape to know who that someone is.

The basis of the system is personalized, or "primary," nursing. Each patient is assigned a registered nurse as his or her primary nurse within twenty-four hours of admission. That nurse is made responsible for and empowered to manage the patient's hospital experience from admission through discharge or transfer to another unit of the hospital. So much care-planning and decision-making has been moved to the frontline that Beth Israel has eliminated two tiers of management in its nursing staff. The nurse is now both care-giver and care-manager.

She (no sexism intended—nineteen out of every twenty nurses in America are women) develops a 24-hour-a-day care plan and has primary responsibility for providing her patients' daily nursing care. She works closely with her patients' doctors, so much so that some patients have been known to call their nurse at Beth Israel instead of their physician when they have questions or problems after being discharged. When she goes off duty, she leaves instructions for the next shifts. When she returns, she updates the plans and makes sure the patients in her care are receiving what they need.

Nursing being nursing, she also handles other duties, helping other nurses with their primary care assignments just as they help her. An average nurse on an average shift will have primary responsibility for two or three patients and may lend a hand with two to four more as time permits. It's a tough pace and a high-burnout profession, perhaps all the more so because medicine has for so long and in so many ways been a male-dominated field, but Beth Israel's frontline workers seem to be thriving on it. The growing nursing shortage notwithstanding, Beth Israel's vacancy rate on staff averages less than 2 percent.

Lest we forget, the old saw used to be that hospitals don't have patients. Doctors have patients. Hospitals have doctors. And doctors were guys who liked their cars comfortable, their tee times guaranteed, and their nurses quiet. Less than twenty years ago, nursing students were still being taught to stand up, and remain standing silently, when a doctor entered the room, and nurses made about the same amount of money as the people who put the filling in Hostess Twinkies.

Much has changed in medicine, and the long-running skirmishing between the sexes has played a role. More women now go to med schools than ever before; men are entering the nursing field in larger numbers. Caught between a complex cost crisis and a growing shortage of cost-effective frontline care-givers, hospitals coast to coast are reevaluating the role of the nurse in providing medical care. That process is leading to both increased professional recognition and more realistic financial compensation for nurses—and, in at least some cases and places, better, more personal care for patients.

Beth Israel is prominent among the hospitals that are systematically changing the personal involvement and professional status of their nursing staffs. The reasoning seems sound: Day to day, hour by hour, it's the nursing staff that does the business of the hospital, from checking vital signs and delivering medications to giving baths and answering questions from patients and family. Good nursing care has a direct, if often subtle, impact on everything from the satisfaction level of doctors (who these days can choose to put their patients in any of a number of increasingly competitive hospitals) to the willingness of a former patient to whistle up a lawyer when something doesn't turn out right.

In addition, in an era of growing cost-consciousness, that $15-an-hour nurse is a very cost-effective way to get the job done. (Even at $20 per, or $30, the nurse's knowledge, training and frontline experience may be too valuable a resource to ignore.) Hospitals are adjusting, and many of them are following the lead of that hospital out in Boston.

All of this transition and change has taken time, and a lot of it dates back to 1966, when a Harvard-trained M.D. and professor of medicine was lured out of the Ivy League classrooms down the road by Beth Israel's board of trustees. Dr. Mitchell T. Rabkin celebrated his first day as president of the hospital by, without fanfare, abolishing the doctors' private dining room. It was an indication of things to come.

It was Rabkin who issued the famous "Statement on the Rights of Patients," which nowadays takes the form of a blue pamphlet titled "Rights" that is given to every patient admitted to Beth Israel as well as to each new employee. Rabkin also instituted an internal hotline that connects patient rooms directly to a hospital service center responsible for everything from burned-out lightbulbs to lumpy mattresses. Under Rabkin a decade ago, Beth Israel put its money ($16 million in mid-1970s cash) where its patients' rights philosophy was by designing a new addition, known as the Feldberg Building, for physical and emotional comfort as well as medical efficiency. With its tastefully decorated rooms, offices, and public areas, marveled *Time* in July of 1976, it was like "a hotel with nurses and operating rooms."

"This is a major teaching and research hospital of Harvard Medical School," Rabkin told *New England Business* a few years ago. "It's world-famous in terms of its research advances, and we're proud of our reputation. That's the high-tech side of what we do, and we have to work hard to maintain our standards. But at the same time we have to realize that we are dealing fundamentally with people, and in an environment of super-special technology, the human issues are increasingly paramount."

It's no accident, then, that Beth Israel has become known as a good place to be a patient. Or a nurse. So successful and permanent has the

Beth Israel primary-nursing model become that in 1986 the hospital established The Center for the Advancement of Nursing Practice, a research and scholarship program dedicated to further refining the role of the professional nurse.

From the conference rooms to the patient rooms, nursing service at Beth Israel is a combination of both patient-care dedication and business smarts. With nurses in increasingly short supply nationwide—the product of years of low pay, long hours, and minimal prestige—Beth Israel is betting that one key to retaining a full and highly motivated nursing staff will be the increased professional involvement its nurses experience. And with issues like overbedding, third-party payment systems, and malpractice litigation to contend with, it has determined that satisfying patients is becoming almost as important as helping them get well again.

With an average daily occupancy rate well over 90 percent, the message apparently hasn't been lost on Beth Israel's "customers."

Beth Israel Hospital
330 Brookline Avenue
Boston, MA 02215

The Mayo Clinic and Hospitals

mayo

A HUNDRED YEARS AGO, MEDICINE WAS PRACTICED BY INDIVIDUAL, INDEPENDENT doctors. Antiseptic technique was a newfangled idea—and certainly not a sure thing to catch on, in the general view. Back then, no one in his or her right mind would have thought of journeying halfway across the continent to the Midwest prairie for medical treatment.

Then a physician who settled in Rochester, Minnesota (about eighty miles down the road from Minneapolis and St. Paul), because that was where the Union Army had sent him to give physicals to new recruits during the Civil War, hung out a shingle with his two sons. A century later, the whole world knows about the Mayo Clinic, the world's largest private medical center.

The essence of Mayo today is the same as it was a century ago: service, an outgrowth of the pioneering group medical practice started in the 1880s by William Worrall Mayo and his sons, Charles and William. The original family practice has grown to more than 860 physicians and medical scientists, plus another 800 medical residents in training, who work on a six-block, twenty-eight-building medical campus that dominates the heart of town and drives the local economy. The medical buildings, hospitals, and even a couple of adjacent hotels are connected by tunnels to protect patients from midwestern weather conditions.

Nearly three hundred thousand patients come to Mayo each year, about a fifth of them traveling more than five hundred miles to do so. Nearly a quarter of Rochester's people work for Mayo or a Clinic-associated business, and about half derive their livelihood from the Clinic and its patients. From admissions clerks to nurses to physicians, they all take the Mayo mystique seriously. That attitude is best summed up in an informal motto attributed to "Dr. Will," as the namesake son is remembered: "The best interest of the patient is the only interest to be considered."

On the Mayo campus, a total staff of more than fifteen thousand physicians, nurses, technicians, and paramedical personnel carries on a tradition of high-quality medical service that puts the patient first, a

153

doctor's wallet (and ego) a distant second. Given that Mayo sees more than a thousand patients a day, and doctors are generally assigned four general examinations daily, that's an ambitious undertaking. Over the generations, Mayo has developed and nurtured a system that continues to deliver on the promise behind its reputation. The key to that system is time.

To put it simply, there's no time limit or norm for how long a doctor spends with a patient. What's more, every doctor is available for consultations, and the Mayo style of group practice makes it likely that more than one physician will be involved in most forms of extended treatment. By tradition, every doctor at Mayo, worldwide reputation notwithstanding, is on salary. There's no incentive to see more patients in order to boost income, and prima donnas seldom are chosen for Mayo's carefully screened staff.

For its part, management is kept lean, and it responds to physician and patient needs, not vice versa. To preserve *that* tradition, Mayo's head administrator is always a doctor chosen from within. Currently it's Dr. Robert Waller, an opthalmologist who came to Mayo as a resident in 1967 and still conducts an active personal practice as well as his administrative duties.

It's a system good doctors love and thrive on—turnover averages less than 2 percent per year. Each year Mayo turns away thousands of applicants to its staff and accepts only one new medical school student for every forty who apply.

Group practice is still the norm, and the term "clinic" is taken seriously. In contrast to major medical centers where patient care is a vehicle for medical research and education, at Mayo and the hundreds of clinics from Cleveland to Scripps developed on the Mayo model, patient care drives research and education. From sophisticated physicals (which at Mayo can take two days or more and may involve a waiting list of several weeks) to complex surgeries, a team of specialists and generalists consults together on diagnosis and treatment. The emphasis is on thorough investigation and clear explanations.

The primary doctor who does your physical, for example, not only does his or her own workup—from weighing you and taking your blood pressure personally to discussing your work and lifestyle—but also spends an average of more than an hour with you before you head home, laying out the results and answering questions.

The Mayo mystique for patient service is no accident. Rather it's a tradition, established occasionally at the expense of other traditions. The Mayos were the first to combine their talents and efforts with other physicians in a group medical practice, a daring and controversial concept to the hidebound medical establishment of the late nineteenth century. They were pioneers in many forms of surgery and sticklers for cleanliness in operating theaters at a time when "serious" medicine was unimpressed by such techniques. They established the country's first graduate school of medicine in 1915, predating the formal founding of the Clinic in 1922. Over the years, the Mayo reputation has been built by generations of successors who have continued the founding family's penchant for research and innovation.

Nor is Mayo resting on a reputation earned in a distant, less competitive past. It's there among *The Best Hospitals in America*. Its monthly newsletter, the *Mayo Clinic Health Letter*, rates right at the top of the growing number of patient-education publications on the market. It's the nation's largest cancer-care center for new patients, with approximately 15 percent of the staff now devoted to the study and treatment of cancer in all its various forms.

It also is the first major clinic to expand its geographical horizons, establishing branch clinics in Jacksonville, Florida, in 1986 and Scottsdale, Arizona, in 1987. Each is staffed primarily by Mayo-trained physicians (also on salary) to assure that quality standards won't be affected by distance. Each was met on opening day with an immediate backlog of patients eager to be treated the Mayo way, evidence once again of the truth of the observation that Mayo may be "the only brand name in the hospital business."

The description is appropriate in light of the sophisticated telecommunications that link the satellite facilities to Rochester's staff and data bases. Through teleconferencing, physicians at any location can confer with their colleagues, often "bringing in" a consultant electronically from a thousand miles away. X-rays, lab readings, and diagnostic info can also be beamed back and forth between Mayo facilities.

Back home in Rochester, Mayo has been a pacesetter in consolidating health care services into more streamlined and cooperatively managed forms, again without sacrificing patient-care standards. After nearly a century of close cooperation, the city's two formerly independent hospitals (the Clinic proper does not include a hospital, and only about 20 percent of Mayo's patients are hospitalized) have been run by the Mayo Foundation since 1986. St. Mary's is the successor to the original country hospital used by the Mayos. Rochester Methodist has been cited by the American Nursing Association as a superior place for nurses to work because of its emphasis on quality patient care. Consistently, over 95 percent of St. Mary's and Methodist's patients pronounce themselves "satisfied" or "very satisfied" in follow-up surveys on their treatment.

Perhaps equally important and as noteworthy as the myriad on-campus medical achievements is the way the Mayo philosophy of medical caring has spread throughout the city it calls home. Rochester today is a bustling town of sixty thousand whose number one industry is Mayo, and it sometimes seems as though the city sees itself as an extension of the

Clinic. Rochester was among the first to install curb cuts on city streets so wheelchairs can move about freely. Its airport is operated by a Clinic subsidiary and has its own fully equipped first aid rooms and trained staff standing by to assist arriving and departing patients and their families.

Friendly, inexpensive lodging for families of patients and visitors to Mayo is a thriving subsidiary industry, from modestly priced motels to modern counterparts of the boardinghouses of generations past, where rooms can cost as little as fifteen dollars a night. It's not stretching the point too far to say that the Mayo medical tradition is taken as seriously off the Mayo campus as it is inside the high-tech medical complex and its associated hospitals.

And then there's the Clinic's long-standing policy on admissions. There is none. No physician's referral is needed. About 80 percent of Mayo's patients come to Mayo on their own initiative, many without having made a prior appointment. Once they arrive, they're continually surprised by another quaint Mayo tradition: No one mentions money until the patient has been treated. Those forms are filled out when you leave, not when you arrive.

At the Mayo Clinic, medicine is still a service.

The Mayo Clinic
Rochester, MN 55905

IT'S HARD TO THINK OF A COMPANY THAT HAD A BETTER YEAR THAN MERCK experienced in 1987. For the second consecutive year, *Fortune* named it America's most admired firm, based on an annual poll of eight thousand executives, financial analysts, and corporate directors (it led seven of eight categories rated; its composite score of nine out of a possible ten was the highest in the survey's six-year history). *Business Month* declared it one of America's five best-managed companies. In *Sales & Marketing Management's* annual peer ranking of the best sales forces within each industry, Merck was the clear leader among pharmaceutical companies. *Working Mother* cited it as one of the best companies for working women.

Good reputation. Good management. Good marketing. Good employer. And customers like it too—witness the 33-percent growth in after-tax profits in 1987, that coming on the heels of a 25-percent increase in 1986. Primarily, those customers are doctors and pharmacists who have learned to trust Merck's intensively trained sales force for both good products and, perhaps more importantly, good medicine.

All that's wonderful, but where does service fit in? Consider that the customers for a pharmaceutical company are not so much the consumers who pay for prescriptions but rather the physicians and pharmacists who must have access to drugs and medicines that can help patients. It follows that giving these customers what they want will involve close attention to their needs, in a strictly product sense, and their perceptions of medical quality, in a more professional sense. Health care professionals want to know that the treatments they are recommending to their patients are effective, carefully tested, and ethically managed. Hollywood stereotypes aside, there's no personal or professional satisfaction in "pushing pills" on patients. The quest is for products that work, ideally sold by people who can explain how and why they work.

A little history: In 1975, Merck was far from a stellar performer. It was well thought of, and profitable, but hadn't been particularly innovative of late, and there wasn't anything in the laboratory that promised to change

that anytime soon. Like most major pharmaceutical companies, its research (i.e., new product development) was broad-based and often
unconnected—make something, then test it in various ways to see what it
might be good for. *Business Month* called it a "traditional shot-in-the-
dark approach to research."

When it approached Dr. P. (for Pindaros) Roy Vagelos—who ironically used to work in his parents' luncheonette about six blocks from the
Merck headquarters complex in Rahway, New Jersey—the company was
looking to change all that, looking for someone who would make an
impact, both on the company and on medicine in general. Vagelos had
worked at the National Institutes of Health in the 1950s before moving to
academia; when Merck came calling, he was a leading biochemical researcher and chairman of the biological chemistry department at Washington University in St. Louis.

Now chairman and CEO, Vagelos joined Merck as director of research, but with a good-sized bankroll and a free hand to do something
with it. What he did was change the research orientation of the company
from shot-in-the-dark to something maybe best described as shot-in-the-
dark-at-a-target-illuminated-by-a-flashlight. In other words, he put
Merck's money into finding drugs that could and would address known
diseases, which is what its customers were looking for it to do all
along.

Nothing happens fast in medicine, and this was no exception, but by
the late seventies Merck's targeted research was beginning to pay off in
promising discoveries. By the mid-eighties, those discoveries had become
tested and approved drugs addressing such conditions as hypertension
and congestive heart failure, high cholesterol levels, high blood pressure,
hepatitis, ulcers, and infections. Meanwhile, the research continues: Merck
Sharp & Dohme Research Laboratories has the pharmaceutical industry's
largest budget, $500 million in 1988 alone, and reports directly to Vagelos
so commercial considerations can't get in the way.

As those new formulations have arrived on the market in recent years,
they have found Merck's fifteen hundred highly trained sales representatives well prepared to bring them to the attention of doctors and pharmacists. This is where the exemplary service comes into the picture. In *Sales
& Marketing Management's* annual ratings, Merck's sales force earned
top marks in six of seven categories, from product/technical knowledge to
reputation among customers. In fact, of the thirteen industry segments
the magazine rated, only Du Pont's chemical sales force earned a higher
score for product knowledge.

That's not surprising. Merck's salespeople are the product of a detailed, three-level introductory training program that is comparable to
paramedical training. Because they must be able to discuss products

knowledgeably with medical professionals who often specialize in highly technical fields, they spend almost a full year learning a lot of what their customers have to know, starting with basic anatomy, physiology, and the nature of diseases. Tests are given weekly during this initial ten-week phase, and it takes scores in the nineties to stay in the program.

But that's just the beginning. From there, new sales representatives spend from six months to a year training in the field, learning how to make effective presentations on the specific benefits of the products they represent. During this second phase, they work in tandem with an experienced district manager every step of the way. Those that survive these first two phases still aren't deemed ready to represent the company. They go back to headquarters for another three weeks of training on medical knowledge, this phase concentrating specifically on the diseases and conditions that Merck's products have been created to treat.

Once in the field, continuing education is frequent and wide-ranging. District-level meetings focus on new treatments, general medical developments, even diseases that haven't yet been solved. At the individual level, sales reps are paired with physicians who act as mentors and take them along on hospital rounds to show them firsthand how the company's products are being used. Every other year, each salesperson is shipped off to a major medical school (Harvard and Johns Hopkins are frequent destinations) for a week of refresher training and an update on the latest developments in the field of medicine.

It's an uncommon degree of preparation for sales work, but the results are visible not just in the media but also at the frontlines where the customers are. Merck's representatives are on call day and night—their physician and pharmacist customers have their home phone numbers—to answer questions or provide for emergency needs.

Through all of it, Merck takes care of them. Compensation is above industry norms, turnover is practically nonexistent, and many entry-level positions open up because the person who used to do that job has been promoted. Promotions, incidentally, are based not only on sales performance but also on medical knowledge and innovation on the customer's behalf.

At Pioneer Hi-Bred International, the agricultural pacesetter in applied science, they used to claim that founder Henry Wallace wanted to increase sales just so he could do more research. Vagelos echoes that same theme. The best thing about Merck's increased sales, he told *USA Today* in 1987, is "so we can support this research expansion."

That, in turn, isn't far removed from founder George Merck's original philosophy of service: "We try to remember that medicine is for the patient. We try never to forget that medicine is for the people. It is not for the profits. The profits follow, and if we have remembered that, they have never failed to appear. The better we have remembered it, the larger they have been."

Merck & Company, Inc.
P.O. Box 2000
Rahway, NJ 07065

LENS*CRAFTERS*®

NOTHING BETTER ILLUSTRATES THE WAY A COMBINATION OF CHANGING MARKET conditions and paying attention to formerly ignored customers can transform business practices than the explosive growth of the optical and "superoptical" stores that promise to make and deliver eyeglasses in one hour. The fact that all this change and growth is happening in the health care field makes it all the more noteworthy. And no superoptical better illustrates how a service-oriented focus can energize rapid growth than Precision LensCrafters (generally known as just LensCrafters), a Cincinnati-based subsidiary of—believe it or not—the U.S. Shoe Corporation.

An outgrowth of two 1978 government decisions, the nation's commercial optical and "superoptical" stores accounted for nearly 30 percent of the $8.8 billion Americans spent on ophthalmic goods in 1987. Not everyone is happy about that, especially the independent doctors of optometry who used to control virtually all of the business, but there's no ignoring what's going on. The biggest thing that's going on is customers looking on eyewear as a fashion accessory—something that can make them look good as well as see well. And where do you buy fashion accessories? Why, in a store, of course.

Just ten years ago, that was heresy. In those days, optometrists "dispensed" glasses to "patients." Although not licensed as physicians, they were every bit as cloistered and controlling as the local medical society, which meant that as a consumer you had to depend on their testing, choose from their limited selection of frames and lens styles, and wait upward of two weeks for your glasses to be prepared at a lab somewhere and sent back to the optometrist's office for you to pick up. Since only the optometrist knew the prescription to which your lenses were ground, and since he didn't have to tell you even if you asked, you were a pretty good bet to come back for your next pair of glasses.

But in 1978, the feds threw optometry, and indeed all of medicine, a couple of curves. First came a Federal Trade Commission ruling that said optometrists had to give patients their prescriptions when they asked for them, a frighteningly radical viewpoint that meant patients could revert back to being consumers and buy glasses from someone other than their optometrists if they wanted to.

As if that wasn't bad enough, the courts weighed in a couple of months later with the idea that professionals could advertise their services. Suddenly, a lot of hitherto closed and mystifying service fields (including law and accounting as well as medicine) became subject to the pressures of a competitive marketplace. The result, in optometry anyway, was to be eye-opening.

LensCrafters makes no medical bones about the business it's in. It "sells" glasses to "customers." By pairing independent optometrists (who either make examinations in the store or next door, depending on local medical regulations) with an on-site lens-grinding lab, and surrounding both with a comfortable showroom stocked with a selection of over 3,000 frames, LensCrafters has grown to nearly 275 stores in some 40 states in just five years. In 1987, it ranked fourth in number of stores but number two in sales for the optical industry as a whole. It's tops in the superoptical category, and if growth continues apace it will lead the entire industry in sales before 1990.

The first store was opened in Florence, Kentucky, in 1983 by Dean Butler, a veteran of many a consumer marketing campaign at Procter & Gamble. (Though the address is across the Ohio River in Kentucky, Florence is actually a suburb of Cincinnati, P&G's home.) Butler, ably assisted by Dan Hogue, another P&G alumnus, figured he could apply many of the tactics he'd learned as a brand manager for such products as Ivory Liquid, Cheer detergent, and Folger's instant coffee to the marketing of prescription eyewear.

First, market research: Customers, he found, wanted dependable glasses, but they wanted a better choice of frame styles than the average small optometrist could afford to stock, and they didn't want to wait two weeks for delivery. Second, product knowledge: Once the prescription is determined, grinding lenses is a simple machine-shop job for a qualified lab, which means the lab can be located virtually anywhere (including close to the customers). Third, marketing challenge: Bring enough customers through the door to keep the on-site lab busy and cost-effective, and you can give them their glasses as fast as the lab can make them. Say an hour, more or less.

For the physical layout, Butler and Hogue found a model in the first small one-hour optical store, which opened for business in New Jersey at about the same time. Within a year they had four stores up and running, at which point U.S. Shoe arrived to bankroll expansion. (Butler and Hogue left the company in late 1987 when their management contracts expired.)

LensCrafters has found a ready market, but it also has taken pains to serve that market capably. To make sure store managers, lab supervisors, and associated optometrists concentrate on product quality, there are now three "campuses" for the company's management training school, grandly known as Precision LensCrafters University. To make sure customers feel confident in the quality of service they are buying, the lab area in each store is placed behind a glass wall and people are invited to watch their glasses being made.

With new stores opening left and right, there are ample opportunities to reward good performers: In its first five years, the company has already promoted more than a thousand "associates" (which is what the company, following a pattern established by J. C. Penney, calls its employees) into store and regional management ranks. During the go-go first couple of years, LensCrafters was opening as many as one hundred new stores a year and hiring sixty to seventy new people a week. Nowadays, forty to fifty new stores a year is "normal." Each issue of *Eyewitness 2000*, the quarterly newsletter published for LensCrafters associates, is packed full of short items on stores that achieve record sales, managers who get promotions, associates who win awards, and people at every level of the company who do "Good Deeds" for their customers and their hometowns.

Take, for example, Cheryl Simpson, a Fort Worth optician who spent a few days with her church group on a Navajo reservation in Arizona doing free vision screening. Or Tina Rexroad, a frame stylist in Cockeysville, Maryland, who used her knowledge of sign language to help a deaf customer select new glasses. Or frame stylist Holly Stewart and Cheryl Vescio, her supervisor at Northtown Plaza in Davenport, Iowa, who braved a windchill of twenty-five below zero to help a woman select and fit a new pair of glasses in her car because she'd broken both legs in an accident and, due to the extremely cold temperatures, couldn't get inside by wheelchair.

Good frontline service is not only regularly recognized, it's also rewarded with tactics ranging from cash bonuses and "President's Pins" to newsletter recognition and an occasional pie in the face. In 1986, for example, LensCrafters debuted the Horizon Club. Each year, throughout the year, supervisors nominate associates "whose horizons of customer service know no boundaries." From the pool of nominees, the company's top managers choose one hundred Club members, each of whom receives one hundred dollars and various psychic goodies. The best ten from the top one hundred are brought back to headquarters in Cincinnati for an annual awards banquet, at which they collect a check for one thousand dollars apiece from president and CEO Ban Hudson. President's Pins are simpler and more numerous. Any time a customer writes a letter to LensCrafters and mentions an employee who provided especially good service by name, that person receives a specially designed lapel pin.

And the pie in the face? Well, first a brief digression about values. LensCrafters is a new business in a new field. It has grown rapidly, which sometimes means running at breakneck pace just to keep up with all the newness and change and growth. In 1986, the company's senior managers stopped for a moment to define what they felt had made them so successful so quickly. The result was a mission statement and a list of "core values," both of which are given to each associate annually. The statement calls for, among other things, developing "enthusiastically satisfied customers all the time." The list includes everything from workstyle to strategic planning, and to make sure it is constantly in mind, it's even reprinted across the bottom of the company's official stationery.

Here's the list: Nurture individuals. Build on people's strengths. Accept mistakes. Focus on winning, not individual scoring. Push ideas. Each store a separate business. Plan for the twenty-first century. Demand highest possible quality. Constantly improve.

And then there's number ten on the list, which was actually added after the first nine had been compiled. Have fun. That explains how Gene Rogers, the general manager down in Austin, Texas, comes to have his picture in the October 1987 issue of *Eyewitness 2000*. Also in the picture is Diana Bishop, an apprentice optician who, the accompanying caption explains, won a "most sold" competition in her store in Austin's Highland Mall, in the process winning the right to throw a pie in the face of the manager of her choice. Guess what she and Gene are doing in the picture?

One column over is a visage that the caption below insists belongs to Chris Coleman, the lab director of the LensCrafters' store in Orange Park, Florida. Without the caption, it's unlikely even his mother would recognize him, what with all the "humble pie" smeared from chin to eyebrows courtesy of his laboratory crew. Chris, it seems, challenged them to attain a breakage percentage at or below 3 percent for a period of two weeks. They did. Then they drew names to see who would get to honor the manager of their choice in an appropriate way.

We can't wait until the organizational development consultants come up with a Ph.D.-level explanation for what that signifies.

LensCrafters
A division of U.S. Shoe Corporation
8650 Governors Hill Drive
Cincinnati, OH 45249

Bergen Brunswig Drug Company

Bergen Brunswig Corporation

IN THE EARLY 1970S, A RELATIVELY NEW CALIFORNIA-BASED DRUG AND MEDI-cal supply wholesaler pioneered the idea of becoming a single source of supply for drug stores and pharmacies. It also harnessed the power of computers to sales and marketing as well as to inventory control and supply; in the process, it advanced the standard of service in its industry several notches by cutting the amount of time and effort needed for those purposes by as much as 75 percent.

Today, wholesalers—all of them highly computerized—account for about 70 percent of the $25 billion pharmaceutical industry, and that market share is expected to grow to 80 percent by the early 1990s. As it does, the company competitors are still trying to match is Bergen Brunswig, the second-largest wholesale drug company in the country. The evidence: In 1987, the company led the pack in the wholesale distribution segment of *Sales & Marketing Management* magazine's annual Best Sales Force survey. The reason was clearly the uncommon level of service, personal and technological, Bergen Brunswig continues to provide to customers.

In a world of chain-store operations, Bergen Brunswig focuses on the independent drug stores that still account for about half of all pharmaceutical sales, both prescription and nonprescription. It also works with chains and with hospital pharmacies, the latter a market of growing importance as hospitals seek to implement better internal systems and maximize revenues in today's tight cost-control environment.

The independents typically are run by a pharmacist who fills prescriptions, provides other health care supplies, and often serves as a source of community health information. To supplement prescription and related health care supply sales, the stores usually offer a mix of other consumer merchandise that can range from diapers and pet-care products to photo processing and greeting cards. Unfortunately, not only is that a tough business, subject to competition from both full-service and discount merchandisers, it's also a business for which people who earn pharmacology credentials often have little training or support.

Enter Bergen Brunswig, which was formed in 1969 through the merger

165

of Bergen Drug Company (previously located in Hackensack, New Jersey) and Los Angeles-based Brunswig Drug Company. The firm is now headquartered in Orange County—the city of Orange, to be exact. Three of its top five officers, including brothers Robert and Emil Martini, Jr. (president and chairman/CEO respectively), are themselves pharmacists who know the retail end of the business firsthand. Consequently, not only does the company provide wholesale products, but it also has created a comprehensive store management service with various levels so retailers can install and use only as much as they need.

"Customers select a distributor based on good service and pricing," notes a December 1987 analysis from Brean Murray, Foster Securities. "These factors require good systems and efficient, high-volume distribution centers. Customers place virtually all orders by automatic order entry directly into [Bergen Brunswig's] computer at the distribution center. The order is picked, increasingly by automation, and delivered to the customer within 24 hours."

In addition, Bergen Brunswig's frontline cadre of qualified salespeople is backed up by merchandising experts who visit participating stores at least once a month to work with owners on sales promotions and management programs. Based on a given pharmacist's needs, Bergen Brunswig can provide everything from co-op advertising and one-stop coupon redemption to sophisticated computer management systems that control inventory and help retailers run their businesses more efficiently.

People are the key: Sales and merchandising specialists alike are called "consultants" in the Bergen Brunswig scheme of things because it's that part of their jobs that the company wants them to take most seriously. To reinforce that commitment, even top executives make a point of making sales calls—Leo Granucci, group vice president of sales, sets a personal quota of a hundred calls a year, *Sales & Marketing Management* reported— and frontline reps are polled at least once a month for customer feedback and market opportunities.

Computers remain an important part of the service package, continuing the tradition of innovation begun more than a decade ago. The level of sophistication ranges from simple order and inventory programs to OmniPhase, the industry's first front-end management system, which incorporates point-of-sale scanning technology for inventory management, cash register operations, financial reporting, and other tasks.

The OmniPhase system is designed to integrate the prescription department, where pharmacists spend most of their day, with cash-register activity in other parts of the store. The combined system uses one computer for information processing, can share peripherals and technical support, and employs the same menus and other computer functions as the cash-register system for consistency. It also automates many functions, such as the relabeling of merchandise on sale, that used to be done by sales clerks. This streamlines operations and simplifies employee training on a par with the automated checkstand systems in use in cost-conscious grocery stores.

Bergen Brunswig supports the system by helping retailers analyze and benefit from the information the computer can collect. Seasonal buying patterns can be tracked, shelf space allocated based on sales performance, price-to-profit ratios optimized, and sales promotions tracked and evaluated, in the process helping the independent merchant hold his or her own against bigger, better-bankrolled competitors.

For OmniPhase, Bergen Brunswig built a complete hardware and software system that integrates TEC registers, IBM computers, software developed by National Data Corporation to the specific needs of retail pharmacies, and its own comprehensive data base of pricing and ordering information. Pharmacy owners can lease or buy the system, and Bergen Brunswig supports them with training designed for both management and new checkstand employees. It also continuously updates and customizes software programs, often based on the experiences of its customers.

Other services are available, again arranged in flexible packages instead of a single, all-encompassing, one-size-fits-all straitjacket. Six hundred of its independent customers use the Good Neighbor Pharmacy program (whose acronym, GNP, not coincidentally connotes revenues), under which Bergen Brunswig handles everything from stocking shelves and arranging displays to monthly sales and advertising flyers. The company offers its own private-label products, supports other merchandise such as a full line of cosmetics and fragrances, and—at no charge—will process coupons and magazine returns (the latter even though it doesn't distribute magazines). A Bergen Brunswig subsidiary, Commtron, is the nation's largest distributor of prerecorded videotapes.

According to *Sales & Marketing Management*, reputation among customers is the number one characteristic of a top sales force. Bergen Brunswig led all competitors among wholesale distributors in that area, as well as three of the other six categories measured in the 1987 survey. The information is no secret to retailers: Bergen Brunswig has built its market share from 6 percent in 1977 to 16 percent nationally in 1987—but an estimated 35 percent in the regional markets where it is most active. Its combination of customer focus, personal involvement, and technological support show how a top service provider can build a profitable niche on a base of even small, independent businesses.

Bergen Brunswig Corporation
4000 Metropolitan Drive
Orange, CA 92668

Shared Medical Systems Corporation

TALK ABOUT BEING PRESENT AT THE CREATION: WHEN THE GRAND DESIGN FOR medical cost-containment known as DRG's (Diagnosis Related Groupings) began as an experiment among 26 carefully selected New Jersey hospitals in 1979, what united 11 of them was client relationships with a ten-year-old healthcare information management company over in Malvern, Pennsylvania, just outside of Philadelphia. Shared Medical Systems Corporation offered an invaluable type of service as New Jersey embarked on the first trial of prospective payments systems because its own information systems already linked clinical and financial data, the underlying tenet of the new billing scheme.

A decade later, SMS is the acknowledged pacesetter in helping hospital administrators and physicians alike keep pace with and survive constantly changing health-care regulations and practices. In a brave new medical world, where as much as 40 percent of a hospital's expenses can be attributed to information-handling in forms ranging from patient care records and billing to staffing and payroll, SMS's services can result in a healthier balance sheet.

That applies to SMS as well. Its net income for 1987 exceeded the net income of healthcare-based computer services offered by all of its direct competitors combined. It has led the industry in growth and profitability for every year of its first twenty years of existence, increasing its dividends to stockholders annually since 1976. It's a record founded on a simple (if anything involving computers can be termed simple) formula of satisfying a special group of very knowledgeable and demanding customers in a very unforgiving marketplace.

And they *are* satisfied customers. As SMS president Graham King told *Healthcare Computing & Communications* in 1987: "Each year we have research conducted to determine user satisfaction levels with SMS and our competitors. Independent research shows SMS' overall customer support is consistently rated higher than that of our competitors and our client retention rate is three times the industry average. We are understandably very proud of these results."

Like most practitioners in modern medicine, SMS is a specialist, not a generalist—in its case, a specialist in managing, analyzing, and coordinating the information flow that monitors the vital signs of the modern business of medicine. Its patients include more than eight hundred fifty hospitals and clinics coast to coast and in six countries, as well as about three hundred fifty physician group medical practices in the U.S. Its crash cart is stocked with complex and highly responsive software that manages patient, financial, and administrative records, not only within departments but—through networking—among them and from one institution to another.

Its staff of more than four thousand employees offers expertise in the design of proprietary information networks, customizes existing systems to special application needs, provides technical training and support, and will even manage the operations of a client's own data center. A network of 26 U.S. and 7 European field offices is linked to Malvern by satellite to provide close personal contact and access to the full resources of the organization. There's also the SMS equivalent of an emergency room: a service center staffed 'round the clock so clients can get immediate attention.

Helping hospitals and physicians come to terms with DRGs—which became the rule for federally financed Medicare payments in 1983 and increasingly include state-specific regulations for Medicaid as well—has been a key element in SMS's growth and success. By the end of 1987, the regulatory compliance aspect of the company's services was supporting 5 generic, 4 national, and 33 state-specific data-reporting formats.

In this, it had a head start, primarily as a result of its foresight in selection and recruiting: Recognizing what the future held for its clients and prospective clients, SMS hired a number of the staff members at Yale University who "invented" the DRG system, which originally was intended to provide a way to review hospital utilization. The insight they provided, along with the wealth of experience gained in serving nearly half of the first hospitals chosen to put the system to work, allowed the company not only to stay close to its customers, but a little ahead of them.

SMS helps clients ride the learning curve by augmenting its more than one hundred software and information management systems with regular updates on changing conditions and in-depth seminars for hospital administrators, physicians, and health-care executives. Advisory groups drawn from users at every level—not only administrators, but physicians, nurses, lab technicians, and department-level managers—review new offerings and suggest ways to improve existing systems. For SMS, staying close to the customer also involves drawing on clients to serve as test sites for new responses to changing health information needs.

SMS adds to its competitive edge by "backloading" client data bases free of charge. In the modern medical business, information is the key to coping, to say nothing of managing. With each successive regulatory change, the hospital's existing information base becomes obsolete—unless it can be integrated into the new rules of the game. Backloading the data converts it into new formats and preserves its value as a guide to past experience.

Both current and new SMS clients have come to value not only that service, but an additional benefit of being part of a larger international data base: regular "case mix" reviews in which individual data bases are compared to the larger data pool to spot problem areas and improvement opportunities that can have a high impact on the bottom line.

Yet the SMS service strategy avoids any tendency toward a "one size fits all" mentality by segmenting business activities according to customers' specific needs. Separate business units for hospital, government, international, and physicians' services conduct their own specific sales, marketing, and product development activities. Each can tailor offerings for customer-specific needs.

In the hospital, for example, SMS' Medical Records Workstation software offers a "paperless" way for medical records and billing departments to use personal computers to work together on a LAN (local area network), and eliminates costly paperwork in the process. Similarly, SMS adapted its existing inhouse and offsite systems to come up with a customized software package that is now used by large multihospital groups to integrate records from each facility operating under the parent company's banner. That allows data processing tasks to be moved from the satellite facilities—which are already stretched thin financially—to a central site, where better-trained personnel and more sophisticated systems can turn the individual pieces of site data into an integrated data base for the entire corporate family.

Though compartmentalized, however, the wheels being invented all roll the same way at SMS. Records-keeping systems for physicians have been consciously designed to be compatible with hospital information management systems, for example. That means doctor and hospital can share a common base of registration and financial information, inpatient and outpatient histories, even clinical records, via terminals miles apart.

It also means a hospital can get a readout on the treatment patterns of different doctors for the same DRG, or track the overall patient patterns of its doctors to make sure it continues to offer the facilities and services they need. And the benefits can involve more than financial savings: With everybody on-line, an emergency room doctor can instantaneously access a personal physician's records on a critically injured patient to learn about drug allergies and the details of previous treatment.

One result of investing in systems that make it easier to stay close to its customers has been an opportunity to bring offsite information management services to the market. More than eight hundred hospital and physician-group clients now beam their information via satellite to SMS mainframes, where processing is handled and records maintained.

SMS also has benefitted from the turmoil of modern health care by virtue of its ability to provide centralized, yet responsive, systems that can help reconcile previously diverse information management practices. That has become increasingly important as hospitals merge, are acquired, combine with clinics and physicians to form new, horizontally integrated provider networks, and struggle to handle information in the manner required by the federal government, state governments, and third-party insurance companies.

At SMS, customers encounter a responsive and highly motivated organizational culture where close to 90 percent of all senior management and technical positions are held by people who've grown from within as SMS has grown. Significantly, a dual career path system allows good technicians to advance without being forced out of hands-on work and client contact.

For all the high-tech gadgetry and systems wizardry, the emphasis—in internal organization, individual performance ratings, and day to day decision-making—is on client service.

Shared Medical Systems Corporation
51 Valley Stream Parkway
Malvern, PA 19355

FINANCIAL

PERSONAL

American Express

H&R Block

BANKING

Citicorp

First Union Corporation

First Wachovia Corporation

First Federal/Osceola

Amalgamated Bank of New York

BROKERAGE

Goldman Sachs & Company

Fidelity Investments

A. G. Edwards & Sons

INSURANCE

Northwestern Mutual Life Insurance Company

Chubb Group of Insurance Companies

Amica Mutual Insurance Company

USAA

```
┌─────────────────────────────────────────────────────┐
│        The Financial Services Industry:              │
│            No More Banker's Hours                     │
│   or Green Eyeshades—the Quest for Quality Is On      │
└─────────────────────────────────────────────────────┘
```

NOT TOO MANY YEARS AGO, THE PHRASE "FINANCIAL SERVICES" WAS SYNONYMOUS with doing business with a bank, perhaps a savings and loan, and just maybe a credit union. Not any more.

A survey of one thousand households conducted by Reichman Research for *American Banker* magazine finds that today over one third of respondents name as their principal financial institution a nonbank bank (the Sears Financial Network, American Express, Prudential-Bache, Beneficial Finance, Merrill Lynch, Fidelity Mutual Funds, Charles Schwab) or a nationwide banking-services company (Citicorp, Bank of America, and others). It is, in fact, getting more and more difficult for consumers to tell what is or isn't a bank. In a financial environment where credit card companies extend credit, banks issue credit cards, department stores sell securities, and brokerage houses have checking accounts, who can blame the consumer for showing a bit of perplexity.

A Little History

How did all this happen? In a word: deregulation. Over the last ten years, successive changes in the rules about who can and can't deliver financial services and where and how those services can be delivered have made the financial services world a bit of a madhouse. Banks have been buying each other up and going into hybrid financial businesses they traditionally were barred from. Many are thinking far beyond their traditional, regulated, geographically defined marketplaces.

As confusing from the consumer's view of the business has been the proliferation of products. Sometimes it has seemed as though the goal of the financial services industry is to see who could offer the greatest number of checking accounts, IRAs, savings plans, and types of loans. At one point competition for IRA dollars was so fierce that an ad for a new plan or a new rate advertised by Bank A on Monday would be cloned— right down to the type style and wording—and reappear the next day on the same page, only this time as an offering from Bank B. Lost in the shuffle were the questions of whether or not consumers wanted or needed all these new products, and how much sense all of it was making to them.

Banks, of course, weren't the only financial services organizations caught up in the helter-skelter of the marketplace. Savings and loan associations took a terrible drubbing in this new competitive environment. Consumers abandoned them wholesale and went on the make for the new products. No small number found themselves unable to compete—and unable to survive. Meanwhile, insurance companies and brokerage firms began offering products that competed with the commercial banks and S&Ls. The Merrill Lynches of the world went into the IRA and checking account business; insurance companies created a baffling array of savings, retirement, and quasi-credit products.

But the latter half of the 1980s has seen a new awareness begin to creep into the financial services business: "If the customer doesn't understand what you are selling, and doesn't believe you can service what you sell anyway, you won't sell much, regardless of the number of shining new products you create."

The differences between types of financial institutions and what they can offer has decreased. The importance of service quality has increased. As the *American Banker* poll makes clear, when customers become disillusioned and look for a new place to house their hard-earned money—something one in five do every year—they do so most often (21 percent of the time) because of poor service. Only 13 percent move their money because they changed residences, and just 12 percent move to get a better interest rate.

A related but independent study of fifteen hundred consumers by Cambridge Reports, the Massachusetts-based research firm, found 44 percent agreeing that "ease of doing business with" is the principal reason for choosing a financial institution. Second came quality of personal service (named by 28 percent) and third, (at 22 percent) was "range of financial services available." In other words, finding an institution that was easy to do business with, being treated well, and having a choice of products outranked location, interest rates, or any of the other nonservice factors used to predict the reasons people choose a bank.

The importance of service quality to financial services customers isn't lost on all providers. The *American Banker* survey found that those organizations gaining most in market share were also those institutions rated highest in service quality by their customers. Credit union customers rated themselves most satisfied with their financial services provider and, sure enough, credit unions experienced the greatest market share gains. Second in gains were nonbank financial services companies. Against this competition, commercial banks and thrifts—savings banks and savings and loan associations—lost market share.

Looking at the data, *American Banker* observed: "Seven out of 10 people use commercial banks, making them America's most popular institutions. Nonetheless, the findings raise questions about the success of bank efforts to get consumers to consolidate all their financial services in one place." This despite the fact that one third of us would like to be able to do all of our financial business—checking, savings, financing, investing, and the rest—with only one institution, according to another *American Banker* study.

The Nonbank Financials

Though nonbank competitors were once sniffed at by banks as hardly worth worrying over, today 48 percent of consumers surveyed in the *American Banker* study use one or more of the banklike financial services offered by nontraditional sources (Sears, American Express, Prudential Insurance, Merrill Lynch, Fidelity Mutual Funds, etc.). They are a force to be reckoned with. Consider just the case of the two best-known of the nonbank financial service providers—Sears and American Express.

Through the Sears Financial Network (Allstate insurance, Coldwell Banker real estate, Dean Witter Reynolds brokerage, plus the Discover credit card), Sears has become a highly visible purveyor of financial products and services. At the same time, American Express has added to its traditional Travel Related Services Company the activities of wholly owned subsidiaries such as Shearson Lehman Brothers and IDS Financial Services. Nine people out of ten, research shows, know Sears as a financial service provider and not just as the home of Kenmore appliances and Craftsman tools. Likewise, 88 percent of consumers know that AmEx does more than issue traveler's checks and charge cards.

Name identification and the fact that one in three Americans visits one of the 833 Sears stores every year (400 have financial service centers) apparently is paying off: 30 percent of all consumers report buying financial products from Sears. American Express has had similar good fortune—11 percent of its customers buy something other than "the card" or traveler's checks from AmEx.

How good is the nonbank financial services industry as a provider of quality service? If one of the services we should judge them by is financial planning skill, the answer is "not so hot." A 1985 test of seven nonbank financial service providers who also advertise financial planning as a service—IDS/American Express, Aetna Life & Casualty, Sears, Shearson Lehman Brothers, Prudential-Bache Securities, Merrill Lynch, and The Consumer Financial Institute—found that "caveat emptor" would be the best advice when dealing with them for that service.

In fall of 1985, *Consumer Reports* sent a couple—a reporter and her husband—out to "shop" these seven companies' financial planning services. The couple met with ten different planners. From the advice they received, *Consumer Reports* concluded: "The plans were, for the most part, disappointing. Almost all the plans contained a serious flaw. They usually suggested that the couple increase its spending on their financial products and services. But with the exception of Aetna's and IDS's, none of the plans analyzed the couple's budget to see where the money for grander investments or better insurance coverage might come from."

A year earlier, the Travelers Insurance Company asked Yankelovich, Skelly and White to find out what consumers expected of financial service providers. The researchers found that the predominant consumer concern was with fairness, defined by four factors:

- *Reliable, professional help* in a technical field where customers feel they cannot or do not want to understand the complexities and want to deal with someone competent and trustworthy.
- *Equal treatment tempered by pragmatism*, stemming from the belief that everyone, big or small, should be treated the same. (There was, however, a recognition of special cases and the need for exceptions.)
- *Responsiveness to individual needs*, including prompt help and continued assistance, especially when problems arise.
- *Giving good service at a reasonable price*, preferably with low prices, but not at the expense of quality in the product or the service support.

If the *Consumer Reports* study is any measure, these four factors can use some attention.

Mutual Funds and Brokerage Firms

Despite the October 19, 1987, market crash, mutual funds are still an important financial service provided by companies vying for the consumer's hard-earned savings dollars. Understandably, the number one criterion for selecting a mutual fund is its track record: the return on investment over the history of the fund. But in the postcrash market, service has become almost as critical a concern. As those who learned the hard way in October 1987 will ruefully tell you, "They can promise you all the growth in the world, but when you can't get through on their [expletives deleted] phone system to sell—well, it's been a nice ride."

What do consumers want from a fund company? According to a study by the Investment Company Institute of Washington, D.C., mutual fund shareholders want to invest in a fund that is part of a "family of funds" (59.4 percent), want to be able to move their money between the funds by telephone (50 percent), and value a toll-free telephone number through which to exercise the option (49.2 percent). Less important, says the study, are having fund reps available to answer questions (37.9 percent), personal check-writing privileges (37 percent), and a consolidated statement (22.9 percent).

According to a survey of eleven thousand mutual fund investors by *Financial World* magazine, only five of the twenty-five major funds knock the ball out of the service park. Those worthy of note, according to its data: Strong Funds, the Vanguard Fund, T. Rowe Price, Fidelity, and Twentieth Century Fund. As an aside, it's worth noting that two of the five service leaders on this poll also had funds with the top returns on investment over the past ten years; Fidelity's Magellan Fund and the Twentieth Century Growth and Twentieth Century Select funds.

Insurance

Few industries suffer cycles of profit and loss like the casualty insurance industry. Temple, Barker & Sloane (TBS), a general management consulting firm based in Lexington, Massachusetts, believed that in such a cyclical industry, attention to good service falters. To test that theory, TBS conducted a survey of two hundred branch offices of national and regional commercial property/casualty insurance brokers to assess the level of service quality they most often experience from the companies whose products they sell.

"At a time when service quality is gaining recognition as a powerful competitive tool," said TBS vice president William A. Sherdan, "our findings suggest that relatively few insurance carriers have actually achieved a reputation for providing it."

The reasons for the inconsistency of service vary, but TBS fastened on two of special note. First, quality as a subject is omitted from most forms of management education and industry training programs. Second, the insurance industry tends to view quality solely in terms of content. But, says Sherdan, "because insurance products generally are simple and the consumer expects perfection in content, *delivery* has become the aspect of quality that truly distinguishes excellent service providers."

The TBS studies showed that clearly by contrasting the difference in approaches to service between carriers given high ratings and the rest:

- Top firms view their service personnel as "a key resource, a competitive advantage and a talent pool to meet future needs throughout the firm." They recruit the best people, train them better, and make them more customer-oriented.
- Top firms also keep turnover to a minimum, averaging 5 percent in areas where industrywide norms exceed 20 percent. The experience and stability of their service work force adds to their edge in the eyes of the brokers who sell their policies.

Unfortunately, Sherdan notes, senior management in the industry has for too long been prone to "reflexively" pursue several predictable courses of action when confronted with a need to improve service—proclaiming that service quality is a major priority for the corporation, adopting a popular quick-fix program, or seeking to place the blame on frontline service workers are time-honored favorites. None of them really addresses the service problem. Organizational changes, not proclamations, are needed. That view is slowly gaining credence in the industry, he adds.

Banks

In the midst of all the change and tumult in the financial services industry, banks have rediscovered the basis of their business—serving customers. Market researchers, sometimes to their dismay, are learning that retail customers are more sensitive to long lines, wrong statements, and snotty loan officers than they are to the array of fine and fancy products a bank offers. In fact, they have discovered that the average civilian in the financial services product wars was put off and confused, not served, by sixteen varieties of checking accounts. As financial writer Sylvia Porter noted in a recent column, "If you ever shopped for the best deal, you know that even Sherlock Holmes would have had trouble."

So the clarion call has gone out in thousands of memos from hundreds of bank CEOs: "Remember, people, above all else our goal is service, service, service!" And though the product scramble continues, and banks continue to buy and sell each other and consolidate operations with little thought to the way their customers view such transactions, a solid conviction has sprung up around service quality. The new belief holds that to be truly competitive in the new, wide-open, deregulated financial services business requires quality products *and* quality service.

The *American Banker* study mentioned earlier tells much of the story about the importance of service quality. But many specifics go into the design and delivery of services that meet the customer's needs. A related study by Travelers Insurance, for example, found that "the key factor influencing customers is trust in the institution"; it goes on to point out that special products are the least influential factor.

Leonard Berry of Texas A&M University maintains that the sort of trust relationship cited by the Travelers' research revolves around good communication. Berry finds six communication glitches common to banks—but obviously germane to all financial service providers:

Overpromising: Promising the customer more than you do or can deliver.

Failing to stay in touch when a problem exists: When problems occur and recovery is critical, customers need but do not always receive more frequent contact with the organization.

Using industry jargon: Bankers may know what an "average daily balance" is, but civilians don't.

Failing to listen to customers: The most frequent customer complaint about a financial institution is that instructions to the organization were not followed.

Telling but not explaining: Common missteps include not teaching customers how to decipher their statements, not explaining the rationale for decisions, and not educating them to the basics of products offered.

Communicating without courtesy: Common courtesy simply isn't common. (We're not picking on banking alone: A study by a shopping service found that 85 percent of retail store salespeople don't bother to say "thank you" to a customer for a purchase.)

Those Who Serve Well

Though considerable room for improvement remains, there has been significant progress in improving service quality in the financial services
industry. We were impressed by the tactics being used by organizations like National Westminster Bank in New York and Meridian Bancorp in Pennsylvania. And we're happy to report that they, like Maryland National Bank and other progressive financial organizations, are finding that service quality, like product quality, doesn't cost—it pays.

But it takes time. As NatWest senior vice president Howard Deutsch puts it in a Bank Administration Institute publication, "Quality improvement is evolutionary, not revolutionary." But as A. Jay Myerson, senior VP of the retail credit division of Cleveland-based Ameritrust told a gathering of his fellow bankers in Atlanta in 1987, "Service companies— including banks—spend 35 percent of their operating costs doing things wrong and then doing them over. We can no longer afford that."

Our exemplars reflect the range of organizations providing financial services these days. On a personal service level, American Express's Travel Related Services Company—the organization behind "the card"— proves that membership does indeed have its privileges. H&R Block, on the other hand, shows how a broad-based service market can be staked out and developed in a relatively short amount of time.

In banking, we easily could have named a dozen or more noteworthy institutions. We've opted to profile five, starting with Citicorp, the national monolith that capably serves more than twenty-five million people worldwide. From the Southeast, where interstate competition is all the rage, come two rival regional banks and a noteworthy thrift. First Union Corporation's story is a classic example of finding out what your customers want you to be, and then becoming just that. First Wachovia Corporation is the last word in relationship banking, having pioneered that approach some fifteen years ago. And First Federal/Osceola, a Florida savings and loan, has developed a fast-paced, sales-oriented culture where growth, not takeovers, is everyone's concern. Finally, we offer union-owned Amalgamated Bank of New York, which inspires fierce loyalty among customers in a city containing more than enough financial options.

Brokerage was a tough call. We can't help thinking that a lot of what goes on in today's financial markets is of dubious value to customers or the economy in general. There are exemplars, nonetheless. Goldman Sachs is a professional partnership where sensitivity to internal customer service has kept people loyal in an era and industry that seem to have lost that quality. Fidelity Investments keeps itself accessible to its nearly three million customers while emphasizing the importance of selecting and training personnel to better serve the clients' needs. And A. G. Edwards & Sons has become the largest brokerage firm not based on or near Wall Street by placing its firmwide emphasis on customer success.

Among insurance companies, we found two outstanding big ones: Northwestern Mutual Life and the Chubb Group of Insurance Companies. We also found two terrific examples of building successful businesses by concentrating on serving specific niches in special ways: Amica Mutual Life Insurance and USAA.

We're not endorsing products here, let's repeat. It's the service provided to cardholders, account-holders, portfolio-holders, and policyholders in a changing and very competitive marketplace that we find noteworthy. For our money, these are winners.

LYNDON DEANE AND CARRIE LEE LEWIS ARE "GREAT PERFORMERS." THEY WORK hundreds of miles apart—Deane in Toronto, Lewis in Saskatoon—but when the son of a customer was injured thousands of miles away while traveling in Brazil with his family, their combined efforts got timely funds to the family and arranged for a flight to bring the boy home for surgery.

It wasn't quite that simple, of course. In addition to the language and currency translations involved, there was also the matter of the paramedic Air Canada decided must accompany the injured boy—a paramedic who needed a visa issued within twenty-four hours, and on a Saturday no less. Nothing daunted, Deane and Lewis stayed on the case and took care of the family and its impromptu traveling companion all the way home, even to providing airport transportation for the paramedic.

Their uncommon concept of "customer service" is unique only in the context of general business practice. Within the specific culture of their employer, it is shared worldwide, and consequently counted on by millions.

Each year since 1982, in the Travel Related Services (TRS) Company that is still 33 percent of American Express, they have celebrated the Great Performers: those employees at every level of the company, but especially on the frontlines, who have led by example in serving their customers. The 1980s have brought acquisitions (Shearson Loeb Rhoades, E. F. Hutton, Investors Diversified Services, Lehman Brothers Kuhn Loeb) and divestitures (most of Fireman's Fund, all of Warner Amex) to American Express, but TRS still produces the dollars—an average growth rate of 18 percent per year over the past ten years—and the service stars for this diversified financial services firm.

For the company behind the card, as for the people who provide service to the members who have one, there are awards and rewards: American Express, *Fortune* reported in December of 1987, earns "the fattest gross profit margins in the credit card business." With more than 27 million cards in circulation (Green, Gold, Corporate, Platinum, and Optima), and some $20 billion in traveler's check sales, TRS produced more net income ($655 million) in 1987 than was reported by the corporation as a whole ($533 million from all operations).

The reason is devastatingly simple. As credit services analyst Spencer Nilson, publisher of *The Nilson Report*, told *Fortune*, "There's no getting around the fact that American Express' service is far and away the best in the industry." Yet with the exception of the Optima Card, which offers revolving credit through a cooperating bank, the family of American Express cards are not "credit" cards in the conventional sense; because of the financial regulations that govern its activities, the company cannot issue credit. Cardholders ("Cardmembers" in American Express parlance) may charge purchases, but each month the entire balance comes due. For that service, members pay from $45 (Personal) to $250 (Platinum) per year, depending on the kind of card they hold.

Why would they do that? Service is the edge: As they do everywhere else in the service economy, customers continue to demonstrate that they will pay a little more for the kind of service that meets their needs and expectations. Among upscale charge-card holders, 60 percent have and use an American Express Card, according to Nilson's figures.

Yet if few people would argue with the premise that American Express's service reputation is well earned, it's worth considering for a moment how it is earned. In the normal run of events, there are very few opportunities to provide service to cardholders: When they apply for a card, when they use it (usually at one of more than two million participating merchants, not for a purchase of American Express services), when they receive a bill, and when there's a problem and they need assistance. That's all, and seldom if ever does a card-carrying member deal face to face with an American Express employee. How, then, can the company win such consistently high marks for service?

It does so precisely because it has learned to manage what few customer contacts it has amazingly well. Most of the Great Performers stories come out of the regional telephone answering centers, where operators are called on to assist customers all over the world. From one minute to the next they may deal with a tourist from Holland who has been robbed of her traveler's checks and credit cards, then turn around and be confronted by a medical emergency in Hawaii.

Those operators earn more than many service workers, but certainly not the kind of wages to put the kids straight through college. Their edge is in the training they receive before and while they are on the job and the extraordinary level of management support they receive as they work on their customer's behalf.

Training begins only after careful selection. Before they put on a headset on their own, telephone service representatives spend five weeks in the classroom, two weeks in on-the-job training, and another three weeks in a training unit. In the process, they learn everything from the company's basic operating policies to the best ways to deal with angry, lost, disoriented, and distressed people who often find themselves in need of immediate assistance while far from home. Through a step-by-step process that includes lecture, practice, listening, and plenty of exercises drawn from past experiences, they systematically develop not only their ability to solve problems but their confidence that solving problems is exactly what their employer wants them to do.

If telephone contact handles the high and low points, written communications define the normal customer-contact style. While the ostensible reason for most of the mail the customer receives from the company is billing and the direct sale of merchandise, American Express maximizes the service opportunity provided in a number of ways.

To begin with, it knows—because it has studied and continues to study its customers—that a large proportion of its Cardmembers rely on their American Express statement for business expense accounts and tax preparation. To assist members in using their account statements for just those purposes, monthly card statements plus quarterly and annual summaries have been designed to provide helpful supporting detail for expense tracking and management. No one asks for that service on applying for the card, but once they have it, they can't do without it.

Other services enhance the value and usefulness of the card. For small businesses, the American Express Corporate Card comes packaged with a quarterly management report that itemizes charges and organizes tax-deductible expenses. It also incorporates travel reservations, ticket delivery, and itinerary information as part of a full-service Travel Management System. Cardmembers of every description have access to some fifteen hundred Travel Service Offices around the world, plus the comfort of twenty-four-hour telephone-accessible service anywhere in the world, whether they need emergency medical assistance or a clarification on a bill.

Interestingly, there's one communication Cardmembers do not receive: Sales offerings and other materials from anyone other than American Express. That's because the company does not, and says it will not, sell or rent its Cardmember list, regardless of the revenue that might be produced from delivering up such a proven audience to other marketers.

American Express also talks to its customers, and listens carefully to their replies. That includes directly interviewing 135 corporate clients of Travel Management Services to gain insight into their customer experiences; studying how top-quality achievers make judgments (those findings were plugged into new training and customer service systems); and following up on 20,000 individual transactions each year as part of a constantly evolving index of customer experiences and satisfaction.

Standards are high, and thorough, and everybody measures performance. The company's "service tracking report" is compiled and circulated weekly, and notes how well norms are being met in more than one hundred separate categories in the U.S. and abroad. New applications, which once were processed in thirty-two days, are now supposed to be processed in fifteen days; in the U.S. in 1986, 100 percent were. Lost and stolen cards are to be replaced the next day; again, 100 percent were in 1986. Similar scores are compiled throughout the operation, from answering the phone in three rings or less and authorizing Cardmember purchases in less than five seconds to replacing stolen Travelers' Cheques within four hours. Bills are supposed to be 100-percent accurate; almost invariably, they are.

And if the Great Performers are the elite, they are not alone in being recognized and rewarded. American Express's various operations use a combination of nearly one hundred reward and recognition programs.

At American Express, it's axiomatic that quality standards must define the product at the level of the *highest* common denominator of customer expectations, not the lowest. "A seamless web of quality emphasis throughout an organization is the only guarantee of uniform service quality at any one point," is how one internal statement of commitment to customer service puts it. Chairman and CEO James D. Robinson III is on record with a simpler imperative, summing up the company's objectives in four words: quality, quality, quality, and quality.

That would seem to cover it.

American Express Travel Related Services Company
American Express Tower
New York, NY 10285

H&R BLOCK®

WHEN THEY ADDED UP THE NUMBERS FOR TAX SEASON 1988, ABOUT A HUNDRED million returns had found their way to the Internal Revenue Service's processing centers around the country. More than 10 percent of them came by way of one of the nearly 7,500 offices of H&R Block, an annual phenomenon that continues to prove how sometimes the most successful services are the simplest. Though it has other, nonseasonal businesses, H&R Block derives more than half of its $800 million in annual revenue from tax preparation work. That's all the more noteworthy when you consider that the average charge for U.S. customers leading up to April 15, 1988, was within a few pennies of $50.

Ironically, in the beginning they did taxes for free. Back in Kansas City, Missouri, in the late 1940s, the primary business of Henry and Richard Bloch was accounting services for small companies that couldn't afford their own accounting staff. The brothers tossed in tax preparation as an extra service. Pretty soon people started coming to them specifically for taxes, and the Blochs obliged, for a five-dollar fee. (The family name, by the way, ends with an *h*, not a *k*: The corporate logo changed the spelling because people kept pronouncing it "blotch.")

The trouble with the tax business, the Bloch brothers soon discovered, was that it meant lots of long, late hours in the spring. So in 1955 they decided to get out of the business entirely, telling their individual tax-return clients they would have to find someone new to do the job. One of those clients was John White, an ad salesman for the *Kansas City Star*. Not only did he not want to find someone else to do what the Blochs had been doing for him, he figured the Blochs could make a full-fledged business out of it—a business they could launch with the help of a couple of ads they could buy from him. For two hundred dollars, which to the Bloch brothers meant drumming up forty new tax returns to break even, the die was cast.

As advertising goes, their two hundred dollars was well spent. The Blochs grossed twenty-five thousand dollars on tax work that year, a seasonal success so startling that they sold their accounting business to concentrate on this new service venture. One key to their initial success was the way they stood behind the quality of their work: If they made a mistake, they guaranteed that they would pay any penalty or interest that resulted. Still, there was nothing in this modest beginning to suggest the first steps of a true service juggernaut. Something else was needed. As it turned out, fortuitously for the brothers Bloch, Uncle Sam provided—by not providing.

In 1955, opportunity's knock sounded suspiciously like a service cut-back from Washington. That was the year the IRS began phasing out its free tax-preparation activities. The following year, encouraged by the initial success in Kansas City to think about growing on a truly ambitious scale, Henry Bloch hung out their tax preparation shingle in New York City by renting small offices as close as possible to the seven IRS locations in town. He reasoned that people walking by on the way to and from not being satisfied by the government might stop in for help, or might decide to pay the five dollars up front rather than standing in line in the IRS office down the street. The Blochs also figured, astutely, that the Big Apple offered better business prospects than St. Louis or Des Moines, the other cities they had been considering.

They were right on both counts. Their homespun tax service quickly found a receptive clientele. But Henry Bloch didn't want to stay in New York, so he put the final piece of the new business puzzle into place by selling a franchise to use the H&R Block name, plus the offices he had opened, to two local CPAs. He even threw in New Jersey and Connecticut to keep the new big-city franchisees happy. Then he headed back home to Missouri to grow the business from its true roots.

Over three decades, it has grown in size, scope, and sophistication. Yet it still bases its fees on the number of forms required for a return, not a percentage that varies with a customer's total income or a commission based on the size of the refund. Small wonder more than 75 percent of all H&R Block customers in 1988 were H&R Block customers in 1987, too.

More impressive than the thousands of offices opened or millions of forms filed is the fact that about three quarters of the forty thousand men and women who work for H&R Block offices each tax season also are repeaters from the previous year. Putting a brand name on tax preparation, Henry Bloch decided (brother Richard has long-since retired, but remains honorary chairman of the board), meant finding ways to train, manage, and assure quality control across the fifty-fifty mix of company-owned and franchised offices the world over. Toward that end, H&R Block uses the familiar combination of good selection criteria, plenty of training, and locally focused management and incentives.

Screening starts in the fall, when H&R Block tax schools spring up around the country. The basic tax course involves seventy-five hours of classroom instruction, which the company figures is the equivalent of two semesters at many colleges. More advanced courses add another forty-five to sixty hours of training in a wide range of tax situations. With tax "reform" bringing continuing changes to forms and schedules of every size and description, tax school isn't just for the new recruits. From preparers to office managers, the average H&R Block worker spent sixty hours in classes getting ready for the new complications Congress added for the 1988 tax season.

Over the years, many people have signed up for the basic classes, which cost up to three hundred dollars, simply to find out how to do their own taxes (half of all Americans still file their own forms), and that's perfectly acceptable. The company's managers run the tax schools both to provide training and to identify promising recruits for their offices. In 1987, for example, more than one hundred thousand people took the classes, but only about thirty thousand of those who tested for jobs at the end were hired. Meanwhile, H&R Block figures the more people learn about doing their own taxes, the less they're really going to want to do them—and where better to take them than to an H&R Block office?

Those who are hired as tax preparers receive a salary paid against a percentage of the fees they generate. Each year, the percentage goes up—a simple device that rewards both productivity and loyalty. They also get an option to buy one share of stock for every hundred dollars of earnings they produce, provided they also work for H&R Block the following tax season. That too builds longevity.

Retaining a large core of people from year to year means each office has its own bank of experience on which to draw. In addition, each has access to regional experts, and the corporation sends constant updates and model forms to its managers to respond to questions and problems as they arise. All this to support a "job" that only lasts from about the first week of January to the middle of April.

The screening process never really ends. Office managers don't become office managers until they have spent three or four seasons working on taxes—which means working directly and extensively with customers. Then they go through company supervisory training and are apprenticed out as assistant supervisors. Once established in their own offices, they are given additional training and supported with a relatively understated policies-and-procedures manual to make sure they assume the actual responsibility for the quality of their operation. Office managers rent their own offices, buy their own furniture, hire their own support staffs. Compensation is tied closely to the number of returns prepared and the profitability of the office. Despite the obvious temptation to take the client list and the experience and go into business for themselves, most choose to stay and grow with the company. They make more money that way, according to H&R Block.

It's not all sweetness and light. Managers who can't or don't measure up are systematically replaced. Franchisees who don't match the standards set in Kansas City are dropped or bought out, despite the cost. The very first franchisees, in fact, were eased out that way. They kept doing things like raising their rates the closer they got to April 15, or charging customers to accompany them to an audit (which the Blochs did for free as part of the service), so in 1966 H&R Block spent more than $1 million to buy back the business Henry Bloch had originally licensed for just $10,000 plus royalties.

No business is infallible, and H&R Block admits to its share of missteps and false starts. At one point, Henry Bloch decided that people should have their taxes done by a different preparer each year, reasoning that a new set of eyes might see new ways to do things and find new dollars for the customer's refund check. The only problem with the idea was that customers hated it. They *wanted* their taxes done by the same person each year. H&R Block did what good service providers do. It listened to its customers and changed its ways to keep them satisfied.

If it's not exactly true that H&R Block is the "customer-friendly" side of the IRS, it is clear that over the years the government agency has become accustomed to the private business's presence. When electronic filing of tax returns debuted in the 1980s, H&R Block offices quickly offered the service. In 1988, the company figures well over 80 percent of the half-million returns filed electronically were filed through H&R Block outlets.

H&R Block also pays attention to the IRS. Responding to the Tax Reform Act of 1986, for example, the company developed its own form, which it dubbed The Tax Forecaster, to help clients relate their 1986 tax form information to the most likely impact of changes the following year. It also confronted the confusion over new W-4 Forms head-on by offering to help people fill them out for free during January of 1987.

But more important than the new systems and the training and the meticulous checking is, in the words of Henry Bloch, a philosophy of listening for the thank-yous. "Our managers go around and listen at the end of an interview," he told *Inc.* magazine in 1987. "Because if the client doesn't say 'Thank-you,' or 'I appreciate what you've done,' we haven't done a good job for him—or for ourselves."

H&R Block
4410 Main Street
Kansas City, MO 64111

CITICORP✦

THE INDIVIDUAL BANK, ONE OF THREE OPERATING AREAS, OR CORE BUSINESSES, of Citicorp, the firm sometimes called "the thirty-foot python among U.S. banking companies," has an interesting problem. It provides consumer services to more than twenty-five million people the world over, including conventional checking, savings, and investment accounts; bankcards of the Diners Club, Visa, and Mastercard genre; and loans for everything from new homes to college educations. In many of those areas—number of bankcards issued, value of mortgages issued, number of student loans provided—it's the largest player in the U.S.

One in five American families does business with it. Some sixty-five thousand people worldwide work in Citicorp's consumer banking areas. Over the five-year period from 1982 through 1986, according to *Fortune*, consumer revenues grew at a rate of 30 percent a year—three times the rate of growth on the wholesale banking side. By contrast, the other two core businesses, Institutional Banking and Investment Banking, taken together have a combined staff of twenty-five thousand. In 1987, the Individual side of the business had net income of $548 million (an increase of just over 50 percent from the previous year), while the corporation as a whole was posting a $1.1 billion loss.

The problem? Complacency. Or, more specifically, guarding against it. "Banks are what the service economy is all about," Richard Braddock told an industry audience at the Bank Administration Institute in Chicago in 1987. As a "sector executive" in Citicorp's management structure, Braddock is responsible for consumer banking operations, so he knows the stakes only too well: "If we can't provide good service, someone else will. In survey after survey, from *The Wall Street Journal* to the *American Banker*, consumers cite service quality at or near the top of their criteria for selecting a bank and maintaining a banking relationship. The implications of *not* providing it are sobering."

A little more than a decade ago, Citicorp, by its own admission, was not providing that level of service. When it decided to consolidate its existing consumer businesses in 1975 and launched what subsequently became a multi-million-dollar overhaul of the way it does business at the consumer level, skeptics were plentiful. The original premise held that a well-served consumer could be a good business proposition. Through the early eighties, there was scant evidence of that; not until 1982, in fact, did the consumer side make money. But since that time, the bank has been on a roll. In the process, it has transformed its parent company: In 1987, the Individual Bank accounted for 60 percent of Citicorp's corporate business, more than double its percentage of ten years ago.

The process of that transformation illustrates how deceptively simple good service can be to describe—and how complex it can be to implement. When Citicorp reoriented its consumer services, it looked long and hard at acknowledged service leaders like Disney, McDonald's, and Federal Express. It also decided to find out from its own customers exactly where they thought things should be going.

By observing those companies that had built reputations, and profits, in their markets based on service, it learned the importance of "service statesmanship" (in essence, the powerful commitment of top management to service quality—"When the fish stinks, it stinks from the head," is a Citicorp axiom). It also picked up on the way those companies established service systems and service professionalism at and in support of the frontlines (the performance of both are measureable). By listening to its customers and the customers of other banking organizations, it turned up a revealing insight: Many of its traditional measures of *good performance* were at odds with what consumers considered *good service*.

Customers, it realized, want and expect banking services to be delivered in a problem-free, competent, and timely manner. "For each service element," according to Braddock, "we've found there's a limit, a wall. The line between reasonable waiting time and the threshold of customer anger can be determined. Goals can be set to meet customer expectations. All it takes is commitment, time, and money."

That's what Citicorp has been doing for the past ten years, and it has taken a lot of commitment, plenty of time, and dollars by the millions—and no one has pronounced the job finished. In that time, however, the commitment and the dollars have yielded visible results.

Citicorp, for example, was the first to introduce automated teller machines (ATMs) on a large scale, and it continues to pioneer new variations on the technology. From the beginning, the intent has been to develop ATM services and hardware that would not intimidate or befuddle the customers they are supposed to benefit. At Citicard Banking Centers in some areas, customers can find multilingual terminals—English, Spanish, and Chinese, with German and French to be on-line before 1990. Touch-screens with typewriterlike keyboard images allow customers to "talk" to the machines, customizing transactions to their own needs—even filing a change of address notice.

The results are encouraging. Nationally, less than half of all banking customers use ATMs for more than 50 percent of their banking transactions; in the New York City area, where one thousand Citicard Banking Centers are in operation, 80 percent of Citicorp's retail banking customers do more than half their banking electronically. On the drawing boards are Citistations, drive-through banks with three to ten lanes, one served by a live teller, the others with ATMs that can be raised or lowered to the level of the customer's car window. If they prove popular, they may become the latter-day equivalent to the corner gas station.

Other systems have been improved. In the bankcard area, for example, customer inquiries over billing discrepancies or questions about policies and procedures once involved several separate contacts, and often ran afoul of limited hours of operation. Now, more than 95 percent of the sixty thousand customer inquiries and problems handled each day are resolved during the customer's first phone call to Citicorp's twenty-four-hour, toll-free service centers.

Predictably, one key to that marked improvement has been increased training and a greater level of responsibility at the frontline. Service representatives are now routinely empowered to do what needs to be done for their customers. At the same time, greater attention has been given to selecting people who are likely to perform successfully in customer service situations, and emphasis also has been placed on retaining top performers to keep them (and their in-depth frontline experience) in the system.

In 1983, Citicorp presented its first Service Excellence Awards to employees who provide meritorious service to their customers. More than seven thousand Individual Bank staffers have won the award over the years—many of them more than once. You can tell the ones who have from the ones who haven't: The normal Citicorp name tag is silver, the name tag of a Service Excellence award winner is gold. The names also are displayed in the lobby of Citicorp's corporate headquarters in Manhattan.

Citicorp continues to talk to, and listen to, its customers, and it makes a point of doing that at the local or branch level so unique situations don't become lost in the greater body of data being accumulated. Based on the continuing research and goal-setting, specific, measureable objectives can then be set at each level.

Managers have service as well as financial goals to achieve. Some targets are measured by the percentage of customers surveyed who report they are highly satisfied with the services that have been provided to them. Others reflect internal standards, generally summed up by the acronym ART: accuracy, responsiveness, and timeliness. In either case, the measurement is from the customer's point of view. When it comes time for their performance to be reviewed, and merit raises determined, customer service ratings are factored in along with financial results and people management.

At Citicorp, measurement is constant and wide-ranging. In the bankcard area, eighty-one separate "quality indicators" are tracked. At the local or branch level, performance against the unit's internal service goals is measured daily. Every month, daily reports in the form of "Service Scorecards" go into the regular reviews of business operations that are sent up the corporate chain of communications. They include the annual goals and the most recent external measures of customer satisfaction as well. Everyone in the branch knows the service satisfaction score and the goals for his or her unit.

Managers are expected to review service performance as often and as seriously as they review financial results. Their own example is also considered vital, and Citicorp makes sure success stories are shared through the various operating entities under the corporate umbrella. That's how Robert Horner's name came up. In 1987, when the St. Louis Cardinals fought their way through the National League baseball playoffs to the World Series, Horner, the head of St. Louis-based Citicorp Mortgage Inc., made sure the people who were most important to the success of his business unit got tickets to the games. He gave the tickets not to business buddies, of course, but to the people in his organization who had won Service Excellence awards.

Citicorp/Citibank
339 Park Avenue
New York, NY 10043

AMONG THE THREE PACESETTING REGIONAL BANKS IN THE SOUTHEAST, FIRST Union often is characterized as "the other bank" in comparisons with First Wachovia and North Carolina National Bank (NCNB). The situation got so obvious that a few years back the North Carolina First Union affiliate started conducting focus groups and research studies to find out what people thought about it—and what they wanted to think about it.

The research, done back in the comparatively peaceful days before interstate banking swept through the region, confirmed First Union's suspicions that its banks had no clearly defined image among consumers or businesses. That can be deadly in today's complex financial services environment, especially with topflight competitors like Wachovia and NCNB working the same turf. The research also clearly documented that what banking customers wanted first and foremost was service, and—happily for First Union's customers—it has provided the data base and marching orders for the company's aggressive, service-focused growth in the region ever since.

Headquartered in Charlotte, North Carolina, First Union is a holding company that now has more than seven hundred banking and five hundred nonbanking offices in thirty-seven states and two foreign countries. According to *Fortune's* 1988 "Service 500," it is the twentieth largest banking company in the country. Its primary banking operations are in North Carolina, South Carolina, Georgia, Tennessee, and Florida, where interstate competition is being tried in a big way.

What First Union boiled out of its research in 1983-84 was a four-part formula for good service *as its customers defined good service*. The formula's elements: speed, convenience, personal service, and simplicity. The formula's complication: According to the research, all four elements had to be in place for it to work. Consequently, First Union has addressed service quality across a broad but well-defined spectrum—and, in the process, achieved noteworthy results in the eyes of both its customers and its employees.

Some of the tactics that have evolved are as simple as renaming products and services with easily understandable, generic titles. You don't sign up for a Modern Lifestyle Financial Funds Management and Processing Program at a First Union bank, you open a No Minimum Checking Account (which, as you might deduce, has no minimum balance). Another example of a simple but effective service enhancement has been bringing on literally hundreds of part-time tellers to cut waiting times during peak periods, such as the lunch hour or on Fridays, when many customers bring in their paychecks for deposit.

Significantly, First Union also embraces the idea that there are internal as well as external customers. Internal systems have been improved to cut down on such irritants as rejected checks (a problem that typically shows up as a customer complaint at the branch teller's window or customer service phone, but actually occurs at a central processing center). The central service center also has reduced the time it takes to respond to inquiries from field offices by 40 percent since 1985.

Other adjustments are more complex. Under a program called ACES (Automate, Centralize, Eliminate, and Simplify), First Union's internal productivity department has attacked the paperwork and procedural snarls that can slow transactions, in the process coming up with more than 130 "enhancements" that have streamlined systems and measurably shortened both internal and customer transaction times (by a factor of several minutes in some cases).

First Union's continuing emphasis on customer research also continues to pay dividends. Every month, for example, every customer who opens a new account is surveyed to get feedback on first impressions and an analysis of the bank's performance compared to the competitor bank the customer used to patronize. Focus groups continue to meet, their members drawn from First Union customers and the customers of its competitors.

Interstate banking has meant plenty of mergers and changes for business customers, and First Union's dizzying growth by merger and acquisition (seventeen since 1985, tripling the holding company's size) has given it more experience than most on the subject. Recognizing the dimensions of this area of potential concern, it has taken the initiative.

When a new bank converts to First Union's systems, its business customers—who have learned over the years to rely on that bank for cash management and other financial services—are visited by a systems specialist who works with the customer company's financial staff to explain and debug any new procedures. And just as many individual customers have personal bankers these days, First Union's cash management customers have an assigned customer service specialist—and a backup for times when the primary account person is unavailable.

There's a truism in service that says first you do it, then you talk about it (a corollary to which would be Don Meredith's old *Monday Night Football* observation, "It ain't braggin' if you can do it.") Now that many of the service-focused enhancements are in place and running smoothly, First Union has begun making a point of its service commitment. Most visible is a simple but tough-minded guarantee: If you open a new account and are not satisfied in the first six months, you can close the account and First Union will refund any monthly service charges you paid starting from day one. The definition of satisfaction is unconditionally left up to the customer.

On a larger level, First Union's commitment to top service is fine-tuned through the use of a third-party research firm that "shops" each branch at least once every quarter to rate it and its employees on a number of service criteria. The tactic has teeth: Those who rate poorly get remedial training; if they're rated poorly a second time, they can be fired. What's more, 20 percent of a manager's annual incentive check is based on his or her branch's customer quality scores.

The evaluations also have a positive side: Employees caught doing something right receive immediate bonuses on the spot, and those instant rewards can run as high as two hundred dollars. Each. When the Laurens, South Carolina, office became just the second branch in the First Union system to earn perfect scores for each person during a quarterly inspection in the fall of 1987, each of its ten staff members pocketed two C-notes.

To build on the local service commitment, branch scores are tracked by city, region, state, and virtually any other way possible, and friendly competition is fostered through incentive and promotion programs like Supercruise '88, the goal of which was to raise average QCS (Quality Customer Service) totals to at least 5.0 on a 6-point scale by the end of 1987. Winners cruised the Caribbean the following spring.

In addition, virtually every First Union employee, regardless of pay scale or job description, is included in at least one of the eighty-five service- and quality-based incentive programs the bank and its offices conduct throughout the year. Customer commendations are also treasured: Internal publications replay the high points of unsolicited fan mail that names employees who have provided outstanding service anywhere in the First Union family.

First Union's success demonstrates that quality customer service can indeed be provided in highly competitive markets, and that rapid growth need not become an excuse for deterioration and disgruntled customers. It also bodes well as a model for other "super-regionals" as regional-level interstate banking spreads in the years to come.

First Union Corporation
First Union Plaza
Charlotte, NC 28288

FIRST
WACHOVIA

IN RECENT YEARS, THE CONCEPT OF "RELATIONSHIP BANKING" HAS BEEN A POPULAR one—at least in the various and sundry marketing and advertising efforts employed by financial institutions of almost every size and description. Too often, unfortunately, what happens is that customers find themselves haphazardly assigned to whichever functionary was on duty on the floor or on the phone bank when they "decided" they wanted to establish a relationship with a banker.

When Wachovia Bank and Trust of Winston-Salem, North Carolina, went the relationship banking route fifteen years ago (long before most banks around the country "discovered" the concept), its managers realized they didn't know what their customers' relationships with the bank were. Accordingly, Wachovia committed itself to integrating everything from bank managers to data processing support staff into the effort.

It also decided the effort would be a long-term focus, not a short-term campaign fronted by a vice president of marketing. By its own calculations, seven or eight years and several million dollars' worth of mid-seventies vintage investment were required to get it right, but today Wachovia is a model of well-run, customer-focused retail banking. It's also one of the top all-around banks in the country.

Wachovia gets top marks for management from industry observers nationwide. In the annual Salomon Brothers' ranking of best-performing banks, Wachovia has been at or near the top throughout the eighties, ranking number one in 1982, 1983, and 1984 (third overall in 1987). In addition, CEO John G. Medlin, Jr.'s, name came up more often than any other in 1987 when *Bankers Monthly* surveyed a blue-ribbon panel of financial analysts, regulators, consultants, and bankers to identify the most effective executives in the industry. "Few managers have as detailed a knowledge of the workings of their organization," one panelist observed, "yet also give their people the freedom to operate."

That doesn't mean Medlin is an unseen, unfelt presence. To the contrary, he answers his own phone, eats lunch in the staff cafeteria (as do Wachovia's other top executives) and is likely to be found wandering

197

through various operations departments or branch banks at any given time of the day.

"You get commendations in letters, but complaints are more likely to come over the telephone," he told the *Greensboro News & Record* a few years ago. "We have a rule: Whoever gets a complaint, whether it is from a customer or an employee, you do your best to respond to it before the close of the day." That "never let the sun set on a problem" attitude is a serious and proven customer service standard throughout the Wachovia organization.

Wachovia makes relationship banking work by making sure its bankers know everything possible about their customers—and their customers know who their banker is and what he or she can do for them. Personal bankers personally do the paperwork on new customer accounts. Their names and phone numbers appear on all customer statements and correspondence. When their customers call or drop by, they can instantly key up transaction records, solve problems, and answer questions.

Their consumer customers value that relationship, as do the businesses large and small in the Southeast and around the country that use the bank's services. These days Wachovia Bank and Trust is approximately half of First Wachovia Corporation, a uniquely run interstate bank holding company with dual headquarters in Winston-Salem and Atlanta (home of the other side of the corporate family, The First National Bank of Atlanta). The combined organization operates nearly 350 full-service banking offices in Georgia and North Carolina, making it the nation's thirty-third largest banking institution, and does it well enough to consistently outperform the bigger-name, bigger-city banks in one of the toughest competitive markets in America.

If that sounds surprising, your regional chauvinism may be showing. Taken together, Georgia and North Carolina would make up the fourth largest state in the country, ranking right after California, New York, and Texas; their combined economies have been growing faster than the national average, and they've become more diversified in the process. And what about that name? Wachovia is the anglicized version of Wachau, the name of the ancestral valley in Austria that was home to a band of Moravian settlers who put down roots in western North Carolina through a land grant in 1752.

In part, Wachovia's success is an outgrowth of that bustling regional economy. Its success also springs from an extraordinary level of competition among the Southeast's three innovative regional banking companies: Wachovia, First Union Corporation, and North Carolina National Bank. The three-way competition obviously has brought out the best in all three players, though in markedly different ways. Wachovia's edge comes from a combination of technology and people-anchored operating standards that continually keeps the bank on the conservative side of the cutting edge, and without cutting up its people, or its customers, in the process.

On the corporate level, for example, Wachovia harnesses computers to capably and cost-effectively provide services, such as cash flow management and pension fund supervision, that other banks can't seem to afford to offer to their customers. It's one of the top banks in the country in providing "lock-box" services (a post office box the bank holds in a company's name for bill collection, with funds being credited to the company as soon as checks are received, thus improving cash flow—and reducing the amount of money a company has to borrow to fund short-term operations). Proprietary, on-line corporate banking services are provided through special terminals installed in the offices of corporate treasurers.

At the same time, consumers have benefitted from that technological capability in the form of well-run variable rate mortgage and credit card programs. Wachovia's pioneering adjustable-rate mortgage model was quickly copied nationwide. Its upscale-class credit card lending (for credit lines of five thousand dollars or more) also uses an interest rate that floats, this one at five points above the prime rate, which means its customers were paying 16 and 17 percent on their balances at a time when finance charges for many competing cards were locked in at 20 percent or more. And Wachovia's in-house data processing capability is so good that many banks around the country hire it to process the student loans they offer to their own local customers.

But none of that would have been effective long-term without the computer-to-people connection. In the late 1970s and early 1980s, Wachovia centralized consumer banking records on half a million customers into a computer system that could be accessed by more than five hundred personal bankers. These key individuals were designated as central contacts for all of a customer's banking transactions—checking accounts, money management planning, installment loans, credit cards, whatever they needed. The system enhances customer service while simultaneously improving account management and providing a sales network for new services (many of which are created based on input from the frontline).

On the national level, Wachovia's fast-rising reputation has been founded on doing well what it decides to do—and not doing things when it isn't positive it can do them well. If that sounds conservative, if it means watching quicker-acting competitors beat it to new business, so be it. Wachovia gets its sense of pride from accomplishment, not acquisition. But it isn't a matter of being conservative for conservatism's sake. One analyst's compromise thumbnail describes Wachovia as "conservative in the fundamentals of banking but creative in terms of new products and systems."

Indicative of Medlin's low-key, quality-based philosophy are these remarks from a presentation to the Bank and Financial Analysts Association's seventeenth annual symposium in New York in 1987: "In these times, success and survival more than ever require a sense of realism and an adherence to basics. First, one must realize that banking is more a qualitative than a quantitative business. Sustainable advances are more likely to be achieved by expanding gradually in manageable increments and patiently maintaining quality standards. Banking also needs patient shareholders who do not expect short-term gains at the expense of long-term values. Despite advances in technology, banking is still a highly personal process of serving customers one at a time. Providing financial services is not like the mass marketing and distribution of soap. Unlike tangible products, the quality of our service is determined by the people selling and delivering them in our stores as well as those processing them behind the scenes."

If that sounds like an executive who both knows and likes the business his business is in, it takes no more than a look at Wachovia's bottom line to determine the return on such an investment.

First Wachovia Corporation
P.O. Box 3099
Winston-Salem, NC 27150

First Federal/Osceola

THE PRESENCE OF REGIONAL SUPERBANKS, NOT TO MENTION THE USUAL ASSORT-ment of local and regional banks and savings and loan associations, plus the generally booming state of the state's economy, makes Florida an attractive and competitive place to run a financial institution. It's worth noting, then, that good service is also an important component in the continuing success of a modest, eleven-branch regional S&L working central Florida. At First Federal/Osceola, the emphasis appears to be on sales. But what makes that emphasis work, in the analysis of *United States Banker*, is "a relentless commitment to service."

First Federal has been a going, and growing, concern for fifty years, but in the last couple it has been posting double-digit annual growth rates and picking up market share at as much as 12 percent a year—all without buying up competitors or rushing out to open new branches on every street corner. The reason is a high-energy, sales-oriented culture in which everyone is expected to help build the business.

The "everyone sells" orientation dates back to 1984, when First Federal brought in a new executive vice president to take charge of marketing and committed itself to playing a more aggressive role in the three central Florida counties where it has offices. Before he moved into financial marketing, Christopher Bell had worked for consumer-goods companies like Revlon, Playtex International, and Johnson & Johnson. Before he moved to Florida, he'd been putting together sales programs for thrifts in California, another attractive/competitive environment. With the blessing of First Federal's CEO, James Davis (whose own multi-dimensional résumé includes stints as a truck driver and a real estate salesman), Bell was told to start making noise.

He started with First Federal's most important audience: its employees. Through that first winter, he met with every one of the thrift's two hundred workers, frontline and backroom, quizzing them about what they thought their employer could do better—and what they personally could do better, if only they had more opportunity, more training, more support, and more rewards. Then First Federal gave them the opportu-

201

nity, training, support, and rewards and turned them loose on the customers. It's a setting tailor-made for high achievers, and First Federal has found it has its share.

You can tell who they are, the achievers. Walk into any of the branches in places like Kissimmee, Cocoa Beach, Winter Garden, or Melbourne and look for the tellers, and the loan officers, and the backroom accounting and administrative people with the little jeweled gold pins on their lapels. You only get those for being the best in a given year in one of eleven award categories.

While you're at it, watch out for someone in a blue blazer. That's the branch's "service ambassador," the person whose job it is to interview a random sampling of customers after they've completed their business and find out how satisfied they are (or aren't), and what they think First Federal could do to serve them better. The thrift uses blue-blazered employees instead of secret shoppers in the belief that it generates more immediate and personal feedback—and because it keeps everyone, employees and customers alike, aware of its visible commitment to good service.

What you won't be able to see are the various bonus and incentive checks that are handed out regularly. For customer sales and service representatives, bonuses are dispensed weekly. For tellers, there are quarterly performance bonuses. (Both service representatives and tellers, by the way, now receive eighty hours of training before they go on the job, and are encouraged to take advantage of continuing education programs, whether provided by First Federal or outside organizations.) For loan officers, there are annual incentives based on production. For everyone, there are twenty-five-dollar rewards paid any time one of their suggestions (like putting express lanes in the drive-through facilities) is adopted.

You also won't be invited to watch while Davis sits down with each individual employee for an annual review. He does. In those sessions, CEO and frontline worker discuss the accomplishments in the preceding year and a written list of excellence goals for the year to come. How's that for a way to reinforce an organization's top-down commitment? Davis also talks to customers when they have a complaint, generally after first asking his staff to brief him on the size of the problem, but not on the size of the customer's account. It's basic First Federal policy that everybody from the president on down answers his or her own phone.

Results pay off personally and professionally: Achievers not only get plaques for their den walls and bonuses for their wallets; they also get first crack at promotions and transfers. And First Federal continues to hire for ability and enthusiasm, often at the expense of paper credentials. For example, Steve Childs, its senior vice president of operations, was hired as a teller back in 1974 with nothing more than a high school diploma. It obviously hasn't held him back. The senior VP of human resources, Judy Williams, started with First Federal as a secretary. She was the thrift's officer of the year in 1986.

It's worth noting that in First Federal's "everyone sells" culture, the operations functions report to marketing, which means technical decisions are judged for their impact on customers and employees as well as accounting. That's why hardware from telephones to the teller terminal system were evaluated by the employees who would have to use them before purchase decisions were made. First Federal also bought equipment that allows it to sort its customers' checks internally instead of contracting that job outside; employees had argued, persuasively, that it would improve customer service.

The advent of regional interstate banking and the prospect that someday financial institutions may be able to expand to national scope have raised fears that only the largest will be left—that smaller, more community-oriented institutions will fade away or be swallowed up into giant, impersonal systems. How can small organizations be expected to survive and thrive in the face of competition from bigger, more expansive adversaries? On the evidence, First Federal/Osceola has one answer: by being visibly and purposely better than the big guys can ever be at knowing and serving their customers.

As the mission statement stitched onto the pockets of the blue blazers expresses it, the secret is "Quality Service Without Compromise."

First Federal/Osceola
2200 Live Oak Blvd.
St. Cloud, FL 32770

Amalgamated Bank of New York
🔼 America's labor bank.

WHAT KIND OF A BANK DEEMPHASIZES PROFITS TO PROVIDE ENHANCED SERVICE to its customers? How about a bank founded by a labor organization in 1923 and still owned by the nearly three hundred thousand members of the Amalgamated Clothing and Textile Workers Union (ACTWU)?

With just four offices around the Big Apple (two in Manhattan, the other two in the Bronx), Amalgamated Bank of New York is no threat to displace Citicorp, Chase Manhattan, Manufacturers Hanover Trust, and the like as a new behemoth among money giants. It's no midget, however: with more than $1.5 billion in assets, it ranks among the top 2 percent of the country's fourteen thousand banks, and it consistently reports a higher return on assets than its bigger and better known competitors, despite (or maybe because of) its notoriously conservative strategy of investing only in short-term government securities, municipal obligations, and other money-market instruments. As a result, Amalgamated isn't subject to market swings or repayment problems in Third World nations. It has *no* nonperforming loans on its books to be expensed at the expense of its customers.

Through the years, Amalgamated has been a consistent innovator in services designed specifically for its customers—primarily middle-class consumers (union and nonunion alike) and organized labor. On at least three separate occasions in recent years, surveys have named it the top bank for consumers in New York. And in an era of tremendous change in the delivery of financial services, it's an example worthy of note nationally as well.

When Amalgamated was created, working men, not to mention women who worked, were considered poor credit risks, and few banks even offered them checking accounts. After all, where was the profit in providing services to people who had very little money and virtually no collateral against which to borrow? With a base of sixty thousand members, the leaders of the Amalgamated Clothing Workers of America (which became the modern ACTWU by expanding into new membership areas over the years) believed they could serve a community need and do so at a modest profit. Thirteen hundred depositors lined up the first day of business to prove their point.

One of the first things Amalgamated did was figure out a way to lend money to people who didn't have collateral. It simply decided not to require collateral—or the double and even triple interest commonly assessed by the loan companies that were the only other source of funds for low-paid working people. Instead, Amalgamated offered people who had jobs unsecured loans at the same rates other banks used for their wealthier clientele. It relied on them to make small weekly payments in a system that is essentially the same one now used for the unsecured installment credit that makes credit cards a fact of modern financial life. Today, Amalgamated continues to make unsecured installment loans for as little as five hundred dollars (it will make loans even to workers on strike) while encouraging its customers to avoid plastic credit and its significantly higher interest rates.

Because many of the union's members were European immigrants who sent part of their wages back across the Atlantic to help those they left behind, the new bank also became a pacesetter in transferring funds abroad. That, in turn, helped its business prospects, since its processes soon became so fast and dependable that several hundred other banks signed on to offer their customers the same service through Amalgamated.

That early orientation toward the smaller customer continues today, and it takes many forms, as befits a progressive financial organization. For example, free checking at Amalgamated is truly free for anyone, regardless of minimum balance. That policy (first introduced in the early 1970s) was reinstituted in 1986, replacing an interim minimum balance requirement that imposed a fee of just $1 when a customer's balance dropped below $100. The fee for traveler's checks (American Express) is fifty cents per one hundred dollars for customers, a fraction of what many competitors assess. The charge for a returned check, which can run as high as $15 at some banks, is just $1.25 to Amalgamated's account holders—a little less than what it "really" costs to process the transaction, according to the bank's figuring, but worth preserving because customers appreciate the courtesy and confidence it displays toward them.

Borrowing is also a lot more customer-friendly, the result of a "consumer prime rate" policy that means Amalgamated, in contrast to most financial institutions, will reduce rates often and in a timely manner when its money costs fall. Interest rates on auto and personal loans are consistently one to three points (sometimes more) below those of competitors: According to *The Wall Street Journal*, Amalgamated was making auto loans at 9.2 percent in 1987 when other New York City banks and thrifts were charging an average of 12.5 percent. Sure, the bank makes a little less, but it serves a little more. And you needn't have an account with

Amalgamated to qualify for the best loan rates. They're the same for everybody who wants to use the bank's services.

On the savings side, the top certificate of deposit and money-market interest rates most financial institutions offer only for hefty levels of investment have been paid on amounts as little as five hundred dollars at Amalgamated since its USAVE program debuted back in 1970. That minimum, by the way, is an *average* figure, not an absolute one, which means a customer's account can dip below minimum without losing interest or triggering a service-charge penalty. Minimum balance for a simple passbook savings account is five dollars, on which Amalgamated pays regular interest and charges no fees.

The bank continues to serve unions and their members, occasionally going bail for striking workers who end up in jail, and helping their organizations make better use of their own financial potential. For example, in 1987 Amalgamated helped three New York locals of the Bridge, Structural and Ornamental Iron Workers Union develop a program to make available some of their pension fund assets as home mortgages for their members. Characteristically, the loans are offered below market rates, and no points are charged.

In all, more than $3 billion of Taft-Hartley retirement funds are under Amalgamated's management—another important part of its services to labor organizations. The bank fields a complete package of financial services geared to the needs of unions around the country—strike funds, trust services, cash management, record keeping and reporting, custodial services, even impromptu loans to keep operations going during job actions. When the National Football League Players Association came knocking during the players' strike in 1982, it didn't have an account with Amalgamated, just a need. Amalgamated came through with $200,000, the start of another satisfying relationship.

As the only bank in the country to be wholly owned and controlled by a union, Amalgamated is constantly conscious of its unique heritage. More than half its officers have come up through the ranks (Edward Katz, the current president, can recall the days when he worked at the bank part-time for sixty cents an hour while attending New York University). All of its board members are union officials, but they don't get company cars or expensive perks, nor do they expect such treatment. The bank's workers, however, do earn higher than average wages. And they're members of Local 153, Office and Professional Employees International Union.

A few years ago, with inflation spiralling higher and making small accounts unprofitable for many larger banks, an executive of Citibank was heard to remark that people with only a couple of hundred dollars in savings shouldn't bother a bank, that they'd be better off keeping their money under the mattress. Amalgamated responded with a full-page ad in *The New York Times*. Its point of view came through loud and clear: "The notion (that small accounts should be turned away) is disgraceful. A profitable bank needn't be so short-sighted as to abandon marginal or even unprofitable services vital to working people. Banks are quasi-public institutions and every facet of their operations need not be determined by cost accounting evaluations." With that, Amalgamated offered a new account, whimsically dubbed "the mattress," for depositors of modest means, no matter how insignificant other banks might consider them.

Altruism? Banks don't stay in business for half a century because of noble intentions. Amalgamated takes care of its customers, whether they are individual accountholders or unions that need an institution in tune with their unique requirements. Either way, it works to promote its customers' welfare and economic interests. And it profits accordingly.

As a story in *New York Magazine* concluded in 1982, "In a city of remarkable banks, the Amalgamated Bank of New York is one of the most remarkable—an institution that is clearly well managed and profitable and yet can serve the smallest customer with friendliness and care."

Amalgamated Bank of New York
11-15 Union Square
New York, NY 10003

Goldman Sachs & Company

Goldman
Sachs

MOST OF US ARE NOT NOW, NOR ARE WE EVER LIKELY TO BE, PROSPECTIVE customers for Goldman Sachs. But among those who are customers of this relatively unobtrusive Wall Street brokerage firm—primarily financial and investment officers at major public and private institutions—this is the standard other companies are measured by.

In the 1987 version of *Institutional Investor* magazine's annual survey of 150 top investment officers at major institutions, the top-rated firm for best overall service was Goldman Sachs. It was also considered best at making key personnel accessible to clients, best at research, best at executing orders and handling block positions, and second most helpful during the market decline of October 1987. In fact, the only two categories of the eight measured where Goldman Sachs wasn't at the top was the one for best foreign brokerage (for which it wasn't eligible) and the one for most improved firm (there's obviously not a lot of room for improvement, but it still ranked fifth out of the top ten major firms named). Goldman Sachs was equally well regarded in 1986, when it also was judged best overall by customers.

In 1987, for the first time, *Institutional Investor* also polled the chief financial officers of the hundred largest companies. Twelve categories were assessed. Goldman Sachs turned up number one in six (for services in equity underwriting, private placements, mergers and acquisitions, research, daily market coverage, and international corporate finance), second in three others (underwriting investment-grade debt, managing pension funds, and underwriting Eurobonds). In 1985, it should be noted, *Euromoney* magazine polled leading brokerage houses around the world to determine their favorites when it came to large-scale trading. The number one U.S. firm: Goldman Sachs again.

In *The 100 Best Companies to Work for in America*, the authors likened Goldman Sachs to the then-powerful and well-respected Dallas Cowboys of the National Football League. The Cowboys have since fallen on hard times, but despite the glitz and glitter (some of it since melted down) of the boom times on Wall Street in this decade, Goldman Sachs has

208

managed to stay true to its own high standards and customer focus. In the aftermath of the October '87 "correction," many high-priced deal-makers and hotshot traders departed their previous employers to start their own firms and preserve environments where they were treated as stars. The defections were not, however, universal.

"Significantly, two major firms still known for strong concern with company culture and teamwork, Goldman Sachs and Morgan Stanley, have been little touched by the recent wave of defections and dissension," noted *The Wall Street Journal* in early 1988. "At many others, though, the old value system to a degree gave way to a culture of cash and indulgence—limousines, corporate jets and dinners at four-star restaurants."

When Beth McGoldrick, an associate editor at *Institutional Investor*, spent nearly two weeks inside the firm a few years ago preparing a report on its corporate culture, she was struck by the way seemingly pious, apple-pie platitudes that inspired cynicism elsewhere—"team spirit," "high standards of professionalism," "pride in what we do," "service orientation"—were taken seriously throughout the organization. "Goldman partners," she reported, "not only extol these virtues, they believe in them and act on them. The principles make up the backbone of Goldman's unique corporate culture. And, as [cochairman John] Whitehead says, that culture really *is* the key to Goldman's astonishing long-run success."

The Goldman Sachs culture is not oriented toward flashy superstars. It's built, rather, on a sense of teamwork that emphasizes results achieved for a client over bonus checks and corporate perks accrued. A few years back, *Fortune* quoted one chief financial officer's concise assessment of what his firm liked and admired about its client relationship with Goldman Sachs: "First, they know their business. Second, they don't seem to have any internal struggles or strife."

A simple but effective Goldman Sachs technique is the "credit memo," an internal missive in which one member of the firm thanks another for his or her help on a project. "An astute young person quickly learns that the way to win here is to send around long memos that give credit loud and clear to everyone who worked on a given task," one partner told McGoldrick. "There are hundreds of these things around here, all noting what a terrific job so-and-so did on your client's deal."

Unlike other major Wall Street firms that have been acquired by larger corporate parents, Goldman Sachs remains a partnership—the traditional form of operation on Wall Street for generations. Partners are chosen only once every two years, and some candidates (a nomination from a current partner is required for consideration) stand for election two or three times before they join the inner circle.

The prospect of an eventual partnership has a trickle-down effect throughout the organization, contributing in often subtle ways to the teamwork clients continue to marvel over. "If [a mergers and acquisitions] group is structuring a merger," *Fortune* pointed out a few years ago, "it will call in people from trading, corporate finance, and arbitrage to offer guidance. They come willingly and are prepared to work half the night; 14-hour days are commonplace. They know that teamwork, along with superb skills in their specialties, is what counts in performance evaluations, which ultimately determine whether they become partners."

Internal systems reflect the need to specialize in today's complex international financial market. Professionals at Goldman Sachs typically enter a specialized field early in their careers with the firm and stay with it, rather than switching around; the firm is determined to grow its future talent from within. One way to look at the tilt toward specialization is to compare high finance to modern medicine: If you want a heart specialist for a triple bypass, you'll look for someone with years of experience in that field rather than someone who might be good in such diverse fields as surgery, pediatrics, and sports medicine—but at the expense of never having become outstanding at any of them.

One measure of the results: *Institutional Investor's* annual "All-America Research Team" contained ten Goldman Sachs members on its first team, the largest representation of any firm in the industry. Another: In 1987, Goldman Sachs was involved as an adviser in seven of the ten largest transactions and in more than eighty transactions with values over $100 million.

Yet there's business that Goldman Sachs doesn't get because its own high standards come first. The authors of *The 100 Best Companies* remarked on its reputation as "the pacifist" of Wall Street because of its long-standing rule against representing a company attempting a hostile takeover. On the other hand, it might just as easily be characterized as the "defense department" because so many firms come to it for help in fighting off unfriendly suitors.

Goldman Sachs rewards the support people who make its continuing strong performance possible. Pay is well above the norm, even for competitive firms along Wall Street, and bonuses can add another 20 percent or more at year-end. The system is designed and managed to build loyalty throughout the corporate staff, and clearly customers benefit from that. Even competitors have been heard to marvel about how "nice" people act at Goldman Sachs. There's very little jealousy, either—the company doesn't own a corporate jet, nor does it provide company cars or limos. It's just not that kind of place.

New York magazine once headlined a story about the company, "Nice Guys Finish First." A few years ago, *Forbes* noted, "Goldman has achieved this eminence with a minimum of infighting that afflicts most Wall Street firms. And when did you last hear of a Goldman partner leaving for greener fields elsewhere? Indeed, this unusual harmony is a major reason for the firm's unparalleled success."

Goldman Sachs & Company
85 Broad Street
New York, NY 10004

Fidelity Investments

AN IMPORTANT CAVEAT: WE LIKE FIDELITY INVESTMENTS BECAUSE OF THE WAY it serves its approximately 6 million individual and corporate customers, many of the former do-it-yourself investors who use its national network of walk-in centers and its various discount brokerage services. We neither like nor dislike, endorse nor discourage personal interest and confidence in Fidelity's *investments* on their own merits. Personal investing is, as the adjective should make clear, personal—whether one or several of the more than 150 different Fidelity products works for you as a financial instrument is something only you can decide.

That said, Fidelity does a lot of things very well for its customers. To begin with, it's accessible: Since February of 1986, customers have been able to call Fidelity via a toll-free 800-number 24 hours a day, 7 days a week, 365 days a year (366 in 1988). What's more, the person who answers the phone, even in the wee hours of the morning, is a "registered representative," a licensed securities dealer who can call up the customer's file, provide price quotes and account information, accept instructions for trades, make exchanges from one fund to another, and otherwise do a lot more than take a message for someone to call back during normal business hours. For the deaf and hearing-impaired, there's TDD (Telecommunications Device for the Deaf) access, staffed by registered reps who have been specially trained to use the equipment.

There are four telephone service centers (in Fidelity's Boston home offices plus Cincinnati, Dallas, and Salt Lake City), and all four are linked by an automatic switching system that routes calls to registered reps wherever they are available. The goal is to answer every call by the third ring, and with a real live person, not a recording that says you have to wait and listen to elevator music until someone breaks free. Fidelity's internal auditing tracks how well that standard is met with the same vigor with which it measures portfolio performance.

One by-product of all that customer contact is the opportunity to monitor the pulse of investors of every size and description and area code. The Fidelity Futures Program regularly collects ideas from the

212

frontline that result in new products and systems or modifications to existing ones. In addition, every week several thousand recent customers are polled by Fidelity's Investor Centers to check out the quality of service provided and the prospect for new services or modifications to existing ones.

A few years ago, for example, Fidelity's continuing customer research turned up a significant blip suggesting that not every customer wants or needs to talk to a live rep. That resulted in the introduction of FAST: Fidelity Automated Service Telephone. It allows customers to use their touch-tone phones to access account information and price quotes, or move money between their various mutual fund accounts. (A number of brokerage companies now offer the service, but none have the range of options that Fidelity offers.)

In keeping with its tilt toward do-it-yourselfers, Fidelity supports customers who want to use their personal computers to track performance and market trends. On-line investors in its Select Portfolio program can trade stocks and options directly to an exchange floor, or track up to nine different, personally variable portfolios at one time. They also have direct access through Fidelity to the Dow Jones News Retrieval Service, allowing them to integrate information from that source with their Fidelity accounts.

On the other hand, not everyone is content with service provided by telephone, whether it involves an individual or a series of beeps. For them, Fidelity offers more than fifty walk-in centers around the country. Each has its own staff of registered reps and support personnel. Each also has a video lending library from which customers can borrow, free of charge, an ever-changing variety of tapes on everything from how a mutual fund operates or alternatives for accumulating college tuition to how to review the performance of their accounts and make best use of financial planning and investment services. In addition to the tapes, periodic seminars contribute to the continuing customer education effort, and sales reps can also send audiotapes and specifically targeted investment newsletters to keep their account holders current on changing market conditions and product offerings.

Fidelity is the kind of business that seems to inspire interesting comparisons. To *U.S. News & World Report* in 1987, "[it] is the L. L. Bean of the fund business, with 1,500 employees taking orders and responding to inquiries over the phone around the clock." Its Investor Centers, said *Institutional Investor* about a year earlier, "with their wall-mounted stock tickers and the mounds of propsectuses lying around, look like a cross between a Christian Science Reading Room and an Off-Track Betting office."

Whatever it looks like, there's no getting away from the fact that Fidelity has offered a number of customer-friendly innovations over the years, many of them a function of its size and stature as a veritable supermarket of investment products, many as well reflecting its penchant for investing in top quality technology when it can enhance service perform- ance. Fidelity was the first investment company to give customers the ability to write checks on money-market accounts (1974). To make it more inviting for customers to switch money between funds, it waived the industry's typical 2-percent sales charge and 1-percent redemption fee in lieu of a simple ten-dollar service charge. Instead of pricing funds based on the closing bell, Fidelity was the first to use computerized information management to price some of its funds by the hour.

Black Monday, October 1987's market meltdown, put a significant dent in Wall Street's confidence, not to mention the quarterly earnings reports of brokerage firms large and small. Significantly, Fidelity didn't duck and hide during the worst of the carnage. Instead, it brought in more than double its normal complement of telephone operators to handle calls and provide updates to worried investors. The three-ring phone answer- ing standard obviously didn't hold up: Some customers reported busy signals for more than an hour, and *Fortune* reported that about 3 percent of Fidelity's 580,000 customers that day (for scoring purposes, 80,000 to 100,000 calls per day is usually the norm) ultimately gave up—but the average call was still answered in about eight rings.

The aftershocks showed up in Fidelity's work force as they did in other brokerage firms. More than 800 Fidelity people were laid off, most of them in volume-sensitive positions like order-taking, mail-processing, and telephone representatives. But in the aftermath, Fidelity has made a point of preserving management and support programs that include train- ing, incentives, and nonmonetary recognition for a job well done.

One of the more revealing stories about Fidelity's inclination to acquire technology in the name of responsiveness traces back to a 1983 power blackout in Boston that led to the two (not one, two) large electrical generators that reside in the basement of the company's headquarters in that city. When the power went down that fateful day, minutes before the market's close, so did Fidelity's computers, the backbone of its customer service system. A maintenance man wandering by told Edward Johnson 3d, Fidelity's chairman, that he could find a back-up generator. Johnson didn't hesitate. The maintenance man got the go-ahead, and Fidelity got the juice—ten minutes before Boston Edison tried to rent the same generator.

To avoid ever putting itself, and its customers, to that inconvenience again, Fidelity now has the two electrical generators in the basement, with a battery pack of some 376 cells next door to take care of things while they power up. If they ever do. The sign on the door says UPS Room: Uninterrupted Power Supply. In Dallas, there's a back-up office.

And another set of back-up software and files is reportedly stored somewhere in Philadelphia. Fidelity may never need that room, or the back-up office, or the back-up files. But they're there, just in case.

Fidelity Investments
82 Devonshire Street
Boston, MA 02109

A. G. Edwards & Sons

A.G. Edwards & Sons, Inc.
INVESTMENTS SINCE 1887

IN 1887, AT THE AGE OF SEVENTY-FIVE, GENERAL ALBERT GALLATIN EDWARDS retired from his job as assistant secretary of the U.S. Treasury to return to St. Louis, the town he'd adopted as home after a tour of duty as a lieutenant of dragoons in the 1830s. There he founded a brokerage company in partnership with his sons. The current chairman and CEO, Benjamin Franklin Edwards III, is the fourth generation of the family to guide the business, which in the intervening century has become the seventh-largest brokerage firm in the country and the largest based anywhere other than near Wall Street.

Ben Edwards professes not to be phased by Wall Street giants with their megabuck image marketing, any more than he is by the discount brokers working the other side of the street. In the end, he reasons, the key to the business is the service-based relationship between client and broker. At the company that bears his family's name, the emphasis is on doing everything possible to nurture that highly personal relationship.

Outside indicators also point to a company with a reputation for excellence that springs directly from the top of the organization. In 1985, *Investment Decisions* cited the company as the nation's best-managed brokerage house. In 1981 and again in 1986, the *Wall Street Transcript* named Edwards himself as the best chief executive in the securities industry, with silver (second-place) awards in 1983 and 1984, and a bronze in 1987.

"[Edwards] has run this retail-oriented firm from the standpoint of satisfying their customers first, rather than making a profit," the publication noted in explaining the 1987 citation. "The relationship with the customer is very important to the company, and therefore to Edwards. Cultivating this association is what makes the CEO so outstanding."

The authors of *The 100 Best Companies to Work for in America* also marveled at an unabashedly unselfish culture where "you are supposed to be accomplishing something for the firm, not for yourself. This is one reason they are able to run a successful branch network. They put a great deal of emphasis on servicing those branches. . . . Edwards is also old-fashioned in that it hasn't built up a huge institutional customer base, doing trades for insurance companies, pension funds, and the like. Its focus is still the little guy."

In an era where most brokerage companies profit from the activities of large institutional investors—pension funds, mutual funds, and other major players—Edwards & Sons still derives from 60 to 90 percent of its income from the individuals who turn to it for investment services. Many of them are in small towns and out-of-the-way places, and they may typically be trading in lots of several hundred shares at a time. No matter: Edwards & Sons prides itself on putting its customers first, regardless of the size of their accounts. Industry analysts point out that the average broker at Edwards & Sons generates less "production" (income to the firm from commissions on sales) than competitors' brokers do. The company sees that as further evidence of its commitment to put customers' profits ahead of corporate profits.

"For example," Edwards told the *Wall Street Transcript* in 1987, "we will not handle the deep discount business because that would tie up our execution forces on the exchange floors or a block desk handling orders at deep discounts. This would mean that they will not be available to handle the orders for which the customers are paying full freight. We feel that if we're going to charge full freight, we'd better give the best handling we can, and we want to have our people available to do so."

Those smaller customers come before even the company itself: Edwards & Sons does not trade for its own account, either before or after rendering services to its investors. Neither does it "manufacture" investment products of its own. If the stocks and bonds it accumulates for sale to its customers, or the mutual funds and tax shelters it could but doesn't create, were actively traded or promoted in order to produce another source of profit for the firm, Edwards & Sons would consider itself in competition with its own customers. That's just not how they do business.

They do, however, do a lot of business—in St. Louis, and in the more than 350 branch offices in 46 states. In marked contrast to most brokerage and financial services firms that had to trim staff and slim operations in the aftermath of Wall Street's October 1987 troubles, Edwards & Sons grew. More than 20 offices were added in the six months after the crash, evidence that even though the firm's clients took their share of hits, their confidence in the broker-client relationships they had established in more halcyon days didn't go down with the market.

That brokers stay and new customers continue to become loyal, long-term clients is testimony to the high level of after-sale service the company provides to its customers. It's worth noting that Edwards himself spent many of his early years in the company in the back-office areas where transactions are processed and account records kept. It's not surprising then that he credits the less glamorous side of the business with helping the firm survive and grow.

"We don't try to tie our customers to the house," Edwards explains. "We don't try to control our sales force. We feel that the important relationship is the one between the customer and the broker. If we can strengthen the broker and the tools the broker has to deal with the customer and give good support, we'll take our chances, then, on keeping the broker and the customer."

The internal systems are designed to support that. Like other brokerage firms, Edwards & Sons salespeople have access to a corporate research and analysis staff that looks at companies, markets, and products and makes judgments on their relative values and prospects. Unlike most brokerage firms, it's not uncommon for brokers and their clients to pick up a phone, ring up headquarters, and—with their broker's assistance—get direct, personal input from the researcher.

In many brokerage firms, about a quarter of the staff is made up of the registered representatives who buy and sell for customers. At Edwards & Sons, about half of the sixty-five hundred employees are brokers. In the industry, broker compensation tends to be equivalent to up to 40 percent of the commissions they generate. Edwards & Sons pays about 10 percent more. To reinforce the loyalty of lower-paid workers—primarily the administrative and support staffers whose accuracy and efficiency are crucial to keeping customers satisfied—the company matches their contributions to the profit-sharing plan at a rate of $2 for $1; for the higher-paid folk, the company contribution is just $1 for each dollar they set aside.

To stay in touch with field operations, both Edwards and his father, chairman emeritus Presley Edwards, make frequent visits to offices throughout the system. While in town, they'll not only meet with branch managers and the office staff, but also with customers. In addition, regional meetings with the sales force funnel feedback from the frontlines back to St. Louis, where systems and support are adjusted accordingly. When brokers relayed customer comments that account statements were hard to read and understand, for example, Edwards & Sons studied and reformatted them—in the process investing in a retooling of in-house computer systems to make the new forms work.

The company also schedules open houses in various branches at which salespeople, support staff, and senior executives (including Edwards himself) can mingle with customers and hear firsthand what's on their minds. That's a crucial form of market research in the Edwards & Sons formula: "It's more important that we listen to the customer than the customer listen to us," is how it tends to be expressed internally.

Accordingly, its twelve regional managers are relatively free to develop opportunities unique to their own markets and the needs of their customers. To remove any tendency to push account activity for any gain other than that of the customer, many branch managers are on salary, with bonuses determined by the firm's overall profitability, not the volume of their particular office. For the same reason, seminars presented to customers are high in information content, relatively low in sales pressure.

The same attitude characterizes corporate management. There's no imperative from a centralized headquarters to force investors lock-step into pet programs—and no indication that the company has any intention of abandoning its prized independence. Companies that have inquired about Edwards & Sons' interest in being acquired have been told there's nothing to talk about. "We think our value is our production people," the current chief executive told the St. Louis *Post-Dispatch* in 1987. "If we put a price on our heads we're putting them in jeopardy."

A.G. Edwards & Sons
One North Jefferson
St. Louis, MO 63103

Northwestern Mutual Life Insurance Company

Northwestern
Mutual Life®

EACH YEAR, FIVE POLICYHOLDERS OF THIS MILWAUKEE-BASED COMPANY ARE selected by the board of trustees to make, at the company's expense, an unrestricted, independent review of operations from headquarters to the frontlines. They go over records, investigate consumer complaints and requests, and have carte blanche to question anyone from president Don Schuenke to agents in the field. A summary of their report is incorporated into the company's annual report; more substantively, their insight has resulted in numerous changes and improvements in the seventy years the novel program has been in existence. It might be merely a coincidence, but this isn't the only evidence of a business working hard on behalf of its customers.

When *Fortune* polled business executives, outside directors, and financial analysts in 1987 for its sixth annual Corporate Reputations Survey (reported in January 1988), the name at the top of the list of life insurance companies was Northwestern Mutual Life. The year before, Northwestern also led the list. And the year before that. In fact, every year since the survey began in 1983, Northwestern has been number one.

In June 1987, *Sales & Marketing Management* reported the results of its third annual Best Sales Force Survey. The leader: Northwestern—in every one of seven categories, from opening new accounts and retaining top salespeople to reputation among customers and holding on to existing accounts.

When Best & Company, the industry research firm that rates long-term performance of insurance products, looked at the performance of the life insurance policies sold to customers twenty years ago by sixty-five companies, Northwestern finished at the top. According to Moody's Investors Service, in an industry where some companies watch 20 percent of their policies lapse in a given year, and where a lapse rate of 12 percent is on the good side of average performance, Northwestern retains nearly 95 percent of its more than two million policyholders year in and year out. Moody's consistently puts Northwestern at the top of the list of insurance companies that keep their customers satisfied.

It makes you think maybe these people are doing something right, doesn't it? They are. While it's the nation's tenth-largest life insurance company in terms of total assets, Northwestern sells only life insurance, disability insurance, and annuities, and those only in specific forms, based on what it considers to be in its customers' best interest. As one insurance industry analyst told *Forbes* in 1988, "The perception [that] Northwestern is genuinely concerned for policyholders is universal in the industry."

All of this didn't start in the 1980s, however. It actually traces back to the 1880s (the company was founded in 1857), when Henry Palmer was in the early stages of his thirty-five-year tenure as president of the company. As related by Frederick G. Harmon and Garry Jacobs in their book, *The Vital Difference*, Palmer established the four basic principles that still guide Northwestern: simple products, low expenses, high risk standards, and cautious investments. During Palmer's term of office, the authors note, "The company's agency field force developed a high reputation for professional skill and an intense loyalty to the company. Northwestern Mutual's agents became noted for high ethical standards and an almost religious zeal for serving the customer."

A century later, that attitude is as much a part of the company as is the view of Lake Michigan from its Milwaukee offices. As Harmon and Jacobs put it, "Service at Northwestern Mutual is not—at least it is no longer— merely a policy or program established by top management and implemented through the company's operating systems. It is an attitude that saturates the entire personality and atmosphere of the company and has become institutionalized as a self-perpetuating custom or culture of the organization."

Stability has a lot to do with that culture: Agent turnover is about half the industry average, virtually nonexistent in the ranks of clerical workers and management alike (4.9 percent and 3.4 percent respectively in 1987).

Productivity benefits from that stability, and in turn encourages it. Northwestern has the industry's lowest ratio of employees per $100 million of life insurance in force—about half the industry average, in fact— which means its workers get more done than their counterparts. In return, they are compensated well: The company keeps pay for its administrative support staff, more than half of whom are members of the Office and Professional Employees Union, in the top 10 percent of the industry. And there *is* such a thing as a free lunch—Northwestern employees have been eating free in the company cafeteria since 1915. A few years ago, *Milwaukee* magazine rated it the best of nearly fifty lunchtime eating establishments in the city.

In the field, Northwestern's top-rated sales force is composed of some sixty-eight hundred agents, all of them independent and all of them on a 100-percent commission system. Extending sales through brokers could expand the company in terms of new policy dollars, the company concedes, but it would inevitably do so at the expense of overall quality and service to existing policyholders. A broker who tries to represent half a dozen different companies will know a little bit about all of them, Northwestern maintains, but not a great deal about any of them. On the other hand, an agent who represents Northwestern will know a lot about its particular products and procedures. At Northwestern, bigger isn't better—*better* is better.

Sales agents are supported with streamlined administrative systems and sophisticated computers that can profile each individual policyholder in a matter of keystrokes. The company's training catalog includes literally hundreds of seminars and courses, all of them designed to improve the performance of the frontline salespeople by helping them improve their selling and business management skills. Evidence of the value the company's agents place on that support becomes visible every July, when thousands of members of the field sales force pay their own way back to Milwaukee for a four-day sales meeting. There they share information and techniques, discuss market trends and issues, and meet firsthand with the administrative staff that supports them in the field.

They also interact constantly with the home office, both informally and through three formal associations of agents. Agent representatives are included on joint committees that review new products and procedures, modify existing offerings, and help the company stay in touch with conditions in the marketplace. It all works because of Northwestern's sharp focus on the customers the company is prepared to serve.

In the end, it still comes back to how well or how poorly a company serves its customers. Northwestern prides itself on interpreting the fine print in the policyholder's favor. In 1980, it startled its policyholders by passing along the benefits of higher interest rates: It increased policy values without hiking premiums. A $100,000 policy taken out twenty years before was revalued at more than $118,000. The rate of increase in cash values for policies with that feature was also increased.

One of the stories Northwesterners tell is the one about the student pilot who purchased a fifty-thousand-dollar life insurance policy. The policy had an aviation exclusion that said no benefits were payable if he died as a result of a flying accident while he was a pilot or crew member. Several years later, he did indeed die when the plane he was piloting crashed. In the wreckage, investigators found his logbook, which showed that just before the crash he had logged his hundredth hour at the controls, making him eligible to apply for a removal of the exclusion. Even though he hadn't, Northwestern paid off on the policy.

A policy statement adopted by Northwestern's executive committee provides a terse summary of the way the company does business: "The ambition of The Northwestern has been less to be large than to be safe; its aim is to rank first in benefits to policyowners rather than first in size.

Valuing quality above quantity, it has preferred to secure its business under certain salutary restrictions and limitations rather than write a much larger business at the possible sacrifice of those valuable points which have made The Northwestern pre-eminently the policyowner's Company."

Right out of the trendy management books of the eighties, right? Well, that depends on which eighties. That statement was adopted not in 1988, but in 1888.

The Northwestern Mutual Life Insurance Company
720 East Wisconsin Avenue
Milwaukee, WI 53202

Chubb Group of Insurance Companies

CHUBB

WHAT MAKES AN INSURANCE COMPANY GOOD IN THE EYES OF AN INDEPENDENT agent or broker? The basic, or core, product of insurance is pretty well standardized among carriers. Rates may fluctuate somewhat, but over time the discriminating factors tend to be in the area of what a study done by the consulting firm Temple, Barker & Sloane (TBS) labels "delivery quality" as opposed to "pure content quality."

The latter is important, to be sure: It includes payment of claims in a reasonable amount of time, accurate billing and record-keeping, and accurate representation of product features. To be an average, run-of-the-mill insurance company, you have to do these things.

But the other quality aspects are a little trickier, according to the TBS study: "*Delivery quality* is more elusive in that it refers to all of the surrounding aspects of dealing with a customer, from initial sales to subsequent servicing." Examples include rapid policy turnaround and prompt return of phone calls, authoritative responses to requests, easy access for inquiries from the field, effective resolution of complaints, general courtesy, and a flexible style of response to the customer.

All of which, in varying levels of intensity, have something to do with the fact that when, in mid-1987, several thousand insurance brokers were asked to rate the quality of service provided by forty commercial property and casualty insurers, the Chubb Group of Insurance Companies got top marks for overall service quality, the second highest frequency of extremely high mentions (9 or 10 on a 10-point scale), and the third lowest frequency of very low scores (5 or less).

Founded in 1882 by Thomas Chubb and his son, Percy, to insure sailing ships and their cargo, Chubb Group today is one of the fifty largest diversified financial organizations in the U.S. About two thirds of its annual revenue comes from its group of eleven wholly owned subsidiary insurance companies, each of which underwrites business, personal, health, life, auto, and other forms of specialty protection on a regional basis. Their policies are sold through a network of independent brokers and agents in the U.S., Canada, and ninety other countries worldwide.

The company prides itself on service as well as sales, especially to customers with special needs. Specialization, in fact, is a basic premise of the business. As expressed by Henry Harder, chairman and president, Chubb's orientation is to "build distinctive and valuable differences into the full range of products and services we offer our customers. We must remember that we cannot be all things to all people, that we can't hope to successfully answer every insurance need that arises in the marketplace. So, it behooves us to find the customers we can serve really well, and then to bend our efforts toward doing it."

Doing it can take any number of forms. In evaluating the "agreed value" to be covered under a homeowner's insurance policy, for example, Chubb-trained appraisers do more than just follow a paperwork process that relies on a formula based on measuring the square footage and counting windows and rooms. Since they often are dealing with a more affluent clientele, they are taught to make personal, on-site appraisals, in the process taking into account fine points of construction and architectural design.

On the business side, Chubb has developed special programs for industry-specific conditions affecting electronics manufacturers, plastic- and metalworking businesses, printing and publishing operations, and small businesses seeking to export their products or services. It also is highly regarded for the property and liability coverage it offers to banks, brokerage houses, insurance companies, and investment firms.

None of which is new. "Service isn't something you graft onto an organization," senior vice president Terry Van Gilder told us. "The CEO can't wake up some fine morning and say, 'Starting today, we're going to be more service-oriented.' The advantage we have is that there's a tradition in this company—you're part of something here, and you're expected to contribute to that. When you come to work here, you see the resources and the will of the organization go in the direction of serving the customer. You see people rewarded for that. You see people praised for that. You get the impression that that's important when you work here."

Like many top service providers, Chubb makes a point of sharing the stories of people who go above and beyond for the sake of their clients, or even their clients' clients. Business coverage, for example, can involve a more active role than simply checking actuarial tables. In 1987 loss control representative Ann Minzner and several coworkers spent months working with an independent agency, its property insurance client, and the city of Boston to improve fire protection for the insured business. The effort began early in the year, when Minzner determined from a hydrant test that the public water supply serving the client's business, which connected via older, six-inch pipe, was inadequate for a building sprinkler system that was connected to a newer twelve-inch main.

Over the next several months, Minzner attended city council meetings and took part in meetings with the water department and city engineers. The sticking point was getting hydrants connected to the new, larger main so the sprinkler system—which was required by local building codes—could operate effectively. By late September, it could. Minzner was there to personally conduct the water flow test on the new hydrant.

Lately, Chubb has been introducing one of the most visible and, from initial results, most successful improvements in personal insurance packaging in many years. Grandly dubbed Masterpiece, it's the result of more than six years of rethinking the way insurance is sold at the frontline, and adds the benefits of modern information technology to the servicing of policyholders and the agents who sell to them.

In contrast to separate insurance products that typically have required several forms each, Masterpiece requires only a one-page worksheet to package a number of separate types of coverage. To accomplish that consolidation, Chubb has eliminated nearly three hundred questions and as many as thirty-three separate endorsements and forms that used to be "normal" in the blizzard of paperwork that had to be completed to initiate an insurance policy. Consequently, the rating manual used by agents to determine coverage offerings and estimate costs is one tenth the size of the previous one.

Both changes are designed to minimize the amount of time an agent or broker must spend on paperwork. The simplification also helps new brokers get up to speed on Chubb's policies faster, and with less training expense, than in the past. When changes have to be made, or a quote is needed, there's a toll-free 800-number with a Chubb service representative waiting at the other end. That eliminates the time- and paper-consuming task of writing up endorsements and new forms.

Policies and forms alike are written in plain English, and customer-specific documents are generated by laser printer and proprietary software. (Chubb boasts that each Masterpiece policy starts from a blank sheet of paper—there are no preprinted versions.) As a result, each individual policy includes only the specific types and amounts of coverage the customer is actually buying. Policies also are accompanied by customer-specific summaries of premiums and coverages, explaining—again in plain English—what is covered and how much each part of that coverage costs. Each time the policy is changed or updated, new documents and summaries are generated.

Under Masterpiece, agents can precisely tailor multiple forms of insurance (automobile, homeowners, personal liability, and coverage for valuable articles) to the specific needs of their individual clients. Or they can use the modular format of the worksheet to write separate, single-dimension policies in any one or combination of those lines. They also can file the policies electronically if they're among the growing number of agents on-line with Chubb headquarters in Warren, New Jersey.

Finally, in a development that threatens generations of number-crunchers, policy records are now computerized by the insured's name, not by a complex and hard-to-find policy number. It's just one more way that the "delivery quality" of its insurance service has been targeted on satisfying customer expectations.

The Chubb Corporation
15 Mountain View Road
Warren, NJ 07061

Amica Mutual Insurance Company

NEVER HEARD OF THESE GUYS, HUH? THAT'S NOT SURPRISING. AMICA ISN'T VERY large: slightly more than four hundred thousand policyholders and about forty offices around the country. It doesn't want to get very large, either, so it doesn't advertise. Basically, that's because it doesn't have to: More than 95 percent of its new business (auto, homeowners, life, marine, and umbrella coverage) comes through referrals from satisfied customers, some 15 percent of whom have been with the company for twenty-five years or more.

Although it's the seventh largest mutual property and casualty insurance company in the U.S. (in a "mutual" insurance company, the policyholders own the business), Amica is more interested in being the best, even if that means it can never be the biggest. Evidence that it's succeeding at its low-key ambition abounds. In 1987 and 1986, it was the best at servicing its customers in the state of New York as determined by an index compiled by the state Insurance Department that divides number of justified complaints by millions of dollars of policy values in force. Amica's rating: 0.25 complaints per million dollars written, *down* from 0.55 in 1986. We won't name names, but the worst performers got 12.35 and 7.32 complaints respectively out of the same million dollars of business in those two years, and the average company among the seventy included on the 1987 list had five times as many customers per dollar complaining about it to the state.

Actually, as good as that is, Amica can do better. During the same two-year period, not one consumer complaint about Amica was received by the Arizona Department of Insurance—something none of the other sixty companies who write about 95 percent of the business in that southwestern state could claim. In 1985, the same thing happened in Virginia: no one complained about Amica. The company is a consistent quality leader in California, too.

Such performance is nothing new, nor is it isolated to a few states. When *Consumer Reports* asked its readers about their claims experiences with auto insurance in 1984 and homeowners insurance the following year, it came up with the same customer quality leader both times: Amica. The company earned a "Satisfaction Index" score of 91 out of a possible 100 points in the ratings of companies providing homeowners coverage, including top marks across the board for access, courtesy, clarity of paperwork, fairness of claims settlements, speed of claims handling, and speed of payment. It had a 93 rating for auto claims (because no one gave it a rating below 92 or above 94—how's that for consistency?), including top ratings for customer satisfaction with non-claims service and one of the lowest likelihoods of dropping customers just because they had a claim.

In 1985, *Checkbook*, a consumer magazine in the greater Washington, D.C., area, compiled ratings from nearly eight thousand readers. Tops for claims handling? You guessed it: 94 percent of its policyholders gave Amica "superior" marks for the courtesy and helpfulness of its claims representatives; 87 percent added superior ratings for speed of claims payment as well. On the nonclaims side, 90 percent also gave Amica superior marks for its helpfulness and speed in making the coverage changes they requested.

Amica gets its name from its original monicker, the Automobile Mutual Insurance Company of America. It was founded in Providence, Rhode Island, in 1907 by a businessman named Adolph Vigneron, who figured that a good insurance company, like any other kind of business, could be built on the basis of providing good service to good customers. Consequently, he focused his insurance venture on people whose character provided evidence of prudence and sound judgment.

In the trade, those are called "preferred risks," and lots of companies claim to want them. Unfortunately, to grow larger companies generally have to broaden their coverage umbrella, both in relation to policyholders and in the number of policy products available, and increasing the quantity often erodes the quality. By staying small and personal, and relying on recommendations from existing customers to prequalify new ones, Amica has retained quality control. (After the laudatory *Consumer Reports* mention in 1984, for example, Amica received more than 150 applications. It accepted just 18.)

For the same quality-conscious reason, it hires its own underwriters and adjusters, all of whom are on salary rather than commission, instead of using independent agents. There's no incentive to write coverage that isn't needed, or to push through a policy for a questionable risk. Amica also has stayed out of the commercial underwriting business to keep itself focused on individual policyholders.

When a policyholder has a claim, however, there's nothing little league about the way Amica's internal systems are primed to handle it. With an unusually high ratio of employees to policyholders (1 to 140 in an industry where 1 to 200 or more is typical), Amica answers each day's incoming mail within twenty-four hours and processes inquiries of any kind within three days. Because policyholders have been carefully screened in advance, Amica also jumps in with wholehearted claims service. Usually only one estimate is requested, from a repair facility of the customer's choice, and Amica's published standard is to cut a payment check within twenty-four hours of agreeing with the claimant on the value of the loss.

It takes quality people to make that kind of a system work, and Amica has put a premium on finding and retaining them. Most professionals (underwriters and claims adjusters) are not only college graduates, but B students or better. Amica doesn't go in for sales contests or incentives, but it does pay a bonus to employees who refer a new person to the firm if that new worker proves to be up to the company's standards after a certain amount of time on the job.

Although training gets constant attention, the most powerful dynamic is "almost a form of osmosis," one near-thirty-year veteran of the company told us: "It's just more or less expected that you go the extra mile for the policyholder. When you work in a day-to-day environment that values the customer, you learn to fit yourself in."

For reinforcement and motivation, each issue of the *Amica News* carries its sampling of letters from policyholders commending, usually by name, Amica employees who have made them feel valued, important, satisfied. Letters addressed to the president are read by the president and responded to personally, whether good or bad. The mailbag serves as the informal but no less important soft-sounding into current customer attitudes that other insurers have to commission third-party research firms to provide.

Still, the most visible form of good service may be the one that has arrived each year since 1908. Since Amica is owned by its policyholders, they stand to share in any profits it realizes. Those profits result primarily from collecting more premium dollars than are needed to pay claims and cover expenses, augmented by returns on the company's investments.

Lots of insurance companies do that every year. Most invest the extra revenue, or credit it against the following year's rates. Amica sends its dividends right back where it figures they belong. In 1987, the company kept $13 million in "operating income" and refunded about $80 million to its policyholders. On average, that meant auto policyholders received about 20 percent of their premium dollars back; homeowner's policies paid a 25 percent dividend.

Lately, service managers in other companies, even other industries, have been calling Amica to inquire into the secrets of its people-pleasing success. Most seem to want an "instant coffee" type of solution; a simple, simplistic silver bullet that can do wonders quickly and with relatively little effort or commitment inside their organizations. Invariably those people come away from Amica disappointed. "It took us eighty-one years to get this good," they're told with characteristic New England crispness, "and we have to work hard every day to meet our standards just to stay that good."

More than three quarters of a century after Adolph Vigneron got together a group of Rhode Island businessmen to form the first mutual company to provide automobile insurance, Amica continues to succeed on the basis of his original operating premise: The quality of the policy-holders ultimately determines the quality of the company.

Amica Mutual Insurance Company
10 Weybosset Street
Providence, RI 02940

USAA

USAA

USAA WAS FOUNDED IN 1922 IN A HOTEL IN SAN ANTONIO, TEXAS, TO SERVE A specific type of insurance customer: officers in the U.S. Army whose highly transient lifestyle made them hard to insure as drivers. The twenty-five founders, all active-duty officers, envisioned an organization run by and for themselves that would provide "protection against loss, liability, lawlessness and lengthy litigation," essentially at cost.

Initially membership in the "United States Army Automobile Insurance Association" (which was headquartered in a converted World War I barracks at Kelly Field in San Antonio) was limited to active duty officers in just that branch of the military, but before long other military officers were added to its service jacket. When Major William H. Garrison, USAA's first president, was transferred to Washington, D.C., in 1923, he invited the Commander-in-Chief, President Warren G. Harding, to become the association's "first" member. Harding respectfully declined, but praised the aviation instructor for trying and wished the new venture well. The wish quickly became reality: USAA signed up a thousand members in its first fourteen months.

These days, USAA (which since 1924 has stood for United Services Auto Association) is made up of thirty-six wholly owned subsidiaries and affiliates that provide everything from personal insurance (property, casualty, life, and health) and financial transactions to discount brokerage and travel agency services. Its 1.7 million members have access to buying services for merchandise and automobiles, can book individual or group travel, and can invest in a growing array of mutual funds, money-market funds, partnerships, and annuities. Still, membership is unrestricted in only four areas: Services provided by USAA Life Insurance, USAA Investment Management, the USAA Travel Agency, and USAA Federal Savings Bank are the only ones available to the general public.

Insurance remains USAA's basic reason for being. It is the sixth largest insurer of automobiles (it ranked sixteenth twenty years ago, when Brigadier General Robert F. McDermott, USAF-retired, became president and chairman) and seventh largest provider of homeowners insurance. Its policyholders are drawn predominantly from the ranks of active and retired military officers (nine out of ten active-duty officers are insured by USAA) and their spouses, but also include officers of several federal agencies, including the FBI, the Secret Service, and the National Guard. And its reputation as a top service provider has not gone unremarked by insurance industry observers and customers alike.

In 1985, *Consumer Reports* looked at how more than two hundred thousand of its readers had been treated by the companies that provided their homeowners insurance. "The two top-rated companies—Amica Mutual and . . . USAA—stood out," it reported, repeating the results of a previous study in 1980. "Both netted scores in the low 90's on our 100-point satisfaction scale. The next-best company scored only in the mid-80's." Like Amica, USAA's policyholders gave the association high marks for fairness in reaching claims settlements, and they gave it even higher marks than Amica's policyholders when the subject turned to helpfulness in nonclaims areas. Billing problems were almost unheard of.

The previous year, some three hundred thousand *Consumer Reports* readers had shared their experiences with more than forty auto insurance companies. Again, USAA ranked second only to Amica in general satisfaction—a rating of 91 on a 100-point scale—and, like Amica, was right down at the bottom of the list when it came to frequency of complaints and penchant for dropping policyholders.

The top ratings were echoed on a regional basis in 1986 by consumer magazines in the San Francisco and Washington, D.C., areas, and are all the more noteworthy in light of USAA's relatively streamlined (some might say spartan) operating style.

Most business is conducted through the mail and over the telephone— the association ranks as the nation's fourth largest mail-order company. In keeping with its emphasis on providing service at the lowest cost possible, overhead is kept to a mimimum. Other than headquarters in San Antonio, there are just five regional offices in the U.S. (plus an administrative office that handles credit cards for the USAA Federal Savings Bank) and two in Europe. The association does almost no advertising and has no sales agents in the conventional sense. Instead, it relies on word-of-mouth recommendations from its members to attract new business—and high-quality service to keep them.

Like other insurance companies, USAA has had to adjust to less than boom times in the eighties. To control costs while at the same time improving services, the association has turned to its frontline people to devise better ways to serve customers. Since 1980, USAA employees have contributed—and been recognized for—more than seven thousand ideas designed to help them "Work Smarter, Not Harder."

One committee suggested creating a booklet to describe the claims process to policyholders; it is now routinely sent to those who file a claim, not only resulting in a better-informed customer but also greatly reducing the number of time-consuming calls the claims center receives from people wondering what's happening to their paperwork—which, in turn, results in even speedier claims processing.

Ruben Cortez, a sales rep for USAA's automobile buying service, recommended converting the manual information files on participating auto dealerships to a computerized database; his suggestion saves twelve thousand hours of time per year—which translates to $113,000 annually, according to USAA's figures—while improving the quality of information being provided to customers and shortening the amount of time they have to wait to get it.

USAA also consolidated six regional functions into four, roughly corresponding to time zones, making business hours more convenient throughout the country. As a result of the overall investment in service improvements, the amount of time it takes for service representatives to respond to inquiries from members has been reduced—in some cases by several days—and the average customer transaction is also going through much faster these days.

That hasn't made service any less personal. In San Antonio, specially trained operators and supportive equipment serve hearing-impaired (a not uncommon occupational hazard in the military) customers over special telephone lines. Medical claims specialists have been known to decorate their work areas with pictures sent to them by the people whose cases they handle.

More recently, USAA has begun converting all incoming mail into electronic images that can replace bulging paper files with micro-thin, highly movable computer records. Despite all the promise and power of the fabled Information Age, the sad fact (as businesses of all sizes and descriptions are constantly reminded) is that paper-based information is bulky, messy, fragile, and inefficient. Paper burns. It gets lost or misplaced. It accumulates in file drawers and boxes and folders that are difficult, and often expensive, to circulate or copy.

Electronic data bases, on the other hand, can be preserved, accessed, duplicated, merged, and manipulated in any number of ways in keeping with the needs of both the business and the company. The file that might take someone several minutes, even several days, to find in a filing system can be called up on a screen with a couple of keystrokes, allowing the customer service representative to have immediate and total access to customer records almost at the moment the customer calls. USAA's service-oriented computer initiative may be the prototype for all kinds of customer service functions in the 1990s.

As the initial system is implemented through 1989, incoming and outgoing mail will be run through scanners to transfer the paperwork to computerized bits that become part of the customer's client history. That will allow service representatives to access a customer's complete file, both policy records and correspondence, from terminals anywhere in the USAA system, in the process reducing the amount of time, and perhaps also the number of people, involved in handling a given customer's needs. Research consistently shows that the fewer the number of people who have to be involved in a service transaction to satisfy the customer, the higher the likelihood that it will have a satisfying outcome in the customer's view.

Good service providers always seem to be looking for a way to do what they already do well even better. USAA is just one more case in point.

USAA
USAA Building
San Antonio, TX 78288

WHEELS

AUTOMOTIVE

Acura Automobile Division

Don Beyer Volvo

Longo Toyota

Jiffy Lube International

TRUCKING

Ryder System

Wheaton Van Lives

United Van Lines

NW Transport Service

Wheels: Keeping the Family Chariot, the Castle's Furnishings, and Business's Goods on a Roll

TEN YEARS AGO WE DID A STUDY FOR THE PARTS-AND-SERVICE DIVISION OF A major automobile manufacturer. The question under consideration: "What does the average consumer expect from the service department of their local automobile dealership?" Our answer was hardly earthshaking. The several hundred Flupmobile owners we interviewed and surveyed told us that when their cars were in need of service, whether emergency or routine, they wanted them to be fixed:

- Right the first time: no repeat repairs please.
- On time: the repair finished when the service writer promised it would be.
- For the price quoted: no dollar surprises please.
- And themselves treated with a modicum of respect.

We were pleased with the clarity of the results, delivered the report, were congratulated by the client, put the fee in the bank, and moved on. A few months later we chanced to mention the Flupmobile study to the head of another research group. "Oh, really? Let me guess what you found—right the first time, on time, within the estimate, and the customer wants to be treated with some respect. Is that about it?"

"Yes," we replied slightly dumbfounded. "How did you know?"

"Easy," he answered, "everyone in the business has done a customer satisfaction study for Flup. They seem to believe they can study poor service out of existence."

That tactic apparently hasn't worked for Flupmobile or any other American automobile manufacturer: When a Louis Harris/*Business Week* poll asked adults in households that had purchased a car within the last five years where auto dealerships need to improve most, guess what they found?

"Getting the work right the first time" 60%
"More willing to tell you when you don't
   need something done" 16%
"Keeping within original cost estimate" 14%
"Do better on completing work when promised" 10%

238

But there are several signs that change is occurring. The automobile marketing pendulum, which has swung back and forth between pushing products and providing service, seems to be swinging toward service once again. All segments of the industry are discovering service is the marketing edge that can provide retailers a profit cushion, whatever the dollar's value vs. the yen or OPEC's price-per-barrel.

A revealing statistic: Only 25 percent of American car-buyers will buy the same brand of car next time, even though brand loyalty for other American products is closer to 65 percent. Why? Most industry observers say the difference is largely attributable to poor service.

There is support for the belief that the 25-percent figure doesn't have to be "just the way it is in the auto business." According to TARP's John Goodman, his organization's studies show that the consumer who reports high satisfaction with the quality of service he receives in the drive lane of his local automobile dealership, whether the dealer is selling American, Japanese, Korean, or Martian-made automobiles, also reports having bought two or more cars from that same dealer.

A 1987 Ford Motor Company study had related findings: Of the 850 largest Ford dealers, those in the top 10 percent on customer satisfaction also had a 3-percent edge in auto market share and a 4.5-percent edge in truck market share compared to all other dealers. In addition, Ford dealers who received the "President's Award" for best customer satisfaction ratings in their respective sales and distribution districts had a return on operating investment 30 percent higher than the national average for Ford dealers. The same study found expressed repurchase intentions (a measure of customer loyalty) to be 61 percent higher for customers who rated themselves "very satisfied" with dealer service, compared with customers who rated themselves "very dissatisfied" with dealer service.

Even Asian manufacturers, who have relied on superior quality to sell cars, are investing in service improvements. Mitsubishi Motor Sales of America surveyed car-buyers at large in 1987 and found 36 percent received postsale follow-up, and 12 percent received service follow-up. The company reacted by starting a follow-up program that trains dealer personnel, provides delivery checklists, and invites customers in for thousand-mile checkups. Results in test markets: a 10 percent increase in customer satisfaction and 10 percent improvement in the condition of used cars.

Ironically, customer-satisfaction surveying is becoming a sensitive issue—because of its success. The publicity given the annual J. D. Power and Associates rankings of customer satisfaction has prompted several consumer groups to suggest that the scores be made public to help buyers choose the best dealerships to work with. Manufacturers are reluctant: They say the ratings are an internal management tool, and their value would be destroyed if published. Dealers, for their part, argue that "bad iron" from the manufacturer reflects on the dealership. "If you get bad product from the manufacturer, there is no way the customer will give the dealer good ratings, no matter how perfect the service," Ron Tonkin, who owns fifteen new-car franchises in the Pacific Northwest, argued in a recent *Wall Street Journal* story.

We tend to agree with the dealers and manufacturers—their arguments strike us as rational, reasonable, and logical. Unfortunately, customers tend not to be rational, reasonable, and logical. The perception that not publishing results means there is something to hide from the consumer could grow.

Attacking Service Problems

The industry not only believes in service today, but has data to show that service quality pays in the short and long term. And carmakers listening to the call for service improvement are coaxing their dealers into action. One U.S. manufacturer is urging dealers to create a new post: an independent customer service manager, totally separate from—and equal to—service department management.

Ford tells its service managers that it can prove quality service makes for better sales, and points to dealers who make it happen. At Family Ford of Waterbury, Connecticut, too many customers bringing back just-delivered vehicles for minor repairs was a red flag. President Edward Shaker solved the problem by awarding a fixed-dollar incentive to service personnel at the beginning of each month. The money is held in escrow, and deductions are made if vehicles are brought back within two weeks of delivery. The program has significantly reduced comebacks, says Shaker.

One of the most service-oriented dealers in the country is Sewell Cadillac of Dallas. In the late seventies, knowing it could no longer compete on car quality alone, Sewell implemented a service program to elevate its relationship with customers to a professional status. Among Sewell innovations:

- Nearly 90 percent of employees have incentive bonuses based on service quality.
- Computers track the time required to deliver the car after the customer has paid the bill, with incentives paid for best average delivery time. The program reduces average delivery time from nearly seven minutes to less than three.
- A fleet of 120 loaner cars is available free to new-car customers who have their Cadillacs serviced at Sewell.
- A 50-item questionnaire goes to all service customers covering all aspects of Sewell's service. Service director Phil Dunnet follows through personally on each one.
- Customers are surveyed by telephone, at the cashier, and in

focus groups to find out what they expect, what they want, and how what they get compares.

The results: In spite of economic problems in Texas due to the slump in oil prices, Sewell has retained a sales position among the top dozen Cadillac dealers in the country. Its service facilities, with 116 bays, are second to none.

Better Systems Needed

While the automotive industry is increasing its emphasis on customer service, it still has a long way to go. J. D. Power found that while nearly every new-car dealer, manufacturer, or distributor has some form of follow-up program to track customer satisfaction, they often are not using the information in an effective fashion. For example, customers surveyed by Power say that a personal telephone contact is the most effective follow-up; the majority of dealer follow-up is through the mail, the least effective method.

New-car dealer service will become even more important in the next five years. Because of a growing oversupply of new cars—by 1990 we may see as many as fifteen million vehicles chasing twelve million buyers—a buyer's market is developing. That means lowballing car prices and interest rates will not be enough to lure customers; all manufacturers will be offering the same promotions. The only meaningful difference between dealers will be customer service.

Increasing Aftermarket Competition

That automobile dealers are taking the service quality challenge to heart is attributable to service profit statistics and the brand loyalty that accrues from good service. But it also owes a debt to greatly increased competition for the automobile owner's after-warranty service business. The average age of the American auto grew from 6.6 years in 1980 to 7.5 in 1985, and has leveled out at just under 8 years.

At the same time, the number of full-service, neighborhood filling stations is down from 225,000 in 1972 to 115,000 today (a 49-percent decrease), according to *National Petroleum News*. And the number of automobile and truck dealerships has also fallen, from 36,000 in 1975 to 25,000 today.

Opportunity abhors a vacuum! Ten years ago if your Flupmobile broke down there were three ways to get it fixed: tow it to the Flupmobile dealer, tow it to the local gas station, or tow it home and struggle with it under the big shade tree in your own backyard. Today there exists a plethora of alternatives.

From parts sales to actual service work, mass merchandisers from Sears

and K mart to Firestone and Goodyear have become forces to be reckoned with. Sears has a 40 percent share of the automobile battery aftermarket thanks to the success of the Sears Diehard; it's also a big player in
the replacement business through its Allstate-brand tires, and it hasn't
done badly in the muffler and shock absorber trade either since it got into
the business back in 1936.

There are nearly eight hundred Sears Auto Service Centers nationwide,
and the business is far from saturated, say Sears officials—which could
account for the company's recent acquisition of Western Auto Supply,
adding almost two thousand outlets (fifteen hundred franchised) to the
system. One key to Sears' automotive success: thirty million people
walking around with Sears charge cards in pocket or purse.

K mart is no slouch either. There are auto service centers attached to
seventeen hundred of its stores nationwide, and plans for more. Also in
the business are Avis Rent-a-Car System (planning seventeen hundred
service centers), Texaco, Ashland Oil, and Quaker State.

A growing form of competition is the specialty "fast fix" business: Oil
change in ten minutes, brake jobs in fifteen minutes, mufflers in twenty, a
complete tune-up in under thirty minutes. Drive in/drive out service is the
norm. Chicago-based Midas International, one of the earliest of the
"McAuto" operations, does about $800 million dollars worth of rapid
"under car" repairs—muffler replacement, brake repair, shock and strut
work, and realignment—out of seventeen hundred domestic and two
thousand worldwide stores.

The newer generation of aftermarket service specialists owe more to
fast-food franchises than the legendary corner garage. More than a dozen
major systems are growing around the country, some specializing (oil
changes, transmission work, glass repair), others targeting a wider range
of fast, uncomplicated repairs and preventive maintenance. The number
of quick-lube outlets alone is expected to reach five thousand by 1990 and
account for nearly 12 percent of the $7.7 billion oil-change business.

With all this quick stop-and-shop service finding increasing customer
acceptance, the next step was probably inevitable. The newest wrinkle in
the auto service business is the "Auto Mall," an attempt to combine fast
and cheap with full service by grouping a collection of McAuto outlets,
typically with an auto parts store thrown in as an "anchor" to attract the
do-it-yourselfer. A 1987 story in USA Today reported two hundred such
auto malls in business already, with some auto aftermarket specialists
predicting two thousand by 1990.

One thing is certain: The service revolution has come to the automobile
industry. Gone are the Gomer Pyles and greasy, ramshackle garages.
Today's auto service center, whether it's in a dealership, a department
store, a specialty shop, or a specialty mall, features spiffy-looking technicians, lots of computer-based gear, and gleaming waiting areas designed

to offer customers comfort and diversion while the family chariot gets life-sustaining attention. Whether the name over the service bays is Precision Tune or Jiffy Lube, Midas or Car-X, Firestone or Goodyear, Sears or K mart, or even Joe's Garage, that hum you hear is an entire industry tuning up its act.

After years of treating service as the back door of the dealership and an aftermarket stepchild, fixing what's broken—and being easy to do business with in the process—has become a major, if not *the* driving force of the industry.

Bigger Wheels, Bigger Problems

There are supposed to be some fairly immutable laws of business economics. They are what give us all hope for the future, as in: "If we can just get the per unit cost down, we're gonna make a bundle." One of the more general of these is the law of supply and demand. When demand goes *up* and supply goes *down*, then prices are supposed to rise. Like strawberries in the winter. The same is supposed to work when the arrows are reversed. Except in the trucking industry—and most dramatically in that special subset of the trucking industry known as HHG, the *household goods* moving segment.

Thirty-eight million, or approximately one in five of us, move from one address to another every year. Why? To keep the real estate agents in business, of course. And about half of that thirty-eight million do their moving between June and September. As anyone who has gone through the household shuffle in the last five years can tell you, if you haven't contracted your move by May, you're in deep sandworms.

So, of course, June, July, August, and September are the months when you can get the *lowest* rates on moving services. The more work available, the greater the discounting that goes on in the industry. Go figure!

Industry observers blame these crazy economics on deregulation: the fact that since the 1980 passage of the Motor Carrier and Household Goods acts, van lines have been more or less free to compete on price and make marketplace innovations on a broader scale than ever before. For the first few years following deregulation, competition meant price-cutting, with discounts reaching as far down as 40 percent of previous, regulated tariffs.

Discounting, say industry experts, reached its zenith about 1985, when, according to the Household Goods Carriers' Bureau, net income from the nation's top moving companies dropped 17 percent. A study conducted by *Traffic Management* magazine in 1987 put the average corporate discount, the price corporations pay for employee relocation moves, in the 25 to 35 percent range, a level Charles C. Irions, president of the American Moving Congress, says provides "a relatively small return on investment."

Predictably, consolidations, buyouts, takeovers, and even bankruptcies have resulted from years of paper-thin earnings. With most of the suicidal price competition bottoming out, the focus has turned to diversification—and improved service.

Nearly all the major household goods carriers now operate separate special products divisions that regularly engage in moving computers and delicate electronic gear, museum and trade show exhibits, art collections, medical equipment such as CAT scanners, computerized machine tools and robotics, and defense systems. It's a good match. The air-ride equipment and crew skill needed to get Aunt Martha's wedding plate and junior's aquarium from Los Angeles to Memphis intact is the same equipment and skill it takes to move a million dollars' worth of telephone switching equipment from factory to field, also intact.

Today, industrywide shipments of nonhousehold goods accounts for 25 percent of HHG fleet business. Burnham Van Services of Burnham, Georgia, reports 70 percent of its revenue from moving electronics, high-value items, and trade show gear, and records one of the lowest operating ratios in the trucking industry.

But one of the discoveries made by companies trying these new market initiatives has been the need to learn to work under new constraints. As one industry insider flatly admits, "It's different than moving furniture. You get your load of households to the new place a day late—so what? Get an IBM exhibit to a trade show a day late and you never work in that business again."

It is an attitude founded on justifiable fear. In 1985, over 40 percent of the complaints received by the Interstate Commerce Commission about regulated carriers concerned late pickups and deliveries, loss and damage, and overcharges by HHG carriers—this while HHG carriers account for only 5 percent of the trucking business nationwide.

At the same time, a few organizations have chosen to focus more tightly on the traditional HHG trade, moving furniture and family goods. These too have found that service innovation and increased niche-marketing has a payoff. Typical is a relocation package called "Connection for Lifestyle Relocation" from a Bekins Van Lines affiliate. It offers financial services, house-hunting help, job-hunting assistance for the spouse, and discounts on hotels and airfares.

United Van Lines will hand-hold a family through every step from packing the china and compiling the tax records to smoothing the move for children and pets and finding the gas and phone company in the new city. Allied Van Lines has an "On Time Pledge" that pays inconvenienced customers $125 for every day delivery is late. And a number of movers have automated their claims process to make the once eternal wait for adjustment a same-week certainty.

Service over the Long Haul

But it isn't only the HHG segment of the trucking industry that has felt the winds of deregulation. Over-the-road freight truckers have had to learn to live in a deregulated environment as well. And after the inevitable rounds of competing through price-cutting and efficiency, the bull haulers and steel movers have discovered service, too.

Reviewing the carnage and evaluating the health of the survivors, *Purchasing* magazine's economics editor, J. William Semich, pointed to a single factor that separated the quick from the dead: "What makes for a survivor in the new deregulated trucking industry? In a word, S-E-R-V-I-C-E."

James W. Lynn, director of marketing for P-I-E Nationwide, the country's largest less-than-truckload (LTL) carrier, agrees with Semich's assessment. "We all understand free market pricing at this point," he told Semich, adding that "buyers have a lot of options. To attract the attention of those buyers, carriers must differentiate the value of their service."

Practicing just that, P-I-E, which had some very shaky years immediately after deregulation, returned to financial health in 1986 on the basis of segmentation and a showering of attention on the information needs of the large shippers it considers its primary market. It was the first to create computer tracking of loads across its entire system and has introduced a PC-based software system for shippers that allows even small customers to generate bills-of-lading, assign carrier and freight bill numbers, and track the status of in-transit shipments.

Other carriers are employing technology to improve service performance. Geostar Corporation of Washington, D.C., and Omninet Corporation of Los Angeles have recently introduced satellite tracking systems that allow dispatchers to see where their trucks are instantly, twenty-four hours a day. An expensive gimmick? Not if you're trying to move parts from one side of the country to the other to meet a manufacturer's just-in-time schedule, or are trucking Defense Department goodies or high-value items, or are interested in knowing where and when a rig goes out of service, or breaks down, or gets delayed en route.

On the other end of the spectrum, NW Transport Service of Colorado enhances its investment in technology with the oldest resource in the business book: people. It runs sleeper cabs with two-driver crews so the loads never have to stop rolling between terminal points. And it lays out terminals, and trains and tracks their crews, to minimize the amount of time goods are off the road while in transit and reduce the number of times they are handled before delivery.

Its service-tracking figures also credit deliveries made ahead of schedule, just as they debit for lateness—and NW Transport regularly wows customers by providing better than 100-percent performance. Time, in the cartage business, is money, big money; knowing how it is being spent and getting the best return as it is spent are both critical to staying in business.

But good service is more than high-tech tracking, user-friendly information systems, and state-of-the-art rolling stock. A couple of years ago, Chemical Leaman Tank Lines, a bulk chemical carrier based in Lineville, Pennsylvania, learned through a series of focus groups that customers have a broad view of what it takes to create exceptional customer service.

According to *Modern Bulk Transporter* magazine, Leaman learned that customers top priorities included: on-time pickup and delivery; the availability, condition, and cleanliness of equipment; good communications, especially about shipment progress; a good safety record as well as driver competence; and self-monitoring through an internal quality-assurance program. In addition, the company learned that customers were "willing to trade off lower rates in exchange for exceptional quality service."

Service on a Roll

In the pages that follow, we profile eight companies: four from the automotive side of what we've termed the Wheels business, four from the trucking segment. Among the latter, Ryder Systems may be the most surprising, if only because most people know it as a renter of busy little yellow trucks rather than for the diversified service firm it has become.

Two of our truckers provide different forms of distinctive service within the household goods segment. Both Wheaton Van Lines and United Van Lines are found toward the end of the alphabetical listings of companies in the industry, but at the top whenever the customers get to vote on who serves them well. Representing the over-the-road segment is NW Transport: It may not rival P-I-E, Yellow Freight, Roadway, or Consolidated Freightways for size or dollar volume, but when it comes to service precision, it leaves everyone else in the dust.

We begin with the smaller vehicles out there on the road—one automobile manufacturer, two service-centered dealers, and a quick-change artist. The maker, Honda's Acura Automobile Division, is off to the kind of new-business launch that business school students will someday be studying in Service 101, whether the course is being taught in English or Japanese. Honda planned it well, positioned it smartly, selected dealers with an eye toward quality, then stocked those brand new showrooms with good product.

Don Beyer Volvo and Longo Toyota showcase service-focused strategies and tactics as different and varied as their East and West Coast markets. And Jiffy Lube is a good example of the fast-growing, people-pleasing businesses carving out a new niche in the automotive field by marketing service as convenience and preventive maintenance rather than as something to be postponed until things are going clunk under the hood.

We hope you enjoy the ride.

ACURA

WHEN YOU START FROM THE BEST YOU'VE GOT, SOMETHING GOOD SHOULD HAPPEN. In the case of the Acura Automobile Division of American Honda Motor Company, it did. And right away. Through a well-conceived strategy of combining outstanding dealers and excellent products, Acura has quickly become a name that pops up with increasing frequency whenever Americans start talking cars.

Formed in 1986 to handle a new, upscale line of Honda-built automobiles (initially just two models, the Integra and the Legend, with a sports car due to be added by 1990), Acura's network of U.S. dealers already has established itself as a rising new service star. The 1987 Power Report, the annual automotive industry rankings compiled by J. D. Power and Associates, put Acura dealers at the top of the list for customer satisfaction, primarily due to their unparalleled attention to the "people service factor." Proving its success wasn't a fluke, Acura topped the Power rankings in 1988 as well.

Power wasn't the only knowledgeable industry observer to be impressed by Acura's debut. The Legend Coupe was *Motor Trend's* 1987 Import Car of the Year; the Integra was second. The top two names on *Car and Driver's* 1988 Ten Best Cars list, chosen from among thirty cars with base prices under $35,000, just happen to be Integra and Legend, too. (In all, Honda made five of 1988's top ten—the Accord, Civic, and CRX are the other three; Ford's Mustang and Taurus, Chevy's Corvette, and the Audi 5000 and Saab 9000 round out the list.) And *Road and Track* called the Legend coupe one of the ten best cars in the world, regardless of price or nationality.

Acura's first-round success isn't an accident. Beginning in the early 1980s, it was planned and plotted at American Honda's headquarters in Gardena, California, then executed by dealers determined to take utmost advantage of a rare chance to make a new first impression on a jaded car-buying public.

American Honda carefully chose the initial network of 150 dealers from among Honda's best performers coast to coast. There are now close to 350 (compared to 900 Honda dealers in the U.S.), and as many as 600 Acura showrooms may be open for business by the mid-1990s, providing production can keep pace with demand. Significantly, more than half of the base of current dealers not only own Honda franchises, but also other luxury-car dealerships (18 percent operate Cadillac showrooms, another third are evenly split among Volvo, BMW, and Mercedes-Benz). Along with their familiarity with Honda's product quality, they brought to the new dealer network experience gained serving their own demanding luxury-car clientele.

But experience was only part of the planning package. To help establish a high-quality image for the new nameplate, American Honda's service-centered strategy called for creating a visible difference between Acura and its competitors, whether foreign or domestic. Accordingly, it mandated that each new dealer would have to establish a separate Acura showroom and service center—an investment of as much as $3 million in some cases—several miles away from its existing Honda dealership. The importance of making a significant investment in topnotch people as well as facilities was ingrained in Acura dealers from the time they started looking for land and thinking about a new letterhead. Acura was to stake out its turf based on Service (with a capital S) to those car-buyers willing to take a chance on an unproven brand: discriminating, upscale customers who would come looking for value instead of Honda's traditional no-and low-frills economy. From the outset, American Honda wanted the Legend and Integra to compete with supercoupes and sporty sedans, not Civics.

Acura's dealers got the service message loud and clear. As measured by J. D. Power, so did their customers. Power's widely quoted CSI (Customer Satisfaction Index) scores are determined by averaging two separate indexes—one measuring people service factors, the other technical service factors. In Acura's first year, its people-service score blew away perennial leader Mercedes-Benz 186 to 177 and outpolled its Honda cousins (who finished second on the overall CSI) by 54 points. On the technical service side, Acura also outshone Mercedes, 106 to 77, though a number of competitors (including Honda, tech-service pacesetter Toyota, Nissan, Mazda, Subaru, and a lone American, Plymouth) posted better scores on that ratings scale.

In its first year, Power concluded, Acura had established itself as a new nameplate "which has found a way to combine Japanese product quality with the finesse of European dealer servicing." The distinctions are significant, since Power's ratings show that Asian carmakers typically perform best on measures of technical service, while dealers representing European manufacturers usually get the best marks for people service. (American manufacturers, alas, perennially fail to distinguish themselves on either measure.)

Acura's high marks are essentially stateless. For example, Power noted, "in the critical willingness of the owners to recommend their dealership service departments, the proportion of Acura owners who 'definitely would' recommend their service department is 30 percentage points above the Asian average, 24 percentage points greater than the Honda average and nearly 10 percentage points more than that of Mercedes-Benz owners. These are happy owners!"

That's the plan. Included in the new dealership network from day one was Acura's own customer research and feedback system that evaluates (and, for the top performers, rewards) sales and service departments on a handful of pointed questions asked of new Acura owners. On the sales side, there are four key questions, starting with whether the new owner was "invited" to take a test drive. Owners also are asked how satisfied they were with their salesperson, how satisfied they were with the way their new car was delivered, and whether someone followed up after the sale to "review [their] satisfaction."

On the service department side, there are only three key questions: How satisfied were you by the delivery condition of your new Acura automobile? If you had a problem, was it fixed promptly? If you had a problem, was it fixed to your satisfaction?

Responses are tracked month by month and year-to-date. Dealers and their department managers know how they're doing with their own customers, within their districts and zones, and against norms nationwide. If they're doing well, Acura's Dealer Recognition Program makes sure they are rewarded. And handsomely. In 1987, the owners of the top fifteen dealerships were presented with a handcrafted, limited-edition crystal sculpture commissioned by Acura from world-renowned Orrefors of Stockholm. Each one is numbered and signed by the artist. To emphasize their value, only fifteen were created, which means there aren't any extras sitting in executives' offices out at American Honda headquarters. You only get one of these for being very, very good. Meanwhile, the fifteen top-performing salespersons, sales managers, service managers, and parts managers received gold signet-style rings—with room for up to three diamonds to be added if they win again in the years to come.

Although new to America's highly competitive auto wars, Acura's fast start shouldn't be that surprising. Its parent, Honda, has been a consistent people-pleaser since it entered the U.S. market in 1971. Once known for sturdy little econo-boxes like the Civic (the Volkswagen Beetle of the 1970s), Honda now accommodates every taste. Its top-of-the-line Acura Legend Coupe, developed in collaboration with Great Britain's Austin Rover Group, commands prices up around $30,000; the simple Civic is still rolling off showroom floors for under $7,000.

Many of its cars are assembled right here in the U.S. in the model automobile production plant Honda built in 1982 at Marysville, Ohio, next door to a 1977-vintage motorcycle assembly plant. A second auto assembly plant is under construction just down the road, and eventually Acura models may be produced domestically.

Honda's U.S. success threatens a lot of instinctive perceptions and prejudices. It now sells more cars in the U.S. than it does in Japan, and expects to be exporting as many as seventy thousand made-in-the-U.S.A. vehicles a year by 1991 (a significant percentage of them outbound to Japan). On the dealer side, Honda now ranks fourth in U.S. passenger car sales, and it's conceivable it could overtake third-ranked Chrysler by the nineties. Some observers have suggested such dynamic success gives the lie to the mournful chant that "U.S.-based" carmakers can't compete by world standards anymore.

Noting that Acura's winning edge in America clearly comes from its dealers, Power, for one, projects an interesting future: "With a product line that appears to be meeting luxury-buyer expectations, Acura's image will soon match that of its more-established European rivals." And even though Acura dealers currently have to import their offerings, the Honda connection, in both Japan and the United States, bodes well for service-conscious car-buyers.

Acura Automobile Division
American Honda Motor Co., Inc.
100 West Alondra Blvd.
Gardena, CA 90247

Don Beyer Volvo

IN 1987, DON BEYER, JR., PRESIDENT OF DON BEYER VOLVO OF FALLS CHURCH, Virginia, made a big impression on his fellow automobile dealers. As recorded by the magazine *Automotive Executive*, while conducting a workshop on customer care at the annual convention of the National Automobile Dealers Association, Beyer rattled off a succession of people-pleasing practices that, in his firsthand analysis, seem to account for a lot of the success of his thriving dealership in Washington, D.C.'s, Virginia suburbs. Where some dealers concentrate on rolling up sales volume, Beyer Volvo works the back door to the showroom: the service department. And far from costing money, the tactic has made both the service department and the dealership overall more profitable than ever.

The typical member of the "Auto Age 500," the sales-based ranking of America's five hundred largest car dealerships compiled by *Auto Age*, generates 12 percent of its annual revenue from after-sale service. At Beyer Volvo, the figure is closer to 30 percent, and Beyer has convincing evidence that satisfied service customers will keep traffic moving for new cars, too—more than 80 percent of 1987 sales were to people who were either previous customers of the dealership or had heard about Beyer Volvo from another satisfied customer.

It shouldn't be surprising, then, to learn that since Volvo initiated its Dealer of Excellence Awards in 1981, Beyer Volvo, a second-generation family business that Don and his brother, Mike, bought from their parents a few years back, has been named among the Scandinavian manufacturer's U.S. elite not once, but every year.

The high satisfaction, and high revenue, figures result from a combination of practices, noted *Automotive Executive*. To begin with, Beyer Volvo's mechanics are all on salary, as opposed to the common industry practice of paying them a flat-rate hourly wage based on the amount of time they actually spend doing repairs.

According to Don Beyer, it's more than a matter of encouraging professionalism in a field that hasn't been known for taking a great deal of pride in itself. Being on salary—the rate was initially set slightly above

252

what each mechanic was making on the flat-rate scale—means there's no incentive to run up time charges, and no objection to coming out from under the hood to talk to customers, or take them on test drives to check repairs, or train apprentices (which is mostly what Beyer Volvo hires these days, since there's almost no turnover among more senior mechanics). As an added incentive, each month the top mechanics—as determined by work quality—can pocket the keys to a $40,000 Volvo 780, which becomes theirs for the next thirty days.

Taking a page from the showroom side, exit test drives are now just as much a given for repairs as they are for new car sales. When the customer comes in to pick up the vehicle, the mechanic (or another service representative if the mechanic has gone off duty) climbs in and off they go to make sure the rattle or thump or slipping or whatever is truly gone. A night shift works service orders until three A.M., so if something was left undone a mechanic will get right on it.

What's more, Beyer keeps more than half a dozen people on duty until eight in the evening so daytime commuters can get home and get their cars without having to leave work early or skip supper. To further tidy up the loose ends, a full-time limousine is available to run customers to and from nearby mass-transit stations during rush hour in the nation's capital; off-hours during the day, the limo will take the customer directly to work or home if need be.

To build the overall skills level of its service staff, Beyer Volvo has employed a full-time service trainer since 1982. The job includes drawing up individual training plans for every technician in the department. In addition to back-shop support, the trainer also conducts free classes for customers, including special sessions for women, owners of diesel-engine Volvo models, and buffs who want to know more about their turbochargers. The response has been so positive that Beyer Volvo salespeople have taken to showing off the training classroom as a regular part of their pitch to prospective new- and used-car buyers.

Nothing is more aggravating to a car owner than having to bring back a car again and again for the same problem. Beyer Volvo puts special emphasis on minimizing repeat repairs. Service writers make a point of asking if anything on the repair order is a repeater. The full-time customer relations representative who calls each service customer two days after his or her car is returned has three questions to ask: Was the repair work satisfactory? Was any of the work a repeat repair? And would the customer recommend Beyer Volvo's service department to others? (Knowing that some people are more comfortable responding on paper than speaking with someone on the phone, the personal letter and return questionnaire that arrives a few days later ask the same three questions.)

Since the service department started pinpointing the problem, the incidence of repeating the same work has been greatly reduced. Still,

Beyer knows that inevitably there will be some dissatisfied customers. For them, there's a special response: the Beyer Volvo Consumer Advisory Board. It's made up of forty-five customers chosen for their ability to provide critical (and valuable) input into the dealership's operations. The board meets quarterly with Beyer and key managers from the dealership, with typical meetings starting over dinner and lasting up to three hours. Discussion ranges freely over any number of consumer issues. Beyer and his people are there mostly to listen and to make note of practical recommendations.

One recommendation that has become standard operating procedure is Beyer Volvo's guarantee of the lowest prices on "genuine" Volvo parts in the metropolitan Washington area. If a customer finds a cheaper price, he gets double his money back. That's happened a grand total of twice—both times due to computer errors in the parts and service data base. Beyer paid up anyway.

Beyer Volvo also makes a point of running an "open" dealership, so much so that any customers who want to are free to spend a day in the Falls Church showroom, during which time the only thing they will not have access to is employee personnel and payroll records. Lunch is on Beyer. Some fifty people have actually spent all or part of a day poking around the place as a result of the offer—and Beyer says another five hundred have called over the years to tell him what a good idea they think it is.

And then there's the goodwill budget. Each year, Beyer Volvo commits about half a million dollars to advertising. It also has allocated as much as one hundred thousand dollars annually to the service department under the heading of "goodwill." There's only one prerequisite: The money has to be spent. And it is—for everything from complimentary car washes to free or reduced repairs when a complaint is decided in a customer's favor.

To keep owners of older models coming back—a noteworthy concern, given the notorious reliability and longevity of Volvos—there's a 100,000-mile club and a 200,000-mile club, with repair discounts of 10 and 15 percent respectively for members. It's not done just to make customers feel good; Beyer figures it brings in repair work that otherwise would go elsewhere, and keeps customers with a marked penchant for not buying a new car aware of the dealership until the day arrives when they're at last ready for a change.

Enough? Not yet. Borrowing from the car rental business, Beyer Volvo offers hurried customers "express" check-in and check-out. Customers can have their service orders prewritten over the phone so they need only "toss their keys on the counter" when they bring the car in. If they've left a credit card in the morning, they can sign off and leave when they come back for their car without ever having to wait for a cashier.

There's also a "My Mechanic" program. This one owes its start to an article on automotive service in which the writer noted that any time someone talks about "my mechanic," it's a lead-pipe cinch that their work is being done someplace other than in a dealership. To become an exception, Beyer Volvo assigns its service customers their own personal mechanic who will work on their car whenever it's in the shop. Every few months, the Beyers throw a "mixer" where customers and their mechanics can meet and mingle over coffee and pie.

Staying in touch with customers also applies to the sales showroom. For four and a half years after a sale, customers can expect a quarterly phone call from their sales representative. They'll be asked how the car is running. They'll be queried about any service problems. They'll be invited to drop by someday soon if they'd like a look at the new Volvos in stock. Their answers will be reviewed for valuable market intelligence and clues to developing problems that can be nipped in the bud.

As Beyer, an unabashed disciple of quality guru Phil Crosby, told *Automotive Executive*, "Quality is free. Any cost associated with improving the quality of our service department will more than flow back to us in increased revenue and increased gross profit."

Don Beyer Volvo
1231 West Broad Street
Falls Church, VA 22046

Longo Toyota

LONGO ≡≡≡
A PENSKE COMPANY
TOYOTA

THE LATE DOMINIC LONGO STARTED HIS TOYOTA DEALERSHIP IN 1963, SETTING up shop in a converted service station in El Monte, California, just east of Los Angeles along the San Bernardino Freeway. As the business grew in import-happy Southern California, Longo would occasionally be asked why he didn't branch out, selling a few thousand units each through maybe half a dozen different locations instead of putting all of his eggs in a single basket at just one freeway off-ramp. The answer was invariably that he couldn't be six places at the same time.

"His was a hands-on operation," recalled Joseph Crown, publisher of *Auto Age* magazine, in a combination editorial and eulogy in December 1987, shortly after Longo's death. "No one screened his calls—he talked directly to anybody who asked for him. He set strict guidelines for his staff that ensured customer satisfaction long before anyone heard of CSI (the Customer Satisfaction Index compiled annually for the automotive industry by J. D. Power and Associates). Dom Longo's reaction to leading the *Auto Age* 500 probably would have been, 'I'm just doing what I like to do best.' "

That he did it well is evidenced by the fact that the business he founded, Longo Toyota, was indeed listed at the top of *Auto Age's* first-ever ranking of the nation's five hundred largest automobile dealerships. In 1987 alone, Longo Toyota sold more than 14,500 new cars worth some $194 million. By comparison, the 1986 new-car volume average for all five hundred superdealers—the largest dealers in the country, remember—was "just" 2,555. In twenty-five years, more than 150,000 southern Californians have bought cars from the dealership. A major factor in Longo's sales numbers: About 60 percent of its volume comes from repeat and referral business—satisfied customers and their friends who keep coming back to El Monte.

The steady growth has moved the business from its first location in an abandoned gas station to a three-acre site, and now to a sprawling twenty-two-acre parcel about a mile closer to the freeway. Parked all over the lot is some $14 million of inventory; over in the service area, 105 bays and a 30-bay body shop are staffed with two shifts to provide after-sale (and after-accident) service from seven in the morning to ten at night.

The sales side of the operation is open from eight A.M. until "close," according to general manager John Clark. Close is whenever customers stop coming in—in car-crazy California, the lights often are still on at two o'clock in the morning. Salespeople are carefully selected and trained. The showroom is furnished with conference tables to handle the various deals being discussed. Three people are assigned full-time to making follow-up calls, assessing customer satisfaction, and trouble-shooting sales and service glitches before they become full-blown problems. Buy a car from Longo Toyota, and within forty-eight hours you can expect a call to make sure you were treated properly, got the car in top condition, and have no problems or lingering dissatisfaction.

Should a problem arise, the dealership's three-person customer relations team enters the fray. Its members have the authority to spend up to five hundred dollars to resolve a customer's gripe (problems that would cost more than that to solve are referred to Clark), which means that scratched paint gets touched up without an argument and other minor glitches are taken care of before they can fester into lingering bad feelings. After all, if you're going to spend several thousand dollars on an automobile, why go back to a dealership that begrudged you a few bucks or a few minutes to make sure you drove away satisfied?

Among the customers who come in every day, there's likely to be a mystery shopper or two. Longo Toyota commissions thirty mystery shops a month and receives an objective rating on everything from the way the telephone is answered to the sales tactics employed on the lot. If a bad report comes in on a salesperson, he's counseled on it—regardless of the volume of business he's generating for the dealership. If the problem is serious or persistent, it's written up and placed in the individual's personnel file.

Among the things that sets Longo Toyota apart is the physical setting in which you negotiate: Instead of claustrophobic little cubicles where you're trapped and isolated while a salesperson and an often invisible manager work to get you to sign on the dotted line, the Longo showroom looks like an oversized cross between a giant's dinette and a church social hall. Tables are set up out in the open, and that's where the deal gets talked and closed. It was like that in the old showroom, and it's like that in the new location, too.

Given that predeliction for fair play, it's predictable that "bait-and-switch," a hallowed auto industry tactic, is a no-no at Longo. "We never advertise price," Clark told us. In the Longo view of the business, it just creates alienation when a customer drawn in by a seductive price arrives only to find that the advertised special was a one-of-a-kind, and, oh golly, it just got sold not fifteen minutes ago. "We have the largest inventory of any dealer anywhere," says Clark. "If you can't find it at Longo, chances are nobody has it."

Not that people can't look around if they've a mind to. In Southern California alone, there are more than 1,000 automobile dealerships— including 77 other Toyota showrooms. Of the *Auto Age* 500, 54 operate in the Los Angeles and Orange County area—including 16 other Toyota dealers—so all those customers didn't drive to El Monte because it was the only game in town. They came, and keep coming back, because they got what they wanted from Dom Longo.

That it's a Toyota dealership they come into is in some ways ironic. Longo was a fight promoter before signing on as a salesman at the Los Angeles Ford dealership owned by Ben Alexander, Jack Webb's former *Dragnet* co-star. His ambition was to save up enough money to buy his own Ford store, but the forty-thousand-dollar bankroll he'd accumulated by the early sixties just wasn't enough for a big-name brand. When Toyota started planning a beachhead on the West Coast, Longo signed up.

Dom Longo's concern for his customers didn't slip as the business grew ever larger. On the evidence of the dealership's sales volume, his concern for the way his customers were treated was basic to that growth. Longo Toyota is now owned by Penske Corporation, the automotive company founded by former race-car driver Roger Penske, but the principles of the business continue to be the ones laid down by the founder.

The success of a company that has been known to send a team of people to a customer's house to wash and wax a car in response to a complaint of a greasy fingerprint left on the dashboard after an oil-change shows how well a top-down commitment to customer service and satisfaction can pay off.

Longo Toyota
3534 North Peck Road
El Monte, CA 91731

Jiffy Lube International

SOMETIMES THE SIMPLEST TYPES OF SERVICE CAN PROVIDE MAJOR NEW BUSI-ness opportunities. Consider changing the oil and oil filter in your car. It's a relatively simple task. It doesn't take long to do. It's good for your car, a simple form of preventive maintenance for what is increasingly a five-figure investment. But it's a nuisance job. And it's messy. There are lots of things you could be doing instead of crawling around under your car and getting your fingers all gooey and black. Face it: While more than 40 percent of all oil changes are do-it-yourself jobs, you yourself just don't want to do it.

That's perfectly all right with W. J. (Jim) Hindman, a volunteer foot-ball coach and founder of Jiffy Lube International, the country's largest and fastest-growing quick-change artist. In less than ten years, Hindman has led his folksy "J-team" to the dominant position in the Grease Bowl competition. With nearly twelve hundred corporate and franchised out-lets coast to coast (and plans to have fifteen hundred in the game by the early 1990s), plus a cooperative marketing agreement with Pennzoil that helps fund continuing growth, Jiffy Lube continues to prove there's still money to be made in the oil business.

The core service is simple: Open the drain plug, drain the oil, close the plug, pour in a few quarts of fresh stuff, twist off the filter ring, replace the filter, tighten the ring, clean up the mess, and send the customer on his or her merry way. Gas stations and garages have been doing that for generations, usually requiring you to leave your car with them for the better part of a day in the process and run the risk when you come back that there'll be grease on the seats as well as the joints, or a whole raft of newly discovered "problems" you might need to get fixed.

Jiffy Lube and the other entrants in the quick-lube field have repack-aged the basic part of that service to make it as convenient and acceptable as running the family chariot through a car wash. In fact, that's exactly what you do when you drive out of many Jiffy Lube service bays—more than 30 percent provide a complimentary car wash, the rest wash the outside of the windows and vacuum the insides, to make sure the visible parts are as fresh as the inner workings.

The company's service standard sounds like a productive gridiron offense: fourteen points in ten minutes, no appointment necessary. In addition to the oil and filter, Jiffy Lube will lubricate the chassis and check the other systems motorists usually can't be bothered to mess with: transmission, differential, brake, and windshield washer fluids; tire pressure; and air filter. Add-on services range from changing transmission and differential fluid to flushing radiators and recharging the air conditioner. The work is done while you wait (which means you can watch if you want to), and when it's done you get your car back right away and can get back about *your* business.

At Jiffy Lube, the work is done while paying strict attention to customer perceptions. The company's managers work constantly to avoid the "grease monkey" image (which is not to cast aspersions on the well-regarded quick-lube chain that operates under that name). Any part of the car that is touched, from seats to door handles to grillwork, is either covered first or wiped off afterward. Technicians pay close attention to cleanliness, from the floor and furniture in the customer waiting lounge to the look of the service bays and the uniformed personnel working in them.

What makes this standard service package into a unique corporate culture is the involvement of Hindman, a self-made millionaire with a weakness for pigskin. During the late seventies, Hindman's nonbusiness time was being spent as the football coach at Western Maryland College, where he turned a team with a 2-6-1 record in 1977 into a small-school powerhouse that won 19, lost 1, and tied 7 games over the next three years. Not only did Hindman return his salary to the school during those years, he also dug into his own pockets to buy team equipment and fund scholarships. One day, one of his more skeptical players scoffed at his stock (if personally valid) "anyone can make a million" viewpoint, so he started looking for a way to do it again.

A former hospital administrator (at one time he was director of medical administration at the Kennedy Space Center) and developer of nursing homes in Maryland and the Midwest, Hindman and several partners were looking around without much luck for new worlds to conquer when a friend noticed the start-up and tentative growth of small oil-change businesses out west. Essentially a piece of fallout from the oil crisis of the mid-1970s that had turned more than half of the country's full-service gas stations into self-service outposts, flower shops, and pizza stores, or vacant lots in the ensuing ten years, the new business didn't need a marching band for Hindman to see the potential.

In 1979, Hindman's group purchased the original Jiffy Lube organization—then eight units, including three franchisees, in and around Salt

Lake City—from local businessman Ed Washburn. They moved the base of operations back home to Baltimore a few months later. In the next six years, as the company's service became better known and its reputation more widely recognized, five hundred new outlets opened for business or were acquired through conversion of smaller chain and independent locations.

There's good marketing judgment as well as entreprenuerial zest at work here. Jiffy Lube selects sites with a lot more attention to being easy to do business with than was ever given to a corner service station. It looks for high-traffic counts in a high-density business area (so customers can slip in over a lunch hour or on the way to or from work or shopping), but conveniently close to residential neighborhoods (a minimum of twenty thousand cars registered within a three-mile radius). Volume is important: the typical three-bay Jiffy Lube can handle eighty-five to more than a hundred cars in a day. It must handle at least thirty a day to break even; forty-five to fifty is about average, and sixty-five is viewed as the new target.

Consequently, work flow is carefully systematized for a three-person crew—one in the common bay area below the service lanes, two above (the second often doing double duty by playing on two teams). The crew member in the bay drains the old oil and lubes the chassis. At ground level, one teammate works under the hood, checking and adding fluid in a motion-economizing semicircle from right rear forward, then back to left rear. Meanwhile, number three checks tire pressures and wiper blades, and does the courtesy cleaning. There's also a shop manager to greet customers, write up orders, and handle payments.

Little customer-oriented touches are built in. Instead of the paper label garages paste inside the door frame, Jiffy Lube uses a see-through sticker that is applied to the upper left corner of the windshield where it will serve as a handy but inconspicuous reminder of the last service date (and mileage) and the next points where a change is recommended. To accommodate more than a thousand local, regional, and national fleet and business customers, the company has a national account system that allows the drivers of courier vans, delivery trucks, cabs, and service vehicles to pull into any Jiffy Lube location, not just the one closest to the company office. Although such accounts make up less than ten percent of the company's business overall, in some areas fleet business accounts for more than a third of the vehicles serviced.

Despite rapid growth in a competitive field, Jiffy Lube has managed to keep on top of quality concerns. Training courses for technicians, managers, and franchisees cover everything from proper service techniques to market analysis and personnel management. Regional managers are expected to be out in the field every day, checking locations in their territory to make sure the standards for everything from the service to the free coffee are being met. A quality-audit program allows Jiffy Lube to send in inspectors unannounced to any location, corporate or franchised, to make sure service standards are being strictly adhered to. As the national organization continues to grow and mature, promotion opportunities have opened up, helping Jiffy Lube keep proven performers and their frontline experience in its system.

Predictably, a number of Hindman's former players have signed up for his new team but, perhaps surprisingly, sports metaphors are not basic to Jiffy Lube's corporate outlook. This is a business, not a locker room, but the sense of teamwork and personal development is no less important. On the field or under the car, Hindman simply believes in people, and maintains that developing them only makes them—and everyone around them—better off.

Jiffy Lube International, Inc.
6000 Metro Drive
Baltimore, MD 21215

RYDER SYSTEM INC

RYDER RENTS TRUCKS. THAT'S WHAT THE OLD COMPANY ADVERTISING SLOGAN used to try to drum into people's minds. But these days, it's hardly an accurate description of this Miami-based transportation services company. Yes, Ryder still rents those school-bus-yellow small trucks and vans for do-it-yourself movers and the like, but that's only about 15 percent of its business. It also leases tractors and trailers for long-haul trucking and hauls automobiles for Detroit (one of every three new cars and trucks in the country is delivered to the showroom via Ryder).

That's not all. It leases whole airplanes, or just the engines, to airlines and aviation companies. It runs municipal bus services for cities from Cincinnati to Sacramento, and is (perhaps fittingly, given the corporate color scheme) one of the largest operators of school-bus systems in the country. It also maintains trucks, buses, and aviation equipment for businesses that would rather put their money into things other than rolling transportation stock, and it provides management services for insurance companies who prefer not to run their own service centers. And it does it all very well.

The most familiar side of the business is Ryder Truck Rental, which has overhauled U-Haul (the family-run company that founded and long dominated the one-way truck rental industry) by focusing on customers willing to pay a little more for the use of newer, more comfortable trucks. The Ryder fleet, noted *Newsweek* in 1987, averages about two years old, compared to a ten-year lifespan for U-Haul. And the yellow trucks are more likely to come with civilized amenities customers want, such as air-conditioning, power steering, automatic transmissions, and more fuel-efficient engines.

To improve services and make them more consistent, Ryder schedules and tracks maintenance by computer and operates centralized telephone reservations centers whose operators are available twenty-four hours a day, seven days a week. They're trained to provide more personal service than gas-station owners and harried dealers. Similarly, emergency road service is provided around the clock. Ryder also fosters a concern for cleanliness and safety as well as courtesy in meeting customer needs, whether those needs are being addressed by its own employees or one of its sixty-one hundred independent dealers (there are about nine hundred company-owned rental locations).

On the frontline, Ryder has worked hard—and successfully—to upgrade performance, and customers aren't the only ones to notice the improvement. The International Customer Service Association (ICSA), a nonprofit organization of more than two thousand customer service professionals in companies of all sizes and descriptions, honored Ryder with its 1987 Award of Excellence on the basis of the company's extensive employee training and incentive programs, overall customer relations policies, and consistent management support.

Two programs were of special interest to ICSA. Ryder's Commitment to Excellence campaign, launched in 1985, establishes uniform performance criteria for one-way rental locations nationwide. There are specific standards for such aspects as facility appearance, truck cleanliness and mechanical condition, customer safety briefings, and speed and courtesy of service provided. Each dealer is evaluated quarterly on distinct criteria for sales, marketing, maintenance, safety, and administration, with point scores adding up to annual awards and incentive merchandise.

The standards reflect regional characteristics and match dealers based on their sales volume to encourage competitive efforts regardless of market size. The criteria are nonetheless ambitious—under Facility Appearance, for example, dealers earn points for meeting "regional standards of neatness and cleanliness in all inside and outside locations visible to the Ryder customer or prospect. The appearance should be such that the Dealer could be used as a model for other Dealers."

People Make the Difference, which dates back to 1984, is an incentive and support program that rewards extra efforts on a customer's behalf. Any of Ryder's twenty-seven thousand vehicle-leasing and service division employees in the U.S., Canada, and the United Kingdom can nominate a co-worker for special recognition. The nomination form requires just a brief description of how the individual "Made A Difference"—and the signatures of the individual's two immediate supervisors (to make sure the good performance hasn't gone unnoticed).

A quarterly newsletter highlights exemplary performers, like Elsie Kohler, "the first lady bus driver for the [St. Charles, Missouri] school district," who has been driving 130 miles each school day for a quarter of a century—that works out to a career of more than five hundred thousand miles—without a single accident. Or Tim Neuppert and Ken Eterno, who organized a caravan of trucks and drivers to rescue computer equipment and office supplies stranded in trailers by a flash flood that engulfed a customer company's offices in Bensenville, Illinois. Or Jim Tipton, a service manager in Lexington, Kentucky, who came to the aid of a West

Virginia family en route to Tennessee when their Ryder rental broke down with a bad fuel pump; Tipton had the truck towed to his house about three miles down the road, where the family could rest while he and another mechanic installed a new fuel pump—and his wife, Rose, put together a homemade meal.

Ryder's other businesses benefit from a similar attention to quality. The trucking side grew out of leasing and renting equipment piecemeal for customers who had a little more business than their own equipment could handle. More than 80 percent of Ryder's full-service truck leasing customers still lease fewer than five vehicles, but increasingly companies such as PepsiCo, Xerox, and Kimberly-Clark have turned over management responsibility for trucking and support systems to Ryder, reasoning that its broad-ranging experience and large scale of operations allow it to provide transportation services more cost-effectively than they can themselves.

Some commercial truck lines and transportation service firms are now using Ryder as the source of "dedicated services," a broad-brush term that can include everything from equipment and maintenance to personnel and management systems. In Chicago, noted *Business Week* in 1987, Emery Air Freight's trucks and the unionized drivers who zip them around town both wear Emery's colors but are actually supplied by Ryder, which also handles the maintenance and plans service routes.

In the air, Ryder is certainly heard from, if not seen in the conventional sense. More than three hundred airlines and hundreds of other customers turn to Ryder for aircraft parts and maintenance, making Ryder, among other things, the world's largest overhauler of jet engines and largest distributor of aviation parts. Some companies lease entire airplanes from Ryder; others lease just the multi-million-dollar turbine engines that literally get air services companies off the ground.

For all the growth and diversification under the general heading of transportation, it's important to see the company for what it is—and what it is not. As president and CEO M. Anthony Burns (who as a boy worked in his father's truck stop in the lonely reaches of Nevada) told *Forbes* in March of 1988, "What we are is a third-party provider of services."

Ryder rents and leases and maintains and manages trucks, in other words, but that doesn't make it strictly a trucking company, any more than it's an airline because it leases and maintains aircraft and aviation parts, or an insurance company because a Ryder subsidiary supports insurance industry clients who need underwriting, claims, auditing, and other services. For Ryder, the key word is "service."

Ryder System, Inc.
3600 NW 82nd Avenue
Miami, FL 33166

Wheaton Van Lines

WORLD-WIDE MOVING

SEVERAL YEARS AGO, *CONSUMER REPORTS* ASKED ITS READERS ABOUT THEIR experiences with the van lines that move personal household goods from town to town across America. Eleven major companies were compared on the basis of nearly twenty thousand moves over a three-year period. The top-rated carrier wasn't exactly a household name: Wheaton Van Lines.

National advertising by larger competitors notwithstanding, the magazine's readers who had used Wheaton clearly felt that it was more interested in meeting their particular needs than did the customers of other van lines. Not only did they give Wheaton the highest marks overall, narrowly edging out United Van Lines, they also went out of their way to praise the way Wheaton's people went out of *their* way to be more accessible, and more courteous, and more professional than they had previously been led to expect was normal conduct by other movers.

"The moving industry provides the only transportation service that deals directly with the public," maintains John Waspi, Wheaton's president. "It is probably the only service that still requires the actual physical movement of materials by a human being." In other words, there's no way yet to automate the packing of china and the carrying of furniture up and down stairs and through absurdly narrow doorways while an anxious customer wonders what's becoming of grandma's antique gilded mirror. "Regardless of the price," he adds, "service is the final product of this business, and repeat customers are essential to the success of the mover."

Service wasn't exactly designed in when the moving industry got its start in the last century. The business began as a way for the people who delivered coal and ice or moved baggage from one railroad to another to pick up a little extra work (which is why many van lines still have "Transfer & Storage" or "Delivery" in their names). Bouncing bags and shoveling coal aren't the kinds of occupations that imbue a strong regard for the fate of what's being moved in the people doing that moving.

In the 1920s, as the horseless carriage became the king of the road, delivery trucks began hauling household goods from one town to the

266

next. The problem with these "long-haul" moves was that the truck came back empty, which is not a promising way to make ends meet. Consequently, local movers began to band together in loose-knit affiliations that used a "return loads bureau" as a clearinghouse. A mover registered his load with the bureau, and the bureau tried to match him up with a return load from an associate in the other city. Today's van lines operate along similar lines; to keep their load factors high, many of them carry both household goods and other commodities, ranging from business supplies and commercial goods to high-tech equipment.

On the other hand, when Earnest S. Wheaton founded a van line service in Indianapolis in 1945, he decided to concentrate all but exclusively on household goods. The only exceptions are high-value items such as computers, where the material being moved needs to be moved with the same style and expertise. Like many van lines, Wheaton is actually an association of independent local carriers, or agencies, in three hundred locations in the U.S. plus several foreign countries. The founder is still active as the chairman of the board, and his philosophy of doing business is still in vogue.

Over the years, Wheaton and its agencies have targeted customer satisfaction, and it shows in a number of ways. Industrywide, about one claim in every three and a half to four shipments is average; for Wheaton, one in five has been typical. In 1987, the average net claim among nearly a dozen major national carriers was nearly $400; without Wheaton's average of less than $220 per claim, it would have been higher. Since 1964, Wheaton also has carried the Good Housekeeping Seal, which means it provides the limited warranty the magazine requires—a promise of replacement or refund if the service is not satisfactory.

All household goods carriers must file an Annual Performance Report with the Interstate Commerce Commission's Office of Compliance and Consumer Assistance. A copy must also be given to every prospective customer. Wheaton's report card for 1987 provides another indication of the company's professionalism. Of the shipments accepted on the basis of a nonbinding estimate (about 80 percent of Wheaton's annual business with individual shippers), 97.4 percent were carried, delivered, and signed off without exceeding the estimate that had been given to the customer. Among competitors, by contrast, nonbinding estimates are exceeded as much as 40 percent of the time.

Fully 99 percent of Wheaton's 1987 shipments were picked up on or before the date scheduled; 98 percent were delivered on or before the date specified in the customer's contract. What's more, 99 percent of Wheaton's shipments did not result in the filing of a claim for damage or expenses in excess of $100 (like most van lines, Wheaton requires its drivers to pay the first $100 of damages on a shipment out of their own pockets).

An aspect of Wheaton's service that *Consumer Reports*' readers respected was the speed with which it paid off in the inevitable event of a claim. Where many carriers habitually took nearly 20 days to settle, Wheaton's average in 1985 was 10.8 days. Times really haven't changed: In 1987, the average number of days between the filing of a claim and the final settlement was 13.4 at Wheaton.

One reason times haven't changed for Wheaton is because of the emphasis placed on multiple communications with customers. Before a move, a sales representative helps the customer fill out a Pre-Move Survey that describes in detail the special requirements of the job. The information helps the local agent plan the job, especially since most household moves involve the shipment of several customers' goods in the same truckload. It also provides a briefing for the driver, helping him determine how many helpers will be needed to pack and load each part of the shipment.

In addition, a Before You Move survey also is filled out, but this one is sent directly to Wheaton's traffic department in Indianapolis, which not coincidentally is where the 800-number "Answer Line" is answered. Before their move, customers receive a wallet-size card with the service center's toll-free number plus the names and phone numbers of the Wheaton agent in their origin and destination cities. By calling any one of the three numbers, customers can find out where their goods are in transit or let Wheaton know that plans may have changed (for instance, that they have been delayed en route to the new address and won't be there to meet their goods when the shipment arrives).

After the move, a Customer's Service Report goes straight to Indianapolis, where it is read not only by the quality control department, but also by the chairman of the board—whose name, you recall, happens to be Wheaton. It contains information on how things went from the time the packing started until the last box was unloaded and into the new residence.

Significantly, there's no confusing five-point or ten-point scale to decipher. Wheaton asks for absolute, clear-cut reactions: Either the Wheaton agent was courteous and helpful or he wasn't; the driver was courteous and efficient or he wasn't; the help was efficient or it wasn't; the customer is satisfied with Wheaton's service or dissatisfied—there's no middle ground. More than 75 percent of Wheaton's customers say yes, the agent, the driver, the help, and the move in general were up to snuff, and more than 85 percent say they'll recommend Wheaton's service to others.

The rating, incidentally, has more than a feel-good purpose. Complaints are responded to directly and discussed with the carriers and drivers involved. If problems persist over time, Wheaton will require an agent to drop an unsatisfactory driver, and it doesn't hesitate to terminate its affiliation with the local agent, either. In 1987, Wheaton's forty-second year in business, four agencies were dropped for failing to meet standards—

but a net addition of 19 agencies brought the systemwide total of affiliates to nearly 330.

That number included five agencies with more than forty years of service under the Wheaton banner: Bucyrus Transfer & Storage of Bucyrus, Ohio; Demary Brothers Transfer in Enterprise, West Virginia; Morris Van Lines of Paris, Illinois; Penn Hershey Transfer of Hershey, Pennsylvania; and Tobin Brothers in Dayton, Ohio. The name painted on the side of the trucks may be Wheaton, but it's their business, too.

Wheaton Van Lines, Inc.
8010 Castleton Road
Indianapolis, IN 46250

United Van Lines

EACH MONTH, THREE HUNDRED PEOPLE WHO HAVE JUST COMPLETED A MOVE VIA United Van Lines get a call from an independent research firm in St. Louis. Their names are selected at random from the shipment information registered with the van line's corporate office in suburban Fenton. Some have contracted with an affiliated United agent themselves, others have seen their household goods loaded in United vans because of their employer's corporate relocation agreements.

Whether they paid for the move themselves or were being moved at the behest (and expense) of an employer, the questions are the same. Even for national account service, it's the individual's reaction to and satisfaction with what happened that tells United whether its services have measured up in the increasingly competitive van line industry.

In 1987, the polling confirmed United's continuing success at pleasing customers. More than 80 percent of its customers pronounced themselves extremely or very satisfied with the friendliness of United's service; the best grade earned by a competitor was a 69. Seventy percent rated the complete service received as extremely or very satisfying, compared to a top score of 55 percent for the closest competitor with whom they'd moved before.

The high marks are one important reason why United has been the fastest growing major van line in the country since Robert J. Baer climbed into the driver's seat as vice president and general manager in 1977 (president since 1982). Another is the way its owners—approximately 135 of its more than 550 van line agents—and their colleagues have shifted into a higher customer service gear, despite (maybe because of) the fact that United has been a consistent top service provider for more than thirty years. Each monthly issue of *Unicom*, United's internal magazine for agents and drivers, carries a regular column titled "Applause, Applause," which shares customer commendations and relates especially noteworthy examples of good service. Most months, the "column" stretches three pages or more.

The customer-focused research, augmented by an annual comparative study that ranks United's service performance against that of competitors, turns up a lot of good news, according to Tonie Lindenberger, United's director of public affairs. But it's the bad news that the van line pays attention to. Relative likes and dislikes provide insight into market trends, enabling United to allocate resources and plan effectively instead of reacting to conditions after the fact.

More importantly, the negative responses that turn up are analyzed and evaluated internally, then acted upon. Departments that aren't measuring up are expected to find ways to improve. Agents whose services have come up short may find themselves visited by a United marketing manager who arrives with a comprehensive performance improvement plan in hand and stays around while it is implemented. "Within a specified period of time, we expect to see results," Lindenberger told us. "When those results don't occur, an agent jeopardizes his or her relationship with the van line. We have an aggressive termination policy for our representatives who do not consistently deliver the level of quality service our customers have come to expect."

Evidence of the strength of that commitment: United used to drop two or three agents a year for service-related problems. Since 1982, when its market share fell seven-tenths of a point to 15.8 percent, it has dumped and replaced nearly one hundred agents—more than fifty in one two-year period in the mid-eighties—and intervened with many more to bring performance standards back into line. By 1987, market share had grown to 17.7 percent (in an industry in which the total number of available moves *declined* 4 percent from 1981 to 1986), making United the new claimant to the title of being the nation's largest mover.

Agents aren't the only ones to feel the zeal United has brought to service. According to the St. Louis *Post-Dispatch*, the prospect of having to stop by company headquarters in Fenton for a session on quality control leaves even normally cocky drivers wishing they were somewhere else. "Drivers who don't meet company standards are called on the carpet before United's Loss Prevention and Safety Committee in Fenton," the paper reported in 1986. "It can be a devastating experience and drivers have been known to break down in tears."

United disclaims any tendency to use the third degree. Rather, it believes—and expects its agents and carriers to believe—that quality is a matter of survival in an industry where overcapacity has led to discounts as deep as 50 percent by some shippers. In return, it gives priority consideration to agent support matters, from dealing with their problems and complaints to providing formal training and informal counseling on operations and productivity. The board of directors of UniGroup, the holding company for which United represents about 90 percent of total business, is composed entirely of professional movers (more than one hundred United agents have served on its board since the company was founded in 1947) to make sure the focus stays on the business. "We have to walk, talk and act on quality," Baer told the *Post-Dispatch*. "That is what will separate the [companies] that stay from the ones who don't."

Perhaps the best example of service quality from the consumer's vantage point is United's Bette Malone Relocation Service, a remarkably comprehensive long-distance planning aide made available to customers by more than 90 percent of United's agents. The service was introduced in 1956, primarily as a woman-to-woman connection for family relocations. Like Betty Crocker of General Mills fame, Ms. Malone is a personification of the company, not a real individual (to avoid any untoward confusion, United changed her original monicker from Betty to Bette). Nowadays, when Malone speaks, it is Lindenberger's lips that move—she's the fourth official heir to the Malone persona, which includes support from a staff of eleven researchers, home economists, and service representatives.

Real or imagined, Malone is one busy lady. This year she'll distribute about one hundred thousand comprehensive relocation packets, most of which will include detailed information on conditions in the seven thousand metropolitan areas worldwide on which her staff maintains a data base. Moving to El Paso, Texas? Malone's six-page backgrounder includes information on population, geography, climate, government, cultural and recreation attractions, even the telephone area code. It also provides addresses and phone numbers for the local water, refuse, gas, electric, and telephone services, plus the four area offices of both the Texas Department of Public Safety (where you go to get your driver's license) and the Texas Employment Commission (which has leads to employment opportunities in the area).

Malone offers helpful—and thoughtfully detailed—advice on the proper way to move almost anything: pets, house plants, antiques, computers and satellite dishes, waterbeds and hot tubs, even the family wine collection. There's a pamphlet of pointers for those who want to do their own packing, another outlining the records that need to be kept for next year's income tax deduction. There are also detailed time schedules for planning each step of the move and conducting a job search in the new city, and a brochure with pointers from psychologists, educators, and family health experts designed to help children make the best of the move to a new home in a strange town.

In recent years, customers and industry observers alike have continued to acknowledge United as one of the van lines most committed to quality. *Distribution* magazine's 1987 "Quest for Quality" ratings gave United top marks across the board for the four categories—service, convenience, price, and sales support—assessed. The readers of *Consumer Reports* ranked it second only to Wheaton Van Lines in describing their overall satisfaction with moving companies in 1985; its sales representatives, they made a point of noting, were more informative than average.

Ironically, thinking of customer convenience accounts for a curious statistical hole in United's customer research data: There's no information generated during the months of November and December. "We don't want to intrude on family plans or activities at such a busy time of the year to solicit information," Lindenberger told us in her official role as director of public affairs.

As Bette Malone, she added, she fully concurs with that basic courtesy.

United Van Lines, Inc.
Subsidiary of UniGroup, Inc.
One United Drive
Fenton, MO 63026

NW Transport Service

TRANSPORT SERVICE, INC.

"YOU CAN'T HARPOON A SUBMERGED WHALE."

That, according to Jeff McMorris, vice president for corporate development at NW Transport Service, is why many competitors still tend to overlook this fast-growing over-the-road transportation system based in Denver, and why many potential customers still are unfamiliar with its highly satisfying service profile.

Current customers, on the other hand, are very aware of the quality of service the company provides. When *Distribution* magazine reported the results of its fourth annual "Quest for Quality" ratings in 1987, the highest numbers on the list of thirty-eight regional carriers belonged to this growing family-run trucker. Its customer-generated service score was an eye-opening 4.64 on a 5-point scale (about 3.5 was average); nobody else came close. It also was the only carrier to earn a score over 4.0 for sales effectiveness (4.71, against an average score of 2.99) or convenience (4.07, with about 3.3 being the norm). That's the equivalent of an Olympic skater winning the long program, the short program, and the compulsories.

And lest you think bigger might be better, consider that *Distribution's* ratings for seventeen national-scale motor carriers turned up not one 4.0 rating in the bunch for any of the four separate categories measured. Leaders such as Yellow Freight, Roadway, and Consolidated Freightways may be (and are) good, in other words, but their customer judges aren't inclined to rate them anywhere near as highly as NW Transport's business audience.

NW Transport is a multiregional trucker handling mostly LTL (less than truckload—the industry acronym for trailer loads made up of several separate shipments from different customers) service through a network of more than fifty terminals in more than twenty states from California and the Pacific Northwest to Ohio. In 1987, it served a total of twenty-five states and was continuing a strategy of controlled growth that calls for adding two or three new terminals a year.

How has a relatively small, privately held company that has "never spent a nickel" on outside advertising managed to keep growing at rates as high as 30 percent per year (15-20 percent being average) through the mid- and late-eighties? The reason, according to McMorris, is the way its twenty-five hundred employees, from the Teamster-organized drivers and loading-dock workers to the computer operators who track shipments all over the country, treat customers.

"We were surprised by the *Distribution* survey," McMorris told us. "We agree, but we were still surprised. The only way to differentiate yourself in this business is through the quality of service you provide." Tempering the pleasant shock of finding out that people are noticing, he added, is the knowledge that customer expectations will be just that much higher as a consequence.

Though the company's roots go all the way back to Utah in the 1880s, NW Transport actually took shape in 1959 when the McMorris family bought into Westway Motor Freight. In those days, the company had three trucks and a few employees, and mostly hauled Coors beer along the seventeen-mile stretch from the brewery in Golden to the distribution center in Denver. Through internally generated growth and quality-oriented acquisitions (significant among the latter, Salt Lake Transfer Company and Colorado-based Harp Transportation), the comparison to a whale has become more accurate. These days, more than two thousand rolling units carry more than five thousand shipments a day over distances that average twelve hundred miles.

NW Transport's success of late reflects its close attention to designing service for the western states where it does most of its business. It's a landscape characterized by long stretches of open road between cities, which puts a premium on speed and efficiency, especially in terminal operations and keeping shipments moving virtually around the clock. The terminal network operates on the increasingly familiar hub-and-spoke principle, with smaller loads being consolidated into full loads, most of them in gleaming new twenty-eight-foot trailers. The system all but eliminates rerouting of shipments and greatly reduces the need for interlining (transferring a shipment to another carrier somewhere along the line).

At the same time, the company has developed systems that minimize the negative side of hub-and-spoke operations, especially "breakbulks"— loads that have to be broken up and reloaded in transit. It's the trucking equivalent to an airline flying planeloads of people from Des Moines, Fargo, and Milwaukee into Minneapolis, where they're unloaded and rerouted to New York and Los Angeles. (We all know how well *that* works from the passenger's standpoint.) The ideal situation results from using computer monitoring and scheduling so that shipments go directly through from their load point to their final destination in the trailer on which they were first loaded—and with the trailer being fully loaded virtually all the way for maximum return.

"Every time you handle the cargo, you inhibit the quality of the customer service," according to McMorris. "It costs you money for the time and labor, it introduces chances for delays, and it increases the number of opportunities when things can be damaged or lost. All of that affects the quality of the service the customer receives."

Most NW Transport loads end up as "truck-trains" of two or three trailers linked behind one sleeper cab and handled not by one driver but by a team of two. The presence of a relief driver allows the trucking equivalent of perpetual motion—and consequently the company's service standards are consistently one to three days faster than many of its competitors—while improving safety as well as service. Meanwhile, computerized administrative and billing systems have eliminated any paperwork that moves slower than the freight being hauled; this further expedites service.

To keep the focus on service sharp, NW Transport recognizes the best terminal in the system each month based on customer quality goals for its various facilities. Part of the company's profit-sharing contribution is also pegged to how well workers in each terminal meet and exceed their annual performance goals.

But NW Transport's service profile continues to rise because most of its loads end up being delivered without delay or damage. The internal numbers bear out the top service scores compiled by *Distribution*. Companywide service reports track on-time deliveries, the time it takes a cargo to move through a terminal, and the condition of the shipment on delivery. It's not unusual for reports to turn up better-than-100-percent performance. How is that possible? NW Transport has a penchant for beating its own schedules, sometimes making deliveries a day or two early. Just as a late arrival would be a negative increment, the early arrival is handled as a credit.

On the damage side, the company's people also excel. In an industry with a claims ratio of about 1.5 percent of revenue for lost or damaged shipments, NW Transport has averaged below .5 percent since 1984. That's a whale of a record.

NW Transport Service
5601 Holly Street
Commerce City, CO 80022

FOOD SERVICE

RESTAURANTS

Shoney's Restaurants

Pizza Hut

Bob Evans Farms

FAST FOOD

McDonald's

Domino's Pizza

Wendy's

HALF OF US WILL EAT A MEAL AWAY FROM HOME TODAY. ONE IN TWELVE OF US will add a second meal out as well. Dinner has replaced lunch as the meal most often eaten outside the home. Over all, says *Restaurants & Institutions* magazine, the industry authority on such matters, 88.9 percent of us eat at least one meal a week away from home, with 40.3 percent of us eating out more than seven times a week. And we spend an average of $31.07 a week for the pleasure of having someone else fix it and dish it up.

Those meals will be served not just in restaurants but in school or company cafeterias and dining rooms, in day care centers, and on airplanes, ships, and trains. Nobody knows for sure how many burgers, pizzas, breakfast sandwiches, and chili dogs are gulped down in the front seats of cars and trucks every day—but it's a bunch, and it counts as well.

Whether it's in a world-acclaimed restaurant or a neighborhood pizzeria, the most lasting negative impression of a restaurant seems to be created by its service. *Chicago Tribune* columnist Mike Royko has written stinging columns about bad restaurant service. In one of the more colorful, he exhorts restaurant corporations to fire all the MBAs and hire some "short Greeks" related to his friend Sam Sianis, who runs the Billy Goat Tavern in Chicago: "He wouldn't know how to read a computer printout, but he'd get drinks in the glasses, food on the table, and money in the cash register." Witty, curmudgeonly—and perhaps wise as well.

In fall 1987, *Money* magazine did a survey of readers and came up with a list of the six rudest restaurants in America. In hopes they've changed, we'll omit their names here. Suffice it to say that the major complaint against the breed was treating customers with disdain and indifference. As one respondent put it, a bad restaurant experience is where "they play favorites; a place where the staff acts as if they are doing the customer a favor; a place where complaints aren't taken seriously."

And while *Money* admittedly was focusing on expensive and trendy restaurants, service is just as sensitive an issue in chains and family-run neighborhood establishments alike.

Preparing and serving food is big business—and an enterprise that can have you talking to yourself in nothing flat. Though the maxim "good times or bad, everybody's gotta eat" has enticed more than a few would-be Burger Barons into the food prep biz, it is a tough, tough business. The challenge of figuring out exactly what new food "concept" will next attract the often fickle appetites and wallets of the Great American Eating Machine has undone more than one of these meal moguls in the making.

As the editors of *R&I's* annual "Tastes of America" survey issue note, "Restaurateurs weathered some difficult times in 1987, but the slump appears to be the result of an overbuilt industry rather than disenchantment with eating out on the part of consumers."

Restaurants, like hotels, are often a matter of personal taste. For some people, as the data suggest, eating out is a way of life. For others it is a special event. To some it is an adventure: "Botswanan native cuisine! Wow, I've never tried that. Let's go!" For still others it is an imposition and a horror to be avoided as much as possible. It is critical for the restaurant industry to know which strokes go with which folks, since as consumers we are by and large loyalists, revisiting an old standby 78.4 percent of the time we eat out.

Some of us value a restaurant because of its ambiance, fine food, and the courtesy of the staff. Being called by name by the maitre d' turns most folks absolutely rosy. Price and predictability are key ingredients for others. And the good old "burger, shake, fries, eat it and beat it" formula is a concept that still others find best fits their tastes.

Where do we go when we eat out? According to *R&I's* 1987 year-end study, hamburger chains remain the most popular type of restaurant, earning visits from 68.3 percent of respondents in the survey. Family restaurants and coffee shops are a distant second.

The Flavor of Service

Because the growth in restaurants has outstripped our appetites, it takes more than a good location and a decent plate of goulash to succeed these days. It takes, you guessed it, attention to service. Says Nancy Ross Ryan, senior editor of *Restaurants & Institutions*: "You'll find service better because the competition is fiercer. There are more places to eat out than ever. Everywhere you look companies are emphasizing training to help improve service as a competitive leg-up."

One aspect of the new service focus is an emphasis on customer treatment. To make the point, the Society for American Consumers made 1987 the "Year of the Waiter." Patrick O'Connell, chef and owner of the Inn at Little Washington in Washington, Virginia—who, along with The Society for American Cuisine, developed the idea—believes that the profession of table-waiting should no longer be seen as a means to an end, but as an end in itself.

His point is intriguing, and perhaps a clue to historical service problems in the industry. "Since waiting tables hasn't been respected, it can't attract the people we need to provide quality service," O'Connell says. "We need to raise their status in the United States before we can have great restaurants like those in Europe."

O'Connell supports a controversial proposal to follow the European practice of adding a mandatory service charge to bills to replace the time-honored and almost universally disliked practice of "voluntary" tipping. His reasoning is that waiters will benefit from finding themselves with a guaranteed income, from feeling their earnings come from the essential worth of the job they do instead of being based on the whims of the unknowing public. The few American restaurants that have implemented the system agree it is a viable way to improve the status of waiters, and believe it could spill over into improved service as well.

On the fast-food front, competition has warranted close management scrutiny of service standards from top to bottom. Ron Paul, president of Technomics, a food service research consulting firm, says consumers increasingly feel fast food is slower than it used to be. According to *The Gallup Report on Eating Out*, fast service means five minutes or less—60 percent of patrons are willing to wait that long.

But as menus continue to broaden, and retaining quality help remains difficult, Paul contends that providing this acknowledged level of fast service is tougher than ever. The chains tend to disagree with the firm's research, but Paul says they are implementing and testing new programs to speed service nonetheless.

Case in point: McDonald's, where double-booth drive-throughs are included at all new stores and in major remodels. Employees also use remote headsets so they can fill orders while taking others from anywhere in the store.

At Taco Bell, which, along with Pizza Hut and Kentucky Fried Chicken, makes up the restaurant segment of PepsiCo's business, the new emphasis on attracting and retaining service-oriented people has taken the form of replacing "Help Wanted" signs with ones that announce "Now Hiring Friendly People." William Martin, associate professor of hotel and restaurant management at California State Polytechnic University, says a strong corporate push at Taco Bell has filtered down to operations and resulted in increased service training budgets. He also anticipates a new customer service approach at Kentucky Fried Chicken, based on PepsiCo's "long history of devotion to quality customer service."

The dinnerhouse/family restaurant segment of the industry also has joined the rush to refine customer service approaches, according to Martin:

At Jax Cafe in Minneapolis, owners breathed new life into a stagnant operation not by altering the menu or interior design, but by retraining the service staff. A consultant updated the restaurant's service style through retraining that covered everything from daily menu briefings and tastings to tips on sales techniques. Instead of just giving a new waitress a uniform and order book and pointing her to the tables, new employees now follow a trained server for up to four weeks, learning the menu and service basics. The retraining effort paid dividends almost immediately— the restaurant reports average checks went up about $4.25 after the retraining.

At the restaurants of Ohio-based Bob Evans Farms, the company has on occasion offered patrons free meals if they were not properly greeted by a host or hostess. "Too many restaurants greet you by saying, 'How many in your party,' or 'Smoking or nonsmoking,' " says Roger Williams, Bob Evans' director of marketing. The last time the tactic was used, just three meals were given away in six weeks— evidence that the company's service standards have been put in place on the frontline from Michigan to Florida. The chain's friendly service and pleasant atmosphere are at the heart of its "Just a few miles from home" ad campaign.

Roy Rogers restaurants have hired Customer Assistance Program (CAP) hosts for almost 80 percent of their locations. Their responsibility is simply to make each customer feel at ease. They greet and say good-bye to everyone, and circulate throughout the restaurant. The job slot is designed specifically for older people, considered ideal because they have more experience in personal interaction than a typical teenage crew member.

One thing the volumes of eating out research make very clear is that consumers (that's us, folks) have specific expectations for specific kinds of dining "experiences." Our expectations of a fast food outlet are very different from our expectations of a family restaurant, and neither of those sets of expectations look much like our idea of a four-star dining experience. Here's a look at the salient differences.

Fast Food. When it comes to the "eat it and beat it" dining experience, says a recent study by the National Restaurant Association, speed and convenience are at the top of the list of customer expectations. That puts a premium on location and accessibility of the outlet.

And that part of the fast-food formula seems to be working well: 75 percent of us, according to the association's study, say we think the industry has done well in locating outlets in convenient places. The same portion of us—three out of four—believe that the food is delivered in a speedy fashion.

We are not, however, quite so pleased with the variety of food being served, the atmosphere of fast-food restaurants, and the quality and price—the value, in other words—of the food we buy there. Just the same, only 6 percent say we never have and never will eat in a fast-food restaurant.

The most substantial trend in the fast-food segment of the industry is takeout. According to *R&I's* 1987 "Tastes of America" data, 57.8 percent of us used drive-through service windows in 1987—up 10 percentage points over 1986—and 63.4 percent of us stopped in for takeout. Home delivery jumped from 19.6 percent to 24.7 percent, and supermarket deli purchases were a rousing 43.2 percent of our purchases of ready-to-eat food. Convenience and speed are indeed important to us.

Coffee Shops and Family Restaurants. The category of full-service chain restaurants is a broad one. A Po Folks, Morrison's, Shoney's, or Bob Evans "store" is quite a different beast than a Bennigan's, Baker's Square, TGI Friday's, or Steak and Ale. The focus and feel are distinctive and different.

Consequently, our expectations of the sit-down chain restaurant not only are a bit different than those for the typical fast-food outlet, but also vary based on the restaurant's "concept"—its distinctive combination of style, size, menu, ethnic theming, and other variables. In the main, though, food quality is more important, as are personal attention, value, atmosphere, cleanliness, and variety.

Fancy Eating. When the topic turns to fancy food and expensive dining, there are more than enough opinions to go around. Food and restaurant critics make a good living inventing their own special vocabulary and divining the differences in the sauces served in $85-a-pop restaurants. But between the extremes of fast-food outlets and world class, budget-busting haute cuisinaries lies "fine dining." And this segment is a nervous place to be in business right now. Says *USA Today*, "Restaurants [of this kind] are starving for customers."

After several years of growth in the "Yup-scale" segment, especially in major metropolitan areas, "sheer saturation has hit the high end of the restaurant market," says Peter Romeo, an editor at *Nation's Restaurant News*. A recent study of eating-out trends by *Consumer Reports* found sales in upscale restaurants were off 18 percent. This drop is attributable, the study author says, to the IRS ruling that business meals are now only 80 percent deductible.

Whatever the reason, the fine dining experience may be on the way to becoming a buyer's market—and no longer a special subspecies of masochism—for the first time in years.

The familiar problem of paying through the nose to be abused by snotty, pretentious waiters and maitre d's is near and dear to the hearts of Nina and Eugene Zagat. Since about 1980, the Zagats have pursued a unique hobby—finding nice places to eat, and telling others about them. Their approach is both dead simple and an extraordinary undertaking. They send surveys to people who like eating out and who are willing to fill out their rating form on the restaurants they eat in. The results are now published annually as the *Zagat Restaurant Survey*.

Actually, there are five editions of the *ZRS*, one each for New York, Chicago, San Francisco, Washington, D.C., and Los Angeles. Reviewers receive free copies of the guide they contribute to. Establishments are rated on food quality, decor, and service—each on a scale of 0 to 30.

The mercifully short commentaries are to the point and sometimes painfully blunt. One restaurant in New York is described, in part, as "snobby and a con game; people eating their public relations." It's the world's largest restaurant grapevine. Perhaps between the Zagats and the business bust that upscale restaurants are experiencing, fine dining will once again live up to its name.

Our Good-Service Menu

Our exemplary service providers are drawn from the same body of organizations *R&I* samples: the chain restaurants and fast-food providers. Certainly, there are many examples of consistently fine service in the fine dining and one-of-a-kind restaurants— service aimed at lofty and specific standards, carefully articulated, and pursued with great vigor and tenacity. At restaurants like Masas in San Francisco, Le Francais in Chicago, and The Quilted Giraffe in New York, the focus is on fine food and creating a memorable dining experience for guests. Their service people come through because the managements of these establishments (and others like them) take pride in creating a unique experience for customers. They manage everyone's efforts toward that end.

But providing good service in a chain restaurant or through a fast-food outlet is an act with many more dimensions simply because of the effort it takes to make service consistent on a nationwide basis. And there are so many more variables to account for and limits to be observed in a corporation than in a one-of-a-kind fine restaurant that the lessons for managers are just that much sharper.

Among the sit-down restaurants, we picked Shoney's, Pizza Hut, and Bob Evans. Shoney's and Bob Evans are both steadfast examples of how dedication to a simple, straightforward concept can work well for both company and customer. They were on our pick list from the start. We also enjoy telling stories like the one about Shoney's CEO J. Mitchell Boyd, who, upon finding a dirty restroom in one of the company's restaurants, doffed his coat, rolled up his sleeves, and cleaned up the mess. No question in anyone's mind how important cleanliness is to the organization's service standards—or how closely managers at every level are prone to focus on details. Pizza Hut, besides being a specialty concept, is an important example of making sophisticated systems work for, not against, employees and customers. It is a story worth pointing to when the critics say automation and service don't mix.

In the fast-food category, we offer McDonald's, Domino's, and Wendy's. Big Mac and Domino's both have made service consistency systemwide goals, and both have succeeded in achieving it—despite ferocious competition in an industry characterized by minimum-wage, entry-level workers and high turnover. Wendy's? Well, you'll have to read that one to find out. It's a service standard backed by interesting people that captured our attention.

SHONEY'S.

"PATRONS *REALLY* LOVE SHONEY'S. SAYING ITS BEST ATTRIBUTE IS GOOD VALUE is a bit misleading because the chain also gets extremely high marks for service, quality of food and cleanliness."

That's how *Restaurants & Institutions* described the top-rated family dining place (it calls the category "Cafeteria/Coffee Shop") in its 1987 "Choice in Chains" study. Shoney's is noteworthy for the close attention it has paid to the nitty-gritty details of restaurant operations since founder Ray Danner launched the business with a part-interest in a Big Boy coffee shop about thirty years ago. Today there are nearly 650 Shoney's in thirty mostly southern and midwestern states. They represent approximately half the sales volume of the company's growing restaurant business, which also includes more than 600 Captain D's seafood houses, about 285 Lee's Famous Recipe Chicken restaurants, and a handful of specialty restaurants and steakhouses. The company also has its own 40-property motel chain, Shoney's Inns.

A 1987 restaurant review from the *Baton Rouge State Times* provides an excellent summation of this Nashville-based chain. "Shoney's," confided newsfeatures editor Freda Yarbrough, "is one of those all-American chain restaurants that doesn't do fancy food. They just do good food at reasonable prices, and they don't mind the kids—they actually give the kids something to read while waiting for food. They even smile when kids take to crawling under the table after things. (It helps when the waitress understands that Mom is not always in control.) And the service is usually prompt; waiting for a waitress is not the norm."

As a secret, that's pretty tame stuff. But it just keeps working from one Shoney's to the next. In a 1984 report on the company, *The New York Times* offered this insight from a Baltimore-based restaurant analyst: "They are far less marketing-oriented than their competitors. A customer brought in by marketing tends to be fickle. Someone who goes to a restaurant because the food is good and they like [the atmosphere] is less likely to be pulled away by a promotion."

To make sure they keep coming back, Shoney's keeps working the details. The typical location, usually along an interstate highway or major arterial, will have about seventy employees, among them as many as seven managers (for competitors, four is about average for a Shoney's-style operation). Generally, those managers are people who started out busing tables and washing dishes. They know they can rise rapidly through the ranks as the company continues to grow, and many do. CEO J. Mitchell Boyd was a Shoney's management trainee who became a franchisee in the Washington, D.C., area and later merged his operation with the parent company. Gary Sharp, division vice president, was once a busboy in a Shoney's. Operations vice president John Clark, awarded Operator of the Year honors in 1987, started out working hourly behind a Shoney's counter in Charleston, West Virginia, back in 1962; his wife, Linda, was named Shoney's Secretary of the Year for '87.

About half the restaurants are company-owned, the other half franchised—but great care is taken in selection of franchisees. To reward managers, there are frequent bonuses, profit-sharing programs, and stock options. At the hourly level, Shoney's uses an employee stock participation plan to provide both a valued benefit and an incentive for everyone to see the value of their work in the company's success. Under the program, each employee has an escrow account into which he or she can put funds withheld from paychecks. Those funds can be used to buy Shoney's stock at a significant discount. From dishwashers to floor managers, people tend to pay attention to that: A $1,000 investment in Shoney's back in 1974 would be worth more than $50,000 today—not counting dividends.

Managers are taught to focus on "R-T-R"—recruiting, training, and retaining—and the importance of the "power of expectations" in building productive, high-quality operations. Expect someone to be barely adequate, they're told, and that's what the person will deliver. On the other hand, expect top performance—and provide the kind of training and supervision and compensation that will make that level of quality possible—and most employees will deliver, both for their managers and their customers.

Decentralized management is the order of the day, with the key being the division-level managers who are responsible for about twenty-five restaurants in a region. "They can paint the restaurants green if they want to," Shoney's president Gary Spoleta told *The New York Times* a few years ago. "We have no strategic planners. No MBAs. We have no layers." That lack of middle management may have served to slow Shoney's growth somewhat (if opening more than one hundred new restaurants a year can be called "slow"), but the company maintains that its success will continue to be measured in quality, not quantity.

To keep even top executives plugged in on day-to-day operations, frequent restaurant visits are normal. Operations managers are expected to spend as many as four days a week in the field. Their visits can get active: Chairman Danner also has been known to personally clean out a dirty washroom—then just as personally clean the collective clocks of the restaurant crew that let it get that way. President Spoleta is remembered for the lunch rush he encountered one day in a Kansas City, Missouri, location. The staff had obviously (given a line of people waiting for tables that extended out the front door) been overwhelmed by an unexpected onslaught of conventioneers. Spoleta promptly shucked his jacket, rolled up his sleeves and started washing dishes; he sent the two regular dishwashers out to clear tables. Meanwhile, the local Shoney's executive he'd arrived with sent the hostess off to get an order pad and help wait on tables while he took over the job of seating customers. As management development, those three hours were considered well spent.

For quality control, Shoney's recruits secret shoppers from among its customers and sends them into its restaurants on a regular basis. In return for a free meal for their families, the customers-turned-inspectors grade the restaurant and its staff on everything from whether the waitress and a glass of water arrived within two minutes to the general quality of the food and the overall cleanliness and appearance of the restaurant. Each month, the reports are added to an increasingly deep and sophisticated data base that helps Shoney's identify both problems and promising managers. In-depth reports circulate through headquarters in Nashville and out to division- and restaurant-level managers; many restaurant managers share them with their own key people, regardless of their job description or pay level.

"We've had only one goal from the beginning," Danner says. "To take one restaurant at a time and make damn sure we're good with that one. And if we're good we'll build another. And if we keep on being good, we'll keep on building. But we'll only get big because we're good."

In 1984, in order to continue to grow into new markets, Shoney's severed its longstanding ties as a franchisee of the Marriott-licensed Big Boy concept because the franchise was limited to just eleven states. If there were any lingering doubts that Shoney's was relying on someone else for its success, they didn't last long. Since the names changed within the system, loyal customers have kept right on coming back to Shoney's, conclusively proving that it's the Shoney's imprint, not a statue of a pudgy kid holding a hamburger platter, that delivers the quality they desire.

Wall Street analysts who have followed the company since it went public in 1969 point to 116 consecutive quarters of increased revenues and pretax operating income through the first part of 1988 in calling Shoney's the best-managed restaurant company in the country. Customers, on the other hand, keep coming back again and again because the food is good and the people are terrific.

Reviewer Yarbrough can testify to that. Her critique was written after a cross-country trek, with children, that included Shoney's stops in: Chattanooga, Tennessee; Huntsville, Alabama; "some woebegon town in Virginia"; and Valdosta, Georgia. The verdict: "Some purists dislike the concept of chain restaurants, since they have to provide menus that will appeal to a large segment of the population. However, after sampling at least three other national chains around the country in a two-week period, Shoney's was the only one which consistently provided good food, good service and low prices, Baton Rouge included."

We can vouch for the fact that the standards are as high north of the Mason-Dixon line: The kids we recently spent a vacation traveling with still remember "Bev" from the Shoney's in Lafayette, Indiana.

Shoney's, Inc.
1727 Elm Hill Pike
Nashville, TN 37202

Pizza Hut

FOR THREE YEARS RUNNING, *RESTAURANTS & INSTITUTIONS'* "CHOICE IN CHAINS" survey has come up with the same favorite purveyor of pizza, arguably America's best-loved food. The winner: Pizza Hut. The external ratings garnered from restaurant patrons track closely with an internal culture that focuses everyone from telephone order-takers and counter help to cooks and waitresses on "creating the perfect pizza *experience*" (emphasis not added by us).

At Pizza Hut, they realize that there's more to good service than just providing good food. Everything counts for the customer, from the voice on the phone to the hot stuff on the table or delivered to the front door, especially when the product involved is the country's favorite food. According to *The Wall Street Journal*, GDR/Crest, a Chicago-based company that follows restaurant trends, has calculated that Americans spent more than $20 billion on restaurant-made pizza in 1987, about 12 percent of the annual total spent in restaurants of all kinds. And growth is continuing, both in dollar volume and percentage. "The Hut" is the biggest, fastest-growing property on that particular block.

A part of the PepsiCo corporate family since 1977, Pizza Hut is still headquartered right back where it started in 1958: Wichita, Kansas. Brothers Dan and Frank Carney (ages twenty-five and nineteen respectively when the business began, and at the time both students at Wichita State University) launched the first restaurant with six hundred dollars they borrowed from their mother. They called it Pizza *Hut* because they wanted pizza in the name and that left room for only three more letters on the building's nine-character signboard. By the time they took the company public in 1969, there were more than three hundred locations and they were on their way to building the largest pizza restaurant chain in the world. The influence of PepsiCo has only further enhanced their original attention to service.

To continue to build on customer-focused core values, Pizza Hut continues to aim high: In 1988 it committed itself to encouraging the delivery of nothing less than "legendary" service. That, according to internal training materials, is "more than just good service, even great service. Legendary service is the unique and powerful sort of personal care and attention that our customers tell stories about. . . . Even though the day to day business of Pizza Hut might look like cooking, cleaning and serving, the real thing we do is provide customer service."

Some of it is the traditional table service the chain started with. But carryout and delivery services also are growing. Inside the restaurant, Pizza Hut took the lead at lunchtime several years ago by promising to put a Personal Pan Pizza on the table in five minutes or give customers a free one for failing to beat the clock. The service, introduced in 1983, sputtered at first—average times often exceeded six minutes, and ten to twelve minutes was unhappily far from uncommon—but Pizza Hut didn't give up. Instead, it worked hard on systems and personnel training to make the standard more attainable, in the process greatly enlarging the lunch trade at the average Pizza Hut, especially among office workers on short lunch breaks. According to company figures, more than 95 percent of its five-minute pizzas are on the table on time these days, and lunch traffic has grown from almost nothing to nearly 20 percent of total sales.

The key to making the "Fast Lunch" system work is making the clock the visible standard of excellence. Lunchtime customers are seated, their orders taken, and then a timer is placed on the table to start ticking down. Almost every time, it's still ticking when the pizza arrives. An eye-on-the-clock orientation also resulted in the second major system enhancement: To make sure paying and leaving are similarly speedy, the revamped system calls for collecting at the table, just as is the practice in a pricier restaurant, instead of forcing customers anxious to get back to the office on time to queue up in front of the cash register.

Many operational details were reworked at the frontlines. Gary Rook, the district manager in Des Moines, Iowa, used a stopwatch and his own firsthand experiences to identify slow spots, in the process streamlining procedures both on the service floor and back in the kitchen. Before long, 97 percent of the customers in his district were rating Pizza Hut's service as equal to or faster than fast food restaurants'. In 1987, Rook was one of nine recipients of the company's Nova Award (from the word in-*nova*-tion), presented annually to individuals whose ideas come to make a difference throughout the Pizza Hut system.

How good has the Fast Lunch system become? Well, consider the experience of Kathy Delaney, manager of a Pizza Hut in St. Charles, Illinois. In 1987, fifty students from a nearby high school descended on the place one lunchtime. All fifty had their pizzas within the five-minute guarantee.

Carryout service, which accounts for about half of Pizza Hut's total sales, was attacked and revamped in 1987, and again measuring time was a key component. Previously, customers who called in an order for pickup were told their pizza would be ready in twenty minutes. As a norm that was fine, but in light periods fifteen minutes or less is possible (meaning customers were getting pizzas "aged in the box"), while in the midst of a heavy rush twenty-five minutes or more might be more accurate (the result being customers waiting impatiently at the counter).

Now most Pizza Huts have a production-time gauge mounted near the telephone. The gauge has a sliding pointer that reflects current conditions, so when customers are told their pizzas will be ready in twenty minutes, that's "real time." How do they know? The computerized order-entry and cash-register system prints the time of the order right on the ticket, allowing the person who cuts and boxes the hot pizza to adjust the pointer accordingly. Good crews pride themselves on being accurate to within a minute, regardless of how hectic conditions may become.

In addition, many Pizza Huts have adopted the Fast Lunch practice of having customers who dine in pay at the table at dinner, too. That reduces congestion at the cash register, since generally the only people there are picking up carryout orders. Customers appreciate that: There's no more agonizing feeling than waiting in line behind a dinner customer paying up while watching a carryout pizza grow cold in a box.

Systems, of course, are useless without efficient teams of workers to make them go. To encourage good people to enter and stay in the system as valuable contributors to its service culture, Pizza Hut has invested heavily in employee selection and development. That includes part-time and seasonal workers as well as full-time staff.

The philosophy, born of the growing shortage of entry-level workers, is that the future of the company will be built with the people who work for it now. That means hiring even the lowest-paid workers in the restaurant with an eye toward their staying power. And it means investing the time and effort to help managers help their people. As Pizza Hut president and CEO Steven Reinemund told area managers in 1987, "We screen our new hires better because we realize the consequences of a bad hire. We are more willing to invest time into 'turning around' our people rather than turning them over."

The results: Turnover among managers has been reduced from 40 percent in 1984 to less than 20 percent in 1987, further improving service and efficiency. (It's worth noting that restaurant managers are evaluated on overall store quality and service, not simply volume or profitability.) Pizza Hut is earning a well-deserved reputation for the way it provides meaningful employment to the handicapped as well.

More recently, Pizza Hut has begun to make its presence felt in the home delivery segment of the market, and with a novel twist that again involves a perceptive understanding of time management. While it works by the same thirty-minute delivery standard made familiar (even legendary) by Domino's, Pizza Hut customers in some areas with delivery service don't need to figure out which restaurant serves their address fastest (or at all). Instead, they call a single telephone number in a computerized customer service center. There an order-taker notes what they want and routes their order to the closest location for prompt preparation and delivery. In other markets, the data base has been installed at the restaurant level so customers can call their nearby Pizza Hut direct.

There's a stereotype of service work as being low-paid and dead-end. In industry after industry, including the restaurant business, the rapid growth of service jobs points up an inherent fallacy of that statement: Someone owns those businesses, someone trains and manages those people, and increasingly those upwardly mobile people are veterans of the frontlines. According to David Zemelman, Pizza Hut's senior vice president for personnel, some 40 percent of the chain's nearly three thousand company-owned restaurants (there are more than six thousand in the U.S. system, nearly seven thousand worldwide) are now managed by people who began as drivers, waiters and waitresses, cooks, hosts and hostesses. Higher-level managers typically learned the business firsthand as restaurant managers. Franchisees report similar career progressions.

Could it be that fast food is a new form of the all-American fast track?

Pizza Hut, Inc.
Subsidiary of PepsiCo, Inc.
9111 East Douglas
Wichita, KS 67201

Bob Evans Farms

WALK INTO MANY, MAYBE MOST, RESTAURANTS, AND THE HOST OR HOSTESS WILL look at you and ask (sometimes, but alas not always, courteously), "How many in your party?"

Walk into one of the approximately 225 Bob Evans restaurants in any of the eleven midwestern and south-central states where the chain operates and more likely than not you'll hear something different: "Welcome to Bob Evans."

That's the official greeting, the first thing you hear, the basis of the all-important first impression that will play a large part in determining if you ever come back. A few years ago, Bob Evans made a contest out of it. Offered a free meal to customers who weren't "properly" greeted. Gave away three meals in six weeks.

It's that kind of attention to service detail that has made Bob Evans a family favorite pretty much everywhere the distinctive red-and-white restaurants are found. Generally speaking, that's on the northern and southern ends of the Interstate 75 corridor that connects Michigan and Florida. The chain, based in Columbus, Ohio, has now crossed the Mississippi at St. Louis and has entered the Southwest through the 1987 acquisition of Texas-based Owens Country Sausage, but it's clearly a midwestern place at heart.

In 1986, *Restaurant & Institution's* annual "Choice in Chains" survey found Bob Evans scored highest for service, food quality, and cleanliness among full-service, coffee-shop-style restaurants. What's more, when its sample was cross-tabulated to compare service ratings among customers of gourmet-style, seafood, ethnic, and specialty restaurants, Bob Evans again got the highest marks for service. And in 1987, Bob Evans was once more right there—with Shoney's—at the top of the charts for customer service, food quality, and value.

For a modest restaurant operation that started out as a fast-food breakfast stop—a place to showcase the fresh sausage made on the Ohio River Valley farm run by, you guessed it, a guy named Bob Evans—that's an enviable record of success. It's all the more noteworthy because there's just nothing fancy to it. From menu selections to decor, Bob Evans is about as basic, simple, wholesome, and unpretentious as a restaurant can get. It's also about as good at those basics as most folks ever experience.

That philosophy started some forty years ago on the original, eleven-hundred-acre Bob Evans farm in Rio Grande, Ohio, about a dozen miles from the Ohio River in the southeastern part of the state. There the original Bob Evans, who retired in 1986, grew his farm business conservatively, only adding what he could pay for, and never turning things over to strangers. It wasn't uncommon for supermarket meat managers to come out to visit the farm to see where all those good sausage products were coming from, and naturally Bob and his wife, Jewell, would invite them to sit down and eat with them. By 1962, they were playing host to so many people that they built a small (seven stools) Sausage Shop to take care of their guests.

It took six years—we're talking *conservative* business practices here—but, emboldened by the pleasure people seemed to get from his growing line of sausage products, Evans decided to open a real restaurant. A site was selected about sixty miles up the road in Chillicothe, the bright red-and-white design was chosen, a fast-food menu featuring sausage sandwiches, hamburgers, fries, and shakes was put together, and the long-awaited restaurant opened—to less than rave reviews.

The problem, it turned out, was service. People wanted it. Uncharacteristically, Bob Evans wasn't providing it. So when business quickly nosedived, a team of employees and managers closed the place down over a weekend, redesigned the interior so customers could sit down, revamped the fast-food offerings into a full-service menu, hired waitresses, and reopened. Their quick work saved the day—and the restaurant chain, as it turned out.

Sausage is still an important part of the business, contributing about a third of corporate sales in 1987. And it's still a business run much as Evans himself used to do things. In nineteen states and the District of Columbia, more than eighty-five route salespeople still make daily direct deliveries to some seventy-seven hundred stores in their areas, stocking shelves, maintaining case displays, and talking to store personnel. In the afternoon, they call the closest of the five Bob Evans production plants with their customers' orders for the twenty-five pork sausage products the company sells. Within twenty-four hours, those orders are made up fresh and loaded on delivery trucks for the next day's run. At Bob Evans Farms, they say that no other sausage company in the country continues to operate in this manner.

Not until the 1980s did the company begin to aggressively expand the restaurant side of the business. When it did, it started from bedrock, turning a down-home personal philosophy into a bona fide corporate

culture. The emphasis remains on substance, not style, good food prepared well and served by people who smile at you and seem to really care
about whether you're enjoying yourself and finding everything to your
liking. No detail is too small, from the greeting you get at the door to the
way they invite you back when you leave.

Among the subtle service aspects Bob Evans measures are the maximum amount of time you have to wait before being seated (ideally no
more than fifteen minutes), how long it takes after you sit down for
someone to come by with water and a greeting (contact to be made in
sixty seconds or less), how long it takes for the food to arrive after you've
placed your order (ten minutes max), and how quickly a vacated table is
cleaned up and made ready for the next customers (no longer than five
minutes).

The universal greeting standard has been relaxed somewhat—it's not
mandatory that the welcome line be used, but hosts and hostesses are
expected to do more than an imitation of airline-style seating ("smoking
or nonsmoking, aisle or window?"). Does that mean that the standard
has been diluted? Not at all. Regular customers, it seems, chafed at the
stock greeting from people they felt they knew. And they said so. At Bob
Evans, they listen to things like that.

Case in point: the Great Cream Pitcher Contretemps. A couple of
years ago, the company decided to do away with its distinctive cream
pitchers in favor of individual portions of coffee lightener. In other
restaurants, after all, that's what they do for customers—it must be more
efficient and cost-effective. So one fine day the cream pitchers disap-
peared from the tables and were thrown away, to be replaced by the
packaged creamer.

It seemed like a good idea at the time. But not for long. Phone calls,
comment cards, and countless questions and complaints from regular
customers made it painfully clear that real cream pitchers were something
people simply *expected* to find at their local Bob Evans. Within a week,
an order had been placed and delivered, the pitchers were back on the
table, and the customers were no doubt enjoying a chuckle with their
favorite waiters and waitresses over the way some people have to be
taught to leave things alone when there's nothing wrong with them.

While the scale of the incident mandated a solution from above, Bob
Evans tries to make sure that most complaints are resolved by the
manager on duty at the time the problem occurred. In addition, it
emphasizes the importance of managers working the floor during meals,
not just exchanging trite conversation ("How is everything tonight?"
"Fine.") but observing and inquiring about clues to dissatisfaction such as
uneaten food and uncomfortable body language that suggests things might
not be going right tonight.

Rather than take a chance on diluting quality standards, the company has kept growth in check—fewer than twenty new locations are added in a typical year—and under its own name and control. "Bob Evans Farms knows it wouldn't be fair to its loyal customers to risk quality by putting their restaurants into someone else's hands," is the official explanation of the long-standing decision not to offer franchises.

Personnel management concentrates on selecting the kind of people who will fit into a Bob Evans operation; people who display the kind of hard work, competence, discipline, and enthusiasm that will appeal to young families and older couples alike. Those who do can move up—witness Julie Briner Mash, 1987 manager of the year. Her father, Ralph, has been with Bob Evans as a sausage salesman for nearly twenty years. She started on the restaurant side of the business in 1975, as a waitress in North Canton, Ohio. Now she manages a restaurant of her own.

Stability and continuity are hallmarks at Bob Evans, as they are in so many good service organizations. The typical restaurant manager has been with the company for more than five years, district and zone managers average at least ten years in the system. Most, like Briner Mash, have come up through the ranks. All are constantly reminded of the company's determination to remain true to its original values. They're in training constantly, starting with a four-month introductory program, but they're also expected to serve as on-the-job examples of the kind of service quality and professionalism the chain expects its customers to experience.

According to *R&I's* annual investigation of the industry, most customers are finding that as distinctive as the cream pitchers at Bob Evans.

Bob Evans Farms, Inc.
3776 South High Street
Columbus, OH 43207

McDonald's

AMERICANS SPEND AN ESTIMATED $50 BILLION A YEAR ON FAST FOOD. MOST often, the food they want fast is a hamburger. When they do, the place they go is likely to be a nearby McDonald's, part of the world's largest food-service organization—those Golden Arches draw more customers each year than Burger King, Wendy's, and Hardee's (numbers two, three, and four respectively in the Burger Wars) combined. In fact, according to a report in *The Wall Street Journal* in 1987, customers in awareness surveys name McDonald's more often than the next *six* competitors combined.

With more than ten thousand locations the world over, about three fourths of them in the U.S., it would be easy to dismiss McDonald's economic success as a function of sheer size augmented by relentless advertising. Easy, but wrong. "We lead the industry because we follow the customers," is how McDonald's chairman Fred Turner is prone to explain it. As restaurant consultant Ronald Paul told *The Wall Street Journal*, "McDonald's is winning on good service."

It's the design of that service system that is interesting. And noteworthy. McDonald's decided early on what it would and would not willingly do for its customers—a common characteristic of many well-run service organizations. The imperative is expressed internally as "QSC&V": quality, service, cleanliness, and value, all of them quantifiable standards. The menu is relatively simple, and it doesn't change much over time. The food preparation and delivery system is based on assembly-line techniques: cook a dozen, two dozen burger patties at a time, decorate them all the same, wrap them up, and keep them in a warming bin so customers can walk up to the counter or slide through the drive-through and get away fast. Yes, you can have it your way (Burger King's most successful, if not quite relevant, point of counterattack), but you'll have to wait, because the priority customers (unlike the more individualized mass production of the Burger King system) are the ones who are content with the standard offering.

Because the service system prizes speed, it has to accommodate customers in large numbers, which means floor managers are constantly trying to maintain a tenuous balance between quality and quantity. Prepare too many Big Macs too far in advance and they'll taste like the box they're sitting in by the time a customer has them in hand. Prepare too few and customers stack up at the counters and in the drive lanes. Yes, you can insist that your order be prepared while you wait (Wendy's point of difference, which also is indeed different but somewhat irrelevant), but again you'll have to wait. Waiting is definitely not what McDonald's is about.

What it is about is consistency. Quality standards are high from the commissary to the counter help. Cleanliness is almost an obsession—McDonald's managers will send their people out to clean up the parking lot of an adjacent competitor to make sure their customers aren't jarred by unpleasant sights. (Wake up a former crew kid in the middle of the night with the admonition, "If you've got time to lean, you've got time to clean," and watch them reach for a rag or a mop out of conditioned reflex.)

Although about 75 percent of McDonald's locations are franchised or joint ventures, the parent corporation in the Chicago suburb of Oak Brook keeps tight reins on quality control. It selects the locations for its restaurants, constructs and owns the buildings most of its franchisees operate, and usually owns or leases the land those buildings are on. To make sure franchisees focus 100 percent of their time and efforts on the business, it bans absentee ownership by corporations and partnerships, and refuses to let its franchisees operate other kinds of restaurants. It doesn't generally supply the food, paper products, or equipment used in each restaurant, but it does require that they be purchased only from approved suppliers who have met McDonald's rigorous quality standards.

Before a license is granted, prospective owners must go through, at their own expense, a training and qualification process that can take up to two years, and they may wait another six months or more before a franchise is made available. Some of that training is in the field, some of it at Hamburger University in Oak Brook, the outgrowth of the management training center McDonald's established in the basement of a unit in nearby Elk Grove Village in 1961.

About three thousand students work on their "B.H." (Bachelor of Hamburgerology) each year. The Oak Brook facility offers eleven different courses taught by twenty resident "professors," all of whom have come up through the ranks. They teach everything from the two-week Advanced Operations Course that hones equipment management, financial controls, human relations, and management skills to the intense, eight-day session in "hamburger marketing" designed for international managing directors, licensees, advertising personnel, and senior operations people. The international classes make use of a United Nations-style simultaneous translations system for non-English speakers.

In the field, training is continuous. The typical manager who works his or her way up through the system to manage a McDonald's restaurant will have spent some two thousand hours in on-the-job training, approximately the same number of hours a college student spends in the classroom earning a bachelor's degree. Maybe that's why McDonald's takes as much pride in the accomplishments of its alumni as do many major universities. After all, founder Ray Kroc was himself a high school dropout. As the success of McDonald's illustrates, it's not how smart the service worker *is*, it's how smart that worker *serves*.

What's true at the frontline is true along mahogany row. Every manager in the system is a Hamburger University graduate, and hundreds have become franchisees with their own restaurants. Half of the corporation's officers are themselves former restaurant managers. On Founders Day (the late Kroc's birthday) each October third, headquarters shuts down, as do the other administrative offices around the world, and the entire corporate staff spends the day in neighborhood restaurants, flipping hamburgers, making milkshakes, cleaning tables, and generally getting back to their frontline roots.

Yet for all the emphasis on uniformity, it's not a one-way relationship. McDonald's listens to its frontline operators, and with good reason: the Big Mac, Egg McMuffin, and McD.L.T. all were invented by individual operators within the system; so was the system McDonald's workers are taught to use to wrap burgers without leaving a thumbprint indentation in the bun.

The first McDonald's was opened in 1948 by two brothers, Dick and Mac McDonald, in San Bernardino, California. The Golden Arches evolved from the exterior style of their drive-in. Kroc was a mixer salesman from Illinois who stopped by to visit one day in 1954 because of the amount of equipment the brothers were buying; he went home as their franchising agent, opening his own McDonald's (now restored and preserved as a museum) the following year in Des Plaines, Illinois. Growth has been an annual story ever since.

In recent years, there has been a trendy binge of "burger bashing," with critics rapping everything from the high sodium and fat content of typical fast-food offerings to the marginal income provided by minimum wage jobs. Given Turner's observation that the company leads by following its customers, it's predictable that McDonald's and its fast-food rivals are now moving toward healthier offerings. Sodium and fat contents have been reduced somewhat, salads are now on the menu, and customer education materials 'fess up to ingredients and their cost in calories and cholesterol.

Meanwhile, as *Time* magazine pointed out in 1987, there's a contrarian viewpoint that looks at the positive impact of companies like McDonald's as providers of basic training for new American service workers. The work culture they're exposed to, often as their first regular employment, values attention to quality, courtesy, efficiency, consistency, cleanliness, and an ability to think on their feet as they interact with customers of all ages and descriptions and demeanors.

At one time or another, said *Time*, McDonald's has employed about eight million people, which works out to about 7 percent of all current U.S. workers. Among other miscellany, that means the group involved in preparing this book is statistically normal—there's a former crew kid among us.

McDonald's Corporation
One McDonald Plaza
Oak Brook, IL 60521

THIRTY MINUTES OR IT'S FREE.

As a service standard, that's about as short and sweet as they come. It defines the service precisely. It defines the standard of performance against which the business promises to measure itself. And it's probably the major reason why Thomas S. Monaghan is running a worldwide chain of more than five thousand pizza stores all over the United States and in seven foreign countries (and rooting for the Detroit Tigers, which he also owns, and for which he once dreamed of playing shortstop) instead of struggling with a handful of pizza parlors up around Ypsilanti, Michigan. That's where DomiNick's was operating in 1960 when he bought into the business.

Today, Domino's is the undisputed pacesetter in the field of home delivery, the entrepreneur's version of meals on wheels. Its food may not win too many taste tests. Its menu (just pizza and cola in most of its stores) gives new meaning to the concept of simplicity. Its legendary service standard has been revised down to three bucks off if the order arrives late (Domino's will, however, provide a *new* pizza free if the customer complains within thirty minutes and returns at least half of the unsatisfactory one). And you can't eat your pizza "there" because there's no seating there, nor will there ever be, according to Monaghan. Doesn't matter. Millions of hungry people clearly are willing to trade off culinary artistry and menu variety for a simple hot meal that almost always arrives at their door less than thirty minutes after they order it.

Even at three bucks' worth of jeopardy, thirty-minute delivery is not as easy as it sounds. Simplicity of consumer choice notwithstanding, a typical Domino's is a pretty sophisticated service operation, one that has to effectively combine choice of location, service radius (in some areas stores are less than two miles apart), order-taking, food preparation, driver training, routing directions, and cash management in the presence of the ubiquitous deadline.

In keeping with its organizational theme of simplicity, virtually all Domino's facilities are built from the same efficient design. All the space is work space. Internal systems are managed for simplicity, and corporate systems support them. For example, the network of twenty-seven commissaries provides all supplies, delivering three times a week to take many of the burdens of inventory management and quality control off the shoulders of store managers while reducing square footage to the bare minimum.

It's the all-important people side of the equation that Domino's delegates to its store managers. Working almost always with a cadre of young, minimum-wage employees, managers (most of them in their early twenties) have to fashion a dependable crew that can function well under pressure. Since 80 percent of all orders are placed during 20 percent of a store's business hours, that means developing an ability to work fast without racing through quality and safety checkpoints. Crews also are extensively cross-trained so employees can do more than one of the five basic jobs—driver, order-taker, pizza-maker, oven-tender, and router (the person who figures out which pizzas go with which drivers to which addresses)—when things get hectic.

Eighty-five percent of that training is on the job, delivered directly by the store managers (albeit from programs developed by a small corporate training staff). Much of it is presented on videotape, with short messages and flashy production values designed to get through to eighteen- to twenty-one-year-old trainees. For managers in training ("MITs" in the Domino's vernacular), who tend to be in their early to mid-twenties, the pacing slows a bit, but video is still the most common and effective medium. The fifth appliance common to *every* Domino's store (after the telephone, cash register, oven, and refrigerator) is a VCR.

Like most fast-food operations, Domino's is relatively low-pay, but there are several incentive systems in place to reward good crew performance, including a national competition each year to crown the fastest pizza-makers companywide. Managers in corporate stores receive 20 percent of their store's profits as a bonus.

The latter also have a longer-term incentive: the prospect of earning the right to buy their own franchise. About 70 percent of all Domino's stores are franchises, but with an interesting twist. In the early 1970s, Monaghan decided to offer franchises only to people who had worked for the company; as a result, 98 percent of the more than six hundred franchisees nationwide are former Domino's employees. Because the operation's start-up and overhead costs are so low, most can and do own a number of stores.

Many businesses use secret shoppers to audit service quality, but Domino's has raised the practice to a science. Its eight thousand inspectors, which it calls "mystery customers," are assigned—two per store per month—to double-check twenty-two different aspects of food quality and store performance. There's no warning or predictable pattern to their impromptu checkups, because they really are customers. Domino's pays them a nominal fee for each evaluation form they submit, but the food they order they also pay for. Thus, their orders are real orders, often placed during real peak periods.

Their reports go back to store managers to be used for both product- and service-quality control, and also are entered into a systemwide database that gives headquarters and regional managers a constant readout on performance levels and norms nationwide. That's one reason they know, for example, that in 1987 the average pizza was delivered in 23.08 minutes.

Among the variables Domino's pulls off each computer-coded form: the times, to the minute, when the pizza was ordered and delivered; the ingredients on the pizza; whether the order-taker used the Domino's name in answering the phone; whether, and for how long, the mystery customer was put on hold; whether the delivery person was neat and clean, and wearing appropriate Domino's attire (including a name tag); whether the pizza was hot, the cola cold, the toppings evenly distributed, the flavor of the cheese and sauce pleasing; and even whether the Domino's drivers seen in the neighborhood of late have been driving safely and courteously.

In addition, periodically each Domino's store manager is expected to personally call back some of a given day's customers and quiz them about their food and service experience with his or her store. The system not only helps evaluate how well the service standards are being met, but also provides direct (if not face-to-face) customer contact. In some regions, supervisors—who typically have responsibility for six to eight stores— have bounceback cards delivered with the pizza as a less-confrontive way of diagnosing service problems and keeping in touch with customers' changing perceptions.

Still others take a more personal approach. Michael Ellis, for example, started working for a Tulsa Domino's as a driver in late 1985. By mid-1986, he was a manager, taking over Store 6480 in Muskogee, where he faced everything from a poor sales record and sporadic delivery problems to a generally negative perception of the Domino's name among customers whose experience up until that time had been less than they had been led to expect.

Instead of turning up the heat on an advertising campaign, Ellis personally went door to door to meet the customers in his service area, introducing himself as the new manager in their neighborhood, inquiring about past service problems, occasionally giving away a free pizza to encourage a skeptic to give the revamped operation a try. To build visibility, he got a small pickup, painted it in the appropriate Domino's color scheme, then sent it out with free Coca-Cola on hot summer days.

Inside, he turned up the heat on operations, making sure product quality and delivery service returned to par. In the space of a year, Store

6480's sales jumped 80 percent in some periods, its delivery time rating (as measured by the mystery customer reports) dropped to under twenty-one minutes, and the store's rating for total customer satisfaction jumped to 98 percent. The tactics and the results led to Ellis being named Manager of the Year for 1986, an award that carried with it a check for ten thousand dollars at Domino's National Awards Celebration the following July. It also made Ellis—since promoted to area supervisor in northwest Arkansas—the author of page nineteen (headline: "Dedication") in the company's 1987 annual report.

From top to bottom, Domino's has survived a period of radical growth (seventy new store openings a month has been "normal") without losing its focus on the service standard that sets it apart. That's largely because so much of the business has been delegated to the individual store managers, the people closest to the customers. "If you don't make it, bake it, or take it, then you're support for those who do," is an operations motto that extends outward from Tom Monaghan's office.

As *Training* magazine reported in 1987, "It appears as though everyone in the corporate management structure within Domino's Pizza, Inc., takes this little saying to heart. They cling to the philosophy that their job is to help their subordinates succeed. CEO Monaghan serves as a role model: Every few months he hosts a national phone-in show, inviting all employees, from drivers to franchisees, to call in with questions about sales, management, corporate goals, and the like."

The "Pizza Tiger" sounds like one smart cat.

Domino's Pizza, Inc.
Prairie House, Domino's Farms
30 Frank Lloyd Wright Drive
Ann Arbor, MI 48106

Wendy's

THE HAMBURGER WARS WERE ALREADY IN FULL SWING WHEN A NEW CHAL-
lenger entered the lists in 1969. McDonald's was clearly the superpower
to be reckoned with. Accordingly, the menu and operating profile
of that first Wendy's in downtown Columbus, Ohio, was designed around
the one thing that McDonald's (and other volume-oriented competitors)
had had to skimp on in the All-American quest to measure service in the
billions—personal service.

The Wendy's formula is deceptively simple: Instead of mass-producing
large quantities of standardized burgers with the same toppings so a large
volume of customer orders can be filled quickly from a central holding
bin, it handles each customer individually, cooking each sandwich to
order. If that means lower counter volumes, so be it. To this day, there is
only one register and one order-taker at the standard Wendy's counter;
the drive-through lane at most of the thirty-five hundred units around the
country (there are about thirty-eight hundred worldwide) constitutes a
second order point. By contrast, the basic McDonald's design can handle
six to ten lines of customers in front of the counter, and drive-throughs
increasingly are built with two windows in succession to speed order-filling.

It makes for an interesting choice between fast food and "not-quite-so-
fast" food—a classic face-off between quantity and quality. Where Wendy's excels is in serving the folks who opt for the latter. It isn't going to
overtake McDonald's in number of stores or average sales per store,
although sometimes in the heat of competition it acts as if it has indeed
decided to accept the challenge on that level. When it stays true to itself,
Wendy's typically succeeds in providing a visibly distinctive level of food
quality and customer service.

Think of it in terms of the physical design: By design, the Wendy's
layout that feeds customers to the order-taker one at a time slows the
rush-hour rush to a trickle. But it means those customers can count on
being greeted and handled as individuals, and will receive hot food
cooked to their specific order. If you don't mind waiting a little longer for
food that's a little hotter and a little closer to the way you might fix it at

home, you're (ahem) Wendy's kind of people. You're not alone, either: *Restaurants & Institutions'* annual "Choice in Chains" surveys have pegged Wendy's tops in the burger class every year since 1982.

Actually, in 1987 Wendy's and Burger King ended up in a statistical dead heat. *R&I* listed Burger King first solely on the basis of the total number of evaluations it had in hand. It strikes us that this is exactly the kind of bigger-equals-better comparison that the Wendy's operating philosophy disdains. For the record, McDonald's finished a consistent and respectable fourth both years.

R. David Thomas, Wendy's founder, learned about service at the frontline. In 1944, at the age of twelve (he claimed to be sixteen), he got a job as a soda jerk in a Knoxville drug store. The owner found out his real age and fired him. He quickly landed another job, working twelve-hour shifts on weekends and as a summer vacation fill-in at a restaurant lunch counter, and he worked hard enough and long enough that this time nobody questioned his age. His formal education stopped when he dropped out of the tenth grade (it's an interesting coincidence that McDonald's Ray Kroc also was a high school dropout). For Thomas, business school involved on-the-job restaurant training that continued through stints as a busboy, Army cook, short-order cook, and eventually Kentucky Fried Chicken franchisee.

When the first Wendy's Old Fashioned Hamburgers restaurant opened its doors in November of 1969, Thomas had plenty of doubters and no real plans for creating a national challenger to the growing burger giants. His only bankroll came from selling back his Columbus Kentucky Fried Chicken outlets for a cool $1.5 million. His new template—carpeting, Tiffany-style lamps, Bentwood chairs, and a simple, made-to-order menu using fresh, not frozen, beef—didn't fit the fast-food mold, and more polished restaurateurs were amused to learn that Wendy was actually his eight-year-old daughter's nickname.

What Thomas had going for him were two things: insight gained at the frontline and his franchising experience with Kentucky Fried Chicken (he had traveled extensively with the Colonel and at one point managed the regional operations of three hundred restaurants). That convinced him to grow the young chain through master franchise arrangements that allowed investors to set up more than one restaurant in their region—usually an entire city, sometimes a quarter of a state.

Today, approximately two-thirds of all Wendy's are franchise operations, but there are only about 250 master franchisees. To maintain quality control, Thomas insisted on one prerequisite: company executives and franchise owners alike have to go through extensive in-store training ("wearing the stripes," in Wendy's jargon—a reference to the chain's original blue-and-white uniforms) to make sure they, like he, have an opportunity to learn the business firsthand.

In all, eleven of the fourteen weeks of the new-franchisee program are spent on the job in a regional training store chosen for its consistently high performance from among Wendy's company-run and franchised operations. A similar training and mentoring system is used to bring new managers up to speed and make sure they imitate good role models when they find themselves on the real firing line.

In recent years, Wendy's has begun to retool a number of its internal systems, including menu offerings, crew training, and regional administration, to more closely support restaurant operations. For instance, under its franchise unit development program, Wendy's develops and builds about two hundred new units a year, then sells or leases them to its top franchisees. The program allows the company to control the pace of expansion and site new restaurants in promising locations, but gives top franchise operators control of hands-on operations and longer-term management. At the same time, more than 150 poor-performing company locations have been closed or sold to franchisees whose track records indicate they can improve operations.

Like others in the fast-food business, Wendy's is facing a growing shortage of entry-level, minimum-wage workers at a time when it is trying to add between three hundred and four hundred new restaurants each year. Consequently, training has been improved across the board as a way of retaining crew members and encouraging the best of them to stay with the company and move up into positions of more responsibility.

Like Disney, Wendy's doesn't have "customers." It has "Guests" (the G is always capitalized). Here's how the Employee Handbook explains it to new employees: "We hope that people who choose to dine at Wendy's will be treated like special Guests in your home. We have invited them by promising quality food served quickly, in a clean and pleasant environment. These customers, our Guests, even pay us for this experience. These are *your* Guests and they reflect *you*. When you smile they smile, and when you thank them for coming they are appreciative. We want to do everything possible so that you and our Guests will have a pleasant and rewarding experience at Wendy's."

On the food side, the emphasis remains on quality. For example, to add a new dimension to its food service profile, Wendy's is betting heavily on the SuperBar, a self-service, health-and-nutrition-oriented buffet that integrates Wendy's existing salad bar with Mexican and Italian dishes. If customers like it, the typical configuration will ultimately offer a choice of more than fifty items ranging from fresh fruits and vegetables to nachos, fettucine, and baked potato toppings (okay, so it's not all health and nutrition oriented). It also will accommodate seasonal and regional variations designed to distance Wendy's from the heavy fried-food fare that more health-conscious consumers are learning to resist.

SuperBar is evidence that Wendy's remains committed to experiment-

ing with new forms and structures, even at the risk of stubbing its
corporate toes. In 1986, for example, it had to cut its losses on a breakfast-
to-order menu, making the service optional in order to protect its lunch
and dinner business. But as long as it is able to keep its focus firmly on
maintaining quality, even if it means sacrificing some quantity, Wendy's
will continue to win kudos from its customers.

Wendy's International, Inc.
4288 West Dublin-Granville Road
Dublin, OH 43017

FOOD SALES

RETAIL

Stew Leonard's Dairy

Vons Grocery Company

Ukrop's Super Markets

SuperAmerica

WHOLESALE

Procter & Gamble Company

Super Valu

Frito-Lay

The Food Industry:
Eating Right and Eating Well

WHEN A SERVICE DELIVERY SYSTEM IS WELL DESIGNED AND FUNCTIONING EFFEC-
tively, it is transparent—essentially invisible to the customer using and
being served by it. Take the modern, self-service emporium where we
buy food and sundries. It may seem that the grocery store as we know it
has been around since the Constitution, if not the Bible—that this is the
only rational way to shop. But it is, in fact, an invention, and a fairly
recent one at that.

Before 1916, groceries were bought over a counter from a clerk who
put them in the shopper's bag or, as an alternative, delivered them later
in the day. But all that changed when Memphis inventor Clarence Saunders,
looking for a new, more efficient way to sell market goods, took out the
counter and invited customers to come help themselves. Thus was born
the basis for U.S. Patent No. 1,242,872, issued to Saunders in 1917 for
"certain new and useful improvements in Self-Serving Stores." It also was
the basis for the first of the three-thousand-store Piggly Wiggly chain.

Twenty years later, yet another service system invention re-revolutionized
and brought the retail grocery biz to its current state of existence. Its
inventor, Oklahoma City grocer Sylvan Goldman, was disturbed that
shoppers in his Standard Food Stores stopped shopping not when their
lists expired but when their hand-held baskets were full. Goldman's
daring solution was to take the load off the shopper's arm, put it on
wheels, and let the customer *push* it around the store until all the
necessary purchases were made. Presto! The shopping cart.

The response, Goldman recalled in a 1977 interview, was underwhelming.
In fact, he had to resort to hiring a cadre of retirees, housewives, and
youngsters to "shop" his stores for ninety days until his bewildered
regular customers gave in and gave this new, radical approach to shopping for food a trial. Today, of course, pushing a shopping cart along a
carefully planned and laid out serpentine of aisleways seems the only
"natural way" to shop for food. The inventions themselves, seen in the
light of history, seem so logical, natural, and chock-full of common sense
that we don't really "see" them. They're transparent.

Selling Healthy

Not all the inventing and innovating to be done in the food business was over and done with in the 1930s and 1940s. The 1970s and 1980s, like the periods preceding them, have been times of growth and change in the grocery business. Today's consumers are interested in both healthier foods and haute cuisine. They crave both convenience and speed in shopping but dote on stores with acres of options. They want the lowest prices, purest contents, highest quality, longest shelflife, and most convenient method of preparation possible.

All those concerns, and more, keep grocers hopping. But according to industry surveys, there is at least one constant on the consumer's shopping list—the desire to be treated well: to encounter a friendly, recognizable face at the cash register and in the grocery aisle.

A 1987 survey by the Food Marketing Institute showed that 93 percent of shoppers rate courteous, friendly employees as an important supermarket feature. During the 1980s, the most successful grocery operations have taken such findings to heart.

- Seaway Foods of Bedford, Ohio, set up a hotline to answer customer complaints and suggestions. The hotline is answered by company executives.
- Stew Leonard's Dairy store in Norwalk, Connecticut, answers every query left in its customer suggestion box. It also distributes copies to every department manager.
- Byerly's, an upscale grocer based in the Minneapolis suburb of Edina, has equipped its nine stores with twenty-four-hour restaurants, card and gift shops, post office services, and roaming home economists who offer free advice on everything from menu-planning to calorie content.
- Southern California pacesetter Vons has created a separate and distinct grocery store chain for the Hispanic customers who now account for close to 20 percent of the region's population.

Increasingly, the industry has discovered the road to success—make that profit—lies in finding ever more innovative ways to determine what the shopper wants, and then be just as innovative in delivering it. Frontline employees are playing an ever larger and more important role as even the biggest chains realize that how their employees interact with customers makes a powerful impression on how the shopper perceives the store.

In 1986, a leading industry trade publication, *Progressive Grocer*, noted that out of twenty dissatisfied customers, only one is likely to say anything; fourteen may simply never darken the door again. Most of the dissatisfied customers never speak up, the magazine said, because they do not believe anyone will take them seriously. It offered ten, if not commandments, then at least helpful admonitions:

- Smile and greet customers; thank them for shopping there.
- Identify repeat customers.
- Learn their names.
- If a customer needs assistance, take the time to really help.
- If a customer questions a store policy, explain it and the reasons behind it.
- If you don't have what a customer wants, apologize and try to find a suitable substitute.
- Pass on customer requests to higher management.
- Treat complaints as opportunities rather than problems.
- Arrange for the customer to talk with a supervisor or manager.
- Invite customer comments.

Giant, based in Landover, Maryland, was second in the Washington area to Safeway in the early 1970s, and a distant fourth to A&P in Baltimore. It has since become the number one grocer in both markets, eclipsing a number of rivals along the way. How did Giant do it? "We have a better mousetrap," answers Alvin Dobbin, senior vice president of operations.

Giant's mousetrap is also a bigger mousetrap—fifty-five thousand square feet compared to an industry average of twenty-seven thousand—and features a gourmet section, the newest grocery trend, which adds another dimension to the chain's already large food and drugstore trade. To build a friendly, personal image that takes the impersonal edge off the scale of the operation, Giant is another company that refers to its employees as "associates;" it also stars them in a TV and newspaper advertising campaign with the slogan, "We care about you."

The tactics are representative of a major and continuing trend in the food business—designing larger stores with more services strategically located throughout. Modern store design puts service departments staffed by knowledgeable salespeople on the perimeter of the store, where they offer specialty merchandise such as flowers, baked goods, fancy chocolates, exotic cheeses, prime meats and seafood, and personal attention.

During the 1970s, when food prices and customer price sensitivities were climbing in tandem, there was a rush to put generic, lower-priced items on the grocery shelves, usually marketed in deliberately garish yellow-and-black or stark black-and-white boxes and wrappings. Today, generics are a much lower item on the shopper's list. According to SAMI/Burke, a New York-based market research firm, generic and store-brand products accounted for 12.9 percent of grocery sales in 1987 compared to 16.8 percent in 1982.

A recent *Consumer Reports* study found that more than 80 percent of its readers prefer national brands to generic or store brands. It reports that national brands, particularly for items such as detergents, toilet paper, soft drinks, and ketchup, are perceived as being of higher quality than generic and store brands.

Generics and store brands are by no means an inconsequential force in real dollar terms, accounting for more than $17 billion in the national shopping cart in 1987. But the price/value balance has clearly tipped back to the latter. The Food Marketing Institute's *Trends* magazine reports that the following items are now deemed very or somewhat important by nine out of ten shoppers: quality produce; good variety or wide selection; quality meat; courteous, friendly employees; good, or low, prices; convenient location; readable and accurate shelf tags.

Trends also notes that while customers generally feel their grocers are meeting their needs, a few areas still need attention. These include many of the same categories listed above, but in a slightly different order: nutritional and health information available for shoppers; good, or low, prices; fast checkout; readable and accurate shelf tags; quality meat; and quality produce.

Some grocers are meeting these concerns in truly innovative ways. When Phoenix radio station KTAR perceived a desire for more information about food and nutrition, it asked ABCO supermarkets to supply someone to host a talk show. The company asked Dave Miller, manager of the ABCO market at the foot of Camelback Mountain, to tackle the job. Miller was formerly a produce merchandiser for Alpha Beta in California, and was regarded by ABCO as being knowledgeable on nutrition and a good talker.

He has had to be: Questions have come in ranging from the use of pesticides in foreign nations to how to cook dandelion greens. So many calls began coming in that the station asked Miller to limit his answers to two minutes or less. There was still a queue of callers, so Miller asked the others to send their inquiries to him by mail. Dozens of letters poured in.

One of the most nutrition-minded supermarkets in the country is Bread & Circus in Boston. The single store opened in 1979 by Anthony Hartnett has grown into a popular chain by selling food containing no preservatives, artificial colors or flavors, refined or synthetic sugars or sweeteners, cottonseed oil, or mostly white flour products. It is pledged to provide organically grown products wherever possible and to eradicate harmful chemical agents from foods if it finds any. The Bread & Circus in nearby Hadley contains a walk-in refrigerator that serves as the company's warehouse, a flour mill that turns out 250 pounds of flour a day for its own bakery, a restaurant, a demonstration kitchen, a deli, and an organic gardening center.

Vons and Giant also have entered the nutritional advice business, the former targeting seniors and other health-conscious customers, the latter placing ads on calcium deficiencies and other health issues and launching a "special diet alert" program that has boosted sales of foods identified as being low in fat, sodium, or cholesterol.

Both companies share with other industry leaders an emphasis on people—both those who shop there and those who wait on them. "You can't make the promises we make and deliver them *most* of the time," says Giant chairman Israel Cohen. "You have to be almost perfect." Cohen, who insists on being called Izzy, reads almost all consumer complaints himself and sends a representative to deal with the more strident ones. The rest are answered by mail and with a telephone call from the company's consumer affairs department.

During the latter half of the 1980s, there has been some sliding away from nutritional concerns toward those of the new quick-delivery haute cuisine interest of the young urban set. *Trends* reported that in 1983, 64 percent of shoppers said they were very concerned about nutrition in food, whereas only 54 percent expressed that concern in 1987.

Giant's entry in the gourmet field is Someplace Special in McLean, Virginia. The store sells triple cream cheese, llama steaks, and other specialty foods. Washingtonians are not the only ones to crave haute cuisine, of course. "Berkeley is full of food snobs," says Bill Andronica, vice president and manager of the three-store Andronica chain in California. Andronica's offers one of the premier gourmet and deli grocery stores in the nation.

"Too often, management thinks delis are drawing cards, not profit centers," says Andronica. "And if you make a profit, they think you're just lucky. To be successful, the deli must be targeted to your market." One of the ways he targeted his deli operations was by hiring one of the West Coast's leading designers, John Sutti, to design two of them. In the Solano store, high ceilings permit food service areas to be canopied by eye-catching metal rods. There are brilliantly-colored panels of material and graphics suspended from the rods. Natural light illuminates the structure.

Andronica also observes that other markets err when they approach delis from a supermarket mentality instead of viewing them as restaurants. He recruited chefs and other people with restaurant experience to staff the deli and operate it as a profit center. Customers took a shine to Andronica's deli, which now averages 11 percent of total store sales.

Others are finding success in the deli and salad bar business. Kings Supermarkets in New Jersey were among the first to offer those services. It offers an in-store cooking school as well. The Kings chain is run by the Bildner family, which also started J. Bildner's, a gourmet operation that has combined with Rich's department stores to meet the never-ending demand for one-stop shopping. Bildner's offers frozen foods such as steak au poivre and duck breasts to go with the store's offerings of designer clothes and other upscale items. Karen H. Brown, a vice president of the

Food Market Institute, says the juxtaposition makes sense. "Today's consumers are very interested in time and convenience," she explains. "The linking of food and department stores really isn't surprising."

The merger of food and dry goods is occurring in middle level markets as well. The latest innovations include the new, bigger-than-ever store called the hypermarket. A prime example is Bigg's of Batavia, Ohio. It has fifty spacious aisles covering the equivalent of more that four football fields, with merchandise rising to the ceiling on almost ten miles of shelves. There are forty checkout counters, including five express lanes. The store is a combination supermarket and discount store, selling steaks, bread, and soda, along with television sets, books, and motor oil.

Bigg's is backed by the French hypermarket company Euromarché. It opened in 1984 and racked up $100 million in sales during its first year, twice what was projected. More hypermarkets are planned by Bigg's, and others—including the French retailer Carrefour, S.A., which owns more than one hundred hypermarkets in Europe and South America—are setting up similar operations. Notable among U.S. entrants to the hypermarket arena are Wal-Mart and the Dallas grocery chain Cullum Cos., which have entered a partnership to create a chain of Hypermart USA stores.

The Good Stuff

The retail food business is not only a big, competitive business, it is a highly varied one. There are more ways to buy our daily bread than you can shake a stick at: Local, regional, and super-regional grocers, convenience stores of every shape and variety, niche specialty stores, and even department stores sell food stuffs. Yet in the era of bigness and national span, family-owned-and-operated corner groceries continue to thrive. In fact, it is the small local and regional grocer who accounts for most of the dollar volume of the industry.

Our exemplars mirror the rich variety of the food business. Stew Leonard's Dairy is a family-owned single-store operation that has become an American business legend—a regular stop on bus tours of southern New England. Vons Grocery Company is a super-regional serving up groceries to the nine million people who live and work in the Los Angeles-to-San Diego corridor of Southern California. Smaller, family-run Ukrop's Super Markets delight shoppers lucky enough to live in the sedate environs of Richmond, Virginia. In the convenience category, SuperAmerica, an Upper Midwest upstart, is taking a good idea and making it better through a focus on service and systems.

Behind the Scenes

Because there is so much more to the great American food chain than the retail grocery store, we also consider the fine service provided by the companies that move the fresh asparagus from field to display case. This generally invisible part of the food industry is a multi-billion-dollar operation of unimaginable complexity—and it works amazingly well.

Three companies give a feel for both the sophistication and variety of the wholesale side of the food and grocery business—and the importance of service quality. Procter & Gamble, though a manufacturer, is nonetheless extremely sensitive to customer views, ideas, wants, and needs. Super Valu, the largest and oldest food wholesaler in the country, defines the crux of its business as retail support. And Frito-Lay is both producer and distributor of the five billion bags of product it vends every year, its service linchpins the route salespeople who serve retailers from the largest supermarkets to the corner convenience mart, with stops at bowling alleys and other establishments as well.

The food biz—be it retail, wholesale, or packaging and producing—is a thin-margin, high-volume, mistakes-can-kill-you-in-a-minute business. It is also as fascinating, intricate, complex, and service-sensitive an endeavor as you can participate in. As we think you'll see, you don't have to give away the store to provide good service to customers.

Stew Leonard's ®

UNLESS YOU'VE BEEN LIVING IN A CAVE FOR THE LAST FIVE YEARS, YOU PROBABLY feel as if you know where to find the butter in Stew Leonard's Dairy store. Here's one guy with one store up there off I-95 in Norwalk, Connecticut—and while it's a big store physically, it doesn't even carry a full grocery line, just about 750 items compared to the 10,000 to 15,000 in a typical supermarket—yet everybody from Tom Peters to Ripley's Believe It or Not has been thumping the drum over what a wonderful job Stew and his crew do at customer service.

Guess what? They're right. Call it simple, call it folksy, call it what you will, Stew Leonard's is the world's largest and most successful dairy store. Sales are approaching $100 million a year (that's about $2 million *a week*, which is more than your typical warehouse grocery store runs through its scanners). Volume per square foot is about ten times the level of conventional grocery stores: The Food Marketing Institute figures $100 million in sales is about normal for a *ten-store* supermarket chain. And profits are $250 per square foot according to *Boardroom Reports*. Obviously, the Leonard family is on to something here.

The three-ton rock out in front of the store is still the best analysis of what. Chiselled into the rock is Stew Leonard, Sr.'s, simple business philosophy (which he credits to a Dale Carnegie course he took when he was twenty years old): "Rule 1: The customer is always right! Rule 2: If the customer is ever wrong, re-read rule 1." Actually the customer is *not* always right, and Stew knows it. Sometimes the customer is 100 percent dead wrong by volume. The point is that even when the customer is wrong, Stew Leonard's people will still treat that customer as if he or she is right. But since all that hairsplitting and backing and filling wouldn't look good inscribed on a three-ton rock, we'll play by Stew's rules.

The success of Stew Leonard's is a result of a good deal more than just determining right from wrong. Leonard calculates that his average customer spends about $100 a week in his store. Multiply that by fifty weeks a year (it keeps the numbers clean and allows for an occasional family vacation), then multiply that total by ten years, and that customer becomes an asset worth $50,000. All of a sudden, passing out free cookies and ice cream to people who have to wait five minutes in line before checking out during peak hours makes sense. So does keeping at least twenty of the store's thirty checkstands open all the time so customers usually won't have to wait at all.

Leonard knows his customers don't like to wait in line. He also knows they appreciate the cookies and ice cream. That's because he listens to them, both informally every day in the store and more formally in focus groups that meet at least once a month. A few years ago, a woman in one of the focus groups observed that she didn't buy fish at Stew Leonard's because it was shrink-wrapped and displayed in a plastic boat. Now fresh fish is displayed unwrapped on a bed of chipped ice (sales doubled after the change), and there's a sampling table at the end of the counter display. Someone else suggested selling muffins in combo packs. Within ten days, Stew Leonard's was doing just that.

Near the front door is a large suggestion box, and customers are encouraged to share their comments, suggestions, and complaints. Each morning the boxes are cleaned out, their contents taken upstairs and typed up on as many sheets of paper as are needed to include them all (one hundred suggestions and comments a day is average). By ten A.M. the comment sheets are photocopied and distributed to all department managers, posted in the employee break areas, and left on the tables in the employee lunchroom so everybody knows how they're doing in the eyes of their most important managers.

There's more. Within twenty-four hours, someone on the store's management team—often someone named Leonard—has followed up with a phone call to thank the customer for his or her comments, explore the details of a suggestion, or discuss ways to resolve the problem. Within forty-eight hours, there's a letter in the mail to follow up yet again. Customers who take the initiative at Stew Leonard's quickly find out how valued their input is considered.

The store also goes to impressive lengths to reward initiative on a customer's behalf among its five hundred employees. A few years ago, for example, a woman wandered up to a young man who had just started working in the lost and found department and inquired whether a gold Cross pen had turned up. It seemed the pen had been her father's, and he had since passed away, and she was feeling a little down and out because of the sentimental value attached. She wasn't even sure she'd lost it in the store, she confessed, but the young man dutifully went from department to department, returning after a while to report he'd had no success in turning up the pen.

Here's where the story gets better. Noticing that the woman was just about in tears by now, the young man reached down under the counter, pulled out three $20 gift certificates (a gold Cross pen costs about $15 to $20, in case you're wondering), signed them, and handed them to her, saying that he knew they couldn't replace what the pen had meant to her, but he'd keep looking and meanwhile maybe this would make her feel a little better.

After the woman left, it occurred to him that, since he was new, maybe he should make sure he had done the right thing in giving away the store's money like that. So he sought out Stew Leonard, Jr., and described what had happened. You be the manager for a moment—how would you have reacted? The younger Leonard took prompt and decisive action.

First, he put the story in the next issue of *Stew's News*, the store's monthly newsletter, with the young man's picture and a glowing description of how he'd done something on behalf of a customer. Second, he gave him a $600 scholarship to attend a Dale Carnegie course because, as he told us, "That's a skill we want developed in our organization."

Similar stories abound. A woman just back from vacation checks through about forty dollars' worth of groceries, then discovers she doesn't have her wallet with her. The check-out clerk, on her own initiative and without a manager's approval, simply writes down the customer's name and address and tells her she can pay the next time she comes in. Happens at your neighborhood grocer's every week, right?

A customer stalks up to the customer service desk, slams down two cases of empty pop cans, and impatiently announces to Marion Murphy, who happens to be on duty there at the time, that he doesn't have time to feed twenty-four cans one by one into an automatic recycling machine and he wants his money right now. Murphy explains that this isn't the can-return department, but since he's in a hurry she'll be happy to get the money out of her purse and feed the machine on her own lunch break to get reimbursed. Nonplused, the customer asks if she's serious. She says yes, it's her job to keep customers happy. The man blushes, picks up the cans, and takes them over to the machine after telling her, "If you've got the time, I've got the time."

On a Friday afternoon, disaster strikes: A computer failure shuts down the cash registers. Most customers wait (munching on free shrimp, courtesy of the management), but one woman leaves, drives thirty minutes to get home, then calls the store and complains to the manager that because of the computer crash, she now has no groceries for her husband's sixtieth birthday party, which happens to be that night. Within an hour, a car pulls up at her house and out pops a Stew Leonard's employee who delivers her groceries—along with a birthday cake that says "Happy 60th, George. Sincerely, Stew." Guess what people talked about at *that* party.

Where does Stew Leonard's find the kind of people who can deliver this consistently high quality of service? *They* find Stew Leonard's. Only one applicant in twenty-five is hired by the store, and the ones who get jobs are those who have demonstrated a positive attitude. The skills, the Leonards reason, can be learned in training.

Interestingly, in contrast to companies with antinepotism rules, about half of Stew Leonard's employees have a relative on the payroll. Rationale: What better way to foster a close-knit, quality-conscious culture? After all, four of the founder's children, not to mention assorted relations, have worked their way up through the business.

Training regularly includes Dale Carnegie courses, even for the frontline workers who start out making seven dollars an hour, about double what many of Stew Leonard's competitors—there are more than ninety other markets within a ten-mile radius of his store—pay. That regional saturation lends itself to a favorite quality-improvement tactic: Every once in a while, they load up a dozen employees from all over the store and drive over to a competitor's business. When they return from the field trip, each person is expected to point out at least one thing the visited store was doing that Stew Leonard's can learn from.

One more simple lesson: the YES principle. Stew Leonard's employees are encouraged to "Think YES," an acronym for "You-Encourage-Support." It works like this: Stew Leonard's wants its employees (the "you") to put themselves in the customer's place and do what they would want done to and for them. It also wants them to "encourage" customers to express their problems and suggestions, because the more information the customer provides, the better able the store will be to meet their needs. For its part, Stew Leonard's promises to "support" its people "in anything you do to better serve the customer."

For all of its fame and success, there's still only one Stew Leonard's. It's still a quintessential family business, a partnership between Stew, Sr., and his wife, Marianne. A second store, to be run by Tom Leonard, is planned for nearby Danbury, and they may actually break ground someday. There's apparently no rush, however, since it has been "planned" since 1985. Meanwhile, customers are getting used to the location, because about six thousand people a day have been stopping by the big tent on the forty-four-acre site to buy fresh produce and garden supplies. Here we go again?

There have been countless inquiries about franchises, and lots of button-down investment types would certainly love to take the company public. To both, the Leonard family has consistently said no. If they did that, they would have to please franchisees and directors and shareholders and the like.

This way, they just have to please their customers.

Stew Leonard's Dairy Store
100 Westport Avenue
Norwalk, CT 06851

VONS

IN THE GROCERY BUSINESS, OWNERS COME AND OWNERS GO AND CUSTOMERS can be every bit as transient. The more competitive the marketplace, the more dire the consequences of a misstep or a missed opportunity, whether it's due to mispricing a line of merchandise or misplacing customer-service priorities because of takeover-induced turmoil at company headquarters.

Case in point: "the nation of Southern California." More than nine million people live and work in the urban corridor from the San Fernando Valley north of Los Angeles to the Mexican border south of San Diego. They're a diverse ethnic mix, most of them émigrés since the end of World War II, but from points of origin ranging from the eastern U.S. to the Far East, the frozen states of the Midwest to the sunny lands south of the border.

All those people put away a lot of groceries, which is grounds for a highly competitive battle among food stores of every size and description, from hardy neighborhood independents to large chains. It's a dogfight that has seen a variety of top dogs—and a series of often messy fights over ownership of the parent corporations—but since late 1986 the leader of the pack has been Vons, the nation's eleventh-largest supermarket chain. From its massive new Pavilions superstores to the conventional Vons supermarkets and the new Tianguis chain that serves Mexican and other Hispanic customers, the company has used, in the words of *Progressive Grocer* magazine, a "combination of high-tech decor, competitive prices and service [to] fight its way back to the top of the Southern California grocery business."

The Pavilions model accounts for fewer than ten of Vons' nearly two hundred stores, but it's a good example of how service, pricing, and design can be forged into a winning combination. In 1984, Vons was still owned by a subsidiary of Household Finance Corporation. A private investor group purchased it in 1986 and the company became public again as The Vons Companies, Inc., in July 1987 through a merger with Allied

322

Supermarkets. (We warned you that supermarket ownership is complicated in California.)

At any rate, back in the HFC era, Vons began looking for ways to break out of the standard mold of large (forty thousand square foot) grocery and nonfood combination stores that were then the state of the grocer's art, Southern California-style. Through late 1984, a research group drawn from all parts of the company and its vendors traveled far and wide, looking at not just grocery store layouts, but also top-performing specialty stores, even department stores. They made a wish list of the good features they would like incorporated into a new prototype.

Without much ado, Household's management gave them the green light for an exceptionally large (seventy-five-thousand-square-foot), high-amenity design that now operates twenty-four hours a day and requires a staff of more than three hundred employees, 60 percent of them full-time (like most Southern California grocers, Vons is unionized). The dream store opened in the central Orange County city of Garden Grove in late October of 1985. It faced competition from twenty different stores in a two-mile radius, yet its combination of size, selection, and service soon had 20 percent of the market.

Personal attention doesn't just happen at the checkstand in a Pavilions. The large layout is designed as a series of specialty "shopping pavilions," each with its own staff and identity to keep the store from feeling like a warehouse. Aisles are shorter than normal and are arranged on either side of a central core that contains the produce department plus a combination of service departments that includes a deli, bakery, coffee corner, and "tortilleria" (which can turn out two hundred dozen tortillas an hour while customers watch).

Personal service is available virtually every step of the way. The deli has a staff of more than fifteen and an extensive menu, from hot Hawaiian chicken to cold zucchini salad. Another fifteen or so staff the adjacent meat and seafood departments, where everything from live lobsters to twenty varieties of made-from-scratch sausage are available. The bakery prepares its own breads and cakes fresh each day, again while customers watch. A floral department near the front of the store can handle anything from a single red rose to full-fledged wedding arrangements.

Sooner or later customers have to pay for their purchases, of course, and here again the service is consistent and far-reaching. Electronic checkstands operate under a "three's a crowd" philosophy—any time three customers are lined up, another register is opened. Cashiers (called "courtesy clerks" in the Vons vernacular) receive training that includes an eight-hour customer service class where typical store situations are acted out and critiqued. Every year, they also can compete in a companywide "bag-off" competition where winners are judged not just on speed but also on item arrangement, even weight distribution, efficient space usage, and courtesy.

Despite their size, Pavilions have very little turnover. They also attract an interesting clientele: Their Royal Highnesses, the Duke and Duchess of York (a.k.a. Prince Andrew and the former Sarah Ferguson) stopped by the Pavilions in Arcadia in 1988, making it the only grocery store ever visited by British royalty.

Bigger isn't the only thing Vons is doing better. To serve Southern California's large Hispanic population (17 percent in the Los Angeles basin), Vons opened its first Tianguis store in 1987. The name derives from the Aztec word for a market or bazaar; it's apt, considering that in a customer-focused design process similar to the one that led to the creation of the first Pavilions, Vons' executives went to Mexico to research food selections, marketing practices, and store designs for the new format, which is on the same massive scale as a Pavilions layout. (When Vons acquired the more than 170 Safeway stores in 1988, it noted that some would be converted to the Tianguis motif.)

Through all the growth and change, the mainline Vons stores also continue to satisfy, as evidenced by the selection of Rick Rivera, manager of a conventional Vons in Alhambra, California, as an "outstanding chain manager" by *Progressive Grocer* in 1987. Rivera started working for Vons as a seventeen-year-old clerk's helper in 1972. He was promoted to store manager in 1983. He's also a reserve police officer, which gives him special insight into community needs—and he proved he can wear both hats capably by being named Alhambra's Reserve Officer of the Year for going above and beyond the call of duty there, too.

In San Diego, registered dieticians from Scripps Memorial Hospitals use Vons stores as a classroom for free guided shopping tours offered to the area's senior citizens. Aisle by aisle, the nutritionists present information on the health value of various foods, show how to read labels, and offer advice on planning healthful menus around special dietary needs and conditions. Vons also publishes a regular series of consumer nutrition pamphlets, called *Nutri-Notes*, that provide detailed information on such subjects as the value of nutrition supplements, healthy options for breakfasts and dining out, and the need for liquids in Southern California's hot, dry climate. Customers are invited to share recipes that are low in salt, fat, sugar, or calories; five-dollar gift certificates are awarded to those that are used.

In awarding Vons its 1987 Fieldmark Award, given annually to companies that make lasting and significant differences in the food industry, *Supermarket Business* praised the company for its "groundbreaking formats, Pavilions and Tianguis, which have set new standards for retailing excellence and innovation." In the growing nation of Southern California, it seems only fitting.

The Vons Companies, Inc.
10150 Lower Azusa Road
El Monte, CA 91731

Ukrop's

THE SCALE OF GROCERY OPERATIONS TO COME MAY BE BEING DECIDED BY LARGE chains serving large markets, but the shape of customer service in the 1990s may turn out to have been pioneered by a nineteen-store, family-run chain serving Richmond, Virginia. Most marketing in the industry is devoted to wrestling for market share, a matter of increasing sales by bringing new people into the store. Usually, according to *Progressive Grocer* magazine, "Programs to cultivate shopper loyalty have taken the back seat to marketing programs that use price, gimmicks and other methods to boost business."

In contrast, under a Valued Customer Program launched in early 1987, Ukrop's has been pioneering a service-focused method that essentially customizes its stores to take care of its "frequent shoppers"—the loyal folks who, like the frequent flyers so valued by the airlines, tend to come back again and again because they already like the place.

The key to the approach is an innovative point-of-sale account-tracking system developed by Citicorp POS Information Services, a Citicorp subsidiary in Stamford, Connecticut. The system ties in to the checkstand scanners and the in-store computer that powers them, opening an account of "electronic coupons" for individual customers that provides discounts on name-brand merchandise without the need to clip and save conventional paper coupons. Ukrop's shoppers who want one can simply sign up for a Valued Customer card. When they present their card at the checkstand, the in-store computer automatically credits them with manufacturers' discounts and the store's own advertised price specials (as many as forty items per month).

The system benefits food manufacturers, customers, and Ukrop's simultaneously. Manufacturers can deliver their sales incentives directly to specific customers who want them rather than circulating coupons by the thousands to reach interested customers by the hundreds. Customers get the savings without the bother of clipping, saving, and then remembering to bring along a wallet full of odd-sized pieces of paper, some of which invariably have expired. For Ukrop's employees, the system means they

326

no longer have to fumble around with odd-shaped bundles of coupons, checking expiration dates and reringing orders to post the discounts.

Of course, customers who *like* the old-fashioned method are welcome to stay with it: When they present conventional coupons, Ukrop's cashiers scan them into the computer system, which compares them to the electronic discounts and credits the one with the greater savings. Savings are also highlighted on the customer's receipt.

For its part, Ukrop's gains valuable insight into its customers and their shopping habits—information that in turn energizes specially targeted promotions to make each store even more satisfying for its loyal shoppers. For all the technology, however, the store works hard to keep the family feeling. *The Scanner*, the company's employee newsletter, contains a regular "Letter from Jim and Bob," the brothers Ukrop who serve as president of the stores and president of food services respectively (their parents, Joe and Jacquelin, started the business in 1937 by mortgaging the family farm to buy a five-hundred-square-foot store in south Richmond).

Customers obviously share that sense of family. They know they're part of a cutting-edge experiment in service, and they've shown no evidence of fearing that all the computerized tracking might someday lead to a grocery store equivalent of Big Brother. The Valued Customer Program, notes Nelson Melton, Ukrop's vice president of administration and finance, "looks very complex to our customers, because they can't actually *see* what goes on. Fortunately, I think Ukrop's has established such a high level of trust that customers simply have faith in us to make the complex processes work for them."

Trust is only the half of it. When Media General Research conducted its biennial study of grocery shoppers in the Richmond area in 1987—a study that's unique because it asks customers what they *dislike* about area stores, not what they like or tolerate—Ukrop's came out best in nine of the eleven categories. Significantly, no one had a negative word to say about the friendliness and courtesy of its employees; they rated the stores tops for produce, meat, cleanliness, good values, wide selection, orderly arrangement, attractive interiors, and fast check-out service as well.

In early 1988, the nineteenth Ukrop's store opened in the Richmond suburb of Laburnum Park. Customers couldn't wait. They lined up at the front door for the official opening. They lined up to sign up for Valued Customer cards. They came in such great numbers that they ended up lined up at the checkstands. Didn't matter. "I've been waiting for years for a Ukrop's to open out here," one customer enthused, "and I don't mind waiting a few more minutes." The only reportable glitch came from uninitiated customers who tried to bag their own groceries—a service Ukrop's still insists on providing.

When the Valued Customer Program debuted at the Ukrop's store in Buford, more than 70 percent of the people who shop there regularly signed up in the first month. Over the next year, the system was extended to each store in the small chain, resulting in the issuing of more than 160,000 cards. So valued has the card become that in one two-week sign-up campaign in early 1988, Ukrop's frontline people took the time to explain the program to more than 113,000 customers, but signed up only 8,300 new shoppers—the overwhelming majority, they discovered, already had Valued Customer cards.

In dollars and cents, Ukrop's holds out the prospect that regular customers can save up to five hundred dollars a year just by remaining regular shoppers. But there's far more involved than just devising a system that frees customers from the burden of clipping coupons. Because the in-store computer system can track individual and segmented buying patterns, Ukrop's is able to provide specific benefits to specific customers.

For example, during one in-store promotion, customers who had regularly purchased Ukrop's store-made pizza over the previous months received a coupon for a free extra topping on the pizza of their choice. Those who had tried the store-made pizza just once received an offer of a free pizza if three others were purchased during the next three weeks. Customers who habitually buy frozen pizza were offered special discounts on the store-made alternative. Pizza sales increased during the promotion, and stayed higher than prepromotion levels after the campaign ended.

Perhaps predictably, the Valued Customer system has changed the way Ukrop's targets its advertising. Instead of regular newspaper ads and coupons for everyone far and wide to clip or ignore depending on personal tastes, the company is now able to use direct mail to reach targeted customers with attractive offers. Customers who make a habit of buying fresh fruit, for instance, can be offered a special discount on other fresh produce. Families with very young children (identifiable from their purchases of diapers and infant formula) can be sent information on periodic specials for cereals, "junior" baby foods, and children's medicines carried by the store.

Response to the program, according to Ukrop's customer research, has ranged from happy to delighted. The first benefit shoppers notice is the obvious one: the convenience of not having to save coupons. In the words of marketing and communications coordinator Carol Spivey, "The system helps us make shopping as painless as possible."

The family-run company was also among the first in the country to offer its customers the use of a modified golf cart, called the Mart Cart, to enable those who have difficulty walking or standing, or who are recovering from an illness or injury, or are pregnant, or otherwise need assistance to retain full access to its stores. The cart has a seat and a motor, with a shopping basket mounted up in front. Customers need merely stop by the store office for a key—which Ukrop's encourages them to keep for future shopping trips—to take out a cart and start cruising the aisles.

It also likes to keep its employees feeling good about the family. In early 1987, Ukrop's faced the "problem" of what to do with nine Caribbean cruises (for two) that it had earned as manufacturers' premiums. "A lot of companies simply have the top executives take premiums home," pointed out Larry Parrent, manager of the chain's store in Ashland. "But that's not the way Ukrop's operates. The company rewards store-level employees."

In this case, it rewarded them by setting up a systemwide competition to reward sales performance at the department level. Parrent's store won four categories outright and tied for first in a fifth. So that March, some familiar faces were missing while the winning department managers were off cruising the Caribbean. Parrent, however, was back minding the store—in typical Ukrop's fashion, he let the people who had done the work enjoy the rewards.

Ukrop's Super Markets, Inc.
600 Southlake Blvd.
Richmond, VA 23236

SuperAmerica

IN THE LATE 1960S, BACK IN THE DAYS WHEN SUPERAMERICA WAS A SMALL CHAIN of gas stations in the Upper Midwest—long before good service was trendy, let alone a national quest for the corporate equivalent of the Holy Grail—the company's managers received a modest little "Customer Satisfaction" leaflet that set out president Dick Jensen's philosophy of doing business. The strength of any organization, it ventured, could very well be measured by the type of service it renders its customers.

"When a customer leaves your station for the first time," the leaflet asserted, "you have made an impression on him. If you have taken a little extra time and made that little extra effort, the impression has been a good one and your customer will return. If he feels he has been treated with indifference, you have probably seen him for the last time."

Though the company he leads has expanded from a corner gas station and car wash in St. Paul, Minnesota, to a multiregional pacesetter in the convenience store field, Jensen has never lost sight of his "service station" roots—and neither has the company informally known as "SA." The basic premise of the business—now a division of Kentucky-based Ashland Oil—continues to be that "customer satisfaction brings them back."

There are bigger convenience store chains in America, just as there are smaller, but it's hard to find one with a more pronounced penchant for innovation and taking care of its customers than SuperAmerica. There were 110 stores when Ashland Oil entered the picture in 1970; there are now more than 500 SuperAmerica locations in sixteen states, all but the two dozen or so in Florida located in a band from Washington and Montana across the midwest to Pennsylvania and West Virginia. Jensen is on record as hating the "*c*-word" label; he maintains SuperAmerica is a hybrid able to offer more than the typical convenience store and faster than a supermarket.

Regardless of the label put on it, one attribute SuperAmerica has earned a right to boast about is quality. In 1987, as it periodically does, the company decided to find out what people in some of its markets thought about their nearby SA, so it surveyed about a thousand customers and noncustomers alike by phone. Two line items in the responses were particularly eye-catching: Asked what they didn't like about SuperAmerica, more than two thirds of the customers sampled said they couldn't think of anything; asked later what items they'd like to have added to the basic SuperAmerica offerings, two thirds again said they couldn't think of a need that wasn't being met.

Perhaps understandably, given its service station roots, SuperAmerica has been quicker to develop the gas part of the gas-and-goods equation than competitors that started from the grocery side of the business. It was the first to put multiple gas pumps out front to make self-service truly convenient (many stores have two dozen pumps or more to make sure customers can get in and out quickly), the first as well to put weather-shielding canopies over the pump islands to protect customers while they gassed up. Microphones are mounted on the posts holding up the canopies so customers at the gas islands can talk to someone in the store if they need assistance, and cleanliness extends all the way down to making sure customers can brush up against a gas-pump hose without dire consequences to their clothing.

Inside, SuperAmerica led the introduction of bakeries and commissary offerings such as sandwiches, salads, and other prepared foods designed to serve busy families. In some areas, customers can now call in a cake order to a central "SuperMom's" bakery and pick it up at a nearby SuperAmerica the next day. The company also was the first to install automated teller machines in its stores—more than 20 percent of its locations now have them—and more recently has experimented with pharmacies and video rental departments because customers said they would use those services in a convenience store setting if only someone would provide them.

People are every bit as important as products to making the service system work. While many convenience store locations get by with one person during slack periods, the basic SuperAmerica crew is always at least two, each running a separate cash register in a central island. Many stores are open around the clock. According to a survey conducted by the National Association of Convenience Stores in 1986, the typical Super-America sells three times more gasoline and about 30 percent more merchandise than the industry average.

Frontline employees are told from the outset that the three most challenging aspects of their jobs will be, in order, customer service, preventing shortages, and accuracy. Regardless of job title or time in grade, the SuperAmerica culture insists that it is every employee's "responsibility to make certain that every customer you serve will want to return to your store again."

They get sixteen to twenty-two hours of training in frontline procedures before going on the job, and on-the-job training continues from there—including a six-hour cashier session taught by the local area manager after they've been on the job for a couple of weeks. One consequence of the latter training is that employees have a chance to meet and speak freely with their boss's boss, which opens up communications even as it makes new hires feel like accepted members of the SA team.

The training emphasis is by design: Regular performance reviews (four in the first year, two the second year, annually thereafter, with merit increases available every six months) are based on observations of about a dozen basic behavioral criteria, from the way customers are greeted and treated to whether the frontline worker calls for backup when a line forms at the register. (Because waiting in line is, by definition, inconvenient, SuperAmerica takes that last item seriously: Store managers are responsible for helping out up front until *their cashiers* tell them their assistance is no longer needed.) The operative standards are "patient respect, courtesy, and appreciation"; SuperAmerica works them into an amazing variety of internal communications materials.

From the corporate perspective, the mindset is that the best store managers are best left alone. SuperAmerica encourages local involvement and the use of local suppliers by its managers, and it supports localized operations with streamlined internal services and procedures. Weekly zone management reports share information, acknowledge contributions, and praise exemplary performers personally. (Interestingly, areas within zones are named for their area managers, not numbered impersonally.) Managers who come up with a good business or promotional idea typically are cited by name, and their ideas described down to the sales dollars they generated so their compatriots can pick up on their success.

The same priority extends to recognizing frontline workers for a job well done. SuperAmerica employees "guilty" of outstanding performance in any of fourteen different areas are written up by their supervisors on the spot (the acknowledgment form notes the date and time, and specific details where pertinent), with copies going to area management as well as into their personnel files. Those forms carry weight at review time and when the growing chain looks for people ready to move up into new responsibilities.

Years ago, a SuperAmerica manager took one of Jensen's informal lectures on customer service to heart and worked out the following equation, which he posted on the wall in the back office of his store. Under the heading, "Why Customers Quit Shopping at a Place of Business or SA," he figured:

1%—Die!
3%—Move away
5%—Start buying from someone they know
9%—Find a more competitive price
14%—Are dissatisfied with the product
68%—Are dissatisfied with the ATTITUDE of a company employee

100%

If the numbers don't help you see service the SuperAmerica way, then consider this definition from an internal presentation on quality service: "From the customer's point of view, if they can see it, walk on it, hold it, hear it, step in it, smell it, carry it, step over it, touch it, use it, even taste it, if they can feel it or sense it, it's customer service."

SuperAmerica
Subsidiary of Ashland Oil, Inc.
1240 West 98th Street
Bloomington, MN 55431

Procter & Gamble Company

IN 1974, A COMPANY THAT AT FIRST GLANCE DIDN'T NEED TO CONCENTRATE a great deal on customer service became a pioneer at a tactic that has since been duplicated far and wide. That was the year Procter & Gamble instituted an 800-number service to keep it in contact with the people who were buying its food and nonfood products (everything from coffee and cooking oil to soaps, detergents, toothpastes, shampoos, and other common household products). The first experiments with calling customers and talking to them directly actually date back to 1971, and not until 1980 did every P&G product have an 800-number printed right on the package, but as it turns out there was nothing new or out of the ordinary going on: Procter & Gamble hired its first consumer affairs expert way back in 1941.

In some ways, Procter & Gamble is a company that learned the lesson of listening to customers at a very early age. As the story is usually told, it was back in 1879 that a soap mixer at the plant in Cincinnati went to lunch without turning off his machine. When he came back, the frothy mixture was almost thrown out, but since it didn't seem to be spoiled it wasn't. A few weeks later, storekeepers up and down the Ohio River were telling the company's salesmen to send them some more of that "floating soap" because their customers couldn't get enough of it. (It wasn't just for novelty value—people washed their clothes, and themselves, in the river so a bar that floated was one that didn't have to be groped for in the muddy depths.) No one anywhere else was getting that kind of response, which helped the company track down the batch that was the source of the shipments—and Ivory soap was born.

Nowadays, Procter & Gamble goes out of its way to talk to, and listen to, its customers. About one million times a year, it phones, visits, or buttonholes customers and potential customers, looking for new market opportunities, ways to improve existing product lines, and clues to help it interpret the ever-changing mysteries of consumer behavior. Some of the research is product-specific, assessing everything from performance to the look of the labels and packaging. Other inquiries are more wide-ranging,

334

including continuing lifestyle and workstyle research that tracks the way people handle the mundane details of daily life—fixing meals, cleaning house, and washing clothes, for instance.

In addition to constant consumer research, the company receives as many as one million customer-initiated contacts each year—about two thirds by phone, the balance through the mails. More than 60 percent are from customers who have a question about how to use a product. Another third involve a complaint. And there are some from customers who are just so happy with whatever it is they've purchased from the company that they feel compelled to provide a testimonial to their satisfaction.

No matter: In Cincinnati, where Procter & Gamble still makes its home, a staff of trained service representatives, segmented by product line and brand name, is ready and waiting to answer the questions, solve the problems, and accept the praise. Monday through Friday, from 9:30 A.M. until 7 P.M. (Eastern Time), the staff of carefully trained customer service reps is standing by. After all, it doesn't make much sense to encourage customer contact and then force people to listen to elevator music while on hold or wait months for a reply to their letters. In off hours, a recorded message provides the service hours for the following day and also offers an emergency number in case first aid is needed.

What kind of training do you need to discuss the finer points of laundry detergent? At Procter & Gamble, product knowledge is just the beginning, but it's an important beginning. Depending on the product area in which they will specialize, customer service people spend four to six weeks in training before ever picking up a receiver or opening an envelope. They get a complete overview of the product areas in which they will be working, from the history of the brand and its current advertising and marketing strategy to the right and wrong ways to use it (and what happens when it is used the wrong way).

There's functional training, too. Those who will be specializing in food products spend time in the corporate kitchens baking cakes. Those who will be fielding questions about hair-care products go out and learn how to give permanents with them. There are visits to manufacturing plants to see how the products are made.

They also get a dose of corporate history and culture that goes back to 1837—when William Procter and his brother-in-law, James Gamble, first went into business together—plus a working understanding of the company's computerized technology and research methodology. Toward that end, several different 800-numbers are used, a different one for each segment of the product line. That assures that the person answering the call will be up to speed on the product about which the consumer is calling.

Product manufacturing and marketing systems are tied in to help them do their job. Each package has a code number that identifies where it was manufactured, and when, sometimes with detail all the way down to which shift or part of the production line was involved. Reference manuals are available on each product, including problems reported and solved in the past, and technical experts can be brought in when matters get complicated.

The objective is to solve the problem on the first contact—in the case of telephone contacts, usually while the caller is still on the line. To make sure the system continues to work, follow-up surveys are conducted with customers who have phoned or written in to see whether Procter & Gamble's response was satisfactory. Division and corporate management receive regular summaries of calls and letters received; product development people get immediate notification of quality-control problems requiring their attention. Testimonials, on the other hand, are not only circulated for their positive reinforcement value, but also scrutinized for clues to why a product is liked, or how it can be strengthened still further.

A few years ago, *The Wall Street Journal* offered this insight from an executive of the American Association of Advertising Agencies: "A lot of people think P&G 'buys' its way into the market with big ad and promotion budgets, or has some other secret to its success. I don't think there's much secret to it. The company simply is tuned in to what consumers want, and it does a good job of making products to satisfy those wants."

The feedback is all the more important now because in today's ever more complex marketing environment, increasing amounts of responsibility for product development, advertising, and sales promotions are being pushed down the pyramid from large divisions to managers of individual brands. That makes it imperative for brand managers to know, in painstaking detail, how their products are being perceived and received in the marketplace.

Regardless of where in the hierarchy (which in the past has been criticized as too large and cumbersome for the company's good) those decisions are made, they will be made by someone who literally has grown up to the Procter & Gamble way of doing business. "Everybody, without exception, starts at Procter & Gamble in an entry-level position," noted a story in the *Washington Post* in 1987, "so that all of its managers come up through the ranks imbued with the corporate culture, rather than joining as hired gunslingers from outside."

Over the years, the P&G penchant for listening to its customers has resulted in new products and inspired changes to the formulation or marketing of existing ones. Customers gave Procter & Gamble the idea of putting a recipe for wedding cakes on its boxes of white cake mix. When people tried to squeeze the last dab of toothpaste out of the tube and the tube leaked, they complained; Procter & Gamble strengthened the tube.

Because they used the products in conditions never anticipated back in Cincinnati, customers also have served as laboratory technicians in discovering that special instructions should be added to recipes when they are being prepared at high altitudes, or that liquid fabric softener would indeed freeze, but could be salvaged and used safely and effectively. When a supplier changed its formulation for a plastic cap used on some fabric softener bottles a few years ago, consumers were the first to notice that the cap was so brittle it splintered while being screwed on and off. Their immediate complaints via the telephone hotline alerted P&G, which not only was able to identify the supplier and correct the situation, but also trace and replace the caps on other products while they were still in the warehouse.

In *Fortune's* 1988 report on America's most admired corporations, P&G cleaned up in each of the eight categories surveyed, its total score of 8.15 on a scale of 10 ranking it fourth among the 306 companies included. In the marketplace, where Procter & Gamble figures it encounters more customers with more frequency than any other business organization, that admiration is expressed at the cash register more than twenty million times a day.

The Procter & Gamble Company
One Procter & Gamble Plaza
Cincinnati, OH 45201

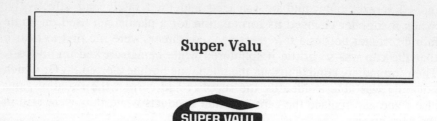

Super Valu

SUPER VALU BILLS ITSELF AS "THE RETAIL SUPPORT COMPANY." TO SHOW YOU HOW much business there can be in retail support these days, consider that this nearly 120-year-old Minneapolis-based firm is the nation's largest food wholesaler; it ranked number one on *Fortune's* annual "Service 500" list of the largest nonindustrial companies in the U.S. in both 1987 and 1988.

But Super Valu isn't noteworthy simply because it's big. It's also very good at providing a host of services, in addition to wholesale grocery and nonfood merchandise, to more than three thousand primarily independent grocery stores in thirty-two states. Meanwhile, its own Cub Foods retail arm is a pacesetter on the no-frills, warehouse-scale side of the retail food business, and its Shop-Ko department stores handle general merchandise.

Super Valu is up-front about what it intends to be and do. Its corporate mission springs from, as the company's Statement of Philosophy (adopted back in 1974) puts it, "a total commitment to serving customers more effectively than anyone else could serve them. We believe the pursuit of this meaningful goal is the continuing and overriding responsibility from which every corporate activity must evolve." The reason: "We believe that customers are most knowledgeable, skilled and capable buyers who will always seek out and do business with that supplier or store which most effectively serves their wants and needs."

Activity is the operative word in the statement above. While most of its actual business volume comes from selling wholesale food and nonfood supplies, Super Valu's independent grocery store customers depend on the company for vital retail services that range from customized advertising campaigns and consumer research to employee training and accounting support.

The premise is clearly service-based. To compete with large, chain-operated food retailers, independent stores must price smart and operate smarter. That's a challenge that in many cases means trying to keep pace with well-heeled mass merchandisers, matching prices and programs and retail improvements head to head, yet without inflating overhead and losing their entrepreneurial flexibility. By helping its customers stay competitive and successful, Super Valu helps maintain and grow the wholesale business that is, to stretch for a metaphor, its bread and butter (85 percent of sales in 1987). And it has been doing that since the 1920s, when the two dominant food wholesalers in the Midwest merged to better serve independent grocers who were struggling to compete with the first surge of chain-store retailers.

The range of services offered is all-encompassing, but store owners can pick and choose what they need. For example, Super Valu will help a retailer plan a new store or remodel an existing one to meet local competitive conditions. Its computerized site-location service, called SLASH, can analyze traffic patterns, area demographics, and the locations of competitors to identify promising market conditions and opportunities. Its legal specialists are available to help negotiate leases and construction contracts; accounting specialists will set up payroll, inventory management, capital improvement, and tax systems.

When the store opens for business, retail counseling programs can track sales and develop plans for the entire operation or specific departments. Super Valu electronics specialists will help customers—the store's management—install and manage point-of-sale scanning systems (about a third of its three thousand retailers are now using scanners); they'll also provide training for the cashiers who must operate them, and handle technical support and maintenance to keep operations trouble-free. For the longer term, the company offers risk-management and insurance programs for the store, and estate- and succession-planning for the owner, to protect the business from the unpredictable hazards of entrepreneurship.

Wholesaling is still basic to the business, and again Super Valu aims to please. A network of eighteen regional distribution centers, most of them serviced by company-owned trucks, fills store orders that are beamed in electronically by customers of all sizes. Many national brand and private-label foods, including more than a thousand frozen foods, are inventoried in the centers; fresh foods such as meat, produce, dairy products, and grocery goods are purchased through Super Valu but shipped straight from their suppliers to cut out handling costs and speed perishables directly to market.

Despite sophisticated support programs and $9.4 billion in sales, the service orientation remains at the independent retailer level: About half of the customers Super Valu serves are single-store operators; two thirds are either individual stores or small chains with no more than three locations. What's more, over 40 percent still run stores of under ten thousand square feet (the average grocery store constructed in 1987 had forty thousand square feet of retail space, according to *Progressive Grocer*). Yet average store volumes continue to be the highest among major wholesalers, providing continuing testimony that Super Valu's services are indeed keeping its customers competitive in a difficult, constantly changing business environment.

To further that end, Super Valu has now launched the Supermarket Directors Institute, a comprehensive training program that brings groups as large as twenty (twelve to fourteen is considered best) into the Twin Cities for a thorough five-week backgrounding in modern commercial operations. Designed to prepare the next generation of independent store managers to compete against their larger, better-financed rivals, the program reflects the importance Super Valu places on helping its corporate customers run the smartest, toughest businesses possible.

Part of the curriculum works the basics. Managers in training take marketing data, make their own analysis of what it says, then build a pro forma for a specific type of store operation that would succeed in that type of market. On the personal development side, they learn time management and how to make effective presentations to employees and community audiences. The premise is that growing the manager helps grow the business—and when that business grows, Super Valu does too.

As for Cub, the food industry stopped and took notice when Super Valu purchased this long-time family-run operation in 1980 and began growing it into a hybrid of warehouse and high-quality retailing operations. A marketing economist at Purdue University who studied Cub's massive, self-service style of service for the Federal Trade Commission called it "the most revolutionary thing to come along in food retailing in 20 years," according to The Wall Street Journal. "Other companies have tried to imitate them, but no one has Cub's impact."

By the end of 1988, there were nearly seventy-five Cub stores—about one third corporately owned—in eight states, and plans call for more than a hundred in operation by 1990. Wherever they operate, Cub stores have gained a reputation for both good value and innovative offerings; in 1988, for example, Cub contracted with Federal Express to deliver its fresh fish overnight.

In keeping with its customer service orientation, however, Super Valu isn't interested in competing with its own customers at the retail level. Rather, it is using Cub as something of a retail laboratory, and sharing the merchandising and systems-management lessons it learns on its own frontlines with other high-volume, low-price operations. That has led to the evolution of a Cub-patterned store format, known as County Market, that is now being used by more than seventy-five independent retailers in nineteen states.

In a business where oversized superstores chock-full of electronic systems and nontraditional, nonfood items sometimes seem to be an irresistible juggernaut, Super Valu has built a thriving business by helping hardy independents and smaller retailers compete and survive. Whether the sign over the door is its own, that of Cub Foods, or one of the many independent names its customers use—Country Market, Sunflower, Hornbacher, IGA, Shop 'n Save, Food Giant, Newmarket, Byerly's, Toddys, Dierberg's, Randall's, Jerry's, Food Town, U-Save, Great Scot, Red and White—Super Valu's thoroughgoing service focus continues to keep food retailers profitable and growing from coast to coast.

Super Valu
11840 Valley View Road
Eden Prairie, MN 55344

EACH WEEK, ABOUT 10,000 ROUTE SALES PEOPLE CALL ON MORE THAN 400,000 COM-mercial accounts across the U.S. In an industry where weekly, even monthly, sales calls are not uncommon, they sometimes visit a customer as many as five times a week. Twice a week is average. The products they represent account for about half of the nearly $7 billion Americans spend annually for salty snack foods. They are manufactured and supported by 27,000 people in 37 U.S. plants.

In the words of Michael Jordan, the company's president and CEO of PepsiCo Worldwide Foods, these people with their "store-to-door service" control the destiny of Frito-Lay. Through them, the company sells more than five *billion* bags of product each year, from a 6 1/2-ounce package of Lay's Potato Chips to a 60-ounce bag of Doritos Corn Chips. Top product price in the line: about $1.98. To those salespeople, and ultimately through them, Frito-Lay makes a quality-driven promise: Whenever any salesperson asks for any one of the company's 150 line items, the product will be available—the right product, in the right quantity—within forty-eight hours. In 1987, 99.8 percent of the time, it was.

In 1985, PepsiCo president D. Wayne Calloway, who spent seven years as Frito-Lay's CEO, building it past $2 billion in annual sales from the $710 million it was producing when he took charge in 1976, described the foundation on which the division's industry dominance is built: "Our salespeople are entrepreneurs of the first order. Over 100,000 times a day they encounter customers who are making buying decisions on the spot. How in the world could an old-fashioned sort of management deal with those kinds of conditions? Our approach is to find good people and to give them as much responsibility as possible because they're closest to the customer, they know what's going on. The entire company is organized to support the people on the firing line."

That involves product development, distribution support, and a personnel environment that encourages and rewards involvement with customers. Unlike many food processors who sell through brokers, wholesalers, and chain warehouses, Frito-Lay sells direct to its accounts. The person who makes the sales calls also puts the product on the shelf, whether that shelf is located in a conventional grocery or convenience store (about 50 percent of total volume) or in a bar, restaurant, service station, or bowling center—"anywhere we can find a door to knock on and make a sale," in Calloway's words. Because the middleman distribution step has been cut out, the product tends to be exceptionally fresh. Because the retailer never has to handle the product until it is rung up at a cash register or point-of-sale scanner, the door is always open.

Almost all salespeople now carry hand-held computers to track orders and reduce paperwork, which means they have more time available in which to sell. The computers calculate the totals (including sales tax and any discounts for special incentives or promotions), can be plugged into printers in the salesperson's truck to print out a sales ticket, and end their day plugged into communication terminals in their distribution centers or homes, where data is beamed back to the company's mainframe for tracking and analysis.

Freshness is paramount for products that go stale in about thirty days. Consequently the sales quality promises Frito-Lay's people make to customers are supported by efficient, responsive production and distribution systems. In addition to the 37 production plants, there are more than 650 trucks and 1,600 trailers, 26 traffic centers, 1,600 distribution centers and small warehouses in the U.S. The system is in constant motion because products can never be stockpiled. The goal is to have no inventory on hand that is more than two days old. If Frito-Lay stopped producing today, the company estimates, its products would be out of stock coast to coast in seven days. Maybe sooner. Because it doesn't, sales of four of its brands—Doritos tortilla chips, Lay's and Ruffles potato chips, and Fritos corn chips—are among the top ten of all dry food brands in the typical supermarket.

That's a long way from the kitchen in the house of Daisy Dean Doolin back in San Antonio, Texas, circa 1932. That's where Daisy's son, Elmer, cooked up the first batches of Fritos. About the same time, over in Nashville, Herman Lay was using his car as a delivery truck for an Atlanta-based maker of potato chips. Up through the end of World War II, their paths never crossed. Doolin moved to Dallas and grew the Frito Company into a force to be reckoned with in the Southwest. Lay eventually bought the Atlanta chip-maker, changing its name to H. W. Lay & Company. According to company lore, both had essentially the same business philosophy: "Make the best product possible; sell it at a fair price to make a fair profit; and make service a fundamental part of doing business."

The eventual merger, which took place in 1961, grew out of the license Frito granted Lay in 1945 to manufacture and market Fritos in its southeastern turf. In 1965, the company merged with the Pepsi-Cola Company to form PepsiCo. There are other divisions these days in addition to Frito-Lay and Pepsi, but it's the crunchy stuff that brings in the green stuff: 41 percent of total revenues in 1987, compared to Pepsi's 32 percent.

Since that time, growth has been the order of the day. The average American consumes twelve pounds of salty snacks each year, which adds up to a lot of customer demand. To make sure it continues to know what its customers' customers want, Frito-Lay twice a year subjects every product to blind taste tests against its regional competitors. That's where the competitive battle is joined. Frito-Lay is the only national marketer of salty snacks. The other 50 percent of the market is divided up among some 150 local and regional companies, many of whom have grown sharper and more sophisticated as time passes. The objective is to be number one across the board.

Ironically, Frito-Lay's well-publicized stumble in 1985 and 1986 owed much to getting away from the basics of the business. In a rush to introduce new products—nearly eighty new items or packages in a dizzying twelve-month stretch—the company overloaded the sales reps with confusing line additions and a flurry of unconnected promotions. Three major new product lines were introduced without benefit of the painstaking test-marketing and consumer research that had long been the key to the success of such mainstays as Fritos, Doritos, Lay's, and Ruffles brand snacks; all were subsequently pulled when Jordan, who had headed Frito-Lay in 1983-84 before being promoted to the parent company, returned as president in December 1986.

Now the emphasis has returned to strong products, aggressive marketing, and effective management—backed by that intense attention to frontline service.

Frito-Lay, Inc.
Subsidiary of PepsiCo, Inc.
Frito-Lay Tower
Dallas, TX 55235

RETAILING

GENERAL

Nordstrom

Parisian

Wal-Mart

SPECIALTY

Liz Claiborne

Avon Products

Home Depot

Florsheim Shoe Company

CATALOG

L. L. Bean

Lands' End

Williams-Sonoma

The Retail Business: Mamas, Don't Let Your Babies Grow Up to Be Shoe Clerks

DESPITE RECENT ADVANCES, LACK OF QUALITY CUSTOMER SERVICE REMAINS THE retailing industry's albatross. In a 1987 *Washington Post* survey of Washington-area customers, a third said they'd stopped shopping at a department store or bought there less often because of service (or the lack thereof). Nationally, one of four shoppers gave similarly low ratings to service at their local retail stores, the *Post* study reported.

A similar study on consumer shopping behavior conducted by Leo Shapiro & Associates, Chicago-based retail consultants, queried over one thousand women in five U.S. cities. It shows the single biggest turnoff for female shoppers is the inability to find qualified help on the sales floor. It's that kind of research that gives people the feeling that, as customers, finding quality service help from America's retailers is much like winning the Publisher's Clearinghouse Sweepstakes—mathematically possible, but not likely.

Yet the flip side—the encouraging news—is that a growing number of U.S. retailers are addressing the problem by implementing programs that emphasize better service and reward employees who perform well. An even better omen for the industry is that, in most cases, the new customer service emphasis is trickling down from top management.

In the early 1980s, when department store sales were robust, most decision-makers focused their attention on cutting expenses. That often meant chopping from payroll and service programs. Although lip service was paid to the value of customer service, the executives intent on getting leaner just couldn't bring themselves to believe that service translated into sales. The fixation with trimming expenses, although valid from the standpoint of the bottom line, began to translate into another, unanticipated reduction at the frontline. Service deteriorated with the morale of those left to provide it, and retailing observers believe it genuinely affected the customer's perception of the shopping experience.

Many of those same decision-makers are now reversing themselves, largely based on the educational experience of watching stores that remained committed to offering outstanding customer service—like Nordstrom's and Macy's—outpace others who devalued the service edge.

A host of new market factors also have conspired to draw retailers' attention to improved service. The emergence and growing success of specialty stores—by nature better geared to serve particular customer needs—on one hand, and the coming of hypermarkets (monstrous general merchandise/food combination stores) on the other have traditional general merchandise retailers backpedaling to reevaluate service philosophies.

The years of lackluster service among mass merchandisers have had their effects. Specialty stores, for one thing, have established a firm beachhead. Because they are less labor-intensive and require less square footage than general-purpose retailers, they have lower operating costs. According to *USA Today*, specialties also produce twice the operating profits of general merchandising stores. In 1986, return on investment for specialty stores was 50 percent higher than for the general merchandisers, it reported.

In addition, retail customers have turned with more frequency to sources other than salespeople for information about products. Sales from both print and video catalogs are growing steadily, as are the retail businesses designed around them. And while retailers may wonder why consumers are willing to go through the extra steps involved in catalog shopping—and psychobabble consultants speculate endlessly about the "unconscious association" with gift-getting and childhood—consumers themselves seem very clear about their own motives.

As a young man in a recent focus group session explained, "It's simple. Who wants to deal with a clerk who knows less than you do about a product, or less than you can learn from a catalog? And when I send something back, nobody treats me like a crook or an inconvenience. I even get a note that says, 'I'm sorry you didn't like the boots. Here's a coupon for 10 percent off your next purchase. Please give us another try!' Now where do you get treatment like that in a store today?" Apparently nowhere generally known—he got a round of applause from the others in the group.

With even specialty retail stores taking on an increasingly homogeneous look and selling similar labels, management is beginning to see more clearly that the differentiating factor for retailers is how they make customers "feel" in the store. And with the rise in two-career families and people working more, customers are looking for a more efficient and pleasing shopping experience. That's particularly true of working women. According to *Stores* magazine, the professional working woman is telling those retailers willing to listen that she will spend more money on higher-priced merchandise, and spend more time in one store, if that store provides her with what she wants. Those stores that are paying attention are reaping the benefits of higher gross margins and a loyal customer following.

At Bullock's in Los Angeles, where customers are predominantly managerial-level working women, the store has redesigned its merchandise areas, instituted wardrobe consultants, eliminated furniture sales, and concentrated on ready-to-wear accessories and gifts. Dayton's stores, the flagship retailing operations of Minneapolis-based Dayton Hudson, now offer "For Your Image" (abbreviated as FYI), a no-charge, by-appointment-only wardrobe consulting service. Its staffers have been trained to identify the customer's needs according to the type of work she does and use the profile developed to find merchandise for her from all around the store. Through such tactics, *Stores* reports that these retailers are not only regaining women they may have lost, but in some cases adding their male companions, who may have shopped elsewhere before.

Couple those factors with a shrinking market for consumer purchases, and customer service takes on new urgency as a competitive tool. Retailers have taken heed and expanded on the experience of two organizations that enjoy much higher sales per square foot than the average: Nordstrom's and Macy's. Much of their sales success can be traced to comprehensive employee-training programs and lucrative sales commission structures that place them among the country's highest-paying department stores. Yet despite big payrolls, Nordstrom's and Macy's remain profitable, indicating that their customers are willing to pay a premium for what is perceived as better service.

Taking that example to heart, Bloomingdale's has redesigned its training programs to give employees additional lessons in dealing with customers. Even those employees who aren't on the sales floor, like bill adjusters, are required to go through the program. Woodward & Lothrop, a department store chain based in Washington, D.C., now enrolls employees in a rigorous self-improvement program, and salespeople are given business cards and personalized stationery as part of a major effort to upgrade their jobs. And at Weinstock department store in Sacramento, California, all of the store's central staff, including data processing, personnel, accounts receivable, merchandising, and advertising people, work the sales floor at least once a year in an effort to keep service at the top of their minds.

Significantly, retailing observers say the national trend is shifting away from a reliance on technical training of sales staff and toward the inclusion of training in the art of human interaction. Woodward & Lothrop's Joseph Culver, senior vice president for personnel and services, says the store is moving its emphasis from merchandise training—how to run a computer terminal or conduct a credit transaction—to "human servicing" techniques such as approaching customers. The objective, he says, is to make sure that frontline people are both knowledgeable and pleasant to do business with.

Retailers that dropped commission and bonus-pay schemes in years past because of high costs are returning to both to improve sales. In addition to providing motivation, incentives seem to reduce employee turnover rates, a chronic retailing problem. Miami-based Burdines experienced 10 percent less turnover in 1986 after introducing a bonus plan in its twenty-seven department stores. Top employees there earn up to thirteen dollars an hour for selling above departmental averages, plus a 1-percent sales bonus that can add up to three thousand dollars or more annually. Retailers are also trying to attract new employees with improved benefits and more flexible work schedules.

Randy Allen, retail industry national director for the accounting firm Touche Ross, says more department stores are now looking at putting salespeople on commission selectively—not necessarily across the board, but rather in those areas such as sportswear and the high-ticket, high-quality women's wear departments where service is the driving force.

There is also a definite trend toward using more full-time salespeople, based on a belief that the additional time they spend on the salesfloor will make them more familiar *with* the merchandise and more familiar *to* the customers who frequent the store. With understaffing and lack of quality help a problem, particularly in the suburbs, retailers seem to be returning to their roots and are again approaching the field of selling as a legitimate profession, with hopes of reaching a different labor pool.

Customer service consultants warn, however, that commission structures and cash incentives alone can't be depended upon to establish a strong sales culture. Stores also need to find nonmonetary ways to acknowledge and reward workers—and many are, giving out everything from special stars on badges to personal recognition from senior management. At Marshall Field, when any employee from sales associate to sales support—anyone with potential for coming into contact with the customer—does something extraordinary, he or she is awarded a "Frangloon," the store's famous Frango mint turned into a pewter coin.

Retail technology is another method by which some retailers are attempting to gain an edge on competitors. To enhance the "service" in their predominantly self-service operations, K mart, Wal-Mart, and Target—the nation's three leading discount chains—are all phasing in scanning equipment at checkouts. They all believe that eliminating delays is the ultimate definition of better service for their particular customers. If the wait at the checkout line is too long, if it takes too much time to locate merchandise, or if it takes too long to get a credit transaction approved, those stores believe a big problem is in the making, and they are right.

Some retailers also are beginning to offer non-traditional services to customers. Macy's operates a convention and visitors center in its Atlanta, San Francisco, and New York stores. The centers provide translation services and make theater, hotel, and restaurant reservations. Other stores are doing such things as installing infant changing tables in men's restrooms to accommodate today's fathers or changing home-delivery schedules to serve customers better on evenings and weekends. And what general department store worthy of the name today lacks a restaurant (the trend is toward two, one trendy and one traditional) or a deli counter?

In the new competitive environment, it's clear that retailers no longer have the luxury of taking any component of service for granted, nor can they ignore it as a marketing opportunity. You need only glance at the Shapiro industry study, which revealed that 50 percent of today's shoppers rank *restrooms* a retail service that influence their shopping choice, to see the validity in that.

According to a *Wall Street Journal* study, adults spend an average of about six hours a week shopping. With consumer spending showing signs of a slowdown, with price discounting expected to continue, and with many retailers cautiously buying only what they can't do without, service excellence will increasingly be the surest way for retailers to set themselves apart in the eyes and hearts of their customers.

Stocking Service

In recent years retail has been a difficult, sometimes downright grim, business. As one exec put it recently, "We have started taking much shorter meetings. After all, if you're locked away in a room for more than an hour, you've very likely missed the latest hostile takeover attempt." Fueled by pressure for profits and high earnings ratios, many retailers have been pushed to the wall looking for ways to cut fat, and some still fall into the trap of doing away with people—and, in the process, the good service that can bring in the customers who will provide the business to get the business flying high again.

At Nordstrom and Parisian, on the other hand, having enough people to provide smooth and satisfying service is the order of the day. In both of these organizations, management has elected to swim upstream against the prevailing currents and street wisdom—and found that it pays off at the bottom line.

Our other exemplar among the generalists is Wal-Mart. How can a discount store be a service exemplar? It can't be if your image of *good* service is constricted to lavishing lots of personal contact on shoppers with the time and money to enjoy such treatment. That, we maintain, is an impoverished view of service. Self-service, when *desired* by the customer and delivered well by the provider, can be as acceptable as the finest kid-glove treatment.

On the specialty end of the retail spectrum, Liz Claiborne has developed a national following by following closely the kind of customer for whom its lines of clothing are specifically designed. Avon is a back-to-basics story that illustrates how success in service quality can be lost and regained. Home Depot offers a case study in making a service-oriented start-up work: It's a "surround the customer with help" story where the marketplace is demonstrating the wisdom of the approach. Florsheim, on the other hand, shows that age and ownership structure need not be deterrents to providing service quality as well as renowned product quality.

Finally, there are the catalog marketers. L. L. Bean is an American business legend that lives up to its reputation. Lands' End aspires to, and achieves, Bean-like ratings from its own carefully researched customers without forsaking its roots—or its whimsical sense of humor. And Williams-Sonoma may be the ultimate example of achieving success through niche marketing, whether the "store" the customer is exploring has a cover or a door.

Nordstrom

ASSEMBLE A FOCUS GROUP OR WORKSHOP FULL OF PEOPLE FROM LARGE RETAILERS and you're sure to hear plenty of reasons why providing good customer service is difficult, expensive, far from cost-effective, and even downright impossible. Then casually mention that Nordstrom is coming to town, and watch the excuses fade into uncomfortable silence. True, there are fewer than fifty Nordstrom department stores, and almost all of them are clustered in just five western states. But in a decade when many well-established department store chains have had to retrench, the steady growth and almost legendary customer service stories that surround this Seattle-based fashion specialty retailer inspire both admiration and dread among competing merchants nationwide.

Admiration because what Nordstrom is doing is working by that hallowed measure of business success: business success. Sales per square foot at Nordstrom were an industry-leading $345 in 1987, almost double the industry average.

Dread because this rising tide is raising consumer expectations in all the other department stores' boats at a time when Nordstrom has crossed the Rockies and begun to establish its first East and Midwest toeholds. The handwriting is on the wall, and it's written large enough and fashionably enough to convince even hardened, cost-conscious skeptics that customers will indeed shop where they find not only the merchandise but the service they desire.

That service, as illustrated by a growing number of "Nordy stories," is sometimes truly extraordinary. Like the one about a sales associate in Seattle who ironed a customer's new-bought shirt so he could wear it back to a meeting. Or the tale of a customer who brought back a pair of shoes a year after buying them to ask if they could be repaired and was given a new pair free instead. Nordstrom employees in cold climates have been known to go out and warm up a customer's car while they finish their shopping. Others have cheerfully gift-wrapped items purchased from a rival store right along with a customer's Nordstrom purchases.

A few years ago, a field researcher for a rival retailer visited a Nordstrom

352

store in California to check out what all the noise from the West Coast was about. Not surprisingly, the report focused on service. To begin with, the researcher reported, Nordstrom's sales associates were outstanding—friendly, outgoing, caring people who clearly impressed their customers as knowing their merchandise inside and out, not just what was in stock in their department, but what was available throughout the store. Salespeople were often heard to ask for customers' home phone numbers so they could call them as soon as something additional came in. Sometimes, long after a customer had left the department, a sales associate would still be looking for related items—and, on finding something, would page the recent customer, just in case he or she was still in the store and might want to come back.

The response to that kind of exceptional service is increasingly something along the lines of joining what you can't beat. West Coast stores now routinely pay sales commissions and higher salaries to retain and motivate the frontline sales associates whose value Nordstrom has so conclusively demonstrated. Many have added personal shopping services and upgraded customer service standards, rising to the level of the competition by offering more assistance on the sales floor, less resistance at the return desk. (At Nordstrom, resistance level is zero: If you don't like it, they take it back.) If it isn't single-handedly transforming department store retailing—if some of the stories (like the one about giving a customer money back for a set of tires, even though Nordstrom doesn't sell tires) have perhaps grown a bit in the retelling—well, Nordstrom is undeniably casting a long shadow.

It's not an illusion. The substance is service. Nordstrom stocks pretty much the same kinds of clothing and footwear found in most other fashion-conscious department stores, though often in more variety and depth. However, its stores are laid out and stocked and staffed to make shopping a satisfying experience for the customer as well as a commercially rewarding business for the company.

In 1986, Larry Senn of Senn-Delaney, a retail consulting firm, speculated on the genesis of Nordstrom's high service standards in *Stores* magazine: "They started in the shoe business," he pointed out. "You fit shoes on people. You go get shoes for them. You put them on their feet. All this makes for a culture that personally serves people. As Nordstrom evolved into a specialty department store it maintained some of that personal attention. Nordstrom people run for the customer. Part of it comes from that. Part of it comes out of the family commitment to service. Nordstrom hasn't had a revolving door with executives with 10 different philosophies. It has a consistent philosophy. And that gets communicated when hiring people."

Founder John W. Nordstrom did indeed start with a shoe store in Seattle in 1901. But while the company grew to become the largest independent shoe retailer in the U.S. by 1963, it has been a growing force in the apparel field for more than twenty-five years now. There's nothing tremendously unusual in the founding father's philosophy of offering the customer "the best service, selection, quality, and value." But the order of those four offerings is noteworthy.

The most obvious factor in Nordstrom's service success is that it does everything it can to prevent the systems and procedures necessary to running an orderly business from getting in the way of the customers. Sales associates routinely walk around the store with customers to help them find what they want. They do that even if what the customer wants is located in a different department. Sometimes they do that even if what the customer wants is located in another retailer's store. Miracles don't just happen on 34th Street—a Nordstrom salesperson really did walk a customer across the mall to Macy's to find just the right dress for her.

Nordstrom also works from a decentralized mindset. Operations are managed regionally. Regional buying groups stock most departments in the stores (shoe departments, however, have a buyer in *each* store) based in part on needs and desires they discern while working with customers on the sales floor. At Nordstrom, buyers are required to spend 20 percent of their time selling; many spend more. In fact, the only way to become a buyer is to work your way up from the sales floor. Consequently, store and regional managers can use their experience and authority to fine-tune inventory and react quickly to trends in their local markets instead of waiting for a ponderous corporate headquarters to pass its hands over their recommendations.

Continuity comes from the service provided. *Stores* recounted an effective illustration, "probably apocryphal," of a Nordstrom sales associate being asked what could get her fired. "Number one, for not taking care of the customer," came the reply. "Number two, for stealing." Again, the order of priorities is revealing.

Not every salesperson on every retail sales floor can provide excellent personal service, or wants to sell on commission. Since Nordstrom wants the kind of people who can and do, it goes to great lengths to hire, train, compensate, and promote frontline people who take care of the customer in the Nordstrom style. To encourage professionalism and commitment, most stores prefer to build their sales staffs almost exclusively from full-time employees. Not only are full-timers going to become more familiar with the merchandise, they're also more likely to be personally available the next time a customer returns to the store.

Some frontline workers, male and female, opt to stay on the frontlines. They like the work. They like the pay: Wages range from $6 to $9 an hour plus commissions that move up from 6.5 percent to 10 percent; top sales associates can earn upward of $80,000 a year, beginners can earn

$20,000. They like the customers, too. And they like working for a company that thinks it's super that its employees like all those things.

Nordstrom likes to reward good performance in more ways than just sales commissions. In 1968, five years after it went into the department store business and long before it had become a phenomenon, the company established the Pacesetters Club as a way of encouraging goal-setting and goal achievement. Pacesetters are sales associates who have set, met, and significantly exceeded personal goals. In recognition, they get new business cards that say "Pacesetter" on them. They get treated (with a guest of their choice) to a night on the town. For the next year, their employee discount on Nordstrom merchandise is upped from 20 percent to 33 percent. About one hundred people a year qualify. Just about everybody tries.

Interestingly, while Nordstrom believes in rewarding outstanding performance, it also likes to reward entire departments, or entire stores. It figures that helps to encourage a greater sense of teamwork among sales associates who might otherwise focus too much on their own personal commissions.

The best evidence that sales is a career track: Every Nordstrom executive started out on the sales floor. Nor is sex a barrier—although the company's five top executives are men (including three named Nordstrom), nearly half of its stores are managed by women, as are six of its thirteen regions; eight of the sixteen vice presidents pictured in the 1986 annual report are women.

It helps that the chain itself is growing, so there are ample opportunities to advance. When the first East Coast Nordstrom opened in the Washington, D.C., suburb of Tysons Corner, Virginia, in 1988, about three thousand people interviewed for four hundred sales openings. None were hired as managers: Those positions, nearly one hundred in all, were filled by experienced Nordstrom folk who transferred back east from stores out west.

Nordstrom, Inc.
1501 Fifth Avenue
Seattle, WA 98101

Parisian

·P·A·R·I·S·I·A·N·

JUST AS WEST COAST RETAILERS LOOK TO NORDSTROM AS A PACESETTER IN THE department store business, folks down south consider Parisian, a nineteen-store chain based in Birmingham, Alabama, an identifiable standard of comparison for fashionable service. From the canopied electric carts that cruise the parking lots around many stores (an amenity especially appreciated by older customers) to the cheerful mini-nurseries strategically located next to the restrooms (a clean, convenient diaper-changing stop for younger shoppers and their offspring), the "Parisian point of view" is that people who enjoy their shopping experiences will seek to repeat them. That they do is evidenced by the fact that only Nordstrom posts higher sales per square foot.

Although it was founded in the late 1880s, Parisian's high-service profile is of relatively recent vintage. For the first sixty years of its existence, there was but one store—in downtown Birmingham—and it sold women's apparel, millinery, and piece goods at budget prices. After World War II, Emil Hess, now chairman of the board but then just the son of the Tennessean who with an associate had bought into the store in the 1920s, began shifting the Parisian image toward one emphasizing more-fashionable merchandise.

In the sixties and seventies, Hess and *his* son, Donald, now the company's president, began to use the store's newfound fashion-and-service edge as a template for expansion by building the second Parisian in a suburban shopping mall on the west side of Birmingham. Other stores slowly followed, growing the business into Alabama's largest independent retailer. Ultimately the state line was crossed (though only by a couple of miles) in 1985, when Parisian added a store in Columbus, Georgia.

Today Parisian operates in four southern states (Alabama, Georgia, Florida, and Tennessee), but growth is limited to two or three new stores a year (one of which is to take the company across the Mason-Dixon line into Cincinnati before 1990). Within its chosen markets, the company aims to be the top-rated name among customers—and its surveys show that it is. To achieve this goal, it focuses on the people who deliver the services that distinguish Parisian from its competitors: the frontline sales people.

About ten years ago, Parisian evolved a system of career pathing, training, and recognition that in essence treats and develops the people on the sales floor much as companies have learned to treat people moving up the management ladder. The process starts with selection. Not everyone thrives on customer contact, or sees sales work as a professional calling, and the odds of finding ones who do among minimum-wage employees are deemed remote. Consequently, Parisian mixes higher-than-average salaries, commissions, incentives, and nonmonetary forms of recognition to attract new people (it recruits on thirty-five college campuses), develop their sense of professional pride, and retain them as valuable service providers.

Once it has identified and hired them, it trains them extensively. Some programs are universal, others voluntary—meaning the employee has to request them—but Parisian pays for them and manages its frontline people along a specific, well-defined career track. New hires start as sales assistants. They get forty-five hours of training before they are turned loose on the customers, and in the course of that preparation they spend at least half a day shadowing a top performer in their department (a tactic that promotes transfer of effective sales habits and fosters a mentorlike relationship for the new hire). After ninety days on the job, the new salesperson is pulled back in for twelve hours of refresher training.

If they meet 80 percent of a store's performance standards in their first ninety days, they move up to sales associates. Those with the skills and drive to move beyond that can work toward senior sales associate, then sales consultant (the equivalent of "vice president, sales," within the store's sales staff, according to a background report in *Stores* magazine a couple of years back). In 1987, Parisian's 275 sales consultants collectively produced more than $50 million in sales.

To make sure shoppers get plenty of attention, Parisian staffs at a higher level than most retailers. It also does almost double the average volume of sales per square foot for department stores nationwide. Goals at every level are clearly defined and measurable. Those who achieve them are rewarded, not only financially but with other forms of recognition, much of it involving their peers and some of it involving their families. Those whose performance deteriorates drop back down the career ladder accordingly. Those who can't meet the standards are told they can't work for Parisian.

Performance standards involve more than sales volume, it should be added. For example, annual reviews give points for a salesperson's ability to work smoothly with others. Prima donnas might pile up impressive sales numbers, but if they tear down the performance of coworkers they really aren't that good in the Parisian point of view.

Parisian also wins kudos for other people-pleasing practices. For example, there's no interest on purchases made on the store's own credit card for six months, and if customers pay the suggested minimum payment, the balance will be paid off before interest charges start to accrue. Parisian has had the policy since the 1940s, and despite the money to be made from revolving credit arrangements the company simply decided to preserve the standard as a way of rewarding its customers.

In addition, gift-wrapping is free, and Parisian will mail gifts free of charge before Mother's Day, Father's Day, and Christmas. To assist loyal customers outside of the metropolitan areas it serves, Parisian maintains a bank of toll-free 800-lines. For customers who want to slip away from the kids for a few minutes of peaceful shopping, most stores offer a "Cartoon Corner," which among other things feature a VCR loaded with cartoons or a family-fare movie.

Does all this customer focus stuff really work? Parisian customers, and customers-to-be, say it does. In 1987, more than eight thousand of them paid five dollars apiece for an opportunity to preview-shop Parisian's first Florida store, located in a Pensacola mall, two days before it officially opened for business. (If they spent twenty-five dollars or more, the price of admission was applied as a discount on their purchases; whether they did or didn't, the money went to four local charities, with Parisian adding another dollar to the pot for each ticket turned in.) Some of those eager shoppers no doubt came for charity. Some came out of curiosity, wondering what they'd been missing for not living in Alabama. Others already knew—since 1984, they'd been driving sixty miles up Interstate 10 to shop the closest Parisian, in Mobile.

Competitors concede that Parisian really is that good, and retailers from other parts of the country have sent observers to Birmingham to find out firsthand how it works. But perhaps the best evidence of the sales culture's effectiveness can be seen in Parisian's annual turnover at the frontline: about 20 percent in an industry where 50 percent is average and 100 percent far from unheard of.

Donald Hess, the third-generation head of the company, let slip the secret of Parisian's success a few years ago in an interview with the Dothan (Alabama) *Eagle*. Ready? "We find out what the customers want and then we provide it. It's a matter of being sensitive to the marketplace—in services as well as in goods."

You just knew it was going to be something hard like that, didn't you?

Parisian, Inc.
200 Research Parkway
Birmingham, AL 35211

WAL-MART

WALK INTO A WAL-MART STORE AND NO ATTENTIVE SALES CLERK RUSHES UP TO personally see to your shopping needs. There are no piano players or cappuccino bars. The floors are covered in utilitarian tile or vinyl, not carpeting. The displays and decor are neat and clean, but there's nothing lavish about them. They're there for function, not for comfort or effect.

This is exemplary service?

Absolutely. Done well, a low-service/self-service strategy can be every bit as pleasing to customers as the high-amenity, high-contact style of a Nordstrom or Parisian store. The trick is to do it well, and Wal-Mart founder and chairman Sam Walton has figured out how to do it very well indeed. His stores are in middle-sized markets—generally fifty thousand people or less—throughout middle America. They lack the flash and filigree of trendier, glitzier competitors. And yet Walton has built the nation's third-largest retailing operation in just a little more than twenty-five years. Only Sears and K mart outsell "Mr. Sam," as the seventy-year-old founder is generally known.

The Wal-Mart formula is deceptively simple: Sell good-quality, name-brand, modestly priced merchandise in a clean, no-frills setting that offers one-stop family shopping. Rather than entice shoppers with an ever-changing array of discounts and sales, Wal-Mart operates from an "every-day low price" philosophy. It sends out few advertising circulars, and the ones it does are positioned as shopping reminders—they contain no off-price specials. Not only does this pricing stability cut advertising costs and contribute to the kind of lean overhead that lends itself to price-competitive retailing, it also creates an image of dependability and, if you will, fair play in the minds of customers. At Wal-Mart, you don't have the nagging doubt that what you're buying might have cost you less last week, or might go on sale next Sunday.

Wal-Mart is another one of those top service-providing companies that seems to function as an extension of its top executive. Walton apparently couldn't care less about the perks and privilege of the wealth he's amassed. He still likes the business, so much so that he's as likely to be found out opening a new store as pushing paper back at corporate headquarters in that Manhattan of the Sunbelt, Bentonville, Arkansas (population: 10,000). That's where he set up shop back in 1950 with a Walton 5&10 after losing the lease on his first Ben Franklin store up in Newport, Arkansas.

At one point, Sam and his brother Bud owned as many as fifteen Ben Franklins, but the five-and-dime business began to give way to bigger things when the first Wal-Mart Discount City opened its doors in Rogers, Arkansas, in 1962. By 1970, there were eighteen Wal-Marts in four states, all of them located in smaller towns.

Lest you think that small towns make for a poor power base, take a moment to count the number of major metropolitan centers (populations of half a million or more) with their oversaturation of strip malls and shopping centers. Then get out the calculator and add up the number of small cities and towns below that fifty-thousand threshold. There's a growth market, yet it hasn't been seen that way by more established competitors.

In the seventies and now through the eighties, as major retailers like Sears, J. C. Penney, and Montgomery Ward have retrenched, closing the doors on their small-town operations in favor of larger stores in big-city shopping malls, Wal-Marts have popped up like prairie flowers all over the Deep South and Southwest, from Texas and New Mexico to Tennessee, Alabama, and Florida. They've also spread up the central plains and river valleys into Missouri, Iowa, Illinois, and Kentucky, and have now entered the frostbelt states of Minnesota, Wisconsin, and Indiana.

All in all, Mr. Sam now operates more than 1,200 stores in some 24 states, providing gainful employment for more than 185,000 people—people, in many cases, who are proud to be part of homegrown success stories in communities that have had precious little to crow about in recent years. Walk into a Wal-Mart store in a town like Decorah, Iowa, and you're likely to find a large poster up near the main entrance detailing the customer service standards. On it you'll find the signatures of everybody who works in the store. People stop by it and point out the names of a neighbor, or a friend, or a relative. It's that kind of place.

And although big-city skeptics have been heard to scoff at Mr. Sam's yeoman retailing strategy, Wall Street has been enthusiastically bankrolling the company since it went public in 1970. The analysts know there's nothing backwoods about Walton (who has a degree in economics from the University of Missouri) or his approach to the retailing business.

People make a visible difference in the average Wal-Mart. They treat their customers like neighbors—which is what they are in many cases—knowing full well that they will share in the success of their store. All Wal-Mart employees are called "associates," but not because it's trendy these days to do that. Walton's first job was in a J. C. Penney store in

Des Moines, Iowa, back before World War II, and he liked what the sobriquet said about his frontline role in the business.

At Wal-Mart, employees are encouraged to take an active interest in the business, from suggesting ways to improve operations to taking steps to cut pilferage and spoiled merchandise. They also get monthly summaries of how well their department is doing, both within their store and compared to similar departments in other Wal-Marts—part of Mr. Sam's belief that the more people know about the business, the smarter they work at it.

That also shows up in a policy referred to as LTC: Low Threshold for Change. Store managers regularly poll their clerks and other associates for ways to improve operations. Practical suggestions get adopted quickly, and actions (and department sales figures) above and beyond can qualify them for bonuses. While Wal-Mart's hourly pay scales aren't going to create a new class of millionaires, no one has been hired at minimum wage for years. Wal-Mart management subscribes to the idea that without the right people, nothing happens. After a thousand hours on the job every employee qualifies for the company's profit-sharing plan (which now has assets of nearly half a billion dollars and dispensed $52 million in 1986).

In simpler times, Wal-Mart executives were expected to learn the business from the inside; the Bentonville staff is still required to spend at least one week each year doing an hourly job in one of the company's stores. And the company continues to value experience and cross-training, even at the highest levels. A few years ago, for example, vice chairman Jack Shewmaker was chief operating officer and president David Glass was chief financial officer; then Walton had them switch jobs, in the process reversing the reporting relationships.

More recently, Wal-Mart has made a point of putting someone from personnel in charge of an operations committee and moved someone from operations over to financial. "We are tearing down those barriers that tend to build up in bureaucratic companies, to make a better organization," Shewmaker told the annual Morgan Stanley Retail Forum in 1987 in describing the company's efforts to remain in control of quality in the face of rapid growth. "So, while the size of Wal-Mart itself is a problem, we are concentrating on people's attitudes toward that size. We want to keep that risk-taking spirit."

One consistent area of risk-taking has been in technology. Small-town demeanor notwithstanding, Wal-Mart has been a pacesetter in harnessing computers as workhorses in providing smooth service. Checkstands in most stores are equipped with electronic scanners that keep inventory records while they add up purchases and print out itemized receipts. Satellite transmissions link each Wal-Mart to headquarters as well as to a network of large field distribution centers strategically spotted to be within a day's drive of the approximately 150 stores they serve an average of five times a week. The on-line data capability cut the time it took to approve bank-issued credit card purchases to six seconds from thirty seconds during the height of the 1987 Christmas rush. Direct-distribution efficiency allows Wal-Mart to make money in small towns that proved unprofitable for retailers who used to truck merchandise in from distant locations.

Walton also takes chances on new retail formats. That's why there are more than eighty Sam's Wholesale Clubs, cash-and-carry membership warehouses, up and running just five years after the division was launched, not to mention the first gargantuan HYPERMART USA (so big, it has to be all caps), which boasts more than two hundred thousand square feet under one roof—in essence a miniature mall, but still oriented to family shopping.

Yet there remains something undeniably down-home and folksy about Wal-Mart and its spry leader. Mr. Sam has never been afraid to make an example of himself if he felt the point was worthwhile. In 1983, for instance, convinced that the company was in for a down year, he promised employees he would do the hula down Wall Street if they managed to beat his downscaled expectations.

They did. And he did, grass skirt and all.

Wal-Mart Stores, Inc.
702 SW Eighth Street
Bentonville, AR 72716

Liz Claiborne

HERE'S A FAMILY BUSINESS WITH A TWIST: ELISABETH CLAIBORNE ORTENBERG and her husband, Arthur, run the largest women's apparel company in the world. It's the fifth-most-admired company on the 1988 roster compiled by *Fortune*, especially for its innovativeness and overall quality of management. In 1987, its sales force outscored competitors and noncompetitors alike in *Sales & Marketing Management's* annual rankings of 100 companies (ten each in ten fields), based in part on an unparalleled reputation among its customers. Its clothes generate about three times the sales per square foot of even the pricey designer lines, a level of performance that pushed the company onto the billion-dollar sales plateau in 1987.

That's nice. But, again, where's the service?

Well, try to find a store with Liz Claiborne's name over the doorway. You can't, unless you know where to look for it—inside somebody else's store. Claiborne brings out six full lines of ready-to-wear clothes a year; most clothiers offer only four lines, one each season. She sells them through major department stores and specialty shops. The extra two lines mean Claiborne labels can change more quickly and adapt more closely to changing market conditions, giving customers what they want almost as soon as they realize they want it. It also means retailers are likely to see their customers more often, because change brings fashion-conscious clothes buyers back to see what's new. And it means retailers can hedge their bets by making smaller buys on a more frequent basis.

Strangely enough, Claiborne has achieved its reputation and success without sending its people on the road to hustle the line, piece-by-piece, to in-store buyers, which is an important part of how most ready-to-wear lines are placed with retailers. Instead, its customers *prefer* to come to New York, where Claiborne's salespeople work out of a centralized design showroom that buyers, and especially retail executives, are prone to visit whenever they're in town (usually several times a year). What's more, retailers must buy the entire line or none of it—no picking and choosing. Both tactics are cut from the same novel cloth as Claiborne's pacesetting six line changes per year in that all three run counter to accepted practice in the retail fashion business.

The reason? Liz Claiborne herself is a designer, not a retailer. Her focus is on the customer who will eventually buy her clothes, and through the years she's built the company and its way of doing business in keeping with that deep, market-focused understanding. Retailers who have bought and profited from her mid-priced but high-quality clothing lines have learned from experience to trust her judgment. They've also learned that the systems included with the clothes work as well for their own employees as they do for their customers.

As a company, Claiborne is built on creating lasting, long-term relationships. Salespeople, noted *Sales & Marketing Management* in June of 1987, don't wine and dine buyers to place product at any costs. They place the line intelligently, based on an overall view of the marketplace, and preferring, in the words of one analyst, to "keep the customers a wee bit hungry" if that results in adherence to Liz Claiborne's own high standards.

Claiborne herself is more than CEO. She works with teams of other designers to create clothes, mostly for working women, although there are Claiborne lines for men and girls, too. She works with manufacturing specialists around the world to get the designs made and shipped while they're still fashionable. She works with established retailers to get those clothes into the closets of women who know what they want and don't want to spend a lot of time buying them, or outlandish amounts of money paying for them.

The company that bears her name may be only in its adolescence, but Claiborne herself is a veteran of nearly forty years in the business. She first started making her mark at the age of nineteen, entering and winning a design contest sponsored by *Harpers Bazaar*. A native of Belgium, she'd divided her early years between Europe and New Orleans before going to work in New York, where she paid her dues on the industry's frontlines, working her way up from a sketcher and model to design assistant to designer.

When Claiborne went into business for herself in 1976, she targeted the legions of women entering and working their way up in the business world. Figuring they would need working wardrobes that were fashionable, comfortable, and affordable, she created three distinct sportswear labels, each designed to offer a collection within a collection. Then she decided to offer those lines to retailers as part of a dependable, full-service package. The company went public in 1981, broke the billion-dollar sales mark in 1987, and continues to impress and delight investors and customers alike.

Today there are more than nine thousand places to buy Claiborne lines, a number of them involving Liz Claiborne "boutiques"—essentially a store-within-a-store—where coordinated fashions, shoes, and accessories are displayed together. Not only is the merchandise Claiborne-designed and made to its specifications in the U.S. and abroad, but so too are the furnishings. Fixtures and displays are built to Claiborne specs, and the people who work there are trained by Claiborne's sales force.

For example, at Jordan Marsh in Boston, *The Wall Street Journal* reported in 1988, the Claiborne boutique boasts fully a dozen salespeople, which is more than twice as many as would be found in most department store sales areas. It was designed by an architect retained and paid by Claiborne, and the people working the sales floor work for "Liz," not Jordan Marsh. The company has a staff of fifteen consultants dedicated to training salespeople in stores coast to coast on the right way to sell the Liz Claiborne lines.

The distinctive level of service appeals to women with finite amounts of time and money available for constructing a working and leisure wardrobe, and also to men who find it easy to shop for the women in their lives, not to mention themselves, with the integrated product lines available. As the menswear side of the business has expanded in recent years, women customers have found the reverse to be true as well—Claiborne styles for men work together as extensively as the women's wear lines.

For the future, Claiborne is broadening its product lines while it continues to build on traditional (if ten years of history is enough to create traditions) strengths. To add accessories to its line, the company acquired an accessory manufacturer in 1986. Claiborne also has its own line of cosmetics, now sold directly to and through retailers after experimenting with a short-lived joint venture with Avon. The long-awaited Claiborne-run retail chain, christened First Issue, made its debut in 1988, but it is being operated independent of the existing Liz Claiborne lines.

In key markets around the U.S., the company has now begun opening a few "prototype and presentational specialty shops." The shops will showcase special Claiborne selections in a setting consumers will likely find very attractive, but there's more to them than selling clothes. They're actually intended to offer Claiborne a unique setting in which to get closer to customers, tracking sales, styles, color preferences, and first-hand perceptions of the company and its product lines. The information will be plugged into future planning and shared with other retailers carrying the full Claiborne line.

For Liz Claiborne, building a culture where people invest themselves in taking personal care of the business is the key to making the business a good fit in the retail marketplace.

Liz Claiborne, Inc.
1441 Broadway
New York, NY 10018

Avon Products

Avon

IF YOU NEED A WORKING EXAMPLE OF THE STRATEGIC MERIT OF "STICKING to the knitting"—focusing a business on what it does best, in the process forgoing costly forays into unrelated and often not fully understood fields of enterprise—consider Avon. In recent years, high-priced acquisitions in retail jewelry, catalog clothing sales, home health care, and medical supplies and chemicals have all come and gone, leaving a residue of dings and dongs on the bottom line. But at what it does best, the direct selling of cosmetics, fragrances, and toiletries that built the business into a billion-dollar success and once again provides about 90 percent of the company's sales and earnings, Avon is definitely a force to be reckoned with.

These days, though, it's not the same old Avon renowned for sending legions of women door to door to sell scents and beauty aids to other stay-at-home women. That's because a funny thing happened to Avon's basic market: It went into the marketplace and got jobs, which meant there often was nobody home when the doorbell rang. That dynamic also affected Avon's sales force. As women looked for careers and for steadier and more bankable incomes instead of the "pin money" of simpler, pre-dual-career times—Avon found itself competing to keep productive salespeople, not to mention recruit and train new ones. In 1982, there were 430,000 women selling Avon products in the U.S.; three years later, their ranks had slimmed to 375,000.

Since that low point, there has been growing evidence that a renewed service focus, both on customers and on frontline sales representatives, has reenergized Avon's direct-sales efforts. The sales force has been rebuilt to a little over 400,000 (there are about 1.4 *million* sales reps in fifty countries around the world these days) as the result of a determined effort to recruit more, train more, and rework marketing programs to address the needs and style of a more modern and professional woman. Sales performance has improved as well: The number of representatives with personal sales over $8,000 rose 8.5 percent in 1987. Turnover, which

368

in good years used to run 140 percent or more, has been sliced by more than half.

As turnarounds go, it's far from a barn-burner. But it reflects some solid, if belated, thinking about how services have to change to keep pace with a customer's changing needs and expectations—and with the frontline salesperson's own changing lifestyle. In the past, for example, Avon used to pay a token $10 bonus for reps who helped recruit new salespeople. That was fitting for a part-time avocation, but it didn't credit the sales force with having very much pride or self-image invested in their work.

Now the recruiter, or "sponsor", gets a 5-percent commission on the recruit's sales for as long as both remain with the company. The tactic has encouraged successful salespeople to network toward longer-term objectives. It gives the new rep an immediate mentor and informal trainer, someone who knows and likes the business and will be comfortable providing tips, problem-solving advice, and encouragement as needed. And it obviously rewards loyalty and longevity. Avon says the program is keeping many current salespeople involved over a longer period of time, and also credits it for bringing back some sales reps who had left the business. That continuity means more customers are being served longer by familiar and experienced salespeople, which in turn results in better sales figures and higher customer satisfaction ratings.

Then there's the product line. For years after women started streaming into the workplace en masse, Avon neglected to expand and improve its offerings or tailor them to the changing tastes of women who saw themselves as professionals on the job as well as individuals with a rewarding personal life. The company seemed oblivious to the fact that Mary Richards might not want the same things June Cleaver had long been satisfied with.

Gradually, moved by declining sales figures and the shrinking sales force, Avon took notice. Product catalogs now include a growing selection of professional skin-care products and more upscale cosmetics and fragrances (including hair-care products for black customers, and Spanish-language sales catalogs for Hispanic women). Fashion as well as traditional jewelry, and accessories designed for working wardrobes, are now regular features in monthly product brochures. There also are products for men, a line that dates back to the realization in 1982 that customers might welcome the opportunity to shop for people other than themselves.

Avon does have a retail sales side, but its activities are restricted to non-Avon brands (unbeknownst to most consumers, cosmetics marketed under such designer labels as Deneuve, Giorgio, Oscar de la Renta, Valentino, and Perry Ellis are Avon's, primarily as a result of acquisitions or joint ventures) and market research. To fine-tune products for its home-sale customers, the company conducts point-of-purchase product tests and comparisons, typically staged in or near a major department store or high-fashion retailer. They give prospective customers a chance to compare Avon products head to head against competitors, and yield valuable market intelligence for the direct-sales network.

Customer service at the frontline has changed in a number of ways, including a redefinition of just where the frontline is. Because two thirds of all women now work outside the home, Avon has diversified its doorbell-ringing fixation, under which each sales rep is allocated a tightly defined territory, by adding a nonterritorial, workplace marketing program. Left to their own devices, Avon sales reps, nearly half of whom work outside the home, were already producing approximately 20 percent of the company's sales from customers they met on the job. A new, formalized program, backed by special training and marketing materials, could conceivably double that percentage by 1990.

Again, the change has multiple dimensions. It allows Avon to continue to reach many of its best customers directly, but in a more convenient and accessible setting. It supports the upgraded product mix by selling to women who have their own income and career ambitions. And it retains as loyal sales reps women who need a larger and steadier source of income but still desire to continue their sales activities.

The company is becoming easier to do business with at the same time that it is targeting a more knowledgeable and demanding customer. In 1988, after several years of testing, Avon debuted a new approach to color. On a four-page color chart in the full-sized quarterly product catalogs that go to regular customers, all 350 shades of Avon cosmetic products are segmented and illustrated within four basic color groups. By matching what she has to the chart, the customer can choose other coordinating shades that mix and match effectively. Avon also has put together training programs to help representatives analyze their customers' skin tones, wardrobes, and personal styles so they can provide useful advice on selecting compatible products.

Across the board, training is now officially recognized as a key component in building both effective salespeople and long-term sales. Trained sales representatives, the company's internal research has shown, are 20 percent more productive and remain active 35 percent longer than those left untrained. Consequently, there are training programs on everything from skin care and fashion trends to personal time management and selling techniques geared for conditions encountered in both traditional one-on-one and more complex workplace settings.

In recent years, Avon has been building a data base on its customers. That's allowing it to take a page from the insurance industry and develop a prototype "stranded customer" program, matching those whose sales reps leave Avon with new reps. Avon estimates that there are, at any given time, as many as ten million American women who would buy its products if only they had a sales rep to turn to. The data base also will pinpoint underserved and underperforming territories and help identify new prospects, who can be assigned to reps looking to build their personal clientele.

And Avon is experimenting with a third channel to direct sales: the telephone. In some metropolitan areas, customers who aren't served by a regular sales rep at home or at work can call an 800-number to make an initial purchase. Deliveries are made by home or workplace reps, thus improving personal service, and matching the new customer with a stable sales rep.

Although Avon has not abandoned or deemphasized its attempts to grow in fields such as retailing or home health care, it has gone a long way toward revitalizing its traditional services while shedding acquisitions that didn't fit right or run well under its banner. Tiffany (the world-renowned jeweler), Mallinckrodt (a health-care and specialty chemicals company), and Foster Home Health Care have been sold off. Avon is still deeply involved in residential health care (Retirement Inns of America and Mediplex Group) and the retailing of its various designer-label cosmetics. But with 90 percent of 1987 revenues coming from the sales generated by individual representatives and their carload (or briefcase-load) of catalogs and samples, personal service seems to be ringing up new success for Avon.

Avon Products
Nine West 57th Street
New York, NY 10019

Home Depot

LOW PRICE AND HIGH SERVICE. IT SOUNDS LIKE A CONTRADICTION IN TERMS, AND for many businesses it has proven an impossible combination. Not so for Home Depot, a chain of nearly one hundred plain-looking, discount-priced, warehouse-style stores that "serve" do-it-yourselfers in search of paint, tools, wood and paneling, plumbing and electrical supplies, nuts and bolts, and other home improvement paraphernalia. Mostly those stores are spread through the South and Southwest, from Florida and Georgia to California, but the Northeast is beginning to see the company's distinctive white-on-orange signs.

In the nine years from its founding in 1979 through 1987, Home Depot grew at a heady compound rate of 80 percent. It wasn't just a matter of opening new stores right and left, either: Sales in existing stores grew by an average of 18 percent in 1987, despite the fact that the company typically faces vigorous price-based competition from other home improvement retail centers in the states where it operates. Noting the competition provided by traditional hardware stores, building-supply warehouses, and large-scale home centers, *Fortune* in early 1988 declared the battle no contest: "Home Depot is the only company that has successfully brought off the union of low prices and high service."

Less than ten years ago, Home Depot was a chancy start-up company organized in Atlanta by three executives who had been sent packing by the new owner of their previous employer. Funding came from a New York City-based venture capital firm, based primarily on the potential of an intriguing phenomenon Bernard Marcus, Arthur Blank, and Ronald Brill had noticed in merchandising experiments conducted in one store of a home improvement chain they had been running. When they marked down merchandise, it seemed, sales volume increased while the cost (as a percentage of sales) of making those sales decreased. In discounting, that's the magic formula that energizes everything from warehouse-sized supermarkets to small, self-service specialty stores. But it's a formula that seldom includes a high level of personal service.

Home Depot's breakthrough thinking came from firsthand knowledge of its typical customer. Do-it-yourselfers now buy more building supply materials than the professionals do—60 percent of 1987 industry volume, according to *Fortune*—but that doesn't make them instantly competent enough (let alone confident enough) to successfully rewire basements, replumb bathtubs, and otherwise redecorate the family castle.

How well they know it. A few years ago, employees in the paint department of the Home Depot in Marietta, Georgia, put up a tongue-in-cheek placard noting that "Husbands are not permitted to select colors without a written note of approval from wife." Most customers reacted with a knowing grin, reported *National Home Center News*—but at least one dutiful husband showed up with a note from home authorizing him to buy paint by himself.

Marcus (now the CEO), Blank (COO), and Brill (CFO) had picked up on that discrepancy firsthand in their previous employer's store, and their understanding of its depths and dimensions grew during the countless hours they all spent on the sales floor in the first years of Home Depot's existence. Consequently they not only built stores large enough to carry twenty-five thousand items (compared to ten thousand in many home centers) but also staffed them with people capable of taking the mystery out of home improvement tasks.

The customer is a key component in the company's strategy for growth. As Marcus and Blank explain it, "The Home Depot's success has been built on our commitment to develop new do-it-yourselfers while serving the expanding needs of our present customers. Our trained salespeople continue to create a new customer base for The Home Depot by encouraging and advising novice do-it-yourselfers. We believe that with proper guidance and instruction, home owners can learn to do their own home improvement projects and repairs, ultimately becoming dedicated do-it-yourselfers."

Home Depot stores place a high premium on hiring workers who are themselves savvy do-it-yourselfers. What they don't know they soon learn, because employee training is continuous. There are handyman skill-building classes each week—employees attend on-the-clock—and Home Depot stores in turn pass that expertise on to customers in the form of free classes on everything from how to build a deck or a cinder-block wall to safe and sane ways to troubleshoot plumbing and electrical systems.

Most stores have a licensed electrician on staff; many also have a licensed plumber in residence or on call. Some stores even tap contractors and professionals who buy their supplies at Home Depot to lead employee and customer classes. Instruction doesn't end when class lets out, either. Customers are told to call at any point in their project if they need help solving a problem or figuring out what to do next.

" 'Our people make the difference' ranks right up there with 'We'll have it for you next week' as the biggest lie in retailing," noted *Fortune*.

"But Home Depot's people clearly *do* make the difference in an industry where the tyro has replaced the pro as the major customer. Part-timers and minimum-wage earners staff most warehouse outlets and many conventional home centers. Home Depot goes the other way. Some 90% of its employees are full time, and they earn higher-than-average salaries with full benefits."

Home Depot's policy is to train its people and treat its people like professional tradespeople. The aim is to build a broad-ranging familiarity with a variety of jobs. And each employee's range of expertise is plainly visible from the badges he or she has earned the right to wear on the company's bright orange apron. (Each badge also represents a ten-dollar bonus.)

The training commitment includes management, too. Top officers of the company regularly spend time in the classroom teaching, firsthand, the practices and skills they expect their regional and store managers to employ. From merchandising practices and time management to safety and security, the Home Depot culture is top-down in the literal as well as figurative sense.

Marcus is on record as saying he'd like to make Home Depot national in scope, the Sears Roebuck of the home improvement industry. That may happen. But it also may not be necessary from the customer's standpoint. According to *National Home Center News*, "There isn't a home center today that doesn't incorporate some of Home Depot's approach."

With industry observers predicting that the do-it-yourself market could grow to $100 billion by 1990, that's service influence on a grand scale.

The Home Depot
2727 Paces Ferry Road
Atlanta, GA 30339

FLORSHEIM®

AT FIRST GLANCE, FLORSHEIM LOOKS LIKE YOUR BASIC, OLD-FASHIONED SHOE store. There are the familiar racks of dress and casual shoes for men and women, the comfortable stores in shopping malls and other high-traffic locations. Corporately, it's one of nearly two dozen apparel, general merchandise, footwear, and furniture companies (including Converse athletic shoes, Central Hardware stores, and the International Hat Company) conglomeratized under the banner of St. Louis-based Interco.

But look again—over there, sitting unobtrusively against the wall in the Florsheim store. Is that an automatic teller machine? Well, sort of. It's a high-tech laser disc (an interactive video system that is similar technologically to the compact discs that are fast replacing LP records) built into a kiosk called Express Shop. In it are all three hundred styles and every different color of shoe Florsheim carries, whether it's in stock in this particular store or not.

If what you want isn't in the back room, not to worry. A Florsheim salesperson can fit you—none of the guessing about width or comfort you'd have to do if you ordered through even one of the best of the mail-order catalogs. Then he or she will turn you over to Express Shop, where your order is sent through on-line to Florsheim's headquarters and administrative center in Chicago. There it's processed, with your order being sent along to the central distribution center in Jefferson City, Missouri, and your bill beamed electronically to your credit card company. Within a week you can expect to receive your shoes, free of charge, via UPS.

Buying shoes through an automatic teller may seem like a strange notion at first, but Florsheim spent two years working the bugs out of the system before implementing it on a large scale. The touchscreen-driven programming is designed to help the customer find what he or she is looking for in whatever way is most comfortable: by size, by style, by color, by seasonal tie-in or lifestyle. Music, photography, and product information are combined in a smooth-flowing presentation that makes the encounter between man and machine far more personal and enjoyable than a confrontation with the typical beeping "money-wall." Customer acceptance in the ten states in which the service has been introduced has been positive. Even in traditional businesses, it seems, change is a constant.

Express Shop is a system Milton S. Florsheim never could have envisioned when he opened a shoe shop in Chicago in 1892. On the other hand, he probably would have been all for it. It was Florsheim who drove the business from a small midwestern retail operation into a nationwide brand name for top-quality shoes. Under Interco, Florsheim forms part of a quality footwear group that also includes Converse; other members of the corporate family include London Fog clothing, Lane and Broyhill furniture, and Ethan Allen showrooms.

In the beginning, some Express Shops were located as freestanding kiosks in shopping malls. From experience and careful consumer testing and observation, however, Florsheim learned that customers would rather have them within the friendly confines of a conventional store. While they appreciate the greater selection available through the electronic system, they also prize the personal service and product knowledge available from the store's staff. Putting the machines inside the stores and training the salespeople in their proper role and operations have provided the best of both worlds.

It's worth noting that not only is Florsheim using videodisc for merchandising, but it also has transformed many of its training programs into disc-based materials. That helps make the most of the hardware investment and encourages salespeople to become familiar with the equipment's operation without the pressure of an anxious customer looking on. Meanwhile, the disc is updated twice a year to incorporate new shoe lines and reflect seasonal changes, but that process is invisible to customers.

There are already more than 350 Express Shops in operation—perhaps the largest and most successful example to date of the futuristic marvels of electronic shopping. As part of the installation process, the company made localized presentations to store managers in company-owned and independent stores, then located the Express Shops in those stores where managers were truly interested and enthusiastic about the program. That further ensures that customers who wander by an Express Shop will receive plenty of support and assistance. Florsheim expects to have more than 2,000 such video kiosks in place in its network of 600 company-owned stores and 7,500 independent dealers over the next couple of years.

More than the technology involved, Express Shop is impressive because of what it represents for customers. In simplest terms, it means no Florsheim customer need ever walk away unsatisfied because a particular size or style or color they wanted wasn't available when and where they wanted it. It also means new styles can be introduced and the product mix adjusted seasonally simply by changing the Express Shop's videodisc.

Ultimately, the company expects the video sales system to be in every store, and some may even be self-service: You'll be able to shop the video display, key in size information and your choice of styles and colors, run a credit card through an electronic reader, and go home secure in the knowledge that exactly what you want will soon show up at your doorstep.

Even better, it should fit just fine.

The Florsheim Shoe Company
Subsidiary of Interco, Inc.
130 South Canal Street
Chicago, IL 60606

L. L. Bean

L.L.Bean®

LEON LEONWOOD. THAT'S WHAT THE INITIALS STAND FOR. HE AND HIS BROTHER Ervin were a couple of small-town storekeepers up in turn-of-the-century Freeport, Maine, partners in a family haberdashery. Actually, it was Ervin who ran the business.

L. L. liked to hunt and fish. He didn't like wet feet. So in 1912 he designed the first pair of Maine Hunting Shoes for himself and had the town's shoemaker put them together, a matter of sewing leather uppers to the rubber soles of a pair of galoshes. They worked out fine. L. L., then thirty-nine years old, astutely decided there might be other hunters and fishermen out there with a similar desire for dry socks.

And that's about as far as small-town entrepreneurship would likely have taken things, except that L. L. Bean wasn't content to sell just in Freeport. (Given that the town today boasts a population of less than seven thousand people, that was a pretty fair marketing decision.) He got a list of people who had bought hunting licenses in the state and started sending out flyers touting his Maine Hunting Shoes. Before long people from all over the region were stopping by the Beans' store for all kinds of sturdy, dependable, and reasonably priced outdoor gear. Over the years, the flyers became catalogs. The mailing list expanded. People who couldn't visit the store started buying through the catalogs. They trusted him, even though they'd never met him. They weren't disappointed.

L. L. died in 1967. The company's greatest growth has come under the direction of his grandson, Leon Gorman, who took over in the 1960s and has built his grandpa's rustic business into the largest outdoor specialty catalog company in the U.S. and the standard against which all other mail order businesses inevitably are compared. L. L. Bean still has just the one company store up in Freeport, but only the Atlantic Ocean draws more tourists to the state of Maine. What has made Bean a coast-to-coast phenomenon are the catalogs—six thousand items offered in twenty-two different mailings in 1987, including four large seasonal editions, eighty-five million copies in all. And the service.

When *Consumer Reports* polled 165,000 of its readers on their mail-

order experiences in 1987, L. L. Bean was the top-rated provider
of the seven merchandise categories (sporting goods, men's
clothes, men's sportswear, women's business clothes, women's sport-
wear, lingerie/ underwear, and luggage/leather goods) where it does business. The highest score it earned on a merchandise satisfaction scale of
100: 97, for sporting goods and luggage/leather goods. The lowest: 94, for
women's business clothing.

Small wonder. Convenience is a Bean byword. Almost anything in any
L. L. Bean catalog can be delivered to almost any location in the U.S.
and Canada in seventy-two hours or less. Bean shipped close to 10 million
packages in 1987 (it figures it can handle 80,000 shipments a day at peak
capacity) and an astounding 99.89 percent of those orders were filled
correctly. In that same year, Bean's service staff handled an estimated 6.5
million orders and customer service calls over its toll-free 800-number,
and sorted through about 5.5 million pieces of mail. So impressive are the
Bean warehouse and shipping operations that Xerox and other companies
have set their service benchmarks based on Bean's delivery speed and
performance accuracy.

The store isn't just for show, either. It still accounts for about 15
percent of the company's annual business ($65 million of 1987's sales of
$490 million), carrying not only everything that's offered through the
catalogs, but also several thousand additional items. As many as 3.5
million people visit the store every year, some to shop, some to see if
there really is a trout pond inside the building. There is.

The people you meet, whether on the phone or in the store, are not
only friendly and cheerful, they're wondrously competent and helpful.
They aren't born that way. Before they go to work on the phone banks,
they spend forty hours training on telephone skills, computer order-
taking, and product knowledge. Whenever a new catalog comes out,
there's new training to go with it, most of it imparted by the product
managers who pick and field-test every product Bean offers. (Incidentally, those are Bean employees, not professional models, in the catalogs.)

Bean's people have built up so much outdoor expertise that the store
regularly schedules about a hundred clinics a year up in Freeport on
everything from bird-dog handling to winter camping. (It figures there's
no point selling something to someone who doesn't know how to use it
properly and hence can't get full value out of the purchase.) Bean still
manufactures more than three hundred of its own items—about 20 percent of the product line—including more than a quarter of a million pairs
of Maine Hunting Shoes annually. It contracts for other items within tight
quality and performance specifications.

The old haberdashery in the quaint seaside town now employs about
2,800 people full-time, another 1,800 during the Christmas season (which
for Bean starts in the fall), when its switchboards may handle nearly

30,000 telephone orders a day. The records through 1987: 75,000 calls in one day, 83,000 pieces of mail. The phone lines, like the store, never shut down. You can call any time of the day or night, any day of the year (including Christmas), and the friendly people at Bean will be there to take care of you.

Taking care of the customers, not the intrinsic charm of the Maine Hunting Shoe, is the reason for Bean's near-legendary success. That's a company trademark that goes back to L. L., whose business philosophy was: "Sell good merchandise at a reasonable profit and treat customers like human beings, and they will always come back for more."

That philosophy was thoroughly tested by Bean's first hundred pairs of boots—ninety of which were returned by dissatisfied customers after the stitching in the leather uppers pulled out of the soft rubber soles. Undaunted, Bean made good on his pledge to refund their money if they weren't satisfied. Then he found a new supplier for rubber soles and borrowed enough money to make some more boots and send some more flyers. To this day, the Bean guarantee is unconditional. Whether you bought it last week or last year, if it doesn't fit, if it doesn't hold up, if it doesn't perform, if it doesn't look good hanging in your closet, Bean will replace it or send you your money back.

Over the years, Bean has nurtured a sense of trust and goodwill in its customers that goes above and beyond the basic routines of a business, and yet has become an important part of the business. "It's as if Bean were family," wrote John Skow in *Sports Illustrated* in 1985, "some sort of mildly eccentric but amiable uncle who lives up in Maine and sends us packages. And people send family photos back to L. L. Bean, generally showing themselves proudly wearing some Bean garment. They chat on the phone to Bean mentioning, perhaps, that they are thinking of sending their teen-agers to Outward Bound, and does Bean's customer-service think this is a good idea? It does. What equipment would the kids need? Bean has a list, and can supply the stuff."

In recent years, Bean has become a mecca for more than just shoppers looking for good value in outdoor clothing and equipment. As noted, from IBM and Xerox to smaller firms, business executives and managers have come to Freeport to try to divine the magic that results in such unparalleled service quality and inspires such mythic loyalty among Bean customers and employees. They tour a bustling distribution warehouse that still relies on people more than computers and automated systems to fill orders. They take in the bulletin boards where letters from customers are posted under the heading "Messages From The Boss." They notice that even temporary workers making less than six dollars an hour get a daily update on what percentage of orders are being shipped correctly.

"Sell good merchandise at a reasonable profit and treat customers like human beings, and they will always come back for more," they are told by Leon Gorman.

Some go away still unconvinced that it can be so simple.

L. L. Bean
Freeport, ME 04033

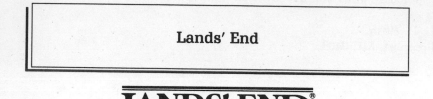

WHEN YOU PLAY IN THE SAME LEAGUE AS L. L. BEAN, YOU HAVE TO BE VERY good to be noticed. When Lands' End went public in 1986, a lot of people started to notice this twenty-five-year-old direct merchant of "cut and sewn" products headquartered in Chicago, but based off in southwestern Wisconsin. Through regular mailings (every four weeks, or thirteen times a year) of its creatively designed and whimsically written catalogs, and through a thoroughgoing emphasis on quality from the vendors who provide the merchandise in those catalogs, Lands' End has established itself as one of the most successful of America's growing number of direct merchandisers. A major reason is service.

The name reflects the company's origins in 1963 as a mail-order supplier of sailboat hardware and equipment. Founder Gary Comer, now president and CEO, had been a copywriter for Young and Rubicam, and it wasn't long before he was putting out distinctive catalogs for the yachting crowd. Then a funny thing began to happen: A clothing section originally intended to complement the boat supplies gradually grew to occupy more and more space. In 1976, Comer and Lands' End decided land was where the business truly was and began concentrating on clothes, accessories, shoes, and luggage as the company's main lines.

Today Lands' End figures it serves a potential market base of twelve million households, a market it expects will expand by another 10 percent or so by 1990. It's a young, well-educated, affluent, quality-oriented market, according to the company's extensive customer research. While about half the U.S. falls into the twenty-five-to-fifty age range, about 70 percent of the Lands' End customer base is to be found there. Nearly 90 percent of its customers have been to college, compared to 35 percent of the country's population at large, and—again compared to the general population—a Lands' End customer is five times as likely to have some level of postgraduate education. Seven out of ten Lands' End customers are in professional and managerial positions, and three fourths of the women who receive its catalogs work outside the home. Over 60 percent of its customers have household incomes above $35,000; median annual income is $46,000. For the U.S. as a whole, $24,500 is about average.

Those demographics dictate the style and content of each catalog from Lands' End: entertaining marketing-oriented stories, colorful pictures, obscurely related anecdotes, lots of product quality and care information, a scattering of personality profiles of people who work for the company in customer service jobs, and, oh yes, prices and ordering information for an average of six hundred different items (some ten thousand options altogether, once you figure in size and color choices).

Consequently, you don't *shop* a Lands' End catalog like a flyer from a discount house. You *read* it like a magazine. The writing style (understandably, given Comer's copywriting roots) is breezy, conversational, sometimes flip, but never pointlessly hip. Lands' End concentrates on supplying staple articles of enduring quality, clothes and accessories that know no time or season, rather than gushing manically over the latest fashion fads.

Its "store"—which it figures measures 10 3/4-inches tall, 8 1/4-inches wide, and 140 pages deep (with "no crowded parking lots, clogged elevators or hidden rest rooms")—is open 24 hours a day, 364 days a year. Unlike L. L. Bean, they take Christmas off in Dodgeville, Wisconsin, where the company now takes in, packs, and ships out the orders. Customers are urged to call toll-free anytime to order. Or just to get acquainted.

It all starts with the order, and Lands' End has put together a winner of an order-handling and fulfillment system. While generically the company is often classified as a mail-order merchandiser, about four out of five sales are rung up over the 800-number. It's a busy one: 4.6 million phone calls in 1987, normally—again according to the company's constant research—answered on or before the second ring by a real live person, not a recording telling you all the customer service people are busy and they'll get around to you as soon as they can.

The customer sales people get seventy-five hours of training before they're allowed to answer the phone and take an order. They have every product in the catalog within reach (which helps a lot when someone wants to know what the mesh knit shirt feels like, or whether the wool flannel trousers have a button on both back pockets or just the one on the left). Between eight in the morning and ten at night (Central Time), they also have the support of the company's extraordinarily helpful team of Specialty Shoppers.

These folks rank right up there with the sales associates in Nordstrom's. Their role is to help customers with questions ranging from figuring out the right size to coordinating the red Shaker sweater on page thirty-nine with the twill slacks on page fifty-four. They're important people in the Lands' End scheme of things, even though a cost-conscious accountant would be quick to point out that they aren't absolutely necessary and things might run as well (well, most of the time, at least), without them. At Lands' End, the point is that things run even better *with* them.

For many loyal customers, it's the Specialty Shoppers who make Lands' End stand out. The slices of life they see are the stuff of Norman Rockwell paintings. A woman loses forty pounds and decides to celebrate by ordering a new wardrobe; a Specialty Shopper spends more than an hour on the phone with her coordinating the choices. The mother of a blind seventeen-year-old who's planning to go off to college delegates to Lands' End the delicate task of picking out a wardrobe of slacks, shirts, sweater, and jacket that can be worn in any combination without making him stand out in a crowd for all the wrong reasons. A bride-to-be whose intended is also a frequent customer calls to request just Lands' End labels; she sews them on her garter to add a surprise twist to the old tradition.

Incredibly, given the mysterious delays and out-of-stock runarounds that have given direct merchandising in general such a bad name in recent years, Lands' End ships most orders within twenty-four hours of receipt. At the height of the 1987 Christmas rush, the longest any order other than those requiring monogramming was "in the house" was thirty-six hours; monograms took another twelve hours. The reason: Lands' End has invested wisely in good computers and good automated systems as well as good people.

In front of each customer salesperson in Dodgeville is a computer terminal on line to the Lands' End mainframe (and backed up by an uninterruptible power supply to avoid having to ever tell a caller "the computer is down momentarily"). Through it, orders are entered, shipping information verified, and even customer credit checked. If an item is temporarily out of stock, the service person says so, sometimes suggesting an alternative, occasionally even referring the customer to a competitor.

If it's in stock, and it usually is, high-speed laser printers kick out order tickets and packing lists for assembly in a highly automated distribution center, where optical scanners route items down a conveyer to the correct packing station and another scanner sorts outbound packages so they can be shipped in the most economical way. Every year for the past six years, Lands' End has upgraded its computer systems to keep customer service standards high despite the strains of growth and competition. In 1987, since the mainframe didn't need attention, it added a computer-controlled garment-moving system so single-item orders that involve hemming pants to customer specifications can still be shipped within twenty-four hours.

Sometimes success breeds excess. And waste. And bureaucracy. Not at Lands' End so far. The plan is to double the company in size, profitably, but over a period of five years, perhaps longer. Initial shareholders got a quick object lesson in how seriously Lands' End takes its quality standards when it throttled back in its very first quarter as a publicly held company, sacrificing volume to maintain service quality. As Comer explained it to shareholders in 1987, " 'Think small' is our credo. Worry about being better, bigger will take care of itself. Think one customer at a time and take care of each one the best way you can."

Significantly, Lands' End put its "principles of doing business" in its first annual report, too. There are eight. All are value- and service-oriented, from number one ("We do everything we can to make our products better. . . . We never reduce the quality of a product to make it cheaper.") through number eight ("We are able to sell at lower prices because we support no fancy emporiums with their high overhead.")

The one most customers notice, and which sometimes seems too good to be true (but isn't) is number three: "We accept any return, for any reason, at any time. Our products are guaranteed. No fine print. No arguments. We mean exactly what we say: GUARANTEED. PERIOD." The 1987 *Consumer Reports* ratings of mail-order companies found Lands' End a close second in four of five different categories (it tied for third in the other one), in every case within two points of leader L. L. Bean on a 100-point merchandise satisfaction scale. It scored 93 or better for all five lines: men's business clothes, men's sportswear, women's business clothes, women's sportswear, and luggage/leather goods.

By the way, in case you're wondering, the apostrophe in Lands' End is indeed in the wrong place. It was a typo in the first printed piece Comer put out for the company back in Chicago in 1963. Even when he found it, he couldn't afford to correct it and reprint the piece. So, since it really didn't make a difference in the quality of the service the company was providing, Lands' End kept it. No one seems to mind.

Lands' End, Inc.
Dodgeville, WI 53595

Williams-Sonoma

"NEEDLESS TO SAY, CHUCK WILLIAMS' POPULARITY WAS BASED ON SOMETHING a little more personal than a supply of Sabatier knives, braids of fresh garlic or eighteenth-century squirrel cage spit turners. What he had—and has—cannot be bought: Good Taste. William Rice, editor of *Food & Wine*, calls it 'Williams' secret weapon.' People who are blessed with the quality are attracted to each other; those who are not so endowed, cluster around the possessor in hopes that the instinct will prove contagious. In that sense Williams is a 'carrier,' and cooks, from master chefs to apprentice egg-boilers, find everything in his stores contagious."

What did people do back in the days when cooking was a chore and not an avocation to be enjoyed and shared? Whatever it was, they did it without the benefit of Williams, of Sonoma, California. Replace the "of" with a hyphen and you have a bona fide business phenomenon. From the quarterly *A Catalog for Cooks* that reaches ten million American homes annually to the growing number of stores (about a hundred in 1988, operating under the Williams-Sonoma name plus Pottery Barn, Gardener's Eden, and Hold Everything), the San Francisco-based specialty retailer has earned accolades from customers coast to coast—among them the financially apt tribute of being "one of the 10 most dangerous stores in the country."

As the opening tribute (from a 1981 story in *Town & Country*) attests, Williams-Sonoma has customers in the same sense that symphony orchestras do. Yes, money changes hands, services are rendered, expectations satisfied. But as Williams-Sonoma president Howard Lester, who has made the financial side of the company work since buying into the business in 1978, explained to *Retailing West* a few years back, "What we are selling is creative cooking and entertaining ideas. That's what we like to think we do in our stores; consumers shop here for new ideas."

In 1956, Williams, the son of an automobile-repair-shop owner whose formal education stopped after high school, was a handyman carpenter who had just remodeled a small commercial building near the town square of Sonoma, up in the heart of California's wine country. Two of the building's three stores were leased, but Williams had to take over the third, a hardware store, himself or let the space sit empty. The problem was, he didn't really like hardware. What he liked was cooking, especially with the kind of Old World cooking utensils he remembered from his German-Dutch grandmother.

Gradually, helped along by summer buying trips in Europe, the nuts and bolts were replaced by knives and pans. San Franciscans with summer homes in the Napa and Sonoma valleys couldn't get enough of the stuff, or the special knowledge and enthusiasm Williams brought to the culinary arts. In 1958, they persuaded the then forty-two-year-old entrepreneur to follow them back to "The City" and set up shop on Sutter Street. He did, and the address quickly proved fortuitous—Williams struck gold in copper pots, cookware, and culinary antiques.

Just as customers energized the first big business move, the second was taken at the urging of another customer-service legend. In 1972, the late Edward Marcus, cofounder of Nieman-Marcus department stores, convinced Williams to issue a catalog based on the Sutter Street store's merchandise and growing reputation. The original mailing list was just ten thousand, most of them spread around the city by the bay. This year, one American home in twelve will be on the list for at least one of the catalogs in the company library.

A Catalog for Cooks is still the mainstay, to be sure, but there are also separate catalogs for Pottery Barn (despite the name, that's actually "pan"-nery and "vase"-ry and home accessories and other posh interior/exterior decor items), Hold Everything (containers and household ideas), and Gardener's Eden (everything for the places around the house where things grow, and the places where you can sit and watch them grow). Each line is separate; each has its own customer targets with multiple mailing lists to segment merchandise according to its unique appeal.

Items are chosen for their basic quality: "We seek out the best product in each category and stock it in depth rather than have a vast assortment of varying levels of quality," Lester explained to *Retailing West*. As much as 50 percent of the four hundred items offered in each catalog and the four thousand products stocked by Williams-Sonoma stores is imported, often because there's no U.S. equivalent. Each operation is run separately, with independent buyers stocking the catalogs and stores.

In its stores and in its catalogs, Williams-Sonoma pays careful attention to customer service, a heritage that comes straight from the founder, who's still active in his seventies as chairman of the company. Store employees are chosen for their own interest in fine cooking, then carefully trained in service standards that include personally greeting everyone who walks through the door. At the hint of a question, they'll help a customer puzzle out a recipe, explain the use of exotic kitchenware such as the Pizelle Iron (which makes Italian wafer cookies that can be left flat, rolled into cylinders, or pressed into a bowl to form an edible ice cream or fruit basket), or point out the fine points of an imported-from-Japan bread baker that mixes and kneads the dough, allows it to rise, and bakes the loaf to a turn in four hours. (To awaken to the smell of fresh-baked bread, just mix the ingredients, put the yeast in the dispenser, set the automatic timer, and toddle off to bed).

A fresh-brewed pot of coffee is always on. Cooking classes seem to fill up as quickly as they're announced. Recipes of all descriptions are handed out constantly (they're also a common feature of every issue of *A Catalog for Cooks*). The popular *Care of Cookware* booklet that Williams-Sonoma developed itself because so few people knew how to take care of fine cooking utensils goes along with every purchase of same. Although most Williams-Sonoma customers are shopping for themselves, gift wrapping is free and a bridal registry is available. Returns are immediate, in full, and hassle-free.

The same attention goes into catalog sales, with telephone sales reps receiving lots of training in ways to help customers pick the right merchandise, or figure out how to use it after they get it out of the box. Williams-Sonoma benchmarked its phone-answering service against L. L. Bean's standards, so it's no coincidence the two operations draw similar rave reviews from customers. And while the company's roots may be in northern California, the distribution center is in Memphis. Why? Well, most of its customers are within closer range of it there (60 percent live east of the Mississippi). And a lot of the merchandise comes in from Europe, so it doesn't make sense to send it all the way to California and then have to send it back. It's essentially the same line of reasoning that brought another noted service provider (you've probably heard of a company that promises to "absolutely, positively" get something somewhere?) to Memphis, although ironically Williams-Sonoma prefers to ship mostly via United Parcel Service.

The company is unique in that unlike mail-order-only stalwarts L. L. Bean and Lands' End, or retail-oriented catalogers like Spiegel and Nieman-Marcus, it has successfully balanced catalog sales with retail store operations. The catalogs, with their intriguing, high-quality selections, bring people into the stores, which can offer ten times as many items. That helps get the stores established—Williams-Sonoma had a base of sixty thousand active mail-order customers in Manhattan alone when it opened its first store in the Big Apple in late 1987—yet it only siphons off about 15 percent of the mail-order business from the store's market area. Some people would call that synergy.

When readers of *Consumer Reports* shared their experiences (more than a quarter of a million purchases from nearly fifty mail-order companies) in 1987, Williams-Sonoma earned a score of 94 on a scale of 100, five points better than its nearest competitor in the kitchen/glassware/

linen category. Williams-Sonoma is accustomed to that kind of enthusiasm. Some businesses take great pride in record sales figures or number of new stores opened. In the company's San Francisco offices, they talk about how Williams is responsible for the appearance of the loose-bottom tart tin in the U.S., or how, by importing exactly that kind of cookware, he set the standard for home chefs who wanted professional-quality omelet and fry pans made of heavy French aluminum. That attitude hasn't been lost on customers.

Williams-Sonoma
100 North Point Street
San Francisco, CA 94133

TECHNOLOGY

ELECTRONICS

Amdahl

Digital Equipment Corporation

3M

AMP

SUPPORT

American Management Systems

Businessland

Dataserv

COMMUNICATIONS

Southern Bell

Southern New England Telephone

CompuServe

Technology: Halftime in the High-Tech Revolution—Regrouping with an Eye on Service

THE AGE OF THE COMPUTER HAS CO-OPTED AND BENT FOR GOOD THE WORD "technology." In its original English language usage, it neither mentioned nor alluded to the microchip, laser beam, or information age. It simply meant "the science or study of the practical or industrial arts." That definition and a dime won't buy coffee on Wall or Main streets today. To the men and women of either curb, technology now is synonymous with computers, lasers, robots, and the heady, and magical, binary-coded, microchip miracles of the last two decades.

The Wonder Years

We have all been party and witness to incredible change the last twenty years. At times it seemed as if we were all about to make reality of the Buck Rogers twenty-first-century comic strip fantasies of our youth. Science fiction writer Arthur C. Clarke has observed that "any sufficiently advanced technology is indistinguishable from magic." To all of us—but most clearly for those of us on the outside of the technology industry looking in—the last two decades have been just that; an era of magical creation. Consider some of the marvels we've come to take for granted:

Twenty years ago spaceships and trips to the moon were the stuff of engineers dreams and sci-fi movies. Today, space is a place where people work and space ships are the buses and trucks that move people and things between there and here.

Twenty years ago satellites were tiny beeping novelties that whirred around the planet and elicited oohs and ahs for their very existence. Satellites today are just another part of the vast world-spanning communications network we all depend on.

Twenty years ago data was something you put in an envelope and mailed across the country if you wanted someone else to see it. Today, each and every day, trillions of bytes of data are transmitted

392

at light-speed, computer to computer, across the country and around the world.

Twenty years ago a computer was something that sat in an environmentally controlled cleanroom, cost millions of dollars, was ministered to by members of a highly trained guild, and was owned by a governmental agency, university engineering department, or *Fortune* 500 company. Today, computers of the same processing power are small, inexpensive, and found on desks, in dens, in classrooms, on Jeep seats, and hanging from the shoulders of busy travelers who can't bear to leave home without one.

Twenty years ago gallstones and kidney stones were an infestation requiring painful and drastic surgical intervention. Today, a focused application of ultrasonic technology makes the cure a simple, non-invasive, outpatient procedure—about as traumatic as curing an upset stomach.

Twenty years ago a robot was a character from *The Day the Earth Stood Still* or *Forbidden Planet*—a chrome imitation of a human being. Today "robotics" is a billion-dollar business and a robot is a silent sentinel that tirelessly welds auto body segments together, tightens nuts to bolts, and spray paints panels and parts with the best of them.

Not every high-tech wonder of the last two decades has involved the creation of something new and never before seen that is just too gee-whiz to believe. Some of the impact has been invisible to the consumer/outsider eye, but just as revolutionary. Take the total makeover of the telephone industry.

A phone call, whether across the street or across the country, used to involve solid copper wires, stepper switches, and a simple electromagnetic analog of your voice. Today a phone call is the end product of a dozen technologies most of us hadn't heard of twenty years ago—lasers, fiber optics, cellular networks, satellite relays, digital switching, voice synthesization, and microwave transmission to mention only a few. Telephony is a high technology and a high art understood completely by only a handful.

The Service Years

While the birth years of the high-tech revolution have been an era of heady invention and innovation, the next twenty—the ones we're heading into now—are quite likely to be the service years, a time in which the code words become reliable, dependable, and responsive. In short, the high-technology industries are discovering service.

In truth, of course, service has been a measure of marketplace distinction in some segments of high tech for a long time. IBM created and originally maintained its role as mainframe computer leader not on technology, but on reliability. Others have promised and frequently delivered more bells and whistles, but few have been as steadfastly reliable and Johnny-on-the-spot with advisors, maintenance and repair people, and general hand-holding as "Big Blue." In the minicomputer business, Digital Equipment Corporation moved the same mountain and reaped the same benefit. DEC's maintenance and equipment service capability is so strong that its technicians routinely service other manufacturers' equipment when it is connected to a DEC network.

Hewlett-Packard, the multi-billion-dollar instrument-and-computer company started fifty years ago by two guys in a garage in the Silicon Valley of northern California—before there *was* a Silicon Valley—stands tall in the marketplace because of service. As one pleased customer told an interviewer for *Electronic Business*, "If you want something that meets the specs and works the first time, and that you don't have to invest the first two weeks learning, you can safely buy HP."

Indicative of its commitment to service is the opening in 1988 of the Hewlett-Packard Customer Support Center in Atlanta: the largest customer service facility in the industry, staffed night and day by technicians who not only solve problems customers are currently experiencing but also devise complex models to predict problems before they occur.

What's new and different is that service and servicing have become much more visible, an increasingly important factor for even the most technically literate customer trying to discriminate among products in the marketplace. Not too many years ago, servicing your equipment was simply a part of the price the big companies paid to be in the business. Today it is a profit center—maintenance is a $10 billion business—for companies of varying sizes and descriptions, many of whom recognize its additional role as a way to stay in touch with the customer.

In 1987 third-party maintenance (TPM) companies— organizations that specialize in fixing for profit what others build—grossed $1.5 billion, and they appear to be increasing business at 10 percent per year. Nearly all U.S. computer manufacturers have entered the TPM business. NCR, Unisys, and Xerox are notable for fast-growing TPM divisions. Companies that don't make the hardware—Bell South, Bell Atlantic, TRW, and American Express, to name some prominent players—also have actively entered the market via acquisition of small TPMs. There is even a fourth-party maintenance industry developing from the suppliers of spare parts and services going into system maintenance work, according to New York-based industry consultant Frost and Sullivan.

TPM companies are decidedly not simple spin-offs of "old" computer company service departments. Their focus, tone, and view of themselves was well exemplified in a talk given at a recent TPM conference by William J. Shields, president of Philadelphia-based Shields Business Machines: "Quality makes all the difference between success and survival. We're not in business for ourselves; we're in business for customers." Shields offered this formula for creating service quality:

- Find out what the customer needs;
- Develop and constantly refine the services that meet these identified needs;
- Learn how and what to delegate to employees on the frontline;
- Provide employees with the training, resources, and responsibility to do the job right.

The new kids on the high-tech block, the microcomputer types, also are learning that service matters. Even in the service morass of personal computers, the race is beginning to go to the swiftest service, not just to the company with the most megabytes for the fewest bucks. Meanwhile, the successful retail chains, such as Businessland and Computerland, have beefed up their post-sales technical support and added classes for customers on a wide variety of software and hardware.

Their larger-scale activities have an individualized counterpart, both in the stores and among the makers of the software that actually runs the hardware. Software marketers such as Ashton-Tate (dBASE IV), Lotus Development Corporation (Lotus 1-2-3), and Aldus Corporation (Page-Maker) now offer, for a fee, special help programs, staffing hundreds of lines with trained tech specialists who can talk most single users through the problems they all too commonly encounter with complex software. Other companies, such as Microsoft and WordPerfect, offer such help lines without a subscription charge (although users calling the free lines tend to be put on hold more).

Ashton-Tate has organized a corporate advisory board to help it improve software design and service. Fort Worth-based Tandy Corporation, one of the earliest microcomputer builders, has the longest-running users' group in the business, and it too has a service component: Created in 1982, the Tandy Business Users Group helps the company improve design and responsiveness to customer needs and problems.

Several dozen such companies offer technical help through electronic "bulletin boards" on national information services such as CompuServe, whose half a million computer-owning members can use their systems to address questions about their hardware and software directly to technical support people—or, because they're sometimes more in tune with nitty-gritty performance glitches, to other users.

Calling for Service

Even the telephone companies, now referred to in the high-technology vernacular as the telecommunications industry, have discovered an advantage in improving not only the core services they provide to business and residential customers but also the quality of the "servicing" those customers receive.

In some respects, that's remedial work. For half a century and more, the American telephone system was the envy of the world. The long distance call we took for granted in the U.S. was an all-day activity in Italy. In Germany, as recently as 1970, you waited months to have a phone installed. Anything over a few days in the U.S. was, and is, likely to send the consumer screaming to the nearest Public Utility Commission. Until 1984, the purveyor of that world-class service was AT&T—at least for about 80 percent of us.

The 1970s brought a rethinking of AT&T's historic telecommunications monopoly. As mandated by federal judge Harold Greene, what had been a business reserved—legally—for one company became a market open to the many. The long-distance telephone call, backbone of telephone company profitability, became a competitive service. Inspired by the gains of MCI and others, more and more companies petitioned for access to the market.

The big bang—or big blow, depending on what happened to your particular phone service quality—came in 1984: court-mandated deregulation. AT&T was forced to divest its family of Bell Operating Companies (BOCs). What had been "the phone company" to most Americans became twenty-two different companies operating in seven different regional groups. In short order, competitors for both "plastic" (telephone equipment) and "juice" (telephone services) multiplied like mayflies.

The American telephone services consumer, business and residential alike, learned quickly that what had been taken for granted could be no longer. Dial-tone quality, long-distance-line access, repair availability, simple billing, and reliability of equipment suddenly became variable features.

If you don't have the slightest idea of what you're doing when you sit down to try to choose a personal long-distance company or package of residential services, consider the plight of the corporate facilities manager who, used to dealing with just "the phone company," must now suddenly comparison shop and pick the "best" telecommunications carrier for an entire company. Career death awaits a mistake in judgment. And if understanding long-distance packages doesn't seem enough of a complication, consider the plethora of weird-science phones and value-added services a buyer must sort through—things like call-waiting, three-party conversations, call forwarding, and cellular car phones. Today's customer must learn to deal with all these variables intelligently, or suffer the consequences.

As a result, telephone and telecommunications companies are resolving that they not only have to improve their technological bells and whistles but also prove all over again that they are easy to do business with, trustworthy, and honest. In advertisements AT&T responds to the need in the person of a sales manager looking eye to eye at you through the screen and intoning, "I'd fire an account rep who would sell you more than you need. We don't do business that way."

The BOCs and their competitors have likewise begun to show a sensitivity to service expectations and frustrations. Southwest Bell has launched a campaign to explain to customers what the company does—and doesn't do—anymore. Likewise Southwest has used ad time to teach customers to test their own phones so they can avoid service calls that are now priced for profitability. For its part, Bell Atlantic, whose biggest customer is the federal government, has marshalled an army of representatives to promote its services—and explain them—to the feds on a one-to-one basis.

At GTE, repair technicians and customer service reps are being retrained and their jobs recast in an effort to make them more knowledgeable, supportive, and empowered to work with customers. At Southern Bell, selection standards and training both acknowledge the need to put service-oriented, knowledgeable, empowered people on the frontline to lead customers through the new technology thicket.

In telecommunications, as in the other high technologies, service is in and important—Ernestine, Lily Tomlin's bun-haired, pompous, and all-too-real phone company bully is fast becoming a figment of the long-past "then" of low-tech yesterday.

Our High-Tech Heroes

We've broken up the high-tech puzzle into three subcategories—electronics (which includes computers and their component parts), support services ranging from basic sales and maintenance to software customization and information management assistance, and telecommunications. Notable by its absence is Big Blue. While IBM, hands down, wrote the book and set the original standard on service with its far-flung network of well-trained technical support specialists, it has of late found plenty of competition for preeminence. The major internal reshuffling underway since 1988 may restore the customer focus and once again make the company as admirable for being easy to do business with as it is for its product and industry leadership.

Until that time, our electronics subcategory offers a couple of companies that, in different ways and on different scales, have successfully taken a page from IBM's book—and added a few chapters of their own. Amdahl and DEC show how paying attention to customers' wants and needs can help smaller competitors meet and beat a big guy on its own turf and on its own terms. In addition, we like 3M (once Minnesota Mining and Manufacturing) as much for its underappreciated excellence in technology as for the familiar consumer products like Post-it notes and Scotch-brand tape that are the more visible result. And AMP is the acknowledged worldwide leader in a big niche, even if its products and services are sometimes very hard to see.

As noted, the umbrella heading of "support" covers a lot of ground. American Management Systems is a creative, respected, and very profitable outgrowth of the electronic tinkering abilities of five former Defense Department techies. Businessland is the computer store both the novice and the experienced microcomputer user love to do business with because its sales and service people go to such great lengths to make things work right—and without making customers feel like technological idiots in the process. Dataserv is a good example of what's afoot in the TPM arena.

In telecommunications, our exemplars come in sizes both large and small. BellSouth's Southern Bell is the big phone company all the other big phone companies tend to study to figure out what business they are in these days (and when the competition finds out, the reaction is a universal, "Wow! They do all that?"). By contrast, SNET—Southern New England Telephone—proves bigger is not always better; its customer kudos are evidence that the good small companies can run service circles around the big ones when they put their minds to it. This category also seems like the best fit for CompuServe, the time-sharing, computerized services company that sets a special standard in user friendliness.

Amdahl

amdahl

"THE WONDER IS THAT AMDAHL MANAGED TO GET OFF THE GROUND AT ALL IN the mid-1970s. To be successful, Amdahl had to demonstrate first and foremost that it would service the customer even better than IBM, no mean feat. Clearly, the company has achieved superiority in responsiveness, both by paying more attention to the customer and by servicing other manufacturers' equipment."

When Amdahl was founded (by Dr. Gene Amdahl, who's no longer with the company) in 1970, the mainframe computer business was a going concern, and the operative color was IBM Blue. The new company didn't have product to ship until 1975, and the industry has been through more shake-ups and shakeouts than anyone wants to remember.

Yet, as indicated by the opening appraisal from First Boston's summary of the 1987 annual survey of mainframe users conducted by Datapro, an emphasis on technical service and responsiveness to customer concerns can be effective competitive strategies. In 1987, Amdahl posted its first billion-dollar-plus revenue year—small change for IBM, but evidence that all those customers who have been saying good things to Datapro about Amdahl's service commitment are buying its computers, data storage products, and data communications systems in ever growing numbers.

Quantitatively, the 1987 Datapro study rated Amdahl first in as many different categories as its four major competitors (IBM, Honeywell Bull, NCR, and Unisys) combined. Qualitatively, Amdahl received the blue ribbon whenever the conversation turned from hardware to service considerations—responsiveness and maintenance effectiveness, troubleshooting, customer education and documentation, applications programs. When asked whether they would recommend the computer system they were using to another user, more than 97 percent of Amdahl's customers said yes they would.

Amdahl operates in only one segment of the computer market, designing and selling to users of large IBM-compatible mainframes that use System/370 software and its extensions. Its customers include large corporations, especially in insurance and manufacturing, public utilities, government

399

organizations, and major universities and research centers. Typically, these customers make a substantial investment in computerization that they then seek to preserve and enhance rather than replace with new systems. Consequently, getting the most out of the hardware and software they already have, and being able to add new bells and whistles as they become available, are important. Amdahl's operating approach is to consider compatibility a starting point, not a boundary, and the customer's existing computer system an investment to be protected, whether or not it currently involves Amdahl components.

The company's 580 series of computers shows evidence of this melding of technological capability and customer adaptability. Since it debuted in 1980, the 580 family has introduced new features, improved speed and broadened applications, and the potential for additional improvements is designed in. As a customer's requirements grow, for example, single-processor configurations can be upgraded in the field to dual- and multi-processor formats. That allows one physical system to do more and more work without requiring customers to buy more or larger systems. The fact that the upgrades can be delivered and installed on site instead of necessitating the removal of old machines and their replacement with new ones means those improvements can be achieved faster, more conveniently, and typically less expensively.

Meanwhile, using the 580/Multiple Domain Feature (MDF), one processor can be "partitioned" and used for multiple computing tasks—in effect allowing one existing system to be operated like four separate computers. That again minimizes hardware and software costs and preserves the customer's investment while providing greater flexibility for users.

But hardware is hardware. Where Amdahl has gained its competitive edge is in the area of service support, both technical and educational. To build a long-term relationship and beat IBM on its own turf, Amdahl knew early on that it would have to listen to what its customers wanted and then deliver. Given the ever-present competition, being a second-best alternative was not going to be financially rewarding.

Yet because of its commitment to being IBM-compatible, Amdahl is necessarily fated to following its bigger rival in new product introductions and manufacturing capability. As a result, delivery times for new computers have been shortened, and Amdahl prides itself on installing new processors "in three days instead of three weeks." Its systems are designed to reliability and performance standards that are every bit as exacting as its competition's, but the tussle for customer loyalty would be no contest if product were the only consideration.

It isn't. "Maintenance service is right up there with reliability in users' minds when they make buying decisions," the First Boston report noted. Datapro measures both responsiveness to service requests and effectiveness in performing the maintenance needed, and Amdahl scores very high in both categories. "Traditionally," First Boston observed, "service has meant the maintenance of installed product, but service is gradually taking on a broader definition in referring to consulting and integration work."

When Amdahl arrived as a viable competitor in about 1976, IBM had things pretty much its own way. If customers had to wait on Big Blue, they waited. Amdahl, being newer, smaller, and deliberately leaner, made speed of service and response a competitive weapon. It was the first to do field upgrades, the first to bring on-line diagnostic services to customers. Those are little details, and far from glamorous in the larger context of a multi-million-dollar product, but customers who depend on their systems being up and running appreciated the effort and attention involved in taking care of them this way.

As it turns out, in focusing on customer support as well as technical service, Amdahl is riding the crest of a wave. Technical support, noted First Boston, "represents the mundane tasks of educating the customer in the use of his computer system, documenting this with manuals, and troubleshooting when glitches arrive." Compared to hardware aspects, education, documentation, and troubleshooting have long been cause for dissatisfaction among mainframe computer users, who, in a situation familiar to legions of buyers of new cars or real estate, often feel abandoned and left to fend for themselves once their purchase decision has been made.

Amdahl recognized the opportunity, and customers haven't missed the way it responds. As measured by Datapro since 1981, no one is in the same league when it comes to troubleshooting: In that six-year period, Amdahl's lowest rating is virtually identical to the *best* rating any competitor has earned. In customer education, its four mainframe competitors were rated right around 2.8 on a scale of 4 in 1986; Amdahl's score was 3.5, the sixth straight year it has received the top score in the category. It also has received the best ratings for documentation (another manifestation of the "easy to do business with" trait) five years out of six.

Amdahl offers an ever-changing mix of product education courses that improve the customer's ability to make the best use of both existing and new computers and accessories. A continuing series of seminars and workshops covers subjects ranging from effective data processing to data communications management. All are provided either at Amdahl facilities or on a customer's site anywhere in the world, depending on what the customer wants. Significantly, more than 60 percent of Amdahl's enrollment comes from users of competitive products.

In addition, Amdahl provides systems consulting services in five areas—performance analysis and capacity management, data processing planning, data center management, network management, and data base/data communications management—to help current and prospective customers develop effective responses to changing information management needs.

What those customers say to Amdahl's people is fed back into the operations loop in the form of regular briefings on field intelligence. Visitors to headquarters in Sunnyvale, California, often find themselves meeting with one or more of the company's management triumvirate: John C. Lewis (chairman of the board), Eugene R. White (vice chairman), and E. Joseph Zemke (good name, but no relation—he's president and chief operating officer).

From the beginning, Amdahl has considered a customer's problem its problem. No matter where in the customer's computer system that problem might occur, or whose brand name it might involve, Amdahl has built a profitable business on providing the services large-scale computer users want and need. The customer service mission statement for its field managers says it best: "In partnership with sales and customers, [Amdahl's mission is to] take a leadership role in providing solutions which give our customers a competitive advantage."

What makes that philosophy go are the two "absolutes" on which it is based. They are, first, that "field management must *understand the customer's business requirements* and develop service plans to support those needs"; and, second, that "field management has the responsibility and authority to solve customer problems and be a *representative of the customer's point of view* with Amdahl."

The emphasis is ours, but even without it the point is obvious. No matter how high the tech, the touch distinguishes the best from the rest.

Amdahl Corporation
1250 East Arques Avenue
Sunnyvale, CA 94088

digital™

EACH YEAR, THE FIELD ORGANIZATIONS OF DIGITAL EQUIPMENT CORPORATION (DEC) conduct surveys of their customers throughout the U.S. In painstaking detail, they ask for feedback on the company's products and services, and the people who provide them. The answers provide not only insight into customer concerns and market trends, but also serve as the primary basis for the company's nonsalaried compensation programs. In other words, at DEC the rewards for good customer service are determined by the customers themselves. From the same source, the company gets its marching orders for future service improvement.

For someone looking for customer problems to solve or service snarls to unravel at DEC, the bad news in the annual surveys is the unrelenting good news coming back from the field. Every year since 1984, the little bar graphs that measure customer satisfaction have continued to rise like the afternoon temperature in the middle of summer. In 1984, typical readings were in the 70s and 80s. Now they're in the 80s and 90s—and for five separate items among the fifty-five variables reported on in 1987, scores hit the perfect 100 mark. The "c-notes" included overall availability (uptime) of Digital hardware, the attitude and manner of DEC's sales and service representatives as well as that of the engineers servicing Digital equipment, the quality of DEC's contractual (on-site) software consulting services, and the quality of the logistics that deliver DEC's educational services.

The surveys are more than a score-keeping tool. They're basic to DEC's management system, long regarded as a model of decentralized operations, although that system more recently has been reformatted within a centralized technical and marketing framework. Management style, with its strong customer focus, is often cited as the primary ingredient in the company's continuing challenge to computer industry leader IBM. DEC was one-fifth IBM's size in 1987, up from one-seventh just two years before. In 1986, *Fortune* called Kenneth Olsen, DEC's charismatic leader, "America's most successful entrepreneur" for the way he

403

built a nondescript start-up company into a multi-billion industrial leader in less than thirty years.

Although the product he did it with was computers, the DEC story revolves around a continuing quest to make the technology more understandable, accessible, and affordable to users. "Aimed at engineers and scientists, DEC's minicomputers changed the way people compute," *Fortune* observed. "Before DEC, all computers were big mainframes housed in special centers, molly-coddled by experts, and used to process large batches of data; DEC's small, rugged, inexpensive machines let individuals apply computing to an endless variety of everyday tasks. DEC laid the groundwork for the personal computer revolution, and many of the revolutionaries discovered the technology's possibilities in DEC products."

Service starts with the sales side. DEC's salespeople are essentially on straight salary, with bonuses of 10 to 20 percent of their salaries awarded for total sales rather than for specific product quotas. That frees them to spend time solving customers' problems and recommending equipment for its ability to meet a need, not a sales incentive goal. Olsen credits that attitude to his father, who sold machines up and down the Atlantic seaboard from a home base in Connecticut; the elder Olsen was respected for talking customers out of buying equipment they didn't really need. When it comes time to figure out stock options for DEC's present day managers, the customer surveys make it simple to pick the people whose success should be rewarded.

While DEC has long prided itself on its entrepreneurial zeal when it comes to finding and satisfying customer needs, the more intensive customer focus dates back to the revamping of the company from 1978 through 1983. Prior to that, DEC was the corporate equivalent of the Balkans—more than two dozen semiautonomous groups focused on individual product lines and competing for time and attention in the same basic region of the marketplace. What worked in the early days started to get in the way as the company grew out of its corporate adolescence. Over a tumultuous five-year period, DEC remade itself into a unified marketing organization more able to function as a mature company in a maturing field.

In the process, it not only kept its customer focus, it enhanced it. "In the early 1980s, for example," reported *Forbes* in 1987, "DEC started building computers to customers' specifications rather than trying to predict their equipment needs from a planning committee. That puts a lot of responsibility on lower-level staff. They must know what customers want, and communicate it to the design team."

Using DEC's Ethernet technology, customers worldwide have been able to attach previously unconnected computers into full-functioned networks that can unite offices, factories, and remote locations anywhere a terminal can be set up. "In the thirty years since the company was founded," explained Olsen in 1987, "we've invested hundreds of millions of dollars in the software and components that make an elegantly simple system for tying together departments, and entire organizations, into an integrated network. By concentrating our resources on one strategy, we've generated a system of networking that has helped Digital achieve high growth during the computer industry slowdown of the last few years. . . . This makes it possible to build and manage fully distributed computer networks that are easy to expand and maintain, protecting customer investments in software, hardware, and training."

The company has concentrated attention as well as dollars: Olsen has been known to order senior executives to spend a day in a warehouse, with hammers and screwdrivers instead of secretaries and telephones, experiencing firsthand—just as customers do—the labor involved in getting the company's products out of their crates and up and running. At special application-development centers around the country, customers can work with DEC engineers and product specialists to design prototype systems that meet their specific needs.

On the service side, DEC has been a quick study. It was the first in the industry to provide a full one-year warranty on its complete hardware line. It pioneered remote diagnostic services for computer hardware in the mid-seventies, quickly expanding the concept to include software services as well. It supports customers who have combined DEC and non-DEC equipment, managing maintenance for any system connected to a DEC system if that's what its customers want. It was also the first to incorporate twenty-four-hour-a-day telephone support for both hardware and software into its standard customer service agreements. A total of fourteen Customer Support Centers (CSCs) are now in place worldwide, each staffed by specialists trained to diagnose and solve hardware and software problems.

The system is designed to operate on one phone call, and one call only. The main CSC in Colorado Springs handles a million calls a year, and has five thousand incoming phone lines to make sure access is immediate from anywhere in the U.S., any hour of the day or night. Other centers are located in Atlanta and Westboro, Massachusetts. No matter which center is called or which system is involved, the first specialist to respond to a customer's request is given complete responsibility for that service call. Whether he or she can solve the problem personally or has to bring in other expert assistance, the customer starts and ends with the same primary contact.

DEC also is known for tailoring its service response to customer convenience. For example, some customers have "eight-hour" service contracts under which DEC provides on-site service during the customer's business hours. Regardless, CSC support is available all day and all night, and if the problem can be solved over the phone, it isn't charged against the contract, no matter when the solution is achieved. On the other hand, if an on-site service call is required, the customer can schedule it in the eight-hour period covered by the contract.

So sophisticated has the system grown that it can solve problems without requiring customers to first identify their causes. The combination of electronic diagnostic tools and people who know the company's hardware and software inside and out can test customer systems on-line, then forward detailed repair instruction to the field service engineer at the customer's location.

DEC also maintains an on-line data base called DSIN (Digital Software Information Network) that a customer can dial into for access to up-to-the-minute information on current software products, including new releases, usage information, and a symptom/solution directory that covers known problems and their proper responses. Artificial-intelligence-based monitoring systems can administer a full diagnostic checkup of a customer's system from hundreds of miles away, with specialists picking up indications of problems before they can develop into a full system failure. That kind of high-tech service makes the image of a repair person arriving with a toolkit in hand to puzzle out a problem for a customer more than a little dated.

Though changing market conditions have the potential to radically alter the industry's complexion on the product side, DEC more than any other computer vendor has been successful in developing technology that can deliver cost-effective service and support to its customers.

Digital Equipment Corporation
146 Main Street
Maynard, MA 01754

3M

MOST PEOPLE THINK OF 3M IN TERMS OF HANDY CONSUMER PRODUCTS: SCOTCH brand transparent tape, audio and videotape, computer diskettes, and those ubiquitous Post-it notes. But to a lot of very savvy businesses in technology-intensive industries from adhesives and manufacturing to health care and photography, 3M is something more: a highly responsive laboratory and development partner and supplier known for a commitment to top quality and an uncommon willingness to experiment and innovate.

While 3M manufactures and markets nearly fifty thousand products and services, loosely organized into about forty-five product lines, most of them are sold to other businesses. That marketing orientation is reflected in a strong business-to-business service culture, whether the product involved is the elastic waistband for disposable diapers or the reflective sheeting used on the faces of traffic control signs.

Case in point: Super-VHS, or S-VHS, the great leap forward in video recording technology that had electronics buffs buzzing long before its introduction. S-VHS represents an improvement of as much as 70 percent in video picture quality—an advance that many industry observers had long predicted could only be realized with metal tape. But in the mid-1980s, 3M engineers came up with a way to improve their company's existing magnetic tape technology. (They had a slight advantage in that 3M invented videotape back in the 1950s.) Recognizing the potential of the breakthrough, they also recognized that there was no point making a videotape that was too good for the current generation of VCRs in the market. Until someone made a VCR (3M doesn't) that could tap the full recording quality of the new tape, the product would have to wait. Or would it?

In recent years, there's been a lot of rhetoric about trade relations with Japan. At times, the impression is that absolutely nothing American gets through an impenetrable trade barrier on the western side of the Pacific. Yet in the 1980s, 3M has successfully worked on mutually profitable joint ventures with Sony, Sumitomo, and a number of other Japanese firms.

This time, it took its new tape technology to JVC, the developer and worldwide licenser of VHS recording technology, where it knew engineers were at work on ways to improve VCR recording and playback capabilities. JVC's engineers promptly seized on the potential of the 3M tape and used it to develop performance standards for the new S-VHS generation of VCRs. Guess who was first in the market with a videotape for the new VCRs when they were introduced in late 1987?

Today S-VHS tapes and VCRs are showing up in growing numbers in electronic showrooms, and industry observers expect them to be the state of the art in the 1990s. For being present at the creation, *High Fidelity* magazine gave 3M's S-VHS tape a Gold Award in its 1987 Product of the Year issue, and *Video Review* noted that as "a sort of silent partner in the development of S-VHS, 3M also deserves credit for the breakthrough, as well as an award for Best Product."

Like many manufacturers, 3M pays attention to maintaining and improving the essential quality of its products. In that context, the official company definition of quality is interesting. "Conformance to customer requirements," is how 3M expresses it. If it doesn't do what the customer wants it to do, in the way and with the reliability that the customer requires, then, technical merits notwithstanding, it's the wrong product for the job.

That's not to say it's a bad product, however. 3M delights in finding new uses for failed and underutilized technologies, so much so that its eight thousand scientists and researchers are informally expected to spend about 15 percent of their time tinkering. Post-its, for example, resulted from research chemist Art Fry's quest for a bookmark that wouldn't fall out of a book, but it took countless hours in the lab to find an adhesive that wasn't strong enough to stick to things permanently.

3M also rewards the technical people who find new opportunities by allowing them to control their own career directions. Lab workers can follow along with a product through development and eventual marketing, or stay in the lab and continue their tinkering; each path offers career and personal rewards. Thus, Fry is still a chemist working on adhesive technologies, while Diane Baum Verploegh is a market development supervisor for the "light management technology" she took off the shelf in response to an automaker's inquiry back in 1982.

A few years back, 3M used to use "We Hear You" as an advertising slogan. In this case, it was literally true. General Motors' Pontiac Division was looking for a dashboard lighting system that wouldn't cast a reflection on the severely angled windshield of some of its new sports cars. When it called 3M, it connected with Verploegh in the lab that specializes in automotive products. She listened, did some searching and tinkering, and eventually found that a plastics technology that had been around the company since 1967 would do the trick. It involved a plastic film that was etched to be transparent, but only at a certain angle. That allowed it to focus dashboard light on the driver while deflecting it away from the windshield.

Verploegh followed the application from the lab to the marketing side, eventually heading a worldwide sales and marketing effort that includes a joint venture with Japan's Sumitomo Corporation. The same basic technology was involved in the drag-reducing tape used on the hull of the 1986 America's Cup winner, *Stars & Stripes*. As Verploeph's progress illustrates, there is no lack of rewards for supporting customers at 3M.

To the Japanese, those legendary modern corporate warriors, 3M is nothing short of a role model. In their 1987 book, *The Challenge of 3M: Managing Creativity*, Japanese management experts Ikujiro Nonaka and Tatsuo Kiyosawa point out that 3M provides a culture where low-ranking research and manufacturing workers, even marketing employees, can bring up development ideas. To them, 3M's expectation that 25 percent of annual sales will come from products that weren't on the market five years ago harks back to the heyday of their nation's economic productivity boom in the 1950s and '60s. (Former 3M CEO Lewis Lehr is remembered for saying, "Perhaps our biggest need at 3M is for people who are uncomfortable without change.")

That creativity doesn't, and can't, start on Mahogany Row. It is a function of frontline people who interact with customers and other technology groups within 3M to find new ways to use existing products and better ways to improve and enhance their value to customers. That's a big reason why electronics manufacturers such as Hewlett-Packard, AT&T, Motorola, and Northern Telecom rate 3M a preferred supplier. Some even route 3M-made components straight to their assembly lines, relying on 3M's own quality-control processes and inspections to assure that the item meets specifications.

The same attention to customer concerns and quality-control detail is given to buyers of products sold under the 3M label. In 1987, for example, 3M's Data Storage Products Division transferred the responsibility of dealing with customer questions and complaints relating to its computer diskettes to the plant in Weatherford, Oklahoma, where those diskettes are made. There, production employees are assigned to follow up on customer inquiries, bringing a level of expertise that isn't often found in customer service centers. One by-product of that expertise was the discovery that about 85 percent of the complaints being received were the result of improper product selection, faulty use, or equipment problems. Based on the frontline input, packaging and point-of-sale displays were promptly improved, and customers have had less to complain about ever since.

3M Company
3M Center
St. Paul, MN 55144

AMP

WHO?

Unless you make electronic equipment, you may never have heard of this Harrisburg, Pennsylvania-based manufacturer, even if it does have sales of $2.3 billion annually and operate more than 170 facilities in 25 countries. If you do, you have. And you know that no matter how small or how complex or how mundane the piece of componentry you want to design into whatever you're designing, AMP will be more than happy to make it—and the complex, often computer-controlled tools that handle it during your manufacturing and assembly process. And AMP will make it so well that you won't even worry about electronically sensitive considerations such as quality control.

In 1987, for the third consecutive year, *Electronic Business* cited AMP as the top maker of components (excluding semiconductors) in the industry. The primary reason: customer satisfaction that rivals leading mainframe computer-maker Digital Equipment Corporation, even though AMP is a fraction the size of DEC and other electronics industry mainstays. More than thirty corporate customers have formally singled out AMP for special recognition as an "outstanding" or "superior" supplier, acknowledging it as the best in its category.

What's its category? AMP's combination of technology-driven quality and service have made it the world's leading producer of electrical and electronic connection devices—in all, more than one hundred thousand types and sizes of terminals, splices, connectors, cable and panel assemblies, switches, touch-screen systems, plus the application tooling to integrate them into larger manufacturing assemblies. The company specializes within a relatively narrow niche, concentrating, as *Electronic Business* explained in its 1986 citation, on "its basic strategies in the interconnection market, which include a continued focus on application tooling and robotic solutions to the problems of surface-mounted device assembly, as well as new packaging techniques in such areas as opto-electronics."

In simplified terms, if you have a computer, chances are the plugs that connect the cables to the ports were made by AMP. If your car is one of the newer models with lots of on-board electronic systems, AMP probably made the central termination system that is designed to handle very complex automotive wiring, but in such a way that it can be easily and reliably installed on the assembly line and serviced by a mechanic at a local garage. The connectors in your home smoke alarm, in the checkstand terminal at your neighborhood grocery store, in the facsimile machine in your office, and in the medical electronics gear in the hospital emergency room across town very likely employ the design AMP evolved from a specialized telephone connector.

Yet what AMP provides is more than manufacturing and design. It places a high priority on "early involvement" as a supplier so it can design what it needs to make in ways that integrate easily into the product the manufacturer will be assembling. Often that improves the end product; not infrequently, it lowers the cost of making it. Customers like that. They also respect the way AMP can play a supportive role in even confidential design and engineering programs, whether that confidentiality is required by government secrecy or intense corporate competition.

That's where the automotive wiring termination system came from—hands-on work with European carmakers Renault and Citroen. AMP also pioneered solderless "crimp" connectors by developing specialized tools for its manufacturing customers and refining existing connector materials and designs; the new system results in a reliable way to reduce production time and increase production consistency. In 1987, more than two thirds of the company's sales came from products that were applied by machines AMP also supplied to its customers.

AMP's early involvement typically leads to long-term involvement as well. Toward that end, the company sees its engineers as its frontline customer-contact people, and they're trained to work with their counterparts in customer organizations worldwide, translating evolving needs into research and development initiatives. Then, whether a new product and tooling is designed, or existing materials that can serve the need are identified, AMP field service engineers follow through by installing and maintaining the application tooling. Meanwhile, technical trainers bring the customer's engineering and production personnel up to speed.

One hallmark of good service companies is that they're easy to do business with. AMP is a good example. There's a hotline information center so customers and AMP field technicians alike can check on the availability, capability, even maintenance requirements of the company's tools and machines. Electronic data interchange helps the company and its customers work together closely, even when physically far apart. Parts for tools and machines typically are shipped overnight and arrive within five days to minimize customer downtime, no matter where in the world they might be.

Meanwhile, active customer support involves everything from highly technical, hands-on training to complete, custom tool kits (for sale or rent, depending on the product and the customer) that contain everything needed to install products such as networking and customer-premise wiring (a growing AMP market). AMP even puts its corporate jet fleet to use for customer service, flying customer personnel to the AMP Institute in Harrisburg for training, or flying the company's engineering trainers out to the customer to provide on-site support.

Decentralization is basic to such a close customer focus. The larger company is made up of the U.S.-based operations of 18 market-focused divisions and a confederation of 25 independent operating companies around the world. They share access to some 150 product lines, but they work in their customers' specific technical and business environments, not to mention their customers' own languages. Internationally, most operations are self-contained: Products for customers in a specific operating company's country or region are designed, marketed, and supported by that particular AMP company.

On the manufacturing side, AMP pays close attention to extremely narrow product tolerances and increasingly exacting customer requirements. Statistical process control and frontline quality control responsibilities have systematically reduced errors and defects to minuscule levels—in the space of just four years, molding rejections have been reduced by nearly 90 percent—yet somehow the percentages of rejections in stamping, molding, and assembly always seem to come out a hair behind their targets. That's because AMP is forever tightening the standards it imposes on itself. Toward that end, several dozen key factors are tracked both manually and electronically to assure that the company's small wonders continue to perform reliably.

On the evidence provided by the marketplace, it's working. In recent years, a growing number of manufacturers have certified AMP products and components for "ship to stock" programs, which means components have been found so reliable that they go straight from AMP to the customer's assembly line without being inspected by the customer for quality compliance. There's a high service quotient in that kind of reliability.

There's also service-focused intelligence in the way AMP has systematically reorganized customer contacts with the company. In the past, for example, technical calls could go to any of literally hundreds of field offices depending on where the customer was and what product he was calling about. Now all calls are routed into five service centers, where technical representatives, product literature, samples, and specs are readily available.

Not even slow-moving paper is immune to AMP's systems expertise. A few years ago, AMP noticed that because of its highly decentralized nature, its various operating groups had evolved no fewer than twenty-two different engineering change systems. That was no problem for the people *inside* a given work group, but it was nothing less than bewildering to customers *outside* the organization. When product change notifications were made, a blizzard of paperwork descended on customers trying to track several different products. In some companies, consolidating nearly two dozen different (and, to their users, comfortable) paperwork systems into even a handful would be a daunting task. At AMP, a product assurance team eliminated twenty-one of the twenty-two, making the last the simple, universal, understandable norm for both employees and customers.

In its first fifteen years of corporate life (1941 to 1956), AMP, which began life as a World War II contractor under the monicker Aircraft Marine Products, managed to grow to annual sales of $32 million. Since the dawning of the age of electronics, it has been on an accelerated upward pace: Sales and earnings have grown at a compound rate in excess of 15 percent annually for the past thirty years. That's bottom-line evidence that customers know a good thing when they see one—even if they do occasionally need to use a magnifying glass to see it.

AMP, Inc.
P.O. Box 3608
Harrisburg, PA 17105

American Management Systems

aMS

THE CHIEF CAUSE OF PROBLEMS, ACCORDING TO THE TONGUE-IN-CHEEK "LAW" coined by former newsman Eric Severied, is solutions. In a service economy, that dynamic can create profitable business opportunities for entrepreneurs adept at spotting the need and serving those who display it. American Management Systems (AMS) is a good example.

The company was founded in 1970 by five civilians who had up to that point been working in the office of the Secretary of Defense, where they had been doing studies and analyses of defense programs. Their expertise lay in solving complex management problems in large organizations, generally by applying computer and systems engineering technology. The computer, they had noticed, was both a part of the problem and a part of the solution. Accordingly, through the 1970s they evolved from a strictly consulting-oriented firm into a service-oriented provider of custom software systems and the expert integration of those systems into an organization's day-to-day business. Whether it involves reducing a bank's credit card losses or cutting the amount of time Navy ships spend in overhaul, AMS's basic service is enhancing the productivity of the client's technology.

Its timing has been pretty good. Over the past two decades, computers have multiplied in number and divided in size and compatibility, creating an electronic Tower of Babel. Anybody can buy a computer. Not just anybody can get it to do everything it is supposed to do, let alone do those things in ways people can control and understand. AMS is one of the businesses those businesses turn to when they want to get the megabytes and the microchips working productively.

The focus is still on large organizations, most of them in five carefully targeted areas: financial services; federal agencies; state and local governments and universities; energy; and telecommunications. Rather than try to be all things to all people, AMS has deliberately worked to focus its services. In 1982, only about 70 percent of its business came from its target markets; more than 85 percent of 1987 revenue came from those five sectors.

To organizations in these markets, AMS offers a turnkey software and service package. Typically, it will license its core applications software to a client, in the process customizing it to the special conditions and needs of the client's business. For large organizations, this turns out to be not only a lot less expensive than developing and painstakingly debugging their own software from scratch, but also preferable to buying a "one size fits all" standardized program. An added advantage of AMS's selective focus is the industry-specific expertise it has developed over the years.

At AMS today, four of the five founders are still actively involved. They have been joined by some twenty-two hundred employees in the U.S. and Canada. The client list reads like an index to *The Wall Street Journal*. Forty of the 50 largest banks in the United States; 4 of the top 6 in Canada. More than 130 financial services firms and credit-granting organizations. Major corporations and universities.

City governments in America's three largest cities—New York, Chicago, and Los Angeles—use AMS-designed systems to manage billions of dollars in annual expenditures for goods and services. The Big Apple also has implemented an AMS-designed system to more effectively process the twelve million parking tickets it hands out each year. No fewer than ninety civilian and defense agencies of the federal government contract for software and services, among them the State Department, the Social Security Administration, the General Accounting Office, the Environmental Protection Agency, all four branches of the military, and the founders' former employer, the Secretary of Defense.

Significantly, AMS earns more than 80 percent of its revenues (which totaled $174 million in 1987) from services. The balance comes from software licensing fees and maintenance of its software programs. The best evidence of how well AMS serves its technology-dependent customers is the way the organizations that do business with it tend to stick around: In 1987, 83 percent of total revenue came from companies that were AMS clients in 1986; more than 50 percent came from clients who have been working with AMS since 1984, when total revenues were only half as large.

According to cofounder Charles O. Rossotti, now president and chief executive officer, a large part of the growth of the company can be attributed to the way it has been able to build and maintain continuing customer loyalty. "Such long-term relationships are not just a major factor in [our] success," he told shareholders in 1987, "they are also, in this business, an ongoing measure of our effectiveness."

How "effective" is effective? The governor of New Hampshire, John Sununu, is convinced the customized financial system package AMS installed on the state's IBM hardware in 1985 has recaptured between 1 and 2 percent of the state's $1.3 billion annual budget. The system, which has created an integrated data base for all of New Hampshire's financial information, handles more than 60,000 transactions and inquiries a day for 27 state agencies via a network of more than 160 terminals.

It has improved budget analysis and cash management. It helps track personnel trends. It identifies funds that perhaps could be transferred from an underused account to a needy one. It also pinpoints spendthrift state agencies with a habit of dispensing most of their funds in the fourth quarter, an indication of money being wasted by use-it-or-lose-it bureaucrats fearful of facing budget cutbacks if they don't manage to spend every allocated nickel.

Sununu is the kind of demanding client AMS thrives on—an engineering Ph.D. from MIT who used to write technical software for clients of his own consulting firm before turning to politics. And the feeling of admiration and satisfaction apparently is mutual. In 1987, New Hampshire and AMS signed a "strategic partnership" agreement under which the state will serve as a beta test site for AMS systems and share the results of its testing with other states.

Another believer is the American Association of Retired Persons (AARP), the largest organization of senior citizens in the world. With twenty-nine million members, AARP's record-keeping and membership-service tasks are immense. As the organization grew over the years, data processing jobs traditionally were farmed out to service bureaus that charged fees based on the number of transactions involved.

Continuing growth, however, made those fees increasingly painful to bear, so in 1985 AARP hired AMS under a three-year contract to build and initially manage a centralized data center. The new system is designed to handle current and future membership files faster and more efficiently, perform additional operations as growth continues and new programs are added, and save the organization money that would previously have been paid to outside vendors. Between operating efficiencies and economies of scale, the AMS center that went on-line in 1987 is expected to realize a return on AARP's investment within three years.

AMS got the job after a lengthy screening process that considered nearly thirty possible vendors. One reason: AMS's commitment to a "life cycle" concept of service. The company's involvement doesn't end at the point of a sale. In many respects, that's just the beginning. From planning and design through implementation and operations management, AMS stays involved.

But that doesn't mean there's no end in sight. AMS is perfectly willing to work itself out of a job, and AARP is a good illustration: As the three-year management contract ended in 1988, AARP took over full ownership and management of the data center AMS built for it—with AMS on hand to assist in making the transition orderly.

If retention of clients is basic to the success of AMS's services, retention of its own people is the key to its future. Significantly, AMS rewards technical talent on a par with management and sales, and the compensation of its senior people is tied to multiyear goals to make sure no one gets too preoccupied with short-term results.

Does it work? Consider that in a firm that was founded just eighteen years ago, the average AMS vice president has been on board for eleven years. It goes without saying that they worked their way up to those positions. What's more, in keeping with the company's priority on specialized industry subject-matter expertise, more than half of the company's mid-level "principals" are in technical, not management, career paths.

It has been said before in a multitude of ways, but the hardware isn't the hard part of the computer. To make it do smart things takes smart input and management by the machine's human masters. AMS provides the kind of critical business-to-business intelligence that often goes unremarked for the exceptional service it really is.

American Management Systems, Inc.
1777 North Kent Street
Arlington, VA 22209

BUSINESSLAND®

"WHAT MAKES BUSINESSLAND DIFFERENT FROM COMPETITORS IS A RELENTLESS emphasis on service—integrating systems and products for its customers, offering them advice on hardware and software selection as well as training. In fact, its direct sales force of 735 is as large as that of many computer companies. Starting with sales of $10 million in 1983, Businessland has grown, internally and through acquisition, into a $600 million (1987 sales) company and seems well on its way to becoming a $1 billion company in the next few years."

The analysis belongs to *Forbes*, circa November 1987. The words may turn out to be truly prophetic or the kind of golden promise that too often has been revealed as base brass in the turbulent computer field. Nevertheless, Businessland's first five years have been marked by steady, even spectacular growth, fueled by customers who have found in this 130-store retail chain (which includes 25 ComputerCraft retail stores acquired in 1988) the kind of sales and service support that are invaluable in making computers function in today's high-tech business and professional environments.

In its own words, "Businessland connects products from multiple manufacturers into integrated office automation systems, and provides the customer ongoing service and support for these complex systems. Businessland is the connecting link between the product users and the product sources."

Several things set Businessland apart from other computer retail operations. To begin with, the company is oriented to process, not products. Rather than push a particular brand or model, sales people and systems engineers are trained to start from the customer's applications need and determine what hardware and software from more than one hundred different manufacturers will function best. They're also trained to know what's available and what it can do—they get update training every month, on company time, to stay on top of a fast-changing industry. Every three months, the company's systems engineers are brought back to corporate headquarters in San Jose, California, for more intensive updates on hardware, software, and evolving user environments.

Before networking and connectivity became buzzwords, Businessland had already tumbled to the fact that an increasing number of sales involved integrating computers from one manufacturer into environments that already had computers from another manufacturer up and running. The software had to mesh smoothly, the data had to be moved without delay or error, and the people had to be able to understand and operate the various systems without loss of productivity. Or sanity.

Consequently, the company turned its odd-lot experiences into a bankable bank of installation expertise and augmented that asset by adding plenty of customer-training programs to make sure the customer's people could make the new and old office automation equipment hum in true harmony. Since that has to be as true in small offices as it is in medium- and large-sized companies (about two thirds of the company's sales come from medium and large businesses, including three fourths of the *Fortune* 100), Businessland has invested in smarts as well as sales: In 1987, while the sales staff stayed approximately even with past years, its staff of systems engineers and field technicians grew by nearly 50 percent.

As a result, Businessland has become a one-stop source of installation, interconnection, and upgrading expertise. Approximately one out of every three new workstations purchased from a Businessland store in 1987 came with host communications adapters to allow the PC to be linked to applications and data residing in a company's mainframe or minicomputer, and the company figures that percentage will continue to grow as customers become more familiar with the ins and outs of computer-to-computer communications.

In the same year, Businessland's technicians installed twenty-three thousand PC-to-mainframe connections, evidence that, increasingly, American companies are learning to combine the operations of all kinds and styles of computer products as information-processing and management needs continue to drive their business activities.

For itself, Businessland practices what it preaches. Its own stores and offices are on-line in one of the largest wide-area networks in the country: the 290-station local-area network at headquarters in San Jose is connected to 120 remote networks in Businessland field locations spread across 33 states, allowing more than 2,100 employees to communicate directly via electronic mail.

Whether customers want to take the new hardware or software back to the office and figure out how to plug it in by themselves, or desire lots of installation assistance, postpurchase warranty and service support, and just plain hand-holding, Businessland is prepared to accommodate them, but it obviously leans toward the latter end of the spectrum. One out of every twenty-three Businessland employees is a trainer, another is a systems engineer, five more are field technicians.

Businessland stores conduct a constant round of training sessions. The company also has developed materials for use by the training departments of its customer companies to further assure that the business can quickly start achieving all the efficiencies and results for which it originally turned to the computer. For individual and networked customers alike, there's also "Solution Line," a subscription-based telephone support service that gives computer-users a place to turn for answers to questions and solutions to problems encountered in their systems.

Local-area network customers who opt for the full service and support package, called the Gold Plan, are assigned a team that includes a systems engineer, a field service technician, a trainer, a technical support specialist, and an account manager. The team offers presale consultation, then helps design the customer's system, installs it, provides documentation and training for it, and supports it through the crucial first twelve months of operation. When trouble occurs, if it occurs, Businessland technicians can provide diagnostic and even repair services via telephone modem.

Finally, all Businessland stores are company-owned, a decision that chairman and CEO David Norman maintains has been crucial to maintaining a focus on service quality, even when the computer industry was suffering through another of its periodic sales slumps and business shakeouts. Because there's no fractious and inconsistent franchise network to manage, Businessland stores coast to coast can be linked together to offer technology support programs such as its series of national conferences and localized executive briefings.

It also can draw on resources throughout the organization on a customer's behalf, even when the scale of the task at hand is a little daunting. For example, when Fidelity Investments moved 600 people across Boston to new offices, Businessland relocated the computers—including 150 PC-to-mainframe connections—without an hour of downtime during trading hours. The move went smoothly because systems engineers from the Boston outlet were involved with the company's people from the time Fidelity began planning the expansion.

Businessland, Inc.
1001 Ridder Park Drive
San Jose, CA 95131

Dataserv

"LIKE MANY COMPANIES INVOLVED IN THE SO-CALLED THIRD-PARTY INDUSTRY dealing in resale of new and used IBM equipment, Dataserv has found success by offering something that IBM is unable or unwilling to deliver. In the parts business, overnight delivery of used IBM components can be worth more than a six-month lag time for new components; the company also stocks new parts from IBM."

That 1985 report from *Computerworld* magazine still offers pointed insight into what makes this Minnesota-based, wholly owned subsidiary of BellSouth tick. Dataserv has built its business on a willingness to do more for a customer than Big Blue will, typically with more built-in flexibility, sometimes at a lower cost, but not uncommonly at a price equal to or higher than the original manufacturer.

Founded in 1969 to trade and lease an early generation of IBM check sorters to financial organizations, it's now the second-largest third-party IBM equipment maintenance organization in the country, and one of the fastest growing to boot. Its spare parts business is second in size and scope only to IBM itself. Its clients include 250 of America's 1,000 largest corporations and 60 of the world's 100 largest multinationals. It posted 1987 revenues of $300 million.

"And all this was accomplished at the expense of IBM, the largest, most sophisticated, and many claim best-managed computer company in the world," according to John Dykstra, Dataserv's director of business planning and development.

The assortment of services bundled under the Dataserv monicker is a little dizzying to grasp at first. The company will service computers—not just IBM models, though a large proportion of the business is in that area—and enhance them with customized software or operator training. It buys up used IBM models to cannibalize for parts, which it then resells to others (it calls itself the "hardware store for the third-party maintenance industry") or reuses in its own maintenance activities. Or it will buy and resell computers that still have years of useful service in them.

It also sells or leases point-of-sale (POS) scanners, again with full maintenance and software support, plus training for operators and management alike; "We're the industry's largest and most competitive remarketer of reconfigured, reconditioned, and recertified IBM and NCR POS systems, too," the company boasts.

In the beginning, much of what Dataserv had to do to build its business involved educating prospective customers to the virtues of the market for "preowned" computers. It's a market markedly different from that for used cars, for example: A computer's value is a product of its functional capabilities, rather than its age. Just because one user has outgrown a given system doesn't mean it can't do a highly effective job of meeting someone else's needs.

On the service side, U.S. businesses spent an estimated $16 billion on computer service and support in 1986. About 85 percent of that was spent with the actual manufacturers of the equipment, according to *Business Marketing* magazine, but third-party suppliers have become such a force that manufacturers, many of whom rely on maintenance and service for as much as a quarter of their total revenue, are lowering prices and making services more customer-friendly to protect what has been a very profitable part of their business.

Dataserv has set its sights on being faster, more flexible, more responsive, and closer to the customer than its competitors can or want to be. Accordingly, business units are kept small and each account is managed as an individual profit center, with incentive compensation of 10 to 15 percent, sometimes substantially more, provided for the *team* serving the account. High performers find they can make two to three times their base salary by taking care of the business of service.

So detailed and thorough is Dataserv's customer focus that it even extends to the design of internal systems. When a new customer signs on, for example, billing analysts are dispatched to the new client company to design, with the assistance of the company's own financial and administrative people, a customized billing system that fits the customer's existing systems and accounting needs.

"The [Dataserv] quality service strategy is fundamental," notes a report on service trends prepared by The Ledgeway Group in 1987, "based on product *specialization*, *stable account teams* and *team accountability*, and *clearly setting customer expectations* [emphasis theirs]. A new team with manager, technicians, and administrative personnel, if necessary, [is] developed for new accounts. In most cases, the customer is involved in personnel interviewing and selection during the recruiting cycle. The team is expected to stay in place and develop a long-term relationship with the customer."

The service rationale is pleasingly simple: The more exposure technicians and service people have to the same types of equipment and operating environments, the more expertise they can develop and the more proficient they can become at satisfying specific customer needs. Consequently, service people often specialize in just one model or design of a product, learning it literally inside and out, instead of becoming marginally familiar with a larger number of systems. That not only reduces training time and expense but also enhances service performance by providing more in-depth and thorough maintenance.

In the vernacular of computers, MTTR (mean time to repair) is reduced, repeat calls for the same problem also are less frequent, and technicians come to see themselves as valuable experts, not just electronic mechanics with a specialized toolbox. That service specialization dictates marketing focus: It's no accident that much of Dataserv's growth—a compound rate of 220 percent since 1983—has come from growing client lists in retail services, banking, and the insurance industry.

If people at Dataserv feel as if they're on a roll, however, it hasn't caused them to lose their freewheeling zest for the business. That's because of a philosophy borrowed from supercomputer pioneer Seymour Cray, who's remembered for saying, "At Cray Research, we take what we do very seriously, but don't take ourselves very seriously." Think number-crunchers are inevitably serious folk? Meet Dataserv computer maintenance's chief financial officer John Harnett, who admonishes one and all to continue to concentrate on the "Four P's"—Pride, Productivity, Profits, and Pfun.

Pfun aside, Dataserv encourages its people to listen to their customers, to learn to think like their customers. "First we fix the customer, then we fix the equipment," is how it's sometimes expressed. "Setting expectations," for example, involves a detailed checklist with more than one hundred individual items ranging from call handling and problem tracking to the customer's desired procedures for managing parts. The checklist is an integral part of the account planning and start-up phase, and many of the key criteria and performance standards it helps identify are written into the client's contract. As Ledgeway observed, "All Dataserv and joint customer/Dataserv responsibilities are understood. They attempt to leave nothing to fall through the cracks of misunderstanding."

Often, Dataserv nurtures on-site user groups. It regularly brings key customer people back to its home office in Minneapolis for additional training and support. What's more, Dataserv sends—through an independent, third-party firm—an annual customer-satisfaction survey to multiple levels in each client company. That results in useful feedback from executive, operations, user, and administrative levels, all of which is carefully scrutinized by the entire account team.

How do customers feel about all this attention? In 1987, Tim Gildea, manager of a retail systems group covering 130 sites in Southern California, was heard to boast that if someone took a survey of his area's customers, 95 percent would rate Dataserv's service "above average" or higher. One of those who heard him was his division's vice president,

John McRae, and he promptly challenged Gildea's claim. Not only that, but McRae also specified that the customer survey had to be administered within thirty days and added that even one "poor" rating would mean automatic failure.

The result? Vindication: 98 percent of the customers in Gildea's area rated Dataserv "above average" or higher; not one "poor" was to be found. As a result, McRae brought the whole service group back to company headquarters for a day so executives could glow all over them. That's how you make good service people into service heroes, role models for the entire organization.

Dataserv
A BellSouth Company
12125 Technology Drive
Eden Prairie, MN 55344

Southern Bell

THE BREAKUP OF THE AT&T NETWORK INTO SEVEN BELL OPERATING COMPANIES (BOCs) with their assortments of local telephone and affiliated service companies in 1983 was a landmark event in American business history. It will take years to sort out all the various ramifications for customers, employees, and shareholders, but one thing's for sure: The disorientation of people within the Bell system was an unappreciated dimension of the breakup.

Suddenly, people who used to know where they stood in the scheme of things were thrown into a strange new world—part regulated, part deregulated, part familiar, part unexplored. Throughout the country, BOCs struggled to figure out just who they were and what their customers expected of them. Inevitably, service standards wobbled. The company that seems to have gotten its act together fastest—from the customer's standpoint—is Southern Bell, part of BellSouth, the BOC charged with serving the southeastern part of the U.S.

Headquartered in Atlanta (which is also the corporate home of BellSouth), Southern Bell provides service in extensive parts of Florida, Georgia, North Carolina, and South Carolina. It includes just under half of the nearly one hundred thousand employees in the BellSouth system, the other major part of which is Birmingham-based South Central Bell, the Bell operating telephone company for parts of Alabama, Kentucky, Louisiana, Mississippi, and Tennessee. According to research conducted by third-party firms tracking changes in the telecommunications industry, Southern Bell's customers give it high marks for responsiveness, installation and repair service, and clear communications (including bills).

An important piece of the service puzzle for BellSouth in general, and Southern Bell in particular, has been recognizing that the breakup left people inside and outside the system without a clear set of values; as a consequence of the massive scale of change, the new corporate culture was undefined. Since deregulation, BellSouth has concentrated on finding ways to establish it, starting with five universal "values" that it maintains can and should serve as a foundation for everything it does. They include the predictable "pursuit of excellence," plus respect for the individual (regardless of where he or she may be in the organizational hierarchy), community-mindedness, and a positive response to change.

All of those come after the number one item on the list, which is titled Customer First. It's defined this way: "We deliver our service in a manner that causes our customers to perceive value added. We will know their preferences and perceptions and market our products and services accordingly. We will judge our performance against the standards of the customer. Only by satisfying our customers are we able to provide an attractive return to our stockholders and opportunities for our employees. A promise to a customer by an employee commits all employees to help fulfill it."

It's that last sentence that's particularly noteworthy. Since 1983, Southern Bell has been backing it up with an internal recognition system designed to focus attention on service delivery and service deliverers. The original program started in Florida; its watchwords were, "I Can Help." By 1988, it had evolved into a systemwide Southern Bell initiative keyed to the phrase, "Count On Me." Under its aegis, the company's people go to interesting and sometimes downright amazing lengths to define and highlight good service, in the process reinforcing the still settling core values of the new culture.

Take Carol Mavigliano, for example. She's a service representative in the Southern Bell office in West Palm Beach, Florida. In the course of a typical day, she handles dozens of calls from current and new customers. In 1988, one of those calls was from the daughter of a seventy-one-year-old man who was living alone and needed to have phone service established. Among other things, he was a diabetic and had a serious heart condition—the telephone represented his lifeline to emergency medical assistance. He also was living on a limited income and didn't have the money for the deposit required. What should she do?

As it turned out, she'd already done the right thing by hooking up with a representative to whom service was more than a job. Not only did Mavigliano get the new-hookup order processed without a deposit, she set it up so the phone would be installed the next day (she called personally on a Sunday night to make sure the phone was working). Mavigliano also contacted the local Chamber of Commerce and medical society to find out how her new customer could reach emergency medical services, and she referred the family to several local organizations, among them the United Way, where special assistance was available for senior citizens.

For her actions, Mavigliano was named the monthly winner of her area's "Count On Me" service accolades and was honored as the quarterly winner for the state. She also was featured as the cover story in Southern Bell's employee magazine.

Perceptively, Southern Bell defines service in the broadest sense: not only the way employees interact with and provide products and services to external customers, but also the things they do internally to help others in the Southern Bell family do their jobs effectively. Southern Bell's employees are encouraged to see every action as having an ultimate effect on the customer, and to see each other as interdependent customers within the organization. To provide a continuing stream of object lessons, teams of employees, drawn predominantly from the frontline positions in the organization, meet regularly to choose "Count On Me" winners who, in the eyes of their fellow employees, their supervisors, or their customers, demonstrate one or more of the five core values in their work.

There's no shortage of ways to nominate people for consideration, and no apparent limit to the amount of time and attention Southern Bell is willing to give to identifying people who ably represent its values around its four-state service area. Any employee at any level can fill out nomination forms (the explanation begins, "Thanks, I knew I could count on you . . .") that describe who did what, when, and why it was so terrific. *Or,* they can call a "Thank You" dataphone that tape-records the details of their service star's noteworthy performance. *Or,* they can call OCTEL, a voice-activated electronic mail system, which also tape-records nomination information. (The recordings are transcribed and distributed in memo form to the appropriate supervisors and review committees.) *Or,* nominations can come directly from customers through letters or telephone calls that commend good service providers to supervisors (that's how Mavigliano came to be recognized).

Each month, the nominations are evaluated and a maximum of five (the suggested norm is three from nonmanagement positions, no more than two from management) selected. Winners receive local recognition, and two or three are passed along for consideration by regional groups within the state (the next level of the company). There, a monthly representative of the district is chosen and forwarded for still further recognition at the state level.

By the time it's through, Southern Bell has identified achievers at the local level (monthly, quarterly, and annually) plus statewide (monthly) *and* companywide (quarterly) winners. Winners receive members-only-style awards—jackets, sweaters, jogging suits, and the like. The top two service providers from the companywide quarterly selections are invited to the annual President's Conference in Atlanta for still one more moment in the company spotlight. Meanwhile, publications at every level inside the company constantly replay "Count On Me" anecdotes and recognition.

It may seem like an extraordinary amount of nominating, and selecting, and recognizing, but for Southern Bell the priority is to set its new values firmly in place while still maintaining a link with its prebreakup past. By focusing on the customer for its various services, it has found a common point of reference for people at every level of the company.

Southern Bell
A BellSouth Company
150 West Flagler
Miami, FL 33130

"PROFESSOR BELL . . . SAID THAT, IN THE FUTURE, TELEGRAPH WIRES AND TELE-phony would be in use generally in dwellings, just as gas and water are supplied—not luxuries but necessaries. Wires would be connected to a central office whence communication could be established with the butcher, the baker, and all calls could be made by telephony and so conversation could be carried on with distant cities for purposes of trade, business, etc., and the message could be quietly sent, as the telephone leaves no record behind it . . ."

In the New Haven, Connecticut, of 1877, this was the cutting edge of the future come to town and displayed on the stage of the local opera house. Folks paid seventy-five cents for the best seats in the house on a Friday evening in April when Alexander Graham Bell made his one and only barnstorming stop in the state. In the audience was the local manager of the Atlantic and Pacific Telegraph Company, and when Bell cut loose with the startling vision recalled above, George Coy sat up and took notice.

Startling? Until that time, the telephone was hardly a versatile instrument. Phones were leased in pairs, connected by a direct line—between a customer's house and his business, for example. But here was Bell himself talking about a wild-eyed system where calls could be "exchanged" through a central switching office. And Coy, with his firsthand knowledge of telegraphy, was just the fellow to figure out how.

Less than a year later, the world's first commercial telephone switchboard, cobbled up by Coy out of carriage bolts, handles from teapot lids, and bustle wire, was in service under a franchise from Bell and his financial backers. The customer base was easy to keep track of: twenty-one New Haven citizens who had signed up to pay $1.50 a month for access to the exchange, through which they could talk with each other whenever they wanted to (provided two other conversations hadn't already loaded the system to capacity).

These days there are 1.5 million residential and business customers signed up for telephone service through Southern New England Telephone, better known in the region as S-N-E-T (snits are what the company works to avoid, so it discourages people from trying to pronounce the acronym). The successor to that first Bell franchise is a hardy, publicly owned, very profitable independent telecommunications company. (In other words, it isn't owned by any of the seven Bell operating companies that emerged from the government-mandated break-up of AT&T in 1983.) More than that, it's widely regarded both inside and outside the industry as one of the true leaders in providing satisfying customer and telephone service.

That it does so is because people from chairman and CEO Walter Monteith, Jr., to former operator (now installer) Mark Gryniuk take seriously SNET's wide-ranging commitment to working hard on the behalf of their customers. As Monteith continually tells SNET's thirteen thousand employees, "Change has become a way of life in our business. And we are finding that many of the ways we've done things in the past are no longer right for today's environment. We must redefine what service means within the context of a new and totally different business place."

One thing that surely is no longer right for today's environment is taking the customer for granted. SNET started the era of deregulation with strong values and high standards, but the company hasn't been content to live in and with the past. Throughout its various operating units, objectives have been systematically toughened—with measurable results.

The objective for customer trouble reports, for example, which SNET benchmarks on 1983 levels, has been chopped in half; in 1987, through continuing efforts to reduce and prevent problems, the standard was achieved and exceeded. A new-customer report system used by SNET service representatives gives those reps on-line access to support groups throughout the company, in the process reducing the amount of time it takes to install new equipment or change existing residential installations.

SNET's on-line expertise shows up in other ways, too. In 1987, SNET debuted a computer program that helps service representatives pinpoint virtually any segment of the millions of cables and wires strung overhead and under the ground, down to the location of any individual telephone pole in front of any customer's house. The computer capability allows service representatives to schedule installations, anticipate system needs, and answer questions that used to require a good deal more time and paper. A corresponding repair service system, dubbed MAPPER, automatically assigns trouble reports to the technicians who can respond the fastest. On the consumer side, SNET also has consolidated its billing and service order offices, which means no more being transferred from pillar to post trying to get an answer to a question. Now one call to one person is generally all it takes.

Blue Cross & Blue Shield of Connecticut has been able to put more than twelve thousand medical professionals on-line to its ProMed Systems subsidiary through an SNET-designed switching network. The service, which Blue Cross calls the Connecticut Health Information Network (inevitably abbreviated as CHIN), is the nation's first statewide system to fully integrate electronic claims, diagnostic, and medical information retrieval service.

To keep in touch with small-business customers, an increasingly important service niche, SNET schedules an annual symposium that brings together business owners and experts in fields ranging from advertising and personnel management to communications technology. For residential customers, local-area advisory boards provide a conduit for information sharing and the constant evaluation of service quality. On a more data-oriented level, every customer who contacts SNET for installation, modification, or repair service receives a short, pointed follow-up questionnaire card that asks, "How are we performing?"

Employee training runs the gamut from standard programs and tuition reimbursement to SNET's innovative Electronic University, which allows employees to attend classes via their home computers. But some things you don't really train employees to do. They perform or don't perform because that's what the culture around them supports. At SNET, it supports service, not the absence of it.

Gryniak's moment of truth came in 1987, back in the days when he was still an operator. He picked up a 911 call one day to encounter a frightened parent desperately seeking emergency assistance for a child who had stopped breathing. Gryniak did more than just dispatch emergency medical assistance. He calmly talked the parent through CPR until the medics arrived.

Ed Lennon, an installer who works out of Hamden, Connecticut, is another example of someone doing just that little bit more that separates the adequate service providers from the truly outstanding ones. One Friday, after finishing the interior installation work on a new business scheduled to celebrate its grand opening the following Monday, he called in to activate the hookup. No way, he was told: The crew responsible for that part of the job had been unable to do its work because construction on the property hadn't been properly finished off. Even worse, the crew had left the site without talking to any of the contractors who might have been able to correct the situation while putting the finishing touches on the building, and now was unavailable until Monday (which meant the company would be without phones up to and including the day of its grand opening).

Lennon could have let the system run on its own momentum. He didn't. On Saturday, the customer was surprised to see an SNET truck pull up and a crew start installing the lines. Shortly thereafter, Lennon stopped by to check things out. It turned out he had talked to his foreman about the situation and they had found a way to get a crew in on Saturday, and the phones switched on that same day.

Then again, maybe the performance of people like Gryniak and Lennon isn't all that much out of the ordinary for SNET. After all, in New Haven they still recall the great blizzard of 1888, during which the city was completely shut down for two days—except for the telephone lines linking it to the outside world. From that century-old event comes the legend of Angus MacDonald, a lineman who put on snowshoes and walked through the storm checking for downed lines. At SNET, Mac-Donald's name and exploits serve as the personification of the kind of service the company still strives to provide.

Southern New England Telephone
227 Church Street
New Haven, CT 06506

CompuServe®

IMAGINE YOURSELF IN A BUSINESS WHOSE MAJOR SOURCE OF REVENUE COMES from the time subscribers spend on-line accessing electronic data bases, bulletin boards, games, and other computer services. Along comes a customer with a whiz-bang new invention: a software program that helps manage on-line connection time, making "sessions" more efficient—and, in the process, invariably shorter. It's akin to running an oil company and having a customer invent an engine that provides more power than existing models while getting a hundred miles to the gallon. If your business is selling gasoline, you really want this idea to spread, right?

You do if you're CompuServe. From its base in Columbus, Ohio, the company has become the country's largest and best-liked on-line computer service. The customer's idea was introduced as "shareware" (software provided by the developer through CompuServe) in mid-1987. It didn't take long for Michael O'Connor's program to attract a good-sized audience, the amount of traffic tipping off CompuServe that something noteworthy might be afoot.

So, in early 1988 the CompuServe Navigator was offered to all subscribers who use Apple Macintosh computers, now backed up with full documentation and the company's own customer service support. The price is modest for software (just a little over fifty dollars), and CompuServe made sure O'Connor stayed in the loop by paying him royalties. After all, when a subscriber cares enough about your service to help you improve it, you want to make an example of him—even if his program helps customers get more for their money.

"Since all of your thinking and reading is done off-line, on-line charges are kept to a minimum," concedes Sharon Baker, product manager for CompuServe's Micronetworked Apple Users Group. "The only on-line costs that are incurred are for the minutes CompuServe Navigator is actually on-line retrieving data. And CompuServe Navigator can access CompuServe and retrieve data much faster than a user could doing the same tasks manually."

Time, in other words, may indeed be money, but satisfied customers are loyal customers. The gamble CompuServe took is that heavy users among its base of four hundred thousand subscribers will reinvest their savings in more services—spend the same amount of *money*, even though they're actually spending more *time* on-line. The company took the same approach in encouraging and cooperating with authors Charles Bowen and David Peyton in the preparation of their independent book, *How to Get the Most out of CompuServe*. CompuServe even included a limited-time special usage credit of $6 for people willing to part with $19.95 for the book—even though it publishes its own user guides and manuals.

CompuServe began in 1969 as a time-sharing data processing service, back in the days when computers were large mainframes and the idea of putting a free-standing, self-contained workstation of comparable power in individual offices and homes was called science fiction. By 1979, which in computer history is eons ago, a consumer service phenomenon was being born. The pioneers of personal computing were looking for ways to hook up their machines and talk to each other, or tie them into larger computer services for access to information. A year later, the business gained access to some deep pockets that could help it grow—and a parent willing to let it alone while it did just that—when H&R Block acquired the company.

These days, connection to an on-line services network is as basic to a computer as a telephone is to a well-run business. CompuServe, along with the other companies in the business of managing information in motion, serves a function similar to the old telephone exchanges: Its network services allow dispersed users, customers, or business branches to connect to a host computer (which can be CompuServe's own main-frame, or a system in another business) and exchange information. That includes "gateway access" to supplemental networks in nearly eighty countries worldwide.

In addition, the company serves as a value-added supplier by creating or providing literally hundreds of packaged options for both consumer and business users. With more than four hundred different products and services to choose from, CompuServe subscribers can use their computers for everything from data base research (more than seven hundred sources in all) and on-line shopping to electronic mail and multiuser games.

CompuServe supports its subscribers in a variety of ways. Service representatives are available by toll-free telephone lines from eight in the morning (eastern) until midnight (two P.M. through midnight on the weekends) to answer questions and solve problems. Via modem, there's a special Feedback bulletin board (which can be entered twenty-four hours a day and used without incurring charges for connect time) where users can leave comments, offer suggestions, and ask questions; CompuServe responds directly and personally via electronic mail, telephone calls, or letters. More than a third of its subscribers left their electronic footprints in the Feedback area in 1987, according to the company's continuing customer research, and two thirds of those who did describe it as nothing less than excellent.

There's also a Questions and Answers area that indexes helpful solutions to common problems and frequently asked questions. And authors Bowen and Peyton have their own *Online Today* forum, where they answer queries and offer advice about using the company's services effectively.

Whether accessed by voice or modem, CompuServe's service reps have developed a first-rate reputation. "Subscribers are so pleased with the help that they've sent our Customer Service representatives thank-you notes and gifts ranging from roses to admission to the David Letterman Show," spokesman Robert Loomis told us. The thank-yous, especially the electronic kind, add up: CompuServe logs more than four thousand such messages a year.

Perhaps one reason is the uncommon amount of interpersonal involvement CompuServe seems to encourage between service reps and their customers. Many get Christmas cards from people they've come to know electronically while unsnarling snarls and resolving technical problems. Fan mail on the Feedback system invariably mentions the CompuServe service representative by name, indicative of the personalization of service possible even with high-tech/low-touch systems.

Online Today, a monthly user guide and support magazine, is sent free to all subscribers and is available on-line as well as on paper. The electronic version is added to and updated both daily and weekly, and readers have their own electronic forum and feedback center through which they can discuss new developments and help each other get more out of the company's services.

The source of the majority of the company's revenue is the on-line service CompuServe provides to corporations as they continue to become more sophisticated in their use of computers. A network of more than thirty sales offices helps more than eighteen hundred business and government customers develop custom programs or make best use of current on-line offerings, backed by an "uptime reliability" that exceeds 99.5 percent. That extends to executives and other subscribers who use their computers for investment services: When the Stock Market "melted down" in October 1987, CompuServe kept its customers on-line to financial data services by switching in another mainframe computer to handle the increased load of log-ons from worried investors.

For both consumers and businesses, the system uses local access points, called micronodes, that feed data into and through the network (which includes specially conditioned telephone lines, fiber-optic cables, and satellites) in the fastest way possible while verifying the accuracy of the information being transmitted. From electronic funds transfer to computer-based teleconferencing, the commercial services offered continue to help businesses harness modern electronics in support of basic communications needs.

The communications network that links retail merchants to the thirteen thousand member banks issuing Visa cards is also provided by CompuServe. It allows merchants to verify whether a card is lost, stolen, or otherwise unauthorized in less than twenty seconds. At the same time, Visa U.S.A. and its member institutions can use the system for electronic mail communications.

By paying attention to commercial as well as personal customers, CompuServe has become the largest vendor of point-of-sale (POS) credit card authorization services and the largest consumer videotext service. It also has developed at least one trapping of its parent, H&R Block— listening for the thank-yous. Take this one from a physician in California: "I'm an old hand at computers though new to services such as CompuServe, and was quite discouraged after a series of problems at the onset. A letter from J. I. Maranville solved the technical problem and was so sensibly friendly that I feel much encouraged to continue."

CompuServe
Subsidiary of H&R Block
5000 Arlington Centre Blvd.
Columbus, OH 43220

MANUFACTURING

Deluxe Corporation

Caterpillar

General Electric

H. B. Fuller

Pioneer Hi-Bred International

Armstrong World Industries

Manufacturing: Where Some Don't Look (But Do Act) Like Service Providers

THE POPULAR NOTION AMONG BUSINESS GURUS IS THAT MAINTAINING AMERica's preeminence in manufacturing industries—or in some cases, recapturing it from foreign incursions—is critical to the continued vitality of the American economy.

America's manufacturers, long the whipping boys of industry experts for slipping product quality and diminished market share, have been answering the call. Forced by foreign competition to slash its labor force and close obsolete plants, the U.S. manufacturing sector has essentially recovered from its 1970s slowdown and is back near a 3-percent growth track. Quality problems have been attacked with a vengeance, both through retraining of workers and through technological developments like statistical process controls that alert workers when a machine starts to produce faulty parts. Countless companies have cut costs by installing just-in-time inventory control, a system in which suppliers deliver quality-guaranteed parts that are used immediately rather than put in stock.

Measured against the competition, however, the improvements are deceiving. The gains in comparative costs American companies have made against the Japanese are primarily the result of the yen's rise and rely on the uncertain fate of the dollar in world financial markets. And improvements on the factory floor have not always been matched in nonproduction areas like marketing, sales administration, and after-sale service systems and support. Nonetheless, undeniable (if sometimes unnoticed) pockets of service excellence exist in the manufacturing sector. The service edge is what sets one company apart from another in what historically have been product-driven fields.

Echlin, a producer and distributor of auto parts, is representative of manufacturers with a service-sector mentality. And it's more than holding its own against burgeoning foreign competition—Japan, Taiwan, and Korea included. Credit a big part of the Branford, Connecticut-based company's success to efficient manufacturing, but give credit also to Echlin's understanding that its business first and foremost is a form of service to other manufacturers.

440

Echlin management long ago realized the parts business is essentially a business where pricing takes a back seat to customer service issues. Pull out your last car repair bill and you'll undoubtedly see the cost of parts as only a fraction of the cost of labor. Remember the hassle of having your car in the shop, and you understand why speed of parts delivery is a critical business test.

According to *Forbes*, an Echlin ignition switch for a 1974 Ford retails for about $34. An off-brand substitute made in Taiwan would go for closer to $25. But foreign manufacturers haven't captured much of the market for the parts. They're too far from their customers—and not just in terms of freight charges. Counter people at Echlin jobbers are taught to use catalogs to help locate parts, and sales are made through customer networks by working directly with mechanics' leads.

Back in the plant, Echlin keeps its factories lean and well motivated. Managers are placed on exact performance standards—specifying, for example, that 95 percent of all orders be filled within forty-eight hours. Each percentage point above or below is worth 5 percent of a manager's pay in terms of a bonus or a bonus debit.

You can easily count about thirty major U.S. corporations that are clearly serious about their manufacturing: Allen-Bradley, GM, Ford, and IBM typically top the lists. But even those companies with excellent records of producing high-quality products are increasingly aware of problems created by ignoring service operations.

IBM has firsthand experience, according to an article in *The New York Times*. By not paying serious attention to customers' frustration with the incompatibility of many IBM machines, it opened customers' doors to Digital Equipment Corporation and other competitors that had funneled research dollars into developing networks that could solve the incompatibility problem. And by abandoning its older PCs to bring to market the PS/2, it turned Compaq into a far-from-compact foe.

A 1987 study conducted by the accounting and management consulting firm Arthur Andersen & Co. forecasts some interesting trends in industrial and commercial customer service. Among the study's findings are these:

- "Value-added" services that provide a pricing or logistical advantage to a product without making it cost more money—for example, inventory management, prepricing, bundling, warranty administration—will be increasingly demanded by customers.
- There will be a dramatic decrease—31 percent—in field sales calls, with a resultant transfer of even more customer contact and sales administration functions to the internal customer service department.
- There will be a significant increase—27 percent—in video catalog ordering by industrial and commercial entities, accompanied by a

slight decrease in ordering from printed catalogs as the video technology spreads.

- By 1995, a typical distributor will be handling 25 percent *more* line items—5,000, up from 4,000 in 1986—but will be dealing with 20 percent *fewer* suppliers, dropping from an average of 50 in 1986 to only 40 in 1995.

The Andersen study also forecasts that just-in-time inventories will double in relative size for both distributors and manufacturers. With the increases, the study reports that America's manufacturers and distributors alike will be expected to improve their "value-added" services to customers.

Close to the Customer

In the future, in other words, manufacturing's customers will have a greater need for a broader base of local inventories, along with a higher response rate in filling orders. And the study makes it clear that manufacturers can ill afford to ignore the competitive potential of distributors. They are big and getting bigger, with mom-and-pop operations on the decline. The new economies of scale will give distributors the advantages of diversity and closeness to the customer.

Case in point: Avnet, the "IBM of distribution" in the electronics industry, voted the world's best distributor by companies surveyed by *Electronic Business* magazine in 1986 and 1987. Avnet prides itself on its ability to incorporate the flexibility of a small company into its operations— it's the biggest distributor in the world—and has developed what is generally considered to be the best computerized inventory system in the industry. And with more than one hundred distribution centers, it stays close to its original equipment manufacturers and its customers.

On a different level, Sun Distributors (an organization we'll deal with at greater length in the Business-to-Business chapter to come) has built a network of stellar regional companies that collectively are blazing a trail based on bringing the brawn of big-company systems to the brains of small, close-to-the-customer specialists.

Spencer Hapoienu, director of New York City-based SAGE Worldwide, the Ogilvy Group's market-consulting firm, says manufacturers are more effective the better they understand the local areas where their products are sold. He cautions corporate managers not to be reluctant to shift decision-making away from headquarters. As American consumers grow more educated and diverse and demand increasingly customized service, Hapoienu says it will be imperative to target local differences cost-effectively.

Caterpillar, the world's largest manufacturer of heavy equipment, is keeping pace with the competition by offering third-party warehousing and distribution services domestically and internationally, as well as management consulting services. After-sale customer service and other support for its dealers—the backbone of its business from the customer standpoint—are both important parts of a new business emphasis, particularly following a doubling of the company's product line in the 1980s.

And from Deluxe Corporation, a financial forms "manufacturer" with a strong service orientation, comes a prototype of decentralization: over sixty regional plants scattered across the country to service its bank customers, and their customers. To live up to its dual goals of error-free printing and two-day order turnaround—which it does about 98 percent of the time—Deluxe believes in placing printing facilities physically close to customers. Each of those plants has a high degree of autonomy, and behaves like a locally owned business.

H. B. Fuller, the biggest independent adhesive company in the world, states that its corporate priorities are customers, employees, shareholders, and the communities where it operates—in that order. It refuses to slight service to those at the top of the list for short-term financial gains on behalf of the folks listed fourth.

Retooling Workers

As service companies have done for years, a broad range of manufacturers are beginning to spend heavily to teach workers new skills and upgrade their old ones. Many companies now give training expenses the same importance as capital costs like plant and equipment.

In 1985, Motorola decided to increase its training budget by $20 million. In a given year, almost a third of the company's ninety thousand employees get a total of two million to three million hours of training, at a cost of nearly $90 million, according to *Fortune*. Motorola training head Bill Wiggenhorn says the results have been encouraging—the rate of return on savings realized from the statistical process control and problem-solving methods Motorola employees have been trained in is about thirty times the training dollars invested.

Increasingly, manufacturers are finding that they are only as good as the delivery and installation of their products. It is an awareness not lost on—and not new to—manufacturers like Grand Rapids, Michigan-based Steelcase. Long the market leader in the manufacture of contract office furniture and systems, Steelcase sells and delivers product exclusively through a network of independent dealerships. Customer perception of service quality is inextricably bound up in the yoked relationship of dealer and manufacturer. As a result, Steelcase works hard to understand the needs of both the office-furniture customer and the company's "partner/customer," the dealer.

When a dealer needs help on an important installation, there is a hotline available with technical advice. Need to know something about marketing a new product or service in your unique part of the world? Chances are a dealer-development person can come help you figure it out. To improve dealer relations, Steelcase sends teams of head office, administrative, and manufacturing people out to call on dealers and learn firsthand how they think it can provide better support.

When it became obvious that service quality was to be a force in the marketplace, it was Steelcase and a group of dealer volunteers who set the standards for quality of installation and ordering—and who determined together how the standards would be measured. It's called "knowing who your customer is," and caring about their needs and concerns.

Manufacturers Who Think Service

A few years ago, this category would have had few entrants. Today there are a goodly number of viable candidates who think first of their customers, second about their internal processes—manufacturers who want to be, and are, "easy to do business with."

Between *In Search of Excellence, A Passion for Excellence*, and *Thriving on Chaos*, Tom Peters has made famous a good number of service-sensitive manufacturers. Milliken, Nucor Corporation, and Tennant Company come quickly to mind, as do 3M, Hewlett-Packard and W. L. Gore & Associates. These names, and others, belong on anyone's "good guys doing good work" list.

For exemplars, we've picked six organizations that seem to us to cover a broad spectrum of types and sizes of manufacturers. Deluxe should be a familiar name by now. Gene Olson, the company's immediate-past chairman, told us once, with some amusement, that the people who write business articles never quite know where to classify Deluxe: "They think we're a manufacturer because we have sixty plants. That's irrelevant. We're in a service business—because we define what we do as a service, not as a product." Caterpillar we've also introduced already, if only briefly. Pay special attention to the way Cat has turned entrepreneurial in developing new services for its dealers.

Two stories about General Electric sold us: the incredible responsiveness to customers that is embodied in the GE Answer Center operation in Louisville, and the more market-specific way the company's jet engine division went from also-ran to king of the skies through superior customer service.

H. B. Fuller, Pioneer Hi-Bred International, and Armstrong World Industries compete in three markets that have almost nothing in common, yet all have capitalized on long traditions of service and paying attention to customers. Even in volatile, highly competitive international marketplaces, their values have not been worshipped from afar. All excel at knowing who the customer is, finding out what the customer expects, and then delivering in highly satisfying ways.

Each of these companies makes and sells products of a physical kind. Yet placed among companies with a higher or more obvious service component, they undeniably belong.

Deluxe Corporation

THERE'S A MYTH THAT GOOD SERVICE CAN'T BE MEASURED IN QUANTIFIABLE terms. There's also a company that disproves that myth: Deluxe Corporation, formerly known as Deluxe Check Printers. If you use checks— and most American families and businesses do—chances are better than fifty-fifty they were printed by Deluxe. How many little red-and-black check boxes do you have around the house and office? If they're red and black, they're almost certainly Deluxe.

What's more, if they were printed by Deluxe, there's more than a 99-percent probability that they were printed right, without defect or error, and about a 97-percent chance they were shipped within forty-eight hours of the time Deluxe received the order. Says who? Says Deluxe. Look it up in the company's annual report. Every year Deluxe reports its service performance as measured against the twin goals of error-free printing and forty-eight-hour turnaround. From the entry-level press operators to the plant managers in Deluxe's electronically linked network of sixty-two printing plants around the country, everybody knows that those are the standards to which they will be held accountable.

At first glance, Deluxe doesn't look like a prototypical service company. After all, checks are a product, aren't they? The answer is yes and no. Yes, checks are physical, tangible, visible. But they also represent an important service for the bank, savings and loan, credit union, or other financial services company with which you do business. Getting them to customers fast and accurately is an important and very visible aspect of the service package the bank is in business to provide. As mergers and acquisitions proliferate in the financial services industry, Deluxe has proven a valuable ally in efficient, accurate, and painless checking account conversions as well.

Think about it from your bank's standpoint. It is putting its good business relationship with you at risk when it turns you over to an outside supplier for financial instruments. The quality of service Deluxe provides to you on the bank's behalf will effect your confidence and satisfaction with your bank, subtly if the order is filled promptly and correctly, more visibly if something goes wrong.

Consequently, the *service* Deluxe provides to your bank is based on an assurance of unparalleled performance quality. On the evidence of more than seventy years in the business, the job is going to be done right the first time, and on time, so that most consumers aren't even aware that they are dealing with an independent company, not their own bank, when they place a check order.

Deluxe was founded on the premise that there was a niche for a printer able to provide exceptionally fast and reliable service to the banking industry. That was in 1915, before the concept of personal checking accounts was even accepted by banks. Today, Deluxe ranks up there with the elite in the fabled *Fortune* 500 in terms of size and net income—yet *Fortune* doesn't list it on its roster of "The Service 500" (the five hundred largest service-providing companies in selected sectors of the U.S. economy). You figure it out.

The formally stated Deluxe definition of good service—that orders are received, processed, printed, and shipped in a maximum turnaround of two days—has been part of the company's culture since founder W. R. Hotchkiss, who pretty much invented the standardized check for business use, put it in writing on August 18, 1936. (You have to like a company with that meticulous a sense of its own history.) There were, to be sure, cheaper ways of running the business, but Hotchkiss didn't want any part of them. "Economy at the expense of service is costly indeed," he decreed.

Over the years, that simple, measurable standard has been built into everything from plant design to computer software. It's the yardstick against which new ideas are measured—not just will it save money, or make it more convenient to do something internally, but how will it effect the organization's customers? If it doesn't serve them, it doesn't happen.

That's the reason there are sixty-two regional plants dappled across the landscape instead of a handful of megaplants in centralized locations. To get the orders in, printed, and sent back out in forty-eight hours, according to Deluxe's reasoning, it makes sense to put the printing facilities close to the customers. Each plant is semiautonomous: It has its own on-site management, P&L, and business plan. Each one feels like a locally owned and operated business. But each is constantly aware of the performance standards set for the entire organization.

Service is a continuing concern, and Deluxe measures it, pokes it, prods it, examines it, and tinkers with it in just about every way imaginable. Predictably, the customer's satisfaction with the transaction is measured and plotted. So, too, is the number of times the phone rings before someone answers it. Each day's orders are processed on a different color of paper—if there's orange (the color for Tuesday orders) in sight on Wednesday afternoons, fur starts flying.

Doing more is nothing extraordinary. To maintain accountability on orders for which the company has promised same-day service, Deluxe attaches a "promise slip" that is initialed, dated, and timed by every person who handles the order. "No excuse will be accepted and no expense must be spared . . . to see that this order is delivered ON TIME," the routing slip proclaims. When inconsistency in the U.S. mails jeopardized turnaround standards, Deluxe lobbied for the "right" of bank stationers to function as postal substations. That meant doing more than before, but it also meant getting the orders filled and shipped—and keeping the customers satisfied.

Personnel management and supervision reflect Deluxe's service imperative. Salespeople are on salary, not commission, because their job is to both sell and service their accounts, and Deluxe wants to make sure one isn't sacrificed for the other. They're backed up at each plant by service representatives equipped with computers that let them track any order in any plant at any time.

Working in close cooperation with its customers, and the customers of its customers, has provided Deluxe with timely market intelligence while making its people much more than one-dimensional order-takers. The company freely credits product innovations such as stubless checks, personalized checks, distinctive colors, and scenic backdrops to its salespeople. The nouveau cliché for that approach is "staying close to the customer." Deluxe has been doing it for generations. No big deal. You think just-in-time (JIT) production management is cutting-edge stuff for the 1980s? Deluxe managers never thought that much about it. They've just been practicing it for decades now.

As might be expected, Deluxe promotes heavily from within, rewarding loyalty and achievement, and fostering a close-knit family feeling (nameplates show not only the employee's name, but the year he or she joined the company). Performance bonuses, on the other hand, are based on company, not personal, results. The priority remains on serving customers, not personal agendas.

Deluxe works very closely with its managers to keep that key audience aligned with the company's core values, business goals, and operating philosophies. It doesn't begrudge time, and money, spent on inculcating a "Deluxe Way" of management that recognizes both performance standards and people's idiosyncracies. That, in turns builds the kind of confidence that greatly impresses customers. Although electronic funds transfer (EFT) is supposed to be bringing about a checkless society—a notion that not once but twice has led *Forbes* to predict Deluxe's demise—the company is still going strong in its core business. It's also diversifying into both financial and other related high-service fields, most notably with the

1987 purchase of another respected provider of good service, Current, the nation's largest direct-mail marketer of greeting cards and stationery.

What Deluxe has created in what initially appears to be a manufacturing environment is a certifiably productive and exemplary service culture, one that can be seen in the day-to-day routine and in responses to circumstances outside the ordinary. It all starts with a thorough, companywide understanding of the way Deluxe defines good service.

Thus, when a midwestern plant was flooded by heavy rains a few years back, the manager wasn't inclined to wait for the puddles to dry before getting back in operation. He knew that, come hell or—literally—high water, he was still expected to meet the forty-eight-hour, zero-defect standard. So he packed up his key people and the magnetic tape containing his plant's order information and headed for a Deluxe plant that wasn't operating at full capacity. The customers never suffered for nature's depredations.

Deluxe Corporation
1080 West County Road F
St. Paul, MN 55164

CATERPILLAR

THE PROBLEM STARTED AT A MINING COMPANY IN KENTUCKY. THE SOLUTION came from Peoria, Illinois. One of two D10s (massive, track-type tractors used in earth-moving work) on the mining site went down with a failed front track roller frame. One machine alone wouldn't be able to keep up with the mine's workload for long. An anxious call went out to the dealership, fifty miles away.

The call came up empty—no such frames were inventoried by the dealer, or by the entire parts network, for that matter. Not to worry, said the dealer, who promptly called the plant where D10s are assembled in East Peoria, not far from the manufacturer's world headquarters. There, workers pulled the vital frame component from a stock unit and had it on its way to Kentucky within twenty-four hours. Operations were shortly back to normal, the mining company started talking about future equipment purchases, and the story was added to the collection of hundreds of similar tales of dealer and product support in the name of responsiveness to customer needs told within Caterpillar, the world's largest manufacturer of earth-moving, construction, and materials-handling equipment and the specialized engines that run them.

You have to look hard to find a company that has been through more adversity in recent years than Caterpillar. Through the 1970s, "Cat" was a juggernaut—a seemingly invincible American manufacturer that so dominated its markets that its very name had become synonymous with product quality. Demand regularly exceeded production capacity for the trademark yellow machines that built roads, dug mines, and generally did the big, dirty construction jobs the world over. Not only were the products first-rate by almost every measure of quality, but the worldwide network of two hundred independent dealerships, including almost a thousand branch stores, was widely respected for its sales savvy and service support.

Internally, employment peaked at just under ninety thousand in 1980, and Cat executives willingly concede that all those years of success had made the company not only complacent, but even a bit arrogant. That

450

changed with almost brutal swiftness. Low oil prices, high interest rates, and a worldwide recession conspired to simultaneously put the brakes on energy exploration, mining, dam building, highway construction, and other large-scale industrial projects. Demand dropped. Competitors, notably Japan's Komatsu, cut prices aggressively in a no-holds-barred fight for business. Cat's bright yellow was submerged in a sea of red ink: The company lost more than a billion dollars in the early eighties.

But Caterpillar survived. In part, it survived because it got leaner: Its worldwide employment has been cut nearly in half, and more than half a dozen manufacturing plants and other facilities have been closed. In part, however, it has survived and returned to profitability because it got smarter, committing more than a billion dollars to modernizing most of its twenty-nine remaining factories under a five-year program ambitiously dubbed "Plant with a Future," and more than doubling its product line, primarily by adding smaller-scale counterparts to its traditional spectrum of huge construction machinery. Encouragingly, overall production employment increased by a net total of thirteen hundred jobs in 1987.

Best of all, it still has that high-quality dealer network, an asset composed of independent businesses that together employ nearly one hundred thousand sales and service workers in North America, South America, Europe, Asia, and the Middle East. After-sale service to customers and new services designed to support dealers are both important parts of the new style of business at Caterpillar, the more so with the doubling of Cat's product line in the 1980s.

Both initiatives reflect a continuation of Cat's traditional corporate commitment to the longer-term, frequently at the expense of enhancing short-term results. "Plant with a Future" is visible evidence of a long-term commitment to heavy equipment manufacturing. Incentive programs to support dealer marketing efforts take nickels out of mutual funds and dividend checks. Other less visible but no less important service tactics are also involved.

Over the years, Caterpillar and its dealers have refined mutual support systems to a fine art. Dealers, for example, can locate and order parts almost instantly for shipment by the fastest available means. That helps their customers reduce downtime. Preventive maintenance and training programs, again implemented at the dealer level, help customers learn how to get the most value for their purchase dollar and control potentially costly repairs. A wide-ranging simplification program focusing on "manufacturability" has streamlined assembly processes and standardized parts and components, resulting in fewer piece parts, fewer tools necessary for assembly and service, and ultimately savings in time and money for both dealers and their customers.

There are payoffs for such an investment. When American Samoa was struggling with chronic power shortages back in 1986, for example, it had its choice of a number of competitive suppliers for power-generating systems. Cat won with a combination of delivering first (through a responsive dealer in California), arranging financing (through a wholly owned subsidiary), and providing a six-month maintenance and training program (again through the dealer) to ensure smooth start-up. Despite intense competition from generally lower-priced alternatives, it's performance like that that makes for loyal Cat customers—customers willing to pay a price often as much as 10 percent higher than some of the competition's for high-quality products and service support.

In the 1980s, in addition to expanding its product line, Caterpillar has turned downright entrepreneurial around the whole notion of service. In recent years, it has added operating units like Caterpillar Insurance Company to arrange insurance programs for its dealers, and Caterpillar Financial Services Corporation (now a wholly owned subsidiary), which provides flexible lease- and purchase-financing options for both customers and Cat dealers in the U.S. and Canada (not to mention American Samoa).

One of the most innovative of Cat's service-oriented ventures is Caterpillar Venture Capital. Formed in 1984, this independent company has Cat's mandate to find and develop new technologies and lines of business by supporting entrepreneurs both within and outside the company.

Internally, Cat Venture Capital is funding, among others, The Caterpillar Service Technology Group, which designs and markets service tools and shop supplies for Cat dealers (who, in turn, provide that critical and satisfying service to the company's ultimate customers), and Custom Machine Products, which modifies standard Cat equipment to meet the requirements of specific customer applications. Outside, one of the most successful new ventures is Advanced Technology Services, a company founded in 1985 by former Caterpillar employees to provide computer maintenance and repair services to both their former company and other businesses.

Since 1987, Caterpillar also has found a way to exploit its huge distribution system through a subsidiary that markets logistics services, including warehousing, transportation, and support. Through Caterpillar Logistics Services, Cat now provides worldwide parts warehousing and distribution for products such as the Land Rover, Range Rover, and Freight Rover vehicles built in Great Britain. Key to making the new service viable was the wholehearted agreement by members of eight United Auto Workers locals to guarantee smooth and continuous operations for outside distribution customers in the event that a strike resulted in a work stoppage at Caterpillar's own operations.

Make no mistake about it: Caterpillar is still first and foremost a multinational manufacturing company. But its broad-brush application of service as an increasingly potent marketing edge is an important component of its worldwide business strategy.

And judging from the balance sheet of late, service is playing very well indeed in Peoria.

Caterpillar, Inc.
100 NE Adams Street
Peoria, IL 61629

General Electric

HOW MUCH DIFFERENCE DOES ATTENTION (OR INATTENTION) TO GOOD SERVICE make for a manufacturing business? Just ask the people who build commercial-airliner and military jet-fighter engines at General Electric— and the managers at Pratt & Whitney, the division of United Technologies that used to dominate those markets, but now finds itself running second to GE.

As chronicled by *The Wall Street Journal* in January 1988, GE overcame years of Pratt & Whitney dominance through "a series of events, some stretching back years and some still unfolding. The story is one of corporate gambles that didn't pay and the deft exploitation of an opponent's weaknesses." The weaknesses GE exploited largely involved service.

Service excellence is nothing new or unusual for GE. On the consumer side, its twenty-four-hour toll-free GE Answer Center is widely considered the state of the art in customer assistance. From Louisville, Kentucky, more than 225 frontline operators and specialists handle nearly three million calls each year, everything from inquiries about product performance to questions about how to get appliances serviced.

Incidentally, the dealers to whom GE refers its consumer customers are those that have provided good service in the past. The practice assures that customers will be treated well and motivates dealers to keep their standards up. The same imperative applies to the more than two thousand field repair technicians who work directly for GE—the industry's only factory-owned and -operated field service organization.

"We realized our technicians had as many as three million contacts a year with consumers," Stephen O'Brien, GE's vice president of sales and service for major appliances, told *Forbes* a couple of years ago. "If the job is done right, it creates terrific brand loyalty." Consequently, the number one criterion for determining the salary of repair technicians and their managers is the grade for customer satisfaction derived from GE's follow-up contacts with service customers.

For commercial customers, there's a counterpart: the Business Information Center, based in Albany, New York, but modeled on the operations of the consumer-oriented Answer Center. It helps new and existing customers navigate their way through GE's various product groups (the company has fourteen "key businesses" making products that include light bulbs, household appliances, railroad locomotives, and plastic parts for automobile bodies).

What does all this have to do with airplane engines? Well, service isn't just a concern of consumers. At stake in this case is a global market estimated to be worth $160 billion in the 1990s, one that includes new engines and spare parts to keep current models flying for both commercial airliners and military aircraft. It's a market Pratt & Whitney used to virtually own. In the early years of jet aviation, Pratt & Whitney held a near-monopoly—both Boeing and McDonnell Douglas used its engines exclusively.

GE's first breakthrough was winning the contract to supply engines for the McDonnell Douglas DC-10 in the late 1970s, but that was an exception to a long-running rule. As recently as 1984, Pratt & Whitney shipped 455 airliner engines to GE's 290; in 1983, it booked 409 new orders to GE's 60. Yet by 1987, a remarkable turnaround had taken place: GE had managed to expand its new-order base by a factor of 22 (1,360 orders), while Pratt & Whitney was still flying in pretty much the same place (467 new orders, down from its high-altitude mark of 494 in 1986). GE shipped 524 new commercial engines in 1987 to Pratt & Whitney's 425.

How did it happen? Some of GE's rise, largely at Pratt & Whitney's expense, involves product design, which in technology-intensive businesses is as much a service component as any other part of the selling process. In the early eighties, GE engineers concentrated on refining and improving two existing engine models, one designed for smaller aircraft, and streamlining technical areas to make the company's engines cheaper to build. Time-tested reliability became an important selling point in GE's sales and marketing vocabulary; snafus encountered while trying to obtain vital spare parts were minimized.

Pratt & Whitney, on the other hand, bet heavily on development of a new, mid-size engine and a replacement for its high-thrust model, which was proving vulnerable to GE's lower-priced alternative. To meet those commitments, each of which required approximately $1 billion, it cancelled development of a smaller engine that would have been matched against GE's other model. At the same time, Pratt & Whitney found itself struggling to keep up with an unexpectedly troublesome consequence of its previous market dominance: maintaining adequate spare-parts inventories for seventeen thousand engines involving sixty different model variations. With fewer models and about one-third the number of existing units in service, GE's maintenance and support demands were easier to satisfy.

Enter market forces. Pratt & Whitney's promising mid-sized engine, designed for the new, more fuel-efficient Boeing 757, had its predictable share of problems on introduction: Northwest Airlines, for example, found twenty different items it wanted fixed, further complicating Pratt & Whitney's service work load. The only "good news": There weren't as many to fix because fuel prices had come down, blunting the 757's fuel-efficient sales pitch and resulting in slower sales of the new plane and its Pratt & Whitney engines. Meanwhile, by focusing on customer needs and redesigning its unchallenged small engine to fit under the wings of the smaller Boeing 737, GE found a new high-flyer for the deregulated skies. About eight hundred 737s with the GE engine have been sold to commercial airlines in recent years.

While design decisions and market developments were problems perhaps not entirely under Pratt & Whitney's control, the issue of after-sale support and service satisfaction was. That turned out to be the company's Achilles' heel and a big part of GE's newfound marketing edge. In addition to product-design considerations, the *Journal* reported, a "record of slipshod service, especially tardiness in supplying spare parts, has also damaged Pratt & Whitney. No mere inconvenience, the late arrival of needed spare parts can disrupt airline maintenance and flight schedules, inflating costs and enraging passengers . . ." With the boom in air travel in recent years, more planes are flying more miles, which means more demand for timely maintenance and repairs. Pratt & Whitney didn't keep up with that important service imperative, despite sometimes vigorous customer complaints. Ultimately, it cost the company business.

In October 1987, for example, Japan Air Lines (JAL) announced it was switching from Pratt & Whitney to GE as supplier of new engines for its sixty Boeing 747s, the largest fleet of 747s in the world. JAL, according to the *Journal*, had grown increasingly intolerant of maintenance disruptions from late spare-parts deliveries. At one point, all forty of the spare engines for its 747s were grounded for lack of those vital parts from the manufacturer, some of them so complex they require a year to produce. When its engineers tested GE, Pratt & Whitney, and Rolls-Royce engines and pronounced the GE model best, JAL bought its first GE engines in twenty-five years. Other GE customers include American and Northwest Airlines, Air France, Alitalia, and QANTAS.

Pratt & Whitney's biggest customer, the U.S. Air Force, also grew weary of repair delays and insensitive treatment in the mid-eighties. After years of relying almost completely on Pratt & Whitney for jet-fighter engines, the Air Force too has turned to GE as a second source. From 1985 through 1987, about half of the engines for its F-15 and F-16 fighters, which originally were totally powered by Pratt & Whitney equipment, came from GE. In 1982, Pratt & Whitney shipped 752 engines to the Air Force. The company's total for 1987 was just 273.

Pratt & Whitney is a good company. It makes good engines and spare parts, and it will undoubtedly continue to compete successfully in the commercial and military jet-engine markets. But those markets have changed in response to service-driven imperatives—forces GE recognized and acted on while Pratt & Whitney didn't. GE has profited accordingly.

Here's some highly instructive math: In 1982, Pratt & Whitney recorded $5.3 billion in commercial and military engine sales; in 1986, $5.5 billion. Its operating profits on those sales grew from $329 million in 1982 to $446 million in 1986, or about 35 percent. In the same period, GE's engine sales virtually doubled, from $3.1 billion to $6 billion, and its operating profit climbed from $344 million to $869 million, an increase of about 250 percent.

There are a lot of ways to interpret the events involved in this market vignette. We would suggest that the numbers show how the results of good service eventually do arrive on the bottom line.

General Electric Company
3135 Easton Turnpike
Fairfield, CT 05431

H. B. Fuller

ville, Kentucky. On the other end of the line, in Macon, Georgia, a valued customer was running out of the glue required for a specialized manufacturing operation. This particular glue, it turned out, wasn't one of the products it bought from the secretary's employer, but since it wasn't working properly anyway, the customer figured maybe someone in Louisville could help.

The prospects were bleaker than they knew: This particular morning, the secretary's boss was out of the country, and the local salesman was on vacation. Time to take a message, right? Instead, the secretary took the initiative. She called the company's regional technical service center in Greensboro, North Carolina, and described the problem. Someone there determined which of the related glues among the company's seven thousand adhesive, sealant and coating formulations would probably do the job. Then he lobbed the ball back into her court: the only stock on hand was in Louisville. Not at all daunted, the secretary walked out of the office, drove her own pickup to the warehouse, loaded up five hundred pounds of product, and headed for the airport. Elapsed time: ninety minutes so far.

At the airport, she encountered another problem. A big one. The air freight company that linked Louisville and Macon had a flight scheduled to leave in thirty minutes, but her employer didn't have an account with it. The bill was going to be pretty close to three hundred dollars, and the freighter wasn't about to accept good intentions in lieu of cash on the counter. Back in a minute, guys. The secretary went to a nearby automatic teller machine and withdrew the money needed from her personal savings. By 2 P.M., the material was in Macon, the manufacturer's production line was not just running uninterrupted, but was operating better than ever (the new adhesive outperformed the one they'd been buying from the other supplier), and the secretary was back in the office.

If you think that story is a little removed from reality, get yourself a copy of the 1985 annual report of H. B. Fuller Company of St. Paul,

Minnesota, the largest independent adhesive company in the world. Turn to page five. The woman pictured by the Instant Cash machine is Lorinda Evans (now Tucker). Her story is nearby. She's still a secretary in Fuller's Louisville offices. She's also a walking illustration of the fact that when Fuller tells anyone who will listen that its priorities are, in this order, customers, employees, shareholders, and the communities where it operates, listeners take it seriously.

Fuller has been saying it formally for more than fifty years, long before it became a publicly held company (in 1968), or a member of the *Fortune* 500 (1984). And it has been practicing that philosophy since Harvey Benjamin Fuller was cooking up glues on his kitchen table back in the waning days of the 1800s. Under the leadership of first Elmer Andersen (who also has served as governor of Minnesota) and now his son, Tony, Fuller has long operated on the theory that the best customer to have is the one you've already got. If the customer is satisfied, he'll come back and order product again and again. He's not going to risk screwing up a smooth operation on a whim, or to pinch pennies.

Consequently, Fuller excels at providing extensive technical support to its customers. Most of its adhesives, coatings, sealants, paints, specialty waxes, and sanitation chemicals are developed or modified to meet specific customer applications for industrial processes. They're a minor part of manufacturing, for example, but usually a critical one—the glue, so to speak, that holds things together. That means they have to work right, and in the manufacturing and customer-use conditions specific to the product.

To make sure of that, Fuller salespeople and scientists alike are accustomed to seeing themselves as part of their customer's company. They spend time on the customer's production lines. They're on hand for test runs of a new process or to troubleshoot problems with an existing one. And they swap stories of their counterparts who have gone the extra mile for customers and, in the process, become part of Fuller's corporate folklore.

Take Arnold Zueger, a sales rep in the Minneapolis offices of the Monarch Products division. In the spring of 1987, he got a late-night call from a customer in Kalamazoo, Michigan, who was, to say the least, very upset over a quality problem that had come up. After discussing the situation with his division manager, Zueger hopped in his car and drove to Kalamazoo (a distance of over five hundred miles) because it got him there quicker than flying. Meanwhile, the division operations manager lined up a technical investigator to meet him at the customer's plant in the afternoon, and another sales rep, Jon Stanwick, flew in to lend a hand.

By six that night a shipment of new product had arrived, and the two sales reps were still there working with the customer's people to clean out the fouled systems and solve the quality problems as they became clearer. One fact emerged early on: The problem didn't originate with the Monarch product. No matter. Zueger and Stanwick stayed on through the night anyway.

It's treatment like that that explains why nearly a dozen companies have been Fuller customers for more than a century, and why many more have been won over in more recent years. But there's also a lesson to be learned in Fuller's more recent history. In the 1980s, Fuller has gone through an extensive reorganization—so extensive that inside of two years more than half of its forty-five hundred employees were doing different jobs—yet it has done so without losing its customer focus.

When Fuller first began to expand to national, and then international, scale, it operated on a philosophy of being physically close to its customers. Plants and technical support centers were sited (or, in some cases, acquired) close to customer facilities so Fuller's technical people could provide plenty of personal service. That closeness and specialization based on customer needs allowed it to succeed against much larger competitors.

In addition, because plants were nearby, no matter where in the world that was, inventories could be kept slim. Whenever a customer needed new supplies, Fuller cooked them up fresh. In international operations, achieving that closeness also meant an emphasis on developing managers and salespeople from the country or region that has made Fuller a model of culturally sensitive operations.

But in the late 1970s, an extensive strategic planning process convinced Tony Andersen that Fuller had reached a point where its own decentralized structure was standing in the way of growth—and could, in fact, make it vulnerable to competitors, most of whom are many times larger. So, beginning in 1982, Fuller restructured itself to focus on customer needs at the industry or market level. Production was shifted from smaller local plants to larger regional facilities, and the number of products was consolidated by as much as half in some categories to gain efficiencies from standardization.

Change on that scale can be disconcerting, both for customers and employees. Fuller, which prides itself on annual turnover of less than 5 percent, kept communications open and made sure change was clearly explained. It also minimized disruptions as much as possible, in some cases taking advantage of opportunities presented by change itself. Rather than closing down the smaller plants, for example, Fuller converted them into an expanded network of technical centers that enables it to continue to keep close, personal working relationships with customers while it integrates production on a larger scale.

Fuller's uncommon corporate mindset and customer-focused manufacturing activities make it a truly exemplary service company. That's clearly a source of pride for Fuller's people, from frontline sales to chemistry labs to secretarial support. And customers benefit accordingly.

"They [employees] have reason to feel good about themselves and the company they work for," Elmer Andersen observed a few years ago. "In a company where product quality is poor and where the customer is being cheated, employees feel ashamed that they have to be involved in such a way to make a living. Pride in one's work and in the company is a great benefit to the company. . . . The ideal of customer service is precious. People will cherish other people who try to serve the customer first."

H. B. Fuller Company
2400 Energy Park Drive
St. Paul, MN 55108

Pioneer Hi-Bred International

WHEN *THE LONG LOOK*, PIONEER HI-BRED INTERNATIONAL'S STATEMENT OF BUSI-
ness philosophy, was written back in 1952, the company sold only two
products: hybrid seed corn and egg-layers. The poultry side of the business is long gone, but seeds (not just corn, but alfalfa, sorghum, soy-
beans, sunflowers, and wheat) have made Pioneer an international
pacesetter in the Green Revolution that has brought improved farm
performance and human nutrition the world over. Through it all, Pioneer
has remained loyal to a rare commitment to make sure the products it
sells and the services it provides increase the efficiency of its customers.
Toward that end, it has become far more than a seed company. It's a
full-service biotechnology firm whose customers have access to the best
modern agricultural science has to offer.

In a world where corporate mission statements make attractive wall-
hangings for the headquarters lobby, Pioneer's is nothing extraordinary to
read through. It outlines three basic commitments: developing new products through extensive research; developing company and industry leadership from within; and working on problems and products "which may
very well be critical to sustaining mankind in the future." It comes with
four operating policies, three of which—trying to produce the best products on the market; trying to deal honestly and fairly with employees,
sales representatives, business associates, customers, and stockholders;
and trying to advertise and sell products without misrepresentation—would
look good in any corporate ethics textbook.

But the fourth one is a little out of the ordinary. And in its light, the
others take on a certain luster: "We try to give helpful management
suggestions to our customers to assist them in making the greatest possible profit from our products." Judging from the evidence visible in farm
fields all over the world, as well as the annual corporate harvest on the
bottom line, how it works is very, very well indeed.

Pioneer got its start in 1926, the outgrowth of Henry Wallace's experiments on hybrid corn dating back to 1913. So seriously is the research
side of the business taken that Pioneer people enjoy recalling the waggish

charges of founder Wallace's contemporaries, who maintained he was only selling seed to fund more research.

But those living laboratory developments could never have realized their full potential without tireless efforts to educate the customers who must buy, plant, raise, and harvest their results. Not only was Pioneer the first company to breed and produce hybrid seed corn, it also has long been a pacesetter in helping farmers the world over benefit from its scientific advances.

The scale of operation is impressive. A network of more than 50 research stations, including 27 corn-breeding stations, across North America; 18 more internationally. Yield trials in progress at more than 250 locations throughout the U.S. and Canada, many of them located on the farms of its customers (some of whom double as Pioneer sales representatives). A staff of about 50 argronomists whose expertise and counsel on everything from market conditions to pest management is made available at no charge to Pioneer customers.

Customer education is vital to the business. When the new corn hybrid designated 3780 debuted in 1973, for example, farmers' confidence in hybrids had been shaken by a drought and brief autumn that had depressed yields from a competitor's top-selling strain. People at Pioneer, reported *Agri Marketing* magazine in 1988, knew how good the new hybrid was, but their customers didn't.

To get the information out and, in the process, counter skepticism in the fields, Pioneer put weigh wagons (grain wagons with a self-contained scale built in) into every sales district. The sales representatives could take the wagons straight to a farmer's fields so corn harvested from equal areas of different hybrids could be judged immediately. The results of thousands of side-by-side comparisons were made available to local newspapers, and the numbers made the case better and more convincingly than any advertising or promotional program could have.

As this vignette illustrates, despite the company's worldwide size and scope, Pioneer's emphasis is local. Chances are the Pioneer corn hybrids a farmer plants, whether his land is in Iowa or Argentina, were produced on a farm within miles of his fields. Before he buys, the farmer has the option of stopping by throughout the growing season to make his own firsthand observations and comparisons. Independent farmers work part-time for Pioneer as combination field testers and sales representatives. They not only sell seed, they serve as mentors and business advisers, offering general assistance on business matters and firsthand information on the best ways to plan, plant, and fertilize the seed variety.

Furthering that local emphasis, Pioneer contracts with farmers in each region to produce hybrid seed corn for sale in their specific part of the country. A seed conditioning plant and warehouse will be nearby, reducing transportation time and spoilage, and assuring a fast response to regionally specific changes and needs. Around that base, sales representatives concentrate their efforts in areas roughly ten miles square, which ensures that they're dealing mostly with their neighbors and friends. Backing up *their* efforts is the team of experienced agronomists.

The agronomists are that extra step that elevates a company that produces products to one that also provides services. Through the expertise available, family farmers and managers of large-scale farms alike can gain access to information and advice that helps them get the highest yields from their crops and the best results from their agribusiness operations.

The key to the program from the customer's standpoint is its local focus. What works in Idaho may not—probably will not—work quite the same way in Georgia. Pioneer's agronomists are specialists in the growing conditions of specific regions. They meet with customers individually, both in countless town meetings and by literally walking their fields. They provide interviews and commentary broadcast by radio stations throughout the Farm Belt. They send out timely publications and even their own localized newsletters with information timed to the growing season and changing weather and market conditions.

The high touch is backed by high tech—an increasingly important aspect of modern agricultural operations. Pioneer has become a source of software as well as seed. Proprietary programs now help farmers manage their finances, track equipment maintenance and tax payments, forecast returns on various crop plantings, and gain insight into changing market and climatic conditions. Pioneer information-management systems are also used by farm managers, agricultural banks, and feed suppliers in the twenty-five major crop-producing states.

In 1986, Pioneer debuted Agribusiness USA, an on-line data base of more than three hundred journals and periodicals devoted exclusively to the information needs of agribusinesses. Each interview prepared for broadcast on farm radio stations is abstracted and available through the service. So, too, are weekly crop-condition summaries and market advisories. Pest-management reports from experiment stations at major agricultural universities are accessible, as are reports from the U.S. Department of Agriculture.

Through carefully managed genetic improvements to seed stocks, especially since the 1950s, agricultural scientists at Pioneer and other agribusinesses worldwide have transformed agriculture. They've developed strains for the specific soil and weather conditions of distinct geographic regions, plants better able to cope with diseases and insects. They've worked with farmers to improve business as well as crop management practices. They've also helped raise corn yields by an average of 1.4 bushels per acre *per year* over the past half-century. At Pioneer, the best part of the story is the uncommon way its people have made sure that farmers the world over can profit from those advances.

Pioneer Hi-Bred International, Inc.
400 Locust Street
Des Moines, IA 50309

Armstrong World Industries

(A)rmstrong

CONSIDER A SIMPLE LITTLE SERVICE WRINKLE THAT SPRINGS FROM ONE PRODUCT line among the many manufactured and marketed by Armstrong World Industries of Lancaster, Pennsylvania. It involves "resilient, no-wax" vinyl flooring, the modern-day descendant of the linoleum formerly sold by the roll for high-traffic floor areas. It shows how even the most basic of consumer products can be enhanced and improved by the addition of a well-designed service component.

Armstrong is a leading manufacturer of furniture, carpeting, and floor and ceiling products, including both rolled and tile products designed for busy families and do-it-yourself home remodelers. Since the introduction of the no-wax product line, the company has tracked periodic calls and complaints from frustrated customers who seemed to assume that no-wax meant no care was required, only to find their once bright and shiny floors dulling over time. Even though detailed care instructions were available through dealers and packed in with the products, it was obvious the word just wasn't getting through. The result was unhappy customers.

In 1983, someone at Armstrong hit on a simple solution: Why not create a way for customers to call a toll-free service center when their no-wax floor was still bright and shiny—like when it was brand new? That way, Armstrong could pass along the proper care instructions, answer the customer's questions—and take an extra moment to personally say thanks for the business.

But how do you get people to call the number? If they wanted help in the first place, they no doubt would have asked for it. If they didn't ask right away, they probably had filed the care instructions with all the other receipts, brochures, and product literature that tend to accumulate in inaccessible places over time.

Armstrong's stroke of service genius was simple, direct, and wondrously effective. It applies an easily removable ink right over the pattern on its various styles of rolled vinyl flooring; the message instructs the customer to call the 800-number printed on the product for information on the proper way to care for the new floor. (For those who can't be bothered

466

with a little more information, the instructions also confide that the ink can be removed with warm water.) Once the consumer calls, the trained customer service representative on the other end of the line can provide all manner of helpful information and advice, and even send literature on additional products.

Since the program debuted, the number of complaints from customers has been reduced from a primary irritant to a minor blip on the graph. In 1987 alone, more than 37,000 customers called to take advantage of the service. That means 37,000 satisfied customers. The system may be simple, but it works.

Though this sharp little service innovation is of very recent vintage, it fits in nicely with Armstrong's traditional high regard for the consumers of its products—and the wholesalers and retailers who sell those products to consumers. The company's first national ad (1917 in the *Saturday Evening Post*) provided interior design ideas that people could use in their homes. As early as 1923, Armstrong was bringing linoleum installers into Lancaster for training designed to help them install the product correctly and learn to be better businesspeople in the process.

The same 800-number inked onto Armstrong flooring is used for far more than a few floor-care and cleaning tips. Armstrong's consumer affairs people personally answered more than 290,000 phone inquiries in 1987 alone, plus another 600,000 pieces of mail. Of those nearly 900,000 customer contacts, only 4 percent involved complaints. The others represented requests for product information, dealer locations, do-it-yourself instructions, even decorating ideas.

To respond effectively, Armstrong's service representatives are available twelve hours a day—generally from 8:30 in the morning to 5 in the evening, regardless of the caller's time zone. In many cases, the twelve-hour shift is job-shared by three people, each of whom works four hours a day, and each of whom has been trained to field questions across the full Armstrong product spectrum. The short shifts keep operators fresh and provide satisfying jobs for people who don't choose to work full-time.

From continuing statistical analysis, Armstrong knows that most contacts are "presale"—that is, made while the consumer is still a *potential* customer. That, according to Andy Armstrong (the last member of the founding family), who directs the consumer affairs effort, is a prime reason for Armstrong's extensive commitment to the service. It's one more point of contact with customers who are making purchase decisions, he points out, and hence one more opportunity to demonstrate Armstrong's commitment to customer satisfaction.

Actually, that's not quite correct. Chairman and president William Adams, who took the helm in 1988, is on record as saying that Armstrong doesn't want its customers to be "satisfied." It wants them to be "delighted."

Consequently, in addition to responding, quickly and helpfully, to each person who calls or writes, Armstrong's people also track them, analyze them, cross-reference them, and communicate their inclinations and interests to product planners and field salespeople. The company also has used the market intelligence generated to open up and reinforce productive communications with architects, builders, and designers who might choose or specify its products in their activities.

One outgrowth of this continuing customer analysis is the development of model Floor Fashion Center showrooms that combine product samples, consumer information, and a computer-controlled laser videodisc player, the last programmed to be operated by shoppers and provide answers to their most frequently asked questions about purchasing vinyl flooring. More than five hundred of the upgraded showrooms have been leased to retailers since the new format was introduced.

To support the wholesalers and retailers who market its products to the public, Armstrong still provides a constant series of training programs designed not to push its particular product lines but rather to help them run their businesses more effectively. Wholesaler sales managers get training in people management skills, credit managers in cash management tools and effective ways for the back office departments to work with frontline people. Their top management can take advantage of courses in personnel management and the importance and influence of top-down activities in maintaining a productive corporate culture.

For retailers, a Marketing Development Center—continuing a tradition that dates back to 1933, when Armstrong sent merchandising "road shows" cross country to help merchants run their businesses better—provides information on Armstrong's continuing research and experimentation in the areas of store-level packaging, lighting, display design and arrangement, self-help instructions, and other consumer-oriented sales tactics. And installers of resilient flooring and ceiling materials are still passing through Lancaster (and other regional training centers) to polish their installation skills.

It all seems to work together in noteworthy fashion. As Andy Armstrong relates, the 800-number inked on to resilient vinyl flooring has done far more than provide a positive alternative to telling a consumer she's a poor housekeeper because she doesn't know how to take care of her floors. It also has provided insight into customer expectations and evolving lifestyles, while demonstrating to dealers that Armstrong stands behind its products.

That, in turn, has made dealers more aware of the care instructions they can provide to customers in their stores and showrooms, further assuring that the product is used and cared for properly. And it has buoyed customer satisfaction, because when the product is used and cared for properly, it looks better and lasts longer, which makes the customer feel better about the purchase—and about the people who made and sold the product.

Armstrong's innovative method of adding value to even the most basic of household products shows how pervasive an advantage service can be in the new American economy. It also demonstrates how well-known, well-established companies can stay on top of their customers' ever-changing needs and expectations, in the process further enhancing their business reputation for providing quality products and services.

Armstrong World Industries, Inc.
West Liberty Street
Lancaster, PA 17604

BUSINESS-TO-BUSINESS

DELIVERY

Federal Express Corporation

United Parcel Service

Sun Distributors

EXPERTISE

Dun & Bradstreet Corporation

Battelle Memorial Institute

Shop'n Chek

DUPLICATING

Quad/Graphics

Xerox

Kinko's

SUPPORT

Safety-Kleen Corporation

Miller Business Systems

ServiceMaster

Business-to-Business Service:
The Bottom Part of the Iceberg

THE BUSINESS OF BUSINESS IS BUSINESS. WALK DOWN THE AISLE OF A CHICAGO-New York shuttle flight—or one between San Francisco and Los Angeles or Atlanta and Miami, for that matter—and ask the passengers, the ones in suits and ties, where they are going and what for. It's a pretty good bet that 80 percent of them will tell you they work for Company ABC and are calling on Company XYZ. Most businesses are in the business of providing goods and services to other businesses.

And as the business world becomes ever more complicated and more tightly interlocked, the quality of the business-to-business relationship becomes ever more important. Price, quality, and service—being well worth doing business with *and* being easy to do business with—are the criteria, with quality and service rapidly becoming the most sensitive of those measures.

There have always been business-to-business service providers. Banks held funds, collected funds, transferred funds, and lent funds to businesses long before they ever discovered consumers. The transcontinental railroads served commerce first, passengers second—and they still do. When "Ryder rents trucks," it rents them mostly to businesses.

Run down the roster of professions. Sure enough, most serve businesses. Architects, computer programmers, clothing designers, management consultants, market researchers, attorneys, accountants—the list is endless.

The newest wrinkle these days is the growing number of business-to-business and professional services that organizations are finding can be better provided by another business—by renting, rather than owning. Companies that once had their own salaried security guards now "rent a cop" from a security firm. Businesses that once invoiced and collected their own accounts, prepared their own payrolls, conducted their own training, or replaced their own vacationing employees now routinely call in another company that specializes in providing as much or as little of that particular product or service as they need.

A decade ago, if you wanted your hospital floors cleaned, needed food prepared for the company cafeteria, or had to add employees to handle a new project, you called personnel and started hiring. Today, you're more likely to call a specialized cleaning service, a caterer, or a "temp" firm with a pool of talented professionals who will work for you as long as you need them, then go away when your need is satisfied. And some of the most common and necessary of today's profitably vended services didn't exist as services at all just a few short years ago. Fifteen years ago businesses didn't have any idea they needed next-day delivery service; now it's a rare business that doesn't rely heavily on overnight delivery by the $5 billion small-package delivery industry.

More, and Better

The last two decades have seen a dramatic improvement in the quality as well as a dramatic increase in the quantity of business-to-business services. From computer maintenance to specialized printing to customized communications, a whole subculture of business support services has grown up around activities that are largely invisible to the public at large, but whose impact is felt indirectly by everyone in America. For all the talk about "low bidding," surveys have consistently shown that service is the more important criterion in selecting vendors.

Some are born great. Others work hard to become so. The business-to-business arena is one such place. In addition to companies whose superb service elevates them from the rest of the pack, there's a new group of fast-growing vendors to whom service, to paraphrase the late Vince Lombardi, isn't the main thing—it's the only thing. In some cases, these service companies come up with solutions to other companies' headaches. Typical is ServiceMaster, the largest contract management firm in the health care industry. Its founders realized that overhead costs were disproportionately expensive for small health care facilities, so they created a program to provide almost all aspects of hospital management more cost-efficiently than a small organization could by doing everything itself. Now they've branched out to other fields.

Other successful business-to-business service vendors perceive a need before anyone else does. If you had polled business leaders twenty years ago and asked whether it would be worth twenty dollars to ship a package across country in one day, the answer probably would have been, "Maybe, once in a while." But once Federal Express launched its high-tech, here-today-there-tomorrow service, businesses found they couldn't live without it. Next-day delivery permitted vendors to service out-of-town customers unavailable to them before. It enabled dramatic growth in the direct-mail business.

Before next-day delivery, for example, you might buy personal knick-knacks by mail, maybe even a small tape recorder. But buy an expensive personal computer, when you'd have to ship it across the country for warranty service? Never. These days, companies such as Texas-based Dell Computer Corporation and New Hampshire-based MacConnection are running multi-million-dollar direct-mail businesses based primarily on their ability to deliver a low-priced, highly reliable product anywhere in the U.S. in a day or two. Customers have learned to expect direct-mail vendors' delivery and warranty service to be provided almost as quickly as going down to their local dealer—maybe faster, because the dealer often sends the unit to the factory anyway.

What one can do, many can do. Federal Express may be the leader, but it's not the only player in the fast-moving overnight delivery field. DHL, Emery, Purolator, and the air freight divisions of the major airlines are all able competitors, and even Greyhound promotes its buses as a way to deliver packages as well as travelers. Meanwhile, United Parcel Service, which virtually wiped out the Post Office's parcel post system by providing better service at lower cost, has introduced a low-cost next-day service.

A service most companies could scarcely do without today is the temporary help business. As legislative fiat and court decisions have made hiring full-time employees a more expensive proposition, temp services have quickly stepped in to make it easier for companies to avoid some of the hassles of hiring while still covering their staffing needs. The industry's growth has been nothing short of meteoric in recent years. Billings for temporary help increased an average of 19 percent per year from 1975 to 1985. The number of temporary workers grew 75 percent from 1980 to 1986.

The fastest-growing segment of temporary help is in the professions. While clerical workers and day laborers still constitute the majority of temp hires, there are hundreds of other types of professionals readily available, including doctors, lawyers, engineers, programmers, accountants, and even corporate managers. The more successful temp services go a step past just testing and calling in temps on demand; they have introduced extensive training programs, especially in word processing, to make sure their temps go on the job already qualified to run customers' hardware and software.

Knowledge Is Power—and Money

As John Naisbitt has long since pointed out, we're not only a service economy, but an information economy. A rapidly growing number of companies are finding that easy and rapid delivery of information is a way to deliver solid profits. Dun & Bradstreet, which has been collecting information on American businesses for almost a century, is a master at repackaging its information in various ways to provide businesses more, and more profitable, information.

Lockhead created Dialog as an on-line service that permits scanning of hundreds of data bases from anywhere in the country. Searching to see if a proposed trademark is clear used to require a D.C.-based patent-and-trademark lawyer and several days' delay, not to mention some big dollars. Now a librarian with a personal computer can search Dialog's Tradesmarkscan, sifting through six hundred thousand entries in thirty seconds for the price of a Big Mac or two. Similarly, the Dow Jones News Service provides an on-line data base that lets companies find out reams of general and financial information on competitors, prospective clients, even merger targets—all within minutes.

Then there are the "hired guns" of the knowledge trade, researchers for rent. The Battelle Memorial Institute's collection of researcher scientists has made significant contributions to the physical and social sciences, not on their own behalf, but for clients who hire their expertise.

Sharper attention to service is also revolutionizing the way very traditional businesses do business with other businesses. Take printing. Technological change in the printing industry has been glacial until very recently. From Gutenberg in the fifteenth century until the end of the nineteenth century, type was set the same way—by hand. After the Linotype machine was developed in the 1890s, it was used almost unchanged for another sixty years. In the last ten years, however, computerized typesetting has all but replaced the clattering linotypes. And that technology, in turn, is being supplanted by desktop publishing and microcomputer-controlled typesetting. In the aftermath of the revolutionizing technology, however, printers are essentially right back where they started from—all using the same type of equipment. Overcapacity is the rule worldwide.

As should have been obvious all along, the only competitive edge available is service quality. Yet printing is an industry where many clients constantly bemoan the absence of good service. Those printers who are determined to provide superb service tend to be successful. One, Quad/Graphics, is so determined that it sends its own customers to "camp" to learn the intricacies and capabilities of modern printing technology. That makes them better customers, and Quad/Graphics profits accordingly.

Serving Those Who Also Serve

Throughout the service 101—not just in this chapter—you can find businesses that serve primarily other businesses: AMP, American Management Systems, 3M, H. B. Fuller, Deluxe, Bergen Brunswig, Shared Medical, Goldman Sachs, NW Transport, Super Valu, Frito-Lay, Ryder. In the main, we've tried to place them according to their industry specialties or unique operating profiles. They could as easily have been considered here—but then this section would have grown beyond manageable proportions.

Among the dozen companies we profile here, we've again gathered exemplars by commonalities, however tenuous. There are three who specialize in delivery (some would say "deliverance"): Federal Express and UPS, plus Sun Distributors. Three more have expertise as a common bond: Dun & Bradstreet in business data, Battelle in scientific areas, and Shop'n Chek in helping another business figure out how well its customers are being treated.

A third trio comes under the umbrella of duplicating: Quad/Graphics is a printer, Xerox sells—and services—copy machines and other office electronics products, and Kinko's runs busy copy centers that feature not just photocopiers but also laser printers and even photographic minilabs. The final three specialize in supporting other businesses: Safety-Kleen by handling the environmentally sensitive yuck that's a by-product of conventional businesses from auto repair shops to dry cleaners; Miller Business Systems by stocking and selling pens and pencils, and office supplies, and office furniture, and designs for that furniture; and ServiceMaster, the industrial clean-up master that continues to evolve into new areas while remaining true to a strong internal ethic.

In every case, their business depends on the success of the businesses they serve—and in their own unique ways, their service contributes to that success.

Federal Express Corporation

FIFTEEN YEARS.

That's as long as Federal Express has existed—just a decade and a half. Before that, no one worried much about how long it took to get a package from one place to another. And certainly no one thought there was a business to be built and a fortune to be earned in charging far more money than Uncle Sam's minions for a level of service that people, especially businesspeople, didn't even know they wanted.

But to Frederick W. Smith, a former Marine Corps pilot in the Vietnam War years, overnight delivery was not only technically feasible, it was eminently desirable. In the bustling Information Age, when microchips and manuscripts were beginning to be viewed with the same importance as machinery, Smith reasoned there was a niche to be found for a company that could "absolutely, positively" get something, anything, somewhere else overnight.

The idea dates back to his student days at Yale in the mid-sixties, where legend has it that Smith earned a *C* for an economics paper outlining a business that combined private planes and a fleet of delivery vans. After two tours in Vietnam, he came home and decided to personally bankroll his idea with the $4 million he had inherited from his father. He raised $72 million in venture capital to launch the business. (Federal Express trivia: The company actually began operations in Little Rock, Arkansas, moving to Memphis is 1973.) He stuck with it, and convinced others to, while his fledgling enterprise was running up $27 million in losses in its first twenty-four months of operation.

You know how it turned out. The marketplace vindicated his service vision. By 1976, FedEx was in the black. In 1985 it flew through the $2 billion mark in annual revenues. It's still the standard by which competitors are judged. As James Barksdale, the company's chief operating officer, told *U.S. News & World Report* a few years ago, "People are so unaccustomed to very good service that when they see it they are dazzled by it."

And it's still the clear leader in service quality. In *Distribution* maga-

477

zine's annual "Quest for Quality" rankings in 1987, the average air express carrier earned ratings of 3.65 (on a 5-point scale) for service and 3.53 for convenience. Federal Express' ratings were a phenomenal 4.44 and 4.21 respectively; well-regarded United Parcel Service was a distant second in each category at 3.86 and 3.77.

When *Consumer Reports* compared air and ground delivery services just before Christmas in 1986, it had its shoppers call for package pickup on December 22. "Federal Express," it noted, "made a perfect showing— never late. The other couriers missed their two-day deadline on one to three deliveries." What's more, the magazine reported, the company excelled at picking them up as well as laying them down: "Federal Express was quickest [at picking up packages] by a couple of hours, on average, and never failed to show up." The other three courier services tested each made at least one of the magazine's shoppers "wait all day in vain."

The stage for Federal Express's success was set with Smith's decision to base the business at Memphis International Airport. Why Memphis? For one, because it's centrally located, within six hundred miles of two thirds of the country's population. It also was largely deserted from midnight to dawn, which meant incoming and outbound aircraft wouldn't be delayed or stacked up in holding patterns. But more importantly Memphis was ideal because to guarantee reliability for a business that depended on airplanes meant making sure those planes had a place to fly into and out of that wasn't going to be regularly socked in by fog or shut down by seasonal weather disruptions. Memphis International gets about ten hours of fog a *year*.

Memphis also gets an average of 65 Federal Express flights a night from a fleet of about 200 planes (about half long-haul jets, half short-hop Cessnas). Most arrive and depart between the hours of eleven P.M., when packages start coming in from all over the country, and four A.M., by which time most FedEx planes have been unloaded, serviced, reloaded with packages that are routed with better than 99-percent accuracy, and sent on their way to cities around the country.

The nightly unload-sort-reload process involves more than 4,000 workers, a million-square-foot, automated complex with approximately 18 football fields' worth of space under its roof, and more than 60 miles of conveyor belts. About 700,000 packages a day pass through Memphis on the hub-and-spoke system Smith copied from the military (and which other air carriers of both commercial passengers and air cargo have since copied for their own operations). That's nowhere near capacity, but it is an amazing expansion from the 50,000 packages the facility was processing when it first opened in 1978.

These days, smaller hubs are up and running in Oakland, California, and Newark, New Jersey, which means that about 30 percent of Federal

Express's volume now bypasses Memphis completely. Brussels, Belgium, is the heart of its growing European operations.

Waiting at airports around the country are Federal Express' fleet of more than sixteen thousand computer- and radio-dispatched delivery vans, each one primed to handle the day's incoming deliveries by 10:30 A.M. Using sophisticated scanners, computer terminals, and on-line information systems, Federal Express drivers can manage their time and routes efficiently and accurately. One by-product of the computers: Drivers can be made aware of overdue accounts and special delivery conditions. The same system allows customers to find out where their packages are within thirty minutes. If FedEx can't find it in thirty minutes, it's delivered free.

But technology isn't the real story behind Federal Express. It's people. In fact, the company's motto is "People, service and profits"—and the order of priorities is no accident. From its very earliest days, Federal Express has placed a premium on hiring, training, and retaining good people. It encourages everyone from the college students who work their way through school sorting packages in Memphis each night to the delivery drivers and staff support people out in the field to take a proprietary interest in their work. It backs that with an uncommon openness and flexibility.

For example, a few years ago, as volume grew in the Memphis superhub, Federal Express confronted a strange challenge to its ability to sort and redirect packages on time. It noticed that things were constantly getting backed up, and no control system seemed able to cope. On further investigation, the company discovered that its workers, mostly part-time college students, had discovered that there was an economic benefit to working more hours—and they were stretching the work accordingly. Rather than a draconian crackdown, Federal Express simply gave them a minimum daily guarantee and announced that those who got done early could leave early, yet would still be paid for the full shift. Inside forty-five days, things were running ahead of schedule. By "beating the system," Federal Express' workers were making the system work better than ever.

They make other systems work, too. Over the years, they've pulled victims from an airplane crash, hunted among thousands of packages for an urgently needed mislabeled one, and spent off-duty hours tracking down a mystery address. These activities aren't found anywhere in the job descriptions of Federal Express employees, but they've tackled them nonetheless. And the company finds various ways to reward this "above and beyond" service while helping employees build a stake in the company.

The Golden Falcon award, for example, is given to employees for notable, even dramatic, achievements, whether on or off the job. It's a direct result of a customer commenting on the service delivered by an employee. Local managers forward customer comments and letters to

Smith and Barksdale, who in turn pass them along to a review committee, which determines those deserving of notice.

Some Golden Falcon winners perform truly heroic acts, like the workers who showed up to help victims after a plane crashed near the Dallas airport a couple of years ago. Other achievements are more directly related to service, like the one involving a courier who spent his personal time tracking down the correct destination for a package from which the shipper had inadvertently omitted the address. The shipper's business had closed for the day, yet the employee managed to track down the correct delivery address, no doubt with the gratitude of the recipients—the package contained the company's payroll.

There's no limit to the number of employees who can win Golden Falcon awards each year, but about eighteen is average. Winners receive a gold pin resembling the Falcon airplane that was a Federal Express workhorse in the early days. The pin can be worn on the employee's uniform as a visible statement to customers and employees alike. In addition, the winner receives an impromptu congratulatory phone call from the chief operating officer and recognition in the employee newsletter. More importantly, to tie it back to a stake in the company, each winner receives 10 shares of Federal Express stock (which was trading at about $44 a share in mid-1988).

A more frequent award is the Bravo Zulu. Named after the Navy signal that designates "well done," Bravo Zulu awards are instant feedback for employees who've gone the extra mile in internal activities, like the back-shop worker who learned and wrote a computer program without professional assistance while maintaining her regular job duties. Managers are given authority to award Bravo Zulu stickers and cash awards of varying amounts to their employees—one hundred dollars or a dinner out on the town are typical. Hundreds of Bravo Zulu awards will be handed out among Federal Express's fifty-eight thousand employees worldwide this year.

The result is a loyal, well-trained, highly motivated work force, paid better-than-average wages and constantly rewarded for meeting and exceeding the company's pacesetting service standards. Package sorters, for example, are expected to make less than one error per twenty-five hundred packages—some of Memphis's champs have been known to sort more than one hundred thousand packages without a mistake. Part-time workers earn benefits that are almost identical to those provided for full-time workers.

An enduring rule of thumb in a good service business is that systems should be transparent to customers. Example: Pick up the phone and dial the local number for Federal Express to schedule a pickup. Depending on where you're calling from, the person who answers that call will be in a regional center that could be several hundred miles away. Other companies would set up an 800-number and make a point of their toll-free largess. Federal Express understands the psychology of a transaction that depends on the customer having absolute confidence in the service to be delivered; it designed its systems accordingly.

If that's a fly-by-night business, Fred Smith will take it.

Federal Express Corporation
2005 Corporate Avenue
Memphis, TN 38132

United Parcel Service

IN ITS EARLY DAYS AS A MESSENGER SERVICE IN SEATTLE, THE COMPANY THAT is now known worldwide by its initials, UPS, was known to deliver everything from hot lunches to telegraph messages, and take on such odd-job assignments as walking someone's dog or escorting a blind man to a funeral, just to keep the fledgling business going. Founder Jim Casey's big break came in 1918, when three Seattle department stores contracted with the service he'd started eleven years previously (at the ripe old age of nineteen) to deliver merchandise to purchasers on the very same day they bought it in the stores.

These days UPS, which began serving consumers as well as business customers in 1953, delivers more packages than anybody, including the U.S. Postal Service, and it matches Uncle Sam's carriers in serving every address in every one of the fifty states. Despite the fact that the organization it considers its major competitor is subsidized and operates tax-free, UPS maintains that its customers—primarily business customers—have made their preference perfectly clear. In 1987, UPS handled 2.3 billion packages; the government's minions delivered 1.4 billion.

And while the Federal Express overnight-delivery air force outguns the company people call "Big Brown" by about three to one, UPS is number two with a bullet, its Next Day Air business building at 30 percent compared to about an 8 percent growth rate for its ground service, according to a *Fortune* magazine report in January of 1988.

"With net earnings of more than $700 million on $10 billion a year," *Fortune* noted, "it is far and away the most profitable U.S. transportation company. Competitors try to emulate the reliability of its service; customers applaud the steadiness of its prices—ground rates have increased only 6.5% since 1982; air rates have stayed the same since the company launched its overnight service more than five years ago. But what makes UPS stand out is its ability to attract, develop, and keep talented people. Top managers, most of whom have come up through the ranks, instill a spirit of winning so pervasive that people who fail are ranked as least best, not losers. Workers, in turn, have almost a Japanese-like identification with the company."

What gives privately held UPS its edge, in other words, what has made it the most admired transportation company in *Fortune's* annual corporate reputations' survey in each of the first four years in which that survey has been conducted, is a bedrock service culture. Others may have brighter colors, fancier technology, bigger advertising budgets. UPS has homely brown trucks loaded, driven, maintained, and supported by exceptionally dedicated people. And if you think unionized workers are incapable of playing a role in providing good service, consider that UPS drivers have been carrying Teamsters cards since Casey invited the brotherhood to organize his company back in 1916.

"Best service at low rates" is how the late Casey capsulized the business some eighty years ago. According to a test of eight package-delivery services during the 1986 Christmas rush, it's a valid description. *Consumer Reports* paired off sixty people in twenty-one states and had them send identical packages via eight different methods. Two (Parcel Post and Priority Mail) involved the Post Office. Two more were UPS's ground and air options. The other four competitors were Emery Worldwide, Federal Express, Greyhound Package Express, and Purolator Courier.

Over short distances (less than five hundred miles), the exercise showed that UPS offered the best service/price combination: Greyhound was a day faster, but at four times the cost; UPS was as fast as Priority Mail at half the price, and a day faster than comparably priced Parcel Post. At distances over five hundred miles, UPS ground service was a day slower than Priority Mail, but cost half as much; it was about twice as fast Parcel Post (and cheaper to boot) and as fast as Greyhound at one-fifth the price.

A similar situation turned up on two-day air service. UPS was on time and anywhere from 35 to 250 percent less expensive at either distance; most of the overnight services delivered overnight, even though two days was the all the speed they needed to provide to satisfy customers. The race is not always to the swiftest.

Since the test was run, UPS has greatly expanded its Next Day Air service. But it also has been in the midst of an uncommon customer-education program since 1985, one aimed at helping businesses determine the most cost-effective and reliable way to get things from Point A to Point B. Not every package that is sent overnight needs to be received the next day, the company reasons, even though next-day service is a comfortable money-maker for a carrier. Consequently, UPS offers its customers a Package Delivery Expense Analysis of inbound and outbound deliveries that is designed to identify cost savings in the level of service, movements within specific geographical regions, and price of service per weight of the package being sent.

In the first hundred such analyses, UPS identified potential savings ranging from as little as $2,200 a year to nearly $1 million annually. In all, it figures the delivery audit—which it provides free to customers willing to provide the internal data needed—has identified total potential savings in excess of $12 million since the service was first tested in 1985. That's money that UPS (and other overnight carriers) could easily realize as income—but at the expense of the quality of service the company promises.

What kind of company helps its customers keep their money? Not one concerned with maximizing short-term return or stuffing nickels into mutual funds, that's for sure. At UPS, however, the people who own and manage the company are the same people who do the work—approximately fifteen thousand managerial-level shareholders own almost all of the stock in the company, subject to a requirement that they must sell it back to the company when they leave or retire. That harks back to Casey's dictum that the business should be "owned by its managers and managed by its owners." One director described it to *Fortune* as an experiment in "managerial socialism." "We have no stars but many bright lights," chairman and CEO John Rogers told the magazine.

Whatever it is, the top-down culture makes UPS one of the most productive service businesses in the world. It works, and works well, despite relatively high wages (package sorters, mostly college students, start at about eight dollars an hour, full-time drivers—most of whom start out as part-time sorters—make about sixteen dollars an hour) and relatively labor-intensive processes. Those processes are carefully monitored: *Fortune* reported that supervisors can estimate to within six minutes how much time drivers will need on their daily routes, but it also noted that many who manage to do the job quicker still get paid for the time allotted to the route.

There's also ample room to improvise. On one otherwise normal night in 1987, a manager discovered that 160 Next Day packages had missed their connecting flights out of Louisville. Given that UPS delivers about half a million air express packages and 10 million surface-delivery parcels every day, 160 left behind doesn't sound like a major mistake. It did to the air operation manager, who promptly chartered half a dozen small Lear jets—at a cost in excess of $30,000—to make sure the packages got where they were supposed to be on time. Average revenue on the 160 packages: about $11 apiece.

That's the kind of service-hero story good service organizations seem to thrive on; and UPS is no exception. Getting the job done means getting it done right. Workers who don't perform don't last. Those who do know there are rewards: Managers can earn an average of $54,000 a year after ten years of service, augmented by another $20,000 or so in stock and dividends. Small wonder turnover among full-time workers is a minuscule 4 percent.

In recent years, UPS has been upgrading technology and adding air power to compete both on the ground and in the skies. The air hub at Louisville is growing, and regional air centers are being planned for the east and west coasts as well. On-board computers are being installed in its fleet of more than forty-seven thousand unobtrusive brown vans and cars. Scanners are showing up in sorting hubs strategically located to serve about a 400-mile radius, with contiguous regions interlocking coast to coast, plus Alaska and Hawaii. (Air service is provided to Canada, sixteen European countries, and Japan; ground service is offered in Canada and West Germany.)

By 1990, UPS hopes to have operations on-line from the delivery vans and cars to the distribution centers and regional hubs. Dispatchers will route drivers from one stop to the next through each vehicle's terminal. Drivers will carry electronic clipboards that will record delivery times and even customer signatures, and can be plugged into a computer and downloaded at the end of the day for record-keeping, billing, and traffic analysis.

But they'll probably keep the outside of the trucks painted brown.

United Parcel Service
51 Weaver Street
Greenwich, CT 06836

Sun Distributors

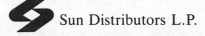 Sun Distributors L.P.

IN THE ARCANE, ACRONYMIC PARLANCE OF MODERN BUSINESS, A VAR IS A "value-added reseller," a company whose basic activity involves taking on any number of standard products, enhancing them with services specifically designed for customers in various niche markets, and then selling both products and services within those markets. As VARs go, the companies that together make up Sun Distributors are among the best.

Sun's stock in trade involves more than one hundred thousand different products sold nationwide through no fewer than fifteen subsidiary companies to customers ranging from original equipment manufacturers (called OEMs) to those serving replacement markets, plus construction firms and maintenance companies. Within Sun's inventory are glass products for automobiles and mirrors, electrical supplies such as light fixtures and cable, fluid power equipment for hydraulic and pneumatic systems, and maintenance supplies from nuts and bolts to chemicals and cleansers.

There's nothing special about the products. In fact, it's their very mundane nature that gives Sun its reason for being. For years, independent distributors have supplied these products to customers, typically with very little strategic thinking beyond price competition. But as manufacturing and other forms of business have become more complex, price alone is no longer a sole (or even most important) determining factor in picking suppliers.

That's where services can add value to the nuts and bolts and chemicals and supplies. For example, just-in-time processes (that's JIT, for acronym collectors) require sophistication off the assembly line as well as on it. Increasingly, companies are turning to VARs for parts and processes that help them do business better and most cost-effectively.

As *Forbes* reported in 1988, "Sun aims not so much to sell pumps and bolts as to sell the engineering and repair services that go with them and the ability to make specialized production runs on short notice. Sun . . . has caught the wave that is changing the U.S. from a manufacturing economy to a service economy. Nowadays the cost of making a bolt or a chemical or even a personal computer may be much less than the cost of keeping it in inventory, delivering it when and where it is needed and making sure it works. As a result, a good many manufacturers are switching to just-in-time manufacturing. This is good news for Sun."

Somewhere along the road to market, distributors handle more than half of the basic products used in American business and purchased by American consumers. Traditionally, they have been small firms that served only one market niche, which means their fortunes rose and fell with conditions in their marketplace.

Enter Sun. In ten years, it has grown by acquisition to become one of the ten largest industrial distributors in the country. It has done so by picking its spots carefully: A mix of entrepreneurial companies within four busy market segments, each with a culture of strong, customer-responsive management and a track record of enhancing basic products with innovative services.

Quality is the key: Sun isn't interested in turnarounds, or picking up lackluster performers just to add numerical growth. On the contrary, Sun provides internal systems support and deeper capitalization, then generally leaves well enough alone, figuring the same management that has been doing things well all along will continue to do so. Consequently, although Sun ranks among the largest industrial distributors in the country, with 1987 sales of more than $425 million and a total employment base of thirty-five hundred, its headquarters staff consists of just thirteen people—chairman and CEO Donald Marshall, four vice presidents, five accountants, and three secretaries for Sun's four operating groups: electrical, fluid power, glass, and maintenance products.

What's more, operating company presidents are never summoned to Philadelphia to report to top management. Instead, Marshall goes to them, and he spends time reinforcing the aspect of autonomy he deems critical to each company's continuing success. "We are selling some 100,000 different products to 120,000 customers across all 50 states," he told *Focus*, a Philadelphia-based business weekly, in 1987. "And the average sale is $250. What that means is that behind our nearly half-billion in annual sales are thousands of employees who've built years-long relationships with thousands of customers. The surest way to destroy all of that would be for corporate-level staff to travel out there imposing a 'generic' model of the distribution business on each of the divisions."

The Sun persona is so carefully downplayed that many customers may not even realize that the attentive, nearby distributor on whom they've come to rely is a member of a much larger family run as a master limited partnership. How do you know if you're doing business with a Sun distributor? Here's a quick look at the roster.

In the fluid power area, Sun companies include J. N. Fauver Company (based in Madison Heights, Michigan), Walter Norris (Chicago), Air-Draulics Company (Phoenix), and Warren Fluid Power (Denver). Each serves distinct geographic markets, providing products (pumps, hoses, valves, and fittings) used in powering and controlling mining machinery, farm and highway construction equipment, steel and chemical plants, and municipal water and sewage treatment facilities. They also add value to those products by offering services ranging from applications engineering and custom fabrication of small hydraulic and electronic systems to repairs for equipment and technical training for the people who operate it.

The glass products group is made up of Harding Glass (Kansas City, Missouri) and Downey Glass (Los Angeles). It also will probably eventually include the operations of Sun Glass, a Chicago-based start-up venture that is designed to grow into a national franchise serving the emerging market for automotive glass replacement.

Electrical products are supplied through American Electric (St. Joseph, Missouri), General Industrial Supply (Fort Worth, Texas), Keathley-Patterson Electric Company (North Little Rock, Arkansas), and Philips & Company (Columbia, Missouri).

On the maintenance supply side, sales and service are provided by Dorman Products (which will be relocating to Warsaw, Kentucky, just across the Ohio River from its current home in Cincinnati, in 1989), Specialty Metals (Lenexa, Kansas), Kar Products (Des Plaines, Illinois), Atlas Screw & Specialty Company (Elizabeth, New Jersey), and Hillman Fastener (Cincinnati).

Sun began in 1977 as a subsidiary of Sun Co., the Pennsylvania-based oil company whose most familiar entity is Sunoco. In 1986, Sun was spun off by its parent and became a master limited partnership, an operating structure of note more to tax accountants than customers. For the latter, the objective is to continue delivering the established level of good service that made each operating company in the family a success in its own right while adding all the administrative enhancements and support that those thirteen busy people in Philadelphia can provide.

Sun Distributors, L.P.
One Logan Square
Philadelphia, PA 19103

Dun & Bradstreet Corporation

D&B

IN A 1986 STORY, *BUSINESS WEEK* ASSIGNED MUCH OF THE CREDIT FOR DUN & Bradstreet's success to its chairman, Charles W. Moritz. "In particular," it noted, "Moritz emphasizes the need for everyone at D&B to serve customers. It is a lesson he learned well in his first job out of the Navy—selling cents-off coupons for what is today a D&B subsidiary [Reuben H. Donnelley]. He keeps a plaque on his desk that says, 'How will it help the customer?' And he meets monthly with small clusters of employees over coffee and rolls to spread the gospel of customer service."

Think of D&B as an information factory. Since the nineteenth century, it has been collecting, collating, analyzing, repackaging, and selling services derived from its data base of credit information on nine million businesses in some 30 countries. In addition, it provides business and credit information in 24 countries. In 1987, Harvard Business School professor James Heskett estimated that a potential competitor would spend $1 billion trying to duplicate that constantly growing asset.

There's more: a collection of other business lines and subsidiaries that all have information at their core. Its Donnelley publishing companies are a mainstay in the selling of advertising and the printing of Yellow Pages for phone companies coast to coast, just as Moody's Investors Service is an authoritative leader in providing analysis of publicly held companies and debt offerings. D&B also publishes the Official Airline Guides and sells travel-related services through Thomas Cook Travel. McCormack & Dodge builds and runs mainframe and minicomputer software programs that provide corporate financial services from salaries and benefits to payroll and personnel information. Dataquest provides market research information in heavy manufacturing and high-technology sectors of the economy.

D&B bought A. C. Nielsen in 1984 to add to its market research capabilities—everything from television ratings to the monitoring of purchases for supermarkets. Early in 1988 it added IMS, a company that specializes in medical publishing and does market research and sales-force evaluations for pharmaceutical companies.

In all, D&B's sixty thousand employees worldwide serve two million customers. That they do so profitably and professionally would be laudable even if their employer did not represent the sum of so many disparate parts. But it's that overall continuity in establishing a distinctive service culture that is even more exemplary.

Moritz credits a comment made at one of the morning kaffee klatsches for putting into words a universal way to express service that has since been applied in every division and at every level of the company. The question: "Where does my work go—and is it really important to anybody?"

As Moritz perceived it, the question was essentially another way of asking, "Who is my customer?" The questioner's work was going somewhere, but he didn't know where, or to whom. As a result, he had no way of knowing whether it was being judged good or bad, complete or flawed, useful or irrelevant. But if he *knew* who his customer was, whether within the company or on the outside, he could investigate, find out more about what was needed or wanted, determine what happened to his efforts next. That could help him improve the quality of his work—not to mention greatly enhance the satisfaction he could derive from the knowledge that it was being done well.

These days, says Moritz, the service imperative at Dun & Bradstreet is clear: "I believe as managers we have a moral obligation to be sure that no person that works for this corporation is unaware of where their work goes and why it is important." His oft-stated objective is for all Dun & Bradstreet employees to be able to express, in their own words and "from the heart," who their customer is. Everyone is expected to know where his or her work goes and why it's important.

In many cases, the customer turns out to be another part of Dun & Bradstreet. By design, each of the company's twenty-five divisions works jointly with at least one other division on projects such as data base and resource development, sales, technology transfer, and new product development. From 1983 through 1987, internal development efforts, both within and between divisions, produced more than seven hundred new products and services; in 1987, over $200 million—or about 7 percent of total corporate revenue—was reinvested in such efforts. That's R&D on a scale similar to that expected of high-tech scientific and electronic products firms.

Externally, in the colorful analysis of *Financial World* magazine in 1987, "Dun & Bradstreet operates like a giant beehive. An army of worker bees constantly gathers tiny pieces of information from clients and potential clients and feeds them to the queen bee, the D&B mainframe computers. When the queen has hatched still more ways to tumble those numbers, another army of bumblebees buzzes back to the field on a marketing mission, to fertilize the client flowers, as it were. The more uses a single fact can be put to, the more efficient and profitable the business becomes. Hence the relentless emphasis on 'customer focus.' "

That, by the way, is what Dun & Bradstreet calls its service-centered recognition program: the Customer Focus Award. It was created in 1987 to formally recognize and internally celebrate extraordinary and innovative business action, or a series of actions, that greatly exceeds the norm. All D&B employees are eligible, regardless of job title or geographic location, or whether their particular customers are internal or external.

Another aspect of keeping service quality and business confidence high comes from the variety of services D&B will not provide. Because some parts of the data base rely on information freely shared by closely held corporations in the interest of assessing commercial credit risk, the company carefully guards the uses to which that information can be put. Lawyers are barred from using information from the D&B data base in lawsuits. Government agencies, including the FBI and the IRS, are not allowed to use it to enforce laws. And unions can't tap it to prepare for collective bargaining and organizing efforts.

Yet for all the high-flying success Dun & Bradstreet has earned over the years, there's just no disguising the fact that much of what its people do every day is simply detail-conscious clerical work. The company may sell "information services," in other words, but that information has to be painstakingly collected, corrected, massaged, and managed to gain or retain its value in the marketplace.

Sometimes, the amount of sheer labor involved in good service goes unappreciated. For instance, in 1986 *Business Week* gave the company a B for profitability and growth, a B for its balance sheet and a B+ for shareholder value. It assigned a D for "efficiency." Sales per employee, it noted, were one-half the level produced at McGraw-Hill and one-third the productivity of the average worker at Dow Jones.

"We don't compare ourselves to them anyway," was D&B's nonchalant reply.

From Moritz (who once was heard to use the word "customer" 93 times in a one-hour conversation) on down, Dun & Bradstreet locks in on the one person without whom its business simply cannot continue, let alone thrive. To make the focus even clearer, some D&B divisions no longer use "Visitor" nametags. The reasoning: A visitor is an outsider, someone who doesn't belong, someone who's only a temporary concern— until he or she goes away.

Now the badges say "Customer." That means everyone who meets and greets them while they're inside a Dun & Bradstreet operation is thinking, "*That's* where my work goes. *That's* why my work is important."

Dun & Bradstreet Corporation
299 Park Avenue
New York, NY 10171

Battelle Memorial Institute

GORDON BATTELLE WAS NOT AN INVENTOR. HE HELD NO PATENTS, WROTE NO books, burned no midnight oil in the laboratory. But his legacy has played a role in everything from the photocopier in your office to the Universal Product Codes on the groceries you buy to the engineering safety system added by NASA in the aftermath of the space shuttle *Challenger*'s tragic ending.

Battelle's legacy is the Battelle Memorial Institute, the world's largest independent research organization—a scientific service center, if you will. Nearly two thousand government and business clients from all over the world—some of the latter industrial giants, others entrepreneurial firms too small to support their own major research divisions—employ Battelle's research and development services each year under individual and joint-venture contracts.

As a not-for-profit entity, Battelle's mission is almost purely research and development, a service that typically involves helping somebody else design and commercialize a new or existing technology. Each year, its researchers file nearly one hundred patent applications, but few of them, if any, will be commercialized under the Battelle name. Instead, they will be brought to market by client firms looking for new ways to apply technology to the challenges of modern life. The service Battelle provides to businesses and government agencies is the vital assistance needed to identify, evaluate, refine, and find a way to market or solve a problem with that promising new technology.

Gordon Battelle lived only 40 years. He died in 1923. He spent most of his years in the various steel businesses built and run by his father, John, around the family's home base in Columbus, Ohio. At one point, he helped nurture the commercialization of a process invented by a former college professor in Missouri to recover valuable chemicals from waste products generated in mining operations.

The experience left such a lasting impression that he inserted a clause in his will setting aside almost half of his estate for a memorial institute "for the purpose of education in connection with the encouragement of creative and research work and the making of discoveries and inventions in connection with the metallurgy of coal, iron, steel, zinc and their allied industries."

At the time of his death (from complications following a routine appendectomy), the idea of industrial research was just beginning to jell. In the early days of the new century, science meant inventing products, often in less than scientific ways. What was needed, noted President Herbert Hoover in 1929 (the year Battelle's legacy became a functioning research institute), was "highly equipped, definitely organized research, not the haphazard product of genius in the woodshed." That was pretty much what Battelle had in mind, too. He might have done the same thing himself, had fate not stepped in.

Sixty years later, the Battelle name stands for more than eighty-two hundred researchers, scientists, and support staffers spread from Columbus to Geneva, Switzerland. At any one time, more than five thousand separate projects worth more than $600 million are underway, their scope, objectives, and budgets set by clients in search of anything from a nonsplitting golfball cover to a way to recycle the plastics piling up in landfills the world over.

Battelle's services are loosely organized into three forms: technology development, technology commercialization, and technology management. In keeping with the original mission, client education and training are woven into all three. About half of Battelle's business results from taking some of its own ideas to businesses who might be able to commercialize them.

No matter where the idea starts, or ends, Battelle's basic systems are set up to respond smoothly to customer needs. Large customers, including government agencies from more than forty nations, typically come to Battelle with full-blown research contracts. Smaller firms and business clients in need of a quick response need merely set up a "task order agreement," an innovative contract system that prenegotiates general terms and conditions and then, once in place, serves as a streamlined template for initiating specific projects of any size. Under the system, a new research or testing program can be launched immediately, and on the basis of something as simple and customer-friendly as a phone call or telex.

One of the legendary customer stories at Battelle involves xerography, the dry heat-transfer technology that makes the modern photocopier an almost universal fixture in every business environment. Battelle scientists got involved in developing Chester Carlson's process in the waning days of World War II—after more than twenty companies turned him away. By December 1946, things were looking promising enough for Battelle to convince the Haloid Company to provide continuing support in exchange for the chance to commercialize the process. In the early 1960s, some of the Institute's 250 related patents were sold in exchange for stock in the company, which by then was known by a different name: Xerox Corporation.

Other evidence of Battelle R&D services are all around us. When the U.S. Treasury was looking for a way to reduce the cost of silver coins, Battelle research led to the sandwich-style copper-and-nickel dimes, quarters, and silver dollars in use today. In medicine, Battelle scientists developed a technique to bind the anticoagulant heparin to the surface of plastic materials used in surgery so complex operations like the repair of aortic aneurysms can be conducted without fear of blood clotting. In the office, that ubiquitous little bottle of white correction fluid began life in a Battelle lab.

Most of Battelle's services are still geared to manufacturers that rely on metallurgy (extracting metals from their ores, purifying them, and turning them into something useful). While most people think HIP is something you try to be, manufacturers know it as hot isostatic processing, a bonding and fabrication process that is becoming a principle technique in manufacturing high-tech alloys and ceramics. Developed at Battelle for the Atomic Energy Commission in 1955, HIP is increasingly being used to make complex-shaped parts and other products that were once impossible to fabricate.

As factory automation and better-managed production processes have become crucial to keeping U.S. industry competitive internationally, Battelle has contributed its share of enhanced computer-based services. To assist small manufacturing companies that specialize in creating and making complex parts and subassemblies for larger firms, Battelle developed a computer-integrated design system cited by *Business Week* as one of the "24 Outstanding Achievements of 1986." The Institute also developed a biotechnology software package that brings computer-aided design capabilities to genetic engineering.

For CTS, an Indiana-based manufacturer of electronic components, Battelle is not only developing the supervisory-control software system that will allow automation of several factory-floor production lines but also is responsible for integrating the control system into the company's new, fully automated manufacturing facility.

Increasingly, Battelle is operating as a common R&D shop for a number of manufacturing firms interested in working together to find solutions to common problems. For the auto industry, a multiclient study is underway to find out if adhesives can effectively replace rivets, screws, and welding in bonding metal and plastic parts together.

Perhaps nothing better illustrates the stature Battelle has achieved than the safety reporting system the Institute is devising under a contract from the National Aeronautics and Space Administration. After the death of seven astronauts aboard the *Challenger*, NASA turned to Battelle to devise a confidential system that would allow the agency's one hundred thousand employees to report potentially dangerous conditions or substandard components without risking their careers, and with confidence that substantive action, not bureaucratic foot-dragging, will result.

Not all Battelle projects involve products or production processes. *Cosmopolitan* magazine commissioned Battelle to conduct an in-depth study of demographic changes over the last fifty years and the way those changes have affected the lifestyles, attitudes, and consumer behavior of American women. The Federal Emergency Management Agency is distributing Battelle-developed safety and education programs to schools and communities in areas vulnerable to earthquake hazards.

Large or small, every client receives a detailed service-and-satisfaction questionnaire at the conclusion of its project; on it, the organization is asked to describe various factors related to the quality of the outcome and the processes and people involved along the way. Even though the unpredictable nature of R&D makes it hard to assess satisfaction, Battelle asks anyway—but it does so in the context of process and expectations, not outcomes. In other words, the research itself may not prove out. It may, in fact, establish that the process or product the client wants investigated won't do what it's supposed to do. But the client should feel that some advantage has come from the knowledge gained, and that its needs were fully and conscientiously attended to.

More than 70 percent of Battelle's industrial clients respond. Well over 90 percent consistently say the lab has met or exceeded their expectations.

Battelle Memorial Institute
505 King Avenue
Columbus, OH 43201

Shop'n Chek

shop'nchek.

AS YOU MAY HAVE NOTICED, A NUMBER OF THE COMPANIES THAT HAVE ESTAB-
lished a reputation for themselves as customer service leaders have left very
little to chance. They create a strategy of good service based on knowledge of what their customers want and what their markets will bear. They
develop systems and hire and empower frontline people in ways that
serve that strategy. And they make sure they are delivering a consistent,
competitive, customer-satisfying level of service, regardless of the business they happen to be in, by checking it out firsthand. Some run internal
audits. Some survey their customers. Some track the quantifiable aspects
of their business—percentage of orders filled inside time limits, shipments
delivered without damage or mistake, and so forth. A number use "secret
shoppers" or "mystery customers" to provide an outside, objective reading on service at the frontlines.

Audits, surveys, and measurements are pretty basic. But where do
mystery shoppers come from? They come from people like Carol Cherry,
president of Shop'n Chek, an Atlanta-based company with eighteen thousand undercover agents strategically stationed coast to coast, plus in
Canada, Puerto Rico, and the Virgin Islands. In the fifteen years since
she bought the customer-checking-service part of her former employer's
business, Cherry has been retained by more than 350 corporations, from
United Airlines and Maytag to Roy Rogers Restaurants and dealers in
Toyota's mid-Atlantic region. In frequencies ranging from single check
visits to saturation surveys requiring as many as three thousand national
visits a month, Shop'n Chek does exactly what its name implies: *shops* the
client's business unannounced, just as any other typical customer would,
and *checks* the service experienced against the service standard. It's an
organized, customer's-eye view of a business—a test employees never
know they're taking, even if they know one's to be given.

The service began in 1973 when Cherry, then twenty-five, went to work
for an inventory management and control service. The company's "Shop'n
Chek Division," she now confesses, consisted of a desk staffed by "a farm
girl from south Alabama." By 1974, the division was a separate company

checking everything from mobile home sales presentations to the effectiveness of in-store marketing of pianos and other musical instruments.

What she noticed was that there was a difference between the way a customer perceived performance and service and the way employees and their managers were prone to grade that service. When it came down to whose viewpoint should carry more weight, internal views often predominated—while customers took their business elsewhere.

A basic Shop'n Chek tenet is that no matter what its mystery shoppers find, it is not the employee's fault. "We're not Big Brother," she tells clients up front, refusing to deploy her field agents to act as spies attempting to catch someone in the act of doing something wrong. In Cherry's opinion, if an employee can't do what needs to be done, the fault lies with the people who hired and trained that person. Either they hired the wrong person for the job, or they haven't provided the proper training, tools, support, and empowerment to make that employee able to perform adequately. Sometimes, she adds, the job itself is designed in such a way that it can't be done right.

What Shop'n Chek *will* do is assess performance against standards that are determined by the client, sometimes lifted word for word out of the training manual that supposedly defines the right way to do something. The criteria-based field design is the difference between sending out miscellaneous people with no more valid standard of judgment than their own likes and dislikes (although on occasion clients have contracted with Shop'n Chek for just that kind of service) and deploying "professional" shoppers who can observe and report knowledgeably and in ways that will be meaningful for clients.

With literally thousands of experienced evaluators in its files—many of whom have been with the company more than five years, some going all the way back to the mid-seventies—Shop'n Chek can meet large-scale and finely detailed needs itself. When repeat visits to the same location must be made, for example, the large talent pool allows a fresh face to be sent in. No work is ever subcontracted.

The work can vary a great deal, however. Manufacturers who often have very little direct control over the way their products are sold at the retail level have used Shop'n Chek to evaluate the way their products are being presented—both in terms of physical setting and the knowledge and quality of the store's personnel. Restaurant chains have mystery shoppers in for lunch and dinner to evaluate the way operating standards for service, quality, and cleanliness are being met in individual properties. Banks and other financial institutions turn Shop'n Chek loose to evaluate the competence as well as the courtesy of their customer contact people.

Shop'n Chek recruits its mystery shoppers from all over the country, many of them recommended by current shoppers, sometimes also by past clients. They work part-time—Shop'n Chek has just 120 full-time employees, most of them in administration and data analysis—but that doesn't mean references aren't checked and educational and professional backgrounds scrutinized. Ninety percent of its shoppers have or are continuing their education beyond high school; more than 70 percent have completed two or more years of college, 40 percent have degrees, and nearly one Shop'n Chek shopper in twelve has a master's or doctorate.

Shoppers are paid as little as five dollars to as much as three hundred dollars for each visit they make, depending on the complexity of the service they must render. For a check visit to a fast-food restaurant, the typical shopper receives five to ten dollars plus the value of the meal. Normally, the clients let shoppers keep anything they buy valued at twenty dollars or less. The higher fee is earned by evaluating more expensive services—buying a car, for example, or returning to a store several times to haggle over the purchase of a major appliance. In those cases, the big-ticket merchandise is returned to the manufacturer.

Shoppers range in age from eighteen to seventy; most of them are between thirty and forty-five. About 60 percent are women. The spread is carefully maintained to allow clients to create customized teams of mystery shoppers. Shop'n Chek shoppers must agree to maintain their confidentiality and are requalified for each assignment. They are also trained in proper techniques, many of them through one-on-one mentoring with experienced shoppers who take them through Shop'n Chek's patient regimen of step-by-step review, follow-up, and verification. When needed, more intensive training may be provided through Shop'n Chek or the client.

If the job at hand is to visit outlets of a fast-food chain to observe food quality and counter service, Shop'n Chek will first make sure that its observers are truly objective: If they, or someone in their family, or one of their friends works for the restaurant chain, they will be eliminated for this assignment. If they've worked for another fast-food chain, their inclusion or exclusion will be at the client's discretion.

Similarly, Shop'n Chek will make sure they enjoy eating at fast-food restaurants and have no objections to the particular kind of fast food the client's operation serves. (In some cases, Shop'n Chek recommends that its clients control virtually every variable, all the way down to determining what the mystery shopper is to order.) Shop'n Chek also will disqualify potential mystery shoppers if they own or manage a business in the immediate area of the client's location, or know anyone who works at the location.

Each shopper is briefed on the client's business and the specific observations they are to make. A detailed survey form also is developed for each client, often using a point system that adds up to 100 so employees inside the organization will be able to understand quickly how they've done.

For some clients, Shop'n Chek will deliberately blow part of its cover: Clients using the Mystery Shopping Incentive Program let frontline employees know in advance that a mystery shopping team is going to be visiting soon and that prizes will be awarded for product presentations or service that meet certain standards. The identity of the shoppers and the time of their arrival stay a mystery until after the visit. Then, if the client so desires, the Shop'n Chek evaluator will reveal his or her identity and personally award the prize (with a written report going back to the client on exactly what transpired). Alternatively, the mystery shopper remains unidentified from the employee's perspective, meeting instead with the manager or another company official, who then presents the award.

With four divisions (manufacturing, fast food/restaurants, retail, and general service) and a growing body of experience, Cherry's company is in a unique position to assess customer service as it's being delivered at the frontline. From her vantage point in Atlanta, Cherry has seen increasing attention to service standards popping up in businesses ranging from automobile dealerships and restaurant chains to health care facilities and municipal government agencies.

If the news her shoppers turn up for clients isn't always good—if often, in fact, the service validates Tom Peters's pointed assessment that "service in America stinks"—she maintains that the willingness of so many companies to pay so much attention to finding out where they are and where they need to be bodes well for the business, and for the American consumer.

"Market research can give them the perception of who their customer is," she told us. "We give the facts about what their customer really experiences."

Shop'n Chek, Inc.
7616 Perimeter Center East
Atlanta, GA 30346

Quad/Graphics

AS NOTED IN *THE 100 BEST COMPANIES TO WORK FOR IN AMERICA*, HARRY R. Quadracci, founder of Quad/Graphics, has been known to talk about his ideas of doing business as "Theory Q." Employees are treated like partners. They all report to him, all thirty-five hundred of them (managers in the Theory Q world are called "mentors" and are expected to teach and lead rather than supervise), but are mostly responsible for their own work within their own press groups. They're encouraged to call him by his nickname, Larry. They also own a substantial part of the business in a style similar to the partnership arrangements in the law firms Quadracci, himself an attorney, was familiar with.

Customers are treated like VIPs, whether they're the print managers for the more than two hundred magazines and catalogs the company handles (from *Time*, *Newsweek*, and *U.S. News & World Report* to *Four Wheeler*, *Black Enterprise*, and *Mother Jones*)or small-business owners with one-time jobs in the plant. Either way, they're given the run of the place and encouraged to visit often. Quad/Graphics employees are accustomed to seeing strange faces on the plant floor at all hours. No matter how strange or out of the ordinary a request their customers might make, they'll deal with it. After all, they figure, the reason customers come to them in the first place is because they believe this Pewaukee (that's a suburb of *Mil*waukee)-based printing company can do things other companies can't or won't.

Quadracci is one of eleven cofounders, most of whom came from a more authoritarian Wisconsin printing company of two decades past. Two of them are also named Quadracci: Harry R., his father, who serves as chairman, and his brother Tom, vice president of manufacturing and president of Quad/Tech. Characteristically, Larry Quadracci explains the company's success as a result of "thinking small"—concentrating on the little things that lead to big success.

Almost from the beginning, for example, Quad/Graphics has operated on a novel three-day workweek: Employees work three twelve-hour shifts in the course of the week, plus every other Sunday (for which they're

501

paid double time), a system that allows the plant to stay up and running smoothly twenty-four hours a day (and boosts productivity about 20 percent over competitors in the process.)

There are no time clocks, no tightly written work rules or job classifications. But there are colorful popcorn wagons parked on the production floor for employees who get the munchies in the middle of a shift. Hourly workers wear blue uniforms (a clean one is provided daily) with their first names over the pocket. Managers wear blue uniforms with their surnames over the pocket. So much for hierarchy. One day each year, the company's managers take part in the annual Spring Fling (or "management by walking away," in *Inc.*'s analysis), a combination of off-site meetings and field trip to an art museum that leaves the plant completely under the direction and supervision of its frontline workers.

In essence, the aim is to build nothing less than "a company without walls." A 1987 report with that title notes that, like a child, a company takes on a life of its own: "What the whole becomes is determined by its most elemental parts: the knowledge, experience, ideas and sweat of individuals joined in the common enterprise. Like the humans from whom it evolves, the new life needs to be nurtured continually in soul and mind and body."

Larry Quadracci first went into the business in 1971 after the bitter labor negotiations he'd handled as manager of a Wisconsin printing company client convinced him there was an opportunity for a venture based on better-run, less-adversarial management. He backed his confidence in his employees-to-be with a second mortgage on his home. He also put his workers in production plants that used the best equipment that modern printing technology had to offer, a tradition that has been continued over the years.

Basic to Theory Q is a belief that knowledge and technology get better as they are shared and spread around (the corporate mission set before every employee is "to learn, to know, to improve and to teach"). Consequently, Quad/Tech, the service-oriented subsidiary company started in 1980 to create sophisticated control systems for pressroom and bindery operations, not only supports Quad/Graphics but also sells its expertise to other printing companies—in essence, Quad/Graphics' competitors.

Stories of responsiveness to customers abound, and they're constantly retold to reinforce the service culture. For example, in late July of 1987 the nation's attention was captured by Lieutenant Colonel Oliver North as he testified before a congressional investigating committee. To chronicle the story, *U.S. News & World Report* put together what turned out to be a 128-page, four-color, perfect-bound special edition.

As the story unfolded, pieces of the issue were sent to Pewaukee piecemeal. On Monday, July 20, Quad/Graphics still had not been given a final page count. The following day, paper was still being delivered to the loading dock. By Wednesday, two full truckloads of the finished publication were on the way to Los Angeles, the first wave of a print run of more than three hundred thousand copies that arrived in bookstores coast to coast while the story was still hotter than the mid-summer weather.

And then there's Camp/Quad, the two-and-a-half-day training program created in 1980 for Quad/Graphics' customers. "Camp" stands for Catalog And Magazine Production. It also accurately describes the breezy program that annually brings several hundred customers and suppliers to Pewaukee for an extensive, expert overview of print processes and technology. From pre-press preparation to finishing and distribution, campers get the benefit of everything Quad/Graphics has learned about its business over the years. Each day's program combines lectures, informal discussions, and teaching tours of various plant operations. Campers also have a chance to meet the people who work on their publications and expand their professional knowledge and contacts within the industry.

Camp/Quad is conducted in the Pewaukee plant and in the Quad/Graphics Technical Center (a converted elementary school) across the street. Campers are lodged in the company's residences on scenic Pine Lake, just west of Milwaukee. Company chauffeurs (actually workers from the plant floor) pick up arriving students at the Milwaukee airport, and other production workers act as "camp counselors" with small groups of customers.

The program has become so successful—and customers so loyal—that in 1986 Quad/Graphics created Advanced Camp/Quad to provide better depth and more detail to campers who wanted to learn still more. If Camp/Quad is an exploratory hike through the printing environment, Advanced Camp/Quad (developed by a press supervisor, Ed Kelley) qualifies as full-fledged nature study. Over four and a half days, it takes its students, who include Quad/Graphics employees and supervisors as well as customers and suppliers, through an actual production job step by step, explaining in technical detail the various processes and technologies involved, and providing valuable tips and techniques designed to help customers get their money's worth from the print services they buy.

The result is a better-educated clientele and more capable and responsive suppliers, all of them more familiar with the processes and technological capabilities Quad/Graphics offers, not to mention more familiar *to* the people who provide those services to them—and more loyal to Quad/ Graphics too.

Quad/Graphics will turn twenty in 1991. Looked at in a figurative sense, you might say the business has just come through its adolescence and is beginning to mature. That's fitting for a company whose working environment, according to Larry Quadracci, owes much to the teachings of Maria Montessori. "If you want excellent preformance," says Quadracci, "you surround people with an excellent environment. We've created not only a place to work, but a place to learn."

Quad/Graphics, Inc.
DuPlainville Road
Pewaukee, WI 52072

XEROX

THERE WAS A TIME, AND NOT ALL THAT LONG AGO, THAT THE NAME XEROX was synonymous with the office copying field. Then came competition, especially from Japan, and Xerox found itself cast as an uncommunicative giant that could not or would not respond to its customers with the same enthusiasm or agility as those companies that coveted its turf. Market share eroded, the baton of leadership seemed to pass to new pretenders to the throne. Meanwhile, the company ventured into financial services with indifferent success.

When you're good, you listen, and you notice, and you learn. On the Business Products and Systems side (which accounted for about 75 percent of its revenues in 1987), Xerox has been doing a lot of all three in recent years. In the early eighties, it took a long, hard look at the company it had once been, the industry it had virtually invented and long dominated, and the strangely difficult straits in which it found itself. In 1985, it launched a thorough restructuring and repositioning of its various office-automation and supply businesses to focus on customer satisfaction above any other determinant of success. In 1986, it gained market share for the first time in the decade.

In 1987, president Paul A. Allaire made it official. Lest there be any lingering doubts, he told employees from top to bottom that the new day at Xerox had arrived, announcing: "I am changing the corporate priorities at Xerox Corporation. Effective immediately, the order is number one: customer satisfaction; number two: ROA (return on assets); number three: market share."

What happened to Xerox, what is happening *at* Xerox, is a case-study example of how even historically successful and admired companies can lose their way. It also illustrates the inherent dangers of America's peculiar "bigger must be better" delusion. But most of all, it shows the essential reality of any service business: There is no permanence to service. Customer loyalties are transient. Each day, the score starts at zero. Stop serving customers well and you can and will lose them. Start serving them well again, and better than your competition does, and you

505

can win them back. Several things about Xerox's renewed customer focus are noteworthy, but we'll concentrate on three: quantitative measurement, benchmarking, and training.

Based on its customer research, Xerox determined that its customers define service based on four criteria: frequency of service needed, response to service calls, length of a service call, and copy quality. From those criteria it has evolved the Performance Measurement System that quantifies service responsiveness in each area. The virtue of measurable standards is that they allow the company to strive for a uniform level of service quality from coast to coast, in large markets and small, regardless of the equipment mix installed.

For example, each Xerox copier model has its own distinct level of service target, an average number of copies it should produce between service calls, based on the level of use it receives. When a customer experiences more frequent service needs, Xerox notices and responds, sometimes by replacing the unit involved. In addition, any time a Xerox representative makes a service call, he or she is trained to do a number of additional diagnostic tests to spot developing problems and nip them in the bud.

Not only does each machine have a "level of service" target, but so too does each customer: every machine, every customer location, has a target response time. When a call is received and a technical representative dispatched, the service center can call up the customer's history by computer and relay information to the service tech while still en route. Service center personnel are also expected to spend a few moments on diagnosis with customers when they phone in for help. If the problem can be solved without dispatching and waiting for a technician, the machine is back in operation that much sooner. Once the technician arrives, Xerox tracks how long it takes to solve the problem.

Finally, Xerox regularly audits its customers' copier quality through a copy analysis and management program. Each month, a random sample of customers is sent a test pattern and survey form. They are asked to fill in the form, copy the test pattern on the company Xerox, and send that copy back for analysis. Each customer-generated copy is checked for image quality, including darkness, background, distortion, deletion, streaks, and spots. Computers analyze the monthly samples and pinpoint developing problems, sometimes before customers are even aware of them.

Xerox first realized the virtues of benchmarking in 1979 when it cross-checked its own manufacturing costs against those of its Japanese competitors and discovered one significant reason why it was getting its corporate socks knocked off. In manufacturing, costs are relatively easy to identify, so the remedial effort was relatively simple. But on the administrative and service side, the problem was a little more complex. Xerox opted to benchmark against noncompetitors on the premise that information would be more willingly shared when it didn't involve the same marketing turf. The first model it chose: L. L. Bean.

What does an office-equipment company have in common with a mail-order clothing retailer? Well, both have warehouse operations whose speed, accuracy, and efficiency have a major impact on customer satisfaction. Both involve handling pieces of varying sizes and shapes, which means neither is easy to automate and must instead rely on human labor. Where computers could get involved was in the area of facility design, work-flow analysis, space utilization, and data management.

Based on what it learned from L. L. Bean, Xerox redesigned its warehouses to shorten the distance the order filler had to travel to reach materials; it now arranges parts according to how often they are needed (the technical term for that is "velocity") rather than by size, weight, color, or habit. According to a report in the *Harvard Business Review*, before benchmarking Xerox was improving productivity at a rate of 3 to 5 percent per year. Since its implementation, gains of 10 percent are common, about half involving continuing excursions to other service leaders in the L. L. Bean mold.

Finally, Xerox has enhanced service to its customers by continuing to enhance its traditionally strong product knowledge and technical training programs. Technical representatives receive up to six weeks of introductory training at the Xerox training center in Leesburg, Virginia. That background is continually enhanced with follow-up, add-on, and refresher courses in the field. From the loading docks to the technical specialists, every Xerox employee has been through a forty-eight-hour course on problem-solving techniques as part of the company's restructuring. The training is designed to build teamwork and awareness of each employee's role in satisfying the customer.

Small wonder that when *Sales & Marketing Management* magazine rated sales forces in 1987, Xerox led the pack in scientific and photographic equipment based on top marks for opening new accounts, holding old accounts, and quality of training. All three contribute to satisfied customers.

In 1987, Xerox put still another piece of the service-quality puzzle in place by instituting an incentive compensation system that is heavily weighted toward customer satisfaction. Sales people, for example, are rated on surveys of their accounts that elicit feedback on everything from the customer's ratings of Xerox products and administrative support to their impressions of the specific sales representative's professionalism and attention to their needs.

No one at Xerox is claiming the task of reestablishing the company as the leader in the office products field is done, or even half done. But it's interesting that in a field characterized by wide-open competition among companies of varying sizes and nationalities, the long-time pacesetter is focusing its future on serving the customer visibly better than anyone else.

Xerox Corporation
800 Long Ridge Road
Stamford, CT 06904

kinko's

PAUL ORFALEA HAS CURLY HAIR. KINKY HAIR, SOME WOULD SAY. WHEN HE opened his first copy center near the University of California campus in Santa Barbara back in 1970, he used his own nickname for the business, an offbeat approach that fit right in with the faculty and students who were his primary customers at the time.

There are now more than four hundred Kinko's around the country and abroad, and the clientele includes plenty of business people in addition to the academic types who still feel welcome. Orfalea and his three dozen partners display a cavalier attitude when the subject at hand involves considerations of how many stores and how many dollars in sales are being accumulated, but there's no similar disclaiming when talk switches to customers. There, the imperative is to combine quality work, prompt and personal attention, reasonable prices, and innovative services to keep Kinko's a pacesetter in its field.

It does, and it is. "Keep the music playing" is the operative metaphor, Orfalea's chosen image for illustrating the harmony, teamwork, and pleasing customer experience a well-run Kinko's shop exhibits externally as well as internally.

Like many quick-copy centers, Kinko's offers fast service for a variety of personal printing needs: small-quantity copies, stationery, résumés, newsletters, flyers, classroom handouts for professors, and bound theses for students. Unlike many such centers, there's continuing attention to customer wants and perceptions, from the courtesy and helpfulness the counter person offers in writing up orders and helping customers select the best papers and printing options to the way the work area is kept clean and jobs run on schedule.

At the store level, Kinko's makes a point of listening to its customers and trying to see its store as they see—or would like to see—it. Mystery shoppers visit each store at least twice a year; their detailed ratings are checked against minimum expectations and shared with regional and store managers to keep everyone current on how they're doing. Customer comment forms are studied and analyzed, and each is personally responded to. While they include the familiar 1- to 5-point rating scales for quality and service, most of the form is blank, encouraging customers to write at length about their experiences, complaints, and suggestions. One question asks, "How could the store be organized to better serve you?"

As the question suggests, Kinko's is always willing to experiment with new options, many of them requested specifically by its customers. Noting that businesspeople often come in to copy correspondence before it's mailed, for example, most Kinko's stores now sell stamps and serve as mail drops.

Capitalizing on the growing popularity of desktop publishing, Kinko's rents time on Apple Macintosh personal computers hooked up to laser printers, and personnel in each store are trained to provide assistance to customers unfamiliar with computerized mice and windows and graphic styling. (In January 1988, *Publish!* magazine recognized Kinko's for providing "the most extensive network of Mac-equipped copy shops.") Some Kinko's have installed one-hour minilab machines to process photos. Others have set up Custom Service Centers to offer more involved services such as wedding invitations, imprinted binders and custom tabs for business reports, banners and signs, and overnight mail.

Kinko's operates under an interesting format. Founder Orfalea offers no franchises in the conventional sense. Instead, he contracts with about sixty regional partners who operate with a great deal of autonomy within a specific territory and under a fluid set of "minimum expectations." (Laser printers, for example, were introduced by some stores as early as 1985; they became a minimum expectation of all stores in 1988.)

Committees representing store managers, regional managers, partners, and the staff of Orfalea's own Ventura-based support company, Kinko's Service Corporation, set expectations, create and modify programs, track quality and performance, and spend a lot of time sharing operational ideas and customer service tactics. There's an almost Scandinavian sense of industrial democracy in the fairly free and uninhibited discussion of minimum standards, system benefits, tips, and tricks that result in better customer service, and new ideas worth considering. "We learn from each other" is a basic tenet of the Kinko's mindset.

That results in operational advances both visible and invisible at the customer level. On the visible end of the spectrum, each Kinko's store in a given area displays the location and hours of operation of other Kinko's locations in that area. Pricing is consistent store to store, and rather than have an individual shop struggle to do a large job itself, the Kinko's culture encourages sharing the overload so the customer gets the finished job as fast as possible.

Information-sharing is less visible, but no less indigenous to the system. For example, in 1987 the "Wattenbarger System" of coding paper stocks became a minimum expectation of all Kinko's stores. The system was invented by Scott Wattenbarger at his Kinko's shop in Stockton, California. It was studied, tested, and endorsed by the Operations Committee as a way of helping stores do a more efficient job of managing the various types of paper they stock for their customers. Most customers couldn't care less what system is used as long as they get the selection and service they want when they want it, but Kinko's worried through the details and decided it would improve quality systemwide, so it was adopted.

The discussion didn't end, however. In an open letter to Orfalea, Frank Perez, a store manager in Denver, expressed his displeasure with the imposition of a system, regardless of how good it might be, from afar. Rather than spark just a one-on-one exchange, Perez's candid views were reproduced as the lead item in *Kinko's News*, the system's monthly internal newsletter (desktop-published and copied by Kinko's Copies, Santa Barbara; printed by Kinko's Graphics, Santa Cruz). Orfalea followed with his own reply. "This is a good business," he explained, "but we have to keep improving if we are to survive in the future. There is no room for complacency."

There is, however, plenty of room for free and unfettered discussion, and subsequent issues of the newsletter returned to the subject and to the larger issue of preserving store-level autonomy while trying to grow based on systemwide quality standards. That's as Orfalea and just about everybody else in the system wants it.

"We want to preserve the managers' independence and discretion as much as possible, but certain requirements must be met," Orfalea wrote. "After all, when a customer has a bad experience at one Kinko's, when the music is too loud or the co-worker can't find the right paper, that hurts all stores eventually. As we balance the different levels of authority in our company, perhaps the most important question is this: Are we one company?"

And then he added the distinctive Kinko's kicker.

"You tell me."

Kinko's Service Corporation
255 West Stanley Avenue, Suite A
Ventura, CA 93002

Safety-Kleen Corporation

YOU KNOW THE SAYING: IT'S A DIRTY JOB, BUT *SOMEBODY'S* GOTTA DO IT. IN the service economy, that's not a gripe—it's a formula for a business. And for more than three hundred thousand businesses in the U.S. and five countries abroad that generate small quantities of hazardous wastes, the somebody who does the dirty jobs, and does them well, is an Elgin, Illinois-based company aptly named Safety-Kleen.

Whether in an auto repair shop or a dry cleaning establishment, an industrial plant or a restaurant, the growing need to handle chemicals and other wastes safely and with an eye toward environmentally smart practices has helped Safety-Kleen compile seventeen years of consecutive growth at an annual rate of 20 percent or better, making it the world's largest marketer of parts-cleaning services (admittedly not a crown a great many entrepreneurs long to wear). Yet the heart of the business is still essentially the same as it was in 1968, when Donald Brinckman—then operating on behalf of Chicago Rawhide Manufacturing, now president and CEO of what has been an independent company since 1974—acquired a Milwaukee inventor's patented "red sink on a drum" system.

The inventor was a gentleman named Ben Palmer, a gravel-pit worker by day, an invcterate tinkerer by night. In the mid-1950s, he had come up with a better and safer system for cleaning the gunk and goo off mechanical parts than the then-popular practice involving a brush and an open bucket of gasoline or solvent. In the vernacular of the time, it was "neat." A washtub was mounted over a barrel of solvent. Inside the barrel was a small electric pump. You put the part to be cleaned in the tub, flipped a switch, and the pump sent solvent up out of the barrel through a flexible hose to dissolve away the crud. On its way back into the barrel below, the solvent passed through a filter which removed the debris. No muss. No fuss. No big deal.

And that's the point. For smaller businesses, parts-cleaning and waste disposal are minor but important aspects of day-to-day operations. It really is a dirty job, and they really don't want to have to do it—especially in an era when the initials EPA (Environmental Protection Agency) have taken on increasing significance.

In 1984, the EPA revised its regulations on toxic-waste disposal to include not just larger businesses that generate more than a thousand kilograms (about a ton) of waste per month, but also smaller enterprises whose wastes amount to a tenth that volume. These companies are not experts when it comes to environmentally sound waste-disposal practices, nor do they want to be. That's when the bright yellow vans start pulling up out back.

As the company explains it, "Safety-Kleen's philosophy of providing services that are too small, or too dirty, or just too mundane for customers to do themselves—plus the company's ever present commitment to resource recovery to help protect the environment from further contamination through indiscriminate dumping of hazardous waste—have proven to be a winning combination."

For customers in the automotive and vehicular repair and industrial sectors of the economy, what Safety-Kleen does is provide full-service parts cleaning and waste disposal service. The cleaning equipment is installed on the customer's premises, then serviced by more than twelve hundred sales and service representatives. The reps visit each customer on a regular basis—more than three million personal customer contacts in 1987 at intervals ranging from a week to two months, depending on a given customer's needs. They not only make sure the machine is working properly and replace the solvent, which is recycled at one of ten Safety-Kleen plants around the country, but also consult on proper waste-handling practices and ways to make operations more efficient as well as more environmentally sound. In addition, they handle emergency repairs and service needs, usually within twenty-four hours of a call.

The table-height sink and drum design is pretty much the same as the one Palmer first devised but is augmented now with a safety lid that has a fusible link closure to provide improved fire safety. The link melts at about 160 degrees Fahrenheit, causing the lid to drop down and smother any fire in the sink. For more independent-minded businesses and do-it-yourselfers, including auto buffs who like to work on their own cars, the company sells a smaller, self-contained unit.

What makes it all work is a network of some 250 branch distribution centers (about 165 of them in the U.S.) located close to customers wherever they may be. The centers operate on a "closed-loop" principle: Solvent delivered to customers from the branch is returned to it after use, where it is accumulated and shipped out for recycling, then brought back to the branch again.

In its early days, Safety-Kleen considered using independent distributors instead of developing its own service and distribution organization. The decision to retain internal control reflected a concern for customer service as well as environmental quality standards. Under environmental regulations, businesses have "cradle to grave" responsibility for the hazardous wastes they produce. Safety-Kleen not only handles and disposes of the waste, it also alleviates customers' fears and uncertainties over proper handling and disposal practices and the regulatory consequences of mismanagement. That peace of mind is as important to the service as the actual disposal work.

Branch distribution centers, originally emplaced to stock parts and solvent, are now proving even more valuable as Safety-Kleen looks for new service vistas. A fast-growing restaurant division cleans air filters, grease hoods and ductwork, fry baskets, and other cooking equipment to keep food-service premises up to fire and insurance codes. To maximize customer convenience and minimize the disruption to a restaurant's business and patrons, cleaning crews are available seven days a week, day or night.

Dry cleaners turn to Safety-Kleen to dispose of the fluid they use; auto body and paint shops rely on the yellow vans to take care of the solvent used to clear spray-gun nozzles and haul away brushes and polishing pads that become saturated with extended use. Safety-Kleen will even service small-volume accounts, routing one of its vans by a company to pick up a drum or two of waste on a regular schedule. The waste goes to one of the processing plants, where it is analyzed and then either recycled or processed into a chemical fuel for industrial use. Anything that can't be reused or reprocessed is incinerated under strict environmental controls. The company also provides new solvent and disposes of contaminated fluids for customers who own their own parts-cleaning machines, regardless of their type or brand name.

All this cleaning up has more than beneficial economic effects on Safety-Kleen's books. According to the company's numbers, in 1987 the yellow vans picked up sixteen million pounds of potentially hazardous waste from dry cleaners alone, from which it recovered about twelve million pounds of reusable solvent. The system used in paint-shop spray-guns—which uses less solvent than conventional methods, resulting in less waste—reduced air pollution to the tune of nearly one million pounds of volatile organic compounds. In all, more than thirty-eight million gallons of spent solvent was not dumped—legally or illegally—in 1987 because of Safety-Kleen. Instead, it was recycled into thirty-five million gallons of reusable material, with the balance disposed of primarily through incineration.

It's worth noting that not so long ago, people were prone to shake their heads and shrug and say that all this environmental quality talk is fine, but it will never be economically feasible. Well, consider that Safety-Kleen is the one and only publicly traded business in American corporate history to grow at a rate of 20 percent or more per year for seventeen consecutive years. Only two others can claim sixteen years at that rate: Automatic Data Processing (ADP) and McDonald's.

As noted in the 1987 annual report, "Safety-Kleen is a dynamic illustration that business and a healthy environment are not necessarily opposing entities. Indeed, they can complement each other for the benefit of everyone."

Safety-Kleen Corporation
777 Big Timber Road
Elgin, IL 60123

Miller Business Systems

"JUST A NOTE TO THANK YOU FOR THE EXCELLENT SERVICE WE RECEIVED FROM Miller Business Systems today. One of our employees misplaced the key to her desk, which held all company checks, deposits, etc., so we were extremely desperate for a key. I called . . . Business Interiors, and requested a key, to which they said it would take two weeks to get. I then explained the situation and within a few hours, 3 keys were not only made but delivered to us. It is really nice to see that a company the size of yours can still provide such personal service. . . . Thank you once again for your excellent service, and please commend your employees. They were extremely helpful and seemed to be genuinely concerned about our situation. Their friendly attitudes and prompt service will be long remembered by Snyder Oil Company."

It has been said—but it's worth repeating—that everything counts for the customer. The comments in the letter reproduced above may be a little out of the ordinary, but they aren't extraordinary for customers of Miller Business Systems in Arlington, Texas. In its files are similar letters from customers ranging from Neiman-Marcus and Dow Corning to Lubrication Engineers and AOA Corporation. They testify to an enthusiastic commitment to service that starts with the owners, Jim and Joan Miller, and extends out to the more than three hundred people who answer the phones, fill the orders, and drive the delivery trucks.

It wasn't always this way. When Jim Miller bought Arlington Office Supply (Arlington is a growing business suburb along the expressway that connects Dallas and Fort Worth) a little over twenty years ago, it had three employees, annual sales of fifty thousand dollars, and was on the verge of bankruptcy. These days it has seven locations (including five walk-in stores and a highly automated warehouse/distribution center) and three hundred employees around the Dallas-Fort Worth "metroplex." Sales in 1987 surpassed $50 million.

One reason this family-run business has become the leading business supply firm in its area is Jim Miller's long-standing guarantee to turn around 95 percent of customer orders in twenty-four hours or less. In

1987, 98.5 percent of all orders met that standard. Another is the wide range of services bundled under the company name: office design and space planning; business relocation management; furniture purchase, rental, and repair (under not one, but three separate plans, including a budget-conscious used-furniture rental service); and more than twenty-two thousand different types, sizes, and styles of computer and office supplies.

A third contributing factor is a culture of customer service that involves smart organization and lots of continuing motivation. For example, in late 1986, to improve service, encourage teamwork, enhance training, and minimize the disruptions caused by periodic turnover, Miller split its customer service people into three teams. Each has four to six members—carefully "drafted" to balance experienced performers and rookies—plus a manager, and all customer accounts are assigned to one of the three teams. Each team has a separate phone number, which is printed on labels in customer catalogs and phone indexes and appears on correspondence and billing.

Team members are charged with taking orders and responding to customer inquiries from their particular base of accounts. Previously, sales reps each serviced individual accounts, but that often meant that a customer calling for a specific rep had to wait because the individual was unavailable or on the line with another customer. Now calls are routed automatically to anyone on the team who's available. That spreads out the work load, encourages experienced people to help their less-seasoned colleagues, and also means that customers get knowledgeable service faster than ever before.

To encourage friendly competition, each group adopted a name (which is why there are Killer Bees, Top Guns, and Silver Bullets manning the phones these days), and Miller then provided each member with T-shirts, buttons, and pennants emblazoned with the name of their team. To make the competition more rewarding, each month members of the winning team (as determined by customer sales and service) earn a forty-dollar bonus.

Does it work? The industry thinks so: *Office Products Dealer* magazine conferred its 1987 Award of Excellence on Miller for its team approach to customer-account management. "We still believe service is the most important part of doing business," Miller told the *Dallas/Fort Worth Business Journal* a couple of years ago. "I have an obsession with it. People get sick and tired of getting poor performance."

To make sure people don't get that feeling from their business, the extended family of Millers and employees (who suggested the current name when the boss held a rename-the-company contest in 1983) uses a variety of tactics. Large contract customers are able to plug in directly to Miller's central computer, placing orders with the assurance that whatever they want is in stock and will be delivered the following day. Smaller customers can use Miller's Tele-Serve program, which matches them over the telephone with professional sales reps who provide planning advice, answer questions, and help them take advantage of price breaks similar to those offered by many discount and mail order suppliers. About 10 percent of Miller's supply inventory consists of items kept in stock for specific customers.

The Business Interiors program includes a computer-assisted design service. Based on a customer's space needs or office configuration, the computer program can call up and arrange various pieces of furniture, then print out a detailed, to-scale layout that notes sizes and colors as well as item numbers, prices, and availability. Miller also inventories furniture for fast-growing clients, storing the customer's as yet unneeded desks, chairs, workstations, and storage equipment in its own warehouse, tracking supplies on a weekly basis as they're used up and need to be reordered, and delivering additional setups as they are required.

Customers of any size are likely to get a personal visit from Jim or his son, Mike, the company's president. While Jim, as chairman of the board, is still the motivating force behind the business, and Joan, as vice chairman, continues to keep tabs on the Business Interiors furniture and design division she founded, day-to-day operations are directed by Mike and his sister, Kathy McKim (vice president). A brother, Greg, is a vice president with a discount office furniture company in Arlington.

In 1987, father and son dropped in on more than two hundred companies all over the Metroplex to find out firsthand about business conditions, identify new opportunities, discuss any problems or suggestions the customer might have, and generally reinforce their commitment to providing a satisfying level of service. The company also holds informal, focus-group-style luncheons monthly at which six to eight customers, chosen to represent a cross-section of large and small companies as well as long-time and relatively newer accounts, are invited in to talk about what they like and don't like with various Miller sales and service managers.

On a larger scale, an annual customer survey has been conducted every year since 1984. Consistently it finds highly satisfied folks around the Metroplex: 95 percent say they're extremely pleased with the service they're receiving. Miller slips a dollar bill in with the survey form as a way of expressing his appreciation in advance for the time the customer will take to tell him how his company is doing. He also sends an update letter that tells them about the steps the company has taken in response to their input.

Picking orders and driving delivery trucks are not the kinds of exciting jobs television tends to glorify in a movie-of-the-week. To keep the customer focus strong, Miller uses various incentive gifts and employee-of-the-month programs in each division, as well as "President's Circle" awards for top sales performers. New employees meet one-on-one with

Jim Miller for a personal orientation, during which he shares his feelings about the company, tells them about the business's history and growth, outlines opportunities for personal growth and advancement, and gives them their own "Success Kit." Included are a bottle of bright green liquid labeled "Enthusiasm," an "I Believe in Myself" mirror, and a piece of string.

To demonstrate his business philosophy, Miller shows them that the only way to keep the string straight and moving in a straight line is to pull (or "lead") it, not push it. He demonstrates the proper use of the mirror, too. Then he drinks the bottle of Enthusiasm.

Whatever is in that bottle, it's clearly the stuff of a family success story.

Miller Business Systems, Inc.
912 113th Street
Arlington, TX 76004

ServiceMaster

*Service*MASTER

"SERVICEMASTER'S BUSINESS IS SIZABLE," NOTED A REPORT IN *FORTUNE* BACK in 1984, "but is so unusual that even its executives have trouble framing a short, sweet description of what the company does. It does supply services, but that isn't too informative. Think of it instead as all-around handyman for corporations, educational institutions, and particularly hospitals. For its hospital customers, ServiceMaster stops short of playing doctor and nurse, but otherwise spreads itself wide, doing housekeeping and laundry, maintaining equipment, ordering medical supplies, preparing food."

While many people associate ServiceMaster with home-cleaning services—it began in 1947 as a furniture- and rug-cleaning service for both homes and offices—health care facilities have been the company's primary customers over the past twenty-five years. Nearly 20 percent of the nation's hospitals are ServiceMaster clients, some under "megacontracts" that bundle together housekeeping and laundry (the two jobs hospital administrators dislike most, according to ServiceMaster's market research), with supply ordering and inventory management, maintenance of equipment and food preparation, and other nonmedical tasks.

The first hospital customer was Lutheran General Hospital in Park Ridge, Illinois, not far from ServiceMaster headquarters in Downers Grove (both are suburbs of Chicago). The salesman who signed up the account back in 1962, Kenneth Wessner, is now chairman of the board. Lutheran General is still a ServiceMaster client. So are more than one thousand other hospitals in the U.S., including two large hospital chains: Voluntary Hospitals of America and American HealthCare Systems.

At first, ServiceMaster had to overcome resistance from administrators who worried that contracting out cleaning services from the kitchen and operating theaters to patient rooms and visitor lounges would imply that they weren't capable of managing the jobs themselves. To ServiceMaster, competence was never the issue. The business of a hospital, figured Wessner, involved doctoring and caring. The rest was support, and it was in those areas that ServiceMaster could do things better and cheaper than internal departments could, thus improving overall operations. Once administrators figured out that bringing in a service contractor made them look good, business took off.

ServiceMaster now manages more than 150,000 workers, some of whom are its own employees, but many of whom are on the payrolls of its clients. There are also about 1,300 ServiceMaster locations around the world, plus more than 3,200 independently licensed franchisees, to provide services to residential and small business customers in the U.S., Canada, Japan, and England. Despite the essential grunginess of the work, morale is high: Two thirds of the people who seek jobs at ServiceMaster are recruited by the company's managers and employees.

ServiceMaster does the jobs a lot of businesses really don't want to do for themselves. But it does them as though the top executives of its client businesses were standing there supervising the work in person. Very little is left to chance. Computers at Downers Grove track preventive maintenance schedules for equipment in hospital, university, and business clients. Other systems manage the inventory of cleaning supplies, or order food for school and hospital cafeterias, or manage home health care for hospitals providing that extended service.

Jobs are broken down into their component parts, often in increments of five minutes, with detailed instructions for what to do at each step. The instruction manual for polishing floors, noted *Business Week* a few years ago, is three inches thick. The floor finish is designed and manufactured to ServiceMaster specifications, which means the worker knows how long it takes to dry. Mop buckets, also built to company specs, are designed to hold only enough water to do a room, ensuring that dirty (sometimes contaminated) water from one room won't be used on the floor next door. Vacuum cleaners, again built to company specs, are battery-powered to eliminate the time previously spent wrestling with lengths of extension cord.

Top managers not only teach in ServiceMaster training classes, they've taken the training themselves. They know firsthand how to wax corridors and disinfect hospital rooms. Workers in many smaller hospital facilities are extensively cross-trained to make them more productive and versatile and keep them from burning out on dead-end tasks. At the same time, computerized management programs designed for those hospitals combine the cross-trained workers from six previously different housekeeping departments into one unified system, reducing administrative overhead and aiding in the quest to control operating costs.

One of the areas ServiceMaster is proudest of is its commitment to training even functionally illiterate workers. The company offers both conventional and unconventional classes, the latter employing color-coded instructional materials and pictorial images to help workers master basic tasks and improve their productivity, the former helping employees upgrade their own skills—a basic step in improving both their self-image and their career potential. It's more than altruism: Turnover is minimized, performance improved, and clients pleased when workers take pride in themselves and their jobs.

"ServiceMaster has given people whose jobs were considered unimportant—janitors, cleaning women, boiler operators, landscapers—new challenges, respect, responsibilities, and career options," noted *Management Review* in 1987. "When ServiceMaster's managers take over a site's maintenance activities, they bring with them a system of defined career paths, so that supervisors and other employees eventually can move up to fill their spots in time. This adds a new incentive for maintenance employees to change and improve their work, and eliminates many of the 'turf' problems one would expect when hired managers come into an established operation. It also utilizes economy of scale by fully tapping the skills and expertise of workers that no one else has, or can justifiably spend time and money to learn."

The task also involves working with managers to equip them with the tools needed to supervise their work forces effectively. When a deaf employee was hired at one ServiceMaster-managed hospital facility, the resident managers took a course in sign language so they could communicate more effectively. The worker quickly became one of the most valued and productive people on the staff and was honored in 1985 by the state of Illinois as the outstanding success story of the year.

In factories, ServiceMaster workers are trained to take care of cleaning everything from shop floors to robotic equipment used in assembling, painting, and handling industrial products. For school districts and universities, ServiceMaster crews clean buildings, prepare lunches, cut the grass, and maintain heating, cooling, and power equipment. In hospitals, ServiceMaster estimates its carefully researched methods and specially developed chemicals and cleaning equipment can cut labor costs as much as 30 percent in some areas while doing a better job than previous methods.

The coming of cost controls has slowed the growth of ServiceMaster's hospital services—though there's been no diminishing of its existing work load in the health care field—resulting in diversification into new fields. Home health care, for example, is a growing phenomenon coast to coast, and ServiceMaster is already one of the leaders.

Outside the health field, the company acquired Terminix in 1986, allowing it to add the services of the country's second-largest pest-control company to its repertoire. It also has placed new emphasis on developing new cleaning business accounts in factories and schools, and through acquisition has gone into food-service management for colleges and universities. Meanwhile, its traditional cleaning services have found a ready market in Japan, where nearly four hundred franchisees are active.

ServiceMaster means both "master of service" and "service to the Master." Founder Marion Wade was a devout Baptist; cofounders Robert Wenger, a Catholic, and Ken Hansen, a Presbyterian, shared his view that a sound business could be built and run as an extension of religious principles. ServiceMaster's number one corporate objective is still "to honor God in all we do." The 1986 Annual Report opens with this admonishment from Ephesians: "Serve wholeheartedly, as if you were serving the Lord, not men, because you know that the Lord will reward everyone for whatever good he does."

Now there's an ambitious service standard: Treat the customer like the Almighty. Well, why not?

ServiceMaster Limited Partnership
2300 Warrenville Road
Downers Grove, IL 60515

PACESETTERS

ENTERTAINMENT

Walt Disney World/Disneyland

Cineplex Odeon Corporation

INFORMATION

The Wall Street Journal

USA Today

PUBLIC

Montgomery County, Ohio

Arizona Public Service Company

Emerald People's Utility District

CARE

Kinder-Care Learning Centers

Chicken Soup

Mini Maid Services Company

SOME ORGANIZATIONS ARE SIMPLY UNIQUE. THEY ARE WHAT THEY ARE, AND comparisons with others are somewhat irrelevant. For some, in fact, no comparison is possible. We've found some common elements among the ten companies who round out our Service 101, and therefore consider them in four somewhat loose groupings.

First, Entertainment. Disneyland and Walt Disney World are part of the theme park industry, but they also are the creators of the industry and an industry unto themselves as well. Virtually every major theme park that has followed is, to some extent, peopled by Disney "graduates," many of whom run extremely fine organizations, real crowd-pleasers, but know that the standard of comparison for the foreseeable future will continue to be you-know-who. That makes you-know-who a pacesetter. The fact that Mickey Mouse now appears in one of the hottest forms of service management training in the country only makes Walt's extended family that much more noteworthy.

Our other great entertainer, Cineplex Odeon, is a Disney on the make—a company reinventing the movie house business on a high-tech, high-amenity scale. When others were writing off the moving picture exhibition business as a dying industry, and fretting over the growth of VCR use, Cineplex set out to make going to the flicks easy, fun, clean, and profitable. Garth Drabinsky's strategy of catering first and foremost to adults who want to see films in a pleasant environment, from seats designed for human comfort, and with feet on floors devoid of melted Milk Duds and stale popcorn, is noteworthy. Adult food, short lines, bigger screens, sophisticated surroundings—most of the new ideas in the motion picture exhibition business seem to show up in a Cineplex property first.

Under Information we've paired two organizations that are seldom mentioned in the same breath—but maybe should be. Both *The Wall Street Journal* and *USA Today* provide valued insight into the world around us in styles at once distinctive and markedly different. Both serve as national newspapers, but for very different reasons.

Mainstream America used to consider the world of business dull, dry, and boring—not to mention incomprehensible. *The Journal* has made it a fit and understandable topic for insiders and observers alike. The business world scoffed that *McPaper* would never make it. It did—and it has changed the newspaper business in the process of proving its doubters wrong. And since no service has more impact than information in the modern service economy, both belong here among the pacesetters they cover.

(Space permitting, we would have added *The New England Journal of Medicine* to this duo: It's the authoritative voice of modern healthcare and its carefully measured words reach subscribers—by print and electronic means—only after rigorous review against uncompromising ethical standards.)

In the public sector, Mr. and Ms. John Q. Public normally have one response to the news that they are going to have to deal with a governmental agency or public utility—a great, grievous groan. Public service, they hold, is an oxymoron, a contradiction in terms. Guess what? There are a growing number of exceptions to that rule of thumb.

At the county and local government level, for example, tax-supported agencies are becoming more responsive, more concerned with the satisfaction of those they serve, and less bureaucratic. (Maybe one message of California's disruptive Proposition 13 got through.) As a key manager in the department of licensing and taxation for a county government puts it, "We don't pass the laws, we just make them work. We aren't even an enforcement agency. We just do the administration and the public knows that. So our job, really, is just to make the whole process as pleasant and painless as possible—for all of us."

Once you start looking, you can find governmental groups from Maine to California, Minnesota to Florida, acting on that belief and making significant improvement in the quality of the service being provided. One of the most determined efforts in the country is in Montgomery County, Ohio, where Claude Malone asks, "If we aren't here to serve, what are we here for? We should do it to the best of our ability. And we should treat our fellow citizens with respect." That's a pacesetter.

A little sympathy, please, for the folks who bring us power, water, heat, and light. The only time they come to our conscious attention is when something goes awry. When do you think of the power company? Sure, when the lights don't work, when the bill shows up, and when they petition the public utilities commission for a raise—a certain formula for eternal damnation.

But many have taken the bull by the horns, so to speak, and started creating new moments of truth: opportunities to show a positive side to the public they heretofore served in relative silence. Most try it through advertising—"Hey! Did you know the real cost of electricity has fallen

16.5 percent in the last 10 years?" A few, like New York Electric and Gas Corporation, Tampa Electric, and Arizona Public Service are doing a whole lot more. Because of some very special circumstances in the markets it serves, we've picked Arizona Public Service of Phoenix to represent them all.

And then there's Emerald People's Utility District of Eugene, Oregon, a small, country power company formed when the people being served didn't like the kind of service they were receiving and decided to take things back into their own hands. How many companies do you know of where the *customers* have a summer picnic?

The final three organizations we consider under the heading of Care. Since 1969, Kinder-Care has been setting the pace for those providing organized, large-scale child care services; the company isn't the only one that seems to be profiting. Chicken Soup takes care of kids, too—kids who don't feel good, and whose moms and dads don't feel much better about leaving them to go to work. And Mini Maid takes care of people's houses and lifestyles while they're off busily working to enhance both; founder Leone Ackerly solved her own quest for satisfactory help around the house by inventing an industry that is, pardon the pun, cleaning up.

In some ways, this section's title is a little misleading. Half the Service 101 qualify as pacesetters in one way or another. Domino's sets the pace for businesses serving people who want their pizza brought to them, just as Pizza Hut does for those cooking it up for customers who want to eat it under someone else's roof. If you're going into the hamburger business, you're following in the big footsteps of McDonald's.

Federal Express, H&R Block, Safety-Kleen, Avon, AAA, and Lens-Crafters are pacesetters in the sense that they pioneered entire forms of business for others to follow. On a smaller scale, growing regional firms like SuperShuttle, Miller Business Systems, Ukrop's, and Home Depot may be national-level leaders the next time someone thinks to look them over. We chose to cover each in the context of an industry group, where the struggle for survival, share, and dominance show them off to their best advantage.

Doing what others don't want to do, or haven't yet thought to do, or flat out don't think can be done, whether within an established industry or out on the frontiers of business, is what makes leaders out of service entrepreneurs and managers. That's what we mean by pacesetter.

Walt Disney World/Disneyland

THERE'S AN INTERESTING PAGE IN A DISNEY MANAGEMENT HANDBOOK, WHICH forms the basis of one of the hottest management training businesses in human resources development these days. On this one page is a statement of management philosophy and tandem ten-point codes of conduct defining the treatment to be accorded to "guests" and "cast members" (which is what they call customers and employees respectively—and respectfully—in the parks).

The guest-relations standards speak of courteous treatment, prompt assistance, a pleasing family entertainment experience. The cast-relations standards equate, point for point. Below the two lists is an eloquent statement: "We believe that guests will receive the quality of treatment we expect them to receive when the members of the cast receive that same quality of treatment." Period.

It's been quite a few years since we saw that page of the handbook. Maybe it's been changed by now. But the underlying philosophy is still alive. And if you think that's Mickey Mouse, stop for a second and try to name a more trusted name in any field of business endeavor in this country. More than twenty-three million people will visit Walt Disney World in Orlando, Florida, this year; another thirteen million will see the sights in the original Disneyland, built in Anaheim in the mid-1950s, when California's booming Orange County was nothing but beachfront and strawberry fields. If Scandinavian Airlines has fifty thousand moments of truth a day, Disney figures it has ten million in that amount of time. Now ask yourself how a company builds a reputation like this, and a thriving worldwide business, using essentially the same eighteen-year-olds that you can't get to pick up their socks.

What Walt Disney invented back in 1955 (Walt Disney World opened to the public in 1971, EPCOT in 1982) was a new business: the modern amusement park. The rides may be designed for kids, but don't kid yourself—this is adult entertainment. Disney people constantly talk about "the setting," the sight and sound and touch and sensation that each attraction is designed to deliver. "You don't build it for yourself," they

529

remember Walt saying. "You know what the people want and you build it for them."

At Disney, they talk about "keys" that "unlock" the product. It starts with the concepts of *show* and *efficiency*. The former involves the sight and sound, the look and feel, the overt and implied messages of the various entertainment experiences inside the parks. The latter is the way equipment and operating systems are designed and deployed within each area. Together, they feed into a concept of *safety*—the safety of the guest is an absolute, uncompromisable standard. The outcome of those three design techniques is Disney's renowned *courtesy*—the company believes quality service is more easily obtained when the setting supports a good show that is efficiently provided and safely managed. On the other hand, obstacles to any of the three basic keys reduces or diverts attention from service quality.

They work in a funny direction at Disney. When they design an attraction for the park, they "imagineer" the entire experience—not just the mechanical parts of a ride, but what you see and hear and sense all around you. If you happen to go through the parks in the off-season, for example, when the crowds are thinner and most of the lines are shorter, you'll find it still takes you about half an hour to get on Space Mountain. Makes no difference how open the walkways may seem, there's always a line at Space Mountain.

The reason will become clear when you've finally wound your way around and down the blue-lit corridors to the platform where they're loading the little rocket cars and you notice that they're running the ride at half capacity. They could run you through quicker, but then you wouldn't have time to look, and talk, and read the signs telling you that pregnant women and people with heart conditions can bail out at this convenient exit over here, and basically get the full effect of the experience the ride is designed to deliver.

Disney has the lowest turnover in the theme park business: 22 percent in an industry where 100 percent per season is not uncommon. For management, it's about 6 percent. Selection plays a big part in that. In a sense, Disney "de-recruits"—it makes it clear that the only way to move up is to start at the bottom, where the standards are tough and uncompromising and personality quirks are subordinated to the entertainment experience and public image they're determined to project.

Whether in the theater or in the park, everybody keeps the set neat and clean, so in the Disney parks everybody picks up paper. Everybody is on a first-name basis, as befits a large, friendly family. A couple of years ago, the annual report pictured Michael Eisner, the high-powered CEO who has reinvigorated Disney since he came on board in 1984, making the rounds in Walt Disney World without a name tag. Now at Disneyland

and Walt Disney World, if you work for the company, you're supposed to wear a name tag anytime you're in the park. Sharp-eyed employees spotted Eisner "out of uniform," so to speak. And they let him know about it. And they weren't afraid to beard the top dog in the Disney menagerie over something as mundane as a name tag because at Disney rank may have its privileges, but it also has the same responsibilities as everybody else.

Selection is a science at Disney. No one gets hired after a first interview—it takes at least two personal screenings by two different interviewers. The first day and a half on the job is spent in a program called Disney Traditions, a full-fledged course in the history, philosophy, ideals, goals, and values of the Magic Kingdom. From there, it's time for on-the-job training—two days to two weeks, depending on the complexity of the job (there are more than a thousand different types of positions in all) to be done.

New employees who don't work out are seldom fired. Instead, the Disney way is to assume that somehow they've put that person in the wrong position, and they'll try retraining and reassigning for a long time before giving up on someone. Those who do work out can gain the opportunity to do a number of jobs within their department and train for new responsibilities that keep them growing and moving within the Disney family.

The training investment is ambitious, and constant. Disney spends four days training the kids who push the brooms and dustbins around the park. Four days. How long can it take to teach someone to sweep up spilled popcorn and candy wrappers, you might ask. A couple of hours. The rest of the training time is spent teaching these lowliest of cast members the answers to the questions that guests are more prone to ask of the sweepers than of the brightly smiling, freshly scrubbed guest relations ambassadors provided for that purpose.

Where's the nearest place to get pizza? What are the names of the Seven Dwarfs? What time is the parade? If I'm standing here in line for Space Mountain and it says it will be forty-five minutes before I get on the ride, how long will it really take to get on the ride? Disney has found through paying attention to its customers that the people with the brooms are five times more likely to be asked these questions than the people ostensibly provided for that purpose. So instead of telling them to tell the guest to go over and ask that girl with the name tag because that's her job, they teach them the answers. That's part of the setting: friendly people who are ever ready to help you. And that, in turn, empowers these workers to truly think of themselves as full-fledged members of the Disney cast and do things for guests in the park.

Training isn't restricted to just one job. Ride the Jungle Cruise long enough, and even the sanest and tamest of people will feed themselves (or perhaps an occasional small and obnoxious passenger) to the artificial crocodiles. To guard against that kind of burnout, Disney rotates its cast members around to different attractions, or gives them a chance to move into the retail shops for awhile.

It also gives them opportunities to move up. Hosts and hostesses, the basic frontline troops who run the rides and make the most extensive public contact, become "lead" hosts and hostesses—essentially the foremen in the parks. From among the leads come the assistant supervisors and the supervisors.

Disney also recognizes the importance of allowing its frontline people to get "offstage" when pressures mount or fatigue starts to set in, and there's no negative consequence for taking advantage of that safety valve. Everybody (at least everybody at Disney) knows that dealing with the public all day is a hard job, and sometimes you get a little frazzled on the frontline.

As the show-biz metaphor suggests, getting offstage is a tactic that allows a cast member to retreat from the public eye momentarily while the mental batteries recycle. Disney managers are trained to watch for signs of stress and tension in their people, and occasionally (though you have to be paying attention to actually see it happen) one will suggest that a worker take a break for a few minutes while he or she fills in and keeps things running smoothly. Since supervisors came from the frontline, they're prepared to do the job without a bump or hitch being visible to the guests.

There is one misconception that we should clear up about Disney, however. Others have written that Disney has a requirement that every year park executives, almost all of whom have come from the frontlines, must spend so many days working in frontline jobs at Walt Disney World or EPCOT or Disneyland. That's not true. They're only *allowed* to work so many days a year in the park.

The vision hasn't changed much since Walt Disney himself was walking the streets of the Magic Kingdom. Once, asked whether his ideas would survive him, he replied: "Well, I think by this time my staff, my young group of executives, and everything else, are convinced that Walt is right. That quality will out. And so I think they're going to stay with that policy because it's proved that it's a good business policy. Give the people everything you can give them. Keep the place as clean as you can keep it. Keep it friendly, you know. Make it a real fun place to be. I think they're convinced and I think they'll hang on after . . . as you say . . . well . . . after Disney."

The words, preserved on page two of "The Disney Approach to Quality Service"—the company's packaged training program that helps outsiders understand the Disney way of doing things and translate it to their own businesses—show that more than twenty years after his death, Walt Disney's vision is still alive.

The Walt Disney Company
500 South Buena Vista Street
Burbank, CA 91521

Cineplex Odeon Corporation

PICTURE THIS: YOU AND YOUR SIGNIFICANT OTHER WANDER COZILY OUT OF A large, comfortable room to find yourselves in a bright, spacious, art-deco-style commons under a skylight some four stories above. You pause briefly by the cappuccino bar to mingle and discuss which restaurant you want to stroll over to for the next part of your evening. Your eyes take in the colorful artwork and period-piece memorabilia.

Sound like a night at a fine theater? It is. A movie theater. In fact, a multiscreen movie theater. But it's obviously not one of those bandbox, spartan layouts down at the shopping mall, where even the popcorn seems economy-class. It's the glitzy Cineplex in Universal City, California—eighteen screens, six thousand seats, $16.5 million invested in making the simple experience of going to a movie theater a form of theater in itself.

The mastermind behind this extravagance (which we'll label, for obvious reasons, a service) isn't some musty throwback to the halcyon days of Hollywood. He's a Baby Boomer, and a Canadian boomer at that. His name is Garth Drabinsky. With 1,650 screens in some 500 locations in 20 states and the District of Columbia, his upstart company, Cineplex Odeon, has come out of nowhere to establish itself not only as the second-largest exhibitor of motion pictures in the United States (it's number one in Canada), but the undisputed trendsetter in an industry that had fallen on pretty hard, not to mention pretty colorless, times in recent years.

Not every Cineplex is or can be as outrageously forward as the Universal City emporium (the world's largest movie complex, for those keeping such statistics circa 1988), but Drabinsky and Cineplex are working on a variety of levels to make a trip to the movies a distinctly more interesting experience than a visit to the corner video rental store.

You remember the VCR, of course. It's the demonic little device that was supposed to sound the death knell of the traditional neighborhood Bijou. And well it might, at least for the dimly lit, indifferently designed, and blandly managed establishments that have cut out everything from cartoons to real butter on the popcorn in their lemminglike quest to turn the excitement of big-screen fantasy into a lockstep little business. Why

534

not rent a cassette when the alternative is five bucks to sit with a couple dozen strangers amid the splendor of carpet swatches on the walls, discarded popcorn tubs on the floors, and a cut-rate sound system you wouldn't put in your rumpus room, let alone the living room where it could be heard by family and friends?

Drabinsky and company want to take you away from all that. Back to an era when going to the movies was both entertainment and experience. When you felt like dressing up and making a night of it, not slipping in for two hours and then running through the drive-through at the burger barn on the way home.

It seems to be working. According to Cineplex, at least, the thirteen-screen "multiplex" (that's movie theater talk for a ton of screens under one roof) in Los Angeles' Beverly Center has the highest per-seat return of any theater in the U.S. In plain English, that means customers are doing what they habitually do by spending their money in places where they like what they're getting in return.

When Cineplex raised ticket prices in Manhattan to six and seven dollars to cover the cost of providing the entertainment, savvy politician Ed Koch, New York's mayor, put in an appearance on the picket line of allegedly outraged consumers that formed out in front. Savvy customers, meanwhile, did what customers habitually do by spending their money in places where they like what they're getting in return, which is why the picket lines quickly gave way to popcorn lines, and other theater chains are now charging that much where they think they can get away with it.

Drabinsky gets away with it by providing an old-fashioned style of service that had all but vanished—and taken with it a lot of the myth and magic from the movies. It's more than fancy decor and some double-digit screen configurations. Even on a smaller scale, say six screens, a Cineplex complex may cost a million more than the $1.75 million invested in the typical no-frills variety. Drabinsky's premise, *Forbes* reported in 1986: Extra in, extra out.

"People don't just like coming to our theaters," Drabinsky told the magazine. "They linger afterward. They have another cup of cappuccino in the cafe or sit and read the paper. We've created a more complete experience, and it makes them return to that location." As those masters of managed entertainment, the Disney imagineers, would put it, "Manage the setting for the experience and you're halfway home." Drabinsky can readily attest that the principle works in settings other than a theme park.

Cineplex theaters are designed to entertain from the time you arrive to the time you leave, not just when they turn the lights out and start showing previews of coming attractions. To make sure his properties are delivering what he is promising, Drabinsky has been known to call or personally inspect as many as twenty-five of his theaters a week. If he sees a piece of spilled popcorn or a discarded candy wrapper on the floor in one of his theaters, he'll pick it up—often while making eye contact with an employee to reinforce the service standard being demonstrated.

Cineplex also uses secret shoppers to check its facilities against rigorous standards for appearance and operational conduct. They time the amount of time they spend in line for tickets or refreshments. They report on the competence and demeanor of employees. They check out the carpeting in the theaters and the cleanliness of the bathrooms. What they find is reported back to headquarters, and anything not up to snuff gets quick attention from the highest levels of the company.

To inspire even greater feedback from customers, Cineplex has lately taken to printing a toll-free 800-number on popcorn cartons. Callers pass along complaints, comments, suggestions, sometimes even impromptu reviews of the movies they've seen or the popcorn they've been served. The comments, good, bad, or indifferent, are circulated around headquarters and out to the field to keep everybody in touch with the people in the seats when the lights go out.

After all, if you're busy putting theater back in the theaters, you have to keep putting people in the seats.

Cineplex Odeon Corporation
1303 Yonge Street
Toronto, Ontario M4T 2Y9

THE WALL STREET JOURNAL.

THE COMMERCIALS PROCLAIM IT "THE DAILY DIARY OF THE AMERICAN DREAM." That's maybe overstating the case a little. But there's no denying that the five-day-a-week business newspaper almost universally known as "the *Journal*" has become a highly valued source of economic and political news, information, and analysis in companies of every size and description.

In this, the fabled Information Age, providing relevant, timely information is itself a service—and *The Wall Street Journal* is by far the nation's most authoritative and relied-upon source of daily business information. That's how you become the largest paid-circulation newspaper in America.

In the process, the *Journal* has set its share of trends in business and general reporting while resisting most of the glitz-heavy and fluff-and-nonsense styles that have turned television news over to talking airheads and daily newspapers into jumbled collections of mismatched news and features. The *Journal* today is still a paper you read rather than look at. Its presses carry only one color of ink: black. There are almost no pictures, let alone bright "color graphics," beyond the occasional line-art sketch, usually of an executive's face. Very little sports—that stereotypical male preserve—other than pointed reporting on the business thereof. The bright success of *USA Today* notwithstanding, the *Journal* disdains color, celebrity watching, quick-scan charts and graphs, lifestyle advice, and less-than-special-interest columns for the news and analysis relevant to taking care of business. With thirteen Pulitzer Prizes to its name, including two in 1987, those are standards clearly worthy of note.

The *Journal* starts from the premise that it's the availability and the reliability of the news that is important to its customers. That's not a matter of overstating the obvious. In the typical daily newspaper, the amount of news you get is relatively proportional to the amount of advertising sold. That's why all those nicely illustrated features show up on days when the grocery stores and shopping malls have something to push. The *Journal* uses a different standard: No matter how small each day's edition turns out to be on the advertising side, it will always include between 130 and 132 columns of news. If the paper grows past 66 pages—which it does frequently on a regional basis—the "news hole" expands, but it doesn't contract. That means readers can count on a consistent news product—and the *Journal*'s more than four hundred reporters and editors can do their jobs with that service standard in mind.

The first place the news shows up actually isn't in the *Journal* at all. It's on the Dow Jones News Service, an electronic information wire fed to forty thousand terminals in banks, brokerage houses, and major corporations nationwide. To make sure its subscribers can get the news they want the way they want it, the News Service is beamed directly to high-speed printers, desktop computer workstations, giant visual display boards, or any combination of the three.

Not every story brief on the News Service will be developed for the following day's *Journal*, but about two hundred stories, both long and short, are evaluated each day. And while many people instinctively associate the *Journal* with "Big Business," the editors and reporters are very aware of the fact that more than 40 percent of their subscribers are in companies with fewer than one hundred employees.

The modern combination of electronic news and in-depth reporting is a far cry from the short, handwritten summaries of financial news that Charles Dow and Edward Jones used to deliver to customers in the Wall Street financial district back in the early 1880s. Dow and first employee Charles Bergstresser were the reporters, Jones the editor. In those days, high-tech meant using styluses to hand-produce up to twenty-four copies of their short financial news reports from a book of tissue-and-carbon flimsies. Messengers ran the bulletins to subscribers, often making several deliveries a day.

Consequently Dow and Jones did what good service businesses typically do—they found a new way to serve their customers by putting together a daily summary of the bulletins, the *Customer's Afternoon Letter*. Their original Dow Jones Average of stock prices debuted in the *Afternoon Letter* in 1884, but it was another five years before the business was ready to take the final step and produce a newspaper. *The Wall Street Journal*, the flagship enterprise of what is now Dow Jones & Company, Inc., first rolled off the press on July 8, 1889.

Today, electronics make sure the *Journal*'s news and analysis gets into the hands of business people the world over. Computers link reporters to editors, editors to typesetters, typesetters to composing rooms and production plants for four U.S. regional (and sometimes subregional) editions designed to serve eastern, midwestern, southwestern, and western readers. Each edition is separately made up from the common news base to accommodate different regional advertisers. Satellites then beam each day's edition to eighteen regional printing facilities in the U.S. and five abroad (where separate editions for Europe and Asia are produced).

Where the U.S. mail can't be counted on to make timely (or satisfactory) delivery to domestic subscribers, the *Journal*'s own National Delivery Service (NDS) staff provides that service to approximately 50 percent of the paper's subscribers. The number has been growing steadily in recent years and is projected to continue heading up, especially in light of rate increases from the U.S. Postal Service. To accommodate morning readers, NDS carriers often roust themselves out of bed and pick up the new day's paper in the wee hours of the morning to be sure of finishing deliveries before ten A.M.

One reason NDS is slated to keep growing: *Journal* customer-service surveys show that readers whose papers are delivered that way rather than through the mail are more satisfied and have a higher subscription renewal rate than those whose paper shows up in the mailbox sometime during the day. Between the *Journal*'s delivery service and Uncle Sam (the latter still handles about 30 percent of daily U.S. circulation; the other 20 percent comes from newsstand sales), more than 99 percent of each day's papers are delivered the day they are published.

The *Journal*'s claims of being a business diary make more sense in the area of news retrieval. It clearly is a newspaper of record, and one whose past reporting is read almost as avidly as this morning's edition. Thousands of readers access the *Journal*'s back issues through on-line computer services; others call the paper's library staff to get the dates when it covered one story or another.

Consequently, Dow Jones, the *Journal*'s parent company, has invested, and continues to invest, in systems and people capable of providing this much-demanded reader service. Through Dow Jones' News/Retrieval Service, the reports of the *Journal*, the News Service, and *Barron's*, Dow Jones's financial weekly, are accessible twenty-four hours a day, often within ninety seconds of their original transmission. Every article, every mention of a company or executive or location on the News Service and in the *Journal* since 1984 is computer-accessible, as are major *Journal* and *Barron's* stories from the past eight years, plus four years' worth from the *Washington Post*.

In the fall of 1987, Dow Jones assured that its News/Retrieval service would remain state of the art by purchasing, for $5 million, two computers that use parallel processing and artificial intelligence technology. Although IBM only gave its stamp of approval to the idea of parallel processing (which is expected to bring still another quantum leap in high-speed information access and processing time) in December 1987, Dow Jones had been tracking the developing technology since early 1986.

Since 1977, the *Journal* has opened each year with a progress report to its readers to let them know where it stands and where it believes its journalistic *and* business responsibilities lie. In January 1988 it defined its mission as meeting its readers' expectations for "the hard news, and also the analysis that helps you tie events together, make sense of issues, and focus on broader trends. It's our job to make events and facts useful and relevant to you—not just in your corporate or professional lives, but also as individual investors, consumers and concerned citizens."

That the *Journal* succeeds in discharging those responsibilities shows up in a number of ways. A 1986 *Times-Mirror* poll named it America's most trusted national news medium. In January 1988, *Fortune* cited Dow Jones as the nation's most admired publishing company, the second most admired for the quality of its products and services, and the third most admired company of any description. Readers, meanwhile, continue to vote with their checkbooks—more than two million loyal subscribers make a point of starting their day with the *Journal*.

From a small financial paper serving the Wall Street district of New York City, the *Journal* has become a world-renowned source of business intelligence. And in the Information Age, *that's* the stuff dreams are made of.

The Wall Street Journal
Publication of Dow Jones & Company, Inc.
200 Liberty Street
New York, NY 10281

IT'S BRIGHT. IT'S BRASH. IT APPEARS TO HAVE BOTH THE COLOR SCHEME AND the attention span of a butterfly. And each weekday, more than five and a half million people pick it up (and sometimes put it down)—a million more than read any other newspaper in the (argh, there's no getting away from the acronym) USA. In its first five years of existence, Gannett's *USA Today* has become a case study of how to provide information as both a service and a business.

The numbers are impressive. From a standing start on September 15, 1982, *USA Today's* readership has grown past 5.5 million. About 1.6 million copies are sold each day through vending machines, on newsstands, and through subscriptions (about 30 percent of total circulation at the beginning of 1988). Advertising revenues grew 35 percent in 1987, evidence that businesses in ever-growing numbers are taking the paper seriously. In May of 1987, after operating losses estimated from $457 million before taxes to $233 million after taxes—but six months ahead of corporate parent Gannett's original projections— *USA Today* posted its first profit; by the fourth quarter of the year it was foregoing bright red ink for basic black on the bottom line.

What those numbers mean is that the service *USA Today* delivers has been judged and found meaningful, desirable, and reliable—and by a pretty sophisticated audience. According to its studies, *USA Today* has more readers in the ranks of top management than the newsweeklies do. That maybe shouldn't be surprising. While early critics of the new publication generally compared it to major metropolitan daily newspapers, what Gannett has actually created is a newsweekly that comes out five days a week. Consequently, its relatively young (median age: thirty-eight), relatively affluent (median household income: $35,900) audience has found in *USA Today's* distinctive quick-read format a running review of developments in news, politics, social trends, business, entertainment, and sports. Taken a day at a time, *USA Today's* stories may indeed lack depth. Piled up through the week, they deliver.

As the novelty has worn off and the business aspects of the publication have proven themselves well conceived, a lot of the early critics have been, if not converted, at least mollified. In its early days, the dizzying collection of brisk, bite-size print items accompanied by big, splashy pictures and colorful graphics earned *USA Today* the nickname "McPaper." This isn't a journalistic dinner, the critics carped. It's fast food for the mind. The analysis being right for all the wrong reasons, the nickname stuck. It also became a backhand source of pride to reporters and editors, who sometimes felt themselves belittled by their media colleagues.

They're not defensive any more. The same nay-sayers who once predicted that the nation wasn't in need of a national newspaper, and certainly not one as allegedly light as this one, have noticed that the media around them, from daily newspapers to monthly magazines to television newscasts, are being changed by it. In the end, customers, not critics, decide how well or how poorly any business performs. And customers haven't been buying the criticism. They've been buying the paper.

Today, even those who are still made uncomfortable by what *USA Today* says about the public's often superficial grasp of issues and events will concede that "The Nation's Newspaper" has made its share of positive contributions. Its tight editing and broad-brush news judgment are now mirrored in newspapers and magazines of every size and description. Its almost obsessive commitment to conversing with its readers has provided new models for involving journalists with their communities. Through person-on-the-street interviews, polls, 800- and 900-exchange telephone hotlines, clip-and-mail coupon questionnaires, even town meetings and a roving bus with Gannett chairman Allen H. Neuharth aboard, the paper contacted or was contacted by more than 280,000 readers in 1987 alone.

And then there's all that color: Almost single-handedly *USA Today* has brought the use of four-color printing technology to the previously dull and lifeless layouts of daily newspapers coast to coast. As Neuharth has said from the paper's very early days, *USA Today* is designed for readers who grew up as viewers—its content and appeal are *supposed to be* visual as well as verbal.

The commitment to use complex forms of editorial color (not just an occasional tint bar, but process photography and complicated illustrations and artwork) is indicative of the risk Neuharth and Gannett took with *USA Today*. It required a significant investment in equipment—more than $200 million worth of color separators compatible with the satellites that beam material to a network of printing plants (thirty-three in the USA, three abroad in 1988) scattered close to readers around the country, plus high-speed presses in each of those plants capable of high-quality color printing. To run them required an equally strong commitment to building teams of skilled and well-trained people that could and would run all that high-tech gear correctly.

"If there is a key to *USA Today's* success in producing a dazzlingly attractive newspaper," *Editor & Publisher* concluded in 1985, "it must be its people and its system. The commitment by top management to highest production quality is reflected in the attention given to detail by highly trained people, working with precision equipment, according to exhaustive standards."

Since the quality of the product is an important component part of the service, everything counts. Machines are calibrated daily. Film processors are monitored hourly. Color ads are carefully proofed. Color densities are checked constantly. Newspapers from each plant are examined daily and evaluated weekly to catch and correct quality deviations among printing facilities.

Editorial draws the same kind of attention to detail. Gannett recruited the bulk of *USA Today's* staff from its own stable of reporters and editors on the more than one hundred newspapers it publishes across the country. Some burned out on the frenetic pace and inevitable false starts of the new venture. Others never made the adjustment from local newspaper to national newspaper mindset. But over time, the style and the staff have settled into more predictable and comfortable patterns as the paper figured out what it was good at.

"Early critics of McPaper wisecracked that *USA Today* could win a professional prize only for the best investigative paragraph," recalled editor John C. Quinn in the paper's fifth annual report to its readers on January 4, 1988. "In 1987 it did—the Freedom of Information Award from the nationwide Associated Press Managing Editors for its investigative paragraphs from every state on the salaries of college presidents, coaches and athletic directors."

Behind it all, driving it through the stormy beginnings and hefty losses, looms Neuharth. In the early days, he was prone to wander the editorial side of the paper, occasionally writing a headline or re-editing a story. He cruised the streets in his limousine, stopping here and there to make sure the ubiquitous blue-and-white vending machines chained to lampposts and anchored to bus benches were filled and working. People who didn't believe as strongly, who couldn't match his investment in time and energy or work with his constant oversight and interference, fell by the wayside. But over five eventful years, his customers proved he was right. There was indeed a niche for a national newspaper.

USA Today
Publication of Gannett Company, Inc.
1000 Wilson Boulevard
Arlington, VA 22209

Montgomery County, Ohio

AMERICA HAS FIFTY STATES—BUT IT COUNTS MORE THAN THIRTY THOUSAND city, village, and township governments. And increasingly it's the counties that are becoming bellwethers for improved government services. As cities lose population, especially their more affluent taxpayers, to suburbs, local area coordination becomes ever more important. More and more counties are stepping in to help streamline overlapping local services even while they take on more of the service-providing character of traditional city governments. When done well, it's an evolution that's both cost-effective and people-pleasing. Case in point: Montgomery County, Ohio.

More than half a million people live in this southwestern Ohio county, most of them in and around Dayton, the city that forms the urban core of the area. But like many counties, Montgomery must balance an urban-rural mix that includes nineteen municipalities, twelve townships, sixteen school districts, and a number of countywide assessment districts. Balancing those different interests is a test in itself. But there's more to it than that.

Like many parts of what's sometimes called the Midwest's Rust Belt, Ohio has seen its share of decay and decline. Small manufacturers that once fed auto parts to Detroit and other manufactured products to other industrial centers in the region have closed their doors. The farm economy is no longer the robust rural engine it once was. The military's presence at Wright Patterson Air Force Base has been scaled down.

Several years ago, Montgomery County decided to stop moaning and start making some positive improvements that might make it more attractive both to its own residents (some of whom were leaving for greener pastures—population has declined about 1 percent since the 1980 census) and to businesses. An areawide economic development plan was hammered out and implemented. The county ponied up a quarter of a million dollars a year for self-promotion. A master-planned industrial park was created, with conditions slanted to high-tech firms. Kodak, Mead, and a dozen others were attracted.

544

What makes all of this a service story is the top to bottom makeover of the Montgomery County government itself. As part of a five-year "Service Excellence" program, the county government has committed itself to changing the perception of government services and the people who provide them. It's clearly not a competition-driven initiative in the sense that people have a choice of where to go for water, sewer, fire protection, or social services. But it is competitive in the sense that service quality affects the overall quality of life—both personal and economic—in the county.

Since the pet project of county administrator Claude Malone was launched in November 1986, every county agency has gotten into an evolving, long-term process. The first step involves identifying its specific "customers." The labels vary: voters, residents, patients, employers, other county agencies. Each agency also has itemized its various services, and many have taken the additional step of surveying their specific publics to find out what people think of them.

That "customer research" is proving to be important. For example, the Department of Human Services (which provides everything from financial assistance and food stamps to counseling and referral services) drew on semiannual surveys of fourteen hundred clients to determine its major service-quality challenges. It found two, both of which are common to many government agencies, both of which were deemed addressable.

The first was waiting time. The research clearly showed that the longer an individual had to wait, the less satisfied he or she was likely to be with the quality of service provided. For those who had been given scheduled appointment times, the waiting game was especially aggravating.

The second service irritant came under the familiar heading of "faceless" bureaucrats. Many of Human Services' clients were already powerless and vulnerable—people in need often are. Wandering through the maze of government offices, they often felt bureaucracy's impersonal touch.

Neither condition is out of the ordinary in government at any level. But for its service customers, the Montgomery County Human Services department decided both could be changed for the better. Accordingly, two new service standards have been formalized. First, all clients now are expected to be seen within fifteen minutes of their scheduled appointment times, and each employee is further expected to make a point of acknowledging that he or she knows they are there and waiting, in the process confirming the time at which they will be called in for their appointment. Second, all employees personally—and personably—identify themselves in both face-to-face and telephone interviews. If you're going to provide a pleasing and professional level of service, the agency reasons, you should be willing to put your name on what you do.

Throughout Montgomery County, this process of diagnosis and change continues to spread. The term "user-friendly" has become a buzzword for spiffing up waiting areas with more professional-looking decor and furniture, and decluttering what used to be unsightly and confusing signage. Publications are being standardized and organized into literature racks. Some agencies are even experimenting with telephone answering recorders, enabling clients to leave personal messages for their specific caseworkers instead of being placed on hold for extended periods of time or encountering busy signals because those workers are meeting with other people.

From an organizational standpoint, services have been redefined and rearranged to make them more understandable and accessible to county residents. For example, all of the various functions of the child support system have been consolidated under the Human Services Department, making it the one-stop source for everything from family assistance to collecting child support from absentee fathers.

Montgomery County also has been working to give frontline people a sense of common purpose, in the process confronting the hallowed interagency problem of "scapegoating" in which workers in one department cover over a service glitch by blaming it on the system or workers in another department. Caseworkers in Human Services have been empowered (and are now expected) to follow through for their clients, tracking down missing checks or misplaced forms, and returning clients' calls with definite answers.

Significantly, the changes in standards have been implemented in management as well. Numerical performance standards that once emphasized volume, frequently to the exclusion of satisfaction, have been amended. Small groups of frontline employees now meet regularly to identify impediments built into the system, often over generations, and recommend solutions.

In the personnel department, for example, about fifteen thousand applicants a year were being seen, typically to fill only about two hundred jobs. Previously applicants were expected to come to downtown Dayton, find a place to park, locate the personnel department, inquire about the jobs available, fill out an application if they were interested in one of them, and wait for an interview that more often than not would lead to rejection. The process has now been modified with the addition of a jobs line so county residents can call first to see what jobs are currently open, saving many a pointless trip and helping those who do come down to arrive better prepared for their interview.

Other evidence of service-inspired change abounds. Workers at the animal shelter now allocate time to calling back county residents who complain about strays and other problems, and field personnel leave a callback card on doors when strays with licenses are picked up and impounded. Annual surveys for all three administrative services departments (the animal shelter plus security and central services) have been expanded, and are now designed by employees instead of the respective department heads.

According to Malone, the service-improvement initiative has become deeply ingrained in county government agencies of every size and description and has prompted a steady stream of phone calls from county governments nationwide who see in the Montgomery County model an image of how government can truly serve its constituents.

Montgomery County
451 West Third Street
Dayton, OH 45422

ONE OF THE SERVICE MAXIMS THAT TRACES BACK TO THE TURNAROUND AT
Scandinavian Airlines System (SAS) in the early 1980s is the idea that
you don't improve service by becoming a thousand percent better at any
one thing; you improve by becoming one percent better at a thousand
different things. A working example of that philosophy comes, strangely
enough, from a public utility company in the Southwest.

Phoenix-based Arizona Public Service Company (APS) provides electric power to about 45 percent of the state's 3.4 million residents. Its
operations, while centered in Phoenix, reach into eleven of the state's
fifteen counties, often requiring it to extend and maintain service in
remote locales and over rugged, unforgiving terrain. At first glance, the
utility business would seem to be insulated from the rigors of a competitive marketplace—as long as the lights light when a customer flips the
switch, how much more service involvement is necessary?

Quite a bit more, as it turns out. The utility business in Arizona is
confronted with a number of different forms of competition, some of
them unique to the region, but others increasingly common around the
country. There's competition for service territory: As Arizona's cities
grow and develop, a combination of large and small power companies is
competing for new and existing service areas that will add cost-effectively
to their current operating turf. When franchise agreements come up for
renewal, local voters have the option of choosing to renew, switch to
another supplier if their service has been less than satisfactory, or form
their own company and buy power directly from generating plants.

There's also competition for new business customers, which tend to buy
more power and be more bankable than homeowners: As companies
relocate to the Southwest, their choice of location is influenced by such
amenities as reliable utility service and cost-control support. And there's
competition for the hearts and minds of consumers, whose support is
important for everything from energy conservation programs to nonadver-
sarial regulatory policies.

Resources and environmental concerns also play an important part in the business. Generating plants are extremely expensive to build. To be cost-effective, power loads have to be as evenly distributed as possible throughout the day. But in the harsh climate of the Southwest, high daytime temperatures make air conditioning a given for most residents, especially older people who have fled colder climes; this means peak loads that can push generating capacity to the limit are followed by off-hours when demand scales way back. Then there's the problem of waste generation and its potential affects on air quality.

What's more, the advent of cogeneration technologies means many businesses now have (or can acquire) the capability to generate some of their power internally; highly efficient plants even raise the prospect that a business could sell back excess power to the utility. Every megawatt of business lost means a utility's fixed operating costs have to be recovered from a smaller customer base. In addition, to encourage efficient operations and keep costs to consumers as low as possible, Arizona's state-regulated energy incentive planning rewards power companies when their plants are operated above 75 percent capacity and penalizes them when operating load runs below 60 percent annually.

For all those reasons and more, APS president and CEO Mark De Michele characterizes the utility business as a competitive, market-driven field where service can and must provide an edge. "Our overriding goal, our most effective weapon against increased competition, is service," he told shareholders and customers at the 1987 annual meeting. "Only through excellent service will we maintain a positive relationship with our customers that will allow for greater acceptance of our prices and help us compete in a very rapidly changing environment."

In 1986, APS was stung when residents of Page, a small city in northern Arizona, withdrew from its service area to form their own local co-op. APS has also been the target of brickbats for building a new unit for its Palo Verde nuclear power plant, and it has campaigned hard against the secession of Gilbert, a Phoenix suburb, from the regional system. Since 1986, these events and their potential ramifications for APS's very future have served to catalyze management's commitment to a thorough, across-the-board upgrading of service quality. Today that commitment involves all eighty-six hundred APS employees, everyone from truck drivers to top executives, under a continuing, broad-ranging effort known as Service Plus.

There's no one major element to Service Plus. Rather, there are lots of individual pieces that all fit into a larger picture of top-quality service. One of the most visible aspects of the program has been with frontline employees, who are empowered and encouraged to be flexible and responsive to customer needs and customer perceptions.

Since 1986, for example, some APS employees have been conducting "Neighborhood Energy *Wattc*h" workshops in their own homes to provide energy-awareness information for their friends and neighbors. APS also participates in area crime-watch programs: Employees who regularly drive visibly marked company vehicles are trained to report any suspicious or potentially dangerous situations they observe, and public service advertising encourages children and adults to ask APS people for help, no matter what kind of help they need.

For Lorraine Ewbank, a resident of Payson, a remote community in the Tonto National Forest northeast of Phoenix, Service Plus took the form of the two-man APS crew that stopped to see if she needed assistance when her car stalled on the road home. Larry Willingham and Derrick Wilson checked the car over, added some of their own gasoline, managed to get the car started—then went more than a few extra miles: Willingham nursed her car home for her, with Wilson following in the APS truck. Neither one worried that an excitable, time-clock-driven supervisor might take exception.

APS employees who speak a second language have formed a Language Bank that is available to customers in person or by phone. The Bank's members have handled inquiries and solved problems in Spanish, Navajo, Japanese, Punjabi, and Tagalog, to name just five of the twenty-eight languages available. For the elderly and the needy in its service areas, the company has compiled a directory of names and phone numbers of agencies that provide special assistance, and employees are empowered to make calls for customers who cannot make them for themselves. APS records also note the names and addresses of customers who depend on life-sustaining equipment such as kidney machines and respirators; in the event of a power outage, their areas receive special priority.

Operating systems have been refined and upgraded in a number of ways, beginning with basic residential electric service—APS offers not one but five separate service levels to allow customers to choose the service that gives them the best value at lowest cost for their particular lifestyle. Like many utilities, APS will do an energy audit for business and residential customers, and like most it charges for that service (usually $15, but $7.50 for customers over the age of sixty). Unlike many utilities, however, APS accommodates people who would rather save the money and do it themselves by providing a free kit that includes the checklist and instruction guide its own inspectors use.

To encourage customers to install energy-saving load controllers, APS finances the devices on a monthly payment plan that starts with no down payment and charges no interest. For realtors, who commonly field a lot of questions about energy use from home buyers, there are special workshops that provide three hours of continuing education credit toward relicensing in addition to pertinent energy information.

To make sure consumer concerns can get through to the people who can do something about them, there's Project VOICE, a consumer advisory panel whose twenty-one members are chosen from customers by an independent selection committee. The panel meets monthly with APS management, and the company provides staff support to allow panel members to follow up on customer suggestions or complaints. That's in addition to the utility's own consumer advocate, who serves as an ombudsman for customers.

One outcome of "civilian involvement" is that APS bills are now more understandable and printed in a larger, easier to read type. Another is that the utility's disconnect policy has been softened to allow more time to resolve problems and differences before service is shut off.

To keep management accessible and up to date on the concerns of business customers and communities in the APS service area, there are regular luncheons with top management for community leaders and business owners. The APS Speaker's Bureau now includes nearly one hundred employees who volunteer their time to talk to community groups (which they did nearly one thousand times in 1987) on energy-related subjects. And APS people are encouraged to volunteer for community programs ranging from the United Way to the annual firewood project sponsored by Cub Scout Pack and Boy Scout Troop 37 in Flagstaff.

What does firewood have to do with running a megabuck utility? Maybe nothing. Then again, maybe quite a bit. Since 1986, tree-trimmers in the APS district around Flagstaff have been hauling the firewood-size ponderosa pine they cut from APS rights-of-way back to their construction yard. A few weeks before Christmas, APS volunteers meet the scouts at the yard to split and load cords of wood for delivery to elderly residents in the area.

Maybe that doesn't show up on the rate base, but it's just one more way that the people of APS provide light and warmth in ways that can't be measured by a meter.

Arizona Public Service Company
Subsidiary of Pinnacle West Capital Corporation
P.O. Box 53999
Phoenix, AZ 85072

Emerald People's Utility District

IN 1978, AFTER EIGHT YEARS OF TIRELESS GRASS-ROOTS EFFORTS, VOTERS IN about 550 square miles of northern and southern Lane County, Oregon (a largely rural service area that surrounds, but doesn't include, the city of Eugene), decided to form their own public utility district to provide electric power. Their rallying point arrived in their mailboxes regularly: bills based on rates that were approximately double what customers of other utilities serving Lane County were paying. They sought to create and control a new system that would put them, the customers, first.

It wasn't easy. Even after winning approval at the ballot box, they had to spend five more years in litigation with Pacific Power & Light Company, the investor-owned utility that had previously provided that service. They struggled over more than a dozen separate issues, including the legality of the election that approved the new utility's revenue bonds, control of existing rights of way, physical assets, and other aspects of the business.

Finally, on November 17, 1983, the Emerald People's Utility District was officially turned on and began serving its nearly fourteen thousand customer-owners. It did it so well so soon that in 1987 Emerald (no business should go through life under the acronym EPUD) received the E. F. Scattergood System Achievement Award from the American Public Power Association (APPA) for sustained achievement and improved customer service.

Emerald, said APPA, exemplifies "the ability of local people to take control of their energy destiny. Its success is due to hard-working, committed employees and consumer owners." In its first four years, APPA noted, the company "provided ever-increasing services, and has upgraded its system to increase reliability. It has widened the difference between its non-profit rates and those of Pacific Power & Light from five to 15 percent. . . . [Emerald's] aggressive pursuit of cost-effective service is based on a foundation of employee development, customer involvement and open communication. Born through volunteer efforts, [Emerald] continues an active program providing consumer-owners meaningful volunteer work in the operation of their electric utility."

The difference in large part involves putting the customer, not profit-minded investors, first. It starts when a customer starts receiving service: Since 1987, no security deposit has been held hostage against the prospect of a bill not being paid on time. But, as befits a "People's" utility district, that's literally just the beginning.

Each month, about 20 customer-owners are invited in for a tour of the new, energy-efficient headquarters and a buffet lunch with Emerald staffers. On the tour, during the orientation, and over lunch, there's plenty of time and opportunity to ask questions, make suggestions, register complaints, and find out what makes the service tick. The Welcome Packet that describes Emerald's services includes a postage-paid card with which a customer can get on the invitation list.

Many customer-owned utilities are actually run by a distant, inaccessible board of directors whose actions are often virtually invisible to the utility's supposed owners and indistinguishable from those of a for-profit board. By contrast, Emerald's five-member board sets rates based on recommendations from a fifteen-member Citizens Rate Advisory Committee. The panel includes representatives for industrial, commercial, agricultural, governmental and low-income residential users, plus area representatives for five subdistricts, the latter drawn—that's right, "drawn," as in put the names in a hat and reach in—from a list of interested customers.

Similar volunteer committees advise the board on finance and conservation matters. More than eighty customers immediately volunteered for the fifteen positions on a new Power Resources Committee when it was formed to study future power development options.

Then there's the utility's annual meeting, which is nothing less than an unabashed summer picnic for ratepayers. It's a laid-back summer's afternoon, complete with pony rides, baseball, bingo, and "the best potluck in the county." Since the customers are the owners, it makes sense to get everybody together for a day of barbequed chicken, music, games, and general fun. In 1987, four thousand people (that's the equivalent of about 30 percent of Emerald's customers) attended.

In the small rural communities that depend on Emerald's service, Emerald people have become familiar sights. To teach electrical safety, the puppets of "The Emerald City" make the rounds of elementary schools, allowing the Tin Man, Scarecrow, and Cowardly Lion to point out potential hazards around Dorothy's home and farm to their second- and third-grade audiences. To further serve as a community asset, Emerald's boardroom is available free of charge to any organization in the communities it serves.

Since public image is important, Emerald likes to keep its bright white-and-green trucks sparkling clean. Accordingly, they're washed once a week. But Emerald doesn't run them through a car wash, or add employees to the payroll to perform that task. Instead, youth groups and other volunteers trot out buckets and brushes every Saturday in return for a donation that funds anything from sports equipment to a high school prom. Emerald gets clean trucks, and the Boy Scouts, Future Farmers, 4-H, volleyball teams, and other organizations around Lane County get a reliable fund-raising opportunity. The wash list often is scheduled as much as four months in advance, and sometimes has a waiting list as well.

It's not all fun and games—you don't stay in business unless you take care of business, too. Being new allowed Emerald to dump outmoded methods and start fresh with customer-friendly, reliable technology. Meters are still read and bills sent monthly, but Emerald takes extra care to make sure its owners know what they're paying for. A user handbook given to each customer describes the typical bill line by line, deciphering the often-mystifying code numbers and pointing out the energy conservation information included in each customer's month-by-month recap of electricity usage over the last twelve billing periods.

Meter readers use hand-held miniature computers that carry information about the usage history at each address on the route (they also provide information on household pets and special service needs, like the presence of life-sustaining health care equipment). Not only are the computers more accurate, they turn out to be more customer-friendly: If the monthly reading doesn't track with the usage history, the computer beeps and the meter reader double-checks the numbers. That alone has cut down substantially on complaints over unexpectedly high bills and misread meters compared to the manual PP&L system Emerald inherited.

At the top of each bill—the part that the customer returns with payment—a place is provided for comments or questions. This simple feedback device helps keep Emerald in touch with customer concerns. In a given month, as many as one hundred send comments along with their checks, so much so that Enid Smith, the district's public information director, has come to recognize a number of "regulars" who seem to consider Emerald some sort of cross between a public utility and a pen pal.

All this close-to-the-customer attentiveness hasn't been lost on Emerald's owners. In 1984, a year after the new utility took over from PP&L, a little less than 60 percent of its customers rated their satisfaction with Emerald's service "excellent to good." After all the struggles and litigation, it's a wonder anyone had much positive to say about the industry at all. Have the old habits and attitudes begun to return? To the contrary: In 1987, Emerald's "excellent to good" rating had risen to an encouraging 83 percent.

Emerald People's Utility District
33733 Seavey Loop Road
Eugene, OR 97405

Kinder-Care Learning Centers

THE ANDERSON FAMILY DIDN'T NEED DAY CARE. WHILE FATHER WAS OUT KNOWING best all day, mom was home taking care of the big, comfortable house and the three bright, bubbly kids.

Times change. Today fewer than one family in nine fits the stereotype of 1950s-vintage television—substantially less, in fact, than the proportion of households headed by a single adult. Family sizes are smaller, and dual-career, two-paycheck marriages are the order of the day: Nearly half the American work force is composed of either couples where both work or single-parent families. And one of every four women on the job has a child under twelve years old. By 1990, there will be an estimated thirteen million children under the age of six with working mothers. So who's taking care of the kids?

In about twelve hundred locations around the country (plus two provinces of Canada), it's people doing business under a trademark belfry reminiscent of the little red schoolhouses of yesteryear. That makes Kinder-Care Learning Centers the largest private child-care provider in the U.S. Founded in Montgomery, Alabama, in 1969, it's a business built on providing an increasingly essential service to a highly demanding clientele.

As with most of the national chains, the key to Kinder-Care is the scale of the service operation. In-home care providers are generally limited by physical constraints to a handful of children, and most homes aren't designed to double as child guidance and recreation facilities. Kinder-Care's are modeled on small-scale schools, providing ample facilities both indoors and out for one hundred or more children of various ages; staffing is done with an eye toward providing much more than a large-scale babysitting service.

At Kinder-Care centers, the TV isn't on all day. In fact, it's seldom on at all. There's a ladder of low-key activities and programs for infants, two-year-olds, three-year-olds, four-year-olds, five-year-olds, and school-age "Klubmates." While programs, materials, and curricula are standardized in a general sense (and make no claims to

556

to prepare the classes of 2001 at Harvard or Stanford), local directors and district managers are expected to customize care and experiences to the needs of their area and its children. Teacher-created materials are in evidence from the toy boxes in toddler areas to the walls throughout the building.

Selection gets plenty of attention. No one is hired on the first interview. At least two are required, one with the center director, one with her manager. After an initial ninety-day trial period, during which on-the-job training is the rule, a more extensive and wide-ranging twelve-week program kicks in. It deals with specific child-care issues, like behavioral management at various ages, and more general concerns, such as room arrangement and safety considerations.

The school motif is taken seriously. Early in the school year, parents are invited in to discuss goals for their children. There are parent-teacher conferences three times a year. Quarterly calendars are sent home to explain upcoming themes and activities. In between, parent involvement is encouraged and impromptu inspections—which, in many states, are a parent's legal right—are invited.

But at heart Kinder-Care is a business, and it works hard at its success. Each center is evaluated twice a year, with points earned for customer relations, programming, and health and safety as well as financial, personnel, and licensing performance. To build espirit throughout the system, "Best of Care" winners in each region are reviewed and rewarded nationally as well. Meanwhile, parents start getting written evaluation forms within three months of enrolling their children, and the same form (not a fresh blank one) is updated three times a year so that any problem areas from previous ratings can be reviewed.

The entrepreneur who launched Kinder-Care is a former commercial real estate salesman who got the idea from a newspaper article on the potential of turning small-scale day-care needs into larger-scale businesses. After some quick and informal research, Perry Mendel talked nine investors into matching his twenty-thousand-dollar bankroll. He used the start-up funds to assemble a team with experience in day care, kindergarten teaching, child nutrition, and early childhood education needs and developed a prototype business that started out with two modest-sized day-care centers in Montgomery. Drawing on his personal knowledge of the real estate market, he picked locations in bedroom communities where he figured the dual careerists who worked at the State Capitol were most likely to be found.

In the early days, Kinder-Care experimented with franchises. That's what drew New Jersey-born Richard Grassgreen to the company about the time the first center was opening. But it didn't take long for Mendel to decide that growth and quality could be managed best by maintaining full ownership and operational control. Grassgreen stuck around in management, assuming the presidency of the company in 1983.

Since then, the Kinder-Care template has been refined and replicated in more than 700 cities, and imitated in countless others. The typical free-standing Kinder-Care center handles about 120 children, from infants to twelve-year-olds, most of them enrolled from within a five-mile radius for the convenience of parents. Programs are targeted to specific ages and learning needs, with breaks for hot breakfasts and lunches plus mid-morning and mid-afternoon snacks.

The day starts whenever busy parents start off to work, but seven A.M. to six P.M. are normal business hours and center directors have to be able to handle arrivals and departures throughout the day. Most have a brightly painted van for field trips and transport to and from school. Some school-age children start the day at Kinder-Care, get on the morning school bus at the center, and return in the afternoon to wait for mom or dad to come home; others are enrolled for after-school hours only.

In an industry where the typical care-giver earns about eight thousand dollars—comparable to the wages of the average parking lot attendant, according to a *Fortune* report in 1987—and turnover averages 40 percent annually, concern has been focused on the quality and qualifications of those who provide child care. Who would work for that kind of money, goes the usual question.

For their part, center operators, including Kinder-Care, point out that the only source of revenue is the fee (approximately half of which is posted against salaries) charged to parents. The checkbook is not fat: The higher prices go, the more families that must opt out of organized programs for smaller, in-home styles of care. In that context, Kinder-Care's attention to management stability and career development continues to pay dividends. By looking for people who genuinely want to work with children, and offering those with the desire an upward mobility track that can lead to better—and better-paying—things, it keeps its service levels focused on quality-based measures.

Kinder-Care's business foundation is also visible in its ability to respond to another evolving force in the day care field: the corporate day-care center. Often located right on a business's premises, these centers are becoming an increasingly sought-after fringe benefit for working parents. In 1981, Kinder-Care set up a separate program, dubbed Kindustry, to work directly with businesses. More than fifty employers now participate in various plans, from the on-site Kinder-Care Learning Center at Walt Disney World to the cafeteria-style child care benefit payments offered to employees of CIGNA.

More than one million children have been taken care of by Kinder-Care since 1969. Though day care sometimes seems like a relatively recent phenomenon, some centers now are starting to sign up the children of parents who attended Kinder-Care centers in their own childhoods. That's one evidence of the quality of service provided. Another comes from the top: all six of the grandchildren of the chain's founder have been or are Kinder-Care kids.

Kinder-Care Learning Centers, Inc.
2400 Presidents Drive
Montgomery, AL 36197

Chicken Soup

FREQUENTLY, THE QUEST TO FIND OUR 101 EXEMPLARY SERVICE PROVIDERS TURNED up quirky, unexpected examples of someone who has found a creative way to build a business out of a hitherto unaddressed customer need. One such example turned up in our own backyard here in the Twin Cities of Minneapolis and St. Paul—a pioneering operation that bills itself as "daycare for kids who don't feel so good."

Created in 1985 and named Chicken Soup by its founders, Ruth Matson (a registered nurse) and Birdie Johnson (an occupational therapist), the service is designed to appeal to businesses as well as parents. According to a survey of working parents commissioned by *Fortune* in 1987, more than 40 percent of the moms and dads sampled missed at least one day's work in the three months prior to the poll to care for family matters like a sick child—nearly 10 percent took three to five days off. Other studies have shown that caring for a sick child is the leading cause of absenteeism among working parents.

The folks at Chicken Soup once calculated that it costs a business in excess of $150 a day when a $40,000-a-year executive stays home to take care of a sick child (and even if they're physically at work, there is no reason to assume that they're as focused and productive as they would normally be). Chicken Soup charges $30 to $40 a day—for four hours or a full day's care respectively—and already nearly a dozen Twin Cities companies have proven themselves willing to pay up to 75 percent or more of that fee to keep key people of varying salary levels in the office, yet reassured that their offspring are being well cared for.

The formula is deceptively simple. Weekdays from six in the morning until six at night, Chicken Soup will take care of mildly ill children between the ages of six months and twelve years old. Most of them tend to be preschoolers with a case of the the sniffles. To protect against cross-infection, the center in downtown Minneapolis separates its charges into three separate illness categories, each of which has its own separate room. A registered pediatric nurse is always on duty in the building; one additional child-care staffer is on duty for every four children in *each*

560

program area. (That's the state-regulated minimum in Minnesota for infants, but Chicken Soup uses it as an operating standard for every age.)

There's the Sniffles Room, for example: It's for children with a variety of upper-respiratory illnesses, most frequently the result of the all-American common cold. For gastrointestinal problems (upset stomach, vomiting, diarrhea), there's the Popsicle Room. For chicken pox, the center goes to a little more trouble—the Polka Dot Room has its own street entrance and a separate ventilation system to avoid exposing the other children.

Unlike conventional day-care centers, there's no pretense of curriculum. Instead, the emphasis is on providing a warm and comforting environment in which children can rest (each child has his or her own cot, the linens for which are laundered daily to prevent the spread of infections), nap, play quietly, or, if they're up to it, participate in some low-key learning activities. Hugging and being held are always on the agenda.

Rather than try to guess what a child needs, the day's schedule is planned individually when parents drop their children off. While they're still there, Chicken Soup's resident nurse does a brief physical assessment (temperature, pulse, respiration, and general symptoms), and care is taken to make sure children have a chance to explore the place before mom or dad leaves for work. At the end of the day, parents receive a daily flow chart of their child's activities, including meals eaten, temperature readings, medications given, and rest periods. With tender loving care on that scale, it's no wonder that 80 percent of the parents surveyed in December 1987 rated Chicken Soup's services "excellent." Fully 100 percent said they would recommend it to others.

The center provides everything from linens and disposable diapers to toys and games, but its charges are also welcome to bring along a favorite blanket or stuffed friend. Breakfast and lunch are served (yes, of course chicken soup is featured on the nutritionist-approved menu), as are morning and afternoon snacks. Parents are encouraged to call as often as they like during the day, or to stop by over lunch or between meetings for a visit. After all, the whole point of the service is to provide maximum peace of mind.

That it does can be seen in the fact that more than half of the children it sees these days have been there before, or have brothers or sisters who have. More than a few happy campers have begged mom and dad to send them back to Chicken Soup, even though they aren't sick anymore. The company is now looking at expansion, including a design that would combine well-care with the current services.

Chicken Soup's service success is evident in the calls that come in almost daily from other parts of the country (and from as far away as Canada and Great Britain) inquiring about how the service works. In response, the parent company, Childcare Management Services, offers comprehensive consulting services and puts on seminars around the country, sharing what it knows about licensing, facilities design, staffing, insurance, admission guidelines, and care levels with entrepreneurs interested in launching similar businesses in their own communities.

To those who call, Chicken Soup has provided information, consulting services, and encouragement based on feedback from some of the country's toughest consumers. Time after time, its little customers clearly have shown appreciation for its services.

Chicken Soup, Inc.
Subsidiary of Childcare Management Services
322 South Third Street
Minneapolis, MN 55415

Mini Maid Services Company

ℳíní 👥₍ℛ₎ ℳaíд

IN THE GOOD OLD DAYS (WHENEVER THAT WAS), WELL-TO-DO PEOPLE HAD MAIDS, often in full-time residence, to keep all the things they'd worked for clean and shiny. Not-quite-so-well-to-do people had a "cleaning lady" who came in once a week or so to perform some of the same services. Domestic work wasn't the kind of high-minded calling that people spent years in preparation for—after all it was, pretty much by definition, the kind of work nobody really wanted to do. Maybe that explains why, until the early 1970s, no one had really looked at cleaning homes and apartments as a bona fide service business.

In just fifteen years, that has changed. Today, cleaning up after affluent professionals and dual-career households has made the residential-cleaning service one of the brightest of franchise opportunities. There are Merry Maids (the biggest national chain), Molly Maids, Classy Maids, just plain "The" Maids, DomesticAides, Maid Brigades, Bucket Brigades, Dial-a-Maids, Maids for a Day, Maids Easy, McMaids—probably even maids in the shade (they get a day off sometime, right?). But the pioneer self-made maid is Leone Ackerly, founder of Mini Maid.

Back in 1973, Ackerly, then twenty-eight, had a comfortable home in Marietta, an affluent community on the north side of Atlanta. She had three daughters, no professional degree or office training, and a husband who had worked his way up to vice president of a security business when she started looking at the old bromide "good help is hard to find" from an entrepreneurial perspective. She was used to doing her own housework because often she couldn't get a maid. Other people probably had the same problem, she reasoned.

So one day she announced to husband Bill that she was going to clean houses and apartments. As a business. The first job took her half a day and wore her out; today, a four-person Mini Maid team using the systematic approach she developed through her own frontline experience (copied and used in some form or another by virtually all of the other maid services now cleaning up around the country) would do the same job in

563

less than thirty minutes. Her first customers weren't sure what was included in her services; in response, she quickly evolved a list of minimum tasks that should be done at least weekly. Minimum Maid Service was the venture's first name—quickly shortened to Mini Maid.

The key to professional housecleaning services, she discovered firsthand, was management of time and motion. Making the service systematic made it more reliable, consistent, and customer-pleasing. From her husband's training in police work, Ackerly adopted the thorough, top-to-bottom, left-to-right, one-room-at-a-time approach, learning to avoid retracing her steps and making sure she had everything she needed with her when she entered a room. She ran a stopwatch on herself as she made beds, cleaned bathrooms, vacuumed rugs, and scrubbed floors. She made individual steps into quantifiable jobs.

That continuing, firsthand learning process taught her, for example, the value of using a long extension cord that only had to be plugged in once instead of making 160 separate bends a day to plug in and unplug a vacuum in eight standard, ten-room houses, which is what she soon figured she should be able to clean. Today, that's a light load for a typical Mini Maid team, which can handle ten houses or as many as fourteen apartments in a seven-and-a-half-hour day.

Ackerly also listened to everyone, from her mother to museum curators, to pick up tips and tricks, many of which eventually found their way into the three-hundred-page operations manual that helps franchisees learn the business side of housework. In addition to the manual, new franchisees get two weeks of training in Atlanta and access to a library of videotapes and other training materials they can use to develop their own professional teams.

It was her mother who helped Ackerly make the real breakthrough in the business: team cleaning. When mom arrived for a visit shortly after the business had started to grow, Ackerly took her along. Her first teammate lasted two weeks doing bathrooms before going back to Florida, but that was long enough for Ackerly to switch from do-it-yourself to divide-and-conquer as a modus operandi. Soon Bill had quit his job to work in the family business, at one point training and running his own three-person team through fifteen thousand jobs before going back to the office to help Leone set up franchise operations.

Pioneering home-cleaning franchises in 1976 turned the Ackerly's innovative little business into a national phenomenon and spawned a host of competitors. No matter: They figure the annual market for housecleaning services is over $7 billion and growing, so there's plenty of room. Mini Maid's turn-key package includes everything from training in the proven internal systems to programs for payroll, tax accounting, personnel management, and promotion. There's also a line of Mini Maid chemicals, all of them noncaustic and developed on the job.

Mini Maid teams come fully equipped with their own cleaning supplies, vacuums, and other necessary materials; they take their used-up supplies with them. In less than an hour, they can clean the standard house top to bottom, then be gone without a trace. That's in marked contrast to the days of sometimes troublesome workers who had to be screened, taught, equipped, and checked up on.

Quality control is built in, from the team members hired (generally housewives and young mothers) to the follow-up phone call Mini Maid managers make the next day to each and every customer. The latter is far from typical, but it's not the only nonstandard practice to contribute to the espirit of Mini Maid franchisees in twenty-four states. For example, unlike many franchises, which assess royalties as a percentage of sales (which means the more successful you become, the more money head-quarters gets), Mini Maid has a flat fee that allows franchisees to keep more of the results of their labors. There's no royalty fee at all for the first two months, which helps ease cash-flow problems during the crucial start-up phase of a new business.

There's also no advertising fee (an assessment that in many franchises can drain away another 2 percent of revenue, or more). Mini Maid lets its franchisees decide how to advertise, and how much money to budget for that purpose; Leone Ackerly also points out that a lot of franchise advertising is done as much to attract new franchisees for the licensing company as to develop customers for existing businesses.

More than once we've run into a business that started out by deciding it was going to become the McDonald's or L. L. Bean of this or that industry. Here's another. Mini Maid aspires to McDonald's-like efficiency, if not similar gargantuan size.

"We still have our first franchisee from 1976," Ackerly told us. "That's because we look for stability in franchising—we're a family, not a factory." When a franchisee encounters an operational problem, the founder herself often lends a hand. Another time-honed tactic is to pair up a new or struggling operation with a nearby franchisee who can provide support and advice. Even when the business is proceeding smoothly, Ackerly still tries to touch base with each Mini Maid operator once or twice a month.

When Mini Maid started, Ackerly set two service standards in place: An opportunity for her customer to inspect her work before she left, and a money-back guarantee if the work wasn't up to snuff. Both standards still prevail, although many Mini Maid teams are invisible to their customers since they come and go while the adults are at work and the kids at school.

Maybe good help isn't so hard to find.

Mini Maid Services Company
1855 Piedmont Road
Marietta, GA 30066

Acknowledgments

THE TITLE PAGE OF THIS BOOK SAYS IT WAS WRITTEN BY RON ZEMKE AND Dick Schaaf. That's a lie—or, at the least, very misleading. The writing of this book was much too much an undertaking for the two of us to have conceptualized, researched, and written it alone. It is, rather, the result of an intensive, eighteen-month team effort.

The team had any number of key players. Julie Hally, our skilled and clever library researcher, did a magnificent job of patrolling the data bases, journal stacks, and general business publications to make this book a timely representation of the state of the art in service quality management. She regularly performed magic by conjuring up real information from the vague references to obscure journals and research projects we brought back from our field work and site visits. And she never once whimpered when faced with instructions to "see if you can find an article in *Trucker*, or *Trucking*, or *Transportation* magazine, something like that—somewhere between 1979 and '82, probably—that talked about the Ryder system and customer satisfaction. Or was it listening? Something like that." She never kicked or hit either, although she was certainly entitled.

Patty Brophy did yeoman work tracking down data on the hundreds of companies we investigated for possible profiling. She spent literally months working with customer service, training, financial relations, and corporate communications people (some of them friendly and helpful, some of them dour and suspicious, and some of them just plain mystified) to surface service data and customer anecdotes, fill in the blanks in our evolving company descriptions, and in general make sure we had the most current information available on our 101 service quality exemplars. She also did her share of tracking down leads on industry data, cajoling reluctant researchers to share their data with us, and reassuring them we would properly acknowledge their work.

Darin Howard and Katie Elton deserve the Performance Research Associates equivalent of Purple Hearts, if not congressional medals, for all the cold-calls they made to industry organizations and associations in

567

search of industry-specific research and reports. Their ability to deal with the tedium of filing, cross-filing, and refiling, hour upon hour, the thousands of clips, stories, articles, and reports unearthed by Julie and Patty also was truly amazing.

To Kristin Anderson and Lisa Wyatt go heartfelt kudos for managing to manage the business of the business while this book was in process, no small feat. In addition, they somehow managed to manage the project budget and keep Part 1 of the book more or less on schedule.

Chip Bell, Jeff Pope, and John Gunkler, though not officially on the project team, were de facto members. That means they didn't get paid for the work they did and the contributions they made. Chip and John spent long hours playing mental handball with us, tossing the key ideas in this book around and about, abusing, twisting, and reshaping them until they passed the critical Bell-Gunkler "makes sense to me" test. Jeff, who has logged more hours in the service-satisfaction mill than anyone we've ever met, spent far too much of his personal time sifting and sorting the professional literature of the field with us, and allowing us to learn the nuances of contemporary customer expectations from the vastness of his experience doing benchmarking, tracking, and comparative satisfaction studies for the clients of his own business, Custom Research, Inc.

Our thanks also to Dave Zielinski, Don Picard, Peter Holste, and Tom Cothran, all of whom were involved in helping us pull some of the final wordsmithing together.

There are dozens of researchers—like Leonard Berry of Texas A&M University and Benjamin Schneider of the University of Maryland—whose work has greatly informed and influenced this book, and to whom we are deeply indebted. We readily acknowledge the debt. There also are countless others who labor as mightily but who do not publish. They, too, were no less willing to share information. Tony Stephens, director of market research with GTE Corporation, Jerry Holmes of the Travelers, and T. A. Rao of Market Probe, are three who come quickly to mind in that regard.

In addition, our work benefitted from the assistance of a special group of people—service gurus, if you will—who, when asked, took the time to nominate organizations deserving of consideration for a list of exemplary service providers. Their kindness was an invaluable aid. Undoubtedly at least some of the very fine companies they named and gave us insights into would otherwise never have come to our attention. So thank you, Karl Albrecht, old friend and past co-author; Ken Johnston, CEO of Kaset; Herb Cohen of MOHR Development; Tom Peters, head of the Tom Peters Group and inspirer of us all; Jim Heskett of Harvard University; and Bob Desatnick of Creative Human Resource Consultants.

Add to those so far mentioned the dozens of men and women who

have buttonholed us after speeches and during workshops, or heard of
the project and phoned or written with the names of companies, associations, nonprofits, and, yes, even governmental offices they believed well
worth our consideration. These too were invaluable and helpful, and
another reason why we hold firm to the notion that this is a "we" effort in
far more than the plural voice of the writing.

Last, but by no means least, we need to thank Gary Luke and the team
at New American Library for taking one very late manuscript and turning
it into one very handsome book.

—Ron Zemke
Minneapolis
July 1988

Suggested Readings and Bibliography

Periodicals, Newspapers, and Reports

Ackerman, Laurence D. "What Makes Successful Service Companies Distinctive?" *IABC Communication World*, October 1986, pp. 17-19.

"America's Best Sales Force." *Sales & Marketing Management*, June 1987, pp. 41-45.

"Auto malls: A growing trend." *Jobber and Warehouse Executive*, August 1987, pp. 25-27, 51.

Bacas, Harry. "Hiring the Best." *Nation's Business*, October 1987, pp. 68-71.

Bell, Chip R. "Coaching for High Performance." *Advanced Management Journal*, Autumn 1987, pp. 26-29, 47.

Bell, Chip R., and Ron Zemke. "Service Breakdown: The Road to Recovery." *Management Review*, October 1987, pp. 32-35.

————. "Do Service Procedures Tie Employees' Hands?" *Personnel Journal*, September 1988, pp. 76-83.

Berry, Leonard L., Valerie A. Zeitham, and A. Parasuraman. "Quality Counts in Services Too." *Business Horizons*, May-June 1985, pp. 44-52.

"The Big Trouble with Air Travel." *Consumer Reports*, June 1988, pp. 362-367.

Block, Peter. "Empowering Employees." *Training and Development Journal*, April 1987, pp. 34-39.

"*Business Month* Chooses 1987's 5 Best Managed Companies." *Business Month*, December 1987, pp. 21-48.

Cebrezynski, Gregg. "Challenges Await Service Businesses." *Marketing News*, November 8, 1985, pp. 20, 24.

"A Customer Service Checklist for 1981." *Customer Service Newsletter*, December 15, 1980, pp. 1-4.

Davis, Herbert W. "Customer Service Strategies for Management." *Davis Database*, June 1985, pp. 1-4.

Denton, D. Keith. "Service Side Productivity." *Industrial Management*, May-June 1985, pp. 23-26.

Elbeck, Matt. "An Approach to Client Satisfaction Measurement as an Attribute of Health Service Quality." *Health Care Management Review*, Summer 1987, pp. 47-52.

"The *Fortune* 500." *Fortune*, April 25, 1988, pp. 357-417.

"The *Fortune* Service 500." *Fortune*, June 6, 1988, pp. 275-317.

Gannes, Stuart. "Strong Medicine for Health Bills." *Fortune*, April 13, 1987, pp. 70-74.

Goodman, John A. "The Bottom Line Benefits of Consumer Education." *Mobius*, October/November 1984, pp. 18-20.

"Goodman's Goods: Effective Customer Satisfaction Surveys." *Service Management*, November/December 1984, pp. 12-14.

Grant, Rebecca A., Christopher A. Higgins, and Richard H. Irving. "Computerized Performance Monitors: Are They Costing You Customers?" *Sloan Management Review*, Spring 1988, pp. 39-44.

Gross, Laura. "Diversified Financial Giants Gaining Consumer Approval." *American Banker*, September 24, 1986.

"GTE's BCOS Tracking Program Measures Customer Satisfaction." *A Total View*, Vol. I, No. 29, pp. 1-2.

Hampton, William J. "The New Super-Dealers: They're Changing the Way Auto Makers Sell Cars—And How You Buy Them." *Business Week*, June 2, 1986, pp. 60-66.

Hartman, Curtis, and Steven Pearlstein. "The Joy of Working." *Inc.*, November 1987, pp. 61-71.

Heffring, Michael P., Ph.D., E. Joanne Neilsen, Marie J. Szklarz, and Grant S. Dobson. "High Tech, High Touch: Common Denominators in Patient Satisfaction." *Hospital and Health Services Administration*, March/April 1986, pp. 81-93.

Heskett, James L. "Lessons in the Service Sector." *Harvard Business Review*, March-April 1987, pp. 118-126.

Hoerr, John, Michael A. Pollock, and David E. Whiteside. "Management Discovers the Human Side of Automation." *Business Week*, September 29, 1986, pp. 70-75.

Hrebiniak, Lawrence G., and William F. Joyce. "The Strategic Importance of Managing Myopia." *Sloan Management Review*, Fall 1986, pp. 5-14.

IFAPA 1987 Passenger Preference Survey Press Summary. Washington, D.C., November 3, 1987.

Increasing Customer Satisfaction Through Effective Corporate Complaint Handling. United States Office of Consumer Affairs in cooperation with Chevrolet Motor Division General Motors Corporation, (available from the Consumer Information Center, Department 606R, Pueblo, CO 81009).

"Is Big Joe a Good Joe?" *Consumer Reports*, September 1986, pp. 566-570.

Jones, Donna. "Auto Malls: More than a Pit Stop." *Venture*, April 1987, pp. 29-30.

Kelley, Robert E. "Poorly Served Employees Serve Customers Just as Poorly." *The Wall Street Journal*, October 13, 1987.

Koepp, Stephen. "High Anxiety and Rage." *Time*, July 20, 1987, pp. 52-54.

———. "Pul-eeze! Will Somebody Help Me?" *Time*, February 2, 1987, pp. 48-56.

Labich, Kenneth. "Winners in the Air Wars." *Fortune*, May 11, 1987, pp. 68-79.

Labovitz, George H., Ph.D. "Keeping Your Internal Customers Satisfied." *The Wall Street Journal*, July 6, 1987.

Leonard, Stew. "Love That Customer." *Management Review*, October 1987, pp. 36-39.

Linden, Fabian. "Value of the Dolls." *Across the Board*, (publication of the Consumer Research Center), December 1985, pp. 55-60.

"Making Service a Potent Marketing Tool." *Business Week*, June 11, 1984, pp. 164-170.

"Mail-order Companies." *Consumer Reports*, October 1987, pp. 607-614.

McAleer, Linda J., and Thomas Dukich. "Customer Satisfaction: Key to Improved Service Planning." *Public Utilities Fortnightly*, June 13, 1985, pp. 40-43.

McCarthy, Michael J. "Stressed Employees Look for Relief in Worker's Compensation Claims." *The Wall Street Journal*, April 7, 1988.

Moosbrucker, Jane, and Emanuel Berger. "Know Your Customer." *Training and Development Journal*, March 1988, pp. 30-34.

Moskowitz, Milton, and Carol Townsend. "The 40 Best Companies for Working Mothers." *Working Mother*, August 1987, pp. 49, 104.

O'Connell, Lauren. "Achieving Quality Service in Your Store Credit Operation." *Retail Control*, November 1986, pp. 56-64.

Pearce, John A. II, and Fred David. "Corporate Mission Statements: The Bottom Line." *Academy of Management EXECUTIVE*, 1987, Vol. I, No. 2, pp. 109-116.

Power, J.D. and Associates. *The Power Report on Automotive Marketing*, August 1987, Vol. IX, No. 8.

Pritchard, Robert D., Steven D. Jones, Philip L. Roth, Karla K. Stuebing, and Steven E. Ekeberg. "Effects of Group Feedback, Goal Setting, and Incentives on Organizational Productivity." *Journal of Applied Psychology*, Vol. LXXIII, No. 2, 1988, pp. 337-358.

"Quest for Quality." *Distribution*, August 1987, pp. 12-32.

Ray, George F. "Productivity in Services." *National Institute Economic Review*, February 1986, pp. 44-47.

"Rediscover the Forgotten Front Line." *On Achieving Excellence*, April 1987, p. 5.

Reingold, Edwin M. "A Homecoming Lament." *Time*, February 2, 1987, p. 55.

Richman, Tom. "Mississippi Motivators." *Inc.*, October 1986, pp. 83-88.

Rudolph, Barbara. "Free-for-All in the Skies." *Time*, March 7, 1988, pp. 50-51.

Schleh, Edward C. "Make Your Executive Decisions Inspire Service." *Management Review*, October 1987, pp. 46-49.

Schlossberg, Howard, and Brad Stratton. "Choice in Chains." *Restaurants & Institutions*, December 24, 1986, pp. 26-112.

Schneider, Benjamin. "The Service Organization: Climate Is Crucial." *Organizational Dynamics*, Autumn 1980, pp. 52-65.

Schneider, Benjamin, and David E. Bowen. "Employee and Customer Perceptions of Service in Banks: Replication and Extension." *Journal of Applied Psychology*, Vol. LXX, No. 3, 1985, pp. 423-433.

Schultz, Ellen. "America's Most Admired Corporations." *Fortune*, January 18, 1988, pp. 32-52.

Schultz, Gregory L. "Rediscovering the Customer." *Service Management*, July/August 1985, pp. 22-26.

Shetty, Y. K., and Joel E. Ross. "Quality and its Management in Service Businesses." *Industrial Management*, November-December, 1985, pp. 7-12.

Shullman, Robert R., Mark D. Willard, and Joel Perelmuth. "Lessons Learned From Service Businesses: The Impact of Service Quality is Measurable—At The Bottom Line." *Mobius*, Fall 1987.

Smith, Robert H. "Productivity in the Services Industry—A Must." *Industrial Management*, November-December 1985, pp. 4-6.

Stallman, Linda, and Nancy McSharry. "Excellent Companies." *Electronic Business*, September 15, 1987, pp. 93-104.

Stratton, Brad, and Lisa Bertagnoli. "America's Choice in Chains." *Restaurants & Institutions*, February 5, 1988, pp. 34-88.

Super, Karl E. "Memorial Hospital Emphasizes Guest Relations to Attract Patients." *Modern Healthcare*, August 29, 1986, p. 42.

Taub, Steven. "Best Broker Survey." *Financial World*, January 12, 1988, pp. 91-92.

"Using a Tracking Study to Keep Your Customers—And Get New Ones." *A Total View*, Vol. I, No. 29, pp. 2-4.

Uttal, Bro. "Companies That Serve You Best." *Fortune*, December 7, 1987, pp. 98-116.

Wehrenberg, Stephen B., Ph.D. "Training—Front-Line Interpersonal Skills a Must in Today's Service Economy." *Personnel Journal*, January 1987, pp. 115-118.

Weinstein, Michael. "American Express Scores on Prestige, But Retail Rating Falls Short of Mark." *American Banker*, September 9, 1986.

———. "Consumers Find Credit Card Interest Too High and Say They Would Switch to Cheaper Banks." *American Banker*, September 8, 1986.

———. "Visa Outranks MasterCard, Survey Finds." *American Banker*, September 9, 1986.

"Where to Stay." *Consumer Reports*, July 1986, pp. 472-478.

"Which Companies Are Best." *Consumer Reports*, September 1984, pp. 566-570.

Zemke, Ron. "Customer Service: Computers Have Their Place but They're not for Spying." *Training Directors' Forum Newsletter*, June 1986, p. 7.

———. "Health Care Rediscovers Patients." *Training*, April 1987, pp. 40-45.

———. "HRD's Crucial Role in Productivity Improvement," *Training*, January 1979, pp. 17, 21, 26, 29.

———. "The Manager as Servant." *Training*, August 1985, p. 8.

Zemke, Ron, and John W. Gunkler. "Organization-Wide Intervention." *Handbook of Organizational Behavior Management*, 1982, pp. 565-583.

Zemke, Ron, and Dick Schaaf. "What Can You Really do About Productivity?" *Training*, March, 1981, pp. 22-31.

Books

Ackoff, Russell L., Paul Broholm, and Roberta Snow. *Revitalizing Western Economies: A New Agenda for Business and Government*. San Francisco: Jossey-Bass, 1984.

Adams, John D., ed. *Transforming Leadership: From Vision to Results*. Alexandria, VA: Miles River Press, 1986.

Albrecht, Karl, and Ron Zemke. *SERVICE AMERICA!: Doing Business in the New Economy*. Homewood, IL: Dow Jones-Irwin, 1985.

Berry, Dick. *Managing Service Results*. Research Triangle Park, NC: Instrument Society of America, 1983.

Block, Peter. *The Empowered Manager: Positive Political Skills at Work*. San Francisco: Jossey-Bass, 1987.

Carlzon, Jan. *Moments of Truth*. Cambridge, MA: Ballinger, 1987.

Crosby, Philip B. *Quality Is Free*. New York: McGraw-Hill, 1979.

Czepiel, Anthony, Michael R. Solomon, and Carol F. Suprenant. *The Service Encounter: Managing Employee/Customer Interaction in Service Businesses*. Lexington, MA: D. C. Heath, Lexington Books, 1985.

Desatnick, Robert L. *Managing to Keep the Customer: How to Achieve and Maintain Superior Customer Service Throughout the Organization*. San Francisco: Jossey-Bass, 1987.

DiPrimo, Anthony. *Quality Assurance In Service Organizations*. Radnor, PA: Chilton, 1987.

Gober, Mary, and Bob Tannehill. *The Art of Giving Quality Service*. New York: Tannehill-Gober Associates International, 1984.

Harrington, H. James. *The Improvement Process: How America's Leading Companies Improve Quality*. New York: McGraw-Hill, 1987.

Heskett, James L. *Managing In The Service Economy*. Boston: Harvard Business School Press, 1986.

Joseph, William. *Professional Service Management*. New York: McGraw-Hill, 1983.

Kanter, Rosabeth Moss. *The Change Masters: Innovation for Productivity in the American Corporation*. New York: Simon and Schuster, 1983.

Levering, Robert, Milton Moskowitz, and Michael Katz. *The 100 Best Companies to Work for in America*. Reading, MA: Addison-Wesley, 1984.

Maccoby, Michael. *Why Work: Leading the New Generation*. New York: Simon and Schuster, 1988.

Nadler, David A. *Feedback and Organizational Development: Using Data-Based Methods*. Reading, MA: Addison-Wesley, 1977.

Normann, Richard. *Service Management: Strategy and Leadership in Service Businesses*. New York: John Wiley & Sons, 1984.

Peters, Tom. *Thriving on Chaos: Handbook for a Management Revolution*. New York: Alfred A. Knopf, 1987.

Peters, Tom, and Nancy Austin. *A Passion For Excellence: The Leadership Difference*. New York: Random House, 1985.

Porter, Michael E. *Competitive Strategy: Techniques for Analyzing Industries and Competitors*. New York: Macmillan, 1980.

Russel, Cheryl. *100 Predictions for the Baby Boom: The Next 50 Years*. New York: Plenum Press, 1987.

Shelp, Ronald Kent, John C. Stephenson, Nancy Sherwood Truitt, and Bernard Wasow. *Service Industries and Economic Development: Case Studies in Technology Transfer*. New York: Praeger Special Studies, 1984.

Sunshine, Linda, and John W. Wright. *The Best Hospitals in America*. New York: Henry Holt, 1987.

Waterman, Robert H., Jr. *The Renewal Factor: How the Best Get and Keep the Competitive Edge*. Toronto: Bantam Books, 1987.

Index

I(T)P Nelson

CANADIAN
Dictionary

of the ENGLISH LANGUAGE